THE PASSING OF AN ILLUSION

The
PASSING
of an
ILLUSION

THE IDEA OF COMMUNISM IN THE TWENTIETH CENTURY

François Furet

Translated by
DEBORAH FURET

The University of Chicago Press • Chicago and London

The University of Chicago Press, Chicago 60637
The University of Chicago Press, Ltd., London
© 1999 by The University of Chicago
All rights reserved. Published 1999
16 15 14 13 12 11 10 09 08 07   3 4 5 6 7

ISBN-13: 978-0-226-27340-2 (cloth)
ISBN-10: 0-226-27340-7 (cloth)
ISBN-13: 978-0-226-27341-9 (paper)
ISBN-10: 0-226-27341-5 (paper)

Originally published as *Le passé d'une illusion:
essai sur l'idée communiste au XXe siècle,*
© Éditions Robert Laffont, S.A., Paris, 1995

The University of Chicago Press gratefully acknowledges the generous contribution of the
French Ministry of Culture to the translation of this book.

Library of Congress Cataloging-in-Publication Data
Furet, François, 1927–97
    [Passé d'une illusion. English]
    The passing of an illusion : the idea of communism in the Twentieth Century / François
Furet ; translated by Deborah Furet.
        p.   cm.
    Includes bibliographical references and index.
    ISBN 0-226-27340-7 (cloth : alk. paper)
    1. Communism—History—20th century.   2. Communism—Soviet Union—
History.   I. Title.
HX40.F86513   1999
335.4'09'04—dc21   98-42109
                                                                          CIP

CONTENTS

vi   TABLE OF CONTENTS

PREFACE

The Soviet regime, having entered the theater of history with great fanfare, left it on tiptoe. Its modest end is surprising when compared with its brilliant career. This is not to say that there is no diagnosis for the debilitating disease that afflicted the Soviet Union, but the disease was concealed by the nation's ideology and international influence. Because of its important role in world affairs, the Soviet Union deserves a place in world history. Furthermore, international public opinion could hardly imagine the possibility of a radical crisis in the social system established by Lenin and Stalin. The idea of reforming this system came up frequently in the last quarter of the twentieth century, giving rise to a multiform and energetic revisionism, which nonetheless continued to maintain the basic superiority of socialism over capitalism. It was inconceivable even to the enemies of socialism that the Soviet regime could disappear and that the October Revolution could be "erased." It was even more inconceivable that such a rupture could be initiated by the single party that held power.

The Communist world was certainly its own undoing. An indication of this self-destruction is that the only Communists left are those who, undefeated, went from one world to another, adapted to another system, became partisans of free markets and elections, or were recycled into nationalists. But not a trace remains of their earlier experiences. Former Communists seem obsessed with negation of the regime in which they lived, even if they carry on the same habits and mores. Class warfare, the dictatorship of the proletariat, Marxism-Leninism have given way to the very things they were supposed to replace—bourgeois proprietorship, the liberal democratic state, individual rights, free enterprise. All that remains of the regimes born of October is what they sought to destroy.

The end of the Russian Revolution, or the disappearance of the Soviet empire, revealed a tabula rasa that bore little resemblance to the state of affairs left by the French Revolution or the fall of the Napoleonic empire. The Thermidorians had strongly supported civil equality and the bourgeois world. Napoleon had certainly been an insatiable conqueror, an illusionist of victory right up to the defeat that canceled out all the gains of this lucky gambler; but after he had lost everything, he still left Europe a vast store of memories, ideas, and institutions, which even his enemies drew upon in order to defeat him. In France, he had founded a state that would last for centuries. Lenin, in contrast, left no estate. The October Revolution ended not by being defeated in war but by liquidating all that it had created. When the Soviet empire fell apart, it was in the strange position of having been a superpower without incarnating a civilization. It was an assemblage of supporters, clients, and colonies; it had constructed a military arsenal and adopted a world-scale foreign policy. Apart from its ideological messianism—which ensured it the adoration of its partisans—it had all the attributes of an international power and was respected by its adversaries. Nonetheless, its rapid dissolution left nothing behind, neither principles, nor laws, nor institutions, nor even a history. After the Germans, the Russians were the second great European nation incapable of giving a meaning to the twentieth century and thus to their past.

To call the series of events that led to the end of the Communist regimes in the USSR and in the Soviet empire a "revolution" is quite inaccurate. Yet that word is commonly used in this context, perhaps because we have no other word in our political vocabulary to describe the collapse of a social system. "Revolution" evokes the idea, familiar to the Western political tradition, of a violent rupture with an earlier regime. In this instance, however, the "ancien régime" was itself born of the Revolution of 1917 and continued to claim ties with that event; so we could also characterize its liquidation as a "counterrevolution," especially since it revived the bourgeois world despised by Lenin and Stalin. The way in which it was carried out surely bore scant resemblance either to an overthrow or to a founding. Revolution and counterrevolution evoke acts of volition, whereas the end of Communism was due to a series of circumstances.[1] What followed its end left little room for deliberate action. From the ruins of the Soviet Union there emerged no leaders ready to carry on, no real parties, no new society, no new economy. There was only an atomized and uniform population. Social clases, certainly, had disappeared: even the peasants, at least in the USSR, had been destroyed by the state. The various ethnic groups in the Soviet Union were not powerful enough to drive out the divided Party elite or to determine the course of events.

Communism thus ended in a sort of nothingness. It did not lead, as so many had hoped and predicted since Khrushchev's time, to a better Communism, which would erase the vices of the earlier one while retaining its virtues—the Communism that Dubcek managed to embody in the spring of 1968 but that Havel failed to achieve in the fall of 1989. Gorbachev had been making its contradictions obvious in Moscow since Sakharov's liberation, but Yeltsin dissipated it right after the putsch of August 1991. The only thing to be found among the debris of Communist regimes was the familiar repertory of liberal democracy. The very point of Communism had been transformed even in the eyes of its former supporters. Instead of being an exploration of the future, the Soviet experience constituted one of the great antiliberal and antidemocratic reactions in twentieth-century European history. The other, of course, was Fascism in its various guises.

One of the distinctive traits of Communism was its inseparability from a basic illusion, which for many years appeared to be validated by Communism's own history, until it was dispelled by that history. By "illusion" I do not mean that the participants and supporters of Communism were unaware of what they were doing and accomplished things beyond what was required of them—which is generally the case. I mean rather that Communism sought to conform to the necessary development of historical Reason, and that the "dictatorship of the proletariat" thus appeared to have a scientific function. It was a different type of illusion from one based on a calculation of ends and means or issuing simply from belief in a just cause; for people lost in history, an illusion of this kind not only gives their life meaning but offers them the comforts of certainty. Unlike an error of judgment, which, with the aid of experience, can be discovered, appraised, and corrected, the Communist illusion involved a psychological investment, somewhat like a religious faith even though its object was historical.

This illusion did not "accompany" Communist history; it made it. Independent of Communist history insofar as it existed prior to experience, the illusion was, at the same time, subject to that history since the truth of its prophecies was contained in its course. Its socket was the political imagination of modern humankind, but it could only survive by constantly adjusting to circumstances. History was its daily bread; the unexpected was continually integrated into its system of beliefs. The only way to get rid of the Communist idea was to stop feeding it. As a belief in salvation through history, it could only be toppled by a radical historical denial, eliminating the need for the adjusting, mending, and patching that were its life's work.

Those constant adjustments are the subject of this book. This is not a history of Communism, even less a history of the Soviet Union; it is a history of the illusion of Communism during the time in which the USSR lent it consistency and vitality. In attempting to describe its evolution over a century, I do not regard it merely as something overtaken by liberal democracy; I see no good reason to substitute one philosophy of history for another. The utopia of a new humanity predates Soviet Communism and will survive it in other forms—without "worker" messianism, for example. What historians of the Communist idea in the twentieth century will find is an entirely closed circuit of the modern political imagination, beginning with the October Revolution and ending with the dissolution of the Soviet Union. Beyond what it actually was, the Communist world always glorified what it wanted and what it would therefore become. With its disappearance, the question of what it would have become has been answered: today, Communism is completely contained within its past.

The history of the "idea" of Communism was greater than the history of its influence, even at the time of its greatest geographic expansion. Since Communism really was universal, touching populations, territories, and civilizations never penetrated by Christianity, a comprehensive study of it would require more expertise than I now command. I shall therefore limit my study to Europe, for it was there that the idea was born, seized power, and, by the end of the Second World War, was at its most popular. There, moreover, it took thirty years to die, between Khrushchev and Gorbachev. Europe was the only place where Marx and Engels, its "inventors," believed it could have a future. The great Marxists, such as Kautsky, thought Russia was too far away to become the movement's advance guard. Once in power, Lenin's only hope for survival was the revolutionary solidarity of the old European proletariats, farther to the west, primarily that of Germany. Stalin exploited the Russian development of the Communist idea to his own advantage, but he never renounced the idea itself, which took on a new lease in life with the anti-Fascist victory. Europe, mother of Communism, was also its principal arena. It was the cradle and the heart of its history.

Europe also provides a comparative perspective; there, the Communist idea can be studied in two different political forms, depending on whether it exerted its power through a one-party system or whether it was spread through liberal democratic public opinion, guided by local Communist parties but extending beyond them in less militant forms. These two worlds were in constant if unequal contact, the former secret and closed, the latter public and open. Interestingly, the Communist idea prospered better in the latter situation, in spite of the spectacle provided by the former. In the USSR, and then in what after 1945 would be called the "socialist camp," it formed the ideology and the language of absolute domination. Simultaneously a spiritual and a temporal power, its will to emancipate did not long survive its will to enslave. In the West, it was also subject to the narrow constraints of international solidarity through its sister parties; but since it was never actually in power there, it retained something of its original charm, dissociated from the character assumed by the Soviet empire at the other end of Europe. Its imaginary path is even more mysterious than its actual history. In seeking to trace its ins and outs, this essay presents a kind of inventory, which is perhaps the best way to describe and analyze a historical consciousness common to both Eastern and Western Europe—two regions long separated by both the reality and the illusion of Communism.

One last word about the author, since every historical work has its own history. I have a biographical connection with my subject: in my youth, I experienced the passing of an illusion as a Communist between 1949 and 1956. My subject is thus inseparable from my existence, and I experienced firsthand the illusion that I am attempting to trace back to the time in which it was most widespread. Should I regret that period of my life as I write its history? I do not think so. Forty years later I judge my erstwhile blindness with neither indulgence nor acrimony— without indulgence because the excuses one often draws from intentions in no way cancel out ignorance and presumptuousness; without acrimony because that unfortunate engagement taught me something. I came away from Communism with a curiosity about the revolutionary passion and with an immunity to pseudo-religious investment in political action. My curiosity gave rise to this study; I hope the book will help elucidate the questions raised in it.

ACKNOWLEDGMENTS

As a newcomer to twentieth-century history, I had the good fortune in writing this book to benefit from the bibliographical advice of friends who are experts in the field. Unfortunately, they are too numerous to be cited in their entirety. Stéphane Courtois, Christian Jelen, Georges Liébert, and Jean-François Revel gave very generously of their time and their erudition. I owe a particular debt to Jean-Louis Panné, the author of a marvelous biography of Boris Souvarine, for having constantly shared with me his immense knowledge of the history of Communism.

Olivier Nora and Mona Ozouf were kind enough to read my drafts and made many useful suggestions. They know how much I value their advice. Finally, I would like to thank my two publishers, who are also dear friends: Charles Ronsac, who came up with the main idea for the book and watched over its progress from start to finish, and Jean-Etienne Cohen-Séat, with whom I maintained a constant dialogue about my subject.

I would like to add that this is an interpretative essay and I have therefore footnoted only the works and articles that I found most useful. —FF

Translator's note. I wish to thank Cristobal Aljovin for tracking down English-language references for this translation. —DF

ONE

The Revolutionary Passion

TO EXPLAIN THE POWER OF THE POLITICAL
mythologies that have filled the twentieth century, we must go back to
the time of their birth or, at least, to that of their youth; only then might
we glimpse their erstwhile glamour. Before being dishonored by its
crimes, Fascism was seen as a ray of hope, seducing not only the masses
but many intellectuals as well. As for Communism, its heyday is still
quite recent, for as a political myth and a social panacea it has long
outlived its failures and transgressions, especially in those European
countries that did not undergo its oppression firsthand. Although dead
among the peoples of Eastern Europe since the mid-1950s, in the 1970s
it was still flourishing in Italian and French intellectual and political life.
The survival of the Communist idea indicates the depth of its roots and
its seemingly limitless capacity to survive experience; it resonates like
an echo of its own golden age, when it was sweeping the world.

To understand the spell cast by the ideologies of Fascism and Communism, we must return to the time prior to the catastrophes over
which they presided, a time when they constituted hope. The difficulty
with such a retrospective overview is that it presents the ideas of hope
and catastrophe within a very compressed period of time. Since 1945, it
has become nearly impossible to imagine the National Socialism of 1920
or 1930 as a promise. Communism, however, can more easily be discussed as a system of beliefs, not only because the victory of 1945 allowed it a longer life, but also because its essential underpinning was the
notion that successive historical periods, interacting with capitalism,
supposedly opened the way to socialism and then to Communism. This
notion is so compelling that it helps us to understand the hope borne by
the Communist idea at the beginning of the century, though we may
thereby risk underestimating or even trivializing the ultimate catastrophe. Fascism fits completely into its own demise, whereas Communism

retains some of the charm of its beginnings: a paradox explicable by the so-called march of history—another name for historical necessity—which takes the place of religion for those who have no religion and is thus so difficult, so painful, to let go of. That, however, is precisely what we must do in order to understand the twentieth century.

The idea of historical necessity gained currency because the duel between Fascism and Communism, permeating it with tragic turmoil, lent it the perfect cover: World War II would assume the role of arbitrator between the two forces that were competing for the succession to bourgeois democracy, the force of reaction and the force of progress, the force of the past and the force of the future. But this vision disintegrated with the demise of the second contender following upon that of the first. Neither Fascism nor Communism turned out to be the ensign of a providential destiny for humanity. They were merely brief episodes, framed by what they had sought to destroy. Produced by democracy, they were interred by democracy. There was nothing necessary about them, and the history of the twentieth century, like that of the eighteenth and nineteenth, could have taken a different course: we need only imagine it without Lenin, Hitler, or Stalin. A true understanding of our time is possible only when we free ourselves from the illusion of necessity: the only way to explain the twentieth century, to the extent an explanation is possible, is to reassert its unpredictable character, an attribute denied it by those most responsible for its tragedies.

What I am seeking to understand in this essay is at once circumscribed and central: What was the role of ideological passions, especially the Communist passion? For those passions were unique to the twentieth century. Not that earlier centuries were ignorant of ideologies; the French Revolution demonstrated their hold over the people, and in the nineteenth century an abundance of world-historical systems were invented or espoused that offered global explanations of destiny in place of divine intervention. Until the twentieth century, however, there were no ideological governments or regimes, although Robespierre in the spring of 1794, with his plan for the Festival of the Supreme Being and the Terror, was not far from such a thing. But even Robespierre's attempt was short-lived; his motivation, moreover, was religious, whereas in the present essay we shall be considering ideologies as systems for explaining the world in which the political actions of human beings have a providential character to the exclusion of divine intervention. In this context, both Hitler and Lenin founded regimes that had no precedent.

Those regimes elicited not just interest but enthusiasm from a segment of post–World War I Europe, not only from the popular masses but also from the educated classes, regardless of the crudeness of the ideas or arguments involved. In this respect, National Socialism—that fuzzy, autodidactic amalgam—was unbeatable; Leninism had at least a philosophical pedigree. Nonetheless, even National Socialism, not to mention the Fascism of Mussolini, counted among the intellectuals clustered around its monstrous cradle some of the great minds of the century—Heidegger for one. What, then, can we say of Marxism-Leninism, which enjoyed hereditary privilege and was watched over from birth to death by numerous philosophers and writers? The latter, it is true, provided only intermittent support, depending on the state of international affairs and the vicissitudes of Comintern policy. Yet if we were to put together all the famous European authors who, at one time or another during the twentieth century, were Communists or pro-Communists, we could constitute a Who's Who of philosophy and literature. To measure the hold of Fascism and Communism over intellectuals in a country such as France, for example—the venerable European homeland of literature—we need only turn to the *Nouvelle Revue Française*, which set the literary tone of the interwar years with Drieu, Céline, and Jouhandeau on the one hand, and Gide, Aragon, and Malraux on the other.

What is surprising is not that certain intellectuals should share the spirit of the times, but that they should fall prey to it, without making any attempt to mark it with their particular stamp. For example, the majority of nineteenth-century French writers, especially of the Romantic generation, were involved in politics, often as *députés* and sometimes as government ministers; yet they remained independent and for that very reason were generally beyond political classification. In contrast, twentieth-century French writers aligned themselves with parties, especially radical ones hostile to democracy. They always played the same (provisional) role as supernumeraries, were manipulated as one man, and were sacrificed, when necessary, to the will of the party. So we are bound to wonder what it was that made those two ideologies so alluring, that gave them an attraction so general and yet so mysterious. It is easier to imagine why a German survivor of Verdun or an anti-Communist bourgeois from Berlin would be touched by one of Hitler's speeches than to understand how that speech would have resonance for Heidegger or Céline. With respect to Communism we find the same thing: the sociology of voting behavior, where such studies have been possible, tells us which milieus were receptive to Leninist ideas but not why those ideas exerted a universal charm. Fascism and Communism owed much of their success to circumstance, that is, to luck: What if Lenin had been detained in Switzerland in 1917 or if Hitler had failed in his bid for chancellor in 1933? Yet the diffusion of these ideologies would have occurred regardless of the political success of their creators or the particular circumstances that brought them to power. That is the unprecedented aspect of ideological politics; the mystery is how it came to take root in people's minds. In a century divided between the theological and the political, the greatest enigma is how this intellectual mishmash could have evoked such strong sentiments and nourished so many individual fantasies.

Rather than make an inventory of this hodgepodge of dead ideas, we should take as our starting point the passions that fueled it. Of all those passions—spawned by modern democracy and bent on destroying the hand that fed them—the oldest, the most constant, the most powerful is hatred of the bourgeoisie. It can be found throughout the nineteenth century before reaching its apogee in our time when the bourgeoisie, under its various names, would provide a scapegoat for all the calamities of the world for both Lenin and Hitler. The bourgeoisie incarnated capitalism, the forerunner (for Lenin) of Fascism and imperialism and (for Hitler) of Communism, which were the origins, respectively, of all they detested. Sufficiently abstract to contain many symbols, sufficiently concrete to offer a convenient object of hatred, the bourgeoisie furnished both Bolshevism and Fascism with their negative pole, along with a supporting complement of older traditions and sentiments. It is an old, old story, as old as modern society itself.

The bourgeoisie is a synonym for modern society. The word designates the class that gradually destroyed, by its free activity, the old aristocratic society founded on a hierarchy of birth. It cannot be defined in political terms, like the "citizen" of classical antiquity or the "feudal lord." The citizen merely held the right to participate in the debates of the City, and the feudal lord was assigned a very precise measure of domination and subordination, which defined his place in the hierarchy of mutual dependencies. The bourgeoisie, however, has no assigned place in the political order, in other words, the community. The bourgeoisie is defined entirely by economics—a category it invented itself with its emergence in the world—in its relation to nature, labor, and the accumulation of riches. The bourgeoisie is a class without status, without a definite tradition, without established outlines; its title to dominate is owed to a single, fragile thing: wealth. Wealth is fragile because it can belong to anyone, and the rich man could as easily have been poor as the poor man rich.

As a social category defined by economics, the bourgeoisie is actually the bearer of universal values. Labor no longer defines only slaves, as in classical times, or commoners, as in aristocracies, but all of humanity.

Labor is the possession of even the most elementary of humans, the individual in primal nudity faced with nature. It is predicated on the notion of fundamental liberty for all individuals in equal amounts for all—the freedom to improve one's lot by increasing one's property and wealth. Members of the bourgeoisie thus conceive of themselves as liberated from religious or political traditions and as undefined as are all men who are free and have the same rights as all others. What concerns them is the future, for they are obliged to invent themselves along with the community to which they belong.

The social existence of these new historical actors is problematical. Here they are, brandishing liberty, equality, and the rights of man—in short, the idea of individual autonomy, in opposition to all earlier societies based on dependence. What new means of association do they have to offer? A society that implicates only the smallest part of their life, since its principal duty is to guarantee for its members the free exercise of private activity and the enjoyment of the things they have acquired. Everything else is up to them: those members may practice the religion of their choice, hold their own conceptions of good and evil, and pursue the pleasures and particular objectives they choose for their existences as long as they respect the terms of the minimal contract that binds them to their fellow citizens. Thus bourgeois society is by definition detached from the notion of the common good. Bourgeois are individuals separated from their counterparts, confined to their own property and interests.

Separated, confined, they become only more so because their constant obsession is to increase the distance between themselves and others. What does growing rich mean if not growing richer than one's neighbor? In a world where no position is determined in advance or acquired in perpetuity, anxiety about the future stirs in every breast and finds no lasting relief. The only repose for the unquiet mind lies in comparing oneself with others, in evaluating oneself through the admiration, envy, or jealousy of others. Rousseau and Tocqueville are the most profound analysts of this democratic passion, the great theme of modern literature. But even that repose is precarious, based as it is on provisional situations and constantly menaced; so even the mind at rest must constantly seek reassurance in the increase of wealth and prestige.

Bourgeois society is thus animated by a corpuscular agitation, constantly driving it forward. Yet this agitation tends to deepen the contradictions inherent in that society's very existence; for not only does the bourgeoisie consist of associates who care little for the public interest, but the idea of the universality and equality of man, which it claims as its foundation and is its primary innovation, is constantly negated by the inequality of property and wealth produced by the competition of its members. Its development belies its principle, and its dynamic undercuts its legitimacy. It produces inequality unceasingly—more material inequality than any other known form of society—while proclaiming equality as an inalienable right of man. In earlier societies, inequality held a legitimate status, assigned by nature, tradition, or providence. In bourgeois society, inequality is an idea that circulates sub rosa in contradiction with the way individuals view themselves; it nevertheless pervades the environment in which they live and in the passions it sustains. The bourgeoisie did not invent the division of society into classes, but by cloaking that division in an ideology that renders it illegitimate, they tinged it with suffering.

And that is why, in this context, the City is so difficult to constitute and, once constituted, so fragile and unstable. The modern bourgeois, unlike the citizen of antiquity, is not bound to a particular country. No lasting status, as was possessed by the aristocratic lord, is to be found at the crossroads of the social and the political. The bourgeois is rich but is thereby guaranteed no definite place in the community—if we can even describe as "community" that degraded place of coexistence, which is nothing more than an accidental product of the movement of society. Deprived of an extrahuman foundation, cut off from its ontological dimension, allotted a secondary role in relation to the social sphere and henceforth furnished with limited attributions, the bourgeois City is a problematical entity. If all men are equal, how is it that they do not all participate equally in sovereignty over themselves? But how can that sovereignty be organized? How can it contain millions of people if not by proxy? Why should the illiterate and the poor, those who are incapable of conceiving of or exercising free will, be let in? How do we "represent" society? What powers should we grant to the representatives placed in different groups by the will of their members? And so on. We shall never be done with all the questions and impasses inseparable from the political constitution of bourgeois society, for to do so we would have to review the entire history of Europe from the eighteenth century on. In the present context, let us focus on the origin of the problem, since its effects have been as visible as ever throughout the twentieth century.

For even though bourgeois society, after an enormous effort, has been constituted as a political will, it is still not at the end of its odyssey. Deprived of a legitimate ruling class, organized by delegation, made up of diverse powers, centered on interests, subject to violent and petty passions, it comprises many of the conditions for the emergence of mediocre and multiple leaders, demagogic agendas, and fruitless agitation.

Its dynamic is the contradiction between the division of labor—the secret of its wealth—and equality, the motto that is engraved upon the pediments of its public buildings. Together, those two elements constitute its reality; it is man's relationship to nature through labor that defines the universality of man. At the same time, however, labor, that historical and social reality, happens to be the curse of the proletariat, which is exploited by a bourgeoisie that accumulates wealth at its expense. If the promise of universality is to be fulfilled, that curse must be broken. And so the idea of equality functions for bourgeois society like an imaginary horizon: by definition unattainable but in constant demand and unceasingly brandished as a denunciation of that society; a horizon which, furthermore, retreats as equality progresses, and is thus ensured infinite utility. The bourgeois' misfortune is not only that the individual is divided within himself but that he offers up one side of himself to the critical scrutiny of the other.

Indeed, does the bourgeois—that concept so dear to all those who detest it—truly exist as someone who belongs to a class possessed of self-consciousness, as the demiurge of modern society? Essentially defined by economics, the bourgeois is but a cog in the machine—a machine that takes its heroes from just about anywhere so that they are easily replaceable. Capitalism was less the creation of a class than of a society in the broadest sense of the term. Its quintessential homeland, the United States, never had a bourgeoisie but did have a bourgeois people, which is quite different. What was very consciously bourgeois about modern France, on the other hand, can largely be explained by political and cultural reaction. The demise of the aristocracy, a demise felt by the entire nation, was not sufficient to constitute a bourgeoisie. That was brought about by the French Revolution, which was not the daughter but the mother of the bourgeoisie: for the whole of the nineteenth century, those in power worried about 1793 starting up again, a ghost that fueled their fear of the popular classes and of republican and socialist ideas. Nonetheless, the French bourgeoisie, which distinguished itself so passionately both from the top and the bottom of society, justifying as nowhere else its designation as the "middle class," had no particular economic project: it disliked the aristocracy but tried to imitate it. It feared the people but shared its inclination to go on living as before. The American people were possessed by the capitalist spirit without ever having had a bourgeoisie; French political society, in contrast, created a bourgeoisie devoid of the capitalist spirit.

The words "bourgeois" and "bourgeoisie" need to be clearly defined. For if they are meant to signify all the things that contribute to the novelty and contradictions of modern society, they ought to be replaced by more general terms that do not automatically posit explanations but that constitute, rather, observations of the new condition of social man in the modern era. All the great minds of Europe in the late eighteenth and early nineteenth centuries were conscious of the arrival of an unprecedented period of history. Depending on their personal perspectives, they called it by different names: the Scots called it "commercial society"; for Hegel, it was the "end of history"; for Tocqueville, it was "democracy." But if Guizot, by putting the bourgeoisie at the center of the definition of modernity, furnished what was to become the most commonly used interpretation, it was not only because Marx would adopt it. It was because he, like Marx—the bourgeois like the "proletarian"—supplied the generations to come with a hero and a villain.

What is so compelling about their reconstruction of the European miracle in terms of the role played by the bourgeoisie is that in their version history has not only a meaning but an agent. That agent was celebrated by Guizot and "critiqued" by Marx but in both cases dominated the scene with its presence, filling it with its collective will. Guizot put an end to class struggle in the name of the bourgeoisie, and Marx pursued it in the name of the proletariat: in this way the conditions and the necessity of their action were personified. Class struggle marked out a huge field wherein the laws of history providentially found their way into wills and passions. Simultaneously, the bourgeois, that deus ex machina of modern society, was seen to incarnate the lie of modern society. The bourgeois offered democratic politics just what it needed—an accountable party or a scapegoat, arriving just in time to portray the force of evil. Celebrated as such by Guizot, the bourgeois could be incriminated by Marx. In fact, the nineteenth century did not even wait for Marx to do so: hatred of the bourgeois was born with the bourgeois.

At first, of course, hatred for the bourgeois was fueled from without, by reference to the old society, which was still quite recent. It came either from partisans of what the French revolutionaries called the ancien régime or from people who, while realizing that history could not be turned back, were nostalgic for the lost world of their childhood. Bonald and Chateaubriand provide an example: the former hated those responsible for the revolutionary destruction, the latter, though he knew they had won, did not like them much either, because he believed they would be incapable of attaining true grandeur—the grandeur of aristocratic times. But both, like many Romantic writers, criticized the bourgeoisie by comparison to what came before it.

The French Revolution, however, had already illustrated the power of a similar though different critique, or passion, aimed at the same adversary but from a different source: the denunciation of the bourgeois from within the bourgeoisie. The revolutionaries had cherished and proclaimed equality for all the French while depriving a great many of them of the right to vote or to run for office. They cherished and proclaimed liberty and yet maintained slavery in their colonies in the Antilles and elsewhere in the name of national commercial prosperity. Those who followed them made use of the timidity or inconsistency of their predecessors in an attempt to carry the Revolution forward in the name of true equality, only to discover ever mounting stakes inherent in the very principle of democracy. If people had to consider one another as equals, what were the poor to think of the rich, the workers of the bourgeois, and the poorest of the less poor? The Jacobins of 1793 were bourgeois partisans of the liberty of production, that is, the market economy, while remaining revolutionaries hostile to the inequality of wealth produced by the market. Using the vocabulary of the old world to denounce the new, they attacked what they called the "aristocracy of wealth." For if democratic inequality keeps reviving aristocratic inequality, why bother to vanquish the ancien régime?

It was this margin of doubt that lent the French Revolution its uncontrollable and unending aspect, distinguishing it from the American Revolution to such an extent that one hesitates to apply the same word to the two events. Both, nonetheless, were animated by the same ideas and comparable passions; they can almost be said to have founded modern democratic civilization simultaneously. Yet the American Revolution concluded in the development and ratification of a constitution that has lasted to this day and has become the sacred ark of American citizenship. The French Revolution produced a multiplicity of constitutions and regimes and gave the world its first look at egalitarian despotism. It gave lasting life to the concept of revolution defined not as a passage from one regime to another—an interlude between two worlds—but as a political culture inseparable from democracy and, like democracy, inexhaustible, with no legal or constitutional limit because it is fueled by the passion for equality which, by definition, has no threshold of satisfaction.

Tocqueville believed that the violence of that passion during the French Revolution remained linked to what the revolutionaries sought to overturn, and that the bourgeois were hated so excessively because they were the unwitting heirs to aristocratic arrogance. The Americans, having never had an ancien régime to vanquish, loved equality as something they had always enjoyed, whereas the French, having once seized hold of equality, were wary of losing it and worshiped it to the exclusion of all else because the specter of the aristocracy continued to lurk behind the spectacle of wealth. Profound and true as Tocqueville's analysis of the two peoples and the two revolutions at the end of the eighteenth century is, it must not lead us to underestimate the strong similarity between the two countries' passions for equality. At the end of the twentieth century, the critique of democracy in the name of democracy is no less obsessive in the United States than in France or elsewhere in Europe. Far from the American version of consensual equality's having informed the Europeans, it seems that the French revolutionaries' obsession with equality seems to have taken over American society.

But the Americans have never used hatred of the bourgeois to fan that originating passion of modern democracy; it has played only a minimal role in their political confrontations, which have played out in other areas and with other symbols. European politics, on the other hand, has been pervaded by hatred of the bourgeois throughout the nineteenth and twentieth centuries. The bourgeois have provided a common quarry for all of modernity's malcontents—those who incriminate the mediocrity of the bourgeois world, as well as those who denounce its lies. French literature, especially during the fifty years following the Revolution, is full of hatred for the bourgeois from both the Left and the Right, from conservatives to social-democrats, from religious believer to philosophers of history. From the religious point of view, the bourgeois are phonies who pretend to be liberated from God and tradition, emancipated from everything, yet remain slaves to their own self-interest. They are citizens of the world but ferocious egotists in their homeland; they are concerned with the future of humanity but are obsessed with immediate pleasures. Up front, they are all sincerity; in their hearts, false. Socialists would agree with this appraisal but—believing as they do in class-free universalism—would add that the bourgeois are unfaithful to their own principles by refusing to grant universal suffrage and thereby betraying the Declaration of the Rights of Man.

Let us not jump to the conclusion that the socialist is a more advanced democrat than the liberal. That type of argument, so often enlisted today to patch up the leaking boat of socialism, is based on an error or a contradiction. For liberals and democrats share the same philosophical world; the socialist critique knows it and so takes aim at both of them. Nineteenth-century bourgeois might refuse to grant universal suffrage, but in doing so they went beyond the limits of their own principles, which they would eventually abandon in any case. What the socialists, from Buchez to the young Marx, criticized about the bourgeois world was the very idea of the rights of man as a subjective foundation of society; they regarded it as a mere cover for the individualism governing capitalist economy. The problem was that capitalism and modern liberty were both subject to the same rule, that of the freedom—

or plurality—of ideas, opinions, pleasures, and interests. Liberals and democrats held that rule in common because it was part of their conceptual foundation; reactionaries and socialists impugned it in the name of humanity's lost unity. In the nineteenth century, it was not unusual for writers who had started out as members of the extreme Right, like Lamennais, to end up on the extreme Left, or for socialist philosophers like Buchez to mix Catholicism with a messianic philosophy of history. For those who would combat the curse of the bourgeois rift, any cultural materials will do. Rousseau's question, revitalized by the immediacy of the revolutionary experience, was on the minds of philosophers on the Right and on the Left and is as pervasive in Bonald as in Louis Blanc: if we are all mere individuals, what sort of society can we hope to form?

What I want to do here is not so much to analyze concepts as to bring a particular sensibility and outlook back to life. In the nineteenth century, people strongly believed that modern liberal democracy was threatening society with dissolution because it atomized individuals, made them indifferent to the public interest, weakened authority, and encouraged class hatred. This was especially true of the French—even more so than the English—because they were the offspring of the absolute individualism instituted on 4 August 1789 and the survivors of a popular revolution that they had only managed to put an end to, and provisionally at that, by setting up a regime even more despotic than the old monarchy. The French never celebrated Utilitarianism as a philosophical guarantee of the social bond; so the bourgeois, in France and elsewhere in Europe, if they were truly property owners, also feared revolution. They shared the fears of their enemies and oriented themselves accordingly. They were particularly worried about a new outbreak of disorder because at that time Europe was more fascinated by the French political experience than by the English constitutional miracle, as we can see by the spread of the revolutionary idea and the way it flared up in 1830 and 1848. And so their contemporaries heaped scorn upon the bourgeois. Their class was represented by Balzac's parvenu, by Stendhal's *coquin*, and by Marx's "philistine." Children of a colossal event, they continued to intimidate its victims and fascinate those who wished to prolong it although the bourgeois themselves were too fearful to assume its heritage. What was great about their past underlined the griefs of their present.

So the bourgeois, transformed by fear, became traditionalists—a negation of themselves which, for all that, failed to endow them with a tradition. They detested revolution, while owing it everything. Aside from revolution, they had only the traditions of others, those of the aristocracy or the monarchy, which always looked bogus when assumed by the bourgeois. They had renounced their historical titles and had no others. At the same time, they had ceased to incarnate liberty and had become authoritarian, tyrannical patriarchs, obsessed with their own comfort and property, as illustrated by Henri Brulard's Chérubin Beyle, described by his son as a combination of aristocratic ego and Jacobin fraternity. In short, all the bourgeois' creations turned against them. They had raised themselves up with money, which enabled them to dissolve the aristocratic "ranks" from within; but that egalitarian tool had transformed them into aristocrats of a new kind, prisoners to their wealth even more than the aristocrats had been to their origins. Possessed of the Rights of Man from the very beginning, they were scared of the idea of liberty and even more so of equality. They had fathered democracy, by virtue of which each person is the equal of all others and is associated with them in the construction of society, and each person, in obeying the law, obeys only himself. But democracy had revealed the fragility of its governments while revealing the danger of numbers, that is, the poor. And so we find the bourgeois quieter than ever about the principles of 1789, which were responsible for their own sensational entrance onto the scene of history.

If the bourgeois epitomize denial, it is because they sprang from a lie. Far from incarnating what is universal, they have but one obsession, their own interests, and one symbol, money. Money is the principal reason they are hated. It is money that unites against them the prejudices of the aristocrats, the jealousy of the poor, the contempt of the intellectuals, the past and the present, and expels them from the future. The source of the bourgeois' power over society also explains their insignificance: a king is infinitely greater than his person, aristocrats owe their prestige to a past more distant than they, socialists preach struggle for a world beyond their lifetime. But the wealthy are merely what they are, rich, and that is all. Money does not testify to their virtue or even to their labors as in the Puritan version; at best, they acquired it by chance, and if their luck turned, they could lose it tomorrow; at worst, they gained it through the labor of others, by miserliness or cupidity, if not both. Money drives a wedge between the bourgeois and their fellows, without bringing that minimum of consideration which would allow them to govern peacefully. The moment when the consent of the governed becomes explicitly necessary to government is the moment when that consent becomes the most difficult to garner.

Nothing better illustrates the moral deficit that afflicts the bourgeoisie from all sides than its aesthetic debasement. In the nineteenth century, the bourgeois began their great career as the antithesis of the artists: they were seen as petty, ugly, miserly, laborious, and stick-in-the-muds, while artists were characterized as great, beautiful, generous, brilliant, and bohemian. Money twisted and lowered the soul, whereas contempt for money elevated the soul to the great things of life; this was a conviction held not only by the "revolutionary" artist or writer but also by the conservative or the reactionary—not just Stendhal, but Flaubert; not just Heine, but Hölderlin. Lamartine remained convinced of this not only when he was a Legitimist but also after becoming a Republican. Virtually everywhere in European culture, the bourgeois were on the receiving end of that mixture of contempt and hatred which was the price to be paid for the very nature of their being and for the manner in which they had entered the political scene. On the one hand, they stood naked in the face of nature, possessing only their productive work in the guise of art and applying their whole being to their utilitarian project without a thought for the beauty of the things they destroyed or created. On the other hand, at least in France, they had overthrown the aristocracy by revolution and had begun their reign with éclat, which could constitute grounds for redemption. But it so quickly became obvious that the bourgeois were incapable of managing the democratic annunciation of 1789 that the revolutionary idea passed to their adversaries. They had exposed their true ambition, which was to institute a market, not a citizenry. And so they would incarnate only the bad part of modernity: they would symbolize capitalism but not democracy.

The bourgeois' dissociation with democracy, however, was neither inevitable nor automatic. The liberty to produce, to buy, and to sell are part and parcel of liberty itself and are affirmed as such when set against the shackles and privileges of the feudal era. The contractual equality of individuals is just as indispensable to the existence of a market as is individual physical and moral autonomy. Nor were these two facets of modern society dissociated in the most democratic culture ever produced by Europe—its American branch. There, free enterprise and human freedom and equality are viewed as both inseparable and complementary. And that dissociation has nothing to do with the progress or the objective drawbacks of the capitalist economy: it would receive its classical and extreme form very early in the nineteenth century in France and Germany, the two countries in which goods continued to be produced according to methods traditional in comparison to those of the burgeoning industrial capitalism in England. In France and Germany, intellectual life was more effervescent than the economy, and the revolution of 1789 had left more permanent and far-reaching traces than in England. The radical critique of the bourgeois would emerge from the flowering of the socialist idea in France and from the left-wing Hegelianism that produced Marx. This is where the evil nature of the bourgeois was revealed, eliciting opprobrium for the following two centuries.

One might be led to believe that, in the virulent denunciation of capitalism's crimes and nature, capitalism itself was less at issue than was the egalitarian radicalism of the French Revolution. In the history of Europe, circumstances were such (and in this anodyne phrase we catch a glimpse of the central mystery of the French Revolution) that the sudden collapse of the largest monarchy and the extraordinary appearance of a new regime followed upon the gradual emergence of a middle class situated somewhere between the nobility and the people. *Post hoc, propter hoc:* credited with an almost divine power by an era that henceforth would need to explain all events by volition, the bourgeoisie would continuously defeat the expectations inseparable from the future it promised. The course of the Revolution had already forced the bourgeoisie to give in—first to Robespierre and then to Bonaparte. The nineteenth century sent it back to its antlike labors amid more memories than it could handle. The era had offered it the role it was least capable of assuming—that of a political class.

Born of democracy, prospering within it, hatred of the bourgeois was only in appearance hatred of the other: it was in fact self-hatred.

So it appears that this society of individuals devoted to pursuing their own interests and pleasures received its political form from without, as a fatal consequence of the inequality of wealth that developed within the society. Class struggle set the rich against the poor, the haves against the have nots, those who profited from bourgeois society against those who survived on its margins, bourgeois against proletarians. This antagonism, though perceived to differing degrees by the various parties, was significant enough to structure the entire political life of the society. Through the poverty or the anger of the workers, as through the former rebuffs of the nobility, hatred of the bourgeoisie received its rational foundation from without.

That sentiment was also fueled, especially in its most violent manifestations, by internal sources, which could be found almost everywhere, even among writers, such as Stendhal, who were neither aristocrats nor socialists. Hatred of the bourgeoisie often provoked conflicts within families—the son's rebellion against his father in the name of liberty as opposed to nature. Its mainspring lay within the bourgeois universe, lodged in the elements that made that universe contradictory. The antibourgeois passion harbored at its core the bourgeois' constant remorse, or their guilty conscience.

How, then, could the bourgeois find peace? They defeated the aristocrats not by wealth alone but by buttressing themselves against the massive stirring of conscience. Many young nobles joined forces with the bourgeois to put an end to the ancien régime because they thought that the idea of universal man, emancipated by reason from centuries of predestination, was both intellectually and morally superior to the voice of tradition. And now where should we find the bourgeois but engaged in a pitched battle with the result of belief in the universality of man. Liberty, equality: unlimited promises that proved problematic as soon as anyone attempted to apply them to society, though this difficulty did not in the least diminish the people's enthusiasm for them. For such abstract promises create an unbridgeable gap between people's expectations and what the society can actually offer them. They kill off, ipso facto, any debate or agreement on the limits of democracy. They nullify the very concept that would have implied a closed future and satisfied participants.

The bourgeois are condemned to live in this open system, which gives rise to contradictory and powerful passions. They are caught between calculating egotism, by which they become wealthy, and compassion, which identifies them with the human race or at least with their fellow citizens; between a desire to be equal and thus like everyone else, and an obsession with difference, which spurs them to pursue even the tiniest distinction; and between fraternity, the horizon of a history of humanity, and envy, an essential part of their psychological makeup. Rousseau explored the two poles of this condition by considering solitude in nature and the democratic logic of the *Social Contract*. But the bourgeois must be content to live in that limbo where one half of a person hates the other half, and where being a good citizen means being a bad bourgeois and vice-versa.

The worst thing about being a bourgeois is being aware of one's misfortune and ceaselessly examining and exposing it in the feverish quest for "self"—the center of the universe but a center possessed of no certainty in its position in the world or in its relationship with the surrounding monads. Autonomous, that self must fashion itself, but to what end? It knows only an endless division which, although it has produced the great literary theme of the era, has done little to reveal the secrets of good government or the path to a reconciliation with itself. Members of the bourgeoisie know neither how to organize their public life nor how to attain inner peace: class struggle and identity crises are part of their destiny. Waving the flag of universality, they also harbor doubts about the truth of what they proclaim, for in part of they believe that their adversaries are right, since the latter speak in the name of the bourgeois' own principles.

Self-doubt has led to a characteristic of modern democracy probably unique in universal history: the infinite capacity to produce offspring who detest the social and political regime into which they were born—hating the very air they breathe, though they cannot survive without it and have known no other. I am not speaking of those who, the morning after a democratic revolution, are nostalgic for the world of their childhood and cling to the memories and customs of that time. What I have in mind is the political passion that constitutes democracy itself, the moral upping of the ante of fidelity to principles that makes just about everyone in modern society, including the bourgeois themselves, an enemy of the bourgeois. The fundamental motif of modern society is not, as Marx believed, the struggle of workers against bourgeois; for if the workers' sole aspiration is to become bourgeois, that struggle is simply part of the general evolution of democracy. Much more important is bourgeois self-hatred, and the rent within them that turns them against what they are: all-powerful in economic terms, in control of things but without legitimate power over others and devoid of moral unity deep down inside. They are creators of unprecedented wealth, but scapegoat of democratic politics; multiplying monuments to their technical genius they betray their political infirmity. The twentieth century would bring all of this to light.

The contrast between the ways hatred of the bourgeois was expressed in the nineteenth century and in the twentieth century is similar to the contrast mentioned earlier in relation to other sentiments or democratic notions. What was manageable in the nineteenth century went out of control in the twentieth. The ingredients of the antibourgeois passion were visible in European culture and politics from the beginning of the nineteenth century, and even earlier if we think of Rousseau. The French Jacobins of 1793, who were supposed to inaugurate the reign of the bourgeoisie, provide the first massive example of bourgeois who detest bourgeois in the name of bourgeois principles; if they were so admired and imitated by the European Left in the following century, it was because they had lent an unforgettable form to the destruction of the bourgeois spirit.

Nonetheless, throughout the nineteenth century, the aristocracy—yesterday's adversary—retained a vestigial splendor: it was Bismarck who unified Germany and Cavour who unified Italy. The monarchs and nobles of Europe largely maintained control of the course of events, while fearing their consequences. Even in France, where the old society had been legally destroyed from top to bottom and civil equality irreversibly instituted on 4 August 1789, the nobility made out very well after the fall of Napoleon. It reigned over polite society and assumed an important role in the national government even after 1830. A degraded version of what classical political thought termed mixed government would take root all over nineteenth-century Europe, with shares going to the monarchy, to the aristocracy, and to democracy. In that hybrid political state, antibourgeois passion was bounded.

The aristocrats disliked the bourgeois, who heralded a world of money and social disorder, but they had witnessed the collapse of one kind of world and realized they had arrived in the bourgeois world and could not turn back. And although the counterrevolutionary idea afforded them an asylum for their memories and a literature for their nostalgia, they would never adopt it as their agenda, in spite of their energetic nature. Because of their excessive hatred of the bourgeois, they forbade themselves a role in public affairs, or, worse still, they shared some of the Jacobins' sentiments and played the Republicans' game, as Chateaubriand tended to do after 1830. And so the survivors of the old world were best off reining in their contempt for the bourgeois in the social life of the new. True to their customs, they easily conserved the mastery of manners that compelled the bourgeois to bow before their past. Subject, however, like all of their contemporaries, to the new god of historical necessity, they adjusted their political activity to the spirit of the times. In sum, the reason the nineteenth century aristocracy was not counterrevolutionary was that it feared revolution.

This is precisely why the bourgeois were political moderates: they could measure the difficulties of their own government by the standard of 1789. They understood the dangers of their historical situation, inherent both in their own preponderance and in the promises of democratic equality. Opting for the happy medium, they resigned themselves to the arrogance of the nobility and the risks of the monarchy in order to govern the people under their wing. Their political pusillanimity, which so exasperated Marx, stemmed from their incapacity—of which they were well aware—to master the forces they had unleashed. On the one hand, that pusillanimity fanned the antibourgeois passion by negating the revolutionary tradition: taking refuge in a mediocre wisdom of petty sentiments, the French bourgeois were all the more hateful because their fathers had participated in 1789 or 1793. On the other hand, it ensured that they remain vigilant to the dangers of the revolutionary tradition, kept them constantly alert to the uncertain "governability" of democratic societies, and led them to reign by proxy in order to avoid the hazards intrinsic to democratic politics.

Nineteenth-century politics, then, were dominated by constant compromise between two worlds, exorcising the thunderclap that had marked the fall of the French ancien régime. The bourgeois were snubbed by the aristocrats, yet governed with or through them. Despite becoming the butt of literature and art, they had thus far experienced only the aggression of their sons. They lived in fear of the masses, but there was in fact more to fear from those like themselves than from the people. Although democratic ideas were gradually penetrating the century, becoming increasingly entrenched, it was not yet a democratic age, and the masses still played a minor role, limited to the repertoire written by the elites. The antibourgeois script, when aristocratic, pertained more to literature than to politics and, when socialist, more to the history of ideas than to social subversion. This scenario is illustrated by the failure of the 1848 revolutions in Europe.

The situation would change rapidly at the end of the nineteenth century. Neither the development of nationalism, nor the explosion of "democratic" anti-Semitism, nor the rise of mass parties like the German Social Democrats makes any sense unless we see such movements as signaling an unprecedented integration of the popular masses into the politics of modern states. But it is only after World War I that we can truly take the measure of that phenomenon.

Time gradually eroded the distance between the bourgeoisie and the aristocracy and brought ideas, tastes, and even life-styles closer together. The cult of the nation, revealed by the war as extraordinarily powerful, welded the two groups together into one common political will, though at the very moment when, by virtue of its course and its conclusion, the war also reawakened a formidable enthusiasm for the idea of revolution. Not only did the war give power in Russia to the Bolsheviks, thus finally allowing them to emerge as successors to the Jacobins and the Paris Commune, but, on the right as well, it opened up a vast new arena for antibourgeois passion by emancipating it from aristocratic tutelage. In frustrated Italy and defeated Germany, that passion was no longer the monopoly of nostalgic or residual classes. Draped in the flag of a nation fallen prey to misfortune, it was passed on to the people—hatred of democracy had become democratic, and it would be taken up by actors new to the public scene: Mussolini and Hitler.

What was new about the political situation in Europe created by the war was the sudden resumption of the revolutionary passion believed extinguished by the nineteenth century. Even on the left, even within the ranks of socialist partisans, even among the Marxists, the idea of revolution had lost its teeth prior to World War I. Blanquism was all but dead in France; in Germany, Social Democracy, once the guiding light of the workers' movement and a Marxist bastion, directed all its energies toward ripening the conditions for the overthrow of the capitalist economy. Neither Jaurès nor Kautsky was still waiting for the "great event"; this, however, was the very idea of revolution revived by the Bolsheviks when they seized power in Russia. Improbable as it was, their success underlined the Bolsheviks' audacity and the force of their will; its extraordinary character emphasized its universal potential.

The most surprising thing about the situation born of the war was that the revolutionary idea was taken up on the right, where traditionally it had met only with hostility. In nineteenth-century Europe, the Right had always detested revolution, first as a plot, then as something inevitable, and finally as a threat. It liked neither those who had desired revolution, nor the air of necessity ascribed to it, nor the fragility attributed to it once the social order had been reestablished. As we have seen, even if the Right was antirevolutionary in spirit, it was generally not counterrevolutionary politically—a counterrevolution would still be a revolution, though moving in the opposite direction. This dual moral position enabled the old nobility to join conservative and even liberal parties, while simultaneously reducing the Right's hostility to the bourgeoisie.

At the very end of World War I, however, antibourgeois sentiment had spread to the Right, growing all the more violent when, instead of being handled with the aristocratic prudence that had characterized it in the preceding century, it was taken up by those who had risen through the ranks in the name of equality and the nation. Like the antibourgeois passion of the Left, that of the Right had become democratized. It had been passed to the people. It was fueled by the antibourgeois passion of the Left, reacted against it, outbid it, and was inseparable from it. The counterrevolutionary idea had been freed from its marriage to the aristocracy; its consequences had been made explicit; it too bore the seeds of revolution.

The subsequent events provide us with a good chronological starting-point: Bolshevism and Fascism are the children of World War I. Although Lenin had already developed his political ideas at the dawn of the century, and many of the components that would eventually form Fascist ideology predated the war, it was the war that enabled the Bolshevik Party to take power in 1917, and Mussolini and Hitler would form their parties in the years immediately following 1918 in response to the national crises produced by that conflict. World War I entirely transformed European life—its borders, its regimes, even its ways of thinking and its mores. It plowed so deeply into the most brilliant of modern civilizations that it left nothing unchanged. It marked the beginning of Western civilization's decline as the center of world power, even as it ushered in the cruel century from which we are now emerging, filled with the suicidal violence of its nations and regimes.

Like any important event, World War I revealed as much about the events that preceded it as it did about the actors—in this case, the monsters—of the future. It is very difficult for us now to imagine what was manifest at the time: today's teenagers cannot even conceive of the national passions that led the peoples of Europe to kill each other for four full years. Through their grandparents, young people may retain a link with that time, but its secrets are lost to them; neither the suffering undergone nor the emotions that justified it make any sense; nor does what was noble or passive about that suffering and those emotions speak to young people's hearts or minds in the same way that even a second-hand memory might do. Historians seeking to reconstruct that extinct world are hardly better equipped. Can pre–1914 Europe really have been the Europe that produced the war? It seemed so civilized and homogeneous compared to the rest of the world that the conflict set off by the assassination in Sarajevo seems almost absurd: a civil war, yet waged between sovereign states in the name of nationalistic passions. This is perhaps why the twentieth century's first war, to the extent that it caused an enormous break with what preceded it, remains one of the most enigmatic events of modern history. Its character cannot be adduced from the era in which it began, and even less can its consequences. That is what distinguishes it from World War II, which was all but inherent in the circumstances and regimes of Europe in the 1930s and was thus filled with that sad, tenacious echo which would extend it right up to the fall of the Berlin wall—in other words, up to our time. We have a complete picture of the causes and consequences of World War II, which has been the fabric of our existence; but World War I exists for us only by its consequences. Ignited accidentally, in a world of feelings and ideas that are forever lost to us, it has this particularity: it remains nothing but an origin—the origin of a world with which we still have contact because we have only just witnessed its conclusion.

Of the two major movements to come out of World War I, the first was the proletarian revolution. It arose like a river that had gone underground in 1914 only to reemerge four years later, swollen with the suffering and disillusion, both individual and collective, produced so lavishly by the war. And if that suffering and disillusion were so visible among the victors, as in France, what about the vanquished? Bolshevism, the accidental and fragile force in control of the czars' empire in the autumn of 1917, had become powerful in Europe after 1914 because of its radical opposition to the war. It had the advantage of making some sense of those awful years by virtue of an earlier prediction it had made, which might seem to have brought the Bolsheviks to the revolutionary victory of October; they offered an explanation and a remedy to the war that equaled it in its violence. Lenin managed to find culprits and scapegoats worthy of the unprecedented scale of the massacre: imperialism, capitalist monopolies, the international bourgeoisie. Never mind that it was difficult to cast the international bourgeoisie in the role of maestro in a war which, to the contrary, had set its various branches at loggerheads. In this way the Bolsheviks recovered their claim to universality—both objectively, because the war, produced by imperialism, would also be the tomb of imperialism, and subjectively, because the enemy was a transnational class that had to be defeated by a world proletariat. August the fourteenth, 1914, crowned the victory of the nation over class; 1917 and 1918, the revenge of class over nation. The war was permeated by nationalism and universalism, twin symbols of the democratic idea that penetrated, by the spilling of blood, into the very depths of the European collective experience.

With democratic universalism, the revolutionary idea reappeared, fortified in all of continental Europe by the French precedent. In the nineteenth century, the memory of 1789 and of the Jacobins had nourished the sense of nationality; of the two competing elements that marked the entire French Revolution—the universal and the particular—European revolutionaries favored the latter, as shown by 1848. The war of 1914 made it clear what massacres could result from the national spirit, when ignited. In the end, that fire would drive people back to the universal. Not that the victors, such as Clemenceau, did not view the forces and frontiers with a cynical (and superficial) eye. But even the victors included the principle of nationality in their guarantees of a new international juridical order: that was the ABC of Wilsonianism. The other face of democratic universalism, and the main reason for its spread, was the social revolution represented by October 1917. There lay the secret of its dissemination. As Europe emerged from the war, what had happened in Russia a year earlier, in 1917, seemed barely Russian. What counted was the Bolshevik announcement of universal revolution. That successful putsch by a Communist sect, directed by an audacious leader in the most backward country of Europe, was transformed by circumstance into an exemplary event, destined to influence the direction of universal history as 1789 had done. The general lassitude left by the war and the anger of the defeated allowed the illusion Lenin had forged of his own accomplishments to be shared by millions of individuals. The Bolshevik leader did not believe he could remain victorious without the support of other revolutions, first of all in Germany. In all of Europe, the revolutionary militants, whether returning from the *Union sacrée* or simply remobilized by the political situation, thought he was offering them a model. Hence the first Bolshevization of a part of the European Left—a Bolshevization that, though it failed to bring its partisans to power, would leave parties and ideas of the same mold all over Europe and, a little later, all over the world. The Russian Revolution was soon to retreat, walling itself in, resigned to existing as an island in the capitalist sea, yet without abandoning any of its universalistic ambition, which, to the contrary, would serve as its principal means of seduction. What was Russian about it would be eclipsed by its universal aspect. From October 1917 on, the Kremlin's red star atop the immense oriental palace of the czars represented the idea of world revolution: with each generation, the twists and turns of history would reduce or dilate the original myth without extinguishing it until Lenin's successors saw to its demise.

Fascism was born of the reaction of the particular against the universal, the national against the international. In its origins it was inseparable from Communism, fighting the latter's goals even while adopting its methods. The classic example is that of Italy, which emerged from the war only half-victorious, frustrated in its national ambitions: it was the first breeding ground of Fascism, and an exemplary case if ever there was one, since Communism and Fascism grew up on the same soil, the soil of Italian Socialism. The founder of the *fasci* in March 1919, Mussolini was a member of the revolutionary wing of the Socialist movement prior to supporting Italy's entry into the war; then, immediately afterward, he found himself in violent conflict with the Bolshevik-leaning leaders of his former party. He supported the mounting nationalism of d'Annunzio at Fiume, but his paramilitary combat groups were only extended nationally in 1920–21 in the battle against the revolutionary organizations of agricultural workers in Northern Italy—a veritable civil war that Giolitti's government was incapable of controlling and that revealed, for the first time in the twentieth century, the weakness of the liberal state when confronted with the two forces fighting fiercely to succeed it.

As for Hitler, the "German Workers' Party" existed before him. But this small Bavarian political group only began to coalesce toward the end of 1919, when Hitler joined it and livened it up with his eloquence. He lacked a socialist past; admirer of Mussolini that he was, however, he gave himself one with the name that made his fortune: National Socialism. In the context of the European political tradition, we should find behind this pairing the paradoxical alliance between nationalism and anticapitalism that we encountered earlier. The association of those two themes served to validate the German people as a community, a nation, which had to be protected against special interests, capitalists, and the nihilistic designs of Bolshevism. In post-1920 Germany, as was the case in Reichswehr-dominated Bavaria, nationalist discourse had no true rivals, since the Bavarian Soviet Republic in Munich was but a bad memory just sufficient to keep anti-Bolshevism going. Hitler's innovation over Mussolini was his hatred of the Jews, those symbols of both capitalism and Bolshevism whom he viewed as a cosmopolitan and demonic force bent on destroying Germany. Judaism fed an ecumenical hatred in Hitler, bringing together two antagonisms usually distinct because they are for the most part mutually exclusive: hatred of money and hatred of Communism. Hitler invented a way of hating both bourgeois and Bolsheviks by means of the Jews, having found such dual hatred within himself before transforming it into the rage of the period.

Thus Fascism reconstituted, along new lines, the nationalistic passion that had been the evil genius of the major European nations on the eve of 1914. The odd thing, of course, is that its destructive character was not revealed by the war itself, even to the people who emerged as losers, mainly the Germans. The Treaty of Versailles, by not opening the way toward a common history for Europe, undoubtedly bears part of the responsibility. But we must not forget that, since 1917, the internationalist solution had been the property of the militant Bolsheviks. This was already clear in 1918. After the last shot was fired, it became more urgent to protect the nation against the Communist revolution than to teach it to reexist, in a weakened form, in a new international order. The urgency of Bolshevism created an urgency for anti-Bolshevism. Fascism was only one of its forms, particularly virulent where the states and ruling classes of the past came out of the war discredited. Unafraid to borrow what they needed from the idea of revolution, they glorified the betrayed nation against the Bolshevik menace. As an unprecedented mixture of familiar elements reemployed in a different context, Fascism became a new ideology by juxtaposition.

Bolshevism and Fascism entered the theater of history almost simultaneously as the latest progeny of the European political repertoire. Today it is hard to realize that they are such recent ideologies, for they seem outmoded, absurd, deplorable, or criminal, depending on the case. Nonetheless, they permeated the twentieth century. One against the other, one supporting the other, they were the subject matter of the century. At once very powerful, very ephemeral, and very evil, how could they have aroused so much hope and so much passion in so many individuals? Those dead lodestars have taken their secrets with them. If we would attempt to unlock them, we must return to the time of their radiance.

The date of their birth and their simultaneous, meteoric character are not the only things that justify a comparative analysis: they were also interdependent. Fascism was born as a reaction against Communism. Communism prolonged its tenancy thanks to anti-Fascism. The war brought them into conflict, but only after linking them to each other. Both movements chose to ignore the space that separated them, although when it served their purposes, they were ready to lay claim to it to facilitate the march toward absolute power—their common rule and ambition. In sum, because they wished to liquidate each other, they were declared enemies, but they were also colluding enemies who, in order to reach a confrontation, had first to eliminate what separated them. When the existence of a common enemy was insufficient to bring them together, they were united by the thirst for combat: this could summarize Hitler's attitude between August 1939 and June 1941. The great secret behind the complicity between Bolshevism and Fascism remained the existence of that common enemy which the two opposing doctrines would downplay or exorcise with the idea that it was on its last legs: quite simply, democracy. Here I shall be using the term in its two classic meanings: the first as a form of government based on the free suffrage of citizens and the periodic competition of parties for the exercise of power and equal rights guaranteed for all; the second as the philosophical definition of modern societies, constituted by autonomous and equal individuals, free to choose their activities, beliefs, and life-styles. In rejecting these two major aspects of modernity, Fascists and Communists were rejecting different things according to their differing philosophical considerations, but rejecting them with equal radicality.

If we were to cite all of both camps' documents denouncing parliamentary rule or political pluralism as so many bourgeois ruses, we should never get to the end of them. That theme, moreover, is as old as representative government itself and appeared in a multitude of more subtle forms in the eighteenth and nineteenth centuries, ranging from denunciations of English elections to critiques of the oligarchic appropriation of democratic regimes, not to mention the great debate between the ancients and the moderns. In the early twentieth century, with Lenin and Mussolini—let alone Hitler—the subject lost its profundity and philosophical interest to the benefit of its propaganda value. It was no longer to be treated as a derivative of capitalist inevitability according to which money, all-powerful money, also dominates politics.

The theme was put forward in order to please, not to instruct. Lenin no longer had the slightest interest in the modern paradox—which had been completely exhausted by Marx, especially in his books on France—that the bourgeoisie was an economic class whose political dominance was by nature unstable and at risk. He saw only the facades and tricks in the political confrontations of the bourgeois parties, which had to be crushed by means of the proletarian revolution whose instruments he had forged.

Anticapitalism, revolution, parties, dictatorship of the party in the name of the people: all of these themes would turn up in Fascist discourse. The obvious difference is that the two discourses did not share the same intellectual genealogy. Lenin, heir to Marx, or his disciple, saw the revolution he was trying to create as the realization of the democratic promise through the emancipation of exploited workers. As a prisoner of his simplified and even simplistic Marxism, he was convinced that the revolutionary dictatorship of the proletariat and the impoverished peasants—the Russian formula for the seizure of power—would be, as he wrote, "a thousand times more democratic" than the most democratic of parliamentary republics. How could it be otherwise, since in such a scenario capitalism would no longer hold a dominant position? Once the exploitation of labor and the alienation of the worker had disappeared, a decisive step would have been taken toward true liberty for man.

The intellectual advantage of Leninist over Fascist discourse was to go beyond the critique of bourgeois democracy and recover the pedestal of liberal philosophy. Even if regimes that laid claim to that philosophy had to be overthrown in order for their promises to be fulfilled, it remained true that the autonomy of the individual was as much on the horizon of Communism as it was at the center of liberalism. This allowed militant Communists to situate their activities in the context of the future and to think of themselves as the heirs and perpetuators of progress. Militant Fascists, on the other hand, had to envision their role as *breaking* the fatal chain of events that constituted modern history's course toward democracy.

Not that we can deduce from the reactive aspect of Fascism that Fascist thought is counterrevolutionary in the way Bonald's thought was. For in Fascism, as in democratic thought, politics had lost its religious mooring, so the Fascists could not claim that they would restore a human community in conformity with a natural or providential order. Like Leninism, Fascism was imbued with immanence; it did not reject modern individualism as contradictory to the divine order, because modern individualism was seen as the fruit of Christianity; if the

Fascists zealously attempted to uproot that conception, it was through the agency of such historical figures as the nation or the notion of race. In that sense, the Fascists' hatred of the principles of 1789 did not prevent them from being revolutionary insofar as they sought to overthrow the bourgeois world, government, and society in the name of the future.

Between these two age-old theories of politics, Marxism-Leninism owes its superior position to two things. First, it flaunted the name of the most powerful and creative philosopher of history to appear in the nineteenth century. When it came to demonstrating the laws of history, no one could beat Marx. Between *Capital* and *The Manifesto,* he offered something for everyone, from the intellectually sophisticated to the least educated. He seemed to be imparting to all the secret of what made humanity divine after God had receded—namely, humanity's capacity to act in history while avoiding its uncertainties, to the extent that revolutionary action reveals and fulfills laws of development. To possess both liberty and knowledge of that liberty: now here was an intoxicating brew for moderns deprived of God—How could Hitler's brand of post-Darwinism or even the exaltation of nation hold a candle to it?

The second major advantage of Marxism-Leninism is, of course, its universalism, which not only allies it to the family of democratic ideas but, better yet, employs the sense of human equality as its psychological mainspring. In order to break bourgeois individualism, the Fascist appeals only to fractions of humanity, the nation or the race. These last, by definition, exclude people who are not a part of them, and even define themselves by those they exclude, in accordance with the logic of that type of philosophy. The unity of the community is forged anew at the price of presumed superiority to other groups and constant antagonism toward them. For those not lucky enough to belong to the superior race or the nation elect, Fascism provided only two options: resistance without hope or enslavement without honor. In contrast, militant Bolsheviks, true to the democratic inspiration of Marxism, aspire to emancipate the entire human race. In the cortège of historical memories that speak to the Bolshevik imagination, the French Revolution is never far. It constituted the first audacious, even heroic, attempt to raise the flag of universal suffrage against monarchical Europe, but it was incapable of transcending the "bourgeois" limits assigned to it by history. As the Jacobins of the proletariat, Lenin and his friends deemed themselves capable of accomplishing the task: they had arrived in the nick of time.

In the nick of time? Not really. From the start, Bolshevik universalism would bump up against the concrete conditions that had surrounded its success. Its leaders had risen to power in the most backward and hence the most unlikely country in Europe. Considering the particularities of their situation, they hadn't a chance of putting old Russia at the fore of human progress or of relieving it of its burden of poverty and ignorance. The Mensheviks had told them so, as had Kautsky, the great oracle of Marxism. So had Léon Blum, in his discourse at the Tours Congress: seeking to do violence to the march of history, the Russians had substituted a Blanquist putsch for what Marx had called the dictatorship of the proletariat. No alarm sounded by European Marxism would have been missed by Lenin. He, in return, had two answers, one doctrinal, one circumstantial. The first, found notably in his riposte to Kautsky, describes the dictatorship of the Bolshevik Party as essentially democratic since it was meant to suppress capitalism, that is, the dictatorship of money. The other emphasized the particular circumstances that brought triumph to the first Bolshevik revolution in Russia, the weakest link in European imperialism. The Bolshevik revolution in Moscow, said Lenin, was but the first proletarian revolution. Others would follow in succession, attesting to the universality of the movement. In the spring of 1919, Zinoviev, president of the Comintern, wrote in the first issue of the *International Communist:* "At the time we are writing these lines, the Third International has as its principal bases three Soviet republics: in Russia, in Hungary, and in Bavaria. But no one will be surprised if, when these lines are actually published, we already have not three but six or even more soviet republics. Old Europe is racing toward the proletarian revolution."

These illusions were short-lived. Before disappearing from the public scene, Lenin had had to come to terms with the decidedly Russian character of the first proletarian revolution. Stalin would substitute the idea of "socialism in one country" for the revolutionary hopes of the post–World War I period, but the universalism of October 1917—whose heritage he took great pains to maintain—was henceforth weakened by its limited territorial incarnation. The French Revolution had always been torn between its universalistic ambition and its national particularity. The Russian revolutionaries started out believing they could escape from this impasse by virtue of the proletarian character of their revolution and its spread throughout Europe. But once that revolution had returned to within the frontiers of the old Europe of the czars, it was caught up in a contradiction even more obvious than the one that had destroyed the late eighteenth-century French adventure.

The Russian revolutionaries had wanted their revolution to be more universal—more truly universal—than that of 1789, because it was to be a proletarian and not a bourgeois one, enfranchising a class with nothing to lose but its chains, a revolution hence freed from all that had made the principles of 1789 abstract in relation to the social reality of the period. But the proletariat they claimed to be championing was so problematical that it could perform its assigned role only through a series of abstract substitutions: the working class was represented by the Bolshevik Party, which was itself run by a small circle of militants, the opinion of the foremost among them always carrying the day. That conception and plan of action were put in place by Lenin before World War I in the course of his many battles within the party, and turned out to be increasingly impractical after October 1917; the dismissal of the Constituent Assembly, the ban on other parties, and finally the ban on all opposing factions within the Bolshevik Party would replace the rule of law with the absolute power of the Politburo and the General Secretary.

No matter that Lenin, just before his death, had perceived the dangers of this regime; it was he who established its rules and logic. In the final analysis, what cemented the system of the revolution was the authority of knowledge, familiarity with historical laws. Authority, knowledge—by definition, repositories of the universal and absent in the French Revolution. But what could be more abstract than knowledge? And what could be further removed from the real interests of society than such an authority? The French Jacobins had hoped that the principles of 1789 would transform France into the home country of humanity; the Russian Bolsheviks expected the same on the basis of their professed understanding of the laws of history. But the country in which they had prevailed, the heritage they had to deal with, the society they had to transform, and the political conceptions they favored all rendered the contradiction between the idea they had of themselves and the image they tried to project even more contradictory than the philosophical ambition of the French revolutionaries. Those French philosophers of history collided with real history before they had even begun to act. Lenin's territorial incarnation of Marxist praxis robbed Marxist sermonizing for a classless society of a great deal of its plausibility.

What was surprising, given these conditions, was not that Bolshevik universalism had quickly produced so many violent enemies but that it found so many partisans and such unconditional ones. Even before its consequences became evident in the field, it was denounced as illusory and dangerous not only by the "reactionaries" but also by the majority of European socialists, by authorities on Marxism, and even by revolutionary Marxists. Nevertheless, if only by virtue of their success and the myth they had constructed of it, the Bolsheviks had already largely succeeded in inscribing October 1917 in the annals of the European Left as a key date in the worldwide emancipation of labor; the ebbing of the Russian Revolution in Europe after 1920 barely tempered the influence of that initial triumph.

The initial ideological success of Bolshevism in Europe remains a kind of mystery, analogous to the one that surrounds the development of Fascist ideas during the same period. The two movements are related as action and reaction, as is obvious from the chronology, the intent of the protagonists, and their reciprocal borrowings. From this interdependent relationship we may hypothesize that the effects of simplification and exaggeration that attended these two ideologies revealed the secret of their attraction. Indeed, both movements exaggerated to the point of caricature the great collective performances of togetherness they had initiated: one became a pathology of the universal while the other became a pathology of the national. Nevertheless, they were the two ideologies that dominated the history of the century. By taking shape in the course of the events they had helped to fashion, they kept aggravating their effects by making their partisans more and more fanatical. Instead of blunting their edges, the test of power would only multiply their crimes and wrongdoing. Stalin would exterminate millions in the name of the battle against the bourgeoisie, and Hitler would exterminate millions of Jews in the name of the purity of the Aryan race. A mysterious evil was at work in the political ideas of the twentieth century.

In order to explore this enigma—the extreme crudeness of the political ideologies of the twentieth century along with their tragic hold on hearts and minds—we begin with some comparisons with the preceding century. The French Revolution, and more generally the birth of democracy, gave rise all over Europe to a wealth of ideas. Few eras have been so rich in intellectual debates of a political sort, or in doctrines or ideologies designed to organize the liberal, democratic, or socialist City. In fact, the old political world survived; the foundation of that City was regarded as in the transcendental order and continued to fuel nostalgia, battles, and even systems of ideas. As the century advanced, Europeans could conceive of the public sphere only by means of the death of God, as a pure creation of human will, destined to ensure liberty for all and the equality of each to all. They developed and refined the extraordinary range of regimes made possible by such premises. Obsessed with mastering a future that was no longer theirs for the taking, they perceived the greatness and unprecedented perils of the condition of modern humanity. Conscious of the problematical character of modern democracy, they included among their numbers many distinguished politicians; the parliamentary debates and the polemics in the nineteenth-century press offer today's reader a taste of a type of discourse incomparably more intelligent than that of the twentieth century. Even their revolutions, though laden with the French precedent, were never prisoners to the

Jacobin catechism or mere copies of the meager language of one party or one leader.

As to celebrating the idea of nation, heaven knows that the nineteenth century went at it with a passion, making it the center of modern historiography and considering it the most powerful source of political activity. The pride of national identity permeates European intellectual and social life; it was the guiding force of the French Revolution and explains why that revolution had been not only admired but feared for the new principles it introduced: its particular aspect authorized each nation, depending on the case, to imitate or resist it in the name of its universal aspect. Yet none of the wars in the nineteenth century—which were in fact very few—evinced the monstrous character of twentieth-century wars. Even in Germany, where the blind and dangerous side of nationalism was revealed with the most intensity, the idea remained couched in that of culture. It never affirmed the particular chosen-ness of the Germans or their superiority as human beings to be something self-sufficient in its pure substance. Rather, the idea was used to exalt Germany's contribution to morality, to the arts, to philosophy, to culture.

In the two centuries of democratic history experienced by European nations, we may imagine a line dividing them roughly in half. Although all the constituent elements of philosophy and of the democratic condition had been conceived during the nineteenth century, and with an extraordinary profundity since we have had nothing to add to them, they have yet to reveal all their potential political effects. Tocqueville, for example, that uneasy thinker always on the lookout for the future, analyzed the secret bond between modern individualism and the unlimited growth of the administrative state, but he did not predict Fascism, let alone its Nazi form. Nietzsche, who announced the death of God and prophesied the moral and intellectual poverty of democratic man, did not foresee the totalitarian regimes of the century that followed so closely upon his heels, much less that his works would be used to justify those regimes. It was in the nineteenth century that history replaced God's omnipotent role in man's destiny, but only in the twentieth that the political follies born of that substitution would emerge.

World War I serves as a convenient benchmark, a fitting overture to the age of European catastrophes. But it too, like all great events, was the revelation of what had occurred earlier: a cauldron of negative passions in Europe—with anti-Semitism at the top—came to a boil at the end of the century in St. Petersburg, Berlin, Vienna, and Paris. Nonetheless, the war was greater than its causes. When it came, it brought death to so many, shattered so many lives, and so irrevocably rent the tissue of nations after having solidified it, that it became the primordial experience of a new era. What resulted testifies to that.

The title of a collection of essays by Ortega y Gasset, *The Revolt of the Masses*,[1] offers a good description of how people felt in the aftermath of the fighting. But we must also understand this title in an analytical sense. The Spanish writer meant that the war had tended to make people feel and act identically, even as it weakened social hierarchies; that it had produced an abundance of political subjects both reactive and sheeplike, inclined more toward great collective emotions than toward critical examination of programs or ideas. In short, the war in its own way had democratized old Europe, which had already been subject to the hidden omnipotence of public opinion for decades. The new element in this type of analysis—a familiar type in liberal thought after the French Revolution and revived in the late nineteenth century—was the discovery that the masses were not, or not necessarily, uniformly illiterate and uneducated. Northern Italy, the first region vulnerable to Mussolini's propaganda, was the most enlightened part of the country. Germany, where Hitler had his first rhetorical successes, was the most cultivated country in Europe. The breeding-ground for Fascism consisted not of archaic societies but of modern ones whose traditional political and social framework had suddenly lost much of its legitimacy. The post–World War I period left those societies in a situation of egalitarian atomization, which Hannah Arendt has seen as one of the explanations for Hitler's victory.[2]

Education and wealth, then, are not necessarily conducive to more rational political behavior. Engraved in the agenda of democracy, the entrance of the masses into modern politics in interwar Europe occurred not as integration into democratic parties but as a revolutionary innovation. In this respect, the Russian Revolution, although it occurred in an entirely different type of society, played a key role in rejuvenating the idea of revolution, lending it a topicality it had not enjoyed since the latter half of the nineteenth century. If we take the part of the revolutionary idea that speaks to the modern imagination—a way of bringing historical time to fruition—we can dissociate the sway it held over the masses from the pragmatic content of its program.

Revolution is a rupture in the ordinary order of days and a promise of collective happiness both within and by virtue of history. What was a recent invention for the French of the late eighteenth century would later become the central and ultimately the universal figure on the European stage. It came to symbolize, above all, the role of volition in politics and was the proof and even the guarantee that people can tear themselves away from their past in order to invent and construct a new society. It was the opposite of necessity. In spite of the fictitious element in its radicality, it would survive all factual refutations because it had lent its pure form to the liberal and democratic conviction that individuals are autonomous. It also affirmed that history was henceforth to be the sole arena in which humanity's destiny would be played out, since history is where the uprisings and collective awakenings that manifest its freedom take place. This constituted an additional negation of divinity, which had for so long been the sole master of the human theater, but it was also a way of reinvesting religious ambitions in politics, since revolution itself is a quest for grace. It offered the only opportunity to combat the penchant of individuals for retreating into private pleasures, and to remake the citizens of antiquity in modern liberty. The revolutionary idea expressed the intrinsic tension of democratic politics, insofar as human liberty and equality constitute absolute promises bearing unlimited expectations—promises therefore impossible to fulfill.

The revolutionary passion transforms everything into politics, which means that everything, starting with humanity, is part of history, and that anything can be attained with a good society once it has been founded. Modern society however, is characterized by a lack of politics in relation to private, individual existence. It is blind to the idea of the common good, since the members of society, consumed with relativism, have their own individual notions of the common good, and modern society can conceive of it only in terms of a taste for well-being, which divides its members rather than unifying them and thus destroys the community supposedly being constructed in its name. The revolutionary idea is the impossible attempt to circumvent that calamity.

The only great thing about the French Revolution was that it illustrated, along with the birth of democracy, the tensions and contradictory passions linked to this unprecedented condition of social man. The event was so powerful and such a rich source of ideas that it sustained European politics for almost a century. But it lived on even longer in the popular imagination, for what the French Revolution invented was less a new society founded on civil equality and representative government than a special way of bringing about change, a certain idea of human volition, and a messianic conception of politics. We must therefore distinguish between what made the revolutionary idea so attractive after World War I and what the late eighteenth-century French were able to accomplish in the realm of historical change; the Bolsheviks, after all, wanted to destroy bourgeois society, while the Fascists wanted to erase the principles of 1789. But both groups remained zealots of revolutionary culture, sanctifying politics so as to avoid despising it.

There is no reason to exclude Fascism from the revolutionary privilege or curse under the pretext that it fought under the flag of a single nation or race, for Fascist doctrines reappropriated the revolutionary spirit to serve an antiuniversalistic project. This was probably one of the secrets of their success. Throughout the nineteenth century, the weak point of the political philosophies or prescriptions hostile to the principles of 1789 had always been their inability to infiltrate themselves into the history they claimed to be refuting. Leaving everything to Providence, they denied the upsurge of liberty experienced by the people. Nostalgic for the old order, they were incapable of realizing that it was from that order that the Revolution sprang. Which ancien régime ought they to have restored if the one whose virtues they boasted of had given rise to the people and ideas of 1789? And how could they erase that revolution without starting another? Fascism provided a solution to these impasses of counterrevolutionary thought and politics by setting up its tent in the camp of revolution: it too was without God and was even hostile to the Christian religion; it too substituted historical evolution for divine authority; it too was contemptuous of law in the name of the political will of the masses; it too ceaselessly fought against the present under the flag of a redemptive future.

All this seems far behind us, and yet it was only yesterday. The peoples of Europe who survived the horrors of war began the twentieth century with the urge to fashion a new dawn; they sought to reinvent their political world around the two great figures of democratic culture, the universal and the national. With these complementary and antagonistic religions, they would create a catastrophe.

TWO

World War I

THE MORE SIGNIFICANT THE CONSEQUENCES
of an event, the more difficult it is to think about it from the perspective
of its causes. World War I is no exception: no one has ever managed to
demonstrate that it was preordained by the economic rivalries of the
great powers. Nor does anyone believe that the peoples of Europe, by
hailing the war with such transports of enthusiasm, actually provoked it
by their respective nationalistic sentiments. None of the links in the
chain of events that led to the war explain what set it off, other than the
diplomatic and political intrigue in which the European royal courts
were embroiled between the assassination of Archduke Ferdinand in
June 1914 and the first days of August of that year, when all the governments in Europe accepted the war and thereby made it an inevitable fact.
The historical debate over who was responsible for what during those
crucial weeks in no way diminishes the rashness of the various participants when we consider what resulted from the decisions they made:
not only a massacre of unprecedented dimension and duration, but also
a gigantic upheaval in the history of Europe.

In this respect, there is no comparison between the beginnings of
World Wars I and II. World War II was inherent in Hitler's accession to
power in 1933. We might counter the idea that the Hitler of 1933 was
somewhat unpredictable with the argument that, according to the conventional wisdom of nations, power supposedly makes men wiser, and
in this case the reverse was true. But it is obvious that from the first two
years—between the terrorized parliament's vote to endow him with
total power and the Night of the Long Knives—the Hitler in power
was the same Hitler who had written *Mein Kampf.* After the Anschluss
in 1938, how can anyone have harbored any doubts about that? Unlike
World War I, World War II was not the improbable or, in any case,

unforeseen product of rivalries between nations that might have been handled more wisely. It was planned and willed by Hitler as a necessary accomplishment of history. From 1936 on, all of Europe saw it coming, and even attempts at arbitration could not stop it, for these merely consisted of successive concessions to the aggressor. In this, World War II was also more ideological than its predecessor insofar as Hitler had sworn death to democracy and had made domination by one race part of his agenda. This is not to say that the participants in the 1914 war were ignorant of the ideological stakes involved and that those of the war of 1939 were blind to nationalistic passions, but in each case the proportions were different. Only World War II can be characterized as an inevitable confrontation between two differing notions of the human being in society: Nazism versus democracy. The tone was set as soon as the author of *Mein Kampf* came to power and proved within the first few months that he was still the man of his book.

There was an ideological logic not only in the triggering of World War II but also in the way it was conducted. To begin with, Hitler made an accord that was all but an alliance with the USSR; after all, the Communists of whom the Western nations were so suspicious were, like them, adversaries of bourgeois democracy. Stalin believed this so strongly that the German invasion of 22 June 1941 took him by surprise. He made the same mistake that Chamberlain had made three years earlier regarding Hitler's loyalty to his projects: Operation Barbarossa was simply the armed pursuit of *Mein Kampf*. That loyalty, moreover, was Stalin's salvation, for if Hitler had been less prisoner to his "ideas," he might have adopted a policy other than extermination in the easily conquered Belorussia and Ukraine; instead of assembling the peoples of the Soviet Union against Nazi Germany, he could have divided and mollified them. There is no other explanation for this blind spot besides ideology. That said, however, Hitler also restored to Stalin the banner that had been his own between 1934 and 1939—the banner of antifascism, which would soon fly above the heterogeneous coalition of British and American democracies with the Soviet Union. More than ever, it is in ideological terms that World War II is recorded in history. No matter what role was played by circumstance, the impetus for the mass extermination of European Jews by the Nazi armies between 1942 and 1944 came principally from a "theory" about the inequality of races and not simply from a national or nationalistic passion.

World War I, on the other hand, owed both its origin and its substance to the rivalries between European nations and the pure patriotism of their citizens.[1] In Paris, Berlin, London, and Moscow, the members of the Second International temporarily renounced the notion that socialist universalism was to take precedence over duty to one's country. Everywhere, groups who had been political adversaries before-hand joined together to form a common front against the enemy, rally-ing unanimously, each to his own flag. They put their political ideas on hold in order to serve their respective countries in a conflict that no one had really foreseen or wanted but that everyone accepted in advance. Of course, they were all prepared for a short war such as those that had occurred in the previous century. Little did they realize that they were embarking on an unprecedented, horrible, and interminable war. But even when this became apparent as the months and then years went by, the allies endured the suffering that the war imposed on them. It was not the mutinies in the French army in 1917 that were so surprising but the fact that there had not been more of them sooner and on a massive scale.

But that was another era. The nations that embarked on World War I were not yet the democratic peoples anticipated by Benjamin Constant or Auguste Comte, living today in wealthy, fin-de-siècle Europe, priz-ing human life above all, preferring the pleasures of well-being to mili-tary servitude and the futile honors of sacrifice. The soldiers who set out to fight one another in August 1914 were not particularly enamored of war, but they respected it both as an inevitability in the life of nations and as a proving ground for courage and patriotism—the ultimate test of civic virtue. What is more, their civilian lives were not so comfortable that they could dismiss out of hand the risks and difficulties of the sol-dier's life as insufferable. Those peasants, artisans, workers, and bour-geois had all been raised as patriots both at home and in school. They belonged to an old, ethical civilization that retained, in the context of democracy, many aristocratic traits. Military heroism found a new jus-tification in service to the nation.

This world of yesterday still touches my own generation through our parents and childhood recollections. Beyond that, however, it has become unintelligible to today's youth. Any young European curious about the future seeks answers from the unified Europe now emerging, obsessed with well-being and no longer interested in national greatness, cultivating human rights rather than military arts. The people who ini-tiated the First World War could not have suspected that they were setting in motion a moral trajectory that would mark the history of twentieth-century Europe, much less the dreadful price it would exact. They regarded the war as a calamity but a familiar one with a known repertoire, as something manageable whose gains and losses could be calculated or wagered on. They reckoned, justifiably, on the patriotism of their fellow citizens—a natural virtue in the old nation-states of Europe. It was in the name of something familiar that they ventured into unknown territory, as generally happens. But in this instance, a massive split soon separated the political universe that had informed their decisions from the one born of the war—a war whose revolutionary nature was unforeseen. Each of the nations involved believed its actions were consistent with its national history, when in fact they were all endorsing the end of an era and inaugurating the first episode of the European tragedy.

When the war broke out, the revolutionary idea seemed overwhelmed by the triumph of nation over class. The socialist parties called off the general strike that had been decided at the Second International, and they adjourned their social war until the end of the conflict. National unity was the watchword everywhere. This did not exclude democratic sentiments. On the contrary, they were to be mobilized for the benefit of the nation. French workers set out to fight German imperialism in the name of the Republic, German workers set out to fight Russian czarism in the name of civilization. Nothing new here: once again in the history of Europe, it was nationalism that crystallized sentiments and loyalties, even when those sentiments and loyalties were sustained by something dating later in time, such as democracy.

It is therefore totally misleading to view August 1914 in terms of partisan politics, as a victory of the Right over the Left, or of counter-revolution over revolution. While the war certainly reduced working-class internationalism to dormancy, it did not extinguish it; that idea survived intact as a promise postponed, and many saw the national passion that had provisionally repelled it as inseparable from the universal image of man and history. Since the French Revolution, the spread of democracy in Europe has been accomplished and experienced as a mixture of revolution and nation. World War I in no way reduced the constraints exerted by this inexhaustible dialectic. On the contrary, the war intensified that dialectic, introducing it into everyone's everyday life through the suffering and deprivation imposed on everyone by the war. The universal test set off by the declaration of war in August 1914 eventually brought into question the very idea of nation, which had engendered and legitimized the war in the eyes of the people. The longer the war lasted and the more human lives it cost, the more deeply it reworked the soil of European politics. It forced even the humblest soldiers to return to their most elementary views about the world. The war transformed the basic tension in modern democracy between nation and revolution, between the particular and the universal, into a matter of inevitable and urgent choice.

World War I was the first democratic war in history. This is not to say that the objectives of the war or the passions it mobilized were new; from the time of the French Revolution onward, national sentiments and the idea of country had been inseparable from armed conflict. What made World War I different from previous wars was that it affected all the citizens of each of the relevant countries, that is to say, all of Europe.

The war actually involved no more countries than did the Napoleonic Wars; nor were the ideological conflicts any sharper than the interminable confrontation between the French Revolution and the European monarchs. But it did plunge millions of people into unheard-of misery for four full years without any of the seasonal intermissions that characterized the military conflicts of classical antiquity. When compared to Ludendorff or Foch, Napoleon was still conducting the same kind of war as Julius Caesar. World War I was industrial and democratic. Its destructive reach was such that few families in Germany or France had not lost a father or a brother. For those who survived, it left unforgettable memories, both potent and contradictory, that would haunt civic life for the years to follow.

Unlike the citizen of antiquity or the knights of the Middle Ages, the modern citizen has no tolerance for war. The pursuit of riches, the taste for individual liberty, and the obsession with private happiness are so characteristic of modern society that many of the best minds of Europe hailed the birth of this society some one hundred and fifty years ago as heralding the end of all wars. "The single goal of modern nations," wrote Benjamin Constant, "is tranquillity and, along with it, affluence, and, along with affluence, its source: industry. Every day, war becomes an increasingly inefficient way to achieve this goal. Its fortunes no longer offer individuals or nations benefits equal to those that result from peaceful labor or regular commerce. . . . War has thus lost its charm and utility. Man is no longer led to engage in it by interest or by passion." [2] The Saint-Simonians thought the same, as did Auguste Comte and many others at the beginning of the nineteenth century, whether liberal or socialist. And the situation they described or imagined is certainly similar to Western Europe today—preoccupied with the work of peace and prosperity; obsessed with the economy, growth, moneymaking, and employment, having created by means of the market a store of common will and common institutions. The wealthy peoples of today are so far removed from the spirit of militarism that when circumstances put them in the way of armed conflict, their first stipulation prior to any engagement is that there shall be no victims, at least on their side—as was demonstrated by the Persian Gulf war of 1991.

Nonetheless, the history of democratic countries has confirmed Constant's assessment—and for how long?—only after a century that witnessed two gigantic wars unprecedented both in scale and in their material and human devastation. Today's observer is struck by the truth of Constant's analysis and, at the same time, by the false implications he draws from it. Throughout the past two centuries, Europeans have certainly been fueled by an obsession with work, wealth, and well-being. But they are also the people of 4 August 1914.

A simple way to solve this enigma is to affirm that capitalist society, far from obeying or conducting a logic of peace between people and nations, bears war in its flanks "as a cloud bears a storm" in the words of Jaurès. Lenin took this idea, which is common to the socialist tradition, and put it at the center of his theory of "imperialism, the highest stage of capitalism."[3] According to Lenin, European capitalism—ever more concentrated in the great monopolies, constantly seeking out new markets with high profit margins—had universalized the world through colonization by the beginning of the twentieth century. In this now-closed universe, the competition, which had grown fierce, among the great capitalist states for territories and markets was bound to lead inexorably to world war.

This "theory" has aged rather badly with the century. Although it may shed some light upon the origins of the 1914 war—colonial rivalries between the great powers with antagonism between Britain and Germany at the fore—it is less useful for elucidating the conflict of 1939: the Hitlerian ambition to dominate the world was more inherent in *Mein Kampf* than in the projects of German capitalism, and the imperialist adventure upon which the Third Reich would finally founder looked more like political madness than economic necessity. Since then, moreover, we have been able to distinguish between capitalist businesses and the states that shelter them; we know that international capitalism is largely independent of particular forms of territorial colonization and has even prospered on the ruins of that colonization. Finally, since the 1960s we have experienced a twofold phenomenon that is inconceivable in Leninist terms: on the one hand, the most rapid capitalist development that the West has ever known, and, on the other, increasing cooperation between the Western nations, whose citizens have become more alike than ever before. If we were to consider only the history of Western Europe since the war, we would be tempted to reverse Jaurès's remark and to view the growth of capitalism as heralding not a storm but peace between nations.

In fact, neither of these ideas is true. The nature and workings of the economy are but one of the elements to be considered in the evolution of international relations and of customs, sentiments, and ideas. *Homo œconomicus* certainly plays a starring role in modern society. But he is alone on the stage or incapable of passions or rationales other than self-interest. Capital certainly has its assigned place in the twentieth century but should not be cast as its scapegoat.

Although one of the causes of the war was undoubtedly the competition among the great powers for control over markets and colonies, it is obvious that the peoples involved, all classes combined, could only have consented to it for reasons of a different order, national or even nationalistic reasons, drawn from an older source. Everywhere, the dominant idea of those who went off to fight was service to the international community, a notion that assumed different forms and varied in intensity depending on the situations or reasons found or invented for it: for the French it entailed Alsace-Lorraine; for the British, the habit of being in charge; for the Germans, the dynamic of revenge on the past; and for the little nations with no state, the possibility of collective emancipation. But all across Europe the idea was a kind of plebiscite on that quintessentially European invention—the nation. A quiet plebiscite, experienced at the time without a sense of contradiction as though it were a simple, almost self-evident decision. The idea that it was an agonizing choice was introduced after the fact by historians, because they knew what later transpired. In fact, when responding to the call of their respective nations in 1914, socialist workers did not feel they were betraying their class, even though, four or five years later, they would come to see August 1914 in a different light. By then, of course, they had been through the war. When it began, the sense of nationality was still the most widely shared sentiment in Europe—a sentiment not necessarily bellicose, though potentially so, but one that carried with it a prior acceptance of the war to the limited extent that anyone understood what was at stake.

If this was the case, the main reason was that the nation preceded "commercial society" as well as democracy in Europe. It was the product of centuries and of monarchs. Centuries shaped its language, its customs, and its mode of coexistence. Monarchs gradually constituted the public authority that would someday lend form to the emerging nation. The peoples gathered around a power that emancipated them from the feudal lords. The aristocracies gradually rallied behind their sovereigns, who eventually incorporated the vassal-type hierarchy into what would become the state. Thus aristocratic societies in the medieval West became monarchical nations at the cost of abandoning their feudal origins: service to the king superseded all other duties. These anciens régimes, of which France and England offer two different but comparable versions, had inherited from earlier times a love of war as the true test of valor. They, too, had clashed many times in another kind of war, wars between sovereigns. This time, however, it was a war between states, and chivalric virtue had become military honor.

French history well illustrates how the passion for military honor outlived the society that had nurtured it, and how democracy adopted that passion at the very moment it was thought to be cutting its moorings to aristocratic society. It had been one of the underpinnings of the revolutionary wars before energizing Napoleon's armies. Bourgeois France remained military: the soldier's heroism remained a means of social promotion. Throughout the nineteenth century, which began with total defeat at Waterloo, France bore the scar of national humiliation, which affected all milieus and all powers. In the first half of the century, the Left was more susceptible to a sort of compensatory nationalism which, after the Second Empire, would become more significant on the right. This observation, though a truism, is accurate; having once acknowledged the canonic division of French politics, however, we must seek to understand the scope, duration, and potency, in nineteenth-century France, of the sentiments and passions born of Napoleon's defeat. We find them in the writings of Stendhal and Chateaubriand, and at the other end of the century in the writings of Clemenceau and Barrès. The Ultras of the Restoration fought the war with Spain in order to obliterate the memory of Napoleon's war; Louis-Philippe discredited his regime because he wanted peace in Europe; Bonaparte's nephew liquidated his own regime by attempting to put a new shine on the French armed forces in Europe; and the Third Republic was uneasy until it had won the Great War in the name of its country.

This is not to say, of course, that the French cult or nostalgia for military glory was provoked exclusively by the nationalistic passion; for the majority of people it was also fueled by the idea of democracy. The French revolutionaries viewed the renewed nation as the avant-garde of humanity and considered its long-drawn-out war with monarchical Europe as an emancipatory mission. But this superimposition of the universal upon the particular did not fool the European peoples for very long, as was demonstrated by the end of the Napoleonic Wars. Although the ideas of 1789 had been cast as the universal means to a collective renaissance, each of the European nations managed to latch on to it to its own benefit and, eventually, to the detriment of France. The heritage of the Revolution was distributed largely on a national basis. By being integrated into the state through modern citizenship, the masses were offered an object of affection above and beyond democracy—namely, the nation. This was a less abstract, older, more spontaneous passion, which could be shared by all, friends and enemies of democracy alike. Even those French republicans of the late nineteenth century who saw their country as the universal homeland were, in their own way, nationalists.

Public opinion, then, generally subscribed to the idea of the nation as something special, and citizens remained receptive to the call to arms that had been the cry of their kings and their republics. The call to maintain "public safety" touched those nostalgic for Louis XIV as well as admirers of Robespierre; it mobilized aristocratic heroism as well as democratic virtue. Not that all the French were thrilled to go to war, as some have alleged for too long.[4] But none shirked their duty to their country, even those who had sworn that they would never fight against their brothers, the German proletariat. When the hour of truth arrived, the call of nation muted that of class solidarity. The Great War revealed the residual sentiments and passions of all times.

And what about the other camp, across the Rhine? The First Reich was also a "commercial society" in full-blown capitalist development. But of all the countries of Europe, Germany was the one that least followed the dictum that the passion for commerce should quell the urge to arms. On the contrary, both the mercantile and the military spirit reigned there, one sustaining the other. Unlike Great Britain, Germany was not an old island nation whose power had been quietly accepted through force of habit; nor was it a nation like France—an old state gradually constructed by monarchy, whose people had never experienced a lasting shift in their territorial base even after the great revolutionary adventure. The German nation, by contrast, only recently unified by the Prussian victories, was more extensive than its state, with offspring to the south and east of its frontiers. A nation at once worldly and idealized, it put more faith in the particular virtues of its people and army than it did in the balance of power among European states or the universal genius of democracy. A military and industrial monarchy, latecomer to world power, it ran into the British flag or British interests all over the world. At the beginning of the twentieth century, Germany remained a nation-state unsure of its foundations and even of its very nature. It was an assemblage of citizens who, though conscious of their collective power, were subjectively enthralled by their conception of it and tempted to abuse it. The European homeland of philosophers and musicians supported an extraordinary economic force as well as a military aristocracy, and the whole mixture was held together by the idea of national superiority and the notion that history was finally ripe. The greatest military power in Europe was also the one most liable to national pathology.

The literary and philosophical exaltation of Germanness had reached its apex by the early twentieth century. Beginning with Romanticism, it was fed by the brilliance of German art and philosophy, the product of an exceptional people in search of the true moral life as opposed to the illusory autonomy of the democratic individual. The "German spirit" stands in opposition to the West as profundity does to superficiality, duty to licence, the community to the society, the organic to the critical, the state as a vehicle for the common good to the liberal state—in sum, as *Kultur* to civilization. Germany had no enemies to the east, for Russia, even in its heyday, had never been more than an imitation of Prussia until it became contaminated by democratic ideas. The Germans' historical disagreement was with the West. Having been cut up, threatened, and humiliated, Germany began to consider itself the aristocratic refuge of its own weakness. Once it had become unified, powerful, and ambitious, it maintained that image as though it were the secret of its strength: its nationhood illustrates another historical path toward modernity that had none of the vices of Western-style liberal democracy. It was this set of circumstances and notions that Thomas Mann would assemble during the war into a bouquet offered in homage to the sacrifices made by the troops: his *Betrachtungen eines Unpolitischen* compares the "ideas of 1914" with the ideas of 1789.[5] For Mann, the miraculous thing about 1914 was that it revealed the German spirit in an apotheosis of sacrifice and unity when confronted by its old adversary, French-style "civilization": "The difference between spirit and politics implies that there is a difference between spirit and civilization, between the soul and society, between liberty and the right to vote, between art and literature; Germanness is culture, the soul, liberty, art; it is not civilization, society, the right to vote, [or] literature."

Nationalism has taken such a toll on human life and has caused so many disasters in the course of the twentieth century that we tend to remember only its misdeeds and forget what was attractive about it. Its strength—visible not only in Germany but just about everywhere in Europe, including Paris and Vienna—lay in its combining the promises of modernity with the reassurances of tradition. When citizens put their own nation-state above others, they can transform it into an incarnation of power, prosperity, and culture. By subordinating everything—even their own lives—to their nation, they recover emotions that help them forget their solitude as individuals. The cult of nation wipes out the civic deficit of democracy. This cult reached its peak just as the major European states were poised to absorb the popular masses through universal suffrage, social solidarity, and general access to education. Nationalist ideology, though it exalted the particular over the universal and the native land over the abstraction of rights, remained the offspring of democracy and in some ways inseparable from it, at once its product and its negation. It presented the individuals that populated Europe's modern societies with a means of cohesion infinitely stronger than their elected representation.

Because of its political and intellectual history, turn-of-the-century Germany provides the best laboratory for observing the phenomenon that would come to weigh so heavily on its own destiny and affect all of Europe as well. It was there that the unique set of ideas soon known as pan-Germanism developed and took root in all levels of the population. A quasi-tribal yet modern version of nationalism, membership in the German nation would turn into a fanaticism of German superiority over all peoples. The Reich was defined less by juridical sovereignty over a territory than by its mission to provide a haven for all Germans and thus to become the spearhead of Germanism in Europe and the rest of the world. The old European sovereigns owed their crowns to God but owed nothing to history. Those who survived the democratic revolution, like the last Hohenzollern in Berlin, received with their crowns the almost divine responsibility of leading a chosen people—a task so oner-ous that Kaiser Wilhelm II found it all but unbearable. The sovereignty of the people is a great deal harder to shoulder than the divine right of kings, for it replaces the judgment of God with that of history.

Pan-Germanism made the particular absolute. A radical rejection of democratic universalism, it nonetheless grew from the same soil, a reli-gion of immanence made available to a single people. Because it con-tained the idea of race conceived along the lines of the survival of the fittest, it had the scientific endorsement of Darwinian evolutionism. By incorporating the notion of race, nationalism draped itself in science, the greatest religious mirage of the nineteenth century. Science imbued it with an exclusionary force that the idea of national superiority alone could not provide: if peoples are separated by racial differences, and if the Germanic race has been elected to dominate the world, there can only be one conquering people, leaving all others without hope. States, and even the German state, are merely provisional juridical semblances at the mercy of conflicts between races or peoples.

To wit, the Jews. In the eyes of the anti-Semite, they represented the quintessential stateless people, drifting for the past two thousand years outside of their territory while remaining intact among the Gentiles, ever more themselves in spite of their homelessness. The reason they were so unified, so clever at weaving their intrigues for profit and domi-nation in the various nations in which they camped, was that they drew their cosmopolitan genius from their extraordinary ethnic, or racial, co-hesion. This then, was the source of their lies and perversity; for be-neath the abstract universality of money and the rights of man lurked the unbreakable will-to-power of a race. They espoused the democratic credo in order to conceal from their victims the secret of their strength. Even as they confirmed the positive obligation on the part of the people they were deceiving to reclaim the idea of race at their expense, they were, in spite of themselves, living proof of that idea.

What was seductive about this sort of anti-Semitism was that it picked up where tradition left off in all of Christian Europe: it turned the Jewish idea of the Chosen People against the Jews. By reversing the sense of their particularity, the Catholic church made the people chosen by God into the people cursed by God. Modern nations saw this wandering people emancipated by democracy as a hidden but formidable threat to their own identities. The Jews retained their accursed alienness in a world in which history had replaced divinity. Their election to the order of misfortune did not end with the coming of citizen equality and the confinement of religion to the private sphere. Indeed, it intensified as the hatred that was so familiar an emotion to the Christian nations of Europe had redoubled.

But what really characterized modern anti-Semitism was the way it articulated with the new passions of democracy. The modern City, removed from all divine foundation, is built upon the will of its members and derives its legitimacy exclusively from their public consent. This said, however, its members are in constant doubt about what they want and even whether a collective will can be extracted from a multitude of separate individuals. The only thing these citizens still believe in is historical action, but at the same time they are uncertain as to what means for collective action remain to them. The idea of nation relieves this anxiety by suggesting a form of unity. An old idea is recycled in a modern context; it is no longer merely traditional, taken for granted as legacy of the past. As required by the democratic credo, it too is woven from multiple wills—positive wills, the wills of all patriots and ultimately of the entire people—but also from negative, evil, alien wills. This is where the Jewish conspiracy comes in.

Why a conspiracy? Because if all political action is intentional, then any conspiracy seeking to undermine the unity of the nation must, by definition, be hidden: otherwise, it would not possess the capacity to mislead, at least temporarily, a large portion of the public. Its clandestine nature explains its efficacy and force. The French Revolution illustrated how the image of conspiracy as antagonistic to the will of the people could take hold in the democratic imagination. Modern anti-Semitism presented a new version, substituting the Jews for the "aristocrats." Why the Jews? Because they constituted a negative example tailored to the nationalist passion; a people of wanderers, scattered, stateless, but staunch in their religion and traditions and retaining, all over the world in varying amounts, something of an identity, thus offering ideal material for imagining conspiracy on a world scale. Having already incarnated the enemy of the Christian God, the Jews offered anti-Semites in democratic times the imaginary material for another malign role—of the nation.

For anti-Semites, it was enough to see how Jews, even when detached from the religion that confined them to the ghetto, even when "emancipated" by civil equality, remained foreigners among whatever nation they lived. Less visible because integrated, they were the more suspect; their particularity, so obvious in Christian times, was now concealed. Jews no longer had any attachment to the world other than money, and no identity other than the generalized abstract equality that had become both their mask and their flag. They were pure bourgeois, separated from their soil and reduced to their essence—the thirst for wealth. Having been persecuted for their particularity in Christian countries, they were despised by modern nations for being creatures from nowhere. In both cases they were outsiders to the collectivity, thus exacerbating their opprobrium. Even a plurality of opinions had no effect on this second accusation, which followed from the first, since the bourgeois were no less detested on the left than on the right.

It is no accident, then, that anti-Semitism spread throughout Europe as one of the strongest public passions at the end of the nineteenth century. At that time, capitalism was developing rapidly, and the masses were being integrated into democratic politics via universal suffrage. Battles for power had no longer had anything to do with the aristocracy since the first half of the century and even beyond. They were now refereed by a far wider audience. The Jew, that incarnation of the bourgeois, that essence of the bourgeois, that *racial* bourgeois, provided the ideal scapegoat for both nationalist exclusionists and the resentful poor. Alone, the Jew would incur democratic contempt, ranging from those nostalgic for the lost community to those anticipating a new national and/or socialist society.

Thus anti-Semitism spread throughout the political life of the major European countries prior to 1914. In Vienna and Berlin, anti-Semitism was already tied to a racist theory through the affirmation of Germanic superiority. But it existed also in France, where it survived the victory of the Dreyfusards as a deeply entrenched feeling immune to circumstances, even though, for the majority of French patriots, the Republic retained the democratic vocation that it had inherited from 1789. In Austro-Hungary, the success of pan-Germanism among the masses can be explained by the structure of the dual monarchy and the effervescence of the stateless nationalities. In the Reich of Kaiser Wilhelm II, pan-Germanism was fanned by different elements but with equal force: the past and the present, backwardness and might—to the point where most Jews themselves were euphoric about their Germanic links. In August 1914, German soldiers were no more hesitant to leave for the front than were the French. In the war that was beginning, they would invest the same courage, fueled by comparable sentiments albeit with a different blend of political traditions. In Berlin as in Paris, the *Union sacrée* was the order of the day, uniting not only all classes but the various stages of nationhood as well. Intellectuals observed this as did the various peoples, equally unaware of the future being opened up by the war. Among those enthusiastic about the war were, on the French side, Barrès and Péguy, Bergson and Durkheim, and, on the German side, Thomas Mann and Stefan George, Freud and Max Weber.

The First World War was basically democratic in nature. Although in the summer of 1914 everyone saw the war coming, everyone let it come, governments and public opinion alike. Between Sarajevo and the decision to order a general mobilization in July 1914, when the future of Europe was determined, the machine set in motion by Austro-Hungary could have been stopped at any time. But no one wanted to— neither Russia, nor France, nor Britain. No matter how responsibility is assigned among the Central Powers and the French-British-Russian coalition, not one of these major countries really tried to avoid the war that the Austrian ultimatum to Serbia had merely made possible. But although, technically, the war broke out for want of political action, it was undergirded by the consent of the people, a consent taken for granted by the public powers. That consent would not, by definition, have been enough to set off the war, but it sufficed to unite public opinion in the various countries behind their governments when those governments faced off, almost like individual combatants, to defend their honor. Triggered by a nationalist assassination, World War I began as a war of nationalities, igniting the collective passions that had filled the preceding century. The peoples and states that participated in it invested not only their power and their glory but also the prejudices they owed to their ranks and histories. This investment explains the sudden eclipse of socialist internationalism.

By its very nature, war is a gamble whose forms and effects are particularly unpredictable. It destroys the balance that the belligerents hope to tip in their favor, though neither side can predict whether its military strength will be adequate or even whether its expectations of victory, when that hour finally arrives, will not have been transformed by the character and duration of the conflict. World War I was the epitome of this general rule. In both camps, it upset all the calculations of military experts and politicians as well as the emotions of their peoples. No prior war had been so poorly predicted in its evolution and consequences.

First of all, there were many technical innovations, which may be summed up in a few numbers. While the French and Germans assumed that, thanks to their stockpile of arms, they would carry off definitive victories within the first few weeks, they in fact exhausted their entire arsenals in two months because the new firepower of the two armies proved so disproportionate to their predictions.[6] Europe of 1914 paid the price of the progress made in arms production since the last major Franco-German conflict, in 1871. That made the war more murderous but would not necessarily have prolonged it if one of the belligerents had managed to get the upper hand. After the Battle of the Marne, however, just the opposite occurred, and the two armies formed two endless, facing lines of trenches from which they shelled one another. The short phase of the war, in which the strategy and clever maneuvers came into play, was over, to be followed by the interminable front, stretching from the Somme to the Vosges in accordance with the terms of the famous communiqué of early September 1914, which had unwittingly announced the grim industry of routinized massacre and futile sorties from trench to trench. We killed thirty thousand men to gain two hundred meters. No previous war had buried, face to face, in trenches, millions of overarmed men—the active mass of two peoples, whose sole purpose was to kill one another from afar or from close up, with no hope of a decisive or immediate victory, nor any respite or winter quarters. The regimes were identical in this respect, and the French Republic was no less prodigal with the blood of its sons than was the German Empire. The conjunction of industry and equal strength, combined with the number of combatants, produced the horrific mêlée symbolized forever by Verdun. The soldiers, buried by the very missiles that had killed them, became the "missing in action." The most famous of them, buried under the Arc de Triomphe, was honored precisely because he was "unknown"; the scale of the massacre along with democratic equality in the face of sacrifice would enshroud these heroes in an anonymous benediction.

The 1914–18 war was democratic because it was a war of numbers— numbers of soldiers, of guns, of dead. For that reason, it was also the business of civilians rather than of the military, a trial undergone by millions of men torn from their daily lives rather than a military combat. Little more than a century earlier, the battles between revolutionary and imperial France and monarchical Europe had initiated the era of democratic war. Yet those wars had never mobilized the entire population as well as the armed forces of a country, not even in France, where so many soldiers made their military service into a profession and converted dangers into decorations. Napoleon's *grognard* was a soldier, but the *poilu* of 1914–18 was a peasant, a craftsman, a shopkeeper, or a bourgeois, while many workers remained at home to produce arms. The war was waged by masses of regimented civilians who traded civil autonomy for military obedience for an unspecified length of time, only to be plunged into a fiery hell where survival was more a matter of perseverence than of calculating, daring, or vanquishing. Military servitude had never appeared less noble than it did to the millions of transplanted men, so recently snatched from the moral world of citizenship.

We could hope for no finer witness of that time than Alain, in his letters from the front to his friend Élie Halévy, written between August 1914 and the beginning of 1917.[7] A philosopher and moralist of democratic humanism, Alain liked neither the war nor the aristocratic values it dragged in its wake. He enlisted at the age of forty-six, on 3 August 1914, as a simple artilleryman so as not to be estranged from the history that surrounded him. As he would say later on, "In order to be happy, I have always needed to go to hell with everyone else."[8] For him, however, war was the political state most alien to the citizen, and World War I conformed to that rule more than any other. The necessary aspect of the war belonged to the realm of passions and was unrelated to interests, which are flexible, and even less to reason, which is conciliatory. The question of honor was resolved within a few weeks and had ceased to be an issue on either side since the Battle of the Marne. After that, the war degenerated into spiritual and moral corruption—an inversion of democratic virtues: it kept its hold by enslaving men under the absolute power of their leaders,[9] by maintaining a generalized atmosphere of fear that lent military action a mechanical aspect, and by the death of the fittest as though a kind of reverse selectivity were at work. The army at war constitutes a social order in which the individual ceases to exist and whose very inhumanity explains the all but indestructible power of its inertia.

Away from the battlefield, Alain found the situation to be no more inspiring. On the contrary, stoically waged by civilians in uniform, the war was a mere spectacle directed by "professional patriots" mouthing platitudes far from the front lines. Alain detested chauvinism, censorship, and the organized conformism of opinion. He couldn't find harsh enough words to describe the intellectuals, journalists, and politicians competing to be the most bellicose. He didn't believe in the "just war." By the end of 1914 he was in favor of peace through compromise; indeed, he followed very closely—thanks to the *Tribune de Genève*, which was sent to him by the Halévys—anything resembling an opening up of negotiations, no matter how fragile the effort. But he had few illusions: precisely because it was so dreadful, so murderous, so blind, and so total, the war was difficult to end. It no longer belonged to the category of armed conflicts that cynical princes could stop when they felt the cost outdistancing the potential gains. It was led by patriots, decent folk elected by the people,[10] daily more locked into the results of the decisions taken in July 1914. The suffering was so severe, the death toll so high, that no one dared act as though it were unnecessary. And how could anyone take such a stand without being labeled a traitor? The longer the war went on, the longer it would continue. It was killing democracy, even though democracy was what perpetuated its course.

Having listened to Alain, let us turn to Halévy's words. Although his responses to Alain's letters have been lost, we can read Halévy's mind through his correspondence with other friends, particularly the philosopher Xavier Léon.[11] These letters make clear the similarities and differences of opinion he had with his artilleryman friend.

To begin with, he was less attached to the specifically French tradition of republican radicalism. Born into a great family of the intellectual bourgeoisie,[12] with Jewish and Protestant ancestry, he was much more cosmopolitan than Alain. His attachment to the Republic was tempered by a passion for British political culture, of which he was a historian.[13] A democrat and no less liberal, he was not a pacifist like Alain. Not that he had the least sympathy for the war, but he didn't see how it could be avoided given the state of European nations and public opinion. Like his friend, he had little patience for the bellicose squawking and cultural anti-Germanism in France; but he believed, nonetheless, that the war was rooted in national rivalries and passions. For him, it was less the product of political intrigues than of the confrontation between pan-Germanism and pan-Slavism in Central and Eastern Europe: public opinion did the rest. Halévy was a more political thinker than Alain. Accustomed, like all great French liberals, to being on the losing side, he had acquired the virtue of active pessimism. He had long foreseen the war, and here it was. It had to be dealt with lucidly.

Although too old to be drafted, he volunteered as a nurse. He was inducted at Chambéry, where he lived "in the clericalism of the ambulance."[14] He immediately grasped—and was probably one of the first in Europe to have done so—that the war had taken on an unprecedented and appalling character after the Battle of the Marne: "I believe—and this is what troubles me—that offensives on both sides have become all but impossible considering the conditions of modern strategy. I don't see how we can get out of it for months and months. I don't see how we can stop it. It is a war between races, rather sordid, lacking in great ideas and brilliant plans." [15] He regarded the war as interminable not because of what was at stake objectively but because of the character it had acquired and the military situation it had created. The course of the war had revealed its nature; it had functioned like a trap. The war had lost any foreseeable end the very moment it ceased to be popular with the troops. It had become merely a sinister arena for fatalism; the soldiers fought mechanically, without calling for peace, because they no longer thought it a possibility. Halévy shared with Alain the fear that this inhuman yet durable condition would destroy civic autonomy. In another letter to Xavier Léon he included this prophetic remark: "The influence that the war could have on the destiny of socialism merits study. Though probably unfavorable to the *liberal* forms of socialism (trade unionism, etc.), the war will, to the contrary, reinforce state socialism, and to a considerable extent." [16]

The great political enigma of World War I was peace, since the conditions of battle obscured its horizon. Halévy had no truck with the simplistic declarations of faith of the revolutionary extreme Left or with intellectuals in favor of immediate peace. [17] He did not believe in a compromise between the belligerents, which was rumored from time to time. To him, the only path to peace was through the defeat of the German military: a long, long route since the battle was so unpredictable and Germany so strong. Halévy saw Germany both as a menace to the balance of power in Europe and as one of the most powerful manifestations of European genius. His pessimism stemmed from the belief that the whole affair could have no lasting outcome unless Germany was defeated, and that any defeat would be a European defeat after so endless a conflict.

"And what lies ahead? In my opinion, a battle with no end in time or in space where time will work for us." [18] A month later, on November 26, 1914, in another letter to Léon, he predicted that "we have ten or fifteen years ahead of us, or thirty years of war. So the second, the last part of our lives will hardly resemble the first." [19]

What was he driving at? Not that the present war would continue for ten, fifteen, or thirty years but that it had inaugurated a new era of instability for Europe—an instability of dispositions of force, national frontiers, regimes. The twentieth century would seem to have born under a black cloud. Let us consider a longer citation from a letter of 27 October 1915, once again to Xavier Léon:

I hold:

1. that the war cannot be considered at an end until the day when we have witnessed the defeat of the Central Powers. I do not know the

details of this defeat. I can hardly see the breakup of Germany; I can better imagine the breakup of Austria, though followed by the absorption in one piece of the eastern part of Austria by the empire of Kaiser Wilhelm II. Whatever. I know what I mean.

2. that the time necessary to obtain this result must be measured not in weeks or in months but in years. When I spoke of twenty-five years, I was not so far off the mark.

3. that when I imagined the possibility of such a prolonged war, I always realized it might be suspended by false armistices, precarious armistices, truces.

4. that subsequently these truces, which will intervene prior to the defeat of Germany, will necessarily include a state of things temporarily favorable to Germany, and thus, momentarily, constitute a victorious peace for Germany.

Halévy notes in closing that a prophet should always cloak himself in "a certain obscurity": a private joke in the guise of a warning to the reader, which detracts nothing from his extraordinary prescience about the European drama of which the First World War was the overture. He may not have predicted the exact scenario, but he grasped the stuff of the tragedy. This historian of the heyday of the British witnessed the disappearance of European liberal civilization, destroyed by its own children.[20]

In the end, it was pessimism that brought Alain and Halévy together: both saw the First World War as a major historical catastrophe after which nothing would ever be the same. Both viewed the great European powers at war as an unexpected return of military despotism in modern times. The increasing control of the economy according to the needs at the front gave governments an extraordinary power over their citizens and suggested a model for potential tyrants. The exclusive pressure of the idea of nation on people's minds, the chauvinism of the elites, the conformity of the masses, and, finally, official censorship was snuffing out democratic life.[21] Civilians could focus on little else but the mail, which might bring a letter from a survivor or the name of a fallen soldier, and communiqués from headquarters, which lied to them on the pretext of keeping up morale. The soldiers could be freer than those on the home front because they were actors in the tragedy. But they were lost in inconceivable violence and could neither see nor understand anything beyond obeying orders: this war was a vast chaos with no place for the mind. The only thing that mattered, as at Verdun, was the animal urge to resist annihilation by enemy artillery. What exceptional determination enabled the troops to hold on? Alain, even before the French mutinies in the spring of 1917, understood the fragility of this compulsory heroism. "We shall pay for all this, believe me; everyone will find out who his true enemies were," he wrote on 13 November 1915.[22]

When the Russian Revolution occurred in February, Alain viewed it in the same light. "I don't know which soldiers you saw," he wrote in a letter of 3 April 1917;[23] "they may have been weak from loss of blood; all I saw were men in a state of revulsion, constantly dreaming of ways of ending the massacre and, when finding no solution, plotting vengeance. One mustn't underestimate it. The Russian Revolution is definitely something to be reckoned with." Here Alain points to the universal turn taken by events in Russia—the fall of czarism took second place to the revolt of soldiers and civilians alike against the war. Who cared about Nicholas II? The misery of war had become the obsession of all Europe. Alain's military experiences as philosopher and artilleryman gave him immediate access to the feelings of many of the troops. During the same period, Halévy expressed a quite different view of the February Revolution.[24] Like the French government, he was preoccupied with the effect of the change of regimes on the way the war was going at St. Petersburg, and hoped that Miliukov would put an end to the chaos in Russia for the good of the allies. To this hope he added a more disinterested and melancholy observation, true to his liberal turn of mind: "This said, is it not a relief for any Westerner deserving of the name to be no longer responsible for the czar and his court?" Everyone "felt this way, in England, in Italy, no matter how conservative. Must France ever remain an enigma to the political observer? Shall we never be able to say whether or not France is liberal to the point of anarchism or hopelessly reactionary?"[25]

Alain and Halévy, then, had very different appraisals of what was happening on the other side of Europe in the spring of 1917. Alain liked the idea of workers' and soldiers' councils, or soviets, as a way of rebelling against the war.[26] Halévy rejoiced in the fall of an ancien régime, while hoping that the Russian revolutionaries would not sign a separate peace with Germany. Nonetheless, the doubts they shared about the future, even the immediate future, united them in the same anxiety: almost three years after the famous summer of 1914, the future of Europe was as obscure as ever. Only one thing was clear: in the war, people had lost whatever control they formerly exerted over history. They were incapable of predicting either the course or the character of that exploit. They knew neither how to conduct it, nor how to end it. The events of February 1917 in Russia, followed by the mutinies of the Chemin des Dames, demonstrated to those willing to see it the price paid by the incapacity of the ruling classes and governments to come up with an

organized exit from the war between the European nations: that price
was revolution, the ancient mother-goddess of European democracy.

From 1814 to 1914, the hundred years of the nineteenth century,
none of the European wars had permanently overturned the international order or brought into question the economic and social regimes
of the warring nations. Admittedly, the French Second Empire died at
the defeat of Sedan, where Napoleon III was taken prisoner. But
his fall wrought no profound transformation on French domestic politics. And although the foundation of the German Empire at Versailles
modified the distribution of power in Europe, it did not essentially
change the general organization of the system as dreamed up by the liqui-
dators of the Napoleonic enterprise: a balance of the great powers—
Austria, Russia, Prussia, and France; a diplomatic clockwork watched
over by Britain, wary of anything that resembled an attempt at continental hegemony. The 1848 revolutions had threatened that balance,
which would nonetheless recover its base a few years later: the invention
of Austro-Hungary, and then German unity under Kaiser Wilhelm II,
would modify its borders but not its spirit. Within this organized group
of powers, the wars that occurred were limited in terms of the objectives, the resources mobilized, and the size of the armies involved. They
brought face to face only voluntary or professional soldiers and not entire peoples. They were brief. The coupling of industry and democracy
had yet to emerge from the shadows of the military heritage of the past.

The First World War would change all that. At its outbreak, however,
it was still in a nineteenth-century mode: the Anglo-Russian alliance, as
was the case during Napoleon's time, held fast to continental power,
if not to expansionism. Germany, not France, was now the dangerous
party. But the war, once declared, eluded its "logic" and its protagonists. The poets would soon write of earlier wars with nostalgia:

> Où sont-ils ces beaux militaires
> Soldats passés Où sont les guerres
> Où sont les guerres d'autrefois.

> Where are they, those handsome servicemen
> Those soldiers gone Where are the wars
> Where are wars of past times.[27]

Indeed, "total war"[28] stripped war of all the intelligence, virtue, and
foresight it had once summoned. In its own way, this new type of war
both confirmed and more appropriately illustrated an observation made
by Benjamin Constant in connection with the Napoleonic Wars. To the
extent that "the situation of modern peoples keeps them from being

warlike by nature," Constant wrote, the war, when it occurred, had changed character. "The new way of fighting, the change in arms and artillery, have stripped military life of its most attractive aspect. The struggle is no longer against danger; only fatality remains. Courage must be tinged with resignation or must consist of insouciance. No longer are we gratified by the exercise of will, by action, and by the development of physical strength and moral faculties that made man-to-man combat beloved of the heroes of antiquity and the knights of the Middle Ages." [29] What prescience on the part of great minds! World War I, as anticipated by Constant, was dominated by fatality and resignation. It turned people into slaves of technology and propaganda—an annihilation of both body and mind.

This is how Ernst Jünger, with the perspective of time, would see it in 1930 when he sought to analyze the unique character of World War I in the history of humanity.[30] That war was not subject to the limits of "monarchical" wars, in which sovereigns, mobilizing their loyal armies but not their entire realms, fought to round out their patrimonies. Kings could be beaten on the battlefield and still retain their thrones. The war of 1914–18 spelled the end of warrior castes and professional armies, of calculations of cost or advantage. The conflict spread from crowns to nations, from armies to peoples; at the same time, lacking clear objectives, it turned into a confrontation between national capacities for labor. Manufacturing of any kind became subordinated to the imperatives of the war, the civil order to the military order. It was the Germany of Hindenburg-Ludendorff, the France of Clemenceau; later it was Lenin's "war Communism," Stalin's Five-Year Plan, and then, eventually, Hitler. The partial wars of the aristocrats and kings were followed by the "total mobilization" of states and "workers"—the last word on the idea of progress and "technical" humanism. Hence the passionless, merciless character of the twentieth century's first conflict, unprecedented in earlier wars. Hence also the outcome, since so many European nations remained too alien to "civilization" to prevail: Russia and Italy, of course, were mired in backwardness, but Austria and even Germany were stymied intellectually and morally owing to the Central Powers' combination of an absolutist tradition with a constantly shackled "liberal" spirit. In this way, Jünger extended the *Kultur-Zivilisation* dichotomy to the interpretation of the entire postwar period.

Let us return to those masses of men who were tossed for years into this "total" battle. They sacrificed everything to the immense machine of modern war as it cut down millions of men in their prime, leaving whole nations maimed and widowed. The parity of forces, massive armaments, the entombment of soldiers in the trenches, and murderous yet meaningless advances and retreats dragged the war on and on. During battle, the soldiers blamed "fate": they had no other choice.

> The emotions of war are similar to those of gambling. Men expect everything from luck. [The soldiers] set out to defend civilization. But that word is starting to grow thin. The war itself is killing it. The war would have had to be brief if the notions attendant on its beginnings were to persist in spite of the war, so that we might rediscover them as if after a bout of delirium. Reduced to their life in the herd, men have lost the power to reflect. There are no more nuances in their lives, no more nuances in their thought. Their willpower too is dying. They are surrendering to discipline, which leads them this way and that, surrendering to chance, which gives them life or death. They feel they are in the hands of fate. This is the very opposite of civilization, for even if they were fighting for civilization, war would be sufficient to rob them of their sense of civilization.[31]

The armistice transformed this stupor into anger. When the cannons finally fell silent, the survivors looked back upon those nightmare years and sought to understand what it all meant and what role had been played by their governments. Politics resumed its functions, heavy with unanimous questioning about the violence and duration of that massacre, trapped in its own immobility.

The immediate origin of the war was the problem of Balkan nationality. Each of the warring powers, however, had clearer objectives of its own. Austro-Hungary was fighting for its survival; Russia, for Slavic influence; France, for Alsace-Lorraine; Germany for its colonies; Britain, to preserve its century-old dominance. The patriotic feelings that led soldiers to the front in August 1914 blurred these objectives in an exaltation of nationhood. The violence of the war led not so much to mounting hatred between enemy armies as to a constant demand from the home front for increased sacrifices on the part of the soldiers. The goals of the conflict became magnified and were then lost in the conflict's very immensity. Like the field of battle, the goals too had became endless.

This is why attempts at negotiation or propositions of compromise were so fainthearted and so soon disqualified, despite the cost of the battles and their incapacity to force destiny. At the end of 1916, even though none of the powers at war had carried off a decisive victory or experienced an irreparable setback, the idea of a peace without annexation or indemnity that was being mooted in the Reichstag was never seriously pursued, even in secret.[32] In suggesting the liberation of the Czechs, the Allies' memo of 10 January 1917 indirectly implied the dismemberment of Austro-Hungary. The negotiations undertaken by the Bourbon princes in the name of Emperor Charles I, moreover, came to nothing.[33]

It was probably in 1917 that the war, having no precise objectives, found its lasting ideological position. The February Revolution in Russia freed the Allies from their obligations to the czarists, obligations that had been brandished by the Central Powers as proof of Franco-British hypocrisy. In April, President Wilson brought the United States into the war, affirming American solidarity with the democratic nations. Wilson hailed the Russian Revolution and suggested that the German and Austrian regimes were doomed: "Prussian autocracy is not and can never be our friend. . . . We are happy to fight for the liberation of nations."[34] The United States' grand entrance into the arena of European politics played to the air of a crusade for democracy, in keeping with the American spirit. The two great forms of democratic universalism, born during the same era, united their messages around the cause of European nationalities. This union lasted no longer than the one that had accompanied the two revolutions of the late eighteenth century. But Wilsonian moralism, by fanning Clemenceau's Jacobinism, sufficed to give the war a significance beyond Alsace-Lorraine or the tonnage of the German fleet—a significance in fact so vast and so intransigent that peace could no longer be achieved short of total capitulation on the part of the enemy. The stakes of the conflict were thus raised to the level of the slaughter they had set in motion. But they were formulated in such a way as to necessitate, on the day of victory, the collapse of thrones and empires in exchange for new republics, the humiliation of certain nations in exchange for the emancipation of others.

Germany would pay the heavy price of defeat. Since Bismarck, it had been the most powerful nation in Europe and was to remain so for the whole of the twentieth century. Twice destroyed, reduced in size, occupied, and even divided, it would twice find its way to a dominant role in Europe, thanks both to its geographic location and to the productivity of its people. The Treaty of Versailles signaled its first humbling. The Reich had to agree to unconditional capitulation. It lost its territories to the west and to the east, abandoning huge numbers of Germans to non-German states. It had to pay out enormous reparations in money and in kind. It was declared the sole party responsible for the war and was condemned to expiate its crime—a moral judgment too categorical to appear unrelated to victory, and one that grated on the vanquished while neither reassuring nor uniting the vanquishers.

Raymond Aron has rightly argued that "the Treaty of Versailles is, to a greater extent than its critics have admitted, the logical consequence of the war, considering both its origins and the ideological significance it gradually acquired during the course of the hostilities." [35] The people who negotiated that treaty (and the series of treaties related to it) were the virtual trustees of promises born of the war. Constricted by the quarrels of "nationalities" and the memories of 1848, which revived half-forgotten passions, they multiplied Slavic states on the ruins of vanquished Germanism, creating everywhere—from Warsaw to Prague, from Bucharest to Belgrade—unlikely parliamentary republics in which the French bourgeois radicals believed themselves to be replanting their traditions though they were merely exporting their form of government. More than a European peace, the treaties of 1919–20 constituted a European revolution. They erased the history of the second half of the nineteenth century to the benefit of a new, abstract division of Europe into small, multi-ethnic states that merely reproduced the shortcomings of the Austro-Hungarian Empire. Those little states were as divided within their new frontiers as they had been within the old, and were separated from one another by even greater hostility than they had experienced under German or Hungarian domination. The Allies had miniaturized national hatred in the name of the principle of nationhood.

What the Allies had tried do with these improvised, poor, and divided states, most of which contained sizable German populations, was to make them the eastern belt of Anglo-French preponderance in Europe. The October Revolution had liquidated Russia's traditional role as an element of European equilibrium, so that Soviet Russia, far from playing—with Britain's blessing—fraternal policeman to the Slavic nations and the great power to the east, had become the pole of the Communist revolution. The new, composite countries carved out of Central and Eastern Europe immediately had to assume a twofold historical function that was too heavy for them: to stand guard both to the east, against Soviet messianism, and to the west, against Germany—a Germany defeated, disarmed, and broken but still to be feared, and occupying a place more central than ever in the politics of Europe.

A final element in this scenario is the total lack of consensus among the three great victors about the new international order they were imposing. Though completely unlike the ambassadors at Vienna who, a hundred years earlier, had remade a European equilibrium destined to endure, they held the same conservative philosophy, and, in order to return post-Napoleonic Europe to a stable base, they resorted to the old recipes of realpolitik. [36] At Versailles, the Allies imposed a Carthaginian peace without a consensus as to its ends, or even its means. The American entry into the war had been decisive, but Wilson's war had only abstract objectives that were almost impossible to translate into political

terms and were hardly appropriate to any arbitration between territorial
rivalries, even if shared by both parties. The French, however, only had
eyes for Alsace-Lorraine and the dismantling of Germany, while Britain
hadn't fought for four years merely to substitute France for Germany
as the dominant power in continental Europe.

Jacques Bainville [37] was one of the most lucid critics of the negotiators
of Versailles, as was John M. Keynes,[38] whose *Essays in Biography* shed
much light on the personalities involved. Sad to say, the French cult of
Clemenceau presents a perfect example of the injustices of collective
memory, for it would be difficult to think of another person as incapable
as was this legendary victor of raising himself to the vision of peace. At
Versailles, the old Jacobin from the Vendée was ignorant, narrow, chauvinistic, and imprisoned in his role as "Father Victory." The persistence
of the commander in war had given way to the blindness of a conqueror.
The aesthete of politics had become a bailiff of peace. This negotiator
was incapable of divesting himself of wartime fierceness. A sarcastic
and passionate old man, exasperated by the political theology of Wilson,
Clemenceau played his greatest role with a combination of cynicism and
naïveté. What did he make of the ruined and revolutionary landscape of
Europe at the end of hostilities? Not much. What was his vision for
Europe? He had no conception of the continent as a whole. With his eye
fixed on Strasbourg, what he liked about the victory was the toppling
of enemy thrones: the flight of Kaiser Wilhelm II and the end of the
Austro-Hungarian Empire. He celebrated the victory of the nationalities and the humiliation of Germany with equal enthusiasm. He turned
the diplomatic instrument with which he hoped to found a new order
into a verdict against a guilty people.

The Europe that emerged from the hands of the victorious powers
in 1919 was conceived even more crazily than the war that engendered
it. Of the four powers that in the nineteenth century had divided up
the territories east of the Rhine for themselves—the Ottoman Empire,
Russia, Austria-Hungary, and Germany—only Germany remained, defeated, disqualified by defeat, but strengthened in the long term by the
disappearance of its rivals and the weakness of its new neighbors. The
French, having become the principal military power in continental Europe, enjoyed this provisional primacy only in appearance; they were
denied it by the British. The Americans had gone back home. Europe
was doomed to fragility even on the side of the victorious nations, let
alone the losers.

The war had mobilized tens of millions of men; several million had
died, several million returned home maimed or debilitated. At the time,
figures such as these were without precedent in the history of war. This

monstrous volume of individual tragedies, when tallied with what had actually been at stake and what resulted, gradually unhinged the societies and regimes involved: the less the peoples in uniform could see an end to their tribulations and recompense for their sufferings, the more they doubted whether the war had had any sense. By drafting all eligible men and requiring supreme sacrifice on the part of one and all, World War I turned everyone, no matter how humble, into a judge of the social contract. In its own way, the war was an elementary and universal test of democracy.

The first regime to give way was also the weakest and the least capable of shouldering the material and moral weight of total war—the last absolute monarchy, the last ancien régime in European history, the Russian autocracy, which had been teetering on the brink since 1905. The crisis had begun with the Russo-Japanese War of 1904–6, and czarism was buried by World War I. Czar Nicholas II attempted to use the war to reinvent a charismatic, peasant monarchy in opposition to the bourgeoisie and the workers. But by setting himself up as supreme commander of an army too quickly defeated, he further undermined his own authority. His throne had become too fragile to be prolonged by the national union of August 1914. The military defeat increased his isolation and precipitated his fall at the beginning of 1917, when, even in the West, the war was petering out before flaring up again. The essential traits of the Russian Revolution can be explained by the national and social breakdown that framed it, which itself resulted from the disintegration of the armed forces. From February to October, the prevailing anarchy was uncontrollable by any one person or party. From crisis to crisis, power moved increasingly to the left, until the Bolsheviks gathered it up from the streets of Saint Petersburg. Not until the summer of 1918 did they truly exercise power domestically, setting in motion the Terror, "war Communism," the Red Army, and the identification of party and state.

The universal character so rapidly acquired by the combined Russian revolutions of February and October 1917 resulted largely from its clamor against the war. That the mujiks were appropriating land hardly impressed the peasant soldiers of the West, deep in their trenches; they had been landowners for centuries. That the czar fell, to be replaced by a provisional government formed by representatives of different parties, was nothing new to them, for they regarded this process as an inevitable consequence of Western history. But the Russian people called for peace: that was how they showed the way out of the tragic impasse in which the governments of the West had allowed themselves to be trapped. Paris and London, gambling first on Miliukov and then on

Kerensky, tried to ignore the heat of the February Revolution for a few months; by April, however, the rout of the Russian military had become inescapable, and the message passing from East to West was increasingly one of peace.

If the bourgeois governments underestimated Russian strength, the victorious Bolsheviks overestimated the revolutionary influence in Europe. Before resigning himself to Lenin's realism, Trotsky—along with the majority of the Bolsheviks—expected a revolt among the various armies, primarily among the Germans. These utopian hopes ended in Brest-Litovsk in March 1918, when a third of European Russia was ceded to Germany. On the western front, the 1917 crisis in morale in the French army had been brought under control. Clemenceau's government, formed at the end of the year, had developed its program for total war. The "revolutionary defeatism" extolled by Lenin since 1914 was still not the order of the day. It never would catch on, not even in defeated Germany. What Russia in 1917 revealed to the European nations was something different: it endowed the idea of revolution not so much with a doctrine as with a universal sense of peace rediscovered. In the absence of a negotiated exit from the war, the events in Russia, no matter how confused, chaotic, and distant they appeared to the West, had at least one clear outcome: they had broken the curse that had locked the wills of the warring nations into an endless bloodbath.

The termination of war, a year later, came about neither through negotiation nor through revolt but through the capitulation of the Central Powers on the eve of a military rout. To the very end, the brute force of arms would have the last word. But although revolutionary defeatism had not done away with war, peace achieved through defeat reawakened the revolutionary idea that had reemerged a year earlier in the czarist empire.[39] Soviet Russia took on the image of avenger of the disastrous domination of the generals. Bolshevism, even before being clearly defined as a political philosophy or revolutionary model, had been fortified by the cessation of hostilities. In defeated Germany, Kurt Eisner seized power in Munich, and Karl Liebknecht insisted on playing Lenin's role in Berlin. In Austro-Hungary, which was coming apart at the seams, Béla Kun triumphed in Budapest.[40]

Peace made revolution the order of the day.

THREE

The Universal Spell of October

WITH WORLD WAR I, THE IDEA OF REVOLU-
tion was returned to the center of European politics. And it was indeed a
return. Democracy in Europe originated with the French Revolution—
that tremendous upheaval whose repercussions would prove so trouble-
some for nineteenth-century politicians. Because its principles, which
had been widely adopted, coexisted with prior institutions, and its ideas
with earlier notions, even by the early twentieth century the Revolution
had yet to reveal all of its consequences. The Europeans of 1914, before
declaring war on one another, made up a mixed political culture; the
democratic idea, universally at work, commingled with the various traditions and forms of resistance within each nation. This blending did
not lead to revolution, however. Even the workers' parties, brandishing the notions of class struggle and the advent of the proletariat, had
already entered the bourgeois parliamentary arena in France, Germany,
and elsewhere.

The one country that did not conform to this scenario was czarist
Russia, whose fragile balance had been exploded by the events of 1905.
During World War I, Russia brought the revolutionary idea back into
European history from its farthest outpost. In its early form, this was a
strange but not improbable occurrence, for in the fall of Nicholas II and
the establishment of a provisional government in anticipation of a Constituent Assembly, the Europeans, especially the French, recognized
their own history. Russia's involvement in the war—as the ally of some,
the enemy of others, important to everyone—made them all the more
attentive to the events in Russia, in spite of the distance. The least likely
thing was not what happened in February 1917 but what came closely
on its heels in October.

With October and the Bolsheviks, revolution assumed a new role. It
no longer bore the standard of the bourgeoisie but that of the working

class. It was under those colors that it sallied forth as if to fulfill Marx's prediction of the overthrow of the bourgeoisie and capitalism. The sticking point was that capitalism had barely had time to exist: the proletarian revolution broke out in the most backward of the great nations of Europe. This paradox engendered an interminable debate within the Russian socialist movement, which even the takeover of the Winter Palace by Lenin's henchmen could not resolve. After all, October might very well have amounted to nothing more than a lucky putsch and therefore have been devoid of "historical" dignity. Following the Mensheviks, Karl Kautsky, the high priest of Marxism, was of this opinion. The Bolshevik revolutionaries' own version of their revolution is not all that credible. Their pretension of inaugurating a new epoch in the history of humanity by the rise of product workers does not ring true when judged either in terms of Russian history or by the radical turn in political circumstances surrounding the February Revolution.

The October Revolution also owed its power over the contemporary imagination to a revival, at a hundred years' remove, of the most potent political image in modern democracy—the revolutionary idea. This revival had long been internalized by the Bolsheviks, who had been discussing the Jacobin precedent since the beginning of the century. Until the First World War, Lenin and his friends had been nothing but a small, extremist group within the Socialist International. They were thrust onto center stage in the fall of 1917 not simply because they had been victorious. It was also because they had adorned with the irresistible spell of victory a mode of historical action in which the European Left recognized its forebears and the Right its enemies. As it turned out, this convergence recurred again and again during the twentieth century, and because of it no territory, no country, no matter how distant, exotic, or unlikely, would be considered ineligible to be a combatant in the universal revolution.

What was so spellbinding about the October Revolution was the affirmation of the role of volition in history and of man's invention of himself—the quintessential image of the autonomy of the democratic individual. After centuries of dependence, the late eighteenth-century French had been the heroes of that reappropriation of the self; the Bolsheviks picked up from where the French had left off. This succession is surprising, not only because it conferred a new dignity upon a nation that had always been at the margins of European civilization, but because Lenin carried out the October Revolution, in Marx's name, in the largest and least capitalist country in Europe. Inversely, it was perhaps the contradiction between belief in the omnipotence of action and belief in historical laws that lent October 1917 some of its power. To the cult of volition—the heritage of Jacobinism filtered down through Russian populism—Lenin would add the certainties of science, drawn from Marx's *Capital*. The revolutionaries thus managed to repossess for their ideological arsenal the substitute for religion that was so sorely lacking in late eighteenth-century France. By combining these two supremely modern elixirs with their contempt for logic, the revolutionaries of 1917 had finally concocted a brew sufficiently potent to inebriate militants for generations to come.

The Russian Revolution would not have had the same significance for the contemporary imagination if the revolutionaries had not cast it as an extension of the French precedent and endowed this break in time with a privileged place in the fulfillment of history by human will. It was as though the ideas of the tabula rasa and absolute renewal were somehow drawing strength from their prior occurrence in history.

To understand how Leninism fits together with the French revolutionary tradition, let us first turn to the Bolsheviks' interpretation of the French Revolution. The Bolsheviks thought it essential to single out the phases that supposedly prefigured the October Revolution while continuing to criticize the universalistic illusions that were inseparable from the "bourgeois" nature of 1789. The "Jacobin" episode—in the broad sense of the term, including the dictatorship of the Committee on Public Safety in 1793–94—was their favorite. It was the most voluntaristic and the least liberal moment of the French Revolution. It also possessed the characteristic, unique until 1917, of fitting neatly and entirely into a single revolutionary ambition as though that ambition were self-sufficient. From mid-1793 on, the Convention had given up the idea of implementing the new constitution that had just been voted for. The Revolution had become its own end and alone constituted the entire political sphere. It must be noted that the members of the Convention had consented to this lawless power on a temporary basis or until peace was achieved; the Bolsheviks, however, turned that exceptional government into a doctrine: they made unregulated power into a rule.[1]

The Bolsheviks were lucky to have been able to claim as their forebears, no matter how imperfect, those French bourgeois of 1793 who had, for a time, put revolution before all else. They even relied on a chronological analogy: just as the Year II had overshadowed 1789, so the October Revolution had eclipsed the February Revolution.

This genealogy, conveniently cobbled together, actually took root in European culture, where it rapidly acquired blue blood. In France, for example, a series of debates on the situation in Russia was organized between 28 November 1918 and 15 March 1919 by the Ligue des droits de l'homme.[2] The Ligue had come to the fore with the Dreyfus Affair and so was beyond reproach from the Left. It brought together an intellectual bourgeoisie that covered the political spectrum from the republican Left to the Socialist Party, and included many famous professors such as Paul Langevin, Charles Gide, Lucien Lévy-Bruhl, Victor Basch, Célestin Bouglé, Alphonse Aulard, and Charles Seignobos. Appraising the very young Soviet Russia was certainly the business of the Left, since the Right needed little information to detest Lenin: How could they entertain the least indulgence for the sort of defeatist escalation he represented, cloaked in the worst of French national traditions, the Terror? The Left, to the contrary, cherished the idea of revolution as an essential part of its heritage. True, in order to establish the Third Republic in the nineteenth century, the republicans found it necessary to dispel the memories of the First. Many, however, never stopped nursing those memories, and 1917 occurred not long after Clemenceau had proclaimed before the French legislature that the French Revolution was a "bloc."[3] Furthermore, revolution designates both a memory and a future. For a people that has undergone that unforgettable experience, their grasp of it has the durable elasticity of a court of appeals for present injustices. Before the Bolsheviks, many of the various families of French socialists had laid claim to the Jacobin precedent, among them Buonarroti, Blanqui, Buchez, Louis Blanc, and Jules Guesde, to cite only the best known.

The return of these hopes and memories was all the more intense because they were called out of the somnolence of pre-1914 political life. To Jean Jaurès, for example, revolution, as a necessary phase in the emancipation of the working class and a prerequisite for a classless society, remained very much on the horizon of history—but there it remained. It didn't impede open strategies or tacit alliances between different leftist groups. The republican idea and the socialist idea are not the same, but they can travel along the same road for as long as the road has priority over the destination. Lenin's October victory, however, signaled the triumph of the opposite conviction, where the objective takes primacy over the route, and revolution per se over what renders it necessary. That victory would be accompanied by an open, violent, and even bitter rejection of any reformism. It would also bring the French Left—both republican and socialist—back to its origins and make its members ashamed of their past. From the exaltation of Jacobin voluntarism the Leninists drew a condemnation of the heirs of that legacy— an effective form of blackmailing for loyalty, which has never relaxed its grip.

The October Revolution of 1917, far from being a replay of the French Revolution, was pure novelty. The characteristics that the Russian event held in common with the Jacobin dictatorship—the fact that it had been hatched by a prior revolution, the establishment of a power exercised by a small, militant oligarchy over a terrorized people, and finally the deployment of lawless violence against its adversaries—only masked the dissimilarities between the two revolutionary regimes.

History has substantiated this difference, for the Bolshevik Party would retain absolute power in what had once been czarist Russia, whereas Robespierre and his friends actually "reigned" over revolutionary France for a mere four months.[4] The comparison with the French Revolution became increasingly untenable as the dictatorship of Lenin's party looked ever more durable. Nonetheless, the comparison held: it turned up, in spite of its increasing absurdity, in attempts to interpret or justify Soviet occurrences. The "new economic policy" liked to refer to Thermidor, even though it in no way modified the nature of the Soviet dictatorship, whereas everything about the French Thermidor, including its name, came from the fall of Robespierre and the end of the Terror.[5] The Bolshevik Party purges carried out by Stalin in the 1930s in the name of the struggle against counterrevolutionary conspiracies were compared to the liquidation of the followers of Hébert and Danton[6] as if those conspiracies were all the more credible for having been originally orchestrated by the Robespierrists; the same argument would be trotted out again to justify the great trials of the 1950s in the "popular democracies" of Eastern and Central Europe. Since 1917, the precedent of the French Revolution—particularly the Jacobin period— has served as an all-purpose means of absolving the arbitrariness and terror that have characterized all of Soviet history, a procedure varying in intensity depending on the period.

Throughout the twentieth century, this biased use of the past was accompanied by a constant leftward shift in the historiography of the French Revolution itself, as the field became increasingly monopolized by Communist or Communist-leaning specialists. For them, the most significant thing about the French Revolution was what it concealed during its course—the fact that one day it would be surpassed. Its true center was thus no longer 1789, but 1793; no longer the rights of man and the development of a constitution, but the social and political condition of the popular classes and the dictatorship of public safety. Albert Mathiez suggested this interpretation but did not go all the way.[7] He gave equal weight to Jacobin universalism and Bolshevik universalism. After him, the French Revolution remained prisoner to its bourgeois condition, which allowed later historians to extrapolate from its most "advanced" period "anticipations" of what would follow. It was seen as having heralded the emancipation of man, yet as being incapable of realizing it. The October Revolution would be cast as the heir of that abandoned promise which, this time, would be fulfilled since the defeated bourgeoisie was no longer there to impede the people's conquests. The successive order of the two revolutions was thus construed as revealing the work of history to the advantage of the Russian event. The Jacobins had their auguries and the Bolsheviks their forebears. By virtue of this imaginary lineage, Lenin's Soviet Union took the reins of human progress and assumed the spot that revolutionary France had been keeping warm for it since the late eighteenth century.

Until the twentieth century, I know of no other examples of a nation whose image was suddenly promoted from a backward country to a guiding light. Yet we find several examples in the twentieth century. When revelations about Khrushchev tarnished the image of the Soviet Union, Mao's China, not to mention Castro's Cuba, took up the torch. The cascade of distant models did not merely signal that revolutionary hopes had narrowed over the course of the century. The fact that such models remained constant, endured, and survived historical refutation reveals the profound roots of those hopes. Deprived of God, our era was to deify history as the advent of a free humanity. The October Revolution was the mythological moment par excellence of this history—a history which, if not the substitute for salvation, had at least become the setting for humanity's reconciliation with itself.

The speed with which October eclipsed February, and the general reluctance, even in the face of reality, to let go of the myth of October, should convince us of that fixation on history. Originally, the events of October certainly dovetailed with the events that had followed the czar's fall eight months earlier; Mathiez, for example, made reference to this when comparing Kerensky to a Girondin and Lenin to Robespierre. Nonetheless, the February republic quickly took second place to the windfalls from the Bolsheviks' seizure of power; moreover, it was all but absorbed by what came after it, squeezed between Nicholas II and Lenin to the point where it would lose any historical identity. Viewed from the other end of the same history, from the decades after Khrushchev when the light of October was in its final decline, the Bolsheviks' revolution survived for a long time in the imagination of the Left in the West, even though it was hated by those who had undergone its consequences. Its reprieve was sustained by a rewriting of history comparable, though at the end rather than the beginning, to the rewriting that had erased the February Revolution: if we separate Lenin from Stalin, we have reinvented a purified October. This is such a tempting procedure that we must not discount the possibility of a posthumous resurrection of "Soviet" mythology. For that mythology has always rested on precedent, thus reconciling the privileges of the totally new with the mental habits of tradition; and therein lies its power.

Without the French reference, the October Revolution retains much of its objective strangeness. Certainly it profited from its coincidence with the moment when many war veterans were wondering, in retrospect, what all the suffering had been for. The Leninist defeatism of August 1914, which had been out of step with the climate of the war years, was able to touch important sectors of the European Left after 1918. Furthermore, the Bolshevik Party considered itself the advance guard of world revolution, nothing more. At that time, Lenin and Trotsky did not imagine their power could survive for long unless taken up by the European working classes; their eyes were riveted on Germany. Nevertheless, neither doubts about the meaning of the war nor an appeal to universal revolution are sufficient to explain why Bolshevism took root in broad strata of Western public opinion.

Russia is remote from Europe. The October Revolution was both geographically and chronologically eccentric. It followed the overthrow of czarism, which, as the last absolute monarchy to be toppled, was itself an expression of that remoteness. Who would have thought that an event symbolic of Russian backwardness would be followed in a matter of months by a second event that prefigured the future of Europe and the world? The Marxists, from the standpoint of their conception of history and with Kautsky at the fore, were the first to denounce such an unlikely ambition. To proclaim that Old Russia, barely emerged from autocracy, was the homeland of the international working class was like standing the world on its head.

But it was quite another story if October was looked at in light of the course taken by the French Revolution. When the known was used to explore the unknown, Russian history was returned to the western matrix, which made it much easier to handle. Revolution, counterrevolution, parties, dictatorship, terror, planned economy were simply a series of abstract ideas, serving as parallels. October following February mirrored the Montagne following the Gironde; the Bolsheviks' dissolution of the Constituent Assembly seemed inevitable if considered alongside the purge of the Convention of 2 June 1793. The constraints of circumstances mattered more than the demonstration of doctrine. This is how the analogical method of reasoning worked, relieving historians as well as contemporary or subsequent public opinion of the need to scrutinize the particularity of events and their participants. Those who reasoned this way acquired an even more extraordinary advantage: they could write off the importance of the past in the analysis of both revolutions: if those revolutions had been so very similar, who cared about the ancien régimes that preceded them!

Another element of the revolutionary idea, the illusion of the tabula rasa, also helped universalize it. The tabula rasa was an expression of the spontaneous "constructivism" of public opinion in the democratic era, and of the tendency to envision social issues merely as products of volition; it represented a rejection of tradition, an obsession with the present, and a passion for the future. The force of this idea surpassed anything Lenin said, wished, or was capable of realizing; it surrounded him with the aura of that other history of a great beginning, that of the French, which had sparked the imaginations of all nineteenth-century Europeans. It mattered little that the Bolshevik leader was a doctrinaire of the dictatorship of a single party, that he abhorred universal suffrage and representative rule, and that he believed Communism was the society of the future, in accordance with a science of history. It mattered even less that he was as much a populist as a Marxist and owed more to Tchernichevski than to Marx. Thanks to the abolition of the past wrought by the revolution, he too had been liberated from the particular determinations of the Russian past. The European Left viewed the Russian Revolution of 1917 less as Russian than as revolutionary; this, rather than Marxism, was what endowed it with universality.

That is why the October rather than the February Revolution assumed its privileged status. The overthrow of czarism in February was still a localized phenomenon, the last episode in an attempt to catch up with the West that had obsessed the Russians since Peter the Great. The huge, semibarbarian nation, long under the thumb of an ancien-régime sovereign, got back in step with Europe. It didn't so much reinvent history as raise itself up to the level of familiar history.[8] Allied with the parliamentary democracies of the West, at war with Germany since 1914, Russia drew from its democratic revolution additional justification for its foreign policy. February had been an exclusively Russian Revolution. In October, however, France and Britain hailed the new republic as the most recent country to follow in their footsteps.

October's uniqueness lay not only in the decree granting land to the peasants but also in the Bolsheviks' wish to find a way to end the war, followed by Brest-Litovsk in March 1918. Although Lenin closed the Russian Revolution by confiscating power within a few months, he started a new revolution against the bourgeoisie in the name of Bolshevism. Blinkered by the comparison with the French Revolution, Aulard and Mathiez would miss this fundamental discontinuity.[9] For these two important French historians, Lenin was not so much the inventor of a new social regime as the politician farthest to the left of a democratic revolution begun eight or nine months earlier. He incarnated not a new doctrine but loyalty to the process of revolution and hence to the revolutionary idea itself.

Thus Lenin became as universal as Danton or Robespierre. He epitomized the "spirit" that had prevailed in France during those extraordinary years and reappeared in Russia in 1917—a spirit which, for want of a better name, is called "revolution" and is difficult if not impossible to define because, unlike the American Revolution, it had neither a fixed point nor a clear outcome and because it was embodied exclusively in the flux of events. The French Revolution had never been more than a succession of "days" and battles around a single idea: the idea that power belonged to the people—a principle both unique and uncontested but incarnated by persons and groups which, one after another, appropriated its legitimacy yet never managed to embody it in durable institutions. The truth of the French Revolution was revealed in 1793, under the Montagnard dictatorship, by the formula that the government of the Revolution was "revolutionary." That tautology reveals the exceptional nature of the power that was without rules and all the more legitimate for being so—even more legitimate than if it had been legal. Therein lies the fascination that surrounded the Bolshevik regime more than a hundred years after Jacobin rule.

Revolution was viewed as not only a special mode of bringing about change, or as a shortcut to the future, but as a social condition and a state of mind in which the unmasking of juridical abstractions at the service of the powerful is achieved by the dictatorship of the true people, who are above all laws since all laws originate with them. This is why the enemies of revolution were so numerous and powerful and all but impossible to diminish. The rule of law never would have its day, except when paired with "reaction," as was the case during Thermidor. In 1920, the Bolsheviks were still stuck on Robespierre; but if revolution as an event could never be anything but a *process*, with no possible consensual ending, how could they have ignored the fact that they were continuing to illustrate the revolutionary spirit in the face of their enemies both domestic and foreign? The French revolutionaries of 1793 had also wished to remain true to the promises of democratic egalitarianism, to descend from political issues to social issues, and to institute a society in which individuals with their selfish interests would give way to regenerated citizens, the only legitimate participants in the social contract. This goal was the revolutionaries' sole claim to power, but what a claim! It was eminent, self-sufficient and superior to any constitution. Lenin would garner the heritage of that claim, attracting the same enemies. He would find himself, like the French in 1793, in a revolutionary situation par excellence, possessed by the passion to eternally pursue human emancipation, and threatened by those who sought to prevent or at least to stall that emancipation.

In order to tease out the comparison between 1793 and 1917, there is no need to establish a hierarchy between the two events and to believe that the second was superior to the first. Lenin held that the Communist revolution, unlike the bourgeois revolution, was truly universal, truly emancipatory. Later, Marxist-Leninist historiography worldwide would posit that the Communist revolution "accomplished" the "portents" of the earlier revolution. In 1918, however, it was enough for Aulard that Bolshevik Russia from 1918 to 1920 "resembled" 1793 France, and for Mathiez that Lenin reincarnated Robespierre. As a staunch republican, Aulard was no Communist, and although Mathiez did join the young French Communist Party at its foundation, he did not remain in it for long, rapidly becoming disenchanted with the dictatorial centralism of the Third International. For him, the Soviet Revolution had stopped short in much the same way as the French Revolution had done. For all that, the two events still shared the grandeur of having been revolutions.

So you could love October without being a Communist and could even cease to be a Communist and continue to love October. Thanks to Lenin, the Russian Revolution was saved from its Russian foreignness, was reunited with the Jacobin precedent, and was reintegrated into universal history. Seventeen ninety-three had not wiped out the memory of 1789, but October certainly erased February. In the French case, the two major episodes of the Revolution have always been recalled and reprocessed both as two distinct elements and as two essential parts of same occurrence. They have been analyzed primarily in terms of their interdependence and their respective effectiveness. The Russian case was quite different: October relegated February to its Russian particularity and seized revolutionary universalism for its own account. The success of that confiscation is due not only to the goal proposed by Lenin—to build a new society—and to mounting calls for international proletarian solidarity. As demonstrated by the reactions of the intellectual Left in France, that success was also due to the insertion of the Russian Bolshevik regime of October into the heritage of the French Revolution by way of the slot left vacant by the Jacobins since Thermidor. Paradoxically, it was precisely when Lenin had broken the Constituent Assembly, liquidated all opposition, insulted his Social Democratic critics, denounced political pluralism, and established the arbitrary rule of terror that he would assume his place in the democratic tradition of continental Europe via 1793. Robespierre, however, had embodied this paradox before him.

The Leninist idea alone could hardly have exercised such a profound influence over contemporary left-wing opinion. That idea was, and would remain, narrow, fanatical and almost primitive. But when fused with the Jacobin idea, it would acquire its mythological force as well as its "bourgeois" credibility. That capacity for synthesis is one of the elements that enabled Leninism to survive the catastrophes it caused as it traversed the twentieth century.

Let us now turn to the characteristics proper to the October Revolution. This formidable appendix to history's chapter on revolutions does not easily fit into the heritage it took as its model. It developed more than a century later, in another country, under different circumstances. It flew a brand-new flag, the flag of the victorious proletariat. The legacy of the French Revolution was rich, varied, diffuse, like democracy itself, which accounts for the diverse borrowings to which it would be subject. The October Revolution elicited a narrower loyalty, which made its universality the more extraordinary but also the more problematical. That universality was recognized by the bourgeoisie but contested by the Marxists.

Hardly had Bolshevism made its historical debut than it overflowed the particular circumstances of its victory and spread into what was formerly the czarist empire. Unknown yesterday, from October 1917 onward it would fill the world with its promise, renewing the mystery of the universality of 1789 after more than a century's hiatus. The message of the French Revolution had always stopped short of Europe's frontiers; the message of the Russian Revolution rapidly moved beyond them, thanks to a knack for extension that would continue throughout the twentieth century. An esoteric theory prior to 1914, Lenin's form of Marxism soon developed into a vast system of beliefs, mobilizing extraordinary passions among both its adepts and its adversaries. It was as if the most eccentric revolution in Europe had cast such a wide-ranging spell through the ideas it incorporated that it touched peoples beyond Europe and the Americas, in places where neither Christianity nor democracy had ever truly penetrated.

The blessing bestowed by history upon an event that did not really deserve it may be traced in large part to the exceptional circumstances of 1917–18. In Petrograd, October 1917 crowned the year in which, for the first time, soldiers collectively demonstrated against the war. A sign of the people's emancipation from the fatality of mutual massacre, the October Revolution achieved what had not even been attempted in February: made inevitable by the peasant soldiers rather than by the "working class," it turned the war against itself—the men of 1918 against their memories of 1914. The October Revolution was sparked by the fire of the tragedy it followed; Europe's most primitive country was now showing Europe's most civilized countries the way forward, though it had never ceased to imitate their history and, until then, had been unable to surpass it. In short, victorious Bolshevism would endow the revolutionary idea, inseparable since 1789 from the notion of democracy, with the added prestige of international peace and fraternity.

The French revolutionaries had themselves laid claim to the causes of the human race and universal peace. But they had made war and led their armies beyond their borders. In the end, they had even chosen a pure conqueror, the most glorious of their soldiers, to head their state. To their nineteenth-century heirs in Europe and Latin America, their national legacy was even more attractive than their teachings about liberty. And the guns of August 1914 had both figuratively and actually buried liberty in the name of the homeland just about everywhere in Europe. The Bolsheviks had seen this coming and had not gone along with the current. What is more, they offered an explanation of the conflict, drawn from the contradictions of capitalism, that ultimate reality hidden beneath the twin figures of democracy and nation. After the fact, their internationalism appeared not as a simple declaration of principle but as a strategic move, which, in the end, paid off. On the tombs of the soldiers, October had united revolution with peace.

The Russian Revolution certainly did not begin to enjoy the fruits of its influence as early as 1917. In February, public opinion reacted much as the various governments did. The allies were torn between the satisfaction of witnessing the fall of the last of the anciens régimes and the fear that the Russian armies would defect; the Germans saw things differently: it was in their interest that Russia should experience major anarchy, and they certainly contributed to Lenin's "revolutionary defeatism." In October, the Bolsheviks' seizing of power sharpened fears and speculation. Russia had entered into the realm of the unknown, and was soon to sign a peace with the Germans under remarkably difficult conditions. Nonetheless, the small sect of Leninism had outstripped a vast movement of opinion that had been perceptible since 1917—notably in the French army mutinies—and flowered in the fall of 1918: the end of the war heightened the survivors' awareness of their suffering and sowed doubts about the purpose of their sacrifices. Once the war had ended, Lenin's radical strategy, which in August 1914 had been the object of little attention or even comprehension, acquired the enormous resonance of pacifism—a sentiment more natural than bellicosity to democratic peoples. Consequently, the Brest-Litovsk peace treaty of March 1918 was regarded no longer as a Bolshevik defection but as the harbinger of armistice. Because the October revolutionaries' first priority was peace at any price, their revolution revealed the profound doubts of all combatants as to the war's purpose. Thus Communist Russia became one of the pillars of the conscience of Europe.

Russia, more than ever, was a part of European history because the Russians could not envision a future without the victorious extension of the Workers' and Soldiers' Soviets beyond Russia's borders, primarily into vanquished Germany. In sharp contrast to the French of 1789, the Russian revolutionaries of October 1917 could only conceive of their success as part of an interactive process with other nations. Lenin, Trotsky, and the members of the Bolshevik Party could not imagine a lasting success without bringing the greatest European nation—and the homeland of Karl Marx—into their camp. To them, the idea of Germany was not a hypothesis, a wish, or a mere strategy; it was something they were certain of, necessary to their survival. Begun in Russia, the weakest point of the imperialist system, the proletarian revolution was doomed unless it spread to the European peoples who had escaped from the imperialist war, starting with the losers. Lenin had no doubt that the fate of October 1917 would be decided outside of Russia with the total political engagement of Communist Russia. Nothing could have appeared stranger or more absurd to him than the idea of basing a lasting strategy on the notion of "socialism in one country."

From 1918 on, the victorious nations contributed to this transnational arrangement of power by lending support to the counterrevolutionary armies that were mobilized in the former czarist empire.[10] This so-called war of "intervention," though never pursued with sufficient enthusiasm for victory, was enough to realize the idea of a bipolarized postwar Europe by reviving old memories; once again, revolution and counterrevolution locked horns all across Europe, as they had during the era of the French Revolution. But in contrast to the unified French of 1792, marching off on their crusade, the nations of 1918 had just emerged from war and had no use for it. This explains why the allied intervention in Russia was branded with particular discredit, as though dishonored in advance, and was carried out as clandestinely as possible. The flag of peace fluttering over the October Revolution continued to provide protection even for the Red Army's attack on the White Army's troops, regardless of whether these were native or foreign. By their interference, the victorious powers demonstrated once more that capitalism tended to lead to war, further supporting Lenin's theory of imperialism.

And so the years immediately following the war, between 1918 and 1921, marched under the sign of Bolshevism, which could be spelled "From war to revolution." This radical motto, a model worth cherishing and imitating, coincided with the hopes of millions of surviving soldiers. It provided them with a rallying point. The clearest example was defeated Germany—the Germany of Wilhelm II—where, as in the Russia of Nicholas II, mutatis mutandis, the early symptoms of military defeat would lead to the sailors' and soldiers' revolt in the autumn of 1918, followed closely by the disintegration of the army and the Reich. The capitulation of November plunged Germany into anarchy; it seemed to have revived the Russian situation of the previous year and promised a revolution led by groups of extreme left-wing socialists in the name of workers' and soldiers' councils. Owing to the radicalization of the opposing camp, which included the general staff and the majority of the Social Democrats, that revolution fizzled. But it demonstrated that the German Revolution was on the horizon of the Russian Revolution. All over Europe, potentially subversive forces sprang up: in Béla Kun's Hungary, in the factory councils of Italy, and even in victorious France, where the Soviets would recognize themselves in the unionizing and political ultra-Left. Resentment against the war, filtered through October 1917, gave the anticapitalist revolution a tremendous boost.

That boost was so visible, and touched to varying degrees such a wide range of countries, whether defeated or victorious, that it may be regarded as one of the general psychological effects of the war. In accordance with the unwritten law whereby people are quickest to condemn those catastrophic situations to which they themselves acceded, the shame of the war intensified when the guns fell silent. Once the extent of the catastrophe became known, the memory of having participated in it assumed the form of "never again." It was this "never again" that made people receptive to the October Revolution, because it added an obsession with remorse to the power of hope. Having accustomed them to absolute violence and subjected them to the constraints of military submission, the interminable war itself had brought the European peoples to revolution. But it had also led them there by another, more obscure path—the return to self. Millions of soldiers who returned to civilian life were caught up in collective remorse over their active or passive roles in August 1914.

This was particularly true of those who voted socialist, voters or militants true to an International whose program, immediately before 1914, was to prevent the war by means of the international workers' movement. But the war broke out after all and was accompanied not by a general strike but by the *Union sacrée*. That de facto rallying, which would open up a huge doctrinal and political split within the Second International, had not been effaced by either Zimmerwald (1915) or Kienthal (1916).[11] Each of those meetings had brought together the small group of militants that had remained true to the resolutions of the Second International but were unable to mobilize their forces around those past engagements—they were relics of another era. It was October 1917 that constituted the massive negation of the *Union sacrée*, something the socialist leaders had a hard time denying: the proletarian revolution had triumphed in the struggle against war.

This admission is not without fallacy, for even though the old Russian regime proved incapable of conducting the war and disintegrated in the face of that challenge, it does not necessarily follow that it was replaced by a "proletarian" revolution. Russia was not even the most likely breeding ground for such an event. But what lent it that appearance, aside from Lenin's assertions, was the February-October sequence, which resembled a two-step devolution of power from the bourgeoisie to the proletariat, and the break with the Western capitalist allies with the signing of the Treaty of Brest-Litovsk. The European Left would see the February-October sequence as a condensed or, rather, an accelerated version of the periods of historical evolution familiar to them from their doctrinal training. With Brest-Litovsk, they once again came face to face with the solemn resolutions of the pre-1914 Second International and, hence, with their sworn faith. In both cases, the October Revolution reunited them with their tradition. The geographical and historical peculiarity of the event was canceled out by the credibility it lent to the corpus of socialist ideas, which had been badly damaged by August 1914. The war had given Bolshevik maximalism the unexpected advantages of orthodoxy and continuity.

The Russian revolutionaries were thus relieved of the responsibility of justifying themselves. That the Revolution took place when it did was sufficient to confirm its necessity, written in black and white in the old resolutions of the Second International. What difference did it make where and how it occurred? If so many looked to the Revolution at the moment when peace had been restored, both physically and mentally, it was less because of its particular reality than because it had mended the link—broken by the war—between their tradition and their imaginings of the future. The proletarian revolution was necessary because it had happened: these were the naive terms, illuminated by a retrospective view on the betrayal of 1914 and the suffering of the war, in which the Bolsheviks recorded not only their victory over Social Democracy but also their expansion in Europe in 1918.

From this time on, the magic of the Soviet phenomenon would exercise a powerful force over the popular imagination, independent of the realities of the regime. Since its greatest justification for arousing enthusiasm was simply that it had occurred, and since its longevity alone had so rapidly endowed it with an almost mythic status, the October Revolution eluded observation and study and was subject only to love or hatred—for heaven knows it was also abhorred, attacked, cursed, and reviled. But these reactionary panics came equipped with their antidotes; admirers of Soviet Russia regarded the virulence of their adversaries as further confirmation of their own sentiments. Marxist-Leninist ideology encompassed and consequently refuted out of hand any contradictory discourse. Thus began the long career of the absurd argument that disqualified by definition anything the Right might say about the Soviet experience.

The Left had less difficulty dodging this sort of suspicion, which Bolshevik propaganda nonetheless tried to pin on it as well, though it was hardly teeming with heretics. It too has a limited arena for discussion, as a result of the polarization of passions in the immediate vicinity of the Russian Revolution not only between the Right and the Left but between factions of the Left. This family quarrel was much more interesting to follow and richer in arguments than the old, familiar confrontation between revolution and counterrevolution. The European Left, socialist or libertarian, that wished to resist the Communist impetus found itself on the front line. In the short term, its survival was at stake, as was its identity. Its house—the "old house" of Léon Blum—was burning, and it had to let the fire run its course and then trace in its ruins a line separating and shielding those rival brothers. It was not enough for them to curse the Bolsheviks, which might have sufficed for the Right, and to brandish the notions of property, order, and religion. Members of the Left had to fight in the name of the doctrinal corpus they shared with the October revolutionaries and thus to discuss, argue, and extend to the maximum the limits of what remained to them.

This was a difficult undertaking, for, at almost every turn in its critique of the October Revolution, the Left that was reticent about or hostile to Bolshevism laid itself open to the accusation that it was defecting to the side of the enemy—a sort of trial of intent that served to prohibit any debate about Communism within the ranks of the Left and was destined to have a long future. This argument, however, deterred neither Rosa Luxemburg, nor Karl Kautsky, nor Léon Blum. Their examples show that it was the leaders of the European Left, once beyond the political and moral blackmailing, who were most capable of constructing a rational critique of Bolshevism. Not that they were better informed than anyone else, but they were familiar with the history of socialism and could situate Lenin's genealogy in that history alongside their own. In contrast to the emotive familiarity with revolution that marked so many militants, they put their trust in an inventory of texts and the democratic tradition of socialism.

Rosa Luxemburg was the first person to criticize the October Revolution in the name of revolutionary Marxism. When expressing concern about the Russian Revolution, prior to her assassination at the hands of the Freikorps, she was more than ever the invincibly independent militant whose words, during the Second International, had expressed an extraordinary combination of libertarian vehemence and Marxist theory. Her entire life, not to mention her death, testified to the virtual cult she devoted to the revolutionary idea. Nonetheless, fearing a monster in the making that would rob her life of its meaning, she balked at October.

As a young Polish Jew, she grew up in Warsaw. She spent her university years in Zurich, dipping into history, political economy, and Marx's *Capital*. In 1898 she moved to Berlin so as to be at the center of the European Workers' Movement in a socialist milieu less factional than that of her native Poland and destined for a prime place in history. Her youth foretold the violence with which, throughout her life, she would attempt to allay nationalist passions, which she viewed as a trap laid for the workers by the bourgeoisie. She belonged to no one nation but entirely to revolution.

In Berlin, she quickly achieved top grades in her education as an activist by refuting the "revisionist" Bernstein, thus gaining the esteem of Bebel and Kautsky. Part of her heart lay with German Social Democracy, of which she was not only the somewhat bohemian daughter but also one of the most gifted orators and most serious minds. But her temperament was too "leftist" for that milieu. A woman in a man's world, a Pole on German soil, a libertarian amid a huge, rule-bound organization, she would always remain at the margin of German socialism, and she rapidly found herself on bad terms with "Professor" Kautsky, although she never sought to found another militant faction.

As early as 1905, she understood that something of historical import was taking place in czarist Russia, that the European revolution appeared to be moving from west to east. So she entered into the debate between the Mensheviks and the Bolsheviks, siding mostly, but not completely, with Lenin. For although, like Lenin, she lived only for the proletarian revolution, she was not prepared to sacrifice the Marxism she had learned from Marx and Kautsky. With her sectarian feelers, she quickly perceived that the dictatorship of the Party would replace the movement of the masses.

From 1904 on, as a young militant writing in the journal *Iskra*, she did not hesitate to express her dissent from the concepts Lenin had expressed in "One Step Forward, Two Steps Back"; for her, those ideas were too authoritarian, too centralist; they linked the Bolshevik leader more to Blanqui than to Marx. The extreme centralization of the Party was in danger of putting the proletariat under the thumb of an oligarchy of intellectuals.[12] Rosa Luxemburg would have other disagreements with Lenin, notably on the question of nationalism. But centralization was the most important issue, because what she said at such an early date was so premonitory; it would resurface fifteen years later, in about the same terms, when the revolution occurred. Imprisoned in 1917 for her antiwar activities, she followed the Russian events as best she could, gleaning news from visitors and scraps of newspapers. She knew enough about what was happening to be concerned for liberty and to write about it.[13] Furthermore, right after being released from prison on 10 November 1918, and during the few weeks before she was assassinated in mid-January, when the revolution was in full swing, Rosa Luxemburg shared not one of the Bolsheviks' illusions about the German revolution. For her, it represented less a rupture or a decisive modification of relative power in Europe in favor of the proletariat than a kind of social chaos whose outcome was completely unpredictable and which could even lead to a victorious counterrevolution. She was therefore also skeptical about the exaggerated optimism of the Bolsheviks and their inclination to seize power under any condition, their willingness to risk isolating and thereby endangering the avant-garde of the proletariat. She exhorted the Spartacists to try to organize and take over the German working class—a prerequisite to the overthrow of Ebert's Social Democratic government.

Rosa Luxemburg's fears about the course the Russian Revolution appeared to be taking and her admonitions to the German militants were based on nothing less than a repudiation of the Leninist conception of revolution, according to which power, when offered by historical circumstances, was to be seized and kept by any means, even by a tiny avant-garde, provided it was well organized and convinced that it represented the interests of the masses. By the end of 1918, almost a year had gone by since the Bolsheviks had forcibly dismissed the elected Constituent Assembly, in which they had lacked a majority. This act was followed within twelve months by censorship of the press, one-party dictatorship, mass terror, and even concentration camps. For Rosa Luxemburg, all these things pointed up the oligarchic character of the Russian Revolution. Her little book, based on what she could gather of the news, revealed the abyss that already separated her from Lenin, who had been in power for only a few months. In mid-January 1919, she died as she feared she would, murdered by members of the Freikorps, before she had a chance to assume the role she was headed for in her last works: that of a critical witness of the Bolshevik Revolution, testifying in the name of popular liberty. No one could have fulfilled that role better than she, fortified by her libertarian genius and a past unsullied by compromise or remorse. Yet even her great voice, I believe, could not have made itself heard against the current, since her death—which confirmed her analyses and admonitions—has not saved her from obscurity. From Lenin's time on, Bolshevism, when victorious, has imposed silence upon its critics even after their death and especially if they took part in its struggles.

Let us now pass from the heroine to the professor and consider Karl Kautsky. The pope of the Second International, the friend and heir of Engels, he was the most famous Marxist theorist before the war. Having been the principal defender of Marxist orthodoxy against Bernstein's "revisionism," Kautsky subsequently turned against the leaders of the ultrarevolutionary Left of the Second International. In opposition to Bernstein, he defended the necessity of a revolution, denying that Marx had ever predicted that capitalism would eventually collapse by itself.[14] He reproached others, Rosa Luxemburg in particular, for their voluntarist illusions that a series of mass strikes, like those that occurred in Russia in 1905, could and should constitute the revolutionary break with the proletarian state.[15] In the prewar years, he increasingly stressed the objective factors of life in society in general and of revolutions in particular. The proletariat will overthrow the bourgeoisie: such is the movement of history. But that movement must be carefully prepared, for it occurs through the political organization of workers in parties and the conquest of power along democratic paths until power falls, like a ripe fruit, into the hands of one or more of the parties of the working class. Kautsky's version of the proletarian revolution bears little resemblance to the huge explosion created by the bourgeois revolution in France at the end of the eighteenth century—an event that in every respect overshot the intentions of its actors, who quickly abandoned themselves to the savage violence of improvisation. The most that could be hoped for from an event of the same magnitude—the one that occurred in Russia in 1905—was the establishment of a bourgeois, democratic order in place of a despotic ancien régime. The proletarian revolution, on the other hand, would derive its strength from a clear sense of history, and Kautsky saw its early signs as lying to the west of Europe, mainly in Germany.

But along came October 1917; the revolution emerged from where Kautsky least expected it, newly clad by Lenin in the theory of "imperialism." Now that this theory, thanks to the transformation of history by the World War, had become the order of the day, it was no longer the most civilized impulse of the West but the child of a Europe gone wild, the product of an unprecedented massacre, emerging from the conflicts of advanced capitalism. Far from having produced the revolution in the democratic countries where the proletariat was numerous and organized, as Kautsky had reckoned in 1909,[16] imperialism had moved the revolutionary flame to Russia, the most backward of European nations. The world revolution would come to pass by way of the weakest link in the chain of the imperialist system, sole offspring of the bloody barbarism of capitalism. In 1918, Kautsky did not believe in world revolution, perhaps because he had long been conscious of the strength of the bourgeoisie and the army in Germany, let alone those in the victorious nations of France and Britain. From the way the various nations had accepted the war in 1914, he concluded that socialism was on the decline and that a failure could not be transformed into a triumph. Like the Mensheviks, he thought that October 1917 was basically nothing more than the crowning of 1905 or the end result of February—the long-delayed outbreak of a revolution with a democratic agenda in a despotic country. But an outbreak of which the little Bolshevik Party, the most radical party of what was formerly the Second International, had taken command, claiming to be transforming its character. This was something Kautsky could not believe.

In 1918 and 1919 he wrote two long essays about the nature of the Russian Revolution: *The Dictatorship of the Proletariat*, which he began in August 1918, and *Terrorism and Communism*,[17] written the following year. As always, one of his objectives was to demonstrate his affinity with Marx, for Kautsky, like Plekhanov, never stopped referring to the basic texts. In this case he managed to come up with a brief reference in Marx to the dictatorship of the proletariat, which he found in a letter criticizing the Gotha program.[18] The phrase was sufficiently ambiguous to allow all sorts of contradictory interpretations. Kautsky saw it as a very broad definition of the social hegemony of the proletariat during the intermediate phase between capitalism and socialism, certainly not as a prescription for a dictatorial government founded on the political monopoly of one party. The latter, however, was the reality of Lenin's Russia behind the increasingly transparent mask of Soviet power; the Bolsheviks had dissolved the Constituent Assembly, fought and then banned the Mensheviks and the revolutionary socialists, and established, from the middle of 1918 on, a reign of terror. The more they cut themselves off from the great masses of the population and treated their former allies as enemies, the more they became isolated and tended toward terrorist dictatorship: an infernal dialectic that could only have worsened with the Russian peasants' inevitable opposition to socialism, once they had been assured that their plots of land were private property.

In one sense, Kautsky was reiterating the critique put forth by his old adversary on the left, Rosa Luxemburg: like her, he denied the Bolsheviks the privilege of representing an entire social class. But while she had at least shared with Lenin the idea that a proletarian revolution was occurring in Russia, Kautsky did not. He believed, like the Mensheviks, that neither February nor October 1917 could escape from its historical determinants; Old Russia was liquidating the ancien régime. What was occurring was not the first socialist revolution but the last bourgeois revolution. The shortcut that Lenin and Trotsky, since 1905, had been wanting Russia to take in order to cut it off from an entire historical epoch could only end in the despotism of one party over the people. It would constitute another experiment in absolute political voluntarism, which French Jacobinism had already shown to be a total failure.

In this way, Kautsky's critique is related to Benjamin Constant's analysis of the Terror of 1793.[19] Under the Directory, the young Swiss writer had interpreted the enigma of government by guillotine in the most civilized country of Europe as an anachronism. For while the French Revolution was moving toward the advent of representative regimes and modern individualism, Robespierre and his cronies thought they were working toward a return to the direct democracy of antiquity, founded on civic virtue. This belief was behind their determination to bend history to their will, and gave rise to the tragedy of the Terror. Kautsky's Lenin, on the other hand, was not looking to the past but was straining so hard toward the future that he too lost sight of what he was doing, if only because of the objective constraints upon his actions. He took a leap not backwards but forwards, in a sort of reverse anachronism whose effects were probably more serious because more lasting: an imaginary reunion with bygone days can never amount to more than a passing illusion, whereas the pursuit of a preordained future maintains the certainty of conviction. The Jacobin Terror and the Bolshevik Terror are part and parcel of the same chronicle of wayward volition, but the second threatened to last longer because it was more resistant to the refutations of experience, and was of greater intensity because it was by definition compelled to go ever farther.

This type of interpretation presupposes, in both Kautsky and Constant, a perception of the stages and direction of history, without which there can be no concept of anachronism. Such an interpretation supports a logical refutation; for if history has a direction and obeys a necessity, then the idea of a revolution taking place outside of or even in opposition to the movement of history becomes difficult to conceive. Such a revolution becomes all the more problematical when the interpreter and the actor share the same philosophy of history, which was the case for Kautsky and Lenin, both fervent Marxists. The only way out was for Kautsky to declare Lenin ahead of the revolution he was conducting, while Lenin reproached his critic for having fallen behind. Never had the concepts of "bourgeois revolution" and "proletarian revolution," so central to post-Marxism Marxist theory, seemed vaguer and more uncertain than during this polemic between Kautsky and Lenin, as each reproached the other for not knowing what he was talking about. The October Revolution, with its implausibility and ambiguous character, exploded the canonical categories of Marxist doctrine. When Kautsky spoke of the bourgeois revolution carried out by the Bolsheviks, he was not just trying to express the contradiction between the objective direction of the Revolution and its actors. He was also implying that Lenin knew no more about the history he was making than Robespierre had done; in the midst of the most frenzied voluntarism, Lenin encountered the uncertainty of historical action. The bitter discovery made by the Second International's professor of Marxism, who had so neatly set out the theory of the passage from capitalism to socialism, was that revolutions break out wherever they can and not where they ought to, and that neither their direction nor their course is predetermined.

Lenin was certainly correct when he fired off an impassioned response to Kautsky,[20] accusing him of backing out like a petty bourgeois "philistine"—the ultimate insult among Marxists—in face of the revolutionary situation that, after all, had been repeatedly foretold and prepared for by the resolutions of the Second International. Lenin had taken the event as it came and had written his response, as it happened, during the first days of November 1918, when the German sailors and soldiers' revolt broke out: now here was the world revolution on the move! While Kautsky theorized his fears, Lenin transformed his impatience into a doctrine: the odd thing is that both antagonists resorted to the same philosophy of political action. Lenin spoke of a coming Soviet democracy, a thousand times more democratic than any bourgeois constitution, although democracy had already become a dead letter by the end of 1918. Kautsky insisted on returning to the idea of revolution, but only to demonstrate that the one he was witnessing was not up to standard. The contradiction that lay at the heart of Marxism was incarnated by the two greatest Marxists of the time, who represented its two extreme versions: the school of revolutionary subjectivism and the school of historical law.

In the end, Kautsky's understanding of the Soviet experiment was less absurd or at least less illusory than Lenin's. He would, moreover, refine it over the years, without altering his initial diagnosis. But at the time, he was almost completely blind to the passions that moved his contemporaries. He said nothing about the war, addressing neither its collapse, which caused the Second International to founder, nor its course, which changed the world. His view of the war was purely abstract—the same view which, in the prewar years, had led him to consider the general strike of the proletariat as a priority. He had no sense or understanding of the collective sentiments that had incited the nations to take up arms against one another, or of the passions that turned the mass of soldiers against the war in the name of revolution, or of the widespread questioning of the sense of those countless deaths. He exemplifies the impasse in which European socialism, the Second International, and German Social Democracy in particular found themselves just after the war—a war to which, if unwillingly or in any case against their doctrines and promises, they had given their collective assent in 1914 and which they dared neither to claim as their own, like the nationalists, nor to condemn, like the Bolsheviks. German Social Democracy was thus divorced from both national and revolutionary discourses, suspended in a state of political weightlessness and condemned to serve one or the other of its adversaries. The German Social Democrats had nothing to say to the survivors of the war. Their leaders were incapable of addressing the nation and speaking of the suffering they had just undergone, even though they had lost everything in the war.

What was left to them? A Marxism that was part of their historical identity and which, in itself, was often of good quality, though it was put out of circulation by the events of August 1914. As this old star faded, the new star of Leninism emerged, Marxism rising from its ashes, consolidated by its victory in "real" history. As a result, the old form of Marxism, which in the face of the new triumphant Marxism was generally in retreat, came to be more of a handicap than an advantage for European socialism. What the old retained in common with the new exposed it to the blackmail of worker solidarity and made it more difficult for the old Marxists than for members of the "bourgeois" parties to participate in democratic coalitions in the government. After its collapse in August 1914, social-democratic Marxism would not have survived so far into the twentieth century if its proponents, confronted with the Bolshevik challenge, had not been compelled to keep swearing allegiance to their origins.

Let us now turn to France, to a debate of a different nature: the debate that accompanied the rallying of militant socialists to the October

Revolution and its "conditions." French socialism never produced a Marxist theoretician with a standing even close to that of Kautsky in the Second International. The French socialists were more heterogeneous, doctrinally and socially, than their German counterparts, and less working-class, less Marxist, more petty-bourgeois, and more interbred with Jacobin republicans. The battle of ideas and power between Guesde and Jaurès had never really been resolved before 1914. Running parallel to it was an autonomous workers' current, revolutionary syndicalism, which was tinged with anarchism and jealous of its autonomy. It was here, in 1915, that the first or at least the boldest opposition to the war originated, the Socialist Party having massively opted for the *Union sacrée* in August 1914. The socialists would be loyal to this fundamental choice until 1917, when the social and military crisis of that year pushed the majority into Wilsonian positions in opposition to the nationalist enthusiasm of Clemenceau. But even then, the French socialists looked at what was happening in Russia without much pleasure, since those events threatened to weaken the allied armies, which is exactly what would occur at Brest-Litovsk.

None of this endeared the French socialist movement to the makers of October 1917. France, moreover, was the great victorious power on the European Continent and thus represented the principal guardian of imperialist interests. The victory itself was what protected the French proletariat from the advances of revolutionary defeatism, which had— *in extremis*, it is true—eventually seduced the German proletariat. German workers, like the British, were corrupted more than ever by imperialism. The politicians who pretended to defend their interests remained chained to the delights of bourgeois parliamentarianism. The Bolsheviks thus had a simple response to the weakness of the French socialist opposition to the war: to put the blame on the entire movement. The political debate between the Russians and the French over the principles of the Third International established in Moscow in 1919 was remarkable for the extreme distance between their original positions.

By the end of the war, the only French socialists Lenin could count on were a few individuals and small knots of militants who, for the most part, were revolutionary syndicalists. He received wider support from members of the CGT (Confédération générale du travail), but that support cooled off considerably when it became clear that the Bolsheviks had relegated the unions to a subordinate role. Then, a little more than two years later, the Tours Congress overwhelmingly voted to adhere to the Third International and to the "conditions" it specified,[21] which went against all the traditions of French socialism. No matter what motivations and second thoughts surrounded this vote, it continues, and for good reason, to symbolize the influence of the Leninist revolution even over the party that was least enthusiastic about it.

I shall not enter into the intrigues surrounding this complex story, which involved a good many intermediaries between Moscow and Paris. It has been meticulously described and analyzed by Annie Kriegel.[22] What concerns us here is both more limited and of wider concern: the movement of opinion that brought French militants to the Moscow theses.

In that movement we find a notion widespread among the whole European Left of the period, that of the imminent end of capitalism, condemned to perish beneath the ruins of the war that had been provoked by its contradictions. In his foreword to a pamphlet by Boris Souvarine that appeared at the end of 1919, Captain Jacques Sadoul,[23] who had remained in Moscow to preach for the good cause among his French compatriots, set the tone for the partisans of the Third International: "Capitalist society is definitively doomed. The war and its consequences, the impossibility, given the resources available to us, of resolving the new problems, have cleared the way for the victorious march of the Third International."[24] These words are followed by a reference to those "great revolutionary forefathers" of the French, whose flame need only be rekindled. This reference can be found in all the activist literature of the time. Even Sorel, though not an unconditional admirer of the French Revolution, had earlier given his blessing to it when he added praise of Lenin to the fourth edition of his famous *Reflections on Violence* (September 1919): "The politicians who maintain, with Clemenceau, that the French Revolution forms a *bloc* are hardly justified in showing severity toward the *Bolsheviks:* the *Bloc,* admired by Clemenceau, caused at least twice as many people to perish as have the Bolsheviks, who are denounced by the friends of Clemenceau as abominable barbarians."[25]

And so Lenin was equated with Robespierre, something we have already seen in the work of Mathiez; but Sorel and Souvarine's Lenin was devoted to a task more universal than Robespierre's: the abolition of capitalism and the bourgeoisie. What is more, the Allies' war of intervention made that task doubly necessary since the October Revolution, born to stop the war, had to stop it for the second time. Lenin was thus situated at the intersection of the Revolution and the armistice, offering French socialists a chance to redeem themselves from the position they had taken on August 1914. In 1919, the war against war was again at issue but under less difficult political conditions.

What was really at stake, even in a France victorious over the Germans, was the question all of Europe was struggling with: how to make sense of the war of 1914. The problem plaguing militant socialists, even French ones, was that of the validity of the *Union sacrée*. Had not France triumphed over Germany? Certainly, but the October Revolution had caused class struggle and revolutions to reemerge from behind the lineup of nations. How could the French socialist Left have ignored this when it was the Right which, in the immediate postwar period, was capitalizing on the political benefits of the victory of 11 November? The debate over the terms of membership in the Third International centered less on the nature of the regime established in Russia than on the Socialist Party's verdict on its past after Lenin's prosecution of that party. The strength of Bolshevism came not from what it was but from the image it offered, once it had triumphed, of what the history of European socialism might have been had its members remained loyal to its resolutions in 1914. It presented another history of the war, one that never took place, which could be compared in the imagination with what had actually happened and had proved to be a cataclysm, even for the winners. The October revolutionaries, those conspirators and suspected Blanquists, could plead nonetheless for the success of, and the respect due to, the positions they had defended. After the fact, they would symbolize the virtues and missions that were betrayed in August 1914.

For this reason, the delegations sent to Russia in 1920 by the French socialist Left—ostensibly on fact-finding missions—looked more like manifestations of allegiance than proof of a desire to know more.[26] The main goal, at least for Cachin and Frossard, was to publicly clinch the deal between the left wing and the center wing of the party—the Committee for the Third International and the majority of "Reconstructors"—at the meeting of the International in Moscow. The debate over the "Twenty-one conditions" went far beyond passing judgment on Lenin's Russia: at stake was the adoption or rejection of Bolshevik principles in the strategy and organization of the international workers movement. It wasn't because they traveled to Moscow that Cachin and Frossard, old politicians that they were, rallied to Souvarine's positions, but the reverse: they made the journey because they already shared those positions. They knew little more than the activists did about the realities of the new Russia. But given the revolutionary enthusiasm of the militants, they sensed that this new Russia was rekindling both their regrets and their hopes.

It was this mental association that Léon Blum sought to destroy with his famous speech at Tours. Blum attempted to dissociate Bolshevik Russia—a particular revolutionary experience—from its pretension to universal value. His argument was Menshevik or even Kautskyist. The revolution, having emerged in czarist Russia, owed part of its character to the world it had turned upside down. In the absence of a strong, preexisting capitalist development and a true bourgeois society, the seizure of power in the name of the proletariat took on the character of a putsch carried out by a tiny party of militarily organized professional revolutionaries. A dictatorship of the proletariat established in this way is liable to be nothing more than a disguise for dictatorship pure and simple, imposed upon an immense population by a minority lacking a mandate. While pointing out the dangers of this scenario without condemning what engendered them, Léon Blum was not contrasting it to a "democratic bourgeois" perspective either legalist, electoralist, or reformist. On the contrary, he attempted to clear the socialist tradition, which he was defending against Lenin, of the suspicion that it was abandoning the revolutionary project for a reform-oriented revisionism. He knew he had to defend revolution all the more vigorously since he himself was critical of the one that had just seized power in Moscow. Revolution? That word, all but sacred, encompassed both the means and the end, the violent seizure of the state by insurrection, and the establishment of a "workers'" regime that would liquidate bourgeois domination. These two convictions, two pillars of the socialist tradition, were hailed by Blum when he declared himself to be more than ever a partisan of the "dictatorship of the proletariat"—another expression central to the resolutions of the Second International. That term was also used by the Bolsheviks, who, as we saw in Lenin's response to Kautsky, wielded it with the accent on "dictatorship" against those nostalgic for bourgeois political pluralism. Léon Blum used it in another, more Jaurrèsian sense: for him, the "dictatorship of the proletariat" was a way of saying that the proletarian revolution, crowning a long social and educational development, was bringing into power a whole enlightened people, with few remaining adversaries. Like Jaurès before him, the French leader was trying to restore to that sacred term the dignity, even the morality, that had been compromised by Lenin's exploit—an exploit Lenin had turned into a doctrine.

The weakness of Blum's position resulted from the failure of his reconsideration of the proletarian revolution and, hence, of the revolutionary tradition to address the rupture in tradition that occurred with August 1914, or to address the war, still the dominant the memory in people's minds. The partisans of the Third International drew their strength from the notion that, in 1914, the Second International had betrayed its mission and its commitments, and from the experience of the trenches and military servitude, whose vicious circle the Bolsheviks had succeeded in breaking. In face of this, how could anyone take seriously a dogmatic discussion masked in semantic ambiguity? If the great majority of militants opted at Tours for the Communist theses without carefully considering their implications, it was because they were caught up in the massive shakeup of all public life provoked by the war years. This was their way of saying "Never again!"

We should not underestimate, however, the lasting symbolism that these debates about dogma, inseparable from interpretations of Marxism, could assume in the workers' movement. This symbolism helps explain how Bolshevism, while owing the greater part of its European influence to an exceptional experience and situation, also found its roots in the reappropriation of a vocabulary and a tradition. What began with the meticulous orthodoxy of Léon Blum became a long, defensive battle over a common inheritance. The socialists who refused to bend to the conditions for membership in the Third International were careful not to lose their rights to the divided treasure of Marxism—an indispensable precaution if the entire territory of tradition were not to be left to the Bolsheviks and their ubiquitous imitators.

To avert the accusation of disloyalty, the socialists hung onto the revolutionary idea all the more firmly. If they impugned the Bolshevik Revolution as a deviation, it was in order to hasten the overthrow of capitalism, which, incidentally, the revolution had accomplished. The measure of fidelity to Marxism they retained, whether by conviction or by necessity, thus made them vulnerable to the Communists' attempts to outbid them. Although this situation is normal of any left-wing party in relation to an extreme left-wing party, the French socialists' intransigent attachment to the Marxist reference proved awkward for two other reasons. First, it limited their understanding of regimes that were difficult to fit into Marxist categories, such as the Soviet one. Second, revolutionary self-affirmation cut them off from center parties without leaving them much leeway on the left, where the Communists were camped. Even when and where they resisted the spell of Bolshevism, the socialist parties paid for it dearly in terms of political autonomy or strategic liberty and were condemned to a narrowly defensive attitude or a shameful alliance with bourgeois parties. Even their youngest and most active militants often had inferiority complexes vis-à-vis their "enemy brothers"; cognizant of the perils that Bolshevism posed for liberty, they admired the organizational capacities and the spirit of sacrifice that it engendered among its partisans.

Thus, in the years following World War I, the Bolshevik Revolution of October 1917 acquired the status of a universal event. It immediately assumed its place in the lineage of the French Revolution, as an event of the same order that also inaugurated an epoch in the history of humanity. In spite of its improbable birthplace, it fulfilled an expectation that had been part and parcel of European political culture ever since the French Revolution: the advent of a society that was sovereign by virtue of the equality at long last attained by its associates. This expectation had been nourished by socialist eschatology throughout the nineteenth century and had drawn renewed strength from the sufferings endured during the First World War. The Bolsheviks' prerogative of universality stemmed both from the European revolutionary tradition and from the exceptional situation of 1918–20.

The birth of the Soviet Revolution was celebrated by countless declarations. The twentieth century opened with a glow surrounding what many contemporaries hailed as a decisive and beneficial break with capitalism and war, bestowing their approval more upon what the October revolutionaries said about themselves than upon actual experience. In rereading all these documents today, one is struck by the volume of peremptory judgments delivered on the basis of so little information. The explanation for this phenomenon applies in both directions: Lenin's Russia was a symbol. It channeled not so much ideas as passions; it stood for universal history. The attempts of Social Democratic theoreticians to contest this stature fell mainly on deaf ears, and although they managed to survive, there is no question that between their brand of Marxism and that of the victors of October, it was the latter's that spoke to the contemporary imagination.

From that period on, however, the Russian Revolution became more than a symbol: it became a history. In one sense—and one only, of course—that history ended with the winter of 1920–21. The war of intervention was over; the Bolshevik counteroffensive failed in the face of Warsaw in 1920; "war Communism" had destroyed the economy and generated famine; the party was all-powerful but isolated and was already ruling through terror and the police. In March 1921, the sailors' insurrection at Kronstadt, invoking the revolution against the Bolsheviks ("power to the Soviets and not to the parties"), ended in a bloodbath. In the same month, Lenin halted "war Communism" and established the New Economic Policy compelled to give a little breathing space to a production that had become asphyxiated by regulation and requisitions. The Russian Revolution entered a period of economic "Thermidor" at the very time when it was making official and reinforcing the apparatus of the dictatorship by which it dominated the country. The Terror could no longer use war—civil or foreign—as an alibi. It had become the way in which the regime functioned on a daily basis. At the Tenth Congress in March 1921, Lenin defeated the "Workers' opposition," which was protesting the identification of the working class with the Party, even as he achieved a vote to ban factions within the Party.[27] Rosa Luxemburg's worst predictions were coming true. The October Revolution was finished, for the workers and peasants had "gone back home"[28] and were henceforth subject to the absolute power of an oligarchy. But it was not finished, insofar as this oligarchy claimed to be the guardian of the spirit of October and was defined exclusively by its loyalty to the ideology it saw as the secret of its victory.

Western intellectuals could certainly have divined the broad outlines of this evolution, in spite of the mystery that so rapidly shrouded the policies of the very recent Comintern. Some, like Bertrand Russell, who in 1920 published one of the best books on Bolshevism,[29] tried to observe what was really happening. The Cambridge logician, one of the great minds of Europe, was also interested in social questions. He was an independent member of the great family of British socialism, which was alien to Marxism, philosophically eclectic, and inclined to the exercise of practical reason. Horrified by the war, he was even imprisoned for saying so, and he dreaded its legacy of "disenchantment and despair," which threatened to lead to what he termed a new religion and seemed to him to be incarnated by Bolshevism. So he decided to go and have a look. He took a short trip to Russia from 11 May to 16 June 1920, at the same time as a British Labor delegation but independently of it. He visited Leningrad, Moscow, and some of the country around the Volga basin. He talked to Kamenev, was received by Lenin for one hour, and also saw the remnants of the Left, the Mensheviks and the Revolutionary Socialists. His was a true study mission, carried out by a keen observer—the exact opposite of the Cachin-Frossard visit to Moscow, which, around the same period, was given up to remorse and rallying.

The days of capitalism were numbered; of that, Russell had no doubt. But on the basis of what he had witnessed in Russia, he returned from Moscow convinced that the Bolshevik path to a new social order was not the right one. In his observations he took account of the particular circumstances surrounding the Russian Revolution: the weight of the past, the country's backwardness in relation to the West, and the war of intervention undertaken by the Allies. Having made this deduction, he saw little of value in the new elements inaugurated by the Russian revolutionary experience. In the domain of economics, the urban–rural circuit had been almost completely destroyed; getting supplies to the cities was problematical; the peasants were unhappy and hostile, the workers passive. Russell's description of daily life in Russia during those years is grim. On the political level, his verdict was even more severe. This British traveler was not fooled for a minute by the "Soviet" myth of direct democracy for the workers. Behind the flag of the Soviets he perceived the dictatorship of the Party; after the popular revolution had receded, the only thing left standing was the omnipotence of a party apparatus. Less than a year before Kronstadt, Russell could already see how disliked and isolated that apparatus had become. He noted that Bolshevism was more popular abroad than at home. In Russia it was detested as a tyrannical regime, whereas outside Russia it was hoped for as a liberation. A failure in the real order of things, it was a success in the realm of beliefs.

The tone of Russell's little book is not polemical but factual. It is a report that assembles stories and descriptions of his experiences, full of awareness of the concrete and the good sense that are a part of the charm of British intellectuals. Even after the fact, the author did not become a fierce adversary of Bolshevism; he was as convinced as ever that history was moving toward the end of capitalism. What he most objected to about Bolshevism was its pretension to universality and its messianic aspect, which threatened to bring the European working class to an impasse; those primitive socialists had nothing to teach the West. They brought only an illusory substance, a false religion, to the hopes of people disoriented by the war. Since he was not a Marxist, as he explains in the second half of his book, Russell, unlike Kautsky or Blum, had no need to defend another version of the dictatorship of the proletariat or to reveal to the century a revolutionary horizon of another type. The experience of history would take care of that. The task at hand was both to analyze the Russian failure, so that other nations could avoid the same fate, and to combat a then-current propensity for Bolshevik messianism.

Russell, who at the end of his life would become less resistant to the attractions of a common front with the Communists,[30] had no trouble at the end of World War I in breaking the spell of Bolshevism. Both as a socialist and as a pacifist, he was curious about Soviet Russia. He went and gathered evidence through observation, like a scientist, and formed his judgment on the basis of that evidence. There was nothing of the passion play in his account, and in this he was quite unusual.

By then, a more common story, of a different sort, was beginning between progressive thinkers and Soviet Russia: a story of belief and disenchantment. At its birth, the Russian Revolution gathered around it a group of admirers and loyal followers. With the passing of the years, would the Revolution fulfill its promises? Could it maintain its fervor? And lastly, how would its partisans' faith survive the course it would take?

FOUR

Believers and Unbelievers

THE FRENCH REVOLUTION, LIKE THE RUSSIAN,
left a long line of admirers in its wake; its supporters and imitators
could be found all over Europe and even beyond. But although both the
Russian and French events were surrounded by the revolutionary spell
proper to the promise of the building of a new world, they kindled different kinds of enthusiasm.

The two countries' historical situations were very different. Eighteenth-century France was the most "civilized" nation in Europe; the
European elite spoke French, and France had always been their cultural
model. The Revolution of 1789 amplified that habit—it neither broke
it nor created it. Russia in 1917, in spite of its enormous progress since
the beginning of the century, remained a newcomer to what European
thinkers called "civilization." Even its ancien régime was recent if we
regard it as lasting until the emancipation of the serfs by Czar Alexander II in 1864.[1] Nonetheless, the October revolutionaries proclaimed
that they were setting an example for humanity and, above all, for Europe. This pretension was not new in Russian history; it had appeared
earlier in the very different guise of Slavophile messianism. But what
lent it novelty in its Leninist incarnation also made it paradoxical: the
idea that Old Russia, barely emerged from czarism, was inventing a
social and political regime that could and should serve as an example
for Europe and the world, yet without a break in its continuity with
Western history. Now, having long viewed peasant and despotic Russia with commiseration, German and other Western European workers
were holding demonstrations to the tune of "Soviets for everyone!"
But although this about-face effaced the Russia of the czars and won
Lenin's Russia its credentials of French-style universality, the regime
still lacked credibility; Social Democratic leaders, among others, with-
held their approval. It would never possess the kind of historical

inevitability that the French had enjoyed, in a west-east direction, in the nineteenth century. Failing the spread of the Soviets, to the limited extent that Russia held a patent on them, this model possessed none of the many-faceted universality of the French democratic heritage. Had "socialism in one country" ever caught on, it would probably have emphasized the non-European side of Russia, thus eliminating concrete historical substance from the model's claim to universalism—a claim that had become increasingly strident as the Russian revolutionaries tried to hang on to its benefits.

At the time when the effects of the French Revolution were spreading in Europe and the world, the Revolution itself constituted an event of the past, with a beginning and an end. The Russian Revolution, in contrast, had only a beginning, which kept recurring. I am not arguing that the "end" of the French Revolution is easy to pinpoint, for the very concept of revolution that emerged with it precludes a clear definition. That ambiguity would dominate internal French politics at least until the Third Republic.[2] But in the end, viewed from Europe or beyond, the events that began in 1789 ended with the fall of Napoleon, when the victorious kings and the restored princes reconstituted a post- and antirevolutionary political and social order. Henceforth, the French Revolution as an event was finished. What remained of it was something else: what contemporaries called its "ideas," which would become an intellectual and political heritage available to all—a heritage that appears to be uniform in contrast to the world of the ancien régime. In truth, that heritage was really quite diverse if we consider the multiplicity of its legacies—the autonomy of individuals, equality before the law, representative government, national laws, democratic dictatorship, and socialism.

Each of these bequests had their partisans and detractors. Some were mutually compatible, some not. None of them were linked to the magic of a name, not even Bonapartism, which—and for good reason—existed as such only in France: the French Revolution eluded the grasp of all who tried to direct it. An event that possessed an extraordinary unitary power and a wealth of contradictions, it would remain so even after it had run its course: a treasure trove of ideas, never the exclusive property of one man or one party; a gold mine for modern curiosity, whether optimistic or apprehensive. The next century would be replete with its questions and accomplishments.

Quite different were the character and destiny of the October Revolution of 1917. Those who seized power in the name of Communism hung onto it in the name of Communism and transmitted it under that same name. In 1787, Mirabeau and Robespierre didn't know they were about to make a revolution. Lenin, however, had always been convinced of it; he was possessed by a single idea, which he believed to be scientific, and he built a party around that idea. For him, October 1917 was to be the appropriation by the science of history and by the Party of a power in escheat. Unlike June–August 1789 in France, October was not the libertarian explosion of a society but the confiscation of state power by a party that made no bones about it, since it immediately dissolved the Constituent Assembly.

I said earlier that the Russian Revolution was over by the winter of 1920–21, with the end of the war of intervention, the mutiny at Kronstadt, the Tenth Congress, and the New Economic Policy. This is true if "revolution" is understood as the more or less heroic founding period of a regime, along with the implementation of radical ideas such as "war Communism," a roughly consensual enlistment of the workers, and a call to international subversion. In this respect, with the Tenth Congress and the NEP, prose certainly followed poetry! But in other ways the Soviet Revolution continued; Lenin was merely carrying out a tactical withdrawal without modifying either his ultimate goal or the Party dictatorship. In this apparent concession to his adversaries, he was truer than ever to the political monopoly of the Party, which in that same year had been reinforced by the prohibition of all opposing groups in its midst. The system adopted in 1917–18 left no room for the people's experience and even less for their choice. It was a regime without accountability, where any change in policy was possible as long as it was decided upon and carried out by the same party, the same men. And so the October Revolution continued, since power remained in the hands of its authors.

Similarly, the revolutionary Terror was defended as merely a necessary response to counterrevolutionary violence—a fiction that had already proved so useful for the defenders or champions of the French guillotine. In 1921, foreign intervention had ended, the Bolsheviks' old adversaries had all gone abroad, the mutiny at Kronstadt had ended in a bloodbath, and the peasants were once again free to produce and sell. It was precisely when the dictatorship of fear appeared less necessary that it was reaffirmed even more forcefully at the 1921 Tenth Party Congress.

The French revolutionaries had never mastered the idea of political representation, one of the thorniest concepts of modern democracy. They had flirted with the essentialist version of representation, which consisted of a pyramid of identities—the people at the bottom, above them the Convention, then the Committee on Public Safety, and the *Incorruptible* on top. This particular conception had never been the object of a real doctrine and had in any case disappeared with 9 Thermidor, which had brought with it the democratic notion of a periodically devolving and thus uncertain power. In contrast, the Bolsheviks, when evoking Thermidor apropos of the NEP, were thinking exclusively of alterations in economic policy. As prisoners of their own historical philosophy, they reasoned as though the only thing that counted was the economy. Their interests coincided with their doctrine. They were in power and there they would stay. In doing so, they added a new chapter to the theory of revolutionary regimes.

The Bolsheviks considered themselves, and themselves alone, to be the guardians of the outcome and direction of the October Revolution through the agency of the Party, which had brought them together under the authority of Lenin. The Party was legitimized not by popular suffrage but by its leaders' knowledge of the laws of history, constantly enriched by "praxis": this was the reason for its unique character and the justification for its monopoly. This was also the reason for the string of tautologies the Bolsheviks substituted for the uncertainties of political representation of the democratic "bourgeois" type: the working class was the emancipator of the people, the Communist Party was the head of the working class, and Lenin was the head of the Party. The idea of a science of history gave rise both to the irreversible nature of the October Revolution and to the necessity for a political oligarchy to watch over that revolution. In his last year, Lenin realized the dangers of the bureaucratic tyranny that was inseparable from this notion of power. But he was the one who had come up with the notion and directed its adoption—it was too late to worry about what his successors would do with it. When the Soviets fell silent, his famous "proletarian democracy" so celebrated by Kautsky was nothing other than the absolute power of a party isolated in the midst of a people exhausted by their ordeal.

Thanks to Lenin, however, the Revolution continued, even though— and perhaps because—his spirit had disappeared among the popular masses. Within Russia, it persisted as a state ideology indispensable to the maintenance of the Party legitimacy; a "strategic pulling-back" of the NEP had to be undertaken, but only so that the final goal of Communism could better be reached, something the Bolsheviks alone could accomplish. And so the idea of orthodoxy made headway, gaining importance because the policies enacted seemed to be moving away from it. Even within the Party, the time of debates and open disagreements was over: the role of guardian of the Revolution was incompatible with factions since they threatened the direction of the Revolution. When the revolutionary tide ebbed, the Bolsheviks shifted from the idea of a Marxist science of history, which had been confirmed by their victory in 1917, to the necessity of a unanimously held dogma. This was the only way they could continue to maintain an iron grip on their interpretation of the past and, inseparable from it, their dictatorship over the present.

An undertaking such as this was all the more difficult because the Russian Revolution had a universal mission from the start. Not only had the revolutionaries reckoned on the support of the international proletariat for their survival, but they had cast themselves as part of something even vaster: the avant-garde of humanity itself. In 1792, the French revolutionaries had employed the same justification for war with Europe, leading to many unpredictable events and implications. The Bolsheviks had made their revolution in opposition to the war. Their notion of proletarian internationalism impelled them not to the armed export of the red flag but to the widespread organization of Communist Parties in their image. Lifted from the tradition of the Second International, though intended to be used against it, the creation of the Third International fulfilled that objective. It was founded on the principle that the Bolshevik Party's ideology and form of organization could be made universal. It was to constitute a centralized command for the world revolutionary movement, with the men of Moscow, holders of the secret of successful revolutions, as the chief strategists. This, of course, implied a separation of the Russian Revolution from the Bolshevik Party: the former would function on a national level, the latter on an international one. But this split occurred only in the division of offices and organizations. Politically speaking, Lenin and the heads of the Bolshevik Party also reigned over the Third International, where the agenda, though presented from another angle, was dominated by questions arising from the situation in Russia.

In short, the Third International was but the institutional extension of the October Revolution in Europe and the rest of the world. That is how it engendered the same problem as had the French revolutionary war of the late eighteenth century: it revealed its particularity at the very moment when it was attempting to substantiate the universality of its mission. Whereas the French, in abandoning themselves to war, risked forgetting their original intentions, the Bolsheviks entrusted the universal destiny of their adventure to the formula that had assured their success at home—a mixture of quasi-military militantism and radical political realism, with a big dose of ideology thrown in. They transmitted to the new International a conspiratorial character inseparable from the extreme voluntarism that had marked their revolution, dressing it in the science of history. This done, they overestimated the probability of new Octobers all over postwar Europe, as was made clear by their strategy in Germany and Bulgaria in 1923. At the same time, however, they managed to plant parties in many places which, by virtue of their common ideology, were subject to a common authority. That ideology would soon have a label: Marxism-Leninism.[3]

In its initial period the French Revolution had been supported abroad by clubs and circles of friends. In its expansionist phase it had created, with the help of local Jacobin groups, sister republics in Italy and elsewhere. But the revolutionaries' baggage, comprising successive layers of ideas, never constituted a homogeneous and unified ideology, much less the cement for a centralized international organization. In contrast, the October Revolution was unitary. It had been prepared, decided, executed, and governed by Lenin and his party, who together directed its entire course and direction. The Soviet experience was constantly filtered through Lenin's Marxism and formed an integral part of the body of ideas that produced it. It was an experience less universal than the French to the extent that it took root in a backward country and offered little of interest to the observer except for a party dictatorship following upon the anarchy of a nation. Yet it was more easily universalized because it was laid each day by its actors in the Procrustean bed of ideology and was thus armed with a preestablished canonical sense prior to being diffused on a world scale by the International. Thus channeled, the catastrophic course of the Russian Revolution came to look like the accomplishment of universal history.

The system's main drawback was rigidity. If the Bolshevik Party was supposed not only to conduct the Revolution but also to determine its direction at any given time, any political disagreement within the Party of the International implied disagreement over its very foundations— its capacity to direct class struggle according to the science of history. The price of orthodoxy was to transform dissent into heresy. But in this case the dogma varied with circumstances, and so orthodoxy had no point of reference other than the Party, which is to say, its leaders. From the start, this weakness lent the Communist world the appearance of an enormous sect with millions of loyal followers but constantly subject to schism. Henceforth, to be a Communist was not so much to be a Marxist as to believe in Marxism as incarnated by the Soviet Union—in other words, the Bolshevik Communist Party's interpretation of Marxism. This belief guaranteed salvation in this world, but it also exposed the believers to the hazards of a belief invested in an experiential object—a revolution, and thus something by definition ephemeral. To be anchored as faith, such a belief would better have been hypostatized as a permanent benefit.

The illusion of a universality that is consubstantial with the revolutionary beliefs of a Jacobin or Leninist type evaporates when the actual course of revolution is examined. The history of Communism was no exception to this rule. On the contrary, it threw it into sharp relief because, on the one hand, it possessed such a strong ideological content and, on the other, it was so full of tragic denials of the promise of collective happiness it flaunted. Even when the movement was quite young and Lenin was still alive, the European Left already included thousands of former Communists who had lost their illusions and their hopes. Throughout the twentieth century, Communism has been like a house that each generation has gone in or out of, according to circumstances. Yet it has also been capable of retaining, for life, militants so unconditional that they would constitute a kind of political species of their own until late in the century. They would never abandon the Soviet Union, which, for them, was inseparable from the revolution. Even during the worst times, even when thrust aside or unjustly suspected of disloyalty, they could conceive of nothing other than service to the cause of October 1917, as though a new world had really been born of it, as giving a sense to their lives.

Let us explore the reasons for this loyalty from the standpoint of three intellectuals who, though belonging to very different worlds, were all born to revolutionary politics with the First World War and the October Revolution and were both united and separated by that experience. These three men were Pierre Pascal, Boris Souvarine, and György Lukács.

One of the first foreign witnesses to the Russian Revolution was a young French intellectual, Pierre Pascal, who kept a diary of what he had seen and thought from 1917 until 1927, the crucial year that marked Trotsky's exile and Stalin's triumph.[4] Pierre Pascal belonged to the generation of young Frenchmen that graduated from the École normale supérieure just before the war (the class of 1910). As a student of the liberal arts, he had been fascinated by Russia, and he visited the country for the first time in 1911. A fervent Catholic, he had read Soloviev, who convinced him of the necessity for a "union of churches."[5] He fell in love with Kiev and studied Russian religious life with great interest. While in Saint Petersburg in that same year, he wrote a master's thesis on "Joseph de Maistre and Russia." In the following year, he returned to Moscow. Even his choice of a thesis topic made obvious his intellectual and moral predisposition toward things Russian. This young Catholic—a close friend of Ernest Psichari, his schoolmate at the École normale—wished to restore to the Catholic spirit its universal vocation and to make it flower again in its communitarian form. He abhorred the modern world's obsession with money and its corollary, bourgeois individualism, the ravages of which had yet to reach the old Russia of peasants and the Orthodox Church. He preferred a Christian monarchy like that of the czar to the lies disguised as the rights of man or the rule of parliament. Pierre Pascal was that rare combination, a Frenchman and a Slavophile. He loved Russia the same way Lamennais had loved Poland—for what remained communitarian and thus Christian about it. By this time he had already decided to do a study of the "old believers," which he would finish much later.[6] Unlike the pacifists or the socialists, he hadn't waited for 1917 to look to the East, because he came from a different and more distant shore than theirs. But for this very reason his testimony is crucial, for it helps us to understand how the October Revolution managed to seduce a huge family of "Catholic" intellectuals who were neither Marxists, leftists, nor even democrats to begin with. Pierre Pascal was but the first of them; Louis Althusser would be the last.[7]

Seriously wounded at the front in September 1914, Pascal then fought in the Dardanelles, prior to being appointed—thanks to his command of Russian—to the French military-diplomatic mission in Saint Petersburg in 1916. There he became caught up in the Revolution, which long detained him in Russia. The daily chronicle he kept for ten years is unique not only because of its documentary value but also for what it reveals about his commitment to Bolshevism and his eventual disenchantment.

He was a "Bolshevik" even before October, as early as February 1917. A Bolshevik of a very particular kind, not a Marxist but a Russian and a Christian Bolshevik; his case illustrates the kind of historical election that Russia enjoyed as the quintessential homeland of Christianity. His official role was nonetheless to combat the defeatist propaganda of Lenin and his cronies, since his job, like that of his colleagues at the military mission, was to keep the fledgling republic in the war alongside France. He even had to spend part of his time exhorting Russian soldiers to this effect. But his professional duties, largely mechanical, formal ones, were already taking second place to his credo of universal fraternity, and in 1918 he refused to return to France, preferring to remain in Russia as a witness to the extraordinary adventure. What drew him to the Bolsheviks between February and October was their attempt to put sense back into Russian history by ending the war that had robbed it of its direction. "The Russian people has a sharp sense of the tragic character of this war, which it does not want, which is absurd, which humanity should not want, and from which it cannot extricate itself" (*Journal* 1:127, 19 May 1917). The Russian peasant as a soldier of humanity against the war was the Tolstoyan vision that pushed Lieutenant Pascal toward Lenin and his comrades in the name of an eschatology taken from Edgar Quinet: "The war is increasingly eluding our governments. We are marching toward a universal social revolution. There will be a European confederation" (*Journal* 1:205, 21 August 1917).

In October, the Bolsheviks took over. "They are the theoreticians," commented Pascal, "but the Russian people, which is socialist or Bolshevik only in name, follows them, because they too live in the future. The people wants to end injustice and unhappiness on earth. Clumsily, sadly, through suffering, it is nevertheless creating that future. The Russian Revolution, no matter what reaction might follow, will have repercussions as massive as those of 1789, maybe even greater: this is no accident, this is an era—one with which Bossuet may well have begun a chapter of his *Histoire universelle*" (*Journal* 1:247, 26 December 1917). Thus "theoretical" Bolshevism was merely the sign of something deeper. It was only superficially anti-Christian because it was not self-conscious. The Russian people took it up as their standard even though its intention was to realize Christianity on earth—a historical stage of a different kind from that of the French in 1789. Of all the different paths Christian ideology might take to meet up with Leninism, Pascal took the one that would ensure that the last would eventually be first. The triumph of October was not etched in the science of history, it was a revenge of the humiliated, the day when wealth would be distributed equally and the Russian people would act according to God's guidance. Socialism was a just but inadequate doctrine because its proponents were unaware—as yet—that it was the instrument of the Christian spirit in earthly affairs.

In the autumn of 1918, Pierre Pascal took the plunge. He remained in Russia against orders. With several others, among whom Jacques Sadoul is the best known,[8] he formed a small group of French Communists in Moscow that would play an intermediary role between the Bolsheviks and the left wing of the French workers' movement in negotiating who should belong to the Third International. Then came the military years, which were also terrible ones—civil war, foreign war, terror in the city and in the country—for young Soviet Russia, cut off from the outside world by the Allies' *cordon sanitaire*. Attacked by the French press as a deserter, worried about what his family was thinking about him, Pascal worked on information bulletins at the People's Commissariat on Foreign Affairs, all the while collecting whatever documents he could find on Russia old and new. The second volume of his Russian journal, which spans 1919 to 1921, is titled *En communisme*, an expression, as he himself quipped, akin to "en religion" (2:7). This period ended in March 1921 with the NEP, which coincided with the beginning of his disenchantment: the Revolution was finished, but one had nonetheless to live with its attendant failures and memories.

The second volume of the *Journal* contains less detail about daily life in Moscow than the first. During these years the author may have had less time to devote to his notebooks, living as he did in precarious material conditions, assailed by the cold and by difficulties in obtaining provisions. Social relations had been torn asunder by the Revolution, and Pascal's world was henceforth almost exclusively political: on one side were the Russian Bolsheviks, of whom he saw little; on the other, a handful of French Bolsheviks who were busy tearing each other to bits—the usual fate of small political groups in exile. Pascal was hard put to counter the accusations of being Catholic that Sadoul leveled at him, hoping to condemn him in the eyes of the Bolshevik leaders.[9] He had to submit to several tests of loyalty, including one before Lenin and his friend Inès Armand. But neither these accusations of nonconformity nor the undivided dictatorship of the Party damped Pascal's enthusiasm. Given his hatred of French bourgeois parliamentarianism, how would he have dealt, for example, with a Constituent Assembly? Had such an Assembly not been dissolved, it would have ended up seating the "younger" party—a creature of the westernized Russian bourgeoisie, flanked by Mensheviks and revolutionary socialists, the former pusillanimous, the latter inconsistent and devoid of ideas. In Pascal we find intact the old distinction, so common in French socialist debates of the nineteenth century, between social revolution and political revolution. What interested our Bolshevized Catholic historian was not so much power and its organization—always subject to illusions and vulnerable to educated lies—but social revolution, the end of property rights and the wealthy. Political liberty mattered little as long as people could recover through the reestablishment and maintenance of equality a new morality of fraternity as announced by Christ and betrayed by the world of money.

Pascal's Bolshevism is closer to Buchez[10] than to Marx. We need only transfer the idea of historical election from France to Russia in order to uncover the messianic overtones of the neo-Jacobin and neo-Catholic prophet of the July monarchy in this neophyte Leninist. Consider the following description of revolutionary Russia, which casts a somber light on the egalitarian apocalypse:

A unique and heady spectacle: the demolition of a society. This is the very realization of the fourth psalm of the Sunday vespers, and the Magnificat: the powerful cast from their throne and the poor man lifted from his hovel. The masters of the house are confined to one room, and each of the other rooms houses a family. There are no more rich people: only poor and poorer. Knowledge no longer confers either privilege or respect. The former worker promoted to director gives orders to the engineers. Salaries, high and low, are getting closer to each other. The right to property is reduced to the rags on one's back. Judges are no longer obliged to apply the law if their sense of proletarian equity contradicts it. Marriage is merely registration with the civil authorities, and notice of divorce can be served by postcard. Children are instructed to keep an eye on their parents. Sentiments of generosity have been chased out by the adversity of the times: the family sits around counting mouthfuls of bread or grams of sugar. Sweetness is now reputed to be a vice. Pity has been killed by the omnipresence of death. Friendship subsists only as camaraderie. (*Journal* 2 : 16.)

Pascal was already worried by the shadow the Cheka cast on daily life, and by the state's weighing ever more heavily upon this Spartan society as the only rule in a lawless world. But he comforted himself by the thought that the police was of the people and that the state was a proletarian one—virtually a nonstate since it was open to "cooks" of all kinds, according to Lenin's prediction. After all, the regime had replaced the word "citizen"—a word with all the juridical coldness of bourgeois individualism—by "comrade," which expressed the concrete fraternity of the world of labor and the triumph of true equality. The Pierre Pascal of 1919–20 looked a little like Péguy: "Head shaven, a big Cossack mustache, kind, ever-smiling eyes, dressed in a peasant smock, and walking barefoot around the town." [11] He manifested the extent to which the Bolshevism of that era managed to garner to its own advantage the emotions and traditions it had formerly had to combat in order to exist: egalitarianism of the poor, Utopian socialism, Christian communitarianism. Pascal, a French intellectual, would clothe these things in a language more recently acquired—that of Lenin—which produced a rather good mixture since the foreign elements were also radically revolutionary and helped consolidate the ideology of the Party, now in power. The intellectual and political adventure of the French lieutenant was one of the first examples of the fascination exercised by Bolshevism over people with very different backgrounds, all of them gripped, in the most rigorous sense of the term, by its historical "presence." [12]

What was the undoing of this presence? What broke the spell of these beliefs, and when and why did they lose their magic? The departure from Communism, an experience inaugurated by Pierre Pascal and frequently repeated in the course of the century, bore all the characteristics

of a loss of faith: the believer's enthusiasm would be replaced by a critical eye, and the very events that had illuminated an entire existence
would lose their source of light. In Pascal's case, we should perhaps
speak of a more recent faith being replaced by an preexistent one, for,
having ceased to be a Communist, he became more Catholic than ever;
he still had religion to succor his soul, exalted by solitude and exile.
Unfortunately, he abandoned his journal in 1921 at the very moment
of his disenchantment. The break with Communism, which moved so
many others to write, halted Pascal's pen. The little he did say makes
clear that what prompted or, at least, fueled his own break in early 1921
was a combination of events: the condemnation of the "Workers' Opposition," [13] the prohibition of all opposing groups within the Party, and
the crushing of the Kronstadt uprising. For him, the Russian Revolution had lost its almost timeless purity as a fulfillment of religion. It was
a power, no longer on the defensive but reigning. The third volume
of Pascal's journals, covering 1922–26, is soberly titled *Mon état d'âme*
("My state of mind").

The author was no longer a Communist, but he still loved Russia and
the Russian people, who had drawn him so far away from his own country long before the Bolsheviks. Recovering the Slavophile myth from
the ruins of Communist mythology, he would go so far as to imagine
"what a good revolution religious Russia might have made, without the
Marxist distortion" (*Journal* 3:40, 2 February 1922). The Bolshevik
Revolution was dead; all it had produced was a bureaucratic state that
took advantage of a newly emerged capitalism. But the Russian people
remained a source of hope. Unlike Western Communists and even Bolsheviks, Pascal approved of the Revolution not *in spite of* its being Russian but *because* it was Russian and therefore Christian. That is what
gave him the strength to remain a member of the French section of
the Bolshevik Party and to work simultaneously for the Soviet government and the Comintern. In any case, he had to go on "writing like a
Communist."

His break with Russia was thus both radical and, of necessity, incomplete. On the one hand, he had "done" Bolshevik politics and had even
gone so far as to investigate its history. In a letter to Alfred Rosmer of
24 September 1925,[14] he traced the origins of the character of the Party
to the famous Second Congress of 1903,[15] which had consisted of fierce
intrigues, byzantine disputes, and a taste for pure force. He was well
aware of the fraudulence of the proletarian state, the political ineptitude
of the Soviets, and the falsehood that surrounded—and would continue to surround—the entire regime, which would prevent him, in
the battles for succession that began as soon as Lenin had been put out

of commission by aphasia, from backing any of the various clans that emerged. He was already too far from the fray of Communist politics to become a Trotskyite. For Pascal, Trotsky—the former head of the Red Army, the man who had advocated the militarization of the trade unions—rivaled Zinoviev or Stalin only in his ambitions, not in his ideas.

On the other hand, where was he to go? By opting to live in Moscow instead of returning to France, Pascal had burned his bridges. Had he gone back to France, he would have had to lie or furnish even more ammunition to the bourgeois and the politicians that he detested and had been fleeing from. He was caught in the impasse of one who had believed in Communism but believed no longer. As his faith eroded, the passion that inspired it remained intact. Feeling as he did about Communism, where was he to channel his hatred of the bourgeoisie? This question went beyond wounded pride, no matter how painful that could be. It brought into play the entire psychological investment in the idea of revolution in the twentieth century. Pascal, when turning away from the Bolshevik Revolution, took great pains to save the convictions that had originally drawn him to it, transferring them from Lenin's failed revolution to the future revolution of the Russian people. Far from creating a new world, the Bolsheviks were restoring the reign of money and of the wealthy. This diagnosis had the advantage of combining Pascal's recent disillusionment with his earlier hatred of the bourgeois. It freed the revolution of its encumbrances and reopened the way for the imagination.

Still before him was the Russian people—egalitarian, poor, religious, Christian, as open as ever to change. Pascal remained loyal to his first love, but he was also aware of the other side of the coin. Tempering press reports with what he learned from rumors and conversations, he described the day-to-day politics of the Comintern and the constant stir they caused in the young French Communist Party. He corresponded with Boris Souvarine, who had been excluded from the 1924 International. From Paris he was sent *La Révolution prolétarienne*, whose founders, Pierre Monatte [16] and Rosmer, had been denied admission into the French Communist Party the year before. Although it was a bit too "Trotskyite" for his taste, he liked the journal. There he found the libertarian spirit and the syndicalists' hostility to factions—some of which were close to anarchism. He offered his services as an eyewitness reporter on the Russian situation. But he felt detached from the battle that was raging from 1925 to 1927 between the factions and the head of the Party. He spoke of it with the tone of a neutral commentator, that is, hostile to all involved. In his eyes, Soviet political life had become as contemptible as bourgeois parliamentarianism. He took no more part in it, concentrating instead on translating Lenin's works into French at the Marx-Engels Institute. But his open-mindedness lent his notes from this last period a freshness that has lost none of its charm. The prose of Pascal disillusioned retains the qualities of the early disciple: simple yet varied, it tends toward the concrete, filled with details of daily life. Furthermore, the "Soviet" divorce between the mythical and the real, once Pascal caught on to it, gave added value to his probing style, which resuscitated real Russian life even as he was already depicting the roles played by Communist mystification. Here, for example, writing as a traveler in the promised land, is what he recorded "on the spot" on 4 September 1927:

> No regime has ever been a regime of lies to this extent. The result is brilliant: a young Frenchman comes to visit the Institute; he is an enthusiastic intellectual who reminds us of the "hero" Sadoul, Guilbeaux, Pascal! and who looks at me with admiration. He has come to study socialist edification at the Communist Academy! He has been here for two months. He is utterly persuaded that we are on the road to socialism; workers' collectives, state factories. . . . He sees nothing, none of the realities. A Communist from the Prombank tells him that our gross national product is greater than that of the United States, and that is enough for him. The Russian assures him that Communism is terribly persecuted in France, and he believes it. He contrasts it to the liberty we enjoy here, and he believes it. (*Journal* 4:190, 4 September 1927.)

Pierre Pascal returned to France in 1933. After his extraordinary detour, he was reintegrated into the civil service in 1936 and assumed a career as a professor of Russian history, winding up at the Sorbonne. Once back in the bourgeois world, although he buried himself more than ever in his love for the history and people of Russia, he seldom spoke again of the Soviet Revolution.[17]

Boris Souvarine belonged to the same generation as Pierre Pascal but to a different social and intellectual universe.[18] He was born in Kiev to a family of Jewish jewelers of relatively modest means, who emigrated and settled in Paris at the end of the nineteenth century when Boris was two years old. His intellectual education consisted of primary school, early apprenticeship to an artisan, autodidactic readings, and socialist ideas. In 1917, he made his entry into politics, writing short reviews for *Le Populaire* under the name he would eventually assume permanently — Souvarine — in homage to Zola's *Germinal. Le Populaire* adopted nei-

ther extreme positions nor revolutionary defeatism. It espoused and defended the minority view of the Socialist Party, searching for a peace
wrought of compromise without winners or losers. When the October
Revolution occurred, the young Souvarine was seized with a passion for
what was taking place in his native land. He supported the Bolsheviks'
wish for peace, feared their dictatorial tendencies, but approved of the
dissolution of the Constituent Assembly,[19] which, for Charles Rappoport—another Russian émigré of his parents' generation—already signaled the failure of the Revolution.[20] But in the end he convinced himself that the dictatorship of the Bolsheviks was indeed the power of
the proletariat; he was thus one of the first French Bolsheviks, in early
1918. He became one of the essential forces in rallying a majority of the
French Socialist Party to Lenin.

    Small, active, intelligent, and dogged, Souvarine devoted as much
energy to celebrating Bolshevism in those years as he would to fighting
it for the rest of his life. He was the kind of person who derived an ironic
pleasure from being right when the majority was wrong—a characteristic as useful in Communism as in anti-Communism. After World
War I, he stood up to the general anti-Soviet feeling of the French public in the same manner in which, after World War II, he would fight
almost single-handedly a no less pervasive pro-Sovietism. He was less
romantic, less sentimental, than Pascal. Like Pascal, he loved the Russia
of the common people, but he loved it because it was not individualistic
like the West, not because it was Christian. It belonged to the world
of his family and his childhood surroundings. His education, largely
acquired outside of school, was wholly democratic and rationalist, less
thorough than that of a professional intellectual, more open than that of
an activist. He worked relentlessly, constantly gathering information,
and had tremendous faith in documents and facts. His passion for the
truth ruled out a political career and remained focused upon the original
object of his enthusiasm, Bolshevism. Boris Souvarine thus made his
way through the twentieth century, not as an internal exile in the manner of Pierre Pascal, but as a despairing witness to the very thing he had
helped bring about.

    As we have seen, he was among those who invoked the French Revo-
lution in defense of the dictatorship born of October 1917. He was also
a participant in the various meetings in favor of the Third International
and against French military intervention in Russia. His militant fervor
would eventually push him to the extreme left of the Socialist Party, far
from his "minority" comrades, whom he found too lukewarm in their
support for the Bolsheviks. He left *Le Populaire* at the end of 1919,
having decided to lead the fight not only against the "majority" but also

against the minority to the point of a complete break. Now here was a real Bolshevik, who was, moreover, in contact with the *missi dominici* sent to France by the Communist International.[21] He was one of their men in Paris. In March 1920, he inaugurated the first of his ephemeral periodicals (he was to publish many of them during his long life) called the *Bulletin communiste*, which sought to introduce Bolshevik politics and thought to the French socialist milieu and to serve as a clearing-house for the reports sent back from Moscow by the Sadoul-Pascal group. In short, it was a sort of new *Iskra* for denouncing the partisans of the *Union sacrée* and breaking with the complacent Center Left.

Souvarine was so far in the vanguard of the socialist extreme Left that he was arrested in May 1920 at the moment when a major strike by the railroad workers, who were accused of conspiracy and anarchistic activities, ended in failure. In an effort of repression, intended to be spectacular, the government cracked down collectively on the strike's leaders—Monmousseau and Midol—and "Sovietist" activists, Monatte and Loriot, along with Souvarine, the leaders of the Committee for the Third International. This amalgam was hardly more justifiable than was the main charge, but it tells us something about the contemporary climate. An anti-Communist mythology was growing up in opposition to the nascent Communist mythology, the former reinforcing the latter by opposing it. The Third International claimed to be the incarnation of the world proletarian revolution, and the bourgeois governments immediately absolved it from that pretension.

So it was from the prison of La Santé that Souvarine would follow the preparation and the meetings of the Tours congress. In his little book *Autour du Congrès de Tours* he described how a chain of activists formed between his prison cell and the outside in order to produce a common text between the Cachin-Frossard group and the Committee for the Third International, in accordance with the wishes of Lenin, who wanted the platform to be both a spectacular disavowal of the past (via the voting of "conditions" set forth by the International) and a rallying of support for the greater part of the old Party in Moscow. This is how, at Tours, by the traditional method of lengthy negotiation between the different currents, they achieved the radical condemnation of that very tradition. This deceptive pact would produce the PCF, of which Souvarine was one of the principal founders, if the least known.

That a man like Souvarine should have become one of the heads of the Party alongside such seasoned politicians as Marcel Cachin suggests how ambiguous the situation was at the time, for he had none of the flowery eloquence of the parliamentarian who brought the house down at socialist banquets. He was a poor orator, ill at ease in electoral campaigns, with a temperament ill suited to that aspect of politics which involved manipulating other people and compromising in the domain of ideas. The irony of history would have it that Cachin, a politician lacking in resolution, the quintessential incarnation of the *Union sacrée*, who had rallied to Moscow at the last minute, would be the one to become the symbol of the Bolshevik turning point of French socialism, whereas Souvarine would be forgotten after being reviled by the very people he had served with such fervor. This was because his attachment to the Third International was more intellectual than political. What drew him to the Bolsheviks was precisely what weakened his commitment, since it was something whole and nonnegotiable. Revolutionary politics is as much a faith as a practice. What is more, in his case that faith in no way extinguished his ability to observe and to analyze.

When Souvarine left prison after his acquittal in March 1921, he was still the man of the International. Neither Kronstadt, nor the turning point of the NEP, nor the Tenth Congress of the Bolshevik Party had discouraged or attenuated his enthusiasm. Unlike Pierre Pascal, he had no inside knowledge of Russian life, and he was not aware of the Bolsheviks' absolute stranglehold on the international movement, as was the old libertarian militant Angelica Balabanova, who had been trying to leave Russia since the summer of 1920.[22] What was most striking about his behavior at the Third Congress of the International in Moscow, as described by his biographer, was not only his devotion to Lenin but also his critical spirit: he gathered information, asked for the program of the Workers' Opposition, talked with Pascal, and was worried by the repression of the anarchists arrested by the GPU (the State Political Administration, formerly the Cheka). Even so, in 1922 he would insist that the revolutionary socialists on trial should be able to choose their own defense, though he stopped short of objecting to the inequity of the trial.

This nonconformist attitude did not keep him from being elected to the Presidium of the International, along with such illustrious Bolsheviks as Zinoviev, Radek, Bukharin, and Béla Kun. At twenty-six, he suddenly found himself at the top, secretary to the movement's Executive, responsible for the follow-through of affairs, notably those of the budding French Communist Party. This is when the great "political" period of his life began, when he got to know the great characters of the Communist pantheon and became Bukharin's friend and Zinoviev's collaborator, an important man, an "international" militant sent on mysterious missions, whose life was tuned to the birth of a new world. When writing or speaking to his French comrades, he was, more prosaically, the man in Moscow or, rather, one of the men in Moscow, since there were others, whom he disliked, such as the Swiss former pastor, Jules Humbert-Droz.[23] He exercised this delegated authority in the same manner in which a provincial member of the Company of Jesus dealt with somewhat distant subordinates, never thinking that his example could be turned against him. At the time, he was indistinguishable from the professional activists of the International. He continued to live on his revolutionary passion in the shadow of the great Russian comrades, happier, no doubt, in their company than amid mediocre intrigues concerned only with the conquest of the young French Communist Party. Like many intellectuals who had stumbled into politics, Souvarine was more interested in influence than in power.

Politics would take their revenge when Lenin's aphasia, in March 1923, set off a crisis of succession in the regime. Souvarine, commenting upon this with an expert air in his *Bulletin communiste*, deplored the way it tended to divide Trotsky from the Bolshevik top leadership through the concerted efforts of the troika consisting of Kamenev, Lenin's closest friend; Zinoviev, the president of the International; and Stalin, who had been elected to the post of General Secretary of the Party the year before. On the one hand, he was pleading for Bolshevik unity, refusing to admit that Trotsky had constituted a "fraction." On the other, he was attempting to dissociate the "Russian question" from the "French question," so that the French might avoid the consequences that had befallen the Russians. Both of these positions are indeed surprisingly naive on the part of someone as familiar with the Comintern as Souvarine. The violence with which the troika and their henchmen attacked Trotsky hardly foretold harmony between Lenin's heirs. And how could Souvarine, who had himself besieged the French Communist Party from Moscow with Trotsky's advice, have imagined that that party could remain neutral in the battle opening up between the Bolshevik leaders? His hopes were quickly dashed and his position reversed. In France, he lost the battle against his rival, Albert Treint,[24] a former schoolteacher who was backed by Zinoviev's envoys to Paris. On an international level, Souvarine was classified as a secret partisan of Trotsky and as one of the leaders of the new "Right" that was active in all sections of the Comintern. When the troika won out in Moscow, it sought to capitalize on its victory and to cleanse the multinational empire of its adversaries everywhere—a formidable innovation, which destroyed Souvarine's fragile positions.

In 1921, the Workers' Opposition had been isolated and defeated by the Bolshevik Party, but neither Shliapnikov nor Kollontai had been expelled from the Party. Lenin had not invented a "Workers' Opposition" on an international scale; it had not occurred to him to assemble all his real or presumed opponents in order to bag them with one net. Three years later, just after Lenin's death in January 1924, the debate in Moscow between Trotsky and the troika, which was largely a rerun of the 1921 debate on "workers' democracy," involved infinitely greater spoils within an even more isolated party. The repercussions it had on all levels of the International imbued it with an extraordinarily abstract quality, since it was necessary to put identical labels on various debates that reflected power struggles rather than ideas. Souvarine was right wing, as was Brandler in Germany, and could also be characterized by such magical epithets as "revisionist," "neo-Menshevik," or "Social Democrat." Saying that Trotsky did not seem to deserve these attributions—which is all he did say—was enough to brand him with the same labels. The International, that is, the troika, already possessed the unstoppable prerogative of an authority that both named the crime and designated the criminal.

Souvarine, when brought before the rigged tribunal that was the Bolshevik Party's Thirteenth Congress in May 1924, and subjected to the invective of the participants, had lost in advance. Even Trotsky, who had already withdrawn, failed to put in a good word for him. The Fifth Congress of the International, which followed in June, investigated Souvarine's case at the request of his enemies in the French delegation, and the Executive Committee recommended that he be temporarily expelled. The recommendation was immediately released in the 19 July edition of *L'Humanité*. He didn't know it yet, but Souvarine's Communist phase was over. Although it had lasted barely five years, it would furnish him with matter for critical reflection for more than sixty years, up to the time of Brezhnev.

Souvarine's expulsion was more official in nature than Pascal's break with Communism. The young *normalien*, caught up somewhat accidentally in the Bolshevik adventure, and more through Russophilia than doctrinal conviction, had never played a role on the political front, nor had he pursued one. The real politician of the French Communist Party of Moscow was Jacques Sadoul. Pascal was a moral witness who saw very quickly—as soon as the civil war ended—that the regime was not only a broken dream but an organized lie. Souvarine, in contrast, had been a militant socialist from a very early age. He played an essential role in rallying the majority of the French Communist Party to the Russian Revolution and had been one of the leaders of the Third International. Thus, his defeat in 1924 bore witness to the political system that he had supported.

From the time the International was established in 1919, Communism had been an internationally centralized system run by the Russian Communist Party. The prohibition on all opposing groups enacted by the Tenth Congress of the Bolshevik Party in 1921, combined with the condemnation of the Workers' Opposition, was a decisive step toward monolithism. What was new about 1924 and the conditions created by Lenin's illness and subsequent death was that the internal crisis of the Bolshevik Party spread automatically to all sections of the International along the lines set by the ruling group: the "right wing" in Moscow henceforth corresponded to the "right wing" in Paris or Berlin. This early entrenchment of party jargon no longer related to commonly perceived reality but constituted a code both esoteric and crude, defining the pecking order and the obligation to submit to it. Once the Party had been hypostatized into a divinity of history, its leaders benefited in their turn from such a privilege, and they reigned by means of humiliation and expulsion. Having accepted the former, those who eventually opposed the system were crippled by the latter; Trotsky provides us with the first example of this in 1924.

Was Souvarine naive to have engaged in such an unequal battle? Or, having measured the stakes and the forces at play, even in defeat, had he sought simply to take a stand for the future? These two hypotheses are not incompatible. The question would recur again and again in the history of international Communism, not only apropos of each leader who was humiliated or thrown out of the Party but also of those who were executed—surely even more numerous. The Souvarine of 1923–24 was very familiar with the political mores of the International and for good reason; he himself had exercised a bit too much control over the French Communist Party from Moscow to maintain any illusions about how debates and decisions were carried out. What was to stop Treint in 1924 from doing to him what he had done to Frossard in 1922? Had he thought himself immune to the rules? Had he overestimated his own influence or "indispensability" to the Russians? So much for the hypothesis that he had been naive. On the other hand, he was also capable of figuring out the implications of Trotsky's first defeat: the end of the "historical leaders" of October, the Party bureaucracy substituted for the Party as guide, a definitive freeze on the Revolution, the reign of lies associated with the police. Souvarine had known Pierre Pascal for a long time and was linked to him by something that predated his Bolshevism: anarcho-syndicalism. Both the arrests of the anarchists by the GPU and the persecution of the revolutionary socialists had troubled these Frenchmen: so much for the hypothesis of a deliberate, conscious choice.

Whatever combination of naïveté and volition we settle on must be supplemented by the particularities of Souvarine's makeup. A former artisan, with no formal education, he had the mind of a historian. He had a passion for documents, for precision, and for the truth found in details. The ebbing of his revolutionary passion revealed his intellectual side, which had been thwarted in his former job. One can imagine him in the summer of 1924 as he left Moscow, beaten but relieved, to return to the little libertarian "commune" in Yalta where he rejoined Pierre Pascal and his companion, the young Nicolas Lazarevitch,[25] and two Italian comrades. Even in the first years of the Soviet regime, those who had served it and bidden it farewell were already explaining their departures with the same argument that Solzhenitsyn would use to break its hold: the worst thing about Communism was not its oppression but its lies. It was this position that brought the Christian Pascal and the Marxist Souvarine together.

Souvarine, however, did not leave the Soviet orbit all at once, and he thus inaugurated what would become the most common method of breaking with the Soviet Union. To the extent that abandoning Communism may be compared to a sort of intellectual detoxification, it was both a precise moment in life, defining a before and after, and a reawakening of the critical faculties which, as they gradually extended to more and more objects, occurred over a longer period of time—the time it took to become accustomed to one's own audacity. Souvarine, who returned to Paris in January of 1925, remained obsessed by the world from which he had just been shut out. He followed the internal battles of the Russian political headquarters very closely and even regained a modicum of hope during 1925 with the collapse of the troika and the shift in alliances. He could not help but see the promise of revenge in the defeat of Zinoviev (who had persecuted him the year before) at the Fourteenth Congress in December 1925, even though it marked a new victory for Stalin, who was linked to Bukharin, over Trotsky, whom he himself had defended. But at the same time his thoughts were turning toward a general critique of the Soviet system in its degenerated state—something which, for him, had begun not with the death of Lenin but with the October Revolution. Even though he was smarting from his temporary expulsion, subject to imminent appeal, and may have thought that circumstances appeared to favor his reintegration into the Party, he was not in the least repentant. He had not stopped writing in either his own *Bulletin communiste*, whose publication he had resumed, or in the journal *Révolution prolétarienne*, published by his friends Monatte and Rosmer, who had their own problems with the International and the

French Communist Parties. That he had fully recovered his critical faculties and his talent for observation is revealed by this "pre-Orwellian" analysis of the language of the International:

> Not one fact, not one quotation, not one idea, not one argument: only impudent affirmations with a half-dozen interchangeable words come from the "heights" (for even *that* is decided in the higher reaches). . . . Take the phrase "for the Bolshevik unity of the Leninist Party"; if you invert the order of the adjectives, you get "for the Leninist unity of the Bolshevik Party"; if you invert the order of the nouns, you get "for the Bolshevik Party and Leninist unity," and so on. Isn't that marvelous? [26]

The man who wrote these lines was already well out of the system in which he had once imprisoned his life and thought. He no longer possessed the fundamental complicity that was the weakness of a Trotsky, a Bukharin, or a Zinoviev. To him, even the Party was fallible, for it was through the dictatorship of the Party's General Secretary that a bureaucratic dictatorship had been established over the country. With his definitive expulsion dropping like a guillotine at the end of 1926, the executive office of the Comintern was certainly taking aim at an adversary, calling him, in its binary vocabulary, a "counterrevolutionary." Suspecting that he was more dangerous than its traditional enemies, they moved preemptively to discredit his reflections and his memories.

Souvarine's break with Soviet Communism was unusual in that it went very quickly from a break to a battle. Souvarine continued for several years to speak of himself as a "nonconformist" Communist, turned his *Bulletin* into a forum for opposition to Comintern politics, called for "honest militants" to react, and evoked the legacy of the Soviets' revolution. But his thinking had already taken a different turn, which would push him beyond factional combat to encompass Soviet history as a whole. This is clear from his obstinate refusal to support Trotsky in 1927–28, immediately before and after his exile. It was not merely a question of pride, or of the passion to be second to none. More important, it was the feeling that his fight was no longer the same as Trotsky's. The former head of the Red Army, even in exile, was still prisoner to Party superstitions whose logic he would replicate tirelessly in the "left-wing" opposition that he sought to revive on an international scale. Souvarine wanted to escape the logic that was part of Lenin's heritage. He was beyond that now, more a witness than an actor; henceforth he was a historian of the failure of Soviet Communism.

Thus, very early on, parallel to and inseparable from the history of Communism proper, a history of the break with Communism was established. And this parallel history was to continue, with each generation, right up to the present.

This phenomenon has touched all kinds of Communists, workers and intellectuals, old hands and neophytes, apparatchiks and grassroots activists, fellow travelers and militants. Intellectuals tend to offer the most interesting examples, if only because they lived the Communist Revolution purely by choice or, if you will, as a belief separate from their social experience, a self-negation in the pursuit of self-realization in the manner of religious ascetics. They epitomized the masochistic pleasure of throwing themselves away for a cause. It was among them, therefore, that the reclaiming of self occurred most brutally. Since writing was their business, their historical testimony is more plentiful than that of any other group.

Many of the militants who left the Third International during the period under consideration departed as if getting off the wrong road or putting a misunderstanding behind them. At the Tours Congress, Frossard had been one of the key men to rally a majority of the French Socialist Party to Lenin's colors. But he had never been converted to Bolshevism. He wanted to channel postwar revolutionary passion into a rejuvenated party shorn of the elements most obviously compromised by the *Union sacrée*. When the International pushed him out in 1922—at the instigation of Souvarine, incidentally—he saw it more as a personality conflict than as a true break. He easily slid back into his old haunts at the Section française de l'Internationale ouvrière. During the twentieth century, many thousands would repeat this painless process. Whether keen on Communism or merely interested in it, depending on the time and circumstances, they would distance themselves without major crises; for them, Communism was just another political movement. It was simply the farthest to the left.

People like Pascal or Souvarine, on the other hand, adopted Communism like a set of beliefs—I dare not say a faith, since Pascal was also a Christian and Souvarine would have rejected the term precisely because he was not. But both of them had hoped that the Soviet revolution would bring about a new kind of human being, finally rid of the misfortune of being bourgeois. They would both pay a heavy price for this: Pascal left his career and his country, and Souvarine went to prison before settling in Moscow as a militant under the command of the heroes of October. They were at the heart of the Revolution, which was the only place they felt was worth occupying; and from there, they witnessed its death. Reading the chronicles and letters they wrote from Moscow, one is surprised at the things they acquiesced to: police surveillance, tests to verify their fidelity to Leninism, the retention of their passports, the opening of their correspondence, the extinction of all free thought—in short, an extravagant sampler of the sort of tyranny that would follow Lenin's death. Both of them finally emerged from their bewitchment, first Pascal and then Souvarine, each in his own way but each radically, and with difficult periods of solitude when they turned in upon themselves, for they were immune to the urge instantly to find a new engagement and to reinvest their dreams in a new figure.

In this respect, they can also be compared to Trotsky, for whom they had sympathy but whom they refused to follow or imitate when he rose up against Zinoviev and then Stalin. Trotsky fought Stalin but not without first submitting to the Party as the guardian of October 1917. He attempted to open up another path yet constantly affirmed that the Bolshevik Russia that had exiled him was a "proletarian state." Driven from the USSR, he attacked Stalin with a flame that his victorious rival could extinguish only by assassinating him. But the very brilliance that his talent as a public speaker and his existence as a victim of persecution lent to this futile battle masked his own blindness about the purpose of his fight. When in power, he was never one to step behind any terrorist measure. Beaten, deported, forcibly expatriated, he continued to share his victorious enemy's idea of an absolute dictatorship of the Party and the necessity of liquidating the kulaks. He fought Stalinist Bolshevism exclusively in the name of a Bolshevism of exile: that is not to say that the two versions were identical, but they were still too close to afford a victory of one over the other. Invincible, indefatigable, and even flamboyant, he was nonetheless at a disadvantage as he fought his executioners even while sharing their political system. With no chance of winning, he prolonged the myth of the Soviets that was intended for those who were disappointed in real Sovietism by offering a fragile support for the idealization of Lenin against Stalin. Souvarine, for his part, rapidly rejected that myth. Consequently he left himself open to the accusations of conformists, who, throughout the century, would reproach him for having renounced his youth, failing to see that this very renunciation was what made him interesting and genuine.

Our third example contrasts strongly with both Pascal and Souvarine. György Lukács came from a completely different background and followed a completely different course. Born in the Hungarian empire of Franz-Joseph, he was a child of German culture. A Bolshevik from the start, like the others, he would remain a Bolshevik to his last hour, in 1971. Not that he could possibly have ignored or underestimated the crises of the Communist movement across the century. On the contrary, he never ceased being both its victim and its dialectician, though he never wavered from the conviction that he would reaffirm on his deathbed: "I have always thought that the worst form of socialism was better to live in than the best form of capitalism." [27]

Lukács thus presents a prime example of a political belief that would survive more than a half-century of observation and even experience, while never ceasing to defend itself before the tribunal of historical reason. The greatest contemporary philosopher of capitalist alienation spent his entire life caught up in Communist alienation. Perhaps the best description of a case like his is this line of Saul Bellow's: "A great deal of intelligence can be invested in ignorance when the need for illusion is deep." [28]

He was born in 1885 among the Jewish aristocracy of Budapest. Both sides of his family were rich, his mother by birth, his father by his own wits. [29] His mother descended from one of the oldest branches of German court Judaism. His father, Joseph Löwinger, learned his trade on the job: at the age of eighteen, he entered banking; by the age of twenty four he had already become head of the Hungarian branch of the Anglo-Austrian Bank and one of the great financiers of the Austro-Hungarian Empire. Soon afterwards he was ennobled by Emperor Franz-Joseph, and, after converting, he changed his name in 1910 to become Joseph von Lukács. Thus, little György, from his tenderest years, found himself equipped with a wealth of identities—Jewish and Protestant, Jewish and noble, Löwinger and von Lukács. A gifted child, precocious and studious, he soon invented an additional identity, electing German culture as the base from which would break with the social philistinism of his milieu. In another era he would have been the erudite son, the family rabbi. But the only thing that the epoch and the milieu into which he was born offered was a magnifying mirror in front of which the classic scene of bourgeois theater could be replayed—the son's attack upon the father. In his case, his mother was the object of his contempt because of her caricatural conformism. His father, a liberal businessman and an enlightened patron of the arts, was a more elusive target for his sarcastic remarks. Nevertheless, the imitative and limited aspects of success for assimilated Jews provided a particularly apt objective for the hatred of the bourgeoisie that he would retain throughout his life. His notes from Heidelberg (1910–13) include a phrase that the young Marx could have subscribed to: "The Jew is the caricature of the bourgeois." [30] Lukács combined two forms of self-hatred—that of the Jew and that of the bourgeois. The former he had inherited, whereas the latter he acquired; in him, they exerted their effects jointly.

His took refuge in the universal—not the universality of modern democracy but that of philosophy, literature, and art. Lukács was a pure intellectual and would remain so all his life, even when caught up in history. Beyond that, from a young age he extended his disdain for the bourgeoisie to everything that he saw as the lies of bourgeois politics, from the sovereignty of the people to rule of parliament. Finally, German culture—his real homeland—led him to tear himself away from the conformism of the masses rather than to devote his life to saving humanity. He lived in the works of Kant, Goethe, Hegel, Schopenhauer, Kierkegaard, and Nietzsche while leading small avant-garde, philosophical-literary circles in Budapest. He had a passion for the theater and was a great fan of Ibsen, to whom he paid a visit. A keen reader of poetry, he flirted for a time with the small, select group around Stefan George. Imbued with the great Greco-German philosophical tradition, he spent many years in Heidelberg, where he became friends with Max Weber. There is no better incarnation of the feverish, abstract anxiety that surrounded early twentieth-century Austro-Hungarian intellectual life than this young, unhappy, wealthy Hungarian Jew. In the semi-feudal, semibourgeois society of Budapest, he was at the center of a small aristocratic, bohemian group that sought its salvation from the menace of modernity even before modernity had really shown its face.[31] The denunciation of the democratic and mercantile West, however, was a theme common to his favorite books from Nietzsche to Dostoevsky.

How did Lukács suddenly go from there to Bolshevism in 1918? For him as for many others, the war interrupted the order of time. This did not immediately affect him, however, for unlike his German friends, he felt no obligation to fight on the side of the Central Powers. He avoided the draft, thanks to paternal connections, and got on with his life. During this period, he was emotionally involved in a very painful marriage, which he endured in an almost sacrificial manner. Even the October Revolution did not coax him out of his political disinterest. But in 1917 his "new life" began with an event in his private life: he found a companion capable of helping him bear his anxiety. He remained hostile to Bolshevism, however, both for moral reasons and because of a Kantian refusal to subordinate ethics to politics. The Hungarian situation of late 1918 was what prompted him to embrace Communism, for he was one of the first to join the Hungarian Communist Party in December, as though he had suddenly been confronted with an unavoidable, urgent choice whose terms and objectives signaled the end of his all-too-long youth.

The Bolshevik Revolution, the German disaster, and the whole of Central Europe faced with a tabula rasa provided the background to the famous lectures that Max Weber gave in January 1919.[32] In these, one of the most profound political thinkers in Germany warned his contemporaries against the temptation to invest history with absolute ends and pleaded for an ethics of responsibility. Weber, the German patriot, caught up in the national catastrophe, kept a clear head, bearing in mind the danger of the Russian contagion, the future role of America,[33] and the future of Germany. But his Hungarian student and friend, whom he had tried in vain to have appointed to a professorship at Heidelberg, gave in to the millenarian tendency prevalent at the time: he relied on history for salvation.

Thus the Great War came between these two men, though it did not affect them simultaneously, in the same way, or for the same duration. In 1914, Weber supported the German justifications for going to war and ignored the risks, whereas Lukács was fearful of the outcome despite his lack of emotional involvement. When the war ended in 1918, Weber assessed the ravages it had wrought on European history; Lukács, in contrast, took that twilight for a dawn.

In its suddenness, Lukács's change of heart was like a conversion. Pascal had been enamored of Russia prior to supporting the October Revolution. Souvarine had been partially linked to the revolutionary extreme Left before settling on Lenin as his leader. Lukács had little taste either for politics or for Russia. Until 1918 he had always been turned inward, engaging in a kind of aestheticizing asceticism by which he attempted to dispel the constitutional derision of the bourgeois. Like the Germans, he saw Russia as a primitive copy of Prussia. For him, the great writers that had managed to emerge from Russia, such as Dostoevsky, were merely rehashing the theme of modern unhappiness. Thus Lukács, in espousing Leninist Communism, did some rapid reshuffling of the philosophical terms in which he posed the problem of his own life. His decision was akin to an enlightenment. The key to his soul no longer lay in moral greatness or art, but in history and politics. The choice was both heroic and irrational; the philosopher thereby affirmed the tragedy of existence while also unwittingly investing it with the masochistic violence that had possessed him since childhood. Bolshevism would henceforth be both his haven and his jail.

As a contemporary witness put it, "Communism found Lukács, not the other way around."[34] He had devised a way out of his philosophical destitution and found a positive form for his existential despair. The passion to appeal to history was very much in the air. Others, in order to break the circle of the German *belle âme*, would be drawn to Fascism, starting from a moral bonding with the redeeming *Volk*. But this Hungarian Jew had ties only to cultural Germanism; with Marx, Bolshevism lent him the support not only of Germany but of universalism, which better suited his needs. He was drawn to it as to a philosophy diffused by the Russian October and the Hungarian Revolution. Those events explain the urgency of his adherence but not its justification, which was drawn from another order of things. When he entrusted his destiny to history, Lukács threw in his lot not with the Russian people, as Pascal did, nor with the Leninist revolution, as Souvarine did, but with two of his great predecessors, Hegel and Marx.

He remained, moreover, a stranger to politics while never ceasing to be its plaything, and he lived through the entire history of Communism, of which he was the greatest philosopher, without ever understanding its nature, which always lay just beyond his field of reflection. Bolshevik militants usually presented the opposite case; they were mediocre philosophers, beginning with Lenin, who managed to combine their ideological simplism with a great deal of savoir faire in manipulating the party apparatus and people in general. Lukács, for his part, knew and worked his Marx as if he were his guardian angel amid the dark shadows of activism, zealously guarding that ultimate reference lest it become obscured in the course of events. This fin de siècle intellectual improvised a bridge between Marx and Lenin—and if that was not virtually impossible, it was nothing compared to the task to follow: tying Stalin to Marx.

That explains the literary nature of Lukács's existence as a Communist, which probably saved him, if not from unhappiness, at least from liquidation. It is true that this existence began with practical rather than intellectual work, for at the age of thirty-three he had just become a novice in the Bolshevik church. Even before reading Lenin, Lukács was deputy commissar of public education in the short-lived Hungarian Soviet Republic, which had been patterned along the lines of the Soviet Union. The son had finally taken up arms against the father. He even served six weeks at the front, across from the Czech and Romanian armies, as a political commissar to the Hungarian Red Army's Fifth Division. We have some extraordinary photographs of Lukács from this time, half-civilian, half-soldier, haranguing "proletarian" soldiers, wearing a long raincoat buttoned up to the chin, from which emerges the fine features of an intellectual looking like a cross between Groucho Marx and Trotsky. I am not putting Lukács down; I am merely attempting to express the somewhat unreal, parodic character of Lukács's first and last encounter with the great politics of Bolshevism—something that would occur only once. The episode, it is true, was unworthy of his moral conversion.

Born of a bad agreement at the top between Social Democrats and Communists, followed by the socialists' resignation, the Hungarian Soviet Republic,[35] haunted by the Russian Soviet precedent and directed by the adventurer Béla Kun, never actually enjoyed any working-class or popular support. The military and political defeat of the regime was greeted with an almost unanimous sigh of relief. After 130 days of intrepid, nonstop activity, Lukács emerged defeated, beset by death threats, hunted, on bad terms with Kun, and despised by Moscow for his leftist excesses.

Thus began his very long exile, from which he returned to Budapest only in 1945. He lived in Vienna, then in Germany, and finally, from 1930 on, in Moscow. If his Viennese years were hard on him, they paled before those spent in Moscow. He was embroiled in petty but fierce battles within the Hungarian Communist émigré community, from which he was eventually thrown out in 1929. But in Vienna, in spite of being harassed by the police and by material worries, he managed to finish his great book *History and Class Consciousness*,[36] published in 1923. In Moscow, he encountered the police once again—this time those of his own regime—and poverty, aggravated by the impossibility of publishing and speaking, even in private. He was assigned, as Pascal had been before him, to David Rjazanov's "Marxist Institute," which was where the Comintern confined suspect Marxists. On a number of occasions he was forced to repudiate his book. His stepson was sent to the Gulag. He would himself be arrested in 1941, accused of being an agent of the Hungarian secret police. Victor Serge, who admired Lukács and had become acquainted with him at the beginning of those wretched years, recalls encountering him, along with his wife, in a Moscow street: "He was working at the Marx-Engels Institute, his books were being suppressed, he lived courageously in fear; almost right-minded, he dared not shake my hand in a public place because I had been ousted and was known as [a member of] the opposition." [37]

What did Serge mean by "almost right-minded"? Serge, who had been in internal exile from very early on, was probably thinking of political conformism, for Lukács never missed a chance to align himself with what was going in the Bolshevik Party. He had no reason to favor Zinoviev, who was a friend of Béla Kun's. He had not been tempted to follow Trotsky, whom he accused of anti-Sovietism. By his very victory, Stalin incarnated world-historical reason, which the philosopher had adopted as his own principle. This explains why Lukács was a Stalinist not out of cynicism but out of wisdom—not the wisdom of resignation but that of philosophy. When he was young, he thought he could escape the fatality of the bourgeois world via the spirit. In midlife he retained the fierce insubordination of his youth but had found a new solution: the Hegelian return from self-consciousness to unity with the whole through the proletariat's revolutionary deeds beneath the banner of Marx.

It is ironic that the 1923 book that he was forced to repudiate in Moscow, where all free thought, especially concerning Marx, was forbidden, contained the theoretical basis for this blind political loyalty. *History and Class Consciousness* resurrected the tone of the young Marx in order to describe the calamities of capitalist alienation, the transformation of men into things by money. If the proletariat, as a universal class, was the only thing capable of ending this "reification" by restoring human value to labor, then the class consciousness of the proletariat becomes a necessary means to that reappropriation. This shift accomplishes in real life what Hegel had conceived of as the reunification of the subject and the object at the end of the history of the Spirit. By restituting that reunion in the manner of the young Marx, Lukács was implicitly criticizing Lenin's theory of consciousness as a "reflection" and Engel's dialectic of nature. Having done this, however, he enhanced the role of the subjective in human emancipation and thus also attributed all but absolute power to the "perspective of class."

Lukács' Marxism was too Hegelian not to expose its author to accusations of idealism by the Kremlin guard dogs. It is true that Lukács, during these Muscovite years, was secretly writing his *Young Hegel,* which was not published until 1948, in Zurich.[38] Nonetheless, his interpretation of Marx was too "subjectivist" not to chain him definitively to the Bolshevik Party, once it had been cast as the conscience of the proletariat and identified as the element that was realizing the entire movement of history. To those around him, therefore, Lukács would never cease to be a dual personality—on the one hand, a cultivated and subtle intellectual,[39] who viewed Marxism as the means to go beyond the contradictions of modernity as set out by the best minds of Europe, and, on the other, someone intellectually hampered by the Bolshevik revolution disguised as the denouement of universal history. Yet he himself felt in no way divided. He never stopped digging for the meaning of Marxism, without ever questioning Bolshevism. Obsessed by the desire to give a more authentic philosophical foundation to Leninism than Lenin himself, he was indifferent to the history of the Soviet Union and almost pleased to be its scapegoat.[40]

Victor Serge's phrase "almost right-minded," was perfect. We can attribute the "almost" to the minor reproaches (never expressed before 1956) that Lukács leveled at Stalin for having counted too much on Party unity, having scorned the mediation necessary for revolutionary action, and having too often subordinated culture to propaganda.

All this was nothing compared to the construction of socialism in the USSR and the necessity of the anti-Fascist battle; Lukács was a "right-minded" man. He had lived through the history of Communism, a militant defeated both by the enemy and by his own people; he had traveled the Soviet Union not as a passerby but as a constant witness. From the time he abandoned the rarefied air of intellectual circles for the fraternity of the masses, he had known little else than disavowal and solitude. Yet he was never tempted to renounce the idea of the essential superiority of Stalinist socialism over liberal democracy or to question the ideological foundations of Bolshevism. The value of his own life had no part in his idea of Communism. Right up to his death, he continually affirmed the sincerity of his various self-criticisms, and we have no reason not to take him at his word. His interpretation of Marx would have been meaningless for him had it come into conflict with the Party that was guiding the emancipation of the world proletariat. That which was most subtle in Lukács's makeup determined his blindest spot. This explains the uneven character of his work, profound when treating Hegel or Marx, but often superficial when it came to idolizing true socialism at the expense of capitalist decadence.[41] It is difficult not to agree with Kolakowski's opinion that Lukács only criticized Stalinism from within Stalinism itself.[42]

The end of his life revealed the internal captivity that had bound him to an idea of the Soviet Union so potent that it had annulled his knowledge of its history. Despite having actively participated in the establishment of the Stalinist dictatorship in Hungary after the war, Lukács came close to being arrested in 1949–50, escaping only by a new series of self-criticisms. It was in this late period that he published his weakest book, *The Destruction of Reason* (1954). Better times were to come after the death of Stalin, when he found some room for maneuvering in a Party divided. But it was not until October 1956 that he openly took sides, accepting nomination as culture minister in the Nagy government,[43] a few days before the arrival of the Soviet tanks. The minister of culture of 1956 would be even more meteoric than the education commissar of 1919, and even more unhappy. He resigned his post almost immediately after assuming it in protest against the end of single Party rule and Hungary's exit from the Soviet orbit. This did not save him from being arrested by the KGB, along with Nagy, as he left the Yugoslav embassy, in which they had both taken refuge during the Soviet invasion. Stoic and sarcastic, the old man shared for a moment the fate of a popular uprising that he had disapproved of as too "bourgeois." Deported to one of the Kafkaesque castles of the Romanian ruling class near Bucharest, he refused to testify in the secret trial against Nagy even though he was politically closer to Kádár than to his ephemeral government boss.[44] His honor was safe, if not his more "proletarian" virtues. Having escaped this last catastrophe, which rekindled his revisionist aura in the West, the philosopher of praxis spent the end of his life on his Olympus, gathering the elements for an "ontology of Marxism." Claude Roy, who met him during this period in his apartment on the banks of the Danube, described his immutable personality thus: "Since he had eluded the last evils of Siberia or the gallows, the old Hegelian rabbi, at eighty, had the last word."[45]

The story of Lukács sheds light, though from the other side of the glass, on the same phenomenon revealed by Pascal and Souvarine in their breaks with the Comintern. In the marketplace of political beliefs, which hold such an important place in the modern mind, Communism is especially long in ideology. This is not so much by virtue of its resistance to experience, common in all militant convictions, which are largely impermeable to facts. Nor is it by virtue of its exceptional longevity, for the Communist faith was lost or broken perhaps even more frequently than any other political belief, to judge by the millions of former Communists produced by the twentieth century. What made it a particularly suitable object for psychological investment is that it appeared to unite science and morals—a miraculous combination of two types of reason drawn from two different universes. Convinced that they are accomplishing the laws of history, militants also fight the egoism of the capitalist world in the name of the universality of man. They swaddle their deeds in a new kind of conscience, exalted as a civic virtue while comparable to the bourgeois philistinism they detest; they are free of the anxieties of living. But with the break from anxieties comes an awakening, which entails renewed solitude. Independently of their "reasons" and pathways, all Communists believed, or still believe, that they are experiencing in advance the reconciliation of humanity with itself. It was the pain and the pleasure of this almost divine assurance that Lukács could never let go of.

FIVE

Socialism in One Country

THE FIRST PHASE OF SOVIETISM DREW TO A
close during the years when Souvarine was expelled from the International and became increasingly detached from it psychologically. He well symbolizes the first Bolshevik diaspora, the first among many, for his case prefigured in microcosm the general tragedy engendered by the Russian Revolution—battle, defeat, exile, and the liquidation of the Bolsheviks of October 1917. Thus the first period of the Soviet experience—though far from homogeneous, including as it did both "war Communism" and the NEP—was distinct from the next because it was led from start to finish by the founder of the regime, the man without whom the October Revolution and, if we go farther into the past, the Bolshevik Party itself would have been impossible.

Since Lenin was the one who lent an existential unity, both practical and mythological, to the Revolution, it mattered little that he initiated contradictory policies. He profited from his extraordinary ability to incarnate one of the great roles of modern democracy: a man who led his people to a new and exemplary future, free of past encumbrances. This image relieved him of having to justify himself, an advantage that extended to the entire Bolshevik Party; responsibility for the Terror or the famine could thus be shifted entirely to the counterrevolution. The formation of the Soviet myth cannot be understood without a grasp of Lenin's role—a role, moreover, to which he really was perfectly suited, certainly more so than Robespierre. The more abstract he was, the more universal he became.

His death would destroy the equilibrium of the revolutionary imagination and almost automatically revive the specter lurking behind every revolutionary creed—the end of the revolution.

That end had already been glimpsed in Lenin's lifetime, right after the invasion and the rout of the Red Army in Warsaw, after Kronstadt, or after the NEP. The retreat of the military signaled the end of the Soviet counteroffensive in Europe. The sailors' mutiny at Kronstadt and the resultant repression marked the "bloody twilight of the Soviets"[1] orchestrated by Lenin and Trotsky. The NEP roused the ghost of Thermidor. Within the Bolshevik Party itself, the Workers' Opposition had already denounced the bureaucratic paralysis of the Revolution. The defeat of that group, followed by the prohibition of all opposing factions, destroyed the only remaining gauge of the state of society and public opinion. Lenin himself, who had spent his life scrapping within his own little group to ensure the predominance of his own line, imposed total submission upon his Party once it had become great and all-powerful. Rosa Luxemburg had long ago predicted that this evolution would be a logical consequence of conceiving the Party as an avant-garde. From 1920–21 on, the old militant Angelica Balabanova and the loyal Pierre Pascal began to distance themselves from the petrified revolution.

But it was later, in 1923, that the illusion of a universal October would be profoundly altered by Lenin's illness and subsequent death. Even the leader's demise became part of the general ebbing of the movement he had succeeded in embodying.

Lenin himself had never been convinced that the proletarian revolution could prevail or even survive for an extended period if it remained confined to backward Russia. He envisioned October 1917 as an overture to a great international event, as international as the war that formed its backdrop: "civilized" Europe, with Germany at the forefront, would follow Russia. This prediction was slow to materialize, for Lenin himself had to fight hard to force his comrades on the Central Committee to sign the capitulation at Brest-Litovsk in March 1918, but it was borne out in part by the November armistice. The similarities between the revolt of the sailors and soldiers in Germany and the falling apart of the Russian army the year before seemed to confirm that a new Soviet revolution was shaping up in the center of Europe in the very homeland of Marxism, whereby the proletariat would compensate for their leaders' treason of 1914. The army had been defeated, the Kaiser forced into exile, and the regime made illegitimate by the defeat. Surely Germany would assume the mantle of the Russian Revolution.

But Germany would produce yet another failed revolution, which continued to misfire—at the end of 1918, between January 1919 and April 1920, and finally in 1923 in central Germany and Hamburg. Perhaps the term "failed revolution," drawn from the 1848 precedent, masked the impossibility of a revolution in Germany. In the sporadic civil war that marked the first years of the Weimar Republic, two extreme parties fought a lawless battle against each other while sharing the same ambition: to destroy the constitutional republic. But what was striking about both the Communists and the Nationalists was not their strength but their weakness. They could bring off ephemeral putsches but were incapable of assuming lasting power. The less weak of the two parties was probably the extreme Right, which drew its support from the hatred of disorder, the fear of Communism, the military tradition, and the sad state of the nation. On the other side, faced with the irregular forces and small groups of nationalists, the Bolshevik-style proletarian revolution could never muster up more than minor elements of the working class and divided leaders, even (perhaps especially) after the birth of the German Communist Party.

During this entire period, the trade union movement and the great majority of German Social Democrats remained resolutely hostile to the Bolshevik Revolution. Taking the opposite political path from the one taken by the Russian Bolsheviks in 1917, they sought to achieve a successful February and to avoid an October. True to Kautskian orthodoxy, they fought for the founding of a democratic republic in a country with a persistent military aristocracy and monarchy. What mattered most to them was to halt the disintegration of the First Reich at the moment when the dissolution of power might create conditions favorable to a German October. Thus they had no qualms about drawing support from the remains of the regular army, the Reichswehr, and even, from time to time, with the army's mediation, from commando units in order to crush the embryonic German Soviets. But this could also backfire: the attempted military putsch by Wolfgang Kapp in March of 1920,[2] supported by part of the Reichswehr, was put down by a general strike called for by the trade unions. These circumstances brought the socialists to the fore in the resistance to a coup d'état from the right.

German Social Democracy was trapped between two currents, one of which deprived it of a national vocabulary, the other of revolutionary prestige. It took the blame for both the defeat and the Versailles treaty and was compelled to fight against the Bolsheviks, with whom it had long fought under a common flag and for the same ideas. Silent on the subject of the war, which it had endured without enthusiasm or resistance, and hostile to the revolution that had come from the wrong side of Europe, Social Democracy had been granted by history the paradoxical mission of founding and defending a bourgeois republic. A novel, prosaic, defensive mission that had no resonance in German tradition, much less in the spirit of the times or in the German political imagination.

Nevertheless, Social Democracy, though ill equipped spiritually, imprisoned in a now-bourgeois Marxism, and caught up in a surprising situation, would eventually prevail. In late 1923, the failure of the Communist insurrection in Hamburg followed by the failure of the Ludendorff-Hitler putsch in Munich signaled the autumn of victory for the Republic. Even the French occupation of the Ruhr had not affected the inequality of forces, as witnessed by the facility with which the rebels of the extreme Left and the extreme Right were put down. If the Social Democrats managed to remain so powerful in spite of such a difficult political situation, it was not because, as the Communist version would have it, they had "put themselves at the service" of the bourgeoisie; to interpret the Bolshevik failure in Germany as a product of the baseness of the Social Democrats sidesteps the main reasons for that failure. Not that subjective factors had nothing to do with it—for example, the republican loyalty of the socialists to the Weimar Constitution, the lack of realism on the part of the German politicians of the Comintern, or the divisions among the leaders of the German Communist Party. But they were certainly less important than the objective factors that had stalled the idea of extending the Russian October to Germany.

Lenin was keenly aware of the exceptional circumstances that had brought him to power—circumstances so exceptional, in fact, that, prior to his return from Geneva and the delivery of his resounding "April theses," none of the Bolshevik leaders had dreamed of the possibility of a second Russian Revolution so soon after February. Right up to the Red Army's takeover of the Winter Palace, some of his close comrades, such as Kamenev and Zinoviev, continued to oppose that audacious endeavor. Nonetheless, with his remarkable sense of timing and the flair for power natural to this gifted man of action, Lenin had won his bet. He understood, however, that his victory was fragile because of the circumstances that had fostered it, and so he resorted to a more orthodox form of Marxism than that of his April theses, a form that brought the laws of social development back into the picture. "It is the fact that we are a backward country that has allowed us to be ahead," he would say in a speech to the Moscow Soviet in April 1918; "and we must perish if we do not hold out until the moment when our revolution receives the effective aid of all the rebels in the world."[3] The International and the Bolsheviks' entire investment in Germany is contained within this statement, which, with the defeat in November of that year, was crowned by the disintegration of the Reich.

The sailors' and soldiers' mutinies, worker agitation, and the resignation of the Kaiser in favor of a bourgeois government that was supposed to make peace as well as create a constitution—the things that made Germany in November 1918 appear to be analogous with Russia in February 1917—had no such effects. German anomie in the autumn of 1918 bore no resemblance whatsoever to the Russian anomie of the winter of 1917. The former was provoked from without and had resulted from a defeat, whereas the Russian Empire crumbled by and upon itself as if it had rotted. In the Germany of Wilhelm II, imbued with the idea that it was the chosen nation, the military capitulation added grounds for a moral disaster. But it did not break the society. It did not tear down the existing hierarchies and traditions. It did not destroy the parties' hold over public opinion. After all, the central place in the political landscape was occupied by the socialist majority, the Catholic Center party, and the liberal democrats, not to mention the role played by the Reichswehr or the remobilization on the extreme Right of the commando units, among whom the aristocratic and military spirit reemerged from amid the national humiliation. Russia, in 1917, had veered toward Bolshevism without encountering any social class, party, or will staunch enough to overcome anarchy and restore some substance to the power of the state. Things were quite different in post–November 1918 Germany. The brief heyday of the workers' and soldiers' Soviets, which, moreover, owed more to Rosa Luxemburg than to Lenin, was crushed by mid-January of 1919, and what emerged during the following months and years of an extreme Leninist Left was more grist for the nationalists' rhetorical mill than a true threat of revolution. For the young German republic, stigmatized from birth by the "stab in the back" legend, the greatest danger remained on the extreme right, as was made plain by the second episode of the triangular battle that lasted from 1930 to 1933.

Lenin, however, never stopped calling for help and for a German revolution. The same thought was uppermost in the mind of the Third International, founded in Moscow in 1919 despite Rosa Luxemburg's warnings. The universalism of October 1917 would first be tested in Berlin. On the one hand, the superficial similarity between the two situations was cause for optimism. On the other, the success of a second proletarian revolution in the epicenter of civilized Europe would rob the Russian Revolution of its exceptional character by reintegrating it into the groundswell of history, as merely the first of a series of revolutions. Finally, the Russian Revolution had been true to its own spirit by inspiring a battle parallel to the one being waged by the commandos against the Weimar Republic. It had itself dissolved the Constituent Assembly after drastically reducing the duration of the "bourgeois" stage that had begun in February with the fall of the czar. The Bolsheviks all remembered that General Kornilov's counterrevolutionary bid in September had opened up their way to power.[4]

Independently of these circumstantial considerations, the Bolsheviks obeyed a revolutionary logic that reduced the political field to two camps. You were either for them or against them, and whoever was not a revolutionary was a counterrevolutionary. The risk to individual liberty carried by this terrible simplification had already been demonstrated by the French Revolution. October 1917 would only aggravate its conditions. Indeed, the Jacobin dictatorship's propensity for branding as "aristocrats" the least bourgeois or most modest of peasants whenever its members feared requisitioning or the drafting of one of their sons received both Marx's and Lenin's philosophical blessing, which lent it the force of a dogma. Since all political conflicts can be deduced from class struggle, and since the postwar order of the day was the proletarian revolution, the struggle for power in the great nations of Europe put the bourgeoisie and the working class at loggerheads; henceforth, there were only working-class parties and bourgeois parties, the former being revolutionary and the latter counterrevolutionary. The October Revolution had shown that the Bolsheviks considered and proclaimed themselves to be the only true representatives of the working class; from mid-1918 on, they remained alone on the scene, having broken even the revolutionary socialists on the left, whose agrarian policy they had nevertheless adopted.[5] Henceforth, all other political forces, from the Mensheviks to the White Guards, were written off as counterrevolutionary shams. Why should things be any different in Germany, from the Social Democrats to the commandos? The Leninist revolution always tended to lump together all that it sought to overthrow.

But the Leninists were well versed in the tactical imperative of using one or another of its adversaries for their own means, should one of them get out of line. In this respect, Germany was a good country for Comintern plots, offering several footholds: the Social Democrats in the government, an extreme Right hostile to the republican regime, an army and a public that would become increasingly nationalistic after Poincaré's France occupied the Ruhr in January 1923. Social Democracy, that "bourgeois" fragment of the working-class movement, occupied a terrain that could be won back by a single-front strategy—and the most reactionary members of the army and the conservative forces could be used to weaken both the Weimar Republic and French imperialism. In the context of 1923, the convergence of interests and an eventual alliance between Communist Russia and nationalist Germany—the big loser at Versailles—were a constant preoccupation for Comintern leaders. Radek, Moscow's eye in Berlin during that crucial year, felt no compunction about humming that particular tune, which was hardly in harmony with the international workers' movement. But at least it allowed Communism to avoid basing its whole future in Germany on the insurrection of October 1923. The crushing of the workers' revolution in the streets of Hamburg did nothing to deter the Soviet state from attempting to seduce the victors.

When the Bolshevik leaders, divided over their German strategy, saw their last hope for a European revolution go up in smoke in 1923, Lenin had already been sidelined. After suffering his first stroke in May 1922, he had sufficiently recovered by the summer to resume working. He wrote his famous "testament" in the last days of the year, just before relapsing definitively into aphasia. He died in January 1924. The Russian Revolution thus lost its leader at the very time when the German revolution, in which it had invested the universal vocation of October, finally died out.

Now began the battle for succession that, after five years (1923–27), would bring Stalin to absolute power. We shall not discuss the vicissitudes of that crucial yet byzantine battle, which ushered in more than a half-century of lies uttered in the confidential language with which a small oligarchy sought to disguise its fierce rivalries. Let us instead consider how Stalin's victory, won through the successive eradication of his rivals, modified the relationship between Bolshevism and the universal, shifting the emphasis from the international to the national. Under Lenin and in the context created by the First World War, that relationship was understandable. But it was obviously more fragile when what we might term the "second Bolshevism" of Stalin was emerging: the war was receding from memory, and the revolutionary cycle had come to the end of its course; now was the time for economic and political stabilization in the capitalist world. The circumstances that had brought the flame of October beyond Russia were no more, and Lenin, who had single-handedly incarnated that flame, was dead.

Perhaps the most fruitful way to trace the history of the transformation, or at least the shift, in the young USSR's relationship with revolutionary universality is from a symbolic perspective, which is generally one of the best ways of studying the evolution of the Soviet world during these years. After Lenin's death, his corpse, in spite of his widow's objections, was embalmed and put on display in the Kremlin for his loyal followers to worship. On the eve of the national funeral, Stalin delivered a ceremonial speech before the Second Congress of the Soviets in the form of a religious sermon, ending with the six solemn oaths of fidelity to the late leader: "When leaving us, comrade Lenin ordered us to hold

high and keep pure the great name of Party member. To you, comrade
Lenin, we swear to carry out your commandment with honor," and so
forth. The former Georgian seminarian rose to the occasion by decking
out the Leninist legacy in liturgical language, which had resurfaced
from his youth. Thus he rendered that legacy more sacred and more
rigid, impossible as it may be to discern how much was attributable to
inner conviction and how much was inspired by manipulative cynicism.
Within the narrow political aristocracy of the Party militants, he spoke
as one cleric to another by raising the pride of caste to a shared promise.
The era of controversies over Marx's texts and of doctrinal debates
about the relationship between the Party and the working class was over.
Henceforth, the Party was a clergy reunited around a church and thus
unanimous. Beneath the surface of the intimidating language borrowed
from a world that predated modern politics, Stalin sought to notify
Trotsky, Zinoviev, and all the others that Party unity was the rule of the
game and that he was now both referee and scorekeeper.

Lenin had devoted his whole life to the Party but had never been
deified. It was he who had originated the theory that the Marxist Party
was the indispensable avant-garde of the working class and its historical
conscience, without which the proletariat could never get beyond the
trade-union level of collective organization. It was also he who, at the
Tenth Party Congress in 1921, had pushed through the prohibition of
oppositional groups. But he had lived his whole life as a militant passionately debating doctrine and politics. He had even sided with the
minority at such critical moments as Brest-Litovsk. He had acquired
preeminent authority in the Bolshevik movement by leading the Party
to power, not by creating a cult. From October 1917 on, moreover,
he had devoted a great deal of time to correcting what he viewed as
the multiple errors of the Party—many of which he attributed to the
cultural backwardness of Russia. His denunciations of this backwardness and his railings against Russian barbarism are too numerous to be
counted, up to and even including his last works. The paradox of Lenin
is that he deliberately established the dictatorship of his party and then
feared its consequences. At the end of his life, this sectarian dogmatist,
this expeditious man of action who had fearlessly put the state at the
mercy of the Party and made terror reign, had second thoughts about
the bureaucratization of the regime he had founded.

Stalin, in contrast, was perfectly at ease with Party bureaucracy and
Russian backwardness. He had been General Secretary since 1922, a job
which, though originally rather uninteresting, he gradually forged into
a formidable instrument of patronage and power. A Georgian, he became more Russian than the Russians, as befitted a man who, born in a

backwater of the empire, had made it to the capital. He had done poorly at school and had read little. Unlike Lenin, who had incorporated a good dose of Russian populism in his version of Marxism while retaining one foot squarely planted in European culture, Stalin had acquired his Marx through Lenin, superimposing his ignorance upon an already simplistic interpretation. He had little taste for discussion and even less for ideas, but he knew that these were part and parcel of the Bolshevik tradition: every little strategy or political move had to be justified by "theory." Since any would-be heir of Lenin had to master this highly particular art, he was led to publish *The Principles of Leninism,*[6] a work consisting of a series of lectures he gave at the Communist university of Sverdlov in April 1924. This was the first appearance of his rocky prose, which often bumped along like a catechism in the form of questions and answers and was concerned with enumerating rather than demonstrating, the various elements of his canonical responses punctuated with "in the first place," "secondly," and so forth. On a doctrinal level, this work was the equivalent of what Lenin's tomb was on a symbolic level. Stalin's commentary was destined to become the sacred word on Lenin's thought. As if better to appropriate the substance of the late founding father, he incorporated many long citations from Lenin into his work. From time to time he threw in a contemptuous remark about an error or an objection on the part of a past or present adversary; indeed, his work must be read on two levels—as a prescription for a political dogma and as a more or less explicit settling of scores. These various elements formed a compact pedagogic treatise lacking in grace but not in clarity; it was, after all, a simplification of Lenin's Marxism, which was itself a simplification of Marx's Marxism. But the author of this peasant catechism did add something original: he peppered his text with praise of the genius of the Russian proletariat and peasantry that would probably have shocked Lenin. The leader of the October Revolution aspired to be a revolutionary in spite of being Russian; Stalin, the Georgian, wanted to be Russian in order to be a revolutionary.

In September 1922, before Lenin's illness had condemned him to silence, the two men had come into conflict over the very issue of Georgia. Lenin had accused Stalin of wanting to restore the domination of Russia over the little republic in which he was born; the country was Sovietized in 1921, against the local Menshevik opposition, with the bayonets of the Red Army. Stalin had backed off, but for him the issue was hardly closed. The new "Union of Soviet Socialist Republics" that was under consideration at the time to succeed the "Russian Socialist Federate Soviet Republic" was intended to guarantee equal rights among the associated nations. But Stalin's own notion of it was closer to the "Sovietization" imposed on sister republics prior to their absorption by the Union under the guise of free association. There, as elsewhere, the uniformity of the Bolshevik Party emptied all substance from any existing national or constitutional pluralism. Greater Russian chauvinism, so often disparaged by Lenin, would unexpectedly find a vehicle in Lenin's party, which had become the sole leader in the name of the proletariat, thanks to one of Lenin's own ideas. And the no less surprising craftsman of this resurrection/metamorphosis was born in Tiflis.

During this period, the same trend was at work within the Third International, an institution conceived by Lenin in 1919 as the new headquarters of the international revolution to replace the preceding one after the failure of its mission in August 1914. It was thus both in conformity with the tradition of the socialist movement and a departure from it: the Third International sought to universalize the revolutionary model of October 1917 and to generalize the victorious party of October, whereas the Second International had been bent on denying their exemplary value. Hence, from the very start, the Bolsheviks enjoyed a de facto, privileged status in the Moscow International, which they had created. This is clear from the membership requirements they imposed on aspirant parties, from the often difficult negotiations that ensued, and from the distribution of responsibilities among the various parts of the institution, which remained under the Bolsheviks' control. Lenin, incidentally, continued to be the supreme authority even after he no longer held official office. But his authority was more political than administrative.

Over time, the institution took on an increasingly bureaucratic cast—an evolution begun under Lenin. From 1921 and 1922 on, the Communist International systematically intervened in the affairs of affiliated parties in a way that had been unthinkable under the Second International. It increased not only the volume of commands but the procedures for controlling militants as well. It sent its clandestine agents, its confidence men, everywhere, sometimes several to the same country where they were supposed either to gather information or to carry out a specific mission. In short, the spirit of Bolshevik centralism also spread to the international level.

After Lenin's death, a new element emerged when the various pretenders to Lenin's heritage sought to use the different national "sections" of the movement for their own purposes. This made it clear that the other parties had become subordinated to the Politburo of the Russian Communist Party—a situation aggravated by the fallout from the succession crisis in Moscow. Trotsky's first defeat by the troika in 1924 set off party purges all over Europe. We have seen how, in France,

Souvarine was no longer allowed to function or even retain his membership in the International—not for backing Trotsky, but merely because he had defended the idea of separating the Russian problems from those of the international movement by means of its different sections. In the following year, Zinoviev's abasement became official, and not even his position as President of the International could save him from defeat in the Politburo. It was thus no surprise that his German protégés, Maslow and Ruth Fischer, who had not wished to betray Zinoviev for Stalin, were forced to step down from the leadership of the German Communist Party.[7] The labels applied to the deviations that enveloped inter-Bolshevik battles spread through the entire international oligarchy of the movement: neo-Menshevism, Trotskyism, Zinovievism, rightism, leftism, social-democratism. And the majority of the Bolshevik Party, manipulated by Stalin, endowed these labels with a significance all the more universal because the strategy of the movement was increasingly subordinated to the singular power of the Soviet state. It was sad indeed to see Stalin's successive opponents fighting within the ideological and political framework he had established, accepting the idea of a Party orthodoxy and thus defeated from the outset.

This rigged battle could be summarized, paradoxically, by the slogan proclaimed at the end of 1924: "socialism in one country." The phrase had several meanings. First, it corresponded to the spirit of the times, after the failure of the German revolution: the postwar period was over and the contagion of Sovietism along with it. It also implied a polemic against Trotsky and his theory of "permanent revolution" according to which the Russian democratic-bourgeois revolution, once completed by the Social Democratic Party (remember, we are back in 1905), would exceed its bourgeois horizon, to the limited extent that it would encounter world revolution. During his lifetime, Lenin had taken issue with this "theory," although it was reasonably close to his own,[8] until October 1917 brought the two men into agreement. In 1924, however, Stalin deployed the idea of "permanent revolution" in a completely different context and transformed it into a doctrine of impotence, according to which it would be impossible to build socialism in the Soviet Union without international support. He thus killed two birds with one stone. At the price of anachronism, he mendaciously reconstructed a scholastic contrast between "Leninism" and "Trotskyism," whereas Lenin had been insisting, since 1917, that if the Bolshevik Revolution were to prevail it was absolutely necessary to have revolutions elsewhere. Stalin had thus assumed the mantle not only of the dead leader but also of the historical honor of the Russian proletariat and peasantry.

The second meaning of "socialism in one country" was the more powerful one and constituted Stalin's nod to Russian chauvinism. By making Trotsky out to be doubly defeatist—on both a national and a revolutionary level, he called forth once more that hubris peculiar to the Bolshevik Party which he had already celebrated upon the death of Lenin. For he was addressing not so much the people, which had long been reduced to silence, as the Party, the sole and isolated master of the nation. The Party was no longer the same as it had been under the old Bolsheviks. Though still run by the old Bolsheviks, it was now largely composed of recent militants who had flocked to the victors by the tens of thousands since October. All of them were, by definition, staff members of the nation's new bureaucracy; most were local potentates, corrupted by absolute power, intoxicated by unbounded authority, bedazzled by Bolshevik discourse about the benefits of "proletarian" violence, and, furthermore, promoted by Stalin and his cronies once the Georgian had taken over the top management of the party machine. They owed him everything, resembled him in crudeness of ideas and morals, and were ready to do anything to sustain and glorify him. The Bolshevik Party had always been a brawling arena, but, from 1924 on, Stalin packed the house, and his partisans increasingly relied on insults and violence rather than argument. It was militants of this type that Lenin had in mind when, in his last lucid year, he had declared himself alarmed by the ignorance of Communist functionaries, their bragging, their treachery: "Every day one hears, and I hear especially, owing to my duties, so many slick Communist lies, so much com-mendacity, that one is nauseated, sometimes atrociously so."[9]

It was to people of this sort—at once servile and omnipotent, quite ignorant but convinced they were in the know—that Stalin served up his ideological cocktail, in which the prerevolutionary debates figured as scholarly discussions despite having led to the Stalinist distillate. How far we are from Marx! Two systems faced off: Leninism, a scientific theory of action, verified by history, incarnated by the Bolshevik Party, but threatened by its enemies from both within and without; and Trotskyism, the sworn enemy, past and present, of Leninism, a mortal danger to Lenin's heritage, a capitulationist discourse masked by internationalist overbidding. Such was the new guise of "socialism in one country." It emphasized a critical element of "Leninist" psychology—the belief that volition, given power, can accomplish anything—and added a new element, concealed beneath the call to activism and manipulated so adroitly by Stalin that no one could reproach him for disloyalty to Lenin: the Great-Russian national passion. Just like the French Jacobins, the late Bolsheviks were entrapped by the "chosen nation" idea, of which they were developing a new version, if a more primitive one. Stalin's formula allowed them to reinvest the traditional chauvinism of the dominant nation in their membership in a totalitarian party.

They were not—not yet, at least—leading a state sufficiently powerful to conceive of extending its frontiers beyond the Union. Within their own borders, however, even more effectively than the czars, they stripped all nationalities of autonomy. Under the pretense of bringing all the peoples in the Union together in the "construction of socialism," they subjected them all uniformly to their lies and their regime. As to the world beyond the USSR, the Communist International henceforth administered residual islands in a space that had shrunk with the ebbing of the European revolution. Its evolution was patterned after that of the Bolshevik Party. The leaders or factions of sister parties became mere numbers in Russian political algebra—pawns moved around according to Stalin's maneuvers; as a result, any survivors in the international aristocracy of Communism were, for better or for worse, integrated into the political system of Moscow. Deprived of autonomy, in the thrall of increasingly abstract slogans, the Communist parties tended to become Russian political enclaves within their respective societies. They were, in their own way, state parties in miniature, except that the state that granted their authority was not their own but "socialist" Russia, the ultimate master of their destinies. Within these parties, the same esoteric language was spoken as in Moscow, and their members lived in fear of being summoned to Moscow. "Bolshevization," a term without the overtones of "Russification," was the initiates' name for this imitative obsession; it continued to evoke something of the universalism of the Soviets, though it actually referred exclusively to the national party in power in Moscow.

In keeping with common practice, I have used the word "totalitarian" to describe that regime because it is the least inadequate. It designates something new in modern politics that goes well beyond the monolithism of a party or a group. It refers primarily to the pretension of a party to be its own end, precluding its members from possessing any other goal in their lives except to serve it to the death. In this pretension, it resembles a religious sect, for it requires of its members the commitment of their public and private lives, their very salvation, while its practical activity is of a purely political order—the seizure and exercise of power. The link between these two orders of reality is furnished by a shared ideology, which the leader of the party is responsible for interpreting and enriching according to circumstances. Policies must constantly be translated into a language both sacred and fictional that separates friends from enemies whenever the need arises. The Bolsheviks were like the clergy of an ideocracy, and when Stalin became the head of that clergy, he was destined to be taken at his word.

This analysis brings us to the famous question of what Lenin and Stalin had in common and what divided them. Partisans of the Russian Revolution have tended and will always tend to distinguish sharply between the two, prepared to sacrifice Stalin in order to save the inventor and the idea of the regime. Adversaries have taken and will always take the opposite position, putting the two successive figures of the Soviet regime in the same bag as master and disciple. But that doesn't prevent our regarding them as both related and separate. The identification of the dictatorship of the Party with the dictatorship of the proletariat comes from Lenin—and heaven knows how much Rosa Luxemburg reproached him for that! The Terror, disdain for the law, confusing of the Party with the state—these too came from Lenin, as did the sectarian caste of ideological debates and the idea of the Party as an aristocracy, which the Bolsheviks had espoused from the beginning. Finally, Lenin invented, sustained, and promoted Stalin almost to the end, at which point he backed off—halfway and too late. Nevertheless, under Lenin, discussion was possible within the Party. It was Stalin who invented the totalitarian Party, a combination of ideocracy and terrorist state, set on liquidating its old guard.

In 1948, Ruth Fischer wrote that in order to understand the origins of Hitlerian Germany one must look beyond the history of Germany and its long quarrel with the West.[10] That, of course, is where the antagonism between Nazism and the western democracies leads us, but we should not ignore the role played by Stalinist totalitarianism in the development of Hitlerian totalitarianism. Stalin's victory, in effect, doubly facilitated Hitler's victory. It provided, after Mussolini, a second example, which was studied and retained in spite of all public imprecations: in terms of brutality, cynicism and duplicity, Stalin cleared the way for the author of *Mein Kampf*. Further, in order to win, Stalin was obliged to inject Russian nationalism into his Leninism, thus inventing a new secret bond with Hitler at the moment when the Communists' aggressive Russification policies were bringing him an ever greater audience from among the German Right.[11]

Thus, the first form of Bolshevism died with Stalin's victory. The new leader had not yet liquidated the veterans of the old party, but he had brought them to their knees, and they were at his mercy. He had driven Trotsky out of the country. His victory crystallized and confirmed the fears expressed by Pierre Pascal as early as in 1921 and by Souvarine a few years later. Over a broken and fear-stricken society, the

Party of October 1917 rapidly inaugurated a terrorist dictatorship completely cut off from the people even though it was allegedly governing in the name and interests of the proletariat. This lie—as Lenin himself eventually realized, although he had introduced it himself—had paved the way for an omnipotent oligarchy. It had fabricated a compulsory and fictitious language insulated from reality and leading inexorably to unity. There, disagreement was tantamount to heresy, and dissent ended up as self-criticism or exclusion. This forced unity, inseparable from the Communist ideology, paralyzed all opposition and manufactured a leader.[12]

The Revolution was dead. Nothing testifies to this more pitilessly than the literary triptych *Vers l'autre flamme*, published in Paris in 1929 by the francophone Romanian writer Panaït Istrati,[13] along with Victor Serge[14] and Boris Souvarine.

Panaït Istrati's first volume, *Après seize mois dans l'URSS*, is not the best of the three. It is a tearful narrative of disappointment: the novelist, invited as a sympathizer to celebrate the tenth anniversary of the USSR, recounts a sixteen-month journey, between 1927 and 1929, across the entire territory of the Soviet Union. The principal interest of the tale, aside from revealing the omnipresent dictatorship of the Party, is that it presents the affective drama of the narrator's psychological break with Communism. The narrator of the second volume, *Soviets 1929*, is the more politically minded Victor Serge, a veteran of revolutionary battles. He was the brother-in-law of Pierre Pascal and, like him, had long nourished doubts about the turn of events—a man much too loyal to the anarchist notion of "neither God nor master" to find the postrevolutionary glaciation the least bit palatable. Indeed, his analysis was radical: the democracy of the Soviets was a lie, and the only reality of the regime was the dictatorship of a corrupt Party, peopled by cynical go-getters who had replaced the militants of the October generation. Serge, in words worthy of Custine, describes how Trotskyism was liquidated: "The atmosphere in which this battle occurred was indescribable. [It was fraught with] mystery, shadows, rumors, anxieties, contradictory assertions, denials, surprises, anguish. People mysteriously disappeared on their way to work or coming out of their homes."[15]

The last chapter of this short book, touching in its mournful lucidity, is devoted to the celebrated Russian writer Maksim Gorky, who had returned to his native country the previous year after his long semi-exile in sunny Sorrento. Hostile to the October Revolution, Gorky had partially supported the regime during the civil war, while maintaining his freedom to criticize and intervene; this is why he left for Italy in 1921. His return, which had been the object of lengthy negotiations,[16] had been meticulously orchestrated by the Party; as soon as he reached the Soviet frontier, he was accompanied by processions, delegations, and banners hailing the "old man with the tough gray jaw" [17] who had willingly inclined his fame to the falsehoods of new times. Now he was paying up, and within a few weeks he had become the dictatorship's propagandist: the man who had once opposed Lenin's October was now bestowing his blessing upon Stalin's Bolshevism. Victor Serge offers a psychological explanation for this aberration—the political naïveté of an old writer taken in by his native land and his vanity. He called it "the Gorky tragedy."

Souvarine's section of the work, *La Russie nue*, signaled the start of his long career as a chronicler of the Soviet disaster. His contribution to this curious trilogy, two-thirds of which was published anonymously, drew the bulk of its factual data from what was obviously a meticulous reading of the Soviet press, especially *Pravda*, and from statistical commentary. This was the author's antidote to the fairy tales of the Soviet journey that were just then catching on. As always with Souvarine, the prose has no literary pretensions, and his narrative is organized in a rather scholarly fashion, from the economic to the political. But from his accumulation of data and facts emerges a portrait of a society that was impoverished both in the cities and in the countryside, and that had not yet returned to its 1913 level. Had this poverty resulted merely from the legacy of the past combined with exceptionally difficult circumstances, it would have been less significant. But Souvarine interpreted it differently: he incriminated the regime's role in this kind of involution of a society constantly beaten down by bureaucratic authoritarianism, corruption, ideological obscurantism, and the dictatorship of a Party that had merged with the national police.

La Russie nue paints a picture of what later would be called "totalitarian" Russia. The elements that Souvarine retained from his very recent past brought him to view what was happening in the USSR as a counterrevolution, a form of state capitalism that was bringing capitalism as such to completion. In his own way, he attempted—like Kautsky, or Blum, whom he had opposed—to construct a Marxist analysis of the failure of the Marxist revolution. But that particular aspect interested him less than the failure itself.

These three volumes presented a radical, lucid appraisal, though their readership at the time of publication was quite limited. The left-wing readers for whom they were written had not engaged in such a sweeping condemnation. They suspected a case of sour grapes—a classic suspicion that was to play into the hands of Soviet Communism throughout the twentieth century, since its real history would be written essentially by former Communists. Because neither right-wing writers, who were too predictable, nor Social Democrats, who were rival brothers, nor former Communists, who were embittered, could be taken seriously, the Soviet Union drew a sort of historical invulnerability from these excluded groups. The Soviets had only to cash in on their own accounts of themselves, even as they rearranged to varying degrees the parts destined for propaganda. Hardly anyone thought that the Soviet discourse was entirely false; this was its best-kept secret, a secret too sad, moreover, to be pursued insistently. The century was still too young for Istrati's book. Since the Soviet Union had lost Lenin, his successor deserved a break.

What happened, however, was that Stalin, having crushed the "left-wing" opposition with Bukharin's aid,[18] turned against Bukharin and the "Right" in 1928. Bukharin, the last survivor of the old Bolshevik leadership of which he had been the youngest member, had been Lenin's pet. But this particular aspect of the about-face is secondary (since Stalin already dominated the Party) in light of its implications. For during this period, in the vocabulary of Leninism, the words "Right" and "Left" concealed the fate of the peasantry, since the position of the dictatorship of the proletariat with regard to the peasantry was at stake. It was an old story, almost as old as the Party itself, having never been far from Lenin's mind. In theory, the interests of the two classes were opposed, since small-scale peasant production, now emancipated from the great landowners, would continue to provide support for the circuits of capitalist production. But the introduction into Leninist scholasticism of the category of "poor peasant" as opposed to "kulak" allowed the proletariat to avoid the impasse of being capable solely of a bourgeois revolution. Through class struggle in the countryside, the workers should have found allies among the poor peasants based upon a transitional program leading toward socialism.

In 1917, these abstractions were shattered by Russian reality. When the Bolsheviks seized power, they were loath to adopt the revolutionary socialist slogan already in use: land for the peasants. In the years of the civil war, the years of "war Communism," they adopted a primitive policy of forcefully appropriating agricultural products for the cities. This terrorist policy, which already brandished kulak sabotage as its justification, alienated the entire rural population and destroyed agricultural production; in 1921, the first great famine killed five million people.[19] Lenin backed off and came up with the New Economic Policy (NEP), which reopened clogged economic circuits and resuscitated rural areas without really making them flourish again. Yet the NEP, no matter how necessary it was, continued to be viewed with suspicion by the Party. A simple tactical retreat, imposed by reality, it had no real ideological dignity despite Bukharin's efforts. Trotsky, never to be outdone in his talent for error, had continually denounced the "defenders of the kulaks" and was soon to be joined in this by Zinoviev. In the interior, "bourgeois" rallyings to the regime, such as Oustrialov's,[20] compromised the new policy by their support. From the outside, the Mensheviks saw it as their chance for intellectual and political revenge: the factual demonstration of the inevitable character of a capitalist and peasant Russia.[21]

This was the situation in 1928 when Stalin, having defeated the leaders of the opposition, sought to revive their anti-kulak program. His crushing of Bukharin was probably only a secondary effect of an operation that was part of a much vaster political perspective. For it was not enough to have proclaimed that the time had come for "socialism in one country": the notion had to be given substance. If not accompanied by a prescription, it looked like a dead slogan. Paradoxically, the renunciation of world revolution, at least in the short term, obliged Stalin to radicalize the course of the Bolshevik regime in Russia. Failing that, he would have found himself in a situation of ideological deficit on two fronts, and eventually deprived of one of the essential supports of the system. The NEP had been a concession to real society, but it had threatened to diminish not only the ideological force of the regime but also Stalin's power. In contrast, "socialism in one country" would bring them to perfection together.

"Build socialism" in the Soviet Union: this expression is emblematic of Stalin's attachment both to the revolutionary tradition in general and to Bolshevism in particular. The idea of "building" a new society upon the ruins of an old one inherited from the past is part of the French revolutionary heritage and, indeed, is the ultimate expression of the French Revolution's novelty—which Burke had found so scandalous. Through their idea of revolution, which was as different from the Ancien Régime as day from night, the revolutionaries of 1789 managed to articulate the fundamental constructivism that haunts modern society. Modern society is a contract between associates with equal rights, a contract produced by their wills and thus secondary to them. This idea is not incompatible with the dictatorship of the revolutionary state, to the limited extent that the state is conceived of, or cast as, the collective agent of citizen volition, in defiance of the powers of the past.

The Bolshevik version of revolutionary subjectivism was even more radical than the Jacobin one, for two reasons. The first is that Lenin, despite his claims to the contrary, made use of the idea of the Party as the avant-garde of class to develop a theory of omnipotent political will.

He did not balk at the obviously absurd idea—particularly for a Marxist—that Russia was the cradle of the proletarian revolution. The second reason is that Lenin, like all Marxists, believed that the will had the serendipitous support of science, though at the price of philosophical aporia. Parties are oligarchies of scholars and organizers, assemblies of people who change the world through their wills, while constantly obeying the laws of history. During the battle for succession, Stalin gradually took on this dual mission as it became increasingly problematical and imaginary. "Build socialism" was the battle cry of the revolution resumed.

These first twelve years of the regime produced a series of absurdities. Lenin established the dictatorship of the proletariat in the most rural society of Europe, and combined the GPU and the NEP. Stalin inherited a terrorized nation that had fallen below the economic levels of 1914, and proclaimed his desire to "build socialism"; in light of the claims of the second Bolshevism, the political undertakings of the first appear almost realistic! Both Bolshevisms were conditioned by ideology, but the second constituted an intensification of the first because it was purely ideological and cut off from economic and social reality. It was, moreover, precisely its links with the original revolutionary promise that lent it credibility: the revolution was provisionally dead in France, and also in China, but it would continue its forward march in the Soviet Union. The specter of a Russian Thermidor accompanying the NEP would be definitively exorcized.

That operation had two facets: agriculture and industry: agricultural collectivization and the Five-Year Plan. Its authors sought to kill two birds with one stone: to gather the capital necessary for industrialization from the labor of the peasants while simultaneously suppressing the peasants as a class of independent producers. I do not intend to depict the cataclysmic character, especially in the countryside, of this program; it has been so misrepresented and we are still so ill-informed about it that its history remains to be written.[22] It led the Soviet Union to introduce a form of mass terror at that time without precedent (except perhaps, though of a different type, the Turkish massacre of the Armenians), and it rang in the hour of the complete, Orwellian totalitarian state. Most surprising of all is that something so excessive should have seemed so ordinary to Western intellectuals and to international public opinion and that something so atrocious should have been hailed as exemplary.

If the liquidation of the peasantry as an independent class by means of the assassination or deportation of several million of them had been clearly announced as such, it would have had no supporters. What lent this program its dark appeal was that it had been enveloped in the abstractions of "revolution" and "socialism," which made it appear as an extraordinary challenge to the human will—something unprecedented even in the history of revolutions and which would usher in a society no less unprecedented. To retain its necessary dignity as an event, however, the revolution required formidable enemies to conquer. Revolutionaries had to have something to hate. Stalin's "great break" in 1929 was no exception: fear of the enemy and its evil spell was the dominant theme of his propaganda. Although the French Jacobins in 1793 had seen the hand of the counterrevolutionary everywhere and extended the category of "aristocrat" in an absurd fashion, at least they were at war with the counterrevolution both within and without their borders. In the USSR of 1929, without a nobility or a bourgeoisie, the enemy of the revolution was something entirely new to the genre—the kulak, the Russian equivalent of the bourgeois and the successor to the big landholder. In 1921, Lenin had set up the NEP; in 1929, Stalin transformed its beneficiaries into scapegoats.

It mattered little that this category had never been clearly defined. The kulak was the class enemy, and that was that. The prerequisites for the category varied with the prevailing degree of egalitarianism—one or two employees, a big house, two cows, and so on. And even when the peasant to be deported was as poor as the others, he needed only be labeled "kulak henchman"[23] for the curse to extend to him. The category was valid not because it was inclusive but because it bestowed authority. It was a cover for a war against the peasants—some of whom were killed, others deported, and still others locked up in huge farms under the auspices of the Party—Kolkhozes and Sovkhozes. Never before had any regime in the world initiated such a monstrous undertaking on such a scale and with such enormous consequences: the elimination of millions of peasants and the eradication of rural life. When attempting to reconcile the nature of the event with the indifference or even praise with which it was received in the West, we have two explanations, not mutually exclusive: either no one really knew what was going on in the Soviet Union at the time because of systematic mystification, or, for many people, the idea of the "collectivization of the countryside" evoked the beginning of a positive utopia linked to the defeat of the counterrevolution. The capacity to mythologize its own history is one of the most extraordinary performances of the Soviet regime. But that capacity would have been less effective if it had not encountered a credulous tendency that is part and parcel of the culture of European revolutionary democracy.

Even with respect to industry, Stalin felt it necessary to invoke the fight against saboteurs, enemies, imperialists, and their agents in order to support his fantastic goals. The saboteur was the kulak of industry: any delay in the implementation of the Plan signaled that there were enemies yet to defeat, hidden somewhere within the regime. The failure of Bolshevik voluntarism to recognize material resistance gave rise to the trials for economic sabotage that multiplied during the 1930s, in which the practice of public confession of the accused emerged, with Vishinski in charge.[24] Organized with the greatest care and after long preparation, staged by means of the psychological and physical torture of the accused, this sinister procedure illustrates the ideological universe of Stalinism, composed of conflicting wills. There were "Bolsheviks" and plotters, and even the economic world, mired as it was in the material sphere, conformed to this dichotomy. The trials, accompanied by confessions, were intended to give maximum publicity to the essentially secret, evil activities of the enemies of "socialism." As Orwell saw so clearly, totalitarianism is inseparable from a constant pedagogy of suspicion and hatred. The economy was just another field of application for this policy-fiction.

It is surprising, in retrospect, that the opposition—or what was left of it—within the Bolshevik Party said nothing. Historians of this period insist that they kept up their internal struggle and even invented new intrigues in anticipation of the failure of Stalin's policies.[25] But the fact is that when tragedy was ravaging their country, they said nothing. Trotsky, for example, from his exile in Prinkipo, made a lot of noise about the persecution of his partisans in the Party but was silent about the terrible famine of 1932 in the Ukraine, which was entirely due to the multiform terror carried out against the peasants. Bukharin, gentle Bukharin, the leader most sensitive to external matters in general and to the future of the Russian peasants in particular, referred in private to "a mass annihilation of completely defenceless men, together with their wives and children."[26] But he too was caught up in the infernal dialectic of the Party, even though it was leading him to his ruin. Stalin had defined the circumstances that formed the background of all political discussion—the reinforcement of class struggle on both an international and a domestic level. The opposition criticized what it continued to call a "line" in Marxist scholastic terms, while not daring, or unable, to take issue with reality.

Even more astonishing was that this deadening of judgment extended to so many people outside of the Soviet Union, for the facts—at least in their massive atrocity—were not entirely mysterious. The history of the genocide of the Ukrainian peasants—five or six million killed, according to Robert Conquest—where ideological folly did not exclude nationalistic hatred, is still not known in detail owing to the inaccessibility of documentation. But it could not be entirely hidden. Menshevik and revolutionary socialist émigré newspapers spoke of it, as did Souvarine.[27] One of the excellent books on the subject was published by Kautsky as early as 1930:[28] in it, he denounced the Terror once again, and predicted famine and the generalization of forced labor under the iron rule of a primitive dictator. His analysis is all the more interesting when we read it today, for had he written it fifty years later, it would have presaged the final collapse we have recently witnessed. Kautsky, as a good Marxist, had no faith in the longevity of a dictatorship that was so reactionary and was reestablishing feudal servitude in a form even worse than before.

Those who wanted to know could have known. The problem was that few people really wanted to. The second Bolshevism—National Bolshevism, Stalinist Bolshevism, or whatever we decide to call it—bounced back from the failure of the first, losing nothing of its mythological power in spite of its national withdrawal. On the contrary, its image swelled in the contemporary imagination just when it was carrying out its most heinous crimes; instead of dissipating, the mystery of the regime's fascination only grew denser.

By this time, the Soviet Union had long emerged from the national isolation of its beginnings. It had recovered its role as one of the great states of Europe, and it had broadened that role as the center of the international Communist movement. This was politics with dual controls, offering the USSR twice the space for maneuvering. It took cynical advantage of this situation, acting as a state distinct from the revolution while in fact subordinating the members of the Third International to its national interests. As was true of other states, its diplomacy was open to adventitious reconciliations with governments of all sorts, depending on its present interests. The Soviet Union, however, since it regarded all other states, being capitalist, as adversaries, continuously denounced them as such, even when negotiating or initiating a mutual accord. Recognition of the USSR's legitimacy was thus a precondition to any rapprochement.[29] The Soviet government used its renewed power to support its regime; to the lies it propagated with the aid of the Third International, its henchmen, and its agents, it added that other instrument of persuasion—brute force.

In the midst of the Ukrainian tragedy of 1932, Herriot, the old French radical leader who had been back on the job for six months, revived the policy of reconciliation with the Soviet Union that he had advocated since the twenties. There was nothing extraordinary about this policy as such, for it was part of the Quai d'Orsay tradition from before World War I. But the other partner was no longer the same. Whereas in the late nineteenth century the republicans had not been compelled to give their blessing to czarist autocracy in order to form an alliance with Nicholas II, Herriot pushed for both a diplomatic accord and an ideological recognition. He took this line in spite of the fact that his vision of the world could not have been farther from what was actually going on in Russia under the absolute power of the Communists of this new era. Nor was he out to make a gesture—as would occur later in French domestic politics—toward the French Communist Party, which was negligible at the time, by making overtures to the East. He achieved his nonaggression pact with the USSR, signed in November 1932, without any consideration of what was occurring there. In the following year, however, when no longer president of the Council, this old boss of French parliamentarianism took a trip to the Ukraine, accompanied by Geneviève Tabouis, one the leading journalists of the day. Upon his return, this is what he had to say:

> I crossed the Ukraine. So! I assure you that it looked like a garden in full yield. You tell me that this land is reputed to be going through a depression right now? I cannot speak of what I have not seen. And heaven knows, I made them take me to afflicted areas. All I witnessed, however, was prosperity.[30]

There is no doubt that this declaration fulfilled a precise political goal, since Herriot took care to deny, with the aid of a seasoned Latinist's understatement, that this "land," the Ukraine, was going through a depression. Moreover, he had traveled to Kiev and Odessa, not to Moscow. But he was not simply lying for reasons of expedience. He had certainly been manipulated, according to a witness.[31] Over the centuries, the Russians had become masters of the art of the "Potemkin village,"[32] and they had almost certainly led him to a made-to-order corner of the Ukraine. Herriot was a left-wing French bourgeois, reared in the republican tradition. Since he was a partisan of the Russian alliance, this diplomatic choice may have affected his appraisal of the Soviet Union. In the course of the century, other temporary allies of Stalin, such as Franklin Roosevelt, would give a democratic seal of approval to his regime. But what reemerged in Herriot at this time was closer to what had been seen in Aulard twelve years earlier, in another context: the idea, in the head of a radical of the Belle Époque, that the Russian Revolution was of the same sort of revolution as the French. The French Communists of the time might well have made left-wing gestures, brandishing, under the orders of the International, the tactic of "class against class"; but this old radical politician, so representative of the bourgeoisie of the democratic tradition, was incapable of dissociating the reality of the Soviet Union from the original message of the Russian Revolution. While Kautsky was denouncing Stalin as a nationalist and counterrevolutionary dictator, Herriot considered him responsible for collectivization and an enlightened successor to Lenin.

This blindness resulted not from mere attachment to tradition but from an inability to gauge and to judge totally unfamiliar phenomena. When the Soviet regime appeared under Stalin at the beginning of the 1930s, it had no historical precedent. Nothing like it had ever existed. Never had any state in the world taken as its purpose to kill, deport, or enslave peasants. Never had one party taken over an entire state. Never had a regime controlled the entire social life of a nation and the lives of all of its citizens. Never had a modern political ideology played a similar role in the establishment of a tyranny so perfect that those who feared it had nonetheless to hail its foundations. Never had a dictatorship possessed so much power in the name of a falsehood so complete and yet so compelling. Not one of these characteristics of the second Bolshevism is intelligible from the examples of the past or from within a familiar conceptual framework.

The same thing would occur apropos of Hitler and Nazism. Between the wars, people had a hard time understanding the unique and, for this reason, monstrous nature—each in its own way—of the regimes of Stalin and Hitler. Lacking a comparable precedent in their experience, the nations of Europe were led astray by false analogies, drawn from the familiar. How much time did it take, for example, for them to understand that Hitler was not a nationalist politician, somewhat more "authoritarian" than the classic German Right, but a politician of a different nature altogether? Chamberlain had still not understood this in Munich, in September 1938. In Stalin's case it was even more difficult to get to the truth, since it was obscured by his position as heir—something he took great pains to affirm and reaffirm. He was Lenin's disciple, the son of the October Revolution, which was itself the offspring of Marxism, fruit of European democracy. The Georgian dictator had concealed his Shakespearean personality in his successive suits of armor, each impenetrable. At the very moment when he was launching the old czarist Russia into renewed national messianism by unleashing unbelievable violence upon it, Herriot, the representative of the French petty bourgeoisie, the left-wing *normalien,* an expert on Madame Récamier, was capable of thinking that he belonged to the same family.

During this period, however, the Soviet illusion found its principal reinforcements in political economy rather than in revolutionary democratic tradition *à la française*. The Great Depression had plunged democracies into a vast collective anxiety. Coinciding with agrarian collectivization and the first Soviet Five-Year Plan, it made the contrast between capitalist anarchy and Communist organization look like that between carelessness and willpower. There is probably no other era of modern Western history in which economic liberalism has been the object of such universal condemnation. Today, when the idea of the marketplace has reconquered the former USSR, it is hard to imagine that the very same idea, less than fifty years ago, evoked almost unanimous condemnation from the general public.

In France, where the critique of economic liberalism was so deeply rooted, the Great Depression seemed to confirm the national pessimism about the market's ability to provide the foundation for a real society. Denunciations of egotistical individualism and the anarchy it engendered were heard everywhere. The crisis seemed to be an object lesson. In contrast, the idea of planning, bolstered by heady statistics released by the Soviet Union, was for social reformers the "chicken in every pot." That idea was further reinforced by Roosevelt's election and the launching of the New Deal in 1934; and for all of its promoters it was inseparable from a certain admiration for Mussolinian Fascism and its achievements, for it presupposed a renaissance of political authority and a reform of the state. It was the spirit of the times in the Paris of those years, shared by intellectual families ranging from the left-wing Catholics who founded *Esprit* in 1932,[33] influenced by Emmanuel Mounier; to dissident socialists who ended up forming a new party in 1933 around Marcel Déat;[34] to "l'Ordre nouveau," the small group that formed around Robert Aron and Arnaud Dandieu[35] and published its bible, *La Révolution nécessaire*, in 1933.

The same period produced a literature much more directly linked to the Soviet experience of industrialization, written by a segment of industrial leaders enthusiastic about the projected or proclaimed outcome of the Five-Year Plan. People like Ernest Mercier,[36] one of the great industrialists of the time, more than a little right-wing in the classic manner, who had been converted to Soviet management techniques by a trip to Moscow at the end of 1935. He was attracted to the USSR, as the German Right had been five or six years earlier, not, of course, by the emancipation of the proletariat, but by the political energy he saw there and the technical mastery of the Russians.[37]

The most surprising thing about this infatuation with Soviet planning—whose functioning or real performance has never really been studied in depth—was that it spread even to the Americans, who, given their tradition, were hardly predisposed to favor state control of the economy. In the United States, which had been so hard hit by the crisis, the Five-Year Plan introduced the Soviet experience into the margins of "liberal" public opinion. Even today, that adjective designates an attachment to the democratic tradition and to social equality. Unlike the Europeans, the Americans didn't have to find another name for the progressive camp, since the critique of capitalism had never mobilized large parties in the United States. Nevertheless, during the Depression, something of what had made the success of the Soviet Union turned up on the liberal agenda. This is how Roosevelt's New Deal was perceived at the time, not only in America but in Europe as well, since it introduced state intervention into the economy. The most liberal liberals, that is, the left wing of the Democratic Party, have often had a weakness for the image that benefited, on its own small scale, the little American Communist Party after the "anti-Fascist" turning-point—the image of a wealthy America that had become poor because of its incapacity to master its economy, in contrast to a poor Soviet Union that was busily organizing its industrial progress through the exercise of will and reason.

We can understand the fraternal resonance that this vision of Sovietism as the controlled conquest of nature by technology might have held for Americans. But the entirely collectivist spirit of that conquest and the confiscation of individual liberties it implied kept this "economic" philo-Sovietism from penetrating liberal public opinion except in the form of a prudent sympathy for the goals of the regime, accompanied by reservations about the means employed.[38] The New Deal and anti-Fascism broadened but did not alter this sympathy. They furnished the American Left with a small dose of socialism, only enough to modify its tradition. While New York intellectuals argued about revolution, Lenin, Trotsky, and Stalin, it was Roosevelt who remained the familiar link to the tradition of Jefferson and Lincoln.

The conviction that the world was moving toward a socialist economy modeled on that of the Soviets was held much more widely in Europe, where the idea had both class reality and doctrinal consistency, which went far beyond the limits of Communist influence. A good example is the British Left, which was alien to the revolutionary tradition of the French kind, more or less resistant to Marxism, attached to the defense of individual rights, and thus less receptive than the French to Bolshevik politics and ideology. British leftists were nonetheless seduced by the Five-Year Plan and what they imagined was the joint success of experimental reason and liberty.

This unstable balance was exemplified by H. G. Wells. A veteran of the Fabian society before the war,[39] he was also a member of the little club founded by the Webbs called "the Coefficients," which mingled ideas of human progress and social reform—a combination they thought the British Empire might universalize, provided it changed direction. For Wells, the inevitability of socialism had nothing to do with class struggle and revolution. Having distanced himself from the Fabians, he tied socialism to an evolutionary philosophy, of which education was the natural vehicle. After the war, his star as novelist shone less brightly in the firmament of English literature, only to be replaced by that of spokesman for humanity, prophet of the global state, as Wells set out on his mission to show the human race the way to salvation.

This mission engendered his enthusiasm for the Soviet experience. When Wells met with Stalin in 1934, he was not on his first pilgrimage to the USSR. He came to see Stalin, but he had already seen Lenin in 1920. As smitten with the idea of the universal as the French were, Wells was no stranger to the kind of status seeking that drew certain men of letters to heads of state so that they might bring home the photograph that would broadcast their rank. Wells, moreover, had some advice to offer. During his first trip in 1920 he had found Russia in a dreadful condition, which he attributed exclusively to the capitalist heritage. He rather liked the Bolsheviks, at least those he designated as "liberals" in his short book *Russia in the Shadows*[40]—Lenin, Trotsky, and Lunatcharsky. Soviet Russia appealed to him as a refutation of Marx's predictions, for Wells, like Pierre Pascal but in a British manner, was an anti-Marxist admirer of Lenin, whom he celebrated as the creator of a utopia.[41]

In 1934, immediately after a sojourn in Roosevelt's America, Wells returned to the place where the future was in the making in order to compare the New Deal with the Five-Year Plan. For him, the rapprochement between the USSR and the United States not only was a product of circumstance, related to the rise of Hitler and threat of the Japanese, but had its source in a more profound evolution—the world crisis of capitalism and the will to reorganize society along rational lines. He defended this idea to Stalin, who honored him with a long interview. "It seems to me that I am more to the Left than you, Mr. Stalin; I think that the old system is closer to its end than you think."[42] The Kremlin leader would have liked to believe this, but how to bring it about? What about the bourgeoisie, the capitalists? What about the proletarian revolution? Wells argued that the Royal Society, queen of academies, was also in favor of the scientific planning of the economy, and that class war, with its insurrectional overtones, belonged to a bygone era. Socialism was the order of the day for all educated men. Stalin, sitting across from Wells, must have been laughing to himself when he heard his enterprise compared to the New Deal. Poker-faced, he trotted out once again the ABCs of Leninism, explained the centrality of political power, class struggle, capitalists and workers, and the necessity of revolutionary violence. He even gave his own version of a basic course in English history. What about the English revolution? Did Cromwell carry it out by obeying laws? Did he behead Charles I in the name of the constitution? The interview ended with the writer's heaping compliments upon the tyrant, declaring that, along with the American president, he was the arbiter of the social happiness of humanity.

Wells knew that there was no such thing as free speech in the Soviet Union. The other purpose of his trip was to establish a bridge between the Soviet Writers' Union and the International PEN Club, and he could see for himself that the Soviet writers were totally enslaved by the regime.[43] But this unfortunate and no doubt temporary situation was secondary to what Wells perceived as Stalin's aspiration to forge a rational society: a curious transference of the idea of a science of human development onto the Bolsheviks by an author who couldn't stand Marx. All he had to do was to mask out, in the name of the end of capitalism, the political status of Soviet society.

Once published, the interview with Stalin prompted acid remarks from another star of British literary life who was an admirer of the Guide, though for other reasons, and who exemplified the diversity of the Fabian "family." Unlike his great compatriot Burke, also an Irishman, Bernard Shaw was a persistent adversary of English parliamentarianism, but an adversary in his own way, which hardly made him an outcast—a status favored by modern writers—since his dramatic works brought him huge success. His hatred for Victorian hypocrisy remained intact, however, as did his disdain for the British political system—that civilized disguise for domination. He directed his famous wit against those things among others, constantly using them as subject matter for his paradoxes. His Fabian socialism was based on his own way of thinking rather than on any doctrine. He had known Wells for years, admired his literary talent, and made fun of his pretensions as universal reformer. Unlike Wells, Shaw had no predisposition against violence, since he prided himself on being a realist. His conversion to Stalin's Soviet Union in 1931 was prompted by the same thing that had moved him to support Mussolini and later Hitler: an efficient government at the service of the nation. In Shaw's eyes, Stalin had broken with the absurd internationalism of Lenin and also, to his credit, had defeated Trotsky, the apostle of the world revolution. Now, with the Five-Year Plan and agrarian reform, Stalin was about to set into motion a Fabian-style Socialist economy and society.

Shaw became a national-Bolshevik of the most improbable sort—a reformist. "Stalin is a good Fabian," he said at the time, "and that's the best that can be said of anyone." [44] Lenin, along with Trotsky, personified the impasses of the Revolution. Stalin was gradually reconstructing a socialist Russia by combining an enlightened dictatorship with a society of producer-consumers. What the British Labour Party seemed incapable of accomplishing,[45] and what the crisis of capitalism revealed to be necessary, had been undertaken by Lenin's successor. The world-famous dramatist hereby showed his high esteem for the latest recruit to the Fabian movement.

Shaw missed none of the comic aspect of the exchange between Stalin, the great man of action, and Wells, the utopia seeker. And, having himself visited Stalin in July 1931,[46] when he formed his idea of the man, he imagined the Bolshevik dictator concealing his amusement as he listened to the lessons of the inexhaustible Wells on the uselessness of class struggle and, more generally, of politics:

> I have never met a man who could talk so well and yet was in less of a hurry to talk than Stalin. Wells is a very good talker; but he is the worst listener in the world. This is fortunate; for his vision is so wide and assured that the slightest contradiction throws him into a blind fury of contemptuous and eloquently vituperative impatience. And to this, Stalin might not have been so indulgent as H.G.'s intimate friends at home.[47]

The rest of this commentary, once the roles of the comic dialogue have been assigned, is devoted to proving the superiority of Stalinist realism over Wellsian utopianism:

> It is evident that Stalin is a man who will get things done, including, if necessary, the removal of Trotsky and the World Revolution from the business of the day. Wells, with his World State without Revolution, he also strikes out of the agenda for the present.[48]

How flexible the Soviet myth was! Wells and Shaw both admired Stalin's Soviet Union as the homeland of an anticapitalist order that was putting an end to the anarchy of profit. But while Wells praised Stalin's civil peacekeeping, Shaw applauded the dictator's toughness. Wells radicalized the "gradualist" tradition; Shaw ignored it, ridiculing Wells's antipolitical otherworldliness. Shaw's own cynicism, however, was no less naive, since he hailed the deportation, assassination, and organized starvation of several million kulaks as the triumph of reason.

It would fall to John Maynard Keynes, one of the most brilliant minds of the time and a true reformer—of capitalism—to dismiss the two writers with one stroke, paying his "affectionate respect to *both* our grand old schoolmasters, Shaw and Wells, to whom most of us have gone to school all our lives, our divinity master and our stinks master. I only wish we had a third, equal to them in his field, to teach us humane letters and the arts." He arbitrated as follows. Communism, he told them, "offered to us as a means of improving the economic situation, is an insult to our intelligence. But offered as a means of making the economic situation *worse*, that is its subtle, its almost irresistible attraction."[49] Why was this so? Because it constituted an ideal in a world obsessed by economics. "When Cambridge undergraduates take their inevitable trip to Bolshiedom, are they disillusioned when they find it all dreadfully uncomfortable: Of course not. That is what they are looking for."[50] If the Soviet political economy evoked such infatuation, it was not only because it formed an almost providential contrast to the spectacle offered by the collapse of capitalism. It was because it revealed a moral idea, a regenerated humanity, delivered from the curse of profit.

Perhaps the most interesting thing about the British reaction to Stalinism is the ease with which the reformist tradition of British socialism clothed the Soviet experience with both science and morality under the cover of a new humanity. That these two ideas are not incompatible was essentially Bernard Shaw's argument: to sustain the Stalinist experience, one had to assume the moral nihilism of Marxism-Leninism in the name of necessity. The end justified the means. Wells, on the other hand, expounded to Stalin the true nature of his enterprise in order to bring him back onto the direct road to individual liberty, which is the moral state of a humanity reconciled. A year later, the Webbs themselves,[51] founders of Fabian socialism, would take this one step farther, bestowing their benediction on "socialism in one country" as though the economic individual of modern society had finally found the scientific means to collective life in the liquidation of the kulaks and the Five-Year Plan.

Although almost in their nineties, the Webbs also journeyed to Russia. Professional optimists, their vast compilation on the USSR, made up of newspaper clippings, academic (especially American) works, travelogues, and official documents, was the crowning glory of a shared life of obsession with the public good. It never seemed to have occurred to the Webbs that some of the things they had collected might have been false. They accepted them as they were, word for word, whether they dealt with the constitution, the judicial apparatus, political organizations, agricultural collectivization, or the Five-Year Plan. They wrote as though a real country could be described and analyzed according to what it said about itself, inaugurating what would be a long-lived academic tradition. They cited neither Russell, nor Souvarine, nor Victor Serge, nor anything that smacked of heresy to Moscow. The result, the two-volume *Soviet Communism,* with its benign spirit and credulity, was one of the most extravagant books ever written on a subject rich in the genre. Nothing was missing, not even a justification of the single party in the name of democracy, for they saw party as acting exclusively by means of persuasion via a pyramid of assemblies through which the population expressed its will. Stalin, moreover, had "not even the extensive power which the Congress of the United States [had] temporarily conferred upon President Roosevelt. . . . He [was] only the General Secretary of the Party."[52] For the Webbs, the USSR was a democracy of associated producers, relieved of the proprietor and the capitalist, producing together, in the name of science, an unprecedented civilization, a new humanity.

These two huge volumes, which have become unreadable for us, now provide the most perfect illustration of how Stalinist Communism could seduce the least revolutionary tradition of European socialism. Like Shaw and, moreover, at his insistence,[53] the Webbs began to view the Soviet Union as exemplary only after 1931; they were too alien to the Jacobin tradition to be interested in Bolshevism and the October Revolution. But in Stalin, the theoreticians of "gradualism" and the proponents of municipal socialism detected a revenge of the experts on revolutionary Marxism; disenchanted with British socialism, they believed their universe was taking shape in Russia. Their friend Bernard Shaw had convinced them of this even before they visited the country. Unlike Shaw, however, they supplemented their conversion with a touch of illusion, a remnant of utilitarian optimism in their socialism; in the Soviet Union they had seen in its infancy the withering away of the state! A mirage, after all, that was common to Manchesterian, reformist, and Bolshevik utopianism and gained Stalin the blessing of the founders of the Fabian Society.

Thus, in the period of "socialism in one country," the Soviet idea had lost none of its mythological capacity. Quite to the contrary. This was the beginning of the Stalinist era, marked by the extermination of the peasants, the absolute enslavement of all under the authority a single man, and the revolutionary posturing of the Comintern parties against the Social Fascists. With the aid of the Depression, however, the USSR of the first Five-Year Plan was still seen as the prime example of utopian humanism.

SIX

Communism and Fascism

BOTH AS MOVEMENTS AND AS REGIMES, COM-
munism and Fascism inhabited the same era—our own. Until the twentieth century, they were absent from the taxonomy of government types.
After World War I, however, they pervaded European politics with their
novelty and their immense ambitions—ambitions at once comparable
and antithetical—proclaiming the emergence of the new humanity, common to both of them, but with antagonistic ideas that set them against
each other. Through their victories, they quickly graduated from movements to regimes, and, from then on, they imprinted European history
with entirely new characteristics. The total political investment they
demanded and celebrated made their battle as incompatible successors
to bourgeois humanity all the more violent: the elements they shared
aggravated their differences.

This conflict presents one of the great problems of twentieth-century
history. Since this history is woven of unprecedented regimes—regimes
unknown either to Aristotle, Montesquieu, or Max Weber—and since
their heterogeneity is what makes this period unique, historians are
tempted to reduce the unknown to the known and to look at the twentieth century through the lens of the nineteenth as another version of
the fight for and against democracy, this time in the form of Fascism vs.
anti-Fascism. This view has had enormous resonance in the political
passions of our time and has become almost sacred since the end of
World War II. It remains a classic example of the particular difficulties
of contemporary and very recent history, for it reveals the intellectual
constraints imposed both by events and public opinion.

In the places where these constraints exercised their greatest influence—France and Italy—they were so powerful that the postulated
equivalence between Communism and anti-Fascism long impeded any
analysis of Communism. Nor did the equivalence facilitate the history

of Fascism. Quickly devalued, like currency in a time of galloping in-
flation, it lumped together Mussolini's regime and Nazism and, ultimately, all authoritarian or dictatorial governments. Indeed, "Fascism"
had to survive its own defeat and disappearance so that anti-Fascism
could continue to irrigate twentieth century history! No other dishonored regime has produced so many posthumous imitators in its victors'
imaginations.

One day, someone should write the history of how these imaginings
were slowly dispelled, and of the respective roles played by political
circumstances and a few original minds. I say "slowly" because we continue to live among the ruins accumulated by such representations; in
Europe, for example, the specter of Fascism is still brought out for display from time to time in order to unite the anti-Fascists—failing other
less abstract objectives. But at least among intellectuals, what remains a
device for politicians is no longer in use. The end of Communism has
made it, too, like Fascism (or Nazism), an object for autopsy. The time
when the great monsters of the century could conceal their battles and
misdeeds has passed. The hour of truth however, was preceded and
prepared by some clear-headed people and books, of which we may now
take stock. These will recur throughout the present work, but here we
should briefly consider certain basic concepts, since they are also the
underpinnings of my analysis.

The first is the invention of the concept of totalitarianism to describe
the new reality constituted by a society almost totally enslaved by a
party-state that reigns through ideology and terror. The word "totalitarianism" emerged when phenomena could no longer be described by
terms like "despotism" or "tyranny." A systematic history of the origins
of the word and its usage would certainly be fascinating.[1] The inade-
quacy of the term "despotism" to describe the modern exercise of un-
trammeled power and its unprecedented reach is an old story. Tocqueville, having taken the term from Montesquieu and the ancients, already
found "despotism" an inadequate designation for something entirely
new to the social democratic state.[2] The word "totalitarian" spread
widely in the 1920s, propagated by Italian Fascism; as early as 1925,
Mussolini exalted "our ferocious totalitarian will"[3] when addressing his
supporters. The word had not yet acquired the dignity of an ideal type,
but it was already loaded with a dual meaning held by no other word in
our traditional vocabulary. On the one hand, it expressed the primacy
of political will over all forms of social organization and the key role of
dictatorial decision making within political movements. On the other, it
designated the extreme point to which Fascism had brought the idea of
the state, developed over four centuries by European political thought:

with the omnipotence of the "totalitarian will," we are no longer referring merely to the absolute power of a despot who is not subject to the
law, but to a state that controls the entire society by absorbing all individuals within it.

No sooner had the word appeared than it became established all over
Europe. It was especially prevalent in Italy, and favored by admirers of
Fascism. In Germany it was used to describe National Socialism, even
though Hitler never employed it—perhaps wary of appearing to copy
the Italians. But it was in Goebbels's vocabulary. In intellectual circles,
Ernst Jünger,[4] as we have seen, used the words *total* and *Totalität* to characterize the mobilization of peoples by their states in World War I; that
massive conflict, by combining the spirit of war with that of technological progress, gave rise to unprecedented forms of political domination.
Carl Schmitt,[5] in his book *Der Hüter der Verfassung* (1931), criticized
Jünger's concept of a "totalitarian state." Schmitt maintained that the
correct distinction was not between the "totalitarian state" and the nontotalitarian state, since all states are entrusted with the legal exercise of
violence, and the Fascist state permitted the survival of a sphere independent of its authority—indeed, it even demarcated such a sphere—
in which private property was the rule. The political philosophy that
provided a framework for Schmitt's thinking justified the Nazi state
in advance rather than pointing to its novelty. However, if we remain
within the German context, the adjective "totalitarian"—which eventually produced its substantive—became current at the end of the 1930s
among anti-Nazi intellectuals and emigrants for analyzing and denouncing Hitler's regime at the same time. Those intellectuals, from Franz
Neumann to Hannah Arendt, were responsible for introducing the term
into the vocabulary of American political scientists immediately after
World War II. We shall return to this.

The inventory of the word in the interwar period does not stop here
however: the adjective "totalitarian" and the concept of totalitarianism,
insofar as they implied something distinct from despotism or tyranny,
eventually passed into scholarly usage in comparisons between Fascism
and Communism and, more precisely, between Hitlerian Germany and
Stalin's Soviet Union. In the article "State" in the 1934 edition of the
Encyclopedia of the Social Sciences, for example, "totalitarian" was used
to describe one-party states, including the USSR. Even without the
neologism, such comparisons had become widespread. In his famous
address to the French Philosophical Association of 28 November 1936,
entitled "The Era of Tyrannies,"[6] Élie Halévy made no reference to the
word "totalitarian" (though it occurred in the discussion following the

lecture).[7] His argument was based entirely on a comparison of the Soviet, Fascist, and National Socialist dictatorships—three "tyrannies" born of the evil marriage between the socialist idea and the Great War. The debate prompted by Halévy's lecture shows clearly that the idea of comparing those three regimes had its source in reflections on the first third of the twentieth century.

The idea could also be found in left-wing political literature, and even in the works of Marxist authors. As early as 1927, Pierre Pascal, on entertaining Tasca in Moscow and listening to him painting a bleak picture of Italian public life under Mussolini, thought that his guest was unwittingly depicting the nature of the Soviet regime. In his writings of the 1930s, to which I have already referred, Kautsky unflinchingly compared Stalinist Communism with National Socialism. He went so far as to deny that the former had the advantage of being better intentioned and holding more emancipatory aims: "The fundamental goal of Stalin, in all countries, is not the destruction of capitalism, but the destruction of democracy and the political and economic organizations of the workers."[8] Henceforth, Soviet Communism was not only comparable to National Socialism but almost identical to it. Even a more "left-wing" author like Otto Bauer, who tended to be indulgent toward the Soviet Union, would write in 1936 that "there, the dictatorship of the proletariat had assumed the specific form of a monopolistic, totalitarian dictatorship of the Communist Party."[9] Thus the founder of the "Internationale 2½"[10] defined the regime with terms borrowed from Fascist vocabulary and implied that Stalinism was unique in the Communist family because of its kinship with the "totalitarian" dictatorships of monopolistic parties, that is, with Mussolini and Hitler.

The concept of totalitarianism, then, is not a recent invention of cold war propagandists seeking to discredit the Soviet Union by identifying it with Nazi Germany, which had been banished from humanity by the Nuremberg trials. Although the adjective "totalitarian" had already become current in the interwar period as a designation for a completely new kind of regime, it had yet to acquire the analytical precision with which Hannah Arendt and the political scientists she inspired[11] sought to endow the term after World War II. It simply implied that "totalitarian" dictatorships had the vocation of exercising a narrower and more complete domination over their subjects than earlier forms of despotism. Depending on the case, the term did or did not include the Soviet regime. But the word itself was not indispensable to the comparison: Élie Halévy, as we noted, still used the old word "tyranny."

Comparing the Soviet Union to Fascist regimes, with or without

using the term "totalitarian," was a common theme in the interwar period, and although liberal thinkers manipulated it with the most profundity, the comparison was used by all political families, from left to
right. Many intellectuals hostile to liberal democracy identified the two
regimes so closely that they vacillated between Fascism and Communism throughout the 1930s. That this idea, which was resisted after
1945, could have been presented as an ideological fabrication born of
the imperatives of the cold war was due to the unexpected angle from
which, at least in the West, it interpreted World War II and the victory
of 1945. Militarily crushed by a coalition that ended up with the Soviet
Union in the camp of the democracies, German Nazism and Italian Fascism alone were cast in the role of enemy of liberty. If Stalin figured
among the victors, that meant that he too stood for freedom—an analogy in keeping with the original lie of his dictatorship, and which was,
furthermore, confirmed by the quantities of Russian blood spilled to
crush Hitler's Germany. The entirely negative idea of "anti-Fascism"
made it impossible to put forward anything positive that might have
reconciled the liberal democracies with Stalinist Communism. It was
both vague enough to allow Stalin to crush democracy everywhere his
armies led him, and precise enough to condemn as blasphemous any
comparison between his regime and Hitler's. The intrepid Hannah
Arendt persevered regardless, as a good heir to German anti-Nazi literature since the coming of Hitler. But just about everywhere in Western Europe, people were intimidated by the choice between Fascism and
anti-Fascism. Even in a country like Italy, where anti-Fascist ideology
had been most influential, the concept of totalitarianism never caught
on. The idea was simply ignored, if not proscribed, in the very place
where it had been invented.

This interpretation does not imply that, from the beginning of the
cold war, comparing Nazism to Communism may not have served as
propaganda to mobilize democracies against the Soviet menace; it certainly did so serve. But the idea predates World War II itself, and its
pertinence is more durable. It was on people's minds again after the war
because the censorship imposed on it by the victory of 1945 could not
erase the history and experiences of the following years. Its influence
depended less on the propaganda of an ideological crusade than on the
rediscovery of a Soviet regime true to type that was snuffing out liberty
in every European country in which its army had planted its flags.

That rediscovery was slow and laborious, greatly hampered by the
heritage of the war. This was the story of the immediate postwar period
in Europe, when Stalinist Communism, victorious over the Fascist dictators, reached its greatest influence. But let us first consider the years

between World Wars I and II. At that time, the relationship between nascent Communism and Fascism, whether as ideological movements or as political regimes, was a very complex one—a relationship of fathering or rejection, of borrowings and confrontations, of shared passions and inexpiable hatred, of tacit solidarity and public belligerence. It produced the darkest quarter-century in European history, from one war to the next. For anyone who would understand this history—so brief, so deplorable, and so mysterious even to this day—a concept like "totalitarianism" is useful only when employed with caution. It best describes a particular state attained by the regimes in question (and not necessarily by all of them) during different periods of their evolution. But it tells us nothing of what those regimes owed to the circumstances of their development, nor of the extent to which they served to engender one another or shared certain hidden complicities.

World War I played the same generative role in the twentieth century as the French Revolution did in the nineteenth, and gave rise to the events and trends that produced the three "tyrannies" referred to by Élie Halévy in 1936. The chronology of the period speaks for itself: Lenin took power in 1917, Mussolini in 1922, and Hitler failed in 1923 only to succeed ten years later. One may thus posit that the passions awakened by these new regimes were contemporaneous and, hence, that the political mobilization of veterans was the key to the undivided domination of a single party.

There is another way of comparing these twentieth-century dictatorships. Instead of analyzing them conceptually at their apogees, why not study how they were formed and how they succeeded in order to define what was specific to each regime and what all these regimes had in common? We must also try to understand what the individual histories of the regimes owed to emulative or hostile relations with other regimes, some of whose traits they borrowed. Imitation and hostility are not mutually exclusive: Mussolini borrowed from Lenin but did so in order to defeat and ban Communism in Italy; Hitler and Stalin offered many examples of belligerent complicity.

This approach, which forms a natural preamble to an inventory of an ideal type such as "totalitarianism," has the advantage of closely following the course of events and the disadvantage of potential oversimplification through linear causality—explaining what came before by what came afterward. Mussolinian Fascism of 1919 can thus be construed as a "reaction" to the menace of an Italian-style Bolshevism that was also produced by the war, patterned more or less after the Russian example—a reaction in the broadest sense of the word, since Mussolini, coming, like Lenin, from an ultrarevolutionary form of socialism, found it that much easier to turn Lenin's own tactics against him. The October 1917 victory of Russian Bolshevism can also be cast as the starting point of a chain of "reactions," with Italian Fascism and then Nazism appearing as responses to the Communist menace, designed along the revolutionary and dictatorial lines of Communism. This sort of interpretation could lead, if not to a justification, at least to a partial exoneration of Nazism, as shown by the recent debate among German historians on the subject:[12] even Ernst Nolte,[13] one of the most thoughtful historians of Fascist movements, has not always escaped this temptation. Such a viewpoint has the additional drawback of attenuating the particularity of each of the Fascist regimes, reducing them not to a single guiding concept but to a single enemy.

Such an approach increases the disadvantages of a less than subtle conceptualization of "totalitarianism." If the Fascist movements are viewed as mere reactions against Bolshevism, they are subsumed by a model that does nothing to facilitate an understanding of their singularity, their autonomy, or the origins and passions they may have shared with their enemy. Putting them into a common, purely negative category impoverishes the analysis of their respective traits and of the relations each of them maintained—whether as movements or, ultimately, as regimes—with the regime they abhorred. Rather than reducing all Fascisms to the same source in order to bring them through the tumultuous course of the century as one group, it is perhaps more fruitful to consider their varied compositions and characters. This is the path taken by the majority of historical works on the question.

For if Communism is indispensable to an understanding of Fascism (and vice versa), it is for broader reasons than might be suggested by the chronology from Lenin to Mussolini, 1917–22, or from Lenin to the early days of Hitler, 1917–23, patterned along a logic of action-reaction. Bolshevism and Fascism occurred in succession, gave rise to one another, imitated and fought one another, but shared the same source— the war—and were products of the same history. Bolshevism, the first to arrive on the public scene, may indeed have radicalized political passions, but the fear it provoked from the Right and beyond does not adequately explain a phenomenon like the birth of Italian *fasci* in March of 1919. After all, the elites and the middle classes of Europe had lived in terror of socialism well before World War I and had bloodily repressed anything resembling a workers' insurrection, such as the Paris commune in 1871; yet nothing comparable to Fascism ever emerged in the nineteenth century. These reactions of rejection or even of panic may explain the people's consenting to one regime or another. They help us understand the antiliberal aspect of a regime founded on fear, but no more. They tell us nothing of its nature, and even less of its novelty.

Born of the war, both Bolshevism and Fascism drew their basic education from war. They transferred to politics the lessons of the trenches: familiarity with violence, the simplicity of extreme passions, the submission of the individual to the collectivity, and finally the bitterness of futile or betrayed sacrifices. It was in the countries defeated on the battlefields or frustrated by the peace negotiations that these sentiments found their quintessential breeding ground. They introduced into the political order the power of numbers, which the nineteenth century had always feared—though it was never really a threat—as the danger of universal suffrage, only to find it coming from an unexpected source: millions of citizens united not by the solitary exercise of a right but by the shared misfortune of military servitude. As many authors have observed, the post–World War I years inaugurated the age of the masses. This new age, however, did not arrive through progressive development and as a natural byproduct of democracy. It burst onto the scene of history through a door that was thought to be barred, since modern societies had been described by many great thinkers of the eighteenth and nineteenth centuries as being entirely oriented toward the production of wealth and the pursuit of peace.

And so the "age of the masses" that ushered in the twentieth century did, in a sense, signal the progress of democracy. It made the great majority—that is, the humblest citizens—an active agent in the nation. On the other hand, the manner in which those citizens were integrated into politics was not, as the optimists had always predicted, through education but through the memories of a war that no one, or hardly anyone, had predicted or wanted, and whose extent, not to speak of its consequences, had certainly been beyond imagining. The masses were not activated as a group of enlightened individuals who gradually became versed in modern politics. They moved brutally from war to peace, bringing the simple passions of the war to the ruins in which the armistice found them. The kind of language that touched them was not that of civilized struggles for power but that of the fraternal community of combat—a discourse claimed on the right as an tribute to tradition, and on the left as a promise for the future; and it was not long after the war's end that the word "socialism," reinvented by the Right, began a new career under the standard of Fascism.

We have noted that the complicity between socialism and antiliberal thought, and even between socialism and antidemocratic thought, is an old one. Since the French Revolution, the reactionary Right and the socialist Left had both been denouncing bourgeois individualism and were both convinced that modern society, deprived of a true foundation, prisoner to the illusion of universal rights, had no lasting future. In the nineteenth century, many European socialist thinkers, such as Buchez and Lassalle, despised democracy and exalted the nation.[14] Conversely, just before World War I, the widespread critique of liberalism brought even the most radical, that is, most nationalist, members of the Right closer to the socialist idea. In theory, it is easy to conceive of an economy liberated from the anarchy of private interests within a national framework, and thus to combine anticapitalist sentiments with a nationalistic passion. Tending in this direction was the Action française during its "revolutionary" years. Charles Maurras perceived very early that "a *pure* socialist system would be devoid of any element of democratism."[15] What he meant was that a system of this sort would bring with it an organic society, free of individualism, reconstituted as a unity of interests and wills—something that complemented rather than contradicted the national idea. Of course, Marxist internationalism had to remain the quintessential enemy of nationalists. "But a form of socialism, freed of the democratic and cosmopolitan element, could go with nationalism as a well-made glove fits a beautiful hand."[16]

The idea of a nationalistic socialism, then, was not new in 1918 or 1920, but when the guns fell silent, it had shed its sophisticated intellectual robe and appeared, in certain popular versions, as an instrument fit to galvanize the masses. Before the war, the socialist-nationalist mix was but an esoteric cocktail for intellectuals. Afterward, it became a widely consumed beverage. Its sudden popularity did not derive from a love-hate reaction to the Russian Revolution or from a scheme to grab a legacy that would help integrate socialism into an anti-Bolshevik program. This had certainly occurred to some ideologues; the National-Socialist (or Fascist) idea, however, had more complex origins and drew its strength from the same source as victorious Bolshevism—the war. Like Bolshevism, it served to mobilize modern revolutionary passions, the brotherhood of veterans, hatred of the bourgeoisie and of money, human equality, and aspirations to a new world. But it prescribed a program other than the dictatorship of the proletariat—that of the national state-community. It thus constituted the second great political myth of the century. Far from being a mere instrument in the battle against Bolshevism—another of its incarnations—it was to take such an important place in the imagination of the time that the European elites were helpless to limit its ravages.

Both Bolshevism and Fascism, as vast collective passions, were personified by personalities who were—alas!—exceptional. This other side of the history of the twentieth century, and its random element, contributed to what was inherently revolutionary about that history. Yet another characteristic common to the three great dictatorships of the era was that each of their destinies was determined by the will of an individual. Obsessed by the abstract history of classes, our century has done everything possible to obscure this rather elementary truth. It has wanted to see the working classes behind Lenin, and to cast the Fascist dictators as the puppets of capital. Countless writers, out of perversity or candor, have made use of this double standard, generally accepting that the Bolsheviks conformed to the idea they made of themselves, yet submitting the Fascists to an interpretation that bore no relation to anything they actually said. The advantage of this learned version of anti-Fascism is that it separates the wheat from the chaff through the sieve of class struggle, thus rediscovering in the gloom of the century the providential thread of necessity. The trouble is, such an attitude explains nothing about the spectacular role played by a handful of men in this tragic adventure. If we were to erase Lenin from history, there would have been no October 1917. Take away Mussolini, and postwar Italy would have taken another course. As for Hitler, if it is true that, like Mussolini, he seized power in part with the resigned consent of the German Right, that makes his autonomy no less disastrous: it was he who carried out the program of *Mein Kampf,* which was his alone.

In fact, these three men took power by breaking weak regimes with the superior force of their wills, which they focused entirely and with extraordinary obduracy upon this unique goal. The same thing could be said of Stalin. Without him, there would have been neither "socialism in one country" nor, by definition, "Stalinism." There is surely no historical precedent for such a concentration of monstrous political wills in such a limited space and time. Each of them triumphed, of course, with the aid of specific circumstances, but their adversaries were people who had already been defeated or who were half consenting. Lenin gathered up power rather than seizing it, Mussolini's Black Shirts entered a Rome that was wide open to them, and Hitler was brought to power by Hindenburg; as for Stalin, any human obstacles to his reign had accepted beforehand the rules of the game that condemned them to defeat.

Once power was theirs, however, they all exercised it rather quickly and in an autocratic manner. Only Lenin seized power according to the classic revolutionary scenario, but all of them made use of it so as to put into practice their conception of the new humanity, truer to their crazy ideas than to their circumstantial backers. Their will to dominate grew and became headier with each success. There is thus little sense in trying to key their actions to particular interests, milieus, or social classes. From Kronstadt on, Lenin's version of the "dictatorship of the proletariat" had little to do with the working class; his rhetoric bore as little relation to what followed as the Jewish genocide did to the program of German big capital.

There is nothing more incompatible with a Marxist-type explanation, including what, in other cases, is true about it, than the unparalleled dictatorships of the twentieth century. The mystery of these regimes can in no way be explained by dependence on social interests—quite the contrary: they were appallingly independent of those interests, whether bourgeois or proletarian. Ironically, historical materialism reached the height of its influence in the twentieth century at a time when its explanatory capacity was most attenuated.

The least inadequate approach to the relationship between Communism and Fascism remains the classic route of the historian—taking stock of ideas, intentions, and circumstances. The investigation may be divided into two long acts, which form two eras: Lenin and Mussolini as the first, and Stalin and Hitler as the second.

Lenin and Mussolini emerged from the same political family [17]—that of revolutionary socialism. Mussolini was *Il Duce* of the revolution before becoming *Il Duce* of Fascism. The title was given him for the first time in 1912, when, with Pietro Nenni, he came out of prison after serving time for his opposition to the war in Tripolitaine.[18] He fully deserved the title. For the entire first half of his life, the years prior to World War I, he gravitated toward the most radical form of revolutionary ideology. He had the same subversive vehemence, the same taste for violence, the same tendency to subordinate all moral considerations to a single end, and even the same passion for ruptures as Lenin: this becomes clear when, during the period of his greatest influence over the Italian socialists between 1912 and 1914, he expelled the moderate elements from the party. His political extremism had other sources besides Bolshevism and was not part of the Russian populist tradition; were we to attempt to describe his antecedents or allies, we should look first among adherents of the republican Risorgimento [19] and revolutionary syndicalism.[20] In pre-1914 Europe, however, Mussolini incarnated a neo-Blanquist version of Marxism that was not remote from the Bolsheviks' version.

Even his famous about-face in October 1914, from an antiwar position to one of an "active and effective neutrality" [21] in favor of the allies, was not a repudiation of the revolution. In the Italian context, its implications were different from those of the rallying of the French and

German socialists to their respective camps. Postunification Italian politics had drawn its inspiration entirely from the idea that Austro-Hungary, its great neighbor to the north, was indispensable to the European equilibrium and was the advance guard of Catholic Europe in the Balkans. The residual territorial contentions between Rome and Vienna were secondary by comparison. Such was the conservative conception that led Italy into the Triple Alliance alongside the Central Powers. On the other hand, Mussolini brandished the heritage of Mazzini[22] against that of Balbo:[23] Italy needed to return to its revolutionary tradition, which had been betrayed by a timid bourgeoisie, and boldly to reconquer the Italian territories still in Austrian hands. Boldly—that is, by breaking with the passivity and shameful pusillanimity that were not worthy of its history. Mussolini's neonationalism thus placed itself in the most revolutionary tradition of the Risorgimento in order, at long last, to accomplish its promise.

With his passion for action, Mussolini could not tolerate Italy's passivity while the rest of Europe was catching fire. In his warlike activism, however, which would gain him excommunication from the Socialist Party, he was careful not to separate the idea of revolution from the renewal of the nation. He intended to use the First World War to regenerate the country, not by opposing it, like Lenin, but by participating in it. Both men rejected pacifism, shared the same disdain for the bourgeois, and were convinced that the war could serve their purposes. But whereas Lenin brought revolution back to life in the context of Marxism, Mussolini made revolution preside over the subversive marriage between socialism and the nation, this last being the substitute for the proletariat in the redemption of the bourgeois world. Like Mussolini, contemporary Italian intellectuals detested the overly prudent politicians and the narrow oligarchy represented by Giolitti—the uncontested master of parliamentary manipulation. For them, interventionism was the way to break both Austria and Giolitti and finally to reconquer Trente and Trieste,[24] the Alsace-Lorraine of Italian patriots. Warmongering thus assumed a place in Italian culture as a revival of the audacities of 1848 and the Risorgimento; Italy's entry into the war in 1915—a veritable anti-Giolittian revolution—also marked the entry of the popular masses into the nation's politics. The Italian case provides the best illustration of the extent to which World War I was associated with a promise both democratic and national.

The war was supposed to be short, but it was long. It was supposed to be victorious, but it was only partially so, quite unable to erase the memory of the Caporetto disaster of 1916. When it was over, it had yet to realize all of Italy's territorial claims, nor had it chased Giolitti and his cronies from power or its vicinity. But the war had so deeply touched national life that it left a great deal of latitude to the chaotic hopes of the interventionists of 1914–15. The state was weaker than ever: D'Annunzio occupied Fiume with his soldiers in September 1919 and refused to leave. The centrist oligarchy of notables that had ruled Italy had lost its constituency. The two modern mass parties, the Socialist Party and Sturzo's brand-new "Popular Party," which reintegrated Catholics into Italian politics, eluded his control. The former, moreover, was beset by a proliferation of revolutionary strikes in 1920, accompanied by factory takeovers, sometimes in confused emulation of the Soviets. In the countryside, during the winter of 1920–21, the rich Po Valley became an arena of violent confrontations between laborers and landowners. The picture was completed by the critical economic and financial situation of Italy, left to balance the accounts from a war that had been too costly. This was the setting in which Mussolini imposed his response to the 1914–15 questionings as to the necessity of an Italian revolution. A list of the elements of that response would constitute a fair definition of Fascism.

Italian Fascism, more directly than any other dictatorial regime of those years, was born of the war. So was Bolshevism, but Lenin acquired power because he had opposed the war, not by harnessing it. National Socialism shared the same origin, although Hitler, orphan of the defeat, had already been beaten once by the Weimar Republic prior to his own victory. Mussolini, having come from the socialist extreme Left, began his march to power as early as 1914 by pushing Italy into the conflict when this could just as easily been avoided. The war was so inseparable from its course that its processes, after the fighting was over, were extended to political combat. Even before becoming a doctrine, Fascism was a paramilitary party backed up by armed organizations. The *arditi*—the Italian army's shock troops, molded in the spirit of warrior aristocratism—furnished the membership of the first *fasci* from their inception in the spring of 1919. What else was there to do for these specialists in incredible risk, these aesthetes of heroic death, threatened, furthermore, with demobilization? Their first "civil" exploit was the sacking of the offices of the socialist journal *Avanti* in Milan, on 15 April 1919.[25] Fascist politics were as straightforward as war: they extended the category of enemy to compatriots.

The passions mobilized and the body of ideology cobbled together by Fascist politics were not simply nationalistic. If this were so, Fascism would have had little more to offer—and even less literature—than did D'Annunzio and his Fiume legionnaires. It constituted a much larger movement and expressed a more profound anger—that of the bourgeoisie and the petty bourgeoisie who had been excluded from the political scene since national unification and demanded their place.[26] Thanks to the war, they had become a part of national life. Caught up in the postwar crisis, they disliked socialism and feared the contagious effect of the Soviet example even more. But they were just as hostile toward the parliamentary oligarchy of their own country, which had confiscated power for so long, incapable of entering resolutely into the European conflict or of obtaining a peace treaty for Italy worthy of its sacrifices and its soldiers. Draped in the values of the war, they brought the means of war into the political arena, bent on preserving the fraternity and violence of those means.

As to fraternity, one of the great themes of the interventionism of 1914–15 was that of discovering the common people. The Fascists, who had rubbed shoulders with proletarian and peasant Italy in the trenches, sought to associate the masses with their conquest of power. As to violence, one of the commonplaces of revolutionary socialism or syndicalism even before it became a leitmotif of the Fascist movement was the denunciation of bourgeois legality. Force took precedence over law. Mussolini had only to remain true to his past in order to feel comfortable in his new role. In the pre-1914 socialist movement, Lenin and Mussolini shared the same hatred for reformists, those shameful allies of the bourgeoisie. Both made a radical distinction between the proletarian cause and bourgeois democracy. But 1914 would divide them: Lenin wanted to oppose the international war by using class struggle; Mussolini wanted to make war abroad in order to take advantage of its internal effects. The two men took contradictory positions in 1914; yet, because of the war, their strategies remained analogous on two levels, technical and moral. On the technical level, they adjusted their political actions to the character of the period inaugurated by the war. All survivors of the trenches had to be touched by their policies, and in order for this to happen, the policymakers had to rely on the kind of simple, massive propaganda to which the terrible years had accustomed them. So much for parliamentary tricks and academic arguments! To transform a society of individuals into one will, to fuse that multiplicity into shared emotions in peace as in war: that was the new secret of democratic politics. Mussolini drew his inspiration from Le Bon,[27] whom he had read and reread. He was also emulating Lenin, whom he admired even while opposing him.

This chemistry had an intellectual and moral price. For the promulgators of such a political discourse, all criteria other than immediate results tended to fall by the wayside as their discourse turned into demagogy, dictated exclusively by the interests of the speaker, no longer bearing any relation to morality in its most universal, elementary aspect or to the observation of the most everyday facts. The "prince's" secrets were out. They were simplified in the worst sense of the word and, as such, were condemned to disappear into the darkness of the all-pervasive lie as the "prince" gave way to the modern dictator, who shared the sentiments and ideas to which he appealed. The dictator retained the Machiavellian desire to seize or conserve power by all means necessary to the exercise of the art of politics. But that art had degenerated. It had been reduced to its capacity to manipulate the masses through words and deeds that played to their dominant passions. Since it implied a broad, subjective identification between the leader and his discourse, it brought to political conflict an emotional violence as well as an absence of scruples and an unprecedented brutality of means.

Just as the nineteenth-century thinkers had expected, the masses erupted onto the European public scene, constituting a political civilization in which the fragile mechanisms of constitutional regimes were short-circuited by primitive forms of popular participation and of parliamentary representation by the identification with a single leader. Before its influence was magnified by anti-Communism, Fascism had been a product of a no less extreme form of the same political passions at work in Communism—in particular, hatred of bourgeois parliamentarianism.

Today, it is hard to imagine the hatred aroused by parliamentary deputies at the time. The deputy was hated as the essence of all the lies of bourgeois politics. He symbolized oligarchy posing as democracy, domination posing as law, corruption lurking beneath the affirmation of republican virtue. The deputy was seen as exactly the opposite of what he pretended to be, of what he ought to be: in theory, the representative of the people; in reality, the man through whom money—that universal master of the bourgeois—takes possession of the will of the people. He was plutocracy disguised as politics. With this image, which in the nineteenth century was shared by everyone from the extreme Right to the extreme Left, the critique of the idea of the "representation" of the people inseparable from modern democracy reached its peak. After World War I, it was reinforced by the psychology of the soldiers who had emerged from that terrible ordeal, a war that had been voted for but not undergone by members of parliament. Even when it took the form of a constituent assembly, ennobled by the French precedent, an elected assembly elicited little indulgence from Lenin in January of 1918. The dictatorship of the proletariat, inscribed in historical necessity and incarnated by the Bolshevik Party, could dispense with the vicissitudes of a vote and the incertitudes of a parliament; Mussolini, decked out in the values of war and fortified by the violence exercised by his partisans in Italy, had merely to bend the deputies to his will.

What was lost in both cases, along with the political abstraction of representation and juridically abstract law, was the idea of the constitutional state. The substitution of a party or its leader for the vote of the citizens or their elected representatives did away with democratic legitimacy and legality. On the one hand, the seat of power was henceforth occupied permanently in the name of its essential identity with a class chosen by history or with a national community superior to all others—an identity of an ontological order, bearing no relation to the empirical contingency of a vote and making nonsense out of political competition arbitrated by an election. On the other hand, the party or person, or both, now in power were no longer encumbered by laws, for which they tended to substitute or superimpose their own will. For them, history was merely the bearer of a law constituting the relationship between the state and its citizens—a dynamic of the forces between classes and between peoples. Revolution was the most constant and natural embodiment of that dynamic.

Disdain for the law as a nominal disguise for bourgeois domination, apology for force as the midwife of history—these themes existed well before the beginning of the twentieth century in Western political thought and were particularly virulent in the decades preceding the Great War, both on the right and on the left. On this subject, Georges Sorel remains one of the most interesting authors of the period, both for the tenacity with which he detested and denounced the pusillanimity of bourgeois parliamentarianism and for the hopes he invested in violence, that great, hidden truth of the modern world. Though an interesting writer, he was never quite to be trusted, for he navigated between revolutionary syndicalism and Action française, was anti-Semitic, and admired both Lenin and Mussolini[28]—which is precisely why we should be curious about his writings. His work is of interest not only on account of its prescient aspect but because it allows us, for once, to measure the distance between theory and practice, and even between intellectuals and real history.

In Sorel's thought, violence is inseparable from creation. Infused by a great idea—the general strike—its role was to tear away the web of lies that covered society and to restore moral dignity to individuals and meaning to their collective existences. As in Nietzsche's thought, it facilitated a reunion of humanity with its own grandeur, beyond the reach of the universal pettiness of democratic times. The bourgeoisie lived in hypocrisy; class struggle brought virtue back onto the public scene to the benefit of the proletariat. It lent violence an ethical goal and turned

the revolutionary activist into a hero. The reason the proponents of the
general strike admired Lenin and Mussolini was that they saw them as
two prodigies of volition who had taken charge of their peoples in order
to realize the new humanity. Poor Georges Sorel! Intellectually a son of
Proudhon, an individualist and an anarchist, he was filled with admiration for the founders of regimes in comparison to which the despised
bourgeois state looked like a libertarian utopia! He saw only the aspects
of those regimes that fit with his own passions and ideas. Lenin was the
successor to the great czars, as revolutionary as Peter the Great and as
Russian as Nicholas I.[29] Mussolini belonged to the betrayed tradition of
the republican Risorgimento. By marrying national renaissance with the
socialist idea returned to its revolutionary vocation, these two "leaders
of peoples"[30] forcibly destroyed the bourgeoisie order in the name of a
higher concept of the community.

In fact, neither the Red Terror that Lenin exercised in order to retain
power, nor the Fascist Terror used by Mussolini in order to gain power,
had much to do with the philosophical idea of violence developed by
Sorel. Lenin's and Mussolini's Terrors were born of an event—the
war—not of an idea. Rather than products of an unprecedented conviction, they were part of a general revival of revolutionary means of domination through fear.

The war generalized the dual habit of violence and passivity. It gave
European nations the worst kind of political education just as it was
mobilizing populations into the military, down to the last citizen. The
Russian Revolution, even the February one, was no exception to the
rule. On the contrary, it combined military defeat, governmental incompetence, and revolutionary ineptitude and was incapable of establishing
a constitutional order. It was the first event to show that the postwar
period was still at the mercy of the passions and expedients of the war.
In October, Lenin seized power not because of his philosophical ideas
but in spite of them. It was circumstance that opened the way to his
inflexible will, in what was a most improbable context for a Marxist.
Mussolini did not triumph in 1922 because he held fast to a doctrine
but because his adversaries were weak, timid, or both. The postwar political world as prefigured by these two men—each of whom claimed
to be its exclusive guide—was not, no matter what they said, one of
Sorelian violence. It was a world of political gangsterism that happened
to be supported by favorable conditions.

Domestic political battles had lost the body of rules that had been
etched into and had become part of the workings of European mores
and institutions during the nineteenth century. Emancipated from civilization's constraints, the passionate wellsprings that animated those

rules grew more powerful and universal than ever. Hatred of money, egalitarian resentment, and national humiliation resonated all the more as the leaders, not to be outdone, fanned the flames. While remaining opportunistic tacticians, the leaders both shared and, at the same time, manipulated the passions liberated by the war. As European politics took a turn for the doctrinal—Bolshevism and Fascism were doctrines, after all—it also became increasingly elementary: first, it transformed ideas into beliefs; and, second, any means were considered acceptable, starting with the elevation of deception and assassination to the status of civic virtues. You could kill your fellow citizens like enemies in a war. They need only belong to the wrong class or to an opposing party. The denunciation of legality as a "formal" lie led to the "real" exercise of arbitrary power and of terror. Whoever was in power had the right to designate the adversaries he needed to exterminate.

Thus, in both Russian Bolshevism and Italian Fascism we find a two-tiered political system in which a philosophy of history coexisted with a political method, the former made up of noble intentions and ideas, the latter of expedience. The former was the poetry, the latter the prose. Fascism lost its poetry with World War II, whereas Bolshevism used it as an opportunity to conceal its prose. In attempting to understand Europe during this period, no historian can sidestep the fact that Mussolinian Fascism was a doctrine and a hope for millions of people. It lacked a great intellectual forebear, but it sought to get rid of the bourgeoisie in the name of the new humanity and, moreover, managed to co-opt a large part of the intellectual avant-garde—the futurists, those nostalgic for the enthusiasm of the Risorgimento, Marinetti, Ungaretti, Gentile, and even Croce if only briefly.[31]

When serving this antibourgeois ambition, the passions aroused by militant Fascism were not the same as those elicited by Bolshevism, but they were of the same nature. Instead of social equality, the nation was reinvented as a communitarian utopia, a renewed seat of great collective emotions; but there was a multiplicity of "passages" between the various obsessions with action. As for the means, those recommended or employed by the Fascist movement were already part of the Bolshevik panoply: anything that served the cause was good.

Fascism, then, was not merely a reaction to Bolshevism. It cannot be reduced to its functional role as a "bourgeois" instrument. To the questions posed by the Communists—How can we rid modern society of individualism? How can we build a true human community? and How can private humanity be absorbed into public humanity?—Fascism proposed a different response, drawn from disparate cultural elements and built upon Italian despair. This doctrine had none of the symphonic beauty of Marxism, but since it was meant to rally the masses, this mattered little. It had to be able to express incompatible things, one after the other. Leninism had opened the way: this is clear if we compare the pamphlet Lenin wrote in 1917 on the eve of October, *The State and the Revolution*, with the way the Bolsheviks actually practiced democratic government a few months later. Mussolini's Fascism presented the same tendencies. With doctrine on one side, propaganda and deeds on the other, the Fascists sought to legitimize their ideas by forcibly seizing power in order to institute a new era of humanity.

The real innovation of Fascism was not that it mobilized a mass anti-Communism, for this had already been done in Germany with the Social Democrats and in Italy with the Christian Democratic Party, but that it invented a revolutionary Right. Fascism of this era, as Renzo de Felice has shown, was a legitimate revolutionary movement with its own ambitions, ideology, and methods.[32] Even after Mussolini had seized power at the price of a tactical compromise with the traditional Italian elites, even after his regime had betrayed his movement, he remained a dictator who had escaped from the control of the governing classes and justice. The Fascist regime was haunted by the ideology of the Fascist movement,[33] and its ultimate destiny, written in the fatal 1938 alliance with Nazi Germany, depended entirely on Mussolini and his henchmen, against all "bourgeois" prudence and to the exclusion of any consultation with Italy's traditional elites.

Fascism, in its classic—that is, its Italian—form, cannot be reduced to a negation of Communism or even to a counterrevolution. The very term "Fascism" draws its strength from the analogy with the French Revolution; to the Bolshevik Revolution it conceded in advance the title the Bolsheviks had adopted as expediently as they had seized power; it was an ideological putsch that contained no more substance than the myth of a "workers' and peasants'" government but which, as we have seen, exercised the same power over the imagination. Fascism, both as a movement and as a body of ideas, was free of the difficulties encountered by the counterrevolutionaries when they sought to define their policies and ideology in the late eighteenth and the nineteenth centuries. The counterrevolution, born of and inseparable from the Revolution, would find itself caught in the contradiction of having to use revolutionary means in order to prevail, while unable to define a goal other than the restoration of an ancien régime, which is where the trouble had started. This was the impasse emphasized by Benjamin Constant as early as 1797, in defense of the Directory. Joseph de Maistre had attempted in vain to exorcize its fatal aspect.[34] Fascism was quite different. It was not defined by reaction to a revolution but was conceived of and intended to be a revolution in itself. Did it not oppose the bourgeois principles of 1789? Certainly, but no more or less violently than it opposed Bolshevism. Did it not seek to destroy Bolshevism? Yes, but not in order to return to something anterior to the October Revolution; it had its own prospective magic.

In Fascism, as in Communism, the idea of the future was based on a critique of bourgeois modernity. This doctrine had a more eclectic genealogical tree than Bolshevism. It arose from a variety of currents and from authors of very different origins, all of whom demonized the bourgeoisie. The doctrine was cast as post-Marxist, not as pre-liberal. It was meant to restore the unity of the people and the nation in face of a society being disintegrated by money. Mussolini was the medium in which all these scattered elements of pre-1914 European culture coalesced. In order for these elements to cease being diverse and contradictory, the war was necessary, binding them into collective emotions. The offspring of Italian revolutionary socialism set the new tone. Fascism was born not merely to vanquish Bolshevism but to break the divisiveness of the bourgeois world. The same ambition and the same ill-being supported both promises and both movements. The Fascists and the Bolsheviks relied on different and even contradictory supports—the one on class, the other on nation—but both sought to dispel the same curse by the same means.

Fascism was not just an outlook or a doctrine but a strategy and, even more, a will to power. Mussolini, following Lenin, was obsessed with the idea of taking over the state and using it to fashion a new people. Curiously, the fascination with Jacobinism had made its way to a country in which the state was weak—almost nonexistent—in both its administrative reality and in the people's image of its authority; this was one of the most spectacular signs of the extension of French-style revolutionary politics into postwar Europe.

Italy presented, for the first time, the spectacle of a three-dimensional battle: a revolutionary Left, a group of "bourgeois" parties, and a revolutionary Right. In this respect, Fascism may indeed be studied as a "reaction" to Communism, bearing out Ernst Nolte's thesis. Not that Mussolini's movement played a significant role in the defeat of what we might term the first Italian Bolshevism, 1919–20. That movement was dormant during the great period of worker agitation, and it kept its distance from the occupation of factories and the inglorious end of socialist "maximalism."[35] It played no part in stopping the "workers'" revolution, but the failure of that attempt opened the way to its own "national" revolution. From the fall of 1920 on, Mussolini developed a dual strategy, which was to serve as a model for the Fascist path to power: terrorize the forces of the Left in order to make the monarchy and bourgeoisie capitulate on the rebound. On one hand, his armed gangs liquidated the agricultural workers' revolts on the plain of the Po and burned the trade union centers on the Peninsula. On the other, *Il Duce* wove his web of parliamentary intrigues, fortified by a reputation as a moderate made for him by the extremists, and taking advantage of the weakness of the liberals caught between two indecisive forces, the socialists and the *populari*.

The young Italian Communist Party made a capital contribution to the victory of the Fascists by reviving the phantom of Bolshevism with its rallying cry, and by directing most of its attacks against the abhorred Socialist Party. Here we see the very beginning of "anti-Fascism." Even though it pretended to be on the front line of the battle against Mussolini, the Italian Communist Party, docile in response to injunctions from the Comintern, which had just helped to legitimize it, defined the Fascist camp as everything not itself. Indeed, the first priority of the anti-Fascist battle was the liquidation of the Socialist Party! By their verbal excesses, the Communists opened the way for Mussolini. The very question "Fascism or Communism?" conceals, under a semblance of radicalism, a de facto consent to the provisional victory of Fascism.

The October 1922 "March on Rome" seemed to confirm the Comintern's thesis, for what turned out to be a military farce signaled the abdication of the king and the liberal parties in face of the *squadristi*, as though the two camps were moving in secret connivance. To all appearances, Mussolini was brought to power by the bourgeois parties, but that was just a facade. To the extent that it was predictable, the dictator's success was acquired during the years preceding the production of the march on Rome. And to the extent that the bourgeoisie consented to that success, it was the product of ignorance and incompetence rather than of complicity.

Fascism had seized power before Mussolini's rise to power. Mussolini was so strong in the fall of 1922 because his troops had been controlling vast regions of the country for months. He appeared inevitable to the soothsayers of Italian politics because he had managed to carve a place for himself in public opinion broad enough to incarnate a renewal of the state. True, his paramilitary gangs ruled more by violence than by ideas. But he understood how to detach himself from them in order to assume a more political stature. The Terror, though it helped him to maintain power, could not, by itself, have procured it for him. Mussolini's strength lay only incidentally in his armed gangs, just as the other extremity of the movement was minimally dependent on his political

talents. What made him so formidable was something else—his ability to give the war, which had been half won and, hence, half lost, a
strong national extension by relying on the major revolutionary thrust
of 1919–20 to turn it around.

In this sense, Italian Fascism did emerge from Communism. Nationalistic frustration alone would not have made a Mussolini. The essential
ingredient was an anti-Communism capable of tapping the opposing
force, which had been diverted from its object. This is how Fascism
escaped from conservatism. It offered the Right, along with its passion
for going to the people armed with old themes in a new form, the secrets
of the Bolsheviks' propaganda and the idea of another revolution, this
one to be carried out in the name of the nation. The energy Mussolini
borrowed from the war was doubled by that which he recuperated from
the Red defeat, whose ruins had been his cradle.

Later in the century, when Mussolini himself had been defeated and,
furthermore, dishonored by his friendship with Hitler, and when the
victorious Communists had retrospectively imposed their version of
events, no one could conceive of Fascism as having ever been anything
but a terrorist version of bourgeois domination—a promise, a popular
hope. The fact that Mussolini had been an anti-Communist was enough
to cast him as the plaything of big capital, as though the only thing
that engendered anti-Communism was self-interest or deceit, leading
straight to dictatorship, or as if twentieth-century bourgeois egotism
was by definition incapable of combining with less selfish causes such as
democracy. The Communist interpretation of Fascism, which has dominated the last fifty years, masked its true nature and its independence,
whether in its relations to the bourgeois world or in its conflictual complicity with Bolshevism.

The Italian example, the first of its kind, was unambiguous. In
October 1922, the Italian political "establishment" had two reasons
to undergo the Mussolinian "experience": first, the Fascist movement
mobilized public opinion and occupied the territory; second, *Il Duce*
inflected his discourse to the Right and thus maintained the hope that
he could be salvaged within the framework of the existing system. Giolitti, the old sage of Italian politics, conscious of the increasing weakness
of the liberal Italian state, thought to use him to parry the socialists and
the *populari*, who were preventing him from governing "as before." But
the dupe of this episode, which bears no little resemblance to Hitler's
accession to power ten years later, was Giolitti, not Mussolini. The Fascist leader, thanks to a mixture of pressure and ruse, seized power not
to consolidate or save the regime but to annihilate it. Far from being

integrated into the parliamentary parties, he used his power to incorporate them into his own battle. From then on, the violence of the Fascist militias against the Communists and the Socialist Left was legal. Fortified by a tailor-made electoral law that awarded two-thirds of the seats in the House of Representatives to the party with the most votes, the Fascist Party controlled the house until April 1924. The crisis provoked by the murder of Matteotti in June did nothing to stop the advance of Fascism, which was crowned in 1928 by the substitution of the Fascist Great Council for the Parliament.

The government established by Mussolini disappointed all Giolitti's expectations as well as those of the liberals and Christian Democrats.[36] They had believed they could tame the revolutionary, who seemed compliant. Barely had he assumed power, however, than he pursued his revolutionary project, if the word "revolutionary" can be applied to absolute state domination conceived as enveloping the entire society. What Giolitti had misunderstood also eluded the Communists: the novelty of the undertaking, unlike anything they had seen before, was particularly mystifying to liberals and Marxists. For, like that of the Marxists, the fundamental building block of the liberals' system, central to modern society, was political economy. The liberals had difficulty grasping how an anti-Communist, no matter how much of a demagogue he might be, would not restore a political role to the moneyed classes by compromising the system of representation. The Marxists believed blindly that infrastructure determined everything: if Mussolini had been put in power by the bourgeoisie, it was because he had become the best defense against the threat of revolution and could be nothing other than the puppet of capital. No one had taken seriously the Fascist critique of political economy, wrapped in the cult of political volition; yet this was the very critique that Mussolini, from 1922 on, would implement.

The mystery of Italian Fascism, as described so clearly by de Felice, was not that it had been eased in by the world of money or that the liberal politicians had, at some point, cleared the way for it.[37] Bourgeois cowardice is well understood. But this tells us nothing about the two major causes of the Fascist dictatorship: first, the success among the masses of the Fascists' ideological preaching, which lent credibility to their pretension to govern; and, second and even more important, the Fascists' political autonomy. What was surprising was not that they compromised with the bourgeoisie but that they remained independent of it. Having gained power with the aid of the bourgeois parties, Mussolini remained true to his determination to liquidate those parties and to establish his absolute power over an absolutist state in order to realize his idea of the nation and of society. He would succeed only partially, and the Mussolinian state was never as "totalitarian" as Hitler's or Sta-lin's, even though the word was invented in Italy.[38] But the fact that civil society managed to safeguard a portion of its liberty does not mean that the government was at all divided about this question. Mussolini con-tinued to be the unique (and popular) master after his first takeover in 1925–1928; in the political order, the king, the bourgeoisie, and the whole traditional framework of the realm had been dispossessed from decision making.

Anti-Communism does not explain much about the rise of Musso-lini, for the "Communist" danger was long past when he became head of the government. Nor, by the same token, does it explain why the ruling classes were divested of power in the space of a couple of years and why Mussolini so gainfully fooled them into a compromise. In order to understand this, we must stop equating Fascism with the bourgeoisie and must restore the movement's unique dimension as a political revo-lution. If Bolshevism did constitute the backdrop for the emergence of Fascism, it was not because it reconciled bourgeois and Fascist politi-cians, since this provisional and circumstantial feature explains nothing about the duration of Fascism or its popularity. What appeared with Bolshevism was something other than manipulation and instrumental-ity: it offered new dignity for politics, a new field for the imagination, and a more profound mooring for the revolutionary passion. Fascism presented itself as both a symmetrical and an opposing reality. Had it been merely a means of containing or annihilating Bolshevism, it would not have left such a grim mark on history. Just as Lenin returned revo-lution to the heart of the European Left, Mussolini presented it to the Right as a reward for rediscovering the people. This engendered an an-tagonism all the more formidable because it was sustained by a belief that the world could be transformed through military action. Thence-forth, there were only partisans and adversaries, the just and the swine. The two opposing camps hated each other not only for what separated them but also for what made them alike.

A most melancholy account of this dual exaltation, at once futile and fierce, can be found in Pierre Pascal's *Mon journal de Russie*, referred to above.[39] It describes a day in 1927, in Moscow, when Angelo Tasca came to visit from his native Italy. Pascal, at the time, was but a disenchanted witness to a Russian Revolution that had turned into police despotism. Tasca, himself a militant of the prewar Italian Socialist Party, had been co-opted by the Third International and was then still a believer:

> He is one of those Italians, full of ardor, sympathetic because of their sincerity, but with little critical spirit. He told us a few stories about

Mussolini, of whom he had been a disciple and even an electoral agent before the war. . . . He naively recounted a mass of facts about the Italian regime that made me want to burst out laughing, so descriptive were they of the Muscovite regime: the newspapers that systematically lie, a public that has forgotten what truth is, and a government that has come to believe its own lies. In the prisons, no newspapers are allowed except for *Popolo d'Italia*.[40] In the army, a Fascist education is given. In a recent speech, Mussolini divided the population into three parts: Fascists, philo-Fascists, and "a-Fascists" ("without party").[41]

The promises of the revolution were different in each camp, but the two regimes were comparable, almost identical, after a few years' time. One side gunned down the bourgeoisie, the other the workers, but both produced a single-party government and the myth of the unity of the people. In describing Mussolinian Fascism, Tasca was unaware that he was also describing the Moscow political scene, right down to its vocabulary. Pascal, who had learned from experience the weight of denial and the value of silence, could not tell him this. Their 1927 encounter in Moscow exemplified, at an early date, what could not be admitted for much of the twentieth century.

Mussolini's victory was only a prologue, however. Ten years after the "march on Rome," the drama would unfold in a more massive theater with far higher stakes. Just when Stalin was definitively establishing his power, Hitler was taking over Germany: the historical relationship between Communism and Fascism was given substance by the twentieth century's two great monsters.

To understand this relationship we may start with what has become an accepted observation: Stalinized Bolshevism and National Socialism constitute the two examples of twentieth-century totalitarian regimes. Not only were they comparable, but they form a political category of their own, which has become established since Hannah Arendt. I am well aware that this notion is not universally accepted, but I have yet to discover a concept more useful in defining the atomized regimes of societies made up of individuals systematically deprived of their political ties and subjected to the "total" power of an ideological party and its leader. Since we are discussing an ideal type, there is no reason why these regimes must be identical or even comparable in every way; nor need the characteristic in question be equally prominent throughout the history of such regimes. Hitler's Germany and Stalin's Russia were two different universes. Nazi Germany was less totalitarian in 1937 than it was in 1942, whereas Stalinist terror was more virulent before and after the war than during the war. But this does not preclude the possibility that both regimes, and they alone, set in motion the destruction of the civil order by the absolute submission of individuals to the ideology and the terror of the party-state. It was only in these two cases that the mythology of the unity of the people in and by the party-state, under the leadership of an infallible Guide, killed millions and presided over a disaster so complete that it destroyed the history of two nations, the Germans and the Russians, making their continuity all but inconceivable. Hitler and Stalin ascended to such heights on the scale of evil that their mystery entirely resists the causal repertoire of the historian. No configuration of explanations and consequences can account for catastrophes of this dimension. But let us attempt, at least, to comprehend their intelligible aspects.

From a "totalitarian" perspective, the relation between the two regimes refutes the apparent simplicity of their comparison along ideological lines. Nazi Germany belonged to the family of Fascist regimes; and Stalin's Russia, to the Bolshevik tradition. Hitler imitated Mussolini; Stalin followed Lenin. Such a classification is supported by the history of ideas, or of intentions, for it distinguishes two revolutionary ambitions—one founded on the particular, the nation or the race, the other on the universal, if we accept that the emancipation of the proletariat prefigures that of all humanity. This classic point-by-point comparison of the two ideologies does not rule out the possibility that either one of them constituted a closed system, based on an immanent interpretation of human history and offering something like salvation to all those suffering the ravages of bourgeois egoism. But if their kinship was the secret of their complicity, it was their antagonism that lent brilliance to their confrontation. World War II, after illustrating their complicity, was the locus of that confrontation, which, in turn, finally made sense of the war.

Nonetheless, "anti-Fascism" offered only a polemical version of the century's history. It barred comparison between the Communist and Fascist regimes from the perspective of liberal democracy. More precisely, it disregarded either the similarity between Hitler and Stalin or the distinction between Hitler and Mussolini. On the one hand, the Hitlerian and Stalinist regimes were the only two truly "Orwellian" regimes of the century; on the other, Italian Fascism was not in the same league as Nazism: it had no totalitarian capacity; it directed but did not destroy the state; and it did not produce—far from it—a national disaster on the same scale as Nazism.[42] The difference may also lie in the realm of ideas and intentions, for if Mussolini and Hitler had at least partial recourse to the same ideas, Hitler put the word "race" at the forefront of his credo, whereas Mussolini was not essentially a racist.[43] Even after his rebellious and tardy rallying to Hitlerian racism, anti-Semitic persecution in Italy could not be compared to Hitler's crimes, either in kind or magnitude.

In the realm of ideas, however, even the distinction between Fascism and Communism is less clear than is often thought, to the limited extent that those ideas are analyzed in the context of the regimes that employed them. With Lenin and Mussolini, the confrontation between class and nation, rather like a replay of the political ideologies of the end of the century, was less radical than it seems, since both men came from the revolutionary socialist tradition, and Mussolini hung onto the Italian Fascist pretension to universalism.[44] Hitler alone would cynically adopt the cult of the particular in the name of the superior race. As for Bolshevism, the victory of the "socialism in one country" proponents lent the movement a national—if not nationalist—accent, which would be incarnated by Stalin and was affirmed over the years. Russia's victory was the prerequisite for the emancipation of the international proletariat. The Soviet Union remained inseparable from a universalist ambition, but the instrument of that ambition was henceforth clearly detached from its end. And this is fairly close to what the idealists have said of Italian Fascists.

In making a special case for the history of the relationship between Stalinist Communism and German National Socialism, we must also consider their totalities, their environments, their dimensions, and their strength. Finally, we must account for the Bolsheviks' remarkable preoccupation with the German question, running parallel with the scorn that Hitler shows in *Mein Kampf* for Russians and Slavs in general. Though situated at the two extremes of the European ideological landscape, Stalin and Hitler shared the same monstrous passions and the same enemy. Evoking the image of Plutarch ruminating on the grandeur of evil, a major English historian, Alan Bullock, has written their parallel biographies.[45] So I shall not undertake their portraits here, clear as it is that these two intertwined lives contain the quintessential horror of the century.

There was a prehistory to this history, which, as we have seen, was already off on the wrong foot: the Bolsheviks had constantly sought complicity with Germany and encountered only failure. They had seen Germany as the condition and guarantee of the proletarian revolution in Europe; all they found was a radical denial of their prediction and hopes. They had been fooled not only by their ideology but by their experience. The "revolutionary defeatism" advocated by Lenin coupled with the disaggregation of the czarist army had seated the Bolsheviks in power. But this formula did not work in Germany. Although the German military defeat had shaken the foundations of the political regime, it failed to turn the people toward Communist revolution, because the Bolshevik precedent had mobilized the remains of the army and the great battalions of the working class, who remained loyal to the old flag of Social Democracy, against the revolution. The failed "revolution" of 1919 had shown that the shadow of the Soviets, far from mobilizing the masses in Germany, united against itself both what was left of the officer corps and their sworn enemies, the Social Democrats. These old adversaries justifiably remained predisposed against one another: they did not share the same vision of the national future. Caught up, however, in the political polarization created by the specter of a Bolshevik-style revolution, they joined forces in order to eliminate the danger of such an event and to remain masters of the future.

Strictly speaking, Russia had not been beaten but had defeated itself. In contrast, Germany had been beaten but not "defeated." The public sentiment that survived the lost war was more than ever one of nationalism, which largely explains the Bolshevik failure in Germany. Indeed, in the years following 1919, Lenin and the Comintern incorporated German nationalism into their strategy, for it might come in handy against French imperialism, which emerged victorious from the conflict. Yet that strategy not only failed to Bolshevize the nationalism of the Germans but legitimized the idea of a nationalistic socialism, hostile to both Moscow and Paris. When Radek, the Comintern's special envoy to Germany, paid tribute to Lieutenant Schlageter, a young Nazi who had been shot by the French in May 1923 for "sabotage,"[46] he did less to advance the cause of the proletarian revolution than to increase support for the founding idea of nationalism.

Postwar Germany was a more radical and tragic version of Italy. The end of the constitutional state and of the half-bourgeois, half-aristocratic monarchy had been accomplished on the battlefields. If the German Empire had been victorious, it would have had to make room after the war for its countless veterans of Verdun and the Somme, a populace unified by trench warfare and in quest of a political order worthy of its sacrifices. Defeated, engulfed by military disaster, Germany could no longer justify the war, and the empire had left no heir capable of responding to this fundamental problem. The social democratic government that succeeded the Kaiser in the throes of defeat represented the men who had gone to war neither loving it nor hating it—an intermediate position that could, unconsciously or subconsciously, have made sense to many of the soldiers but which, at reckoning time, disarmed those who had been responsible for the war. Nor did these last possess the resourcefulness to invoke Wilsonian democracy as an end of the conflict; that was the winners' argument. The men who formed the government of the vanquished were socialists: in Germany, socialism had deeper roots than democracy.

Yet the "socialist" response to the problem of making sense of the war came from elsewhere—the October Revolution. To avert the potential of revolution and to save Germany from a Bolshevist-type impasse, the Social Democrats could not rely on the debris of the traditional army. What defeated both Bolshevism and the Social Democrats during those years was not so much the traditional leadership as another revolutionary force that emerged from the war, this one on the right— the military or paramilitary groups born of the German disaster and indispensable to the new republic. Theirs was a quite different spirit than that of the old army. It was forged in the camaraderie of the trenches and battles—egalitarian where that of the old army had been hierarchical, communitarian rather than dominated by caste, independent rather than programed to obey. These new-style soldiers disdained the law if it issued from Parliament and had no use for the politics of representation. Their sentiments might have brought them closer to the Bolsheviks if the blood spilled during the war had not created an uncrossable abyss between them.

The German militias had the same force of revolutionary conviction as the Bolsheviks but used it to encourage nationalism instead of transforming it into an instrument for the overthrow of the social order. So the Bolsheviks were at the head of their hate list. Unlike the socialists, they broadcast an interpretation of the war that was all the more dangerous for being charged with their revolutionary zeal, leading straight to the negation of Germany. The members of the irregular forces and the various nationalist associations had to drive home the idea that the war had been lost because Germany had been betrayed, but that it would eventually defeat its internal enemies in order to accomplish what had been interrupted by their betrayal. When the revolutionary idea came to the aid of German conservatism, endowing it with new passions, the stab-in-the-back legend provided it with the very image of the enemy.

The war radicalized the idea of Germany's particular historical mission, and the defeat did not extinguish that idea. Indeed defeat, along with national malaise and the Bolshevik menace, lent it new luster. In this new dual between *Kultur* and *Zivilisation*, the socialists had little to say, and their spiritual and political weakness is one of the great dramas of the era. As democrats and the principal supporters of the Weimar Republic, they represented, like the Catholic centrists, a western orientation for Germany, that of *Zivilisation;* but that orientation, which went against the nationalist tradition, also meant alignment with the winners. As socialists, they belonged to the same family as the Russian Bolsheviks, and although unceasingly exposed to the Bolsheviks' hostility, they opposed them with a bad conscience, as though engaged in internal divisions. Too Marxist for the bourgeois elements they had assumed, and too bourgeois for the Marxist elements, the socialists were hated or despised by both the Communists and the revolutionary Right. So much so that even their political victories of 1919–23 over both Bolshevism and the nationalists lent no additional legitimacy to the republic.

It is within this context that the body of ideas and images launched by Hitler becomes intelligible. In the aftermath of the war, Hitler was steeped in this burgeoning of nationalist and revolutionary organizations in the name of the little German National Socialist Workers' Party that he would eventually lead. Unlike Mussolini, he had no political past. He was not, like Stalin, heir to a party or a system. There was nothing in his earlier life to distinguish him from anyone else; and the age, that is, the prewar period and the war itself, had flowed right through him, in a sense defining his anonymity. Even after the war, this man-in-the-street remained indistinct except for his excessive investment in collective passions: more than anyone else, he interiorized odium for the "November criminals" and the signers of the Treaty of Versailles. Historians, reluctant to attribute to such an ordinary man the extraordinary crimes that marked his reign, could have been tempted to assign him only a contingent or secondary role: seen in this light, Hitler would merely have personified a capitalism that was moribund and thus all the more violent. There are many factors, as we shall see, that lent credence to such a preposterous interpretation. But one of them was the need to dispel the incongruity of one insignificant man in relation to the cataclysmic character of his deeds.

Even more than to capitalism, Hitler gave voice to German passions after the defeat. This man, who had started from so little and who was the most improbable chancellor, was brought to power mainly by his capacity to incarnate the ideas and fears common to millions. He cursed democracy in democratic terms. He destroyed it in the name of the people. His dictatorial program was neither obscure nor surprising, since he both preached it and had laid it out in a book. *Mein Kampf* is therefore one of the better ways to pry open the enigma of his triumph.[47] To understand what created Hitler, a study of the fascination that ideas exert on passions is a more reliable guide than an analysis of interests.

This, in fact, is what he himself says when referring to "popularity" as the first foundation of authority.[48] He intuitively understood the greatest secret of politics: that even the worst tyranny needs the consent of the tyrannized and, if possible, their enthusiasm. A secret as old as history and even more effective in democratic times, when everything is subject to public opinion: it is ideology that, through common sentiments, enables isolated citizens to unite and recognize as their leader one who knows how to translate imperatives into collective emotions. In this respect, Hitler was a pure ideologue. His discourse was fashioned exclusively for purposes of manipulation and power (in this sense he was a radical nihilist); yet he identified totally with that discourse, believing, along with his crowds of supporters, his own prophecies. He proclaimed what he was going to do, however grim, before doing it, thus adding an element of mystery to his success. The Bolsheviks, for instance, had seized power in Russia in the name of secondhand slogans such as "land to the peasants"; no sooner in power, they quickly dropped any notion of putting into practice the various points of their ideology. Hitler never stopped calling his shots. History offers few other examples of exploits so closely tailored to an ideological program from start to finish.[49]

Not that Hitler's ideology owed nothing to intellectual tradition, as had Leninism in both its primitive and its Stalinist forms. But the Bolsheviks had a single intellectual lineage, and Lenin, like Stalin, could always hide behind Marx—an inexhaustible economic, historical, and philosophical guarantee. Hitler had no such reference. He had no great designated philosopher and claimed no forebears. He was self-sufficient. Alone, he set himself up in a role that the Romantics had fashioned for themselves in the previous century—that of mediator between the people and ideas.[50]

By so doing, Hitler discredited all the ideas he employed in advance, simply by using them. A man of the crowd, addressing the crowd, he appropriated the treasures of the past in a primitive form, uprooting them at will, reinventing them. He personified a nation torn from its tradition by a lost war—Germany as tabula rasa. The Germans had staked their entire history on the war. It was as if the defeat had cut them off from themselves without offering them a plausible future; in the end, it left them with nothing but the "ideas of 1789," so foreign to the national spirit. Bolshevism, that alien product of Russia, was even more foreign—a primitive offspring of the French Revolution, in spite of the Russo-German connivance that might have come of their common hatred for French imperialism. As for the "ideas of 1914," they had survived their historical discreditation in the irregular forces, but only after becoming caricatures of themselves and bones of contention in the civil war. German society became democratic at the very time when it lost its center of gravity as a nation. It was this situation, much more than Wagner or Nietzsche, that provided the basis for Hitlerian ideology.

I shall not attempt here to list the writers and the ideas recycled by this ideology. Hitler, moreover, never quoted anyone, so convinced was he of the absolute originality of his pronouncements. What is intriguing is how such a collection of heterogeneous materials could ever have produced the illusion that a new political order was being founded. One of its elements had already been discovered by Mussolini in 1915: to unite the nation with the working class by tearing the former away from the bourgeois and the latter away from the Marxists. A national socialism in the sense Spengler had in mind when speaking of Prussian socialism[51] would have been one way of recovering both anticapitalist passion and revolutionary hopes and putting them in the service of the historical chosenness of Germany, betrayed by Weimar. This meant giving prime importance to the dual role that the Social Democrats, so powerful in pre-1914 Germany, had been incapable of fulfilling during the war—that of being both a revolutionary and a nationalist party. After the war, the Social Democrats dropped both roles, having gone over into the service of the Weimar Republic and become bourgeois. Hitler had sensed the existence of this enormous vacuum, which the Communists could not fill in the name of the Moscow International.

If he had stopped there, the only thing to distinguish Hitler from Mussolini would have been the virulence of German national frustration. Italian Fascism contained the same hatred for bourgeois liberalism, the same obsession with the unification of the people in the state, the same emphasis on renewing the society, the same imitation of Bolshevik methods. But Hitler was more than a German nationalist or even a pan-Germanist, more than an enemy of democracy or a Fascist. He was, as Hermann Rauschning put it,[52] a prophet of nihilism. Unlike Mussolini, he opposed Christianity in the name of natural selection. He meant to reverse the entire tradition of Europe in order to substitute the reign of the strong over the weak. He wanted to destroy democracy in the name not of class but of race. In this way, the Nazi idea went beyond the limits of even an extreme form of nationalism such as that of the Italian Fascists. It was less a surge of the nationalistic pathology, from which it nonetheless drew much of its persuasion over public opinion, than an abstraction drawn from social Darwinism that had become a promise of world domination.

If Hitler's preachings coincided with many pan-Germanist commonplaces fashionable at the beginning of the century, such as the conquest of the Slavic countries or the inevitable decline of France, they possessed the particular characteristic of being centered on a transnational or even an a-national idea, the idea of race. Not that this idea was new, since it had already been elaborated in the late nineteenth century.[53] But now, reemployed in a systematic fashion, made into the centerpiece of a political program, and substituted for the idea of the nation as a force both more elementary and more universal, it transformed the nature of nationalist ideology.

The same was true for Hitlerian anti-Semitism. Hatred of Jews, of course, was nothing new in European history. In its many forms it was inseparable from the Christian Middle Ages, from the age of absolute monarchy, and even from the so-called "emancipation" period. It resurfaced widely at the end of the nineteenth century, notably in the Vienna of Hitler's youth. The author of *Mein Kampf* had no need to search deeply in his memory in order to come up with portraits of plutocratic Jews, defined exclusively by their wealth, strangers to the state, parasites of collective labor, scapegoats of the Right and the Left. He had only to add a new role, that of Bolshevik agents. Whereas the pre-1914 Jews were bourgeois or socialist, postwar Jews were also Communist. In that role, they offered the unique advantage of incarnating both capitalism and Communism, liberalism and its negation. Through money, the Jews decomposed societies and nations; in Bolshevik guise, they threatened their very existence. Jews personified the two enemies of National Socialism—the bourgeois and the Bolshevik,[54] who were also the two figures of *Zivilisation,* the two versions of *homo oeconomicus,* and the two forms of modern materialism. Hitler did not miss a single item on modern anti-Semitism's long agenda.[55] He used the Jews to fill all the roles furnished by the Left and the Right at the beginning of the century.

The distinguishing characteristic of Hitler's anti-Semitism, even more than its capacity to unite opposites, was its radicality. It constituted the core of the Nazi political prophecy, without which it would have lost all direction. In fin de siècle nationalistic ideologies, Jews figured, to varying degrees, as scapegoats of various evils that compromised or overwhelmed the life of a nation; but the solution was merely to limit their influence in order to save the nation from corruption. It was a question of maintaining or defending the integrity and, hence, the strength of a country in an internationalized world victimized by increasingly fierce competition. The expansion of the nation, and not the extinction of the Jews, was the goal. The German anti-Semitic program, if no different in nature from the others, certainly had a violence that has given rise to a vast historical literature.[56] More than any other major European nation, the Germans quickly gave an ethnic cast to their vision of the nation, tending to an aggressive or arrogant stance toward the outside world. In German politics, the notions of the master race, pan-Germanism, world conquest, and *Lebensraum* had appeared at the end of the nineteenth century and provided fertile ground for anti-Semitism. A search for the origins of German anti-Semitism, however, should not distract us from recognizing how uniquely sinister was Hitler's hatred of the Jews.

Unlike Italian Fascism, Nazism was not basically nationalistic. It superimposed on nationalist passions, from which it continued to draw most of its strength, a racist ideology that constituted a world system. The Aryan race, destined by its intrinsic superiority to dominate, stumbled upon the Jews, who, as antiprinciple of this natural order, were their principal antagonists. The "Aryan" destiny became universalized through the Jews because they ruled over the West by means of money and over the Slavic masses by means of Bolshevism, bent on threatening or destroying the master race. As a pure race that took care to perpetuate itself as such, the Jews lived as parasites in all nations, possessing a talent for both imitation and deception. Hidden behind the false universalism of the liberal bourgeoisie and the workers' movement, the Jews, like Aryans, also sought to govern the world but were in no way entitled to do so: from thence the inevitable world confrontation, of which Hitler claimed to be both prophet and instrument. The Jews had succeeded in annihilating Germany in 1918. Hitler represented counteroffensive and victory.[57]

I must admit that I have never grasped the significance of the historiographical discussion, fashionable in studies of Nazism, between the "intentionalist" and the "functionalist" interpretations of Hitler. In researching the causes of the Jewish genocide, for example, the intentionalists emphasize Hitler's intentions, while the functionalists stress the bureaucratic workings of the system. I don't see why these two interpretations should be mutually exclusive. It is obvious that the extermination of the Jews by Nazi Germany had its primary source, in the chronological sense of the word, in Hitler's hatred of the Jews—a hatred so pathological that it dictated his vision of the world. But in the implementation of the genocide, that hatred in no way rules out the role of German customs and attitudes, which tended to unconditional obedience to authority or to what Hannah Arendt has called "the banality of evil."[58] This second type of causality may have been used to erase the first because it touches the social and moral tissue of the country and hence appears more "profound" in an age when we are obsessed with "structure" to the detriment of "events," and because historians are careful to downplay the role of individuals and ideas in history. This tendency has falsified a part of the historical literature on Hitler's Germany, to say nothing of studies of Stalin's Russia, where it has wreaked havoc.[59]

Just as Hitler would not have become master of Germany if there had been no Hitlerian ideology, so Hitler, having become master of Germany, remained Hitler the ideologue, the primary source of the extermination of the Jews. One of the extraordinary features of the two major twentieth-century totalitarian dictators was their continued dependence on the ideologies that served as their foundations. Even Stalin, who claimed to have his roots in Marxism—that is, in a learned philosophy of a democratic sort—transformed that heritage into an instrument of absolute government over men's minds. In his hands, an enlightened (in the sense of the *Aufklärung*) body of ideas degenerated into an instrument of terror. As for Hitler, his message never varied. For both dictators, ideologies were not mere stepping stones to the conquest of a party or a state, to be put on the back burner when no longer needed, as bourgeois politicians naively believed. Ideologies are quite different from programs or declarations of faith. They are the stuff of belief and of volition, the chapbook of action. Even political voluntarism, which held such a spectacular role in both dictators' philosophies, was subordinate to their ideologies; the call to political action was meant to realize objectives predetermined by ideology. The construction of socialism implied the liquidation of the kulaks; the organization of National Socialist Europe, the liquidation of the Jews. Both of these undertakings, each in its own way, were crazy, inhuman, and criminal. But they were decided upon and carried out. The totalitarian ideologies of the twentieth century were distinguished from all other ideologies by the uncannily narrow constraints they exercised upon the actions of those who professed or followed them, from party leaders to rank and file, from rank and file to the people at large.

There was also the element of luck, or circumstances, by definition independent of will. Luck was supposed to be the special gift of opportunistic politicians adept at seizing opportunities and profiting from windfalls, experts in the possible and in adjusting promises to realities. Luck, however, turned out to be a field of maneuver in which Stalin and Hitler—and Mussolini before them—outclassed the craftiest of bourgeois politicians. What could Herriot do when faced with Stalin? Von Papen or Chamberlain, when faced with Hitler? Independently of their incontestable individual talents for political maneuvering, both dictators had a radical advantage over their rivals: they were not burdened by the least moral sentiment. Ideology, by equipping them with a set of beliefs, rid them of any scruples about the means they employed. True, by the time they appeared on the stage of history, the art of politics had been separated from morality for hundreds of years; reasons of state had long had their own set of rules. But international rivalries and even conflicts were contained by means of membership in the same European civilization, and power struggles within individual states also obeyed accepted rules. What was new about Hitler and Stalin was what Friedrich Meinecke, in an attempt shortly after World War II to express his horror at Hitler's moral nihilism, called a "Machiavellianism of the masses."[60]

Bolshevism and National Socialism shared a religion of power, the most openly professed in the world. To conquer and retain power, any means were good,[61] not only against enemies but against friends as well, even assassination—a common practice for both parties, regimes, and dictators. Nevertheless, even this precious power originated in a superior logic—the end it was intended to fulfill, that of fulfilling history, hidden in the tumult of conflict, revealed by ideology. Terror, no longer reserved for real or imagined reprisals against the enemy, became a daily practice of government. The purpose was to impose universal fear, the key to realizing the future, whose secret was the exclusive possession of the Supreme Leader, followed by the Party.[62] The fact that Communism and Fascism assigned contradictory roles to history and reason—the emancipation of the proletariat versus the domination of the Aryan race—mattered little. Though not insignificant on a philosophical level, that distinction detracts nothing from the similarity of the nature and workings of the two political systems.

In many thundering discourses, Hitler expressed his respect, if not admiration, for Stalinist Communism and its leader. Abhorring Bolshevism as the last manifestation of the Jewish conspiracy, Hitler made the fight against the German ambitions of the Bolsheviks one of his first priorities, though he shared the Bolsheviks' disdain for liberal democracy, along with the revolutionary conviction that the age of the bourgeoisie was over.[63] The starting point of the Jewish conquest, its deepest roots, lay in modern liberalism and, before that, in Christianity, another thing the Communists wanted to uproot. So the confrontation between National Socialism and Bolshevism was not the most important item in the ideological order. Stalin, moreover, cast off the old guard, partially Jewish, of Lenin's buddies: Trotsky, Zinoviev, Kamenev, and Radek had all been driven out or subdued by 1927. "It is not Germany that will turn Bolshevist," predicted Hitler to Rauschning in the spring of 1934,[64] "but Bolshevism that will become a sort of National Socialism. Besides, there is more that binds us to Bolshevism than separates us from it.

There is, above all, genuine, revolutionary feeling, which is alive everywhere in Russia except where there are Jewish Marxists. I have always made allowance for this circumstance, and given orders that former Communists are to be admitted to the party at once. The *petit bourgeois* Social Democrat and the trade-union boss will never make a National Socialist, but the Communist always will."

As shown by the rest of Rauschning's text, this statement in no way modifies Hitler's intention eventually to attack Russia in order to conquer the fertile Slavic lands. The idea of founding an Aryan German Empire would certainly bring Hitler into confrontation with Stalin, especially since the idea of territorial expansion was also part of the political imagination of his rival. But the existence of a common will to crush the liberal democracies allowed the Führer to envision a provisional alliance with Stalin's Russia, at least until they had beaten France; this is clear from the 1934 talks.

Before being a quasi alliance, which it would become in 1939, this unavowed kinship was already visible as a conflictual complicity during the post–World War I years. It pertained primarily to the general situation, for both Germany and Russia found themselves in the losers' camp and consequently inimical to the Treaty of Versailles. The Comintern hoped to channel German hostility toward French imperialism, and some members of the German Extreme Right, which sought to pursue the path opened at Rapallo,[65] looked favorably on the young Soviet Union. Their approval may have been purely circumstantial, attributable to the postwar situation, though it often seemed to have deeper roots, in the old Germano-Russian complicity against the West.

Written during the year of Rapallo, Moeller Van den Bruck's *Third Reich* predicted, like Spengler, a "Prussian-style" socialism—antiindividualist, corporatist, hierarchical, in short, "organic." More optimistic than Spengler, the nationalistic professor saw it as the means to a renaissance of *Kultur* versus *Zivilisation*. Like all of the German Right, he was equally repelled by liberalism and Marxism and was hostile to class struggle, "Judaic" internationalism, and the dictatorship of the proletariat. But he was also pro-Russian and an ardent admirer of Dostoevsky—another prophet of hatred of the West. This explains how he could hate Marx while intermittently retaining a weakness for Bolshevism: to see the regime founded by Lenin as a kind of socialism peculiar to the Russians and in keeping with the somewhat primitive genius of that nation was enough to bring it into the fold of the *Volksgeist*. Like the Social Democrats but with opposite goals, the German revolutionary conservatives uncoupled Marxism and Bolshevism in order to celebrate the latter at the expense of the former.[66] We have seen what the Bolsheviks got for their trouble. In 1923, when the French were occupying the Ruhr, Communists and National Socialists together celebrated Schlageter as a national hero.[67] Nevertheless, the reasons both groups devoted so much energy to controlling public opinion was to gain power and to destroy one another. But they overestimated their own strength or underestimated that of their common enemy, who enjoyed the support of the army. The Communist insurrection of Hamburg was as easily crushed as was Hitler's putsch in Munich.

At the beginning of the 1930s, this triangular conflict intensified once again when the economic crisis gave the Comintern renewed hope for an anticapitalist revolution and offered Hitler a new opportunity to seize power. The relationship between Bolshevism and Nazism was simpler than it had been from 1918 to 1923. It provides a test case: On the one hand, Stalin had triumphed in the USSR. He had purged both the Comintern and the leadership of "brother parties." The German Communist Party,[68] one of the great stakes in the USSR's power struggle between 1923 and 1925, had been brought into line by Ernst Thaelmann's iron rule.[69] From then on, Soviet policy took precedence over everything else. On the other hand, nationalist and German antidemocratic zeal of the immediate postwar period had finally found its principal outlet in Hitler's party, which unopposedly dominated the entire German Right, bringing it new blood.

Thus began the key period—a little more than two years' time—during which Hitler would take over the state. He employed a strategy similar to the one used by Mussolini ten years earlier, combining the paramilitary violence of the SA (Sturm Abteilung),[70] a propaganda and indoctrination campaign unprecedented in modern politics, with parliamentary intrigue and the manipulation of the ruling classes. Like Mussolini, Hitler was brought to power by the legal authorities in Germany—in the person of Hindenburg—and first formed a coalition cabinet with the conservatives and the Reichswehr, which thought to make him their hostage. Just the opposite occurred, however, and even more rapidly than in Italy. "We have reached our goal. The German Revolution has begun" wrote Goebbels on 30 January 1933 in the published version of his journal.[71] He was familiar with the program: to sew up the totalitarian dictatorship in the months ahead. Although it is true that a certain conservative milieu—principally von Papen, Kurt von Schleicher,[72] and Hindenburg—helped Hitler into the saddle,[73] it is absurd to view this as proof that the new Chancellor was the tool of the "bourgeoisie." When voted "full powers" in March 1933, he was not,

even indirectly, anyone's delegate; what he obtained was his own freedom to act. In other words, the secret of Hitler's triumph lay not in the
omnipotence of one class but in the consent of a nation.

Since this subject is far too comprehensive to be treated here, I shall
limit my discussion to the relationship between the German Communist Party and the National Socialist Party in the years leading up to
1933. The backdrop of this period was the economic crisis that had engendered universal doubts about the persistence of capitalism. In Germany, the critique of the liberal-capitalist universe occupied a major
place in the national political culture. This situation fed into old convictions, on the left and the right and, above all, among the Communists
and the Nazis, both avowed bourgeois-haters. The Marxists, especially
if they were Leninists, were watching the general crisis of capitalism
they had been counting on for so long, and were waiting for the political
upheaval. The position of the Right was summed up by Spengler in *The
Hour of Decision*, written between 1932 and 1933:

> We live in momentous times. The stupendous dynamism of the his-
> torical epoch that has now dawned makes it the grandest, not only in
> the Faustian civilization of Western Europe, but—for that very rea-
> son—in all world history, greater and by far more terrible than the
> ages of Caesar or Napoleon. Yet how blind are human beings over
> whom this mighty destiny is surging, whirling them in confusion, ex-
> alting them, destroying them! [74]

For the German historian, the collapse of capitalism was simply bringing the era begun in the eighteenth century to a close, that of liberal
democracy, along with its last-born, Bolshevism. The Nazis thought
much the same thing.

The issue of power thus appeared at both ends of the political
spectrum and was reinforced from 1930 on by the German electorate.
With the elections of September 1930, the Nazi Party, with 102 deputies, became the second-largest party in the Reichstag after the Social
Democrats, which had lost seats since 1928, whereas the Communists
increased their electoral capital by one-third. The economic crisis compounded the disaffection suffered by the Weimar Republic since its inception. It pushed public opinion to the two revolutionary poles of
the political scene, while the Communists did little to prevent Hitler's
ascent. To the contrary, the "anti-Fascist" proclamations disguised a
policy more like support than opposition.

The more combative the proclamation, the more popular it was in
some circumstances. This was one of the best-kept secrets of twentieth-

century Communist politics. Take, for example, the German Communist Party during this period. Manipulated by Moscow during one of the most sectarian phases of the Comintern, its sole strategy was to fight for the proletarian revolution under the Comintern's banner. This done, after the fashion of the Italian Communist Party, it made no distinction between liberal democracy and Fascism or, for that matter, Nazism. They were both forms of bourgeois dictatorship, one hidden, one open. Both were detestable, both condemned. It was even possible that Nazism was the inevitable prelude to the "proletarian" revolution. The Communists' battle had a special target: not the Nazis or the democrats but Social Democracy, which they labeled "Social Fascism." It mattered little that the socialists had done their best to fight the Nazis. Facts could not hold out against ideology: their crime was to have "divided the working class," that is, to have been hostile, in the name of political democracy, to the Leninist vulgate of Marxism. The Bolsheviks had learned from Lenin that the first prerequisite for their success was to crush the Mensheviks. A fortiori, they had to liquidate the German socialists, who were responsible for defending the Republic of November 1918 against them, thanks to agreements made with the Reichswehr.

By attacking Social Democracy as the "principal social support of Fascism," the German Communist Party did more to weaken the anti-Fascist coalition than to reinforce its own cause. Indeed, the Communist/Nazi alternative proposed by its members countributed to Hitler's success for two reasons. First, it pushed into the Nazis' arms, along with the socialists, all the so-called bourgeois parties, whether those of the Catholic Center or the Democratic Party, which supported the republic, or the two right-wing parties, which were not originally supporters of Hitler. Second, and even more important, this comparison tended to make Communism the exclusive center and stakes of the anti-Fascist battle. This played right into the hands of Goebbels, who constantly conjured up the specter of the Bolshevik Revolution while the members of the German Communist Party were marching around the streets with their flag. Goebbels had more room to maneuver than Thaelmann: he could make more headway in the terrain of "national" opinion in a republic born of defeat, unable to put down roots. On the contrary, Thaelmann was merely the representative of a revolution that had already been defeated in 1919 and 1923 and was no more likable under Stalin than it had been under Lenin; the social democrats, moreover, continued to keep a closer watch than ever.

The Communists drew their persuasive force less from who they were then from what they were rejecting—Hitler. This statement is also valid in the opposite sense: the Fascists—and that is all that Hitler was at that point—drew more public benefit from what they rejected—Stalin—than from their own ambitions. The two camps helped each other through a common negation of all that existed between them. They organized their complementary and reciprocal belligerence by loudly proclaiming themselves to be the only fighters in the ring, the only ones with solutions to the crisis. But in this match, which precluded democracy, Hitler was the only one to cash in on his capital of rejection. The Communists couldn't do so, for in fighting against Hitler exclusively for the sake of the Bolshevik Revolution, they forfeited the benefits of embodying a broad anti-Nazi front. Their role was limited to offering Hitler, who would turn it into a powerful weapon, the advantage of being the quintessential incarnation of a "national" anti-Communism. The more they affirmed the necessity and imminence of a German October against the bourgeoisie, the more they opened the way to power for the Nazis.

There is a second version of this story, which is not incompatible with the first but complements it in a purely Machiavellian way: it is the one told from Stalin's viewpoint.

In those crucial years 1930–33, when Hitler was proceeding with his great maneuvers for the conquest of power, Stalin was already the absolute ruler of the Bolshevik Party and hence of the Communist International and all of Soviet politics. He had just brought Bukharin, his former ally and last potential rival, to his knees. The old guard was crushed or submissive; "socialism in one country" reigned supreme; and the cynical Georgian had just taken over the left-wing line that had been expounded in opposition to him by Trotsky and Zinoviev a few years before. The NEP was dead and buried. Now was the time for the great class struggle between the kulaks and the Five-Year Plan.

The Comintern was no longer merely one of the keyboards on which Stalin tinkled the international tune of the USSR. From the beginning, the Communist revolution, international by definition and thus internationalist by doctrine, oscillated between its native country and the ones it wanted to take over. During Lenin's time, the Russian Bolsheviks had already laid their hands on the entire Comintern administration and, from there, ruled over their "brother" Communist parties. But the ultimate goal of their actions, as we have noted, was to provoke yet another revolution, primarily in Germany: they were convinced that this was the condition for the survival of the regime born in October 1917. Although Stalin had inherited the omnipotence of the Russian Bolsheviks over the International, he advocated a rolling-back of the construction of socialism in the USSR. The brother parties' principal duty was to close ranks around the besieged fortress. Should one of them prevail, however, it would threaten the absolute power of the General Secretary, who would then have to share his authority with another victorious revolutionary party. How could he not fear a Communist Germany? How could he have lived with a victorious German Communist Party in a central European nation that had so often served as an example for the Russian czars and had also been Lenin's great hope? The German Revolution did not figure in Stalin's agenda.

What did figure in it, and more than ever, was hatred of Social Democracy. That passion and that policy were the original features of Bolshevism. They became extreme in the early 1930s with a turn toward the left and the strategy of "class against class." Parliamentary democracy and Fascism, as was constantly reiterated by loyal representatives of the Comintern, were false alternatives. They were two equally abhorrent versions of the dictatorship of capital, though the latter, by virtue of the violence to which it openly laid claim, was pedagogically superior to the former because it revealed the truth of bourgeois domination. The key battle was that of the proletariat for the proletarian revolution, which implied the destruction of the Weimar Republic—yet another reason for attacking its principal backer, Social Democracy. Stalin's prime target was what Hitler wished to liquidate as the party of the "November Revolution" of 1918: the heart of the 1918 counterrevolution, the pillar of the bourgeois Republic, and the harbinger of Fascism. Social Democracy was a Marxist party for the Nazis, a Social Fascist party for the Communists. It nonetheless led both parties to hate the same thing—an independent, popular political force, anchored in the West.

The German Social Democrats, founders and saviors of the November Republic, which they endowed with its first president, Friedrich Ebert, were largely responsible for the republic's ability to compromise between social classes, unions, and political parties. They constituted its principal supporters, thanks to their involvement with labor, and until 1930 they participated in its governments. While constituting a regime of social compromise and pluralistic democracy, the Social Democrats embraced a foreign policy oriented towards the West, toward Anglo-American capitalism, whose support was one of the conditions for national economic reform. Finally, those Marxists were the intransigent partisans of political pluralism. Doctrinaires as well as politicians or union leaders, their only vision of socialism was as a crowning of democracy. Their old mentor Karl Kautsky, moreover, had been the most thorough and perceptive critic of the Bolshevik experience ever since 1917. The irony of the history of Weimar was that the liberal tradition of the West, the bête noire of the German Right and of Russian Communists—*Zivilisation* for the former and capitalism for the latter—was represented by the socialists, who drew their inspiration from Engels's appointed heir—a situation that would occur again during the course of the century, knocking democratic socialism off its professed path and turning it into the defender of "bourgeois" liberties. The German case was typical in that Social Democracy, between 1930 and 1933, was the preferred target of both the extreme Right and the extreme Left. For Hitler, it embodied both "Marxism" and the bourgeois republic: he killed two birds with one stone. For Stalin, it represented a betrayal of Marxism and thus a perfect instrument both of capital and of Hitler, which proved that Leninism led only to Hitler. Each camp wanted to liquidate the entire Western tradition by annihilating Social Democracy.

Stalin's ideological complicity with the Nazis, maintained via a preferential hatred for the Social Democrats, cut across mutual national interests that were well established at the time and destined to last; the young Soviet Union had long maintained close relations, though largely secret, with Germany on economic and military matters. Since Rapallo in 1922, those relations had continued to grow:[75] the USSR equipped itself with products of German industry, and the Reichswehr clandestinely rearmed itself with matériel produced in Russia by German firms. In turn, the Red Army received part of its training from German instructors, reviving an old tradition. This collaboration was very favorably received in German leadership circles, whether military, industrialist, or diplomatic. Such milieus were traditionally inclined to hostility toward the West: conservative deputies in the German Reichstag allied with the Communist Party in order to block the Locarno Treaties and the Dawes Plan. They despised the Russians but feared them less than ever in their Bolshevik version, which served their own designs. They had been the staunchest supporters of a pro-Russian foreign policy; it did not take them long to perceive Stalin as less a revolutionary leader than a national dictator.

The coming of Stalin, indeed, consolidated the sympathy that the "conservative revolutionary" German Right had been harboring, to varying degrees, for the USSR since 1919.[76] The Georgian, in spite of his origins, appeared to have lent a Russian twist to the Soviet revolution, restoring its national verity. He had driven the Jews from power in Moscow, beginning with Trotsky, the most visible of them. He had set the first Five-Year Plan in motion and had undertaken the collectivization of the countryside—real challenges to Western capitalism. As a new czar, he acquired absolute power, which he exercised with an iron fist for the benefit and in the name of the Russian nation. The image of

Bolshevism had changed, and the curious "National Bolshevik" German Right identified all the more with its passions, transposed into the framework of primitive Russia, subject to the will of one man. Hatred of the West, the omnipotence of political decisions, rejection of Christianity, the aristocratic nature of the party in power, the cult of labor and workers, the organic nature of the society that was coming to birth: Stalin's Russia was seen as a kind of primitive neo-Prussianism, a Russian socialism organized like a military camp. Even the Soviet Revolution could be included in the long list of Russian borrowings from Prussia!

This bric-à-brac of ideas could be found, for example, in the work of Ernst Niekisch, once an extreme left-wing militant, president of the Bavarian Soviets in February 1919 after Eisner's assassination, who became a nationalist out of hostility to the pro-Western foreign policy of the Weimar governments. Niekisch retained the idea of the historical chosenness of the working class along with his new convictions; but the worker, who once held the role of emancipator of humanity, now became the incarnation of the nation, the symbol of reasons of state.[77] October 1917 gave itself Marxist colors only in order to affirm its Russian nationality, which was being eroded by Western capitalism: "Leninism is simply what remains of Marxism when a brilliant statesman uses it for purposes of national policy." Stalin was the true, sole heir of Lenin. "Firmly tied to the very essence of things Russian," he possessed what was, according to Niekisch, the most precious gift of politics: "the fanaticism of reason of state."[78] Not surprisingly, our author returned from a trip to Russia in 1932 full of enthusiasm for the Five-Year Plan, which, in mobilizing an entire people, he saw as a prodigious voluntarist challenge to technology.[79] Since he detested liberal democracy, the reasons for his enthusiasm were a little sounder than those of Herriot or Pierre Cot, supporters and defenders of liberal democracy. Still, it is hard not be perplexed by the strange capacity of the Soviet experience to engender such contradictory illusions.

National Bolshevism was not just the concern of writers and intellectuals. It had resonance in many youth associations and even in the left wing of the Nazi Party. Goebbels had always tended to be pro-Russian, even pro-Soviet, because he hated the West, as was Otto Strasser because of his revolutionary radicalism. Several groups went along with the German Communist Party out of a conviction that Communism, even if provisionally victorious, would eventually open the way to *völkisch* socialism. The Communists thought the same thing in reverse: the workers or petty bourgeois who had strayed into Nazism formed a kind of Communist reserve, and even if the Nazis seemed to be on top for the time being, they would actually have worked for the final success of Communism. That was what the "Declaration-Program for the National and Social Liberation of the German People," published by the German Communist Party on 25 August 1930, was all about: this document, quite anti-Versailles in tone and in the direct line of "Schlageter" policy, sought to dissociate the Nazi voters from the leaders of the movement so as to regain them for the Communist revolution. Otto Strasser's break with the Nazi Party, which occurred shortly afterward, fueled such a hope. The illusion lasted until Germany's defeat.

Stalin was, of course, behind the policies of the German Communist Party, of which his vassal Ernst Thaelmann became sole leader in 1932.[80] The German Right didn't have to be National Bolshevik for Stalin to prefer it to the liberal bourgeoisie, let alone the Social Democrats. He had been dealing with it long enough to know that it shared his interests and motivations rather than his ideas. Industrialists, major landowners, army officers: what little he knew of Marxism convinced him that he was dealing with the only powers that counted. Quite naturally, he shared their conviction that he was capable of controlling the Nazi movement when the time came. Furthermore, he regarded everything to the right of the Social Democrats as bourgeois; it was better to side with the pro-Russians. To wave the flag of Communist revolution, to oppose the Social Democrats, and to favor the German Right were three parts of the same policy. Such was Stalin's contribution to Hitler's triumph.

Today we are tempted to add even more items to the inventory of advantages that the Nazi regime managed to draw from the Georgian dictator's calculations. After all, Hitler, whether friend or enemy, was going to be the most formidable ally of Stalinist Communism, facilitating its territorial spread—first as an associate and then as an adversary—as far as the center of Europe, not to speak of Nazism's imminent role as chief propaganda target for the Comintern and, subsequently, the Cominform for fifty years. But we would be overestimating Stalin's political intuition if we were to credit him with such Machiavellian prescience. What is certain is that he immediately perceived that a "bourgeois" world torn apart by the appearance of a Germany governed by the extreme Right and thus determined to smash the international order established by Versailles would bring a great deal of flexibility to Soviet politics. There, Russia found unexpected room for maneuver between Germany and the victorious nations, with France at the fore; it would fill that vacuum immediately. In this sense, the long complicity between Stalin and the German Right, along with Stalin's isolation at a critical time for the German Communist Party, was the overture to the pact of 1939.

A major facet of the politics of the 1930s, and one that led to the Second World War, was the character of Hitler's regime. Postwar Europe, without realizing what was happening, saw the birth and development of Soviet totalitarianism. Europeans observed Mussolini's victory in Italy with a generally favorable eye. In 1933 came the last political innovation: Hitler's Germany. It was the Italian scenario all over again with a faster beat. The Nazis' revolution occurred from within, after their leader became chancellor. But instead of extending over several years as was the case in Italy in 1922, it bore down like a tornado. Its deliberate strategy was to liquidate isolated adversaries that had already been beaten. From late February on, less than one month after Hitler's accession to the chancellorship, thousands of Communists were arrested and constitutionally guaranteed liberties abrogated following the burning of the Reichstag. On 5 March, amid a mass of propaganda and open violence, the elections gave more than half the votes to the nationalist coalition, with 40 percent to the Nazis—the preamble to the liquidation of Weimar's political institutions. Before the end of March, the Reichstag gave in to intimidation and granted full powers to Hitler. Next, the *Länder* were brought to heel, henceforth to be controlled by the central state, unions and parties were prohibited, and all powers devolved exclusively to the Nazi Party. Between the end of January and the beginning of July 1933, the first revolutionary wave had cut down all obstacles. The second wave, in the following year, would clean out the revolutionary party itself. On 30 June 1934, Hitler ordered the assassination of one hundred of his partisans, beginning with Ernst Röhm, the head of the Sturm Abteilung and one of his oldest comrades.

The savagery of these executions says more than anything else about the character of the regime being established. Their point was less to eliminate opinions at variance with those of the leader than to liquidate men who showed, or were suspected of showing, a spirit of independence. Hitler did not have Röhm killed because he was further to the left than he: such distinctions, drawn from another political universe, are meaningless here. The man he killed was a potential rival, had known Hitler from the start, and enjoyed the personal fidelity of his troops. The Night of the Long Knives, played out like a settling of scores among gangsters, made Matteotti's murder look like a minor tragedy: the Italian socialist deputy had been killed by disavowed henchmen, and his assassination gave rise to enormous public indignation. In contrast,

Hitler himself conducted his henchmen's attack, and the army supported it with the backing of the public.[81]

What is more, this behavior seems to have gained him Stalin's admiration. The General Secretary was a connoisseur; yet in this area he would be a mere imitator. At the time, he had not yet killed or ordered the killing of the old Bolsheviks but had merely exiled them or put them at his mercy. The Night of the Long Knives, however, gave him new ideas: less than six months after the liquidation of Röhm and his followers came the death of Kirov, the number two man in the Party, in Leningrad. Stalin did not behave like Hitler. He took the pretext of a murder[82] to set off an operation even vaster and more lasting than Hitler's mission of 30 June—the massive repression of members of the Bolshevik Party.

Thus the two regimes, almost simultaneously, revealed the two traits that distinguished them from civilized humanity—the rule of a single party over the state, and the undivided domination of that party by one man. They were political systems without fixed rules, with nothing to protect anyone, and with a political police that could arrest and liquidate any of its citizens except for one. This universal terror had long been one of the pillars of the Soviet regime, but it was based both on doctrine and on pretext—the war, the counterrevolution, class struggle, the kulaks. The massive, blind repression set off all over Russia by the death of Kirov, seventeen years after the Revolution, was unique because of the diminishing credibility of the excuses or the ideological explanations that were offered. The "dictatorship of the proletariat" was already a generation old, and its victims were no longer its alleged enemies but its oldest supporters. Henceforth, for Stalin as well as for Hitler, the Terror nourished itself. It increased by virtue of its own impetus and perpetuated itself by the very irrationality of its exploits, which was indispensable to the omnipresence of fear even among those who were spreading it—except for "Big Brother." This regime had nothing to do with the class dictatorship that Lenin had spoken of, or with the "total state" advocated by so many German professors under Weimar.[83]

This brings us back to the starting point of this chapter: the similarity between the two men was not wasted on keen observers of the period, even though not all such observers used the word "totalitarian." Another testimony is perhaps all the more eloquent for having come from an author less well known than Élie Halévy or Karl Kautsky. Waldemar Gurian was a relatively obscure German writer, neither a liberal like Halévy nor a socialist like Kautsky, a Jewish professor converted to Catholicism who was forced to emigrate by the brown terror. In 1935 he published a little book on a subject surprising for someone driven out of Germany—*The Future of Bolshevism.*[84]

The author was not an anti-Nazi admirer of the Soviet Union but, rather, a radical critic of the Russian regime, which, according to him, came out of the same mold as Nazism. For Gurian, Bolshevism could not be equated with a negation of Christianity, or, as the bourgeois saw it, with the destruction of property, or with the reversion of Europe to barbarism, as Spengler feared. For all these reasons, Bolshevism had lost the magnetism it had possessed immediately after World War I, for it had been defeated, and even seemed to have been exterminated, first by Italian Fascism and then by National Socialism. The reason for its powerful presence in the twentieth century—a reason hidden by the volley of reciprocal insults—was that Hitler was the ideological younger brother of Lenin. There is a more philosophical manner of expressing this secret kinship, insofar as we can extend the concept beyond the Russian regime with its geographic marginality and historic backwardness. For if the essence of Bolshevism was not to be found in Marxism or in the Russian or Russo-Asian heritage but, rather, in the absolute priority given to the political order and the molding of society, then the regime born in October 1917 represented the first appearance of the party-state, imbued by ideology with an eschatological mission.

In Russia, that appearance took its form from Marxism because there were no other ideas to guide it into modernity, and because recourse to Marx helped fire the masses with revolutionary hope and the power of science and technology, that nineteenth-century religion. In the rest— the heart—of Europe, on the other hand, the people and the parties who were convinced that they had the same vocation as the Bolshevik Party in Russia could not act in the name of the nineteenth century. They too were absolutists of political will and ideology, but they wanted to resist nineteenth-century notions and, hence, both liberalism and Marxism, including its Russo-Asian version. That was the function of National Socialism, the "brown Bolshevism."[85]

Gurian's comparison of Nazism with Communism originated in the same principle that had led some members of the German extreme Right, prior to Hitler's arrival, to sympathize with the USSR. To Gurian, both regimes were indeed born of a passionate rejection of liberalism, of which Marxism in Russia was but a circumstantial philosophy. Both sought to liberate technology from its enslavement to capital. Gurian, a Catholic philosopher, was no liberal either. He also thought the Bolsheviks and Nazis were both products of the crisis of bourgeois Europe, whose death, between 1914 and 1918, resulted from its inability to go beyond itself. But he feared that crisis for precisely what the National Bolsheviks liked about it. He saw the anti-Roman, anti-Catholic spirit they celebrated as a sign of moral decadence. For him, the philosophy of life, the savagery, the cult of force that they hailed as a renaissance were all indications of the decline and even the suicide of civilization. He was afraid that nationalism, the source of their strength, was democratic poison. Gurian adopted under new circumstances (since Hitler was now in power) the National Bolsheviks' analytical approach, but he did so in order to denounce what they had praised.

"Red" Bolshevism was thus seen as an augury of the century's totalitarian regimes, though in the garb of another age. What it prefigured was realized in a modern form by Hitler. Germany not only was not lagging behind in technology and industry but was overdeveloped in these areas. Gurian saw excessive economic development as one of the reasons for the huge increase in corporate interests and pressure groups, and he raised once again the classic objection that had been leveled by many German conservatives against the Weimar Republic: that it was nothing more than a arbiter between lobbies. Whereas the Russian Bolsheviks had taken power through anarchy, the German Nazis did the same thing by playing on the fear of anarchy in the name of a strong and unified state, personified by a leader.

The logic of this comparison should not lead us to conclude that Gurian harbored any indulgence for the regime that had driven him from his native land. On the contrary, both Bolshevisms, the red and the brown, were part of the political dissolution of European civilization. His chapter on the Hitlerian state makes this quite clear. In contrast to the Soviet regime, which functioned under a democratic camouflage, Hitler's regime declared where it stood; but it followed essentially the same rules: the party had subordinated the state and, by means of the state, controlled all of society and public opinion, beginning with the churches. Just as there was a Soviet people, so there was a National Socialist people: anyone outside it was an antisocial individual. Unity was constantly celebrated and reaffirmed publicly, above all in ideological pronouncements. Its supreme form was the cult of the leader, the Führer. The masses were thus in compulsory and permanent communion with the party-state. Beyond that, there were only enemies of the people—a category both elastic and repetitive at the disposition of the Führer; for Lenin, this meant the bourgeois; for Hitler, the Jews. The existence of a plot had to be emphasized at all times in order for the people to remain vigilant and the regime eternal. The literal distinctions between the two ideologies and the different circumstances behind the two regimes mattered little by comparison with their similarity and novelty.

One question remained, and Gurian met it head on: Could these two totally hostile regimes have shared the same moving spirit? With his response, he took aim at German anti-Nazi conservatives, who, under the pretext that Nazism was less radically nihilist (especially in its hostility to Christianity) than Bolshevism, were skeptical about such an identity. Neither of the two ideologies, he retorted, should be judged as a philosophy. They were instruments of action, historical forces, aiming for the same goal, which revealed their essence: the absolute political power of the party reigning over a unified people—the secret of twentieth-century societies. To that extent, it was Nazism that "most clearly embodied Bolshevik ideology"[86] because it was pure nihilism and lacked the distant attachment that Bolshevism, via Marxism, had retained with the universalism of reason. The discourse of Nazism was vital force, power was its only end, and violence was its only means. By camouflaging its means by its ends through the use of Leninist language, it betrayed its origins, like vice paying hidden homage to virtue, as it continued to declare that the reconciliation of humanity was its goal.

The Nazis' hostility to Russian Bolshevism was fueled less by the reality of Stalin's regime than by what Stalinism retained of Marxism. Only Hitler and his partisans revealed the cult of force and power in its naked form, detached from any nineteenth-century-style utopia. To a society justifiably terrified by the threat of Communism, the Nazis offered protection and renewal, at the price of the same means used by Communism but in an ideological version that radically suppressed any idea of morality. Russian Bolshevism sought to break with the past, whereas many German conservatives and bourgeois believed that Nazism, on condition that the idea of nation should be superimposed on that of race, was a way of insuring continuity with tradition. But they were completely wrong: Nazism was a form of Bolshevism turned against its initial form. The later form had the advantage over its predecessor of having renounced utopia, with the additional benefit of a superior technical and intellectual environment: here, Germany was way ahead of the Soviet Union. Hitler did a better job than Stalin of accomplishing Lenin's totalitarian promise—better, too, than Mussolini, who left the monarchy intact as well as the church and civil society. It was in Nazi Germany that Bolshevism was perfected: there, political power truly absorbed all spheres of existence, from the economy to religion, from technology to the soul. The irony, or tragedy, of history was that both totalitarian regimes, identical in their aim for absolute power over dehumanized beings, presented themselves as protection from the dangers presented by the other. The most convincing part of their propaganda came from hostility to what resembled them.

Was Nazi Germany less dangerous than the Soviet Union for the future of the world to the extent that it did not proselytize on an international level? No, replied Gurian; to the contrary. It was condemned to expansion, whereas the USSR, primitive and full of potential riches, had its frontier within its own territory. If Bolshevism in its two forms was the child of the century, born of the disintegration or apathy of the bourgeois world, it is hardly surprising that Nazism, the truly modern form, should have caught on and triumphed.

Compared to Russian Bolshevism, then, Nazism possessed a superior potential for evil. Gurian's analysis deprived his contemporaries of the comforting idea that Hitlerism was a known type of regime. If Hitler were merely a dictator, dictatorships fade away along with the social circumstances that made them necessary; and if he were merely the puppet of big capital, he could at least be expected to evince a certain docility with respect to his silent partners and, thus, a minimum of rational circumspection. Gurian suggested that such an interpretation concealed the enigma of Hitlerism's power over the Germans. Hitler was outside any conscious, organized social force. Both before and after his victory he eluded the nation's elites—an unusual trait. At bottom, neither liberal nor Marxist theories of Fascism account for the essential feature of European history since 1918: that politics during this period, in several major countries, had escaped from the bourgeoisie. Not only do they not explain this fact but they obscure it. In the case of Hitler's victory in Germany, the phenomenon is especially striking: power was confiscated, in the name of the "masses" by a party of adventurers in the most civilized country in Europe, from large, powerful, and educated elites, without producing anything like the social disintegration of the Russian debacle of 1917. The mystery lies less in the parliamentary circumstances of January 1933 than in the way that the Nazis managed to reduce the country, including the bourgeoisie, to absolute obeisance in just a few months.

Many German intellectuals agreed with Gurian's analysis. Thomas Mann, abroad when the Reichstag was burned, refused to return to Munich. The Nazis did not hesitate to threaten even the greatest names in German culture. The man who had warned his compatriots against "the ideas of 1789" in the name of the "ideas of 1914" may well have been an unconditional patriot as well as one of the most famous writers in Germany and in Europe, but his mere existence as an independent witness made him suspect. He noted in his *Journal* on 27 March 1933: "It was left for the Germans to stage a revolution of a kind never seen before; without underlying ideas, even against ideas, against everything nobler, better, decent; against freedom, truth, and justice. Humanity has never seen its like. Accompanied by vast rejoicing on the part of the masses, who believe that this represents their true desires, when in fact they have been duped with insane cunning."[87] Before Nazism, no government had ever shown such contempt for noble ideas, or even for ideas themselves. It was as though German culture had turned on itself. Nevertheless, Hitler's regime did have two precedents, "the antidemocratic upheaval in Russia and the one in Italy,"[88] for, like them, it had originated with the war; its population had been "democratized" by defeat and humiliation and had not been able to deal with that explosive encounter. Nazism was a German form of Bolshevism.[89] The sorry novelty of Hitler's regime was the extremism it revealed in matters of cultural and moral indignity, as if Germany were paying for its historical chosenness with extraordinary degradation. In the eyes of the man who wept over the "ideas of 1914," the war that had produced the Nazis had been nothing more than the madness of a bunch of adventurers, destroying the nation.

A few years later, during the dark time of the Hitler-Stalin pact, Thomas Mann took to groaning about a Germany "perhaps forever cut off from the West, fallen back on its Oriental side"—in short, about the end of Germany. "In Germany, a revolution with a profound effect has occurred; it has completely *de*nationalized the nation, according to all the traditional ideas about the German character, by giving itself 'national' airs. Nazi Bolshevism had *nothing* to do with the German character. The new barbarism most naturally found contact with Russia, which appeared to be opposed to it."[90] And the author of the *Considerations* wished that "civilization" could be sufficiently intact and powerful to outlast the two allied monsters. He recovered his earlier mistrust of the overly "civilized" West at the very moment when there was no other recourse for him against Nazism, vanquisher of *Kultur*.

The best counterpoint to this clear-sighted despair of a few great Germans, uncertain about the survival of their nation, can be found in the thinking of some fine minds to the west, notably Élie Halévy. Treading the same path as Gurian and Mann, Élie referred to that time, in his famous 1936 lecture, as "the era of tyrannies."[91] He chose the word "tyrannies," rather than "dictatorship," as the term that most closely described the situation, in order to indicate the enduring character of the Russian, Italian, and German regimes. Dictatorship was a provisional stage on the political state's path to liberty, whereas tyranny lacked that horizon. Tyranny was self-sufficient and rejected any other end. It was born of the degeneration of democracy and the contradictions of socialism; its ambition was to take their place. The First World War had been its cradle. As to the particular form of tyranny, Mussolini imitated Lenin, prior to providing and example for Hitler. As to its foundation, the modern structure of the state offered unlimited means for domination over society to totalitarian parties. Finally, the history of the three tyrannies of the twentieth century reduced the ideological distance between the three as Communism became increasingly national and Fascism increasingly social. Thus Élie Halévy's analysis tends to attenuate the differences between the two kinds of tyranny in favor of their similarities; Marcel Mauss described this neatly: "The Communist Party remained camped in the middle of Russia, just as the Fascist Party and the Nazi Party camped, without artillery or a fleet but with a complete police apparatus." [92]

Yet it was precisely during this period that Communism was attempting to redefine itself by fighting Fascism.

SEVEN

Communism and Anti-Fascism

IN THE FIFTEEN YEARS FOLLOWING ITS BIRTH,
Soviet Communism assumed many different guises. It embodied the
armistice, the international revolution, the Jacobin revival, the workers'
homeland, bourgeois-free society, humanity no longer alienated, capitalist anarchy vanquished, and the economy returned to the producers. Though issuing from a common source, these images were hardly
identical. Depending on the domestic and foreign affairs of what the
USSR had become by 1922, they varied in intensity and persuasive capacity; the revolutionary idea had flowered again and was no less unpredictable than it had been in the eighteenth century. In the 1930s it
had been worn away by time and events. Stalin had succeeded Lenin,
Trotsky was in exile, the disaffected had begun to manifest their criticisms, and the Communist parties were either dormant or defeated.
"Socialism in one country" had altered the agenda of revolutionary
Bolshevism; what was left was more closely related to economics than
to politics: the Western world, prey to capitalism's most universal crisis,
provided a tailor-made negative example for the propaganda surrounding the first Five-Year Plan. But if that comparison helped to hide the
horrors of "de-kulakization," it was also a sign that the influence of the
Communist Revolution issued less from itself than from the hardships
wrought by capitalism, which it had brought to an end.

The same thing occurred in the realm of politics. Having once drawn
most of its influence from the capitalist crisis, Stalinist Communism
would find a new political arena in anti-Fascism.

Even before the reign of Stalin and with Mussolini's first steps, the
Communist International had always been anti-Fascist. There were,
however, two sorts of anti-Fascism in the Communist world; the first, as
was illustrated by the German Communist Party's reaction to Hitler,
saw Fascism as a mere variation of bourgeois capitalist dictatorship.

From this perspective, the only real anti-Fascist battles were those fought by the Communists, since they were the only ones set on uprooting capitalism and the bourgeoisie. All other strategies were illusory and intended to divert the popular masses from the proletarian revolution. A good example of such diversion was Social Democracy, whose influence over the workers made it an important enemy and the main roadblock to the establishment of the dictatorship of the proletariat. These strategic conceptions indicate the strength that voluntaristic Leninism attributed to its enemy: the Bolsheviks' hatred of the bourgeoisie was fueled by a sense of its formidable power. Whether democratic or Fascist, the bourgeoisie remained in control, manipulating a subservient Socialist Party.

All things considered, the bourgeoisie was perhaps easier to defeat in its Fascist form; the Communists, inclined to rationalize anything that happened as inevitable, tended in retrospect to view the triumphs of Fascism as so many "supreme stages" of bourgeois domination—"supreme" in the sense of more dictatorial than ever but also more fragile—and as the last stages of history, unconsciously bringing in the proletarian revolution. For Marx, the "ultimate" form of bourgeois dictatorship was the Second Empire;[1] for the Bolsheviks, it was Fascism. They had come to power with World War I, and its dialectic of misfortune had long ago prepared them for the tragedies that would produce their victories.[2] As we have seen, to these doctrinal considerations, which amounted to an acceptance of Fascism in the guise of a fierce battle, Stalin added circumstantial reasons drawn from international policies of the Soviet Union, which favored relations with the German Right. Hitler's accession to power put a brake on the great project of Bolshevism—the German proletarian revolution—at the very outset.

In the following years, a second form of Communist anti-Fascism emerged, alternating with rather than replacing the first, and fleshing out Stalinist strategy. This second form no longer lumped together all that was not Communist. It conceded that liberal democracy and Fascism were not the same thing, and it consented to defend the former, at least temporarily, along with the bourgeois parties and Social Democracy. It had not changed its colors and even less its essence, but it had changed its tactics, which were no longer simply deduced from its doctrine. This change, however, did not preclude a return to a more rigid interpretation under different circumstances. Leninist-Stalinist ideology possessed an admirable capacity to combine opposing strategies under the injunction of the Great Interpreter.

This shift can be explained by two series of events, the first related to the international situation of the USSR, the second to the policies of the Communist International. They were of unequal importance because, in the era of "socialism in one country," the fruits of the battle would first be seen in the USSR, which modified but did not obviate the need for the international proletarian struggle. Stalin had never publicly implied that he had a role in the Comintern. He wanted to appear distant from that cosmopolitan forum, which, before he got his henchmen Molotov and Manouilski to infiltrate it, had long been in the hands of his rivals—Zinoviev, and then Bukharin. Henceforth, the position of the International was set. It had long ceased to be involved in the internal questions of the Bolshevik Party and its sister parties, as we know from Souvarine's experience of 1924–25. But it was still trying to define the revolutionary strategy of the proletariat. When building socialism in the USSR became the top priority, the affiliated parties became little more than defenders of the central bastion, while Soviet foreign policy became the ultimate goal of the world proletariat. Inherent in the nature and functioning of the Comintern, this evolution was to transform the Communist leaders of the world into an international organ run by the Kremlin. During the period under consideration, the transformation was just about complete: Stalin would soon be manipulating the foreign Communist parties the way Hitler was manipulating the Germans outside of Germany.[3]

Hitler's accession to power in Berlin threatened to modify the European situation: the author of *Mein Kampf,* who claimed the Slavic lands in the name of German *Lebensraum* and shouted out incendiary harangues against the order of Versailles, was hardly a reassuring partner for anyone, whether in the West or the East. Yet Stalin, like all practitioners of European realpolitik, must have believed that Hitler, once in power, might modify his ideas and projects. In any event, Stalin remained silent during all of 1933, even after the Reichstag had burned and the German Communists had been banned—even when it became clear that the new chancellor had not changed his National Socialist colors. After March 23, Hitler had made it clear to the Reichstag that German foreign policies did not obey the same logic as domestic policies, and that he wished to maintain the same friendly relations with the USSR as long as the Communist question remained an internal affair.[4] Stalin had no trouble understanding these terms, since they were the same as his own. Both leaders understood that the spate of unclouded relations between the USSR and the German Right was in the balance; each side was holding its breath.

In January 1934, Stalin finally reacted publicly at the Seventeenth Congress of the Bolshevik Party, a quintessentially solemn occasion. What he did not say was as important as what he did: not one word about the burning of the Reichstag, the Leipzig trial, or Dimitrov, which were at the center of a gigantic campaign orchestrated by the Comintern, but he did make some motions in the direction of the League of Nations, which Hitler's Germany had quit in October 1933 and which the Soviet Union would join once again in September 1934. This precaution should not be interpreted as rallying to the Europe of Versailles, nor as an act of hostility toward anyone in particular: Stalin had understood that Hitler was threatening world peace, perhaps irremediably, but he was careful to define the limits to which he was prepared to go. Hence this pronouncement, which expressed his basic ideas: "In our time, the weak do not count, only the strong count. . . . We were no more oriented toward Germany yesterday than we are oriented today toward Poland or France. Yesterday and at present, we are oriented toward the USSR and only the USSR."

One word to the wise is enough! In international matters, the Soviet Union would be guided exclusively by its own interests and count only on its own strength. Stalin said nothing, watched, and redirected his strategy toward a rapprochement with France. The heyday of the Franco-Russian alliance was not that far in the past, and geopolitical constraints took precedence as Germany found its strength. On 2 May 1935 in Moscow, the odd couple of Stalin and Pierre Laval signed the Franco-Russian Treaty of Assistance. It stipulated that the two countries had to aid one another "in case of an unprovoked attack on the part of a European state." But the agreement was not as clear as it seemed. France, to temper Britain's concern about an overly rigid obligation, specified that the "attack" in question had to be authenticated by the Council of the League of Nations, a tribunal whose star was already on the wane: the Italian invasion of Abyssinia, in the fall of 1935, would deal it a death blow. The Soviet Union, for example, was not covered in the case of an attack by the Japanese, and the Western Allies' troops were not guaranteed safe passage through Polish territory—indispensable for the defense of France in the event of an attack—because it brought Polish sovereignty into question. Unlike the Franco-Russian agreements of 1891–92, the treaty was not really meant to cover either hypothesis. Laval sought a more aggressive French diplomatic policy and turned to Moscow after making overtures to Italy. He gave the Radical Party what it wanted and delighted in the prospect of getting back at the French Communists. Nor did the Soviets seriously consider the military option. The interest of the treaty was that it constituted an obstacle to a Franco-German rapprochement or, more precisely, precluded French support for a Nazi attack on the USSR.[5] This would be borne out by the arrangements for a military collaboration discussed over the next four years: neither party pushed for a military confrontation in the face of Polish ill will.

Although the 1935 Treaty of Assistance had no military implications, it did have political ones. Pierre Laval, prior to returning to Paris, managed to get "Monsieur Staline" to issue the famous communiqué legitimizing the national defense of France. The declaration took a stance contrary not only to the antimilitarism of the workers' movement but, more importantly, to the tradition that had produced the French Communist Party. This brings us to the other side of the story: Stalin was now not only the head of the Soviet government but the head of world Communism. In the second role he was less visible, hidden behind the Comintern, but as sovereign as ever: the very nature of the regime was defined by the existence of these two allegedly separate organs, which were nonetheless run by a single leader with a single policy.[6]

Stalin controlled the Comintern, just as he controlled the USSR's foreign policy. In the Comintern, Dimitrov and Manouilski were at his bidding; Litvinov served this function in the Ministry of Foreign Affairs. At this time, moreover, the Communist parties were absolutely subordinate to the International. They were subject to minute surveillance from Moscow's envoys, who sent frequent and detailed reports to the "center"[7] and were "sections" of a highly centralized movement in the fullest sense of centralization.[8] It is therefore remarkable that Soviet policy underwent a second shift during this crucial era.

To understand this second shift, we must return to the era prior to Hitler's accession to power, when the International Congress of Amsterdam opened on 27 August 1932, organized around the theme of "how to oppose Fascism and the war." The Comintern played a central role, thanks to Willi Münzenberg, who was the great orchestrator of the event. With Münzenberg, the drab fate of Comintern functionaries assumed the tragic allure of a novel. Not that we should regard him as an anti-Stalinist hero just because he ended up breaking with Stalin; threatened with liquidation in the caves of Loubianka, he really had no choice. Until 1937, he had been a loyal underling like any other militant in the vast Jesuitical bureaucracy of Moscow. History, however, would afford him the perfect role: during the anti-Fascist shift he had served the Comintern as a kind clandestine minister of world propaganda with a special concentration on Western Europe. This function perfectly suited his totally modern talent for political publicity and the manipulation of images and words. None of the many writers, artists, and intellectuals he had used or fooled could bring themselves, in retrospect, to dislike him. What is more, he was lucky enough to have been captured by two great portraitists, erstwhile collaborators who became disenchanted with Communism but not with their former boss—Arthur Koestler and Manès Sperber.[9] For people like them, this child of a Thuringian innkeeper whose father was the illegitimate son of a baron brought a touch of class to the life of a militant worker.

Even as an adolescent, Münzenberg had won his spurs in the aristocracy of great revolutionary autodidacts as head of the "Youths," that future reserve of the German Socialist Party. A radical antimilitarist, he spent the war years in Zurich, where he met Lenin. Expelled by the Swiss in 1917, he returned to Germany and joined the Spartacists prior to becoming one of the founders of the German Communist Party in 1919. Then Lenin summoned him to Moscow: it was not the best place for him, but it was the one most appropriate to his ideas. Although the intensity of his revolutionary faith made him a Bolshevik, he was more interested in propaganda than in theory. Having little taste for the debates and issues that brought the leading players of the Party into conflict, and maintaining his distance from internecine struggles, he also differed from the others because he was extroverted and entirely oriented toward proselytizing. If he had been an American, he would have been another Hearst. As a German, a member of the proletariat, and a revolutionary militant, he brought to the Bolshevik cause a talent that would have made him rich and influential in the bourgeois world.

He had quickly made his mark. In 1921, Lenin made him responsible for a vast operation to aid the starving population of the Volga. He also founded the "International Workers' Aid" organization. In each case he had to mobilize energy, emotions, and means to aid the October Revolution. "Willi," as everyone called him, was an international activist but of a particular sort. He had risen rapidly to the head of a network of geared-down corporations that sought to magnify the Soviet experience and popularize it everywhere through a variety of channels—the press, movies, theater, soup kitchens, humanitarian associations, intellectual gatherings, solidarity petitions. So the huge "Münzenberg trust" ended up administering to a world of sympathizers, from Western Europe to Japan, who were lulled over the years by the propaganda of a boss acting as though he were independent of the Comintern. Willi was the great orchestrator of "fellow travelers"—typical members of the Communist world and, at that time, of the Fascist world as well, not Communists but thereby all the more dependable when fighting anti-Communism. His usual quarry was the intellectual, who had more influence and more vanity than the ordinary mortal. He compelled writers, philosophers, and artists to sign in as bona fide combatants, so that he could mobilize them instantly.

By living on the edge of Communism and lavishing his charm on external sympathizers, the propaganda king carved out a lifestyle for himself, adulated by his émigré entourage, conscious of the superiority of his talents, proud of the difficulty of his particular art *in paribus infidelium*. Viewed with vague suspicion by the apparatchiks in Moscow, and particularly disliked by the German group, which consisted of the future leaders of East Germany, he enjoyed only a few good years, 1934–36, in the Paris of the Front populaire. Summoned to Moscow in 1937, during the Great Terror, he hung back, fell ill, and finally remained in France, contenting himself with sending a letter to Stalin.[10] By 1939 he no longer had a homeland: both Germany and the Soviet Union wanted his head. The French interned him in a camp as a German. When he escaped in June 1940 to flee Hitler, there is reason to believe, although there is no proof, that he was assassinated by an agent of the GPU (the Russian secret police).[11]

But let us return to the beginning of his happy period, the "Amsterdam-Pleyel" time, for that is when his talent and cult of loyalty were most visible. The International Congress against Fascism and War, which met in Amsterdam in the summer of 1932 and was largely the product of his ceaseless activity, deviated not one iota from the Comintern's line. It was not an "anti-Fascist" meeting of the sort that would be mobilized a year or two later in opposition to Hitler. Its goal remained "the fight for peace" that had been at the forefront of Soviet policy since 1929; in this context, "Fascism" was understood in a very general, vague sense as something related to the militarization of capitalist countries. Of those capitalist countries, Great Britain and, to a lesser extent, France were considered the most threatening, since they were the triumphant imperialisms of 1918. The more peace-loving they pretended to be, the more dangerous they were. One of the great themes of Amsterdam was denunciation of "Genevan pacifism"—in other words, the League of Nations. Under the guise of defending the armistice they were actually defending the Soviet Union, cast as the only peaceful power because the only one free of capitalism. This defense was all the more urgent because the Congress declared that an anti-Soviet war was imminent.[12] From the beginning of 1932 on, an impressive array of Comintern publications stressed the imminence of a war against the USSR;[13] this likelihood was linked to the end of capitalist stabilization and manifested by the Japanese invasion of China a year later.

The fact that the Soviet Union signed nonaggression pacts with Finland, Latvia, Estonia, Poland, and Herriot's France during that same year in no way modified the Comintern's delirium over the anti-Soviet war being readied in the West. This was another illustration of the split-level character of Communist policy, both levels working toward the same goal—world revolution. The USSR's foreign policy was carefully aimed to protect the fortress of the international proletariat against any military aggression; the Communist International defined the revolutionary goals and slogans of its local sections. The battle against Versailles, bourgeois pacifism, and imperialism fit neatly with a "class against class" strategy. On 14 January 1933, at Thaelmann's side, Thorez addressed the Berlin Communists in these terms: "We, the Communists of France, are fighting for the annulment of the Treaty of Versailles, for freedom of choice for the people of Alsace-Lorraine even should that choice include separation from France, and for the right of all German-speaking peoples to unite freely."[14]

Two weeks later, Hitler became chancellor of the Reich. For Comintern strategy, 1933 was a watershed year. Hitler's accession to power transformed the international playing field, though not in one stroke, nor in one day, for it took time to see how the Hitler-Hugenberg tandem would evolve.[15] The Communists had believed both in Hitler's identity with the German Right, and in the provisional nature of the Nazi phenomenon. They were rapidly disillusioned by events, although Stalin, as leader of the Soviet Union, remained prudent: it may have taken the Night of the Long Knives to convince him of Hitler's omnipotence in Germany.[16] Through the Comintern, however, he reacted more quickly. The burning of the Reichstag and the ensuing terror provided the first justification for a new and massive anti-Fascist campaign. Moscow's usual targets—the Treaty of Versailles, the League of Nations, French imperialism, and Social Democracy—were no longer adequate. Now, there was another imperialist on the scene—Hitler, enemy of liberty and a new threat to world peace.

At first, the new threat looked like a great show, put on in Paris by Willi Münzenberg, the tailor-made Cominternist. For him, the burning of the Reichstag was the opportunity of a lifetime.[17] With his genius for propaganda, he crushed Dr. Goebbels—another specialist in the field—in a head-to-head match, and invented the new face of Stalinism: anti-Fascist Communism. Let us turn to Koestler's account of this key episode, which occurred when he had returned, a somewhat disabused Communist, from a long stay in the USSR. He would be heartened by the Leipzig trial:

I arrived in Paris in the middle of the Reichstag Fire Trial, which was holding Europe spellbound. The day after my arrival I met for the first time Willi Münzenberg, Western Propaganda Chief of the Comintern. The same day I started work at his headquarters, and thus became a minor participant in the great propaganda battle between Berlin and Moscow. It ended with a complete defeat for the Nazis—the only defeat which we inflicted on them during the seven years before the war.

The object of the two contestants was to prove that it was the other who had set fire to the German Parliament. The world watched the spectacle with fascination, and with as little understanding of its true meaning as small children have when they watch a complicated thriller on the screen. For the world was not yet accustomed to the stage-effects, the fantastic swindles and cloak-and-dagger methods of totalitarian propaganda. And in this case there was not one producer of the show, as later in the Moscow trials, but two, who played out their tricks against each other like rival medicine men before the assembled tribe.[18]

The Nazi medicine man, Dr. Goebbels, was well known, and loudly declaimed his own role. Münzenberg, on the other hand, manipulated public opinion, hiding behind an "International Aid Committee for Victims of Hitlerian Fascism," which was championed by international democratic celebrities and issued innumerable pamphlets and tracts.[19] Goebbels proclaimed that van der Lubbe was a Communist agent; Münzenberg said he was a Nazi provocateur.

> The world thought that it was witnessing a classic struggle between truth and falsehood, guilt and innocence. In reality both parties were guilty, though not of the crimes of which they accused each other. Both were lying, and both were afraid that the other knew more of the actual facts than he really did. Thus the battle was really a blind-man's bluff between two giants. Had the world understood at the time the stratagems and the bluffs involved, it could have saved itself much suffering. But neither then nor later did the West really understand the psychology of the totalitarian mind.[20]

In this reconsideration of his life, in which, with resigned compassion, he reflected upon the side he had taken in that propaganda battle, Koestler may have attributed too much talent to the Cominternist. The "total defeat" of Goebbels that Koestler had witnessed had graver consequences, which were quite ably exploited by Münzenberg though not his creation. Nazism was more easily identified than was Communism as an enemy of democracy, since hostility to democracy was part of its credo. In the West, the Reichstag fire signaled the Nazi Party's turn toward undivided power. The Communists arrested along with van der Lubbe looked like heroes of democracy in the face of dictatorship. At the Leipzig tribunal in September, the Bulgarian militant Dimitrov brilliantly opposed Goering. He was already prepared to support any cause that had the least support from Moscow; here was one that would put him on the world stage and show him to his best advantage, and he would prove himself equal to the situation. Perhaps he knew that his fate would be directly decided by Hitler and Stalin.[21] The trial turned into a Comintern triumph because both the leading actor and the director, Dimitrov and Münzenberg, were unwittingly costumed by Hitler in democratic ideas. Faced with the Nazi revolution that had destroyed all other political parties in the space of a few months, Münzenberg's "International Committee" called for the indignation and the support of all freedom lovers.

Although the "democratic" glorification of Dimitrov incontestably bore Münzenberg's imprint, there is no reason to conclude that it was merely a personal political initiative, or that the great agitator had been ordered to put a new policy in motion. Stalin kept watch over Dimitrov, whom he repatriated to Moscow in February 1934 a few weeks after he was acquitted, thanks, no doubt, to a secret deal with Hitler. But he took care to withhold his voice from the world campaign orchestrated by Münzenberg. The Comintern, for its part, was also cautious about public declarations. In Moscow during 1933 and part of 1934, both parties felt strongly that the cloudless sky of relations between the USSR and the German Right was at stake. Could this situation, advantageous to both parties, which had lasted since Rapallo, continue? Transposed from Soviet state lingo into the language of the Communist International, the question could be formulated in a twofold manner: Was it possible that the Soviet Union, if attacked by an imperialist state such as Nazi Germany, for example, could find support from another imperialist state such as France? And, if that were the case, could the French Communist Party be brought to support "its" bourgeoisie, in the name of interests superior to the those of the proletarian revolution?

This question seems byzantine only for those not within the Marxist-Leninist universe; insiders saw it at work in the Western Communist parties' strategies and debates born of the condemnation of the treason of 1914 and obsessively concerned with the struggle against their own bourgeoisie, their own imperialism, their own army. Opposition to war, inseparable from capitalism, was still a way of militating for the revolution that would end the curse of war; it entailed being true to class struggle and redoubling the domestic battle through international solidarity with the USSR. Nothing within the concept of Fascism as it was conceived and used by the Comintern for years—that is, as a quasi-normal product of bourgeois democracy supported by Social Democracy—could either justify the real differences in the way various imperialist states were treated or lead to the notion of a democratic war against Fascism: a fortiori if this meant singling out Germany as the principal adversary, whereas it was still the major victim of the Treaty of Versailles. The Amsterdam movement had set its sights on Versailles, and the meeting held at the Salle Pleyel in Paris in June 1933 in no way modified that orientation. The fight "against Fascism and war" had remained above all a war against bourgeois pacifism and the chauvinistic anti-Fascism of the affluent powers. That is why the Amsterdam-Pleyel movement failed to draw a crowd around its cleverly camouflaged Communist nucleus.

Even at the end of 1933, as the Dimitrov trial came to a close, the thirteenth session of the Executive Committee of the Communist International had nothing spectacular to announce.[22] The old Bolshevik Kuusinen, who gave the report, interpreted the crisis of world capitalism as the sign of a new era that promised profound changes—various forms of Fascism, wars, revolutions. His text contained the same traditionally apocalyptic accents of Leninist philosophy along with the notion of an ultimate redemption by the proletarian revolution. Fascism and war were part of the grim practice of capitalism, but they also augured its end. Hitler's National Socialism was no exception to this rule: it was accompanied, like the first years of the Third International, by a renewed promise of a German proletarian revolution. The call to battle against the bourgeoisie and the "Social Fascists"[23] was thus livelier than ever. It was not until June 1934 that the "Internationals" of Moscow came up with a new orientation. During this period, Stalin considered a rapprochement with the West, which paved the way to the USSR's entry into the long-reviled League of Nations in September. A year after his arrival in Moscow, Dimitrov was installed as Secretary General of the International—a sign that the supreme ruler, although he had remained silent, had not underestimated the political capital of the Leipzig trial. Indeed, in the report he prepared for the Seventh Congress of the Comintern in July, Dimitrov proposed that the term "Social Fascist" be dropped and that the strategy and tactics of the movement be modified, moving toward replacing the "class against class" slogan with a united front. We are now in the midst of the "shift."

Events helped. In Germany on 30 June 1934, the Night of the Long Knives left no doubt, had any remained, that Hitler was determined to reign as absolute master. In France, between 6 and 12 February of that year, the Communist Party had been forced to a reconciliation with the Socialist Party;[24] the Comintern henceforth focused its attention and efforts on France. In the absence of a more precise chronology, given what we presently know, let us say that the second half of 1934 marked the shift: on 24 October, Thorez, who was under the guidance of Fried, his immediate boss in the International, proposed to the Radical Party at its Congress in Nantes an anti-Fascist "Popular Front" even more extensive than the SFIO (Section Française de l'Internationale Ouvrière). Fried is supposed to have come up with the term "Popular Front," which was destined for a great future.[25] Ceretti, however, in his *Memoires,*[26] recounts how, on that very morning of 24 October, Thorez received a Comintern delegation at his home in Ivry, composed of Togliatti, Gottwald, and himself. Fried was also there but said nothing. Togliatti, it seems, sought to dissuade the General Secretary of the French Communist Party from going to Nantes to initiate his project. It is thus possible that two "lines" continued to coexist at the time. It was not until 9–10 December that the new policy was made official by the Executive Committee of the International: Thorez was invited there to present his report on the model experience of the French Communist Party.

The most obvious sign of the shift was the signing of the Franco-Soviet pact on 2 May 1935. More significant than the pact itself, which was just a diplomatic instrument, was the communiqué that Laval managed to extract from Stalin, which amounted to a directive for the international Communist movement. The Communist parties, especially the French, saw the anti-Hitler front becoming the center of their battle, even if it meant provisionally collaborating with their own bourgeoisies. This about-face was all the more brutal because it entailed a reorientation of the international struggle against the losers rather than the winners of Versailles at the price of a new definition of Hitlerian National Socialism. The question was considered from all angles by Dimitrov in his report to the Seventh World Congress of the Communist International on 2 August 1935.[27]

The new Secretary General of the International was faced with the problem of how to provide a Marxist theory of Fascism that would distinguish not only between "Fascism" and generic "bourgeois domination" but also between German National Socialism and generic Fascism. The typology of political regimes was a classic puzzler of Marxist thought, as we can see by the way Marx treated Bonapartism. In the bourgeois era, all power that did not assume the typical—or British—form of representative government remained difficult to decode in terms

of class domination. When considering the first and second French Bo-
napartisms, Marx oscillated between several prognoses: the state would
reconcile hostile factions within the bourgeoisie; the rural masses, having
become the state, would short-circuit the political elites; the state would
become hypostatized once it had become independent from society.

Dimitrov himself superimposed on the tyrannical character of the
Fascist regime the idea of class fraction. Fascism in power was the "open
terrorist dictatorship of the most reactionary, the most chauvinistic, the
most imperialist elements of financial capital." This definition descends
directly from *Imperialism, the Highest Stage of Capitalism*, the Leninists' bible. It allowed Dimitrov to identify the particularly imperialist
elements within that sector that were the real manipulators of the regime. He next sought to differentiate German National Socialism, distinguished by its particular brutality in international and domestic
matters, from other varieties of Fascism. He affirmed rather than analyzed this distinction, by means of an implicit comparison with the Italian case, but what counted, in contrast to the past, was precisely that
affirmation. With Dimitrov's report, "Fascism" in Communist thought
was no longer a mere political tendency at work in bourgeois democracies and Social Democratic parties; it was now seen as embodied in a
distinct dictatorial regime in several European countries—Mussolini's
Italy, Pilsudski's Poland, and Nazi Germany. Hitler provided an ideal
type; it was as if National Socialism at last offered a focus for the International's policies.

The true focus was the defense of the Soviet Union, bastion of the
world proletariat. Hitler, however, replaced all the beneficiaries of the
Treaty of Versailles in the role of principal adversary of the USSR and
of peace. As the advance guard of the counterrevolution, he furnished
Dimitrov with both an enemy of Communists of whatever nationality
and with a person bent on destroying the Soviet Union through war.

Communism and Fascism faced each other as revolution versus
counterrevolution, a relationship familiar to European political culture.
Nazism would bring that confrontation to a head. The two opposing
regimes were closely linked, for Fascism was in many ways a response
to the threat of the proletarian revolution. In the final analysis, their duel
delimited the battle lines of the twentieth century: in this sense, anti-
Fascism was simply a revolutionary camp. In another sense, however, it
encompassed, at least in its primary stage, the partisans of pluralistic
democracy side by side with the Communists, and included not only
socialist, anarchist, Catholic, and unorganized workers but also bourgeois parties and freedom-loving peasants. The new tactic adopted by

the Seventh Congress was to make the unified front of the working class the spine of the coalition and to surround it with the anti-Fascist Popular Front, in which the Communists posed temporarily as champions of the bourgeois heritage. The dictatorship of the proletariat and the overthrow of the bourgeoisie were still the ultimate goal; the prescribed path, however, was different. The French experience of 1934–35, lauded by Dimitrov, was henceforth the model for the International. The Popular Front had replaced the "class against class" approach.

The strength of the new arrangement lay in its extraordinary flexibility. On the one hand, the goal of the workers' revolution was firmer than ever, not as a distant horizon for Communist efforts, but as the natural outcome of the anti-Fascist battle. If financial capital was the last resort of Fascism, then the defeat of Fascism was also the defeat of capitalism in its "highest," or ultimate, stage. Dimitrov had rediscovered a classic dialectic in the history of Marxism: the more the bourgeoisie needed for dictatorship, the nearer it was to its end. The Communists alone thought they knew the true meaning of the anti-Fascist offensive. They made it their first priority because they had no idea that they were simply working for the restoration of bourgeois freedoms.

On the other hand, their struggle had changed its name. Henceforth, Communist militants identified not with Soviet republicanism but with democratic anti-Fascism. This in no way implied a rejection of the original myth: the Soviet Union remained more than ever the homeland of all workers, wherever they were. The unconditional defense of its territory was its primary imperative. Nonetheless, blind solidarity with the USSR was altered slightly when it became identified with anti-Fascism; it lost part of it foreignness and crudeness and affirmed its raison d'être and political morality. The "third phase" militants had faith in Stalin because he hated the bourgeoisie and passionately wished to hasten its end. The anti-Fascist Communists joined the army of the proletarian revolution principally to defend and guarantee liberty against Hitler. In both cases, the fight was draped in philosophical dignity, for each group sought eventually to emancipate all of humanity from exploitation. The priority of the battle against Hitler lent that abstract idea relevance while softening the "third phase" character of class struggle.

Hitlerian racism seemed to confirm ipso facto the patent on democratic universalism claimed by the Bolshevik Marxists under Stalin as well as under Lenin. Here was proof, more powerful and tangible than any philosophical proclamation, that Stalin was Hitler's adversary. The issue of the Soviet regime's true nature was put on the back burner, whether because the anti-Fascist policy of the USSR and the Comintern were sufficient proof of the regime's democratic character, or because the priorities of the anti-Nazism battle mitigated or suppressed doubts about the status of freedom in the Soviet Union. Ultimately, this argument blamed Nazism for what was admitted about the Stalinist Terror—especially the trials; like the Jacobins, the Bolsheviks were merely striking out at the enemy, that is, Hitler's agents in the USSR.

With anti-Fascism, the Communist movement shed the narrowest and most sectarian aspects of class struggle as it had been conceived and practiced, for example, between 1929 and 1934. The "working class" became truly national and drew the benefits of the traditions and virtues of patriotism. It had gained many allies to its right, well beyond the socialists. Except in the Fascist states, the Communist Parties had multiplied their members and deputies all over Europe. Although France, homeland of the Popular Front, provides the most striking example, in many countries the movement to stop Hitler gave Communism its most glorious moment and its militants whatever nobility illusion could endow.

The anti-Fascist aspect of Communist culture at the time did, however, expose the entire movement to a certain vulnerability. In the autumn of 1939, the USSR's foreign policy made an about-face, and doubt arose over the militant identity itself of these disciples of Bolshevism. The only thing that survived the tempest set off by the German-Soviet pact was the Communist Party apparatus. The anti-Fascist mobilization of the mid-1930s had in no way checked the subordination of international Communism to Stalin. The weakness of the international movement—the flip side of its strength—was that its rootedness in a specific territory and history constantly threatened the universality of its character. Thus, in 1935, the Soviet Union was subject to the most widespread state terror ever imposed. In December 1934, Stalin made the assassination of Sergei Kirov[28] a pretext to unleash unprecedented repression of the "enemies of the people," who were arrested, killed, or deported by the millions.[29] At the time, Hitler was a mere sorcerer's apprentice on the scale of mass terror. Compared to the liquidation of the Bolshevik Party between 1935 and 1938, the Night of the Long Knives appears a minor incident.

Anti-Fascism, however, diverted attention away from the USSR toward Nazi Germany, which since January 1933 had been rife with causes for indignation on the part of friends of freedom, an indignation stimulated less by factual observation than by ideological tradition: Hitler won glory by crushing democracy, thereby furnishing his adversaries with a cause. Stalin was quick to exploit this situation. By means of the abstract negativity of anti-Fascism, which was devoid of substance, the new face of democracy permitted a union of democrats and Communists. In the guise of an alliance between equals, Communism sought to spread its influence by relying upon something that Lenin had always detested and had sought to outlaw once and for all in October 1917. Hitler was decrying the principles of 1789, while Stalin was promulgating the new Soviet constitution of 1936 with great pomp. Through anti-Fascism, the Communists had recovered the trophy of democracy without renouncing any of their basic convictions. During the Great Terror, Bolshevism reinvented itself as a freedom by default. Even while drawing strength from what it despised—the homage of vice to virtue—it was intimidating its adversaries by spreading the rumor that anti-Sovietism was the prelude to Fascism. Not only was Hitler useful in reviving the idea of democratic Communism, but he also provided a pretext to incriminate democratic anti-Communism. The Comintern's great shift of 1934–35 orchestrated in its own key the reorientation the Soviet Union's foreign policy.

After a year or so, Stalin had sized Hitler up like a connoisseur. Unlike the British leaders, he wasted no time asking what the Nazi dictators "really wanted." He understood what no one in the West wanted to admit: that *Mein Kampf* was a government program. The USSR was consequently in danger and needed to ensure that it was not alone in opposition to Hitler; nor indeed, was it going to be the first country attacked. This is why the USSR joined the League of Nations and made overtures to the West—especially to France. The Comintern then played the same tune in another key: ideology, by definition, amplified and transformed the rationale of realpolitik. Broadly, antibourgeois Communism was followed by anti-Fascist Communism, "class against class" Communism was followed by Front populaire Communism, and insults to Briand were followed by attacks on Hitler. Nazism provided the Russian Revolution with a means of enriching its universal character at the very moment when it was more "Eastern" than ever. Stalin, for his part, played off both sides: he used Dimitrov to animate the propaganda of democratic Communism and Litvinov to gauge the intentions and means of the great European powers.

There is no reason to believe that Stalin only had eyes for "grand" international politics and that he scorned or neglected the Comintern "shop."[30] He may not have been present in person, but Manouilski ruled in his name. Although we are gaining an understanding of the activities and functioning of that enormous international revolutionary bureaucracy, we still know little about how it was pieced together at the top, how Manouilski was subordinated to Stalin. We also know little about the way decisions were made at the summit of the Soviet Union during this era. What is certain is that Manouilski, like Litvinov in the diplomatic sector, had no margin of autonomy vis-à-vis the all-powerful Secretary General, whose cult was taking off in the Soviet Union as well as in the associated parties.

This would suggest that the history of the 1934–35 shift did not signal the shelving of the Comintern but the very opposite—a vigorous reappropriation of the entire international apparatus, which had become more indispensable than ever. During the worst phase of the Kremlin's bloody dictatorship, only the Comintern militants could provide the appearance of unitary anti-Fascism that would help win democratic hearts.

As would become clear in 1939, Stalin himself did not subordinate his policies to the battle against Fascism. The new period that began in 1934 provided him with a popular slogan and a political space that allowed him to implant a vast apparatus of revolutionary subversion, entirely devoted to him, all over Europe. In 1939, and in 1940 when he had become Hitler's ally, he did not abandon his "international" Cominternians of the anti-Fascist period, provided they had remained loyal when the pact of August 1939 was signed. After 1945, many of them, having spent both war periods in Russia, before and after 20 June 1941, would reveal the secrets of Stalinist anti-Fascism as they in turn, throughout Eastern Europe, became instruments, at once servile and omnipotent, of Soviet totalitarianism.

So as to avoid getting ahead of ourselves, let us return to Paris, just before the mid-1930s, as we seek to understand the spell cast by anti-Fascism over the contemporary imagination.

During this period, Paris was in all respects the ideal place to observe anti-Fascist Communism.

Since 1917, the Soviet Communists had made a major investment in Germany. Even after 1923, when Germany no longer represented the Soviets' supreme hope, Germany remained their favorite field for maneuvers as well as their most useful ally. Presided over by Hindenburg from 1925 on, the Weimar Republic retained the alliances forged at Rapallo. After the economic crisis however, the regime lost stability, and a dozen or so years after the earlier failed attempts it again became potential prey for revolutionaries. In 1933, Berlin ceased to be the second most important Communist capital after Moscow: Hitler had put an end to that long-standing illusion.

The German Communists took refuge in Paris, where they were

reunited with their Italian comrades. A large number of militants who had been driven out of Central or Danubian Europe by right-wing dictatorships were also living there. During this period, France was open to victims of political persecution, and it was in Paris that the International reestablished many of its European activities. As we have seen, Münzenberg, as early as the summer of 1933, managed to stir up the Parisian proletariat with stories of the misfortunes of German Communists. What had begun with the Amsterdam-Pleyel movement was now pursued on a new and wider scale, since the main battle front had changed.

The resident host in Paris was the French Communist Party in the midst of a crucial year. After its glorious departure from Tours in December 1920, the French section of the Communist International had long been vegetating. In the heat of the immediate postwar period, it had incorporated so many elements alien to the spirit of Leninism that it quickly shrank to a few thousand militants, kept vigilant by Moscow against the opportunistic tradition of French socialism and obsessed with domestic attempts to exaggerate the working-class character of the Party and the "correctness" of its revolutionary line. The movement's electoral base remained extremely localized and quite limited, having shrunk even more by 1932 than it had in 1928, even though the French Communist Party was in the process of attaining its historical dimension.

With respect to internal affairs, let us not enter the maze of internal intrigues in Paris and in Moscow that led, in 1931–32, to the elimination of the "Barbé-Célor Group" and to the selection of those who would furnish the lasting core leadership of French Communism—Thorez, Duclos, Marty, and Frachon.[31] All these operations were organized and carried out by Manouilski and his headquarters. Thorez, moreover, was supervised by Eugen Fried, one of the first young Slovakian veterans and a survivor of the Béla Kun adventure of 1910, who had joined the bureaucracy of the International in 1924 and had become a member of the Czechoslovakian Party Politburo in 1928, eventually to be installed in Paris as a plenipotentiary.[32] In France, he represented what Robrieux called the "glaciation," the complete and direct takeover of the French Communist Party by the International.

This internal glaciation, accomplished in 1932–33, barely preceded the external shift, the policies of the Front populaire—policies common to the entire Communist world but paradigmatic in France, since France would constitute the ultimate terrain for the development and success of those policies.

We have already noted the role of the French situation in the shift effectuated by the Comintern during 1934. That shift was hardly an accomplished fact at the beginning of the year, contrary to Thorez's affirmation, against evidence to the contrary, of the political autonomy of the French Communist Party. The events of 6 February 1934 and the following few days would prove the opposite: the French Communists did demonstrate against the extreme right-wing Leagues on the 6th, but not in favor of the Republic or of democracy;[33] this was also true on the 9th, when the slogan remained "Soviets everywhere" or even "Government for the workers and peasants." Although on 12 February the French Communist Party, after the Socialist Party had already done so, finally supported the anti-Fascist general strike decided upon by the Confédération générale du travail, they nonetheless continued their attacks on Social Fascism for some months. The policy of unity with Social Democracy against Fascism, defended at the time by Doriot and Barbé, was condemned by Thorez as "opportunistic" in several articles that appeared in *Humanité* in March and April 1934. At the end of May, Doriot was expelled from the Party after he refused to go to Moscow for arbitration by the International. Thorez, for his part, would obtain his rival's head. Although hitherto loyal to the strategy of "class against class," he made no moves toward the policy recommended by Doriot until late June at the National Conference of the French Communist Party at Ivry, motivated by written instructions from Moscow.[34]

Things started moving quickly. On 15 July, a large Socialist-Communist union meeting took place, organized jointly by the Parisian regional directors of the Communist Party and the two SFIO federations. So many showed up that the room proved too small; the meeting was moved to a gymnasium. The meeting was followed by a pact of united action, signed on the 27 July by both parties, committing them to join forces against Fascism and to abstain from mutual criticism during the "common undertaking" that was to be headed by a coordinating committee drawn equally from the two groups. In early October, the reunification of the Confédération générale du travail and the Confédération générale du travail unitaire was set in motion. On 9 October, Thorez launched the phrase *Front populaire du travail, de la liberté et de la paix* ("Popular front of work, liberty, and peace"). He would reiterate it at Nantes on the 24th, rallying the Radicals to the anti-Fascist cause. The Radical Party had long worked for a Franco-Soviet rapprochement; Herriot, as we have seen, had labored for it, though in a blinkered manner, while Anatole de Monzie and Pierre Cot (among others) on his left were advocates for the Soviet regime, both of them having been engaged in the Amsterdam-Pleyel movement and the RUP (Rassemblement universel pour la paix), two missions manipulated by Moscow.[35]

It was as if French Communism, far from escaping from the mandatory logic of Comintern strategies, constituted the Comintern's most fertile field. Once Germany was firmly under Hitler's thumb, France became more important to Stalin than when it had merely represented victorious imperialism at Versailles. His own Communist Party, which had been in perpetual renovation from the start but more especially since 1931, had finally acquired a lasting leadership invested with a capital task: to be the advance guard of the anti-Fascist shift, having become a truly Stalinist party. But if the French Communist Party did not escape from Comintern law, it brilliantly pioneered the anti-Fascist role. The special envoys that succeeded one another in France throughout 1934—Manouilski himself, Anna Pauker, Gottwald, Togliatti, not to mention Fried—had not toiled in vain. They had unceasingly discussed, consulted, and argued; the Communist world combined a taste for the "theoretical" palaver with the security of voluntary servitude. This time, however, contrary to what had occurred in Germany, they had planted the right seed in the right soil: Germany had rejected them; France would come to heel.

Since 1918, France had been living in the shadow of war. In every household, a photograph of a deceased father, brother, or husband stood enshrined on the mantle; every village had its war monument in the main square, engraved with a long list of the fallen—a moving sight even today. No one knew that this formidable military victory would be both the first and the last of the century, but all were aware of its price, which they continued to pay from their stock of memories. The slaughter decimated the younger generations. It had destroyed not only the losing nation but a victorious nation as well, and not one of the strongest. The French, whether on the right or the left, wanted to be done with massacre. So they tended either to exalt the strength they had lacked or to make war against war, even if that meant war against their own government.

Postwar patriotic fanfares or antimilitarist proclamations, I suspect, contained something of this passion—something of the "never again!" The French of that time had paid so dearly for victory that it had paralyzed their wills. The retrospective fear of their ordeal led them to a sort of collective abdication—unfamiliar even to them—which accounts for the somewhat dismal character and inglorious end of the French interwar period.

In the 1920s, however, animosity toward war had produced violent sentiments on the left. That hatred was by no means a weak emotion, for it was inseparable from revolution. We need only reread the famous texts of the Second International, which had been betrayed in 1914; the culprits had been designated beforehand—capitalist interests, the imperialist system, the bourgeoisie. Four years later, their crimes were multiplied by the experience of the survivors of the trenches. Denunciation of the imperialist war became the favorite theme of revolutionary extremism, with the French Communist Party at its center, though there were other peripherally associated groups, such as the remaining revolutionary syndicalists, pacifists, radical antimilitarists, and the intellectuals of *Clarté* (the movement founded by Henri Barbusse in 1919).

Pacifism, from that time on, kept a low profile. On the winners' side, the idea of maintaining peace by maintaining military superiority would justify a reoccupation of the Ruhr by the French army in 1923; that idea would die of its internal contradictions and because it wore the mask of war in a time of renewed peace. The dominant desire of French public opinion was to preserve the hard-won peace by setting up a defensive network of alliances and an international system of obligations and sanctions. The definitive barring of arms in the settlement of international conflicts depended not on revolution but on unanimous agreement about democratic juridical processes: the League of Nations was conceived as an arbitrational tribunal. That particular form of pacifism was denounced as a product of the Treaty of Versailles, a pacifism of the winners, imperialism in disguise. Yet the League of Nations was democratic and nationalist and thus expressed the ambiguous sentiments of a large number of citizens.

The two types of pacifism had opposite principles. If we simply consider the League of the Rights of Man,[36] that bastion of the left, it becomes obvious just how conflictual the debate about the armistice was, despite the shared ideals and sentiments from which it started. In early 1927, for example, a discussion was launched about the Paul-Boncour law on the "general organization of the nation in times of war"—a document that provided, on the one hand, for a strictly defensive military organization against Germany and, on the other, for various arrangements concerning the government and mobilization of the country in the event of a conflict. Although the majority of the members of the League approved of the democratic spirit, the very hypothesis of war was enough to arouse the indignation of radical pacifists: "Since 1914," thundered Michel Alexandre, "we know how laws are made and that any risky war may be dubbed a defensive war."[37] Alexandre was a philosopher, a disciple of Alain's, for whom his firebrand periodical, *Libres Propos*, offered a monthly forum. He belonged to the small group of young intellectuals who were publicly opposed to the war from 1916 on, and for whom that opposition constituted the very fabric of their lives. Vehemently against the lies of warlike propaganda, hostile to Versailles, to French imperialism, and to the League of Nations, scornful of patriotism and the army, they had long ago lost their illusions about the Socialist Party, which continued to make antimilitarist pronouncements long after betraying their spirit.

The views of these intellectuals inclined them, to varying degrees, toward Communism, which many of them knew little about, other than that it had eliminated capitalism and, hence, the cannon merchants. The Soviet Union, which in 1918–20 had been the victim of the war of intervention and hated by the great imperialist powers, lent one of its faces to their passion, but the Soviet Union's other face was less attractive: as individualists and libertarians they disliked the closed aspect of Communism. The Party itself distrusted intellectuals and had forgotten nothing of Lenin's criticisms of even the most intransigent pettybourgeois pacifism. The Communists' negative attitude went even further: for them, among all possible pacifist positions, it was the most extreme ones that they were most suspicious of. If supporters of those policies called for revolution, it could very well have been one different than their own and a threat to them by eliciting hatred of the state instead of adoration. If they were hostile to all wars, regardless of the circumstances and participants, they could one day pose as class adversaries, as events would bear out.

Although the "fight for peace" was certainly at the forefront of Communist battles and was another name for the condemnation of capitalism, it had particular significance in this context, since it was based solely on an evaluation of the relations between the USSR and the capitalist world. Hence the dramatization of the imminence of an anti-Soviet war constantly used by Stalin to justify revolutionary vigilance, the unity of the Bolshevik Party, and strict discipline within the entire movement. With the world economic crisis and the progress of German National Socialism, Stalin added something new, superimposing the increasing possibility of interimperialist wars upon the "aggravation of contradictions" between the Soviet Union and world imperialism.[38] This impeccably Leninist hypothesis opened up room for diplomatic maneuvering between the capitalist powers. It underlay both the organization of the Amsterdam-Pleyel movement (and its evolution from Amsterdam to Pleyel, between 1932 and 1933) and the idea of a rapprochement with France, which had gradually become one of the goals of Soviet foreign policy.

Completed and made official in 1935, the anti-Fascist shift was accompanied by Stalin's declaration to Pierre Laval at the signing of the Franco-Soviet pact. Stalin, in his usual sober style, expressed his approval of "France's policy of national defense in order to maintain its armed forces at the level of its security." On the Soviet side, this little

phrase marked a reorientation of "the fight for peace" which would provoke a general outcry from the French public, especially among Communist and left-wing members of the French press. In its anecdotal aspect, this affair had the theatrical charm of surprises and reversals. What
made it important, however, was that it constituted a fundamental reworking of the image of Communism in French public opinion.

This reworking falls into two phases—the rupture with "hard-core"
pacifism, and the launching of a unitary, even nationalist, pacifism by
means of anti-Fascism.

From 15 May 1935 until 1939, the French Communist Party broke
with the antiwar militants and with the policy of peace at any price,
including concessions to Hitler. Those who continued to be obsessed
with opposition to Versailles and to their own bourgeoisie and army
were no longer in the Party's orbit and were often its adversaries. They
saw the pact concluded with Stalin, vague as it was, as a resurgence
of the Russian alliance that had preceded the First World War. In the
Party's dropping of its opposition to French military budgets, they detected a return of the *Union sacrée.*

People of this mind became increasingly opposed to a war against
Hitler, even when Hitler's ambitions and the probability of war became
clear. Persuaded that the German chancellor could be appeased by
means of negotiation, if only because he too was struggling against the
results of Versailles, they were the conduit for a strong current of leftist
opinion, notably among teachers, whose union they dominated. Moreover—and something sadly revealing about the era—the more illusions
they had about Hitler, the clearer they became with respect to Stalin:
the friends of Soviet Communism turned into its prosecutors. They
began denouncing Soviet tyranny. They also suspected that the inevitability of war with Hitler that they had so passionately challenged was
part of Stalin's calculations, and that the true goal of the Secretary General was to divert the Nazi menace toward the West. In such chapels of
antimilitarism as the Teachers' Union, and among such remnants of
revolutionary syndicalism as Alain's disciples, Stalin's carefully weighed
words to Laval signaled the march toward war. All these people remained opposed to Hitler, but peace took precedence over the crusade
against Fascism.

The Communist Party, when faced with attacks of this sort, defended
its new line *in the name of peace* and did not dissociate the anti-Fascist
battle from the fight for peace. This was already the case during the
Amsterdam-Pleyel movement, but Fascism was not specifically German
at the time; it was a tendency of all imperialisms, beginning with
the victorious powers of 1918. In 1935, fascism had found a country,

Germany, as well as a proper name, Hitler. How could French public opinion, no matter how weary of the horrors of war, have been oblivious of such a striking Germanization of Fascism? By making German rearmament official, by increasing the risks of a new conflict, Hitler's conquest of absolute power had also made the fight to maintain peace even more indispensable. In 1932, when the Communist International spoke of the imminence of an imperialist attack against the USSR,[39] it was believed only by those who were already convinced. Not that the earlier situation gave cause for pessimism, but no one in France at the time could have imagined that they were on the eve of an armed mobilization against the USSR. In 1935, however, Nazi Germany revived a more familiar image of the war; after all, memories were fresh. In spite of Hitler's protestations,[40] the French, who could not help fearing a tragic repeat, were all the more determined to head off renewed hostilities. The new German situation thus lent a credibility to the fight for peace that denunciations of French imperialism never could have done. Supported by the League of Nations as well as the USSR and filled with new respect for the international order and the treaties signed by France, the French Communist Party gave a more bourgeois tone to its pacifism.

The Party's new adversaries, soon to be joined by Doriot,[41] who had been expelled in 1934, accused it of having consented to the war beforehand by means of the Franco-Soviet treaty. It was a reasonable suspicion, for it certainly pointed to Stalin's strategy and to the origin of the Communist shift. On the other hand, the Soviet Union had returned to the League of Nations; it had turned over a new leaf on the international front and seemed to have been converted to a diplomacy of "collective security" that formed a common foundation for Herriot's and Blum's foreign policy. Fascism, eternally stalking the corridors of capitalism, found its principal incarnation in the hereditary enemy of France—the defeated Germany of 1918 but the same old Germany. So defending peace could be justified not just as an anti-Fascist measure but as a nationalist one. From the long-forbidden word "nationalist," still distrusted or abhorred by members of the pacifist Left, the Communists would fashion a new weapon. They needed only to attune it to class struggle so as not to expose themselves to the charge of no longer having any internal enemies. Thus, against all evidence but by virtue of a sort of rhetorical and "objective" necessity, they aimed their fire at what they called "French Hitlerians."

An invention of the Communists, French "Hitlerism" was all but impossible to find in French political life before 1939. The closest thing to such a movement was Doriot's PPF (Parti Populaire Français), between 1938 and 1939 after most of its best-known members—Drieu, Pucheu, and Jouvenel—had already left it. The existence of a true form of French Fascism is questioned by historians of this period. But there was clearly a "magnetic field"[42] of Fascist ideology in French politics, especially in its Mussolinian form. Its effects can be listed and measured among the Croix-de-Feu of Colonel La Rocque on the right, and among Déat's neosocialists, Bergery's *frontistes,* or Communist renegades such as Doriot on the left. French intellectual life, for its part, offered many similar examples, but on another plane. On a political level, admiration and imitation of National Socialism collided with the constraints of the domestic and international situation: the French, weak victors of the last armed conflict, were not drawn to nationalistic bellicosity, and Hitler was their potential enemy in a war of revenge encouraged by his regime. Even those who detested liberalism, parliamentarianism, and Communism saw nothing exemplary in National Socialism. What brought it supporters or at least indulgent spectators was the idea of signing a pact with Hitler; but since this prospect precluded an upping of the nationalist ante, they could not form a real Fascist movement.

Across from them, the Communists had donned nationalist garb. They had yet to demonstrate their democratic colors—something not all that easy for a party that was a section of the Communist International. The Moscow trials that began in 1936 would constitute a window on the Terror. A vast repression that hit well-known people was more difficult to hide than the liquidation of the Ukrainian kulaks a few years earlier.

A first line of counterargument consisted of pleading the radicalization of the combat: Nazism made no distinction between adversaries. With one sweep, Hitler liquidated the German Communist Party and the Weimar Republic. He had put the Communists and Democrats, all the various parties, in the same bag. Consigning German militant Communists to the first internment camps, he offered the Comintern a strategic and ideological advantage by simplifying the combat into two camps: Fascism and anti-Fascism. The identification of liberal democracy and Marxism, so familiar to German thought and so basic to Nazi ideology, was confirmed in one sense by what happened in 1933, even to the minds of those who thought it incoherent or absurd. In the end, Hitler imposed that identity even upon his enemies by forcing them to unite against him. If Marxists could be persecuted along with liberal democrats, must they not share something more important than their disagreements? Surely this indicated that they ought to unite against the common enemy. In general, the democrats did not linger over the philosophical implications of the first question, preferring to fall back on the second; the urgency of their situation obscured the contradiction. The Communists were far too subtle political maneuverers to push an argument about constitutional order or democratic pluralism further than necessary. So it was through a negation that the various groups facing Hitler united with his alleged French henchmen: anti-Fascism was an umbrella cause for parties and people holding contradictory ideas about democracy.

That negation, however, had partially reintegrated Communism into the democratic order, postulating that it belonged there. To separate liberalism from democracy had been a tendency familiar to France since the French Revolution. In a more elaborate version than a simple defensive reaction, anti-Fascism also contained an initial response to the philosophical problem of modern democracy. By simplifying the political universe into two camps, it implicitly led to the idea that the camp fighting against Hitler was not just a collection of temporary allies, disagreeing about everything and united merely by circumstances, but consisted of people who represented two eras of the same emancipatory movement, bourgeois democracy and proletarian democracy. The idea of a chronological connection was part of the socialist legacy. Although Blum and his friends, preferring liberty to unity, refused to extend this connection to the Bolsheviks during the Congress of Tours, they did not put an end to the debate on the relationship between the Soviet regime and democracy. Even as the French Communists were tracing a sharp line between themselves and the capitalist world, constantly fighting socialists and radicals, the left wing of the bourgeois world, many members of the Left continued to treat them as estranged but not totally lost brothers.

Let us take a backward glance at the 1927 National Congress of the League of the Rights of Man, that sanctuary of the Republic and the republicans. The order of the day was a debate on the "principles of democracy"[43]—another resumption of the eternal French discussion about the relationship between liberty and equality, formal and real rights, democracy and revolution. A delegate of the section from Courbevoie asked if republican legality could "be given a vacation" in the name of progress and equality, or socialism. This question reawakened the specter of the "dictatorship of the proletariat," to which most republicans, in the name of liberty and the rights of man, remained hostile. But the president of the League, the old Dreyfusard Victor Basch, could not reconcile himself to such a legalistic profession of faith and concluded the discussion by opening up a revolutionary future to the Republic itself:

Not for political principles—we shall not let ourselves be lured onto that field—but for the principles of liberty and equality that are our own, the very principles of 1789, I say that insurrection could become our most sacred right and the one most indispensable to our duties.

Oh! comrades, let us not be afraid of the word revolution! And let us acknowledge that all revolutions are necessarily a vacation from legality. *(Applause.)*

We ourselves were born of the Revolution, our Republic was born of a revolution. Do you really think that the era of revolutions has been ended forever? . . . Do you really believe that just because one class has acquired the position, thanks to that revolution, to which it had justifiably laid claim, the classes that did not benefit from the Revolution will be eternally content with the humiliating position provided for them in the present social organization? No! Don't believe it for a second!

Revolution was probably the key word that linked the democrats of the League of the Rights of Man to the Soviet experience, though they knew a little about its despotic character and were critical of it. They certainly had the same memories of the revolutionary origin of French democracy as the Russian Bolsheviks. Distant as that origin was, it kept reemerging from the past, its legend renewed by events. For the whole of the nineteenth century, French-style revolutionary politics accompanied the history of France and continental Europe, as demonstrated in 1848. That politics was present at the rendez-vous with Russian Bolshevism, and we have already seen how the French Left in the period immediately after World War I viewed the October Revolution through the prism of 1793.

The French Revolution could be brandished as a precedent even by those who sought to erase its legacy. To a Marxist, and even more to a Marxist-Leninist, there was no doubt that it marked the arrival of the bourgeoisie, along with its trail of political illusions. Still, the Revolution had also produced Jacobinism, a heroic moment, while the bourgeoisie was concerned only with utility; it represented the ultimate thrust of willpower, while the bourgeoisie preferred economics to politics; it was an egalitarian adventure, while the bourgeois dreamed only of wealth; it was democracy without liberty, while the bourgeoisie did as it pleased. It was an episode that rehabilitated the guillotine in the name of public safety, having justified it in advance in the name of equality; the French Revolution thereby furnished the elements of its own extension well into the following centuries.

The Russian Bolsheviks of the 1920s never abandoned their Jacobin lineage any more than the French Communists did. A perusal of *L'Humanité* reveals numerous references to the Jacobin example, even during the most sectarian periods of the history of the French Communist Party. This is not surprising if we think of Jacobinism as a precedent to Bolshevism in the category of terrorist dictatorships exercised in the name of the people. Until condemned by historians of the second half of the twentieth century as "totalitarian democracy,"[44] Jacobin democracy was celebrated either as the dictatorship of public safety[45] or as the ephemeral prefiguration of the power of the people mobilized against its foreign and domestic enemies.[46] In both cases, especially the latter, the precedent of 1793 was essential to the legitimation of the "dictatorship of the proletariat" as conceived by Lenin—the Robespierre of the proletariat—and carried out by means of terror from 1918 onward.

But the Russian 1793 did not end with civil or foreign wars. After defeating and eliminating its enemies, the terrorist dictatorship of the Bolshevik Party continued. Even as it was perpetuating itself as an absolute power based on ideology and fear, increasingly monolithic and concentrated in a single pair of hands, it was launching itself into unprecedented ventures such as the collectivization of the countryside. It no longer fought its enemies; it set up straw men and liquidated them. For this reason, with the passage of time and as the Soviet regime affirmed its omnipotence, it lost some of its "Jacobin" legitimacy as well as its fragility. Between 1927 and 1932, Moscow could talk about the imminence of an anti-Soviet war all it liked, but the result was more a general mobilization of the extreme revolutionary Left against each of the imperialist bourgeoisies than a reconstitution of public safety within the USSR.

Once again, it was Hitler who turned this situation into a gift for Stalin by threatening the USSR as soon as he took power. Not that the new German chancellor immediately launched himself into aggressive overbidding in matters of foreign policy—quite to the contrary. But the Leipzig trial put him on the world stage as the central person in the fight against international Communism. Stalin perceived what the British and French leaders had long closed their eyes to: that this time it would be war with Hitler, and that the fate of the USSR depended on the nature of the conflict. So it was natural that Stalin should start talking about public safety, and that Hitler's adversaries in Western Europe, especially in France, should recognize the tone. If the battle between Hitler and Stalin was a replay of the fight between revolution and counterrevolution, it could hardly have been unfamiliar to them.

Stalin spoke of mounting foreign perils, of intensifying domestic class struggle, of the purging of traitors, and of a general mobilization to save the socialist homeland: these "Jacobin" themes concealed the mass terror he had set into motion in 1935, which had nothing to do with a national defense against Nazi Germany. Yet these themes were bound to stir the militants of the French Left, which had been used to justifying the Jacobin Terror by reference to counterrevolutionary plots. It was from this historical "analogy" that the Stalinist Terror, having entered one of its worst periods, drew part of the support it elicited or the enthusiasm it aroused. From 1918 on, the pretext of circumstances had served to idealize the character of the Russian Revolution. In the mid-1930s that role was renewed, and vastly extended, by the Nazi menace. By demonizing Communism and designating it as the main enemy, Hitler earmarked it for democratic goodwill, and his hatred earned Communism a democratic certificate of merit. In France, along with Fascist-leaning pacifists, there were now Communist-leaning democrats.

At the core of the Comintern's anti-Fascist ideology was the idea of using the bipolar division of the political world promoted by Nazism as a decisive weapon against Nazism. Hitler drove the Soviet Union into the camp of liberty. It was not enough for him that the Soviet Union had become, through the force of circumstances, the natural ally of democracy. By the logic of ideology, the USSR was supposed to be democratic, not, like France, because it was Communist, but because it had suppressed capitalism. The French Left did not have to search long in its own tradition in order to come up with a name for a nation that was seeking to create a new social order and had to defend itself against reactionary forces: it was a revolutionary democracy. Precisely because of this situation, the Soviets could not enjoy all the luxuries of liberty. Hitler had managed to give a revolution long paralyzed by bureaucratic terror the innocence of a fresh start.

Reactions to the great Moscow trials a year later would seem less extravagant and mysteriously novel since they too had precedents in the French Revolution.[47] Like Stalin, Robespierre had to expose the enemies of the Revolution hidden within the Revolution. Let us look, for a moment, at the little book published in 1937 by the Communist historian Jean Bruhat, *Le Châtiment des espions et des traîtres sous la Révolution française* ("The punishment of spies and traitors during the French Revolution").[48] It begins with an evocation of the dangers of war that hung over the Soviet Union because it was surrounded by capitalists, and with citations from Stalin himself comparing anti-Soviet plots to the foreign machinations against revolutionary France. In both cases, revolutionary personalities were bought by a "foreign conspiracy" in order to hasten the end of the Revolution. Robespierre's trial of Danton was reenacted by Mathiez, for whom it was nothing other than the punishment of a corrupt man and a traitor by revolutionary justice. Dumouriez, the traitor's protector, was the precursor of men such as Zinoviev and Kamenev, and Saint-Just was the dispenser of justice prefiguring Vishinski. To make clear what he has in mind, Bruhat reviews the generals of the French Revolution who were executed for "treason"—now we are but a short step away from Tukhachevsky and his Nazi complicities. "Why should what was true in 1793 become an odious calumny in 1937? Do we think that the Fascist powers have a less violent hatred for the first workers' and peasants' Republic than the hatred that animated the feudal states with respect to the French Revolution?"[49]

Anti-Fascism, then, functioned on two levels: on the one hand, it was supposed to mobilize not only the Communist and socialist Left but democrats and even patriots as well—in short, that huge nebula the Comintern called the "popular masses"—against Hitler and, hence, against Mussolini. On the other, it needed the entire working class as its core and the Communist parties as its leaders. For them, Fascism was but a late political form of capitalism: it would be dead when the domination of capital was done away with. Anti-Fascist rallying was thus part and parcel of a revolutionary strategy, as would become clear after World War II in the Central and Eastern European countries which, under this flag, became "popular democracies." The strategy first required a defensive period devoted to defeating Fascism with the help of all democrats. Thus, with useful ambiguity, depending on the combatants' degree of initiation, anti-Fascism could adopt the entire "democratic" (in the Marxist sense) spectrum—defense of the Republic, human rights and liberties, and even the fight for the Soviet model, with respect to which these slogans were supposedly no longer meaningful since class struggle no longer existed. In mass demonstrations, anti-Fascist defense slogans replaced the Parisian proletariat's cries of "Soviets everywhere!" Even so, the final objective had not been lost. The idea of "revolutionary democracy," resurrected from 1793 by the French Communists, appeared just in time to cover up the ambiguities of an anti-Fascism both liberal and antiliberal, defensive and victorious, republican and Communist.

The history of the French Front populaire does not fall within the boundaries of the present work; our focus is the circumstances and strategies that rendered it possible, as well the group of political images that made it the shining moment of the French Left in the interwar period. The French example most clearly illustrates the Comintern's political shift in 1934–35 and the full complexity of anti-Fascism— both as an ideology taken from Communism and as the cement of the rediscovered unity of the Left.

During these years, the effects of the Nazi takeover of Germany exacerbated the French crisis—an economic crisis that occurred later in France than in the United States or Germany but lasted even longer. There was also a latent but much-discussed political crisis evidenced by the events of February 1934, its most obvious symptom a widespread antiparliamentarianism on both the left and the right. That sentiment may have pointed to a more general malaise on a national scale. France, huddled under the umbrella of a victory whose benefits it was afraid of losing even though it rejected responsibility for its conditions, was a nation that had lost its will, faced with a Germany bent on recovering its own. This disparity helps explain the fascination that Fascism and, consequently, anti-Fascism exercised in French politics.

Fascist ideas, whether manifested by disdain for parliamentary regimes, antipathy for bourgeois individualism, or glorification of the national community, were very much in the air at the time. They coincided with long-familiar French themes on both the left and right. On the right, in the Leagues, for example, Fascist ideas collided with anti-German feelings; on the left, with attachment to the Republic. These ideas slowly undermined both sides without creating a stable ideological basis for anyone. After 1933–34, even a militant anti-Fascist like Bergery almost unconsciously imitated Fascist techniques for fighting and propaganda. Having begun as a supporter of the Amsterdam-Pleyel movement, this radical politician gradually moved away from the Front populaire, gaining sympathy for Italian Fascism and peace at any price.[50] Christian Jelen has given us an excellent account of the ambiguities of prewar French pacifism, describing how the movement combined even the extreme Right and the extreme Left.[51] A telling example is Léon Blum's Socialist Party, which since 1920 had been torn between doctrinal intransigence and participation in bourgeois governments. It had to remain Marxist to avoid ceding too much territory on the left to its Communist rival, but in forbidding itself to govern with the Radical Party it totally disarmed the Left, as happened, for example, after the elections of 1924 and 1932.[52] Blum's party was split in 1933 by a confrontation between a socialism dedicated to national union and a socialism adhering to the labor tradition. Although it governed Front populaire France in 1936, it had not initiated the movement. For Léon Blum, anti-Fascism at last provided a sufficiently urgent reason to govern or, in his own parlance, to "exercise" power.[53] He eventually parted ways with the Communists over the Spanish Civil War; his party remained fundamentally pacifist, readily approving the Munich agreements.

In contrast, the Communist Party had made anti-Fascism into a duplicate of itself. So identified with the Revolution had anti-Fascism become that it was now the sole object of the Communists' strategy. The militants were not at all shocked by its narrow connivance with the defense of the Soviet Union; on the contrary, anti-Fascism was just another name, an international one, for loyalty to the workers' homeland. So the Communists remained shielded from the contagious effects of Fascism, wary of any leanings toward it. Leninism had already taught them the accuracy of certain Fascist critiques—of the corrupt deputy or the capitalist profiteer, for example. They had long been settled into their own territory, immunized against the trouble-making passion for "community" that had ravaged Germany and may have been threatening France; they intended to be the sole manipulators of that passion. The Fascists were their greatest enemies since they had stepped onto their territory, but they were also to be their last enemies since they opened the way to the final revolution. "Well grubbed, old mole!"[54] as Marx had said in different circumstances. The mole had done a pretty good job in the twentieth century as well. It had presented Stalinist Communism with the flag of anti-Fascism, and the victory of the Front populaire in France would fabricate memorable souvenirs of that occasion so brilliantly exploited by Lenin's heirs.

Since its origin, the Comintern had lost nearly all of its battles, whether in Europe or in the East.[55] The German revolution, which had always been the Comintern's top priority, had failed continually—in 1918, in 1923, and when the world economic crisis again made it a possibility. All this would culminate in Hitler. The French spring of 1936 reversed the current. The electorate gave a clear majority to the candidates of the three parties united in the Popular Front, singling out the Communists, to whom they gave the greatest increase since 1932[56]—poetic justice, since the Communists had fathered the Front populaire. Fifteen years after the split at Tours, after many internal purges and much revolutionary verbiage, the French Communist Party had finally reached the "masses"; its slogans coincided with the masses' political aspirations.

Nonetheless, in keeping with good Leninist doctrine, an electoral victory was a test too bourgeois to be significant. The strength of the Party was measured not by votes but by the influence it exerted over the working classes and the discipline of its cadres. As to the cadres, the die had been cast: the apparatus had been constituted, inspected, verified, almost never to budge again. But with respect to the workers, 1936 was still the decisive year—by virtue not of the April-May elections but of the strikes in June.

Events themselves, however, did not spring from Communist initiatives. The first work stoppages, accompanied by factory takeovers, occurred before mid-May in steel mills in Toulouse and in Paris. Sparked by a movement of solidarity with workers who had been dismissed for having taken a day off on May 1, the stoppages quickly achieved success. The movement spread during the following weeks, especially after Monday, 25 May, the day after a huge demonstration at the wall of the Fédérés. If the traditional tribute to the martyrs of the Commune managed to bring together hundreds of thousands of Parisian workers, it was because it was caught up in the exceptional atmosphere of the electoral victory of the Front populaire candidates on 3 May. Left-wing France lived in a state of grace, with the working class at its core: the two parties claiming to represent the workers were at the head of a united movement—the Communist Party because it was the initiator, the Socialist Party because it furnished the troops. It was the first time in French history that the proletariat was thus honored, propelled by French voters to the forefront of the nation, no longer the tragic figure of an ephemeral insurrection like that of June 1848 or of spring 1871, but the trailblazer of a coalition summoned by universal suffrage to govern the Republic. The subtle but powerful sense of a force at long last unified and liberated contributed to the extraordinary contagion of the strikers' movement at the end of May and in early June 1936, the very moment when Blum was forming his government. The working class, the great forgotten member of the Third Republic, made a spectacular entrance onto the scene of French history, bringing something of the spirit of February 1848.

One of the most penetrating commentators on this era was a young philosopher who sought deliberately to understand, from within, the wretchedness of the "worker's condition."[57] Simone Weil, a *normalien*, burned from an early age with two gifts that would eventually consume her—philosophical intelligence and compassion. When still quite young, she had become familiar with Monatte's *La Révolution prolétarienne* and with what remained of revolutionary syndicalism. She was a friend of Souvarine's. A teacher at the lycée Du Puy in 1931, soon to be associated with local trade unionism, she went to work in a tool-and-die factory in 1934–35. Her "Factory journal," which she kept daily, constitutes the best testimony to the material and moral poverty of the French workers' world of this period: harried by foremen, dazed by the rhythm of production, humiliated by the chain of command, the proletariat was submerged in alienation. Imprisoned by the fragmented character of production, workers could not even see what they were making. What Simone Weil observed in the mid-twentieth century was the condition of the proletariat of the nineteenth, aggravated by Taylorism. Echoing Rousseau, she described the negation of man's human nature: "Nothing paralyzes thought more than the sense of inferiority necessarily imposed by the daily expectations of poverty, subordination, and dependence. The first thing we must do for [modern factory workers] is to help them to recover or to retain, depending on the case, their sense of dignity." [58]

Not that Simone Weil was a revolutionary, for she had much too strong a religious sense to invest unreasonable hopes in the here and now. Compassion never obscured her ability to think, and this saint in search of a faith never ceased to argue like a logician. She expected nothing good to come of Communism, having divined its true nature. Nonetheless, class spirit seemed to be a reasonable means to progress, since it rid the workers of complicitous submission and brought them liberty. Weil passionately wanted to be useful. In the first six months of 1936 she kept up a remarkable correspondence with one of the directors of the factory who had a little social compassion. She tried to persuade her correspondent to allow her to educate his eight hundred workers and to hire her as well, at the humblest rank, to work in his factory.

Ironically, the project for a cultural factory journal that she would have written, intending it to be an instrument of worker's pride, was destroyed in 1936 by the reality of class struggle. A few days after the "Matignon accords," [59] Weil wrote to her correspondent of the joy that she had felt as she followed the movement and success of the strikes. Not that she expected any political result: "As for the future, no one knows what it will bring, nor whether the current workers' victory will, in the end, constitute a step on the way to a Communist totalitarian regime, or to a Fascist totalitarian regime, or (and this is what I hope, although, alas, I don't believe in it) to a nontotalitarian regime." [60] But this clear-sighted pessimism about the period was accompanied by true moral joy at the sight of the reversal of powers achieved by the strikes:

> If the strikers' movement had brought me pure joy (a joy rather quickly replaced, however, by the anxiety that has never left me since the distant time when I understood the catastrophes toward which we are headed), it is not only for the sake of the workers, but also for the sake of the bosses. I am thinking right now not of material interests . . . but of moral interests, of the salvation of the soul. I think it is good for the oppressed to have been able, for a few days, to affirm their existence, raise up their heads, impose their wills, obtain advantages due

to something other than condescending generosity. And I think it is also good for the bosses—for the salvation of their souls—to have been obliged, in their turn, for once in their lives, to yield to force and to be submitted to humiliation. I am happy for them.[61]

The great Simone Weil, probably the most original voice of her time, put her finger on the deepest collective emotion issuing from the victory of the Front populaire—the much heralded entry of the workers into national politics. This philosopher understood the sources, at once Christian and democratic, of her feelings: the workers had reappropriated their humanity by revolting. Most of her contemporaries, when not giving in to class panic, felt or expressed the same emotions in a less developed but no less sincere way, some through history, some through ideology.

The Third Republic had little indulgence for the workers. Unlike the Second Republic, the Third was not born in a burst of social fraternity but, on the contrary, emerged in a conservative spirit in the aftermath of a terrible repression in the streets of Paris in the name of a bourgeois order. The executioner of the Commune was also the founder of the Republic. His successors paid almost no attention to the workers' plight; for them, the French only existed as defined by civic equality and the patriotism of one and all. Despite Jaurès's efforts, the workers' movement reemerged less through an alliance with a republican Left than through a form of class-based socialism or unionism in a Guesdiste or anarcho-syndicalist version. What is more, a radical like Clemenceau was no better disposed toward the movement than was an opportunist like Jules Ferry: in the workers' memories, Clemenceau was responsible for the shootings of Draveil and Villeneuve-Saint-Georges.[62] Finally, the *Union sacrée* of 1914, concluded on the barely sealed tomb of Jaurès, turned out to be nothing but a forced rallying of the workers' movement to republican bellicosity: its true nature would be revealed at a terrible price, as French socialism, after 1917, groped around in search of a compromise peace, while the opposite political strategy—victory at any price—found its champion in the most Jacobin of republicans.

The Republic had won the war, but without altering the workers' exile within the nation. After the Congress of Tours, that exile found a special interpreter in the young French Communist Party. Born of the reaction against the *Union sacrée*, obsessed by the "rightist" drift, mistrusting the intellectuals, and jealously watching over its proletarian composition, the Party underscored the things that radically separated it from bourgeois parties and their accomplices, the socialists. In a country like France, with its broad and deep-seated democratic culture, the

Party affirmed the primacy of the workers' revolution as something quite distinct from bourgeois democracy and entirely dependent on its own action. Similarly, Leninist instruction, hammered home by the Comintern, exaggerated a preexistent worker-oriented tradition. With Bolshevik Marxism, that instruction supplied more than an example and a doctrine: it provided a culture and a party, making workers' messianism look like a science and a future. The socialists also fancied themselves a proletarian party and had no intention of allowing their rival brothers to monopolize the term. But their deputies were all bourgeois, their revolution was increasingly problematical and without known precedent, and, finally, no one saw *them* going to work in factories.

All this became clear in June 1936. Not that the Communists were the sole instigators of the movement, which was much too big to have been set off by a single party. But they were the only ones to welcome, organize, and take charge of it, as though history was finally fulfilling their predictions. The April–May elections had just endowed them with the influence of a major party. More important to them, the strikes confirmed their status as guides to the workers, of whom they had claimed to be the only true representatives since Tours. The Communists were the most visible beneficiaries of the two great moments of the Front populaire in France; even though they had refused to participate in the Blum government as the active element of the victorious anti-Fascist coalition, they had made their entry into national politics. Furthermore, they were responsible for the hundreds of thousands of strikers who had occupied their factories in the elation of renewed power but not in the name of the dictatorship of the proletariat.

Paradoxically, Stalinist Communism took root in France by virtue of events alien to its repertory—democratic elections and protest strikes. At a time when anti-Fascism was providing Communism with a vast socialist and even bourgeois electorate during both rounds of voting, the success of the June strikes allowed French Communism to enlarge its working-class vocation in the framework of the anti-Fascist union. Thus it won on two counts: as a "democratic" party and as a Leninist one. Its revolutionary credentials shed their somewhat conspiratorial character in 1936, but their promise remained undimmed. Established legitimately in the memories, emotions, and passions inseparable from 1936, Communism had given a new historical substance to worker messianism, of which it was more than ever the guardian.

Indeed, it mattered little that the French Front populaire never lived up to the public enthusiasm it had generated. Neither its economic policies nor its military or foreign policies really responded to the needs of the day, and it is best remembered for its policies on social welfare. In the end, the victory of a united Left in 1936 and the first socialist-led government in French history stood out from the humdrum routine of French politics, and not least because it changed the moral and material situation of the nation's workers. In this respect, 1936 constituted a key date in the psychological history of the French Left and in the history of the French Communist Party within the Left. This first string of happy memories, inseparable from the workers' solidarity and popular support for it, would provide a quarter of a century's political capital for the French Communists. The enormous benefits they brought to France earned them the right to forget or ignore the horrors they had approved in the USSR. Better still: they rendered such horrors all but unthinkable. By turning their backs on a revolution in France in favor of the forty-hour week and paid holidays, the Communist Party had sweetened the Soviet Revolution. Social progress and totalitarian dictatorship were wrapped up in the same workers' mythology as were the accordions of the Front populaire and the assassins of the secret police.

Contemporaneous with the French Front populaire, events in Spain would constitute the second great test of the Comintern's new political line. Paradoxically, the civil war set off by the military insurrection of July 1936 would provoke the first public disagreements within the French Front populaire, while permitting Communist anti-Fascism to enlarge its international resonance.

The Spanish affair crystallized an international crisis, lending it an ideology drawn from the confrontation of parties on the local scene. The Spanish Left had won the February 1936 elections—barely by votes but handily in seats. Even though it was highly fragmented, unified only by electoral obligations (except for the anarcho-syndicalists), its victory signaled the first success of a "Popular Front" in Europe. In reaction, the Right mobilized, with the Falangists and the military to the fore, drawing support from reactionary social forces and the Francoist *pronunciamento* on 17 July 1936. This course of events—simplified for our purposes here, but accurate—provided an ample scenario for the Comintern to play Fascism against anti-Fascism.

Hitler and Mussolini, not about to miss an opportunity, publicly supported General Franco in August by almost immediately lending him military aide in the form of men and equipment. So Franco's progress was linked to Hitler's success, just as his setbacks would consecrate a victory shared by democracy and Communism, united under the flag of anti-Fascism. Stalin reacted from within the ideological framework he had occupied since 1934: he affirmed the support of the USSR for the Spanish Republic, although he would wait until early autumn to send political or military advisers and equipment, while the Comintern took the initiative of the "International Brigades." Britain and France, on the other hand, decided to follow a policy of nonintervention, backed by an international arms embargo on Spain.

The disparity between the attitudes of the Russians and the Western democracies gave the moral advantage to the USSR, for it lent Soviet policies the appearance of perfect consistency in words and deeds. It even put Russia into the category of international democratic solidarity—which for the European Left amounted to a certificate of good conduct: having long denounced the policy of "collective security" as an imperialist lie, the "workers' country" was now upping its obligations. In contrast, Léon Blum, head of the Front populaire government, appeared to be betraying his own ideas, whereas in fact he was prisoner to both the pacifism of French public opinion and to the alliance with Great Britain. The nonintervention policy meant resigning himself to an inglorious abandonment of the Spanish Republic, concealing what little aid he had sent to it. On his left, the French Communist Party was giving him lessons in international democracy. This absurd situation was experienced by the leader of the French Left as moral torment, the anti-Fascist idea, in its false simplicity, functioning as a trap.

In reality, neither international politics nor the Spanish situation was entirely subsumed in the opposition between Fascism and anti-Fascism. Through Spain, the Second World War threatened to spread to all of Europe, as almost everyone was aware. Now, however, the war was progressing by means of three actors rather than two: Hitler, Stalin, and the democracies. British leaders, whose decisions dominated French foreign policy, had their reasons for refusing to come to the aid of the Spanish Republic: as conservatives, they did not really like the revolutionary hullabaloo issuing from Spain, and they liked even less the idea of being prematurely drawn into a confrontation with Hitler. Even though Stalin came to the aid of Spain in hopes of pressuring France and Britain to intervene even indirectly (by lifting the arms embargo, for example) so as to contribute on an international level to a potential setback for Germany, the British, who had little hope for a liberal republic in Madrid, were in no hurry to intervene at Stalin's side against Hitler.

For the British, the defeat of the pro-Franco forces in Spain signified a step forward for Communism in Europe. Since the Conservative government, for good reason, did not feel involved in the choice between Fascism and anti-Fascism, it could retain dangerous illusions about the new German regime as well as its realistic prejudices about Communism. British noninterventionist policy was located at the intersection of these two attitudes, indicating a consensual impotence, lacking an option clearly in keeping with national interest. When Communism spread to France, it collided with ideas and promises that had constituted the basis of government for the Front populaire. Just a few months after his victory, Léon Blum had agreed to a nonintervention treaty in Spain, shattering the anti-Fascist union that had brought him to office; that, at least, was how the Communists saw it, and they told him so immediately. Thereafter, they constantly compared the USSR's attitude toward the Spanish Republic with that of Western democracies: the former had indicated seamless solidarity on the part both of the Soviet State and of the Comintern via the International Brigades; the latter, in contrast, had adopted a lax abandonment of liberty in Spain under the cover of a fictitious embargo, and had opened up the way to a victory for Hitler and Mussolini with the mediation of Francoism. Thanks to this interpretation, the Spanish Civil War would become the key event of the 1930s, an early confrontation between the international forces of Fascism and those of liberty. The democracies of the West had missed the boat, whereas the Soviet Union had come running with men, arms, and fanfare. In this event, Communist anti-Fascism forged both its history and its mythology.

Some of the myths were true. Nonintervention might well have been an effective policy as well as a wise one, as long as it was imposed upon everyone. If not, it was merely a cover for weakness, or partial complicity with Franco and his foreign protectors. This brings us back to the roots of the British attitude, based on an antipathy for Communism stronger than any mistrust of German Nazism. Not that British Conservatives were entirely misguided in their anti-Communism: the tragic side of the story, the cause for a still-lingering bitterness, is that the British, unlike others, who were blinded by generosity, saw Stalin for what he was, and for less than magnanimous reasons. Their mistake when faced with Hitler was to allow anti-Communism to dominate their foreign policy. British Conservatives committed the opposite mistake from the democrats, who were pro-Communist because they were anti-Fascist; the British leaned toward the Fascist powers because they were anti-Communist. More precisely, for they were little given to ideological debate, they wanted to show Stalin that they would not let themselves be dragged into a confrontation with Hitler, and to show Hitler that his true enemy lay to the east. Unable to judge which of their enemies was the worse, they hoped to see them annihilate each other. This sentiment was not unknown in Paris, especially on the right, even if not shared by Léon Blum. Committed to nonintervention in Spain, the head of the Front populaire government, aligned with London, reluctantly but fairly confidently relied on the pacifism of the Left. In any case, for three long years this hypocritical and risky policy clearly symbolized the moral weakness of the democratic nations in face of Fascism, a weakness leading to political and military abdication.

This unfortunate situation explains only the bad reasons for nonintervention; there were better reasons, related both to the nature of the Spanish Civil War and to the ambiguities of Communist anti-Fascism.

At the time of the Civil War, Spain had for centuries been at the political periphery of Europe. Locked into its own past, eccentric and violent, it had remained Catholic, aristocratic, and poor. It retained a powerful ancien régime, which engendered revolutionary passions. The monarchy had been discredited by a series of bad kings, the army was feared as a tool of dictatorship, and there was little social support for representative democracy. Even national unity was problematical, and the diversity of national parties compounded those of the Catalonian or Basque separatist movements. The elections of February 1936 lent this archaic, fragmented schema a misleadingly simple appearance since the votes were split between two camps—for and against the Frente popular—and seemed to mirror the French situation of the same era. Beginning in July, the Civil War sealed up the division with the blood of fallen soldiers, as if old Spain, after a long exile, had assumed a central role in European history only to become the symbol and the battlefield of twentieth-century ideologies. The intervention of the Fascist dictatorships on Franco's side was tantamount to a confirmation of the strange telescoping of twentieth-century European passions with nineteenth-century Spain.[63]

Spain in 1936 was one of the least appropriate European countries for an analysis in terms of Fascism/anti-Fascism. The July 1936 insurrection was an army revolt supported by the Catholic Church, monarchists, landowners, and all the most traditionalist powers in Spain. The only strictly "Fascist" elements were the remains of José Antonio Primo de Rivera's Falange and his social program;[64] that Francoist "Left," however, would rapidly be stripped of power along with the legitimist Right. The new Falange that resulted from the insurrection's progress accompanied rather than spearheaded the victory. As for Franco, a less charismatic leader, less comparable to Il Duce or the Führer, would have been hard to find. This general, no more or less famous than his peers, was a crafty oligarch, the Louis XI of the counterrevolution, totally without talent for stirring the masses. Hitler and Mussolini saw him less as a peer than as a pawn for spreading their influence in southern Europe; Spain was to be a test of Franco-British intentions. A few years later, Franco himself felt no obligations toward them either. By staying out of World War II, he relativized his links to Fascism as well as the international repercussions of his victory.

Taking a look at the other side, we are struck by the mass of contradictory ideas and parties that espoused anti-Fascism. To begin with, the strong anarchist movement in Spain—represented by the FAI (Federación Anarquista Ibérica), which was highly influential within the CNT (Confederación Nacional del Trabajo)—had rejected the Popular Front program as too conservative while leaving those loyal to it the liberty to support it through their votes. Hence, the government that resulted from those elections, which was dominated by the center and left-wing republicans, had no hold on the social movement that followed upon the electoral success, as had happened in France. Even more than in France, the working and peasant classes had major grievances to avenge. The terrible repression that followed the workers' insurrection in the Asturias was still a recent memory, yet the government was incapable of ending the labor strikes and the peasants' land seizures. This libertarian social revolution was also millenarian in spirit, appropriate to the Spanish anarchistic genius and promoted by the powerful union directed by the left-wing socialists, the UGT ("General Union of Workers"), which was hostile to an alliance between the workers' movement and the liberal republicans. The small Communist Party, barely emerging from its "class against class" phase, did its best to navigate between the revolution and the Popular Front government and had little effect upon the course of events.

Nonetheless, the July military insurrection, true to the character of the twentieth-century European Right, justified itself with the claim that Spain must be saved from Communism. In the Spanish case, the nonexistent Communist threat was the pretext for a counterrevolution of the classic type, but it also served to designate a truly popular revolution, to which the army revolt gave new strength. Spain offered the spectacle of a conflict older than that of Fascism and anti-Fascism; there, revolution confronted counterrevolution.

The military uprising radicalized the social movement in the opposite direction, accentuating its revolutionary character, at the very time when the new republican government, moderate as it was, was compelled to rely on popular organizations such as unions and parties. Since all of the government's political means—the army, the majority of the police force, and many of the civil servants—had gone over to the rebels, the government had to fill the deserted administration with an improvised personnel, characterized more by the desire to fight Franco and his henchmen than by competence or discipline. This was the moment when the anarchists, or the armed militia of the Spanish revolutionary syndicalists, restored order in the large cities that had remained loyalist; when countless committees of the people accelerated peasant self-rule over domains that had been torn from the hands of the large landowners. Aristocratic and bourgeois Spain, when not in sympathy with the insurgents, was lying low. In many places, the Catholic Church paid the price of its connivance with the ancien régime. The government of Professor José Giral retained only nominal power. The committees and militias of the CNT and the UGT had taken charge of the safety of the Republic in the name of the revolution.

But that revolution, which the army revolt brought to a boiling point, had many different faces. The anarchists, descendants of Bakunin and revolutionary syndicalism and especially strong in Catalonia and Andalusia, hoped to make it the violent prelude to a society of small, self-governed, autonomous communities, which were urged to join together freely at the regional or national level to exchange their products. The churches would be shut down as so many symbols of obscurantism, to be replaced by universal education for the regeneration of humanity through liberty and fraternity. This utopia, which reemerged from the nineteenth century, contained nothing that could rally the socialists, let alone the Communists. The former were torn between a Right that was oriented toward the center and a Left that was looking to Bolshevism; the old reformer Largo Caballero fancied himself the Spanish Lenin, and the socialist youth organization (JSU) was caught up in the fusion with its Communist equivalent. The Spanish Communist Party, still weak in terms of activists and voters, had been taken in hand again by envoys from Moscow, as had all sections of the International. It, too, was behind the winning initiative of the Frente popular in February. Amid all this revolutionary effervescence, it boasted a policy of republican defense. To this centrifugal diversity of political forces we must add the statutes of autonomy accorded to the Catholic and reactionary provinces such as the Basque countries and the Navarre, and the unpredictable behavior of the Catalonians: for in Catalonia the middle and petty bourgeoisie, both urban and rural, found itself caught between the anarchists demands and centralization from Madrid.

Given the Spanish political situation in July 1936, the only way to avoid a republican triumph as the outcome of the revolution seemed to be a second civil war to decide the true winners of the first: Would it be the anarchists, the Trotskyists, the socialists, the Communists, or even one of the various autonomous movements? As the unity of the Republic openly disintegrated from the army revolt, the national crisis brought out a profusion of different Spains born of conflicts that had been accumulating for generations. Behind the apparent simplicity of the two camps—officers and clergy on one side, workers and peasants on the other—lay general dislocation, local powers improvised at gun point, violence, and assassinations. To this multitude of tiny revolutionary or counterrevolutionary republics, the notions of Fascism and anti-Fascism lent some kind of ideological consistency.

The banner of Fascism brought a modern orientation and the promise of victory to the Spanish counterrevolution. For the Spanish Revolution, it was anti-Fascism that lent it what unity it could muster. The counterrevolution brought together primarily the army and the traditionalistic church. The revolution united forces which, though they were almost all revolutionary, were heterogeneous and even hostile to one another and thus irreparably divided by their common ambition. In the summer, Italian and German aid to Franco, followed by the mobilization of the Comintern in the opposite direction, locked the Civil War into the two totalitarian languages. Henceforth, Spain became a central target of Soviet policy and Comintern activity, providing us with one of the best vantage points from which to reflect on the nature of the new anti-Fascist strategy.

What did Stalin want? During this period, he was obsessed with isolation, for his top priority was to avoid a head-on conflict with Nazi Germany. The treaty signed with France the year before provided scant reassurance since it carried no military commitments. For the French, it was a domestic policy maneuver to the same extent that for the Russians it was a signal to Hitler more than a commitment to the French. Stalin had seen through the strategy of the British Conservatives and a portion of the French Right precisely because he had similar intentions, though directed in the opposite direction: he wanted to blow the Nazi storm toward the West. The Spanish Civil War was the opportunity he had been waiting for: should it reach international dimensions, it would anchor the Fascist powers in the far West of Europe, with a good chance that France, where the Left was in power, would be dragged into the conflict. The war, of course, had to last a while, so the Republic had to be provided with additional means for it to keep up the fight. If Franco should eventually win, Stalin would have anchored the battle between Fascism and anti-Fascism far away from the USSR, minimizing its risks. If he should lose, a bloodless Spanish Republic would remain, which would become a Soviet satellite—good currency for any purpose. In both cases and for a minimal investment, Spain was an anti-Fascist showcase for Soviet propaganda as well as a coded message to Hitler.

At the end of August, Stalin joined the nonintervention pact so as not to cut himself off from the international community, especially the Western powers. On the other hand, he did not respect the terms of the pact any more than did the Germans and the Italians, whose first deliveries of arms and aircraft in early August surely played a decisive role in the initial success of the insurrection. Even as he signed the pact, Stalin used its fictitious character as an argument to intervene and send more of his own people than weapons and more political personnel than soldiers. Just as the Moscow show trials were getting under way, the Spanish Republic was being occupied by a extensive Soviet mission based in Barcelona and Madrid.

The Soviet intervention in Spain now had a dual objective, military as well as political. On the military side, it sought to stop the progress of the insurgent army, already in control of the northwestern half of Spain and Andalusia. The Soviet Union had furnished—or rather sold, for the Spanish Treasury's gold—arms, aircraft, and tanks, which were operational in October. The Comintern had also established the International Brigades. In November, the Francoist columns were stopped at the gateway to Madrid. The terrible battles around Madrid in the winter of 1936–37 evidenced a balance of forces that augured a long war.

Stalin's price for his services had become clear: he expected republican Spain to accord special priority to his men in the conduct of the nation's affairs. This aspect of the Spanish affair has long been taboo and to some extent remains so, despite the many accounts and studies confirming it, most of which have been met with silence:[65] it was too damaging to the image of anti-Fascist Communism. Indeed, the aid to Spain given by Stalin and the Comintern was accompanied by an increasing hold over the political orientation of the Spanish government. Once in Spain, after October 1936, Soviet personnel and their affiliates were installed all over the country in the usual half-public, half-clandestine forms—an embassy, the NKVD, military and civil advisers, remote-controlled fellow travelers. The Soviet Union controlled the International Brigades, which were under the command of confirmed Cominternians, as well as the Spanish Communist Party, which had risen to prominence from its very small beginnings, thanks to Moscow's aid to the Republic. In September 1936, it was at the Party's insistence that Giral, weakened and buffeted by the winds of the Spanish Revolution, ceded his seat as chief of the government to Largo Caballero, the old socialist whose rhetoric was much prized by the Spanish public. But Caballero, although he managed to reestablish a minimum of unity in the running of the country, was not sufficiently docile for the Communists. He opposed the fusion of the Socialist and Communist parties—

a Comintern technique destined for a great future but which, in its trial run, was a failure, effectively sealing Caballero's fate.

The Communist strategy involved two apparently contradictory tactics that were in fact complementary. It celebrated the anti-Fascist union along with a larger-scale reunification of all republicans, from revolutionary workers to liberal bourgeois. Next, it called for a strong central government, to run the war effort, and a moderate welfare policy, the precondition of class unity. This strategy reveals what separated the Communists from all the various branches of the anarchists and, above all, what distinguished them from the intransigent partisans of worker and peasant self-rule or of the redistribution of great properties to the communities of residents, to say nothing of the church burners. The Spanish Communists were even more opposed to the ever-mounting revolutionary tone of militants who had come through Communism and had left it, disappointed but without losing any of their subversive fervor. This was the case with members of POUM (Partido Obrero de Unificación Marxista), which was born in September 1935 of the joining of the two dissident groups of Communists and even included one of Trotsky's old followers.[66] It would prove a difficult gathering for Stalin's envoys, occurring as it did during the first Moscow show trial.

They had no difficulty, however, in using the need to unite the republicans to justify their condemnation of Leftism. The exigencies of the hour seemed sufficient to put right on their side. Their policies had a second facet that was concealed by the idea of public safety: the control of the Republic they had come to defend. One should read Burnett Bolloten's two books to realize how deeply the Communists had penetrated the Spanish republican state administration and how that state, from the fall of 1936 on, was increasingly subject to the injunctions of the USSR's representative. In Spain there was a miniature Soviet government, headed by a representative of the NKVD named Orlov,[67] who took orders directly from Ezhov and Stalin, executing them by means of a vast network of intermediary institutions and associates or docile accomplices. Franco-British nonintervention gave Stalin a monopoly on blackmail, using military aid, while the campaign to save Spain served as a cover for its transformation into a Soviet satellite state.

Everything about this operation, including a mixture of brutality and prudence, bore Stalin's mark. Unlike Mussolini, he did not risk an overt takeover—he sent his secret services to buy and deliver arms to Spain with cash or gold. The International Brigades were the mainstay of the Comintern. A great many Russian advisers took the road to Spain, but no one saw them at the front; they had to remain in the shadows. Finally,

Stalin imposed his conditions on a weak partner surrounded by his en-voys and their local henchmen. In November, when the nomination of the supreme commander of the republican army came up, it was Gen-eral Berzin, one of the chiefs of the Soviet mission, who put forth the name of José Miaja, a weak, vain man, not particularly left-wing and thus all the more malleable. Was it necessary to name a junta for the defense of Madrid during the period when fighting was going on in the university residence halls? Koltsov, the *Pravda* correspondent, took care of everything, relying on the socio-Communist youth groups. Better still, the substitution in May 1937 of Juan Negrin for Caballero as the head of government was largely the result of Soviet intrigue; to the old leader of the socialist Left, who was not always very docile, the Russians preferred a brilliant university graduate who came from the right wing of the Socialist Party and was more easily manipulated and less anti-Communist than the leader of his group, Indalecio Prieto, the next in line for the job.

Stalin's goal was neither to salvage liberty nor to come to the aid of revolution in Spain. Nor was it the defeat of the Francoist insurrection; he would probably have been satisfied merely to bar Franco from victory so as to maintain the European war in a place that allowed him to hedge a bet and fix the Germans' attention on the West. His objective was to put republican Spain under the Soviet influence and to make it a "friend of the USSR"—an expression that implied leaving the bourgeoisie in place so long as it was pro-Soviet. It was the Comintern version of the Popular Front on an international scale. This strategy was neither de-fensive nor offensive but both, since it could serve either as a basis for negotiations in case of a setback or as a chance to move toward a Soviet-style "revolution" of the sort that would occur under different circum-stances in Central and Eastern Europe after World War II. In 1936, the order of the day was defense. In any event, though far from home, Stalin had marked out his territory.

The most typical event in his seizure of the Spanish Republic was the repression of the non-Communist revolutionary Left in Catalonia, which he controlled from Moscow in the spring of 1937 just before Negrin took over the government. The famous "May days" in Barce-lona have been recounted by Orwell in his *Homage to Catalonia:*[68] trig-gered by a Communist attempt to take over the anarchist-controlled telephone exchange, the May days dug the Spanish Revolution's grave. Starting 3 May, the great working-class city built barricades, while the Catalonian government, supported by the republican Left and the Com-munists, more or less maintained its hold over the bourgeois neigh-borhoods. The libertarian uprising eluded the control of the CNT and the FAI, who sought a political escape from the situation. The anarchist youth groups, the POUM, the Trotskyists, and the "Friends of Durruti"[69] did their best to control things, calling for the dissolution of the legal authorities and for a Catalonian Constitutional Congress made up of the basic committees. The crisis was partly resolved after 5 May, with the formation of a new Catalonian government from which the minister of the interior, who had covered the attack on the *telefónica*, was excluded, but its political composition was hardly different from what had preceded it. On 6 and 7 May, the arrival of the troops sent from Barcelona by the Valencian government ended the fighting: the victory of the republican bourgeoisie and the Catalonian Communists would also be paid for by a receding of provincial autonomy.

The problem that had hung over everyone's head since the victory of the Spanish Popular Front in February 1936 was decided in May 1937 in Barcelona by the victory of Marx over Bakunin, and of "socialism," in the broadest sense of the term, over anarchism. The difference between February 1936 and May 1937 was that, in the meantime, "socialism" had taken on an increasingly Communist cast. The little Spanish Communist Party had become great and powerful, fortified by the conjuncture of the Civil War, Italian and German intervention, Western passivity, and Soviet aid.

The Party had increased its sway over public opinion—especially moderate public opinion—by presenting itself as having subordinated everything to victory over Franco, while anarchist anti-Fascism, by making the overthrow of public authority its top priority, called into question the very existence of the state and the waging of war. But the argument in the name of public safety, which the Communist Party frequently invoked, took into account only its official actions and not its hidden motivations. Though the Spanish Communists, in their propaganda, benefited from Soviet aid to the Republic, they were also the intermediaries of the Soviet advisers' investment in Spain. Russian aid was proportional to the Spanish government's willingness to follow the "advice" of the envoys from Moscow. Thus the Spanish Republic became more and more subordinated to its powerful ally, to whom it had opened up its military, diplomatic, and police establishments, with guaranteed impunity for its nationals' actions.

Histories of the Spanish Civil War, whether written from the left or from the right, all confirm that these conditions prevailed in the Spanish Republic in the spring of 1937. Perhaps the most remarkable aspect was the constitution of an apparatus of repression directly controlled by Soviet services with procedures, agents, and prisons, independent of the Spanish state. Indeed, in the repression that liquidated the POUM after the May demonstrations in Barcelona, everything bore the Soviet stamp: the accusations of "Hitlerian Trotskyism," the particular hatred reserved for the extreme Left, the blatant lies, the extraction of confessions by torture, the assassinations. At the very same time as the Tukhachevsky trial, Orlov was proceeding in Spain just as Ezhov was doing in the USSR, since he had his own private prisons there. Take, for example, the June 1937 assassination of Andrés Nin, a former Bolshevik, secretary to Trotsky, then founder of the "Communist Left" in Spain, and finally one of the leaders of POUM—all of which qualified him as a prime candidate for Stalin's torturers and assassins. The Soviet contribution to the atrocities committed during the Spanish Civil War was distinguished by the deliberate effort to lump its victims together with those of the Moscow trials. The POUM was labeled Trotskyist, hence Hitlerian, hence Francoist.

In many ways, Stalin's experience in Spain was more political than military. The Spanish Civil War has repeatedly been described as the first testing ground for the coming world war. Historians have drawn comparisons between arms, tanks, and airplanes. Hitler's *Blitzkrieg*, however, emerged only in September 1939, when the Panzer divisions rolled into Poland. What was being tested in Spain was the political technique of "popular democracy" that would flourish in Central and Eastern Europe after 1945.[70] Its theoretical basis was already in place: the Spanish democratic republic, which the Communists professed to defend in the name of anti-Fascism, was in fact a new type of republic with a unique social content; it was not yet entirely proletarian, but the roots of the bourgeois order had already been destroyed or were being destroyed.[71] This byzantine theory said two contradictory things: that anti-Fascist Communism was defending bourgeois democracy, and that it was suppressing it. But, as was often the case with Communist language, it was advantageous to say what in another respect was concealed: that "consistent" anti-Fascist Communism ought to have brought political predominance to the Communists. I do not agree with Hugh Thomas's contention that, after the anarchist defeat of May 1937 and the formation of the Negrin government, two counterrevolutions were face to face—one led by Franco and the other led by the Spanish Communist Party in the shadow of the new prime minister.[72] The term "counterrevolution" is appropriate for Franco but not for the other camp. It is indeed true that the Communists crushed a revolution in Barcelona, but only in order to substitute their own.

The Spanish Communists lacked one form of decisive support enjoyed by their Romanian, Polish, Hungarian, and Czech counterparts during the postwar period—the Red Army. This was another reason for infiltrating the police and military security services and for taking control of the Ministry of War and of most on-site military commands. It would be erroneous to claim that they spearheaded the "anti-Fascist" battle, but they did divide and weaken the Fascist movement by imposing their own goals, constantly pursued through the political disqualification or physical elimination of adversaries within their own camp. When they were at the height of their influence in the spring of 1938, when Negrin's second cabinet was being formed, the military situation was still tolerable, for the armies had victoriously defended Valencia and would soon turn to the offensive on the Ebro. But pressure from the Communists, which may have been effective in the unification of the military organization, ended up destroying the political foundation of Spanish anti-Fascism. When they finally got their old adversary Prieto removed from the Ministry of Defense, all that the Communists controlled was a political stage littered with ghosts: they had killed the popular revolution, destroyed the POUM, reduced Catalonian autonomy, enlisted the anarchists, alienated the left and right wings of the Socialist Party represented by Caballero and Prieto, and compelled Azaña to follow them;[73] thus was the flame of the Spanish Republic extinguished. The authority it had finally mustered to beat Franco was less republican than pretotalitarian. "For a long time I have been saying," Luis Araquistáin wrote to his daughter, "that whether we are defeated or whether we win the war the independent Socialists will have to emigrate, because in the first case we shall be assassinated by Franco or in the second by the Communists."[74]

This testimony detracts nothing from the wrongs wrought, on the part of Britain and France, by the policy of nonintervention, which had in reality been pure passivity. On the contrary, by turning a blind eye to Italian and German support, and by leaving republican Spain all but alone with Stalin as far as military aid was concerned, the Western democracies aggravated the Soviet blackmailing of Caballero and Negrin. I see no reason to retract the condemnation of Anglo-French passivity toward Hitler, even if the role played by public opinion was generally underestimated. Nonintervention in Spain, as practiced by London and Paris, followed the cowardly submission of 7 March 1936 and prefigured the spirit of Munich.

To condemn the Anglo-French policy, however, is not to imply that the British and the French, rather than consenting to or suggesting territorial gains to the east to Hitler—something particularly delicate for the French, given its system of alliances—should have participated in Moscow's anti-Fascist logic. It was one thing to know how to hierarchize the various perils and another to succumb to the mirages of ideology.

London and Paris were guilty of having attempted to play Hitler against Stalin, not of having mistrusted Stalin. Like them, the Georgian was playing a double game. We may make endless conjectures about what Stalin, in his heart of hearts, disliked more—National Socialism or the Western democracies. What is certain is that he was not taken in by the pacifists' nonsense. He was increasingly sure that war was imminent, and he was haunted by the USSR's isolation. The hypothesis of a war between the imperialist powers, however, had always been part of the ABCs of Communism.

In Moscow, eyes were also trained on Berlin. In his memoirs,[75] the Soviet agent Krivitsky, who had defected to the West in 1937 after being a "resident" NKVD in Holland with an eye on Eastern Europe, affirmed that Stalin had actually been seeking an accord with Hitler since 1934. His rapprochement with France, and then with the Eastern European states, was but a detour on the way to his goal. A Soviet envoy to Berlin sounded out the possibility of a pact in February 1937 but returned empty handed.[76] The least one can say is that Stalin had kept two irons in the fire; he let this be understood from 1934 on, and stated it clearly after Munich. He knew very well that European international life had three poles, not two as implied by anti-Fascism. The problem was that the three poles formed three antagonistic pairs, precluding any true alliance.

The Spanish Civil War was no exception to this rule. Britain, followed by France, wanted nothing to do with the mounting revolutionary tide, let alone anything that would risk a war with Hitler. Stalin, for his part, was also extremely wary of being drawn into a major conflict with the German dictator. If we can believe Krivitsky, what Stalin really wanted to do was to show Hitler that he was a good interlocutor. Another theory is that he wanted to draw Britain and France onto a battlefield that would "fix," by means a long war, the explosive aspect of the international situation at a price the USSR could afford and far from its borders. Hugh Thomas has described this strategy in three sentences:

> [Stalin] would not permit the republic to lose, even though he would not necessarily help it to win. The continuance of the war would keep him free to act in any way. It might even make possible a world war in which France, Britain, Germany, and Italy would destroy themselves, with Russia, the arbiter, staying outside.[77]

In all these cases, Spain was a pawn in the hands of the Soviets.

History, however, would have it differently. Earlier than anticipated, the war in Spain would be relegated to a secondary position in the international situation. In 1938, the European crisis shifted from Spain to Austria and then, in summer, toward Sudetenland. Hitler had more important maneuvers in mind than military aid to Franco. He was considering repatriating the Condor legion (an idea he eventually gave up). The British were in discussion with the Italians. The French were also, for the Italian alliance, ailing from Mussolini's massive intervention in Spain, was an old idea of the Quai d'Orsay. Stalin was preoccupied with Hitler's threats to Central Europe and was trying to reduce his involvement in Spain. Negrin himself was making advances (which came to nothing) toward Franco for a compromise peace, failing which the republican army fought the terrible battle of the Ebro, which was raging at the time of the Sudeten movement in September 1938. The Franco-British capitulation at Munich pushed Stalin toward an accord with Hitler—a possibility he had never abandoned. It provided him with one more reason to pull back from Spain, as symbolized by the retreat of the International Brigades in the fall.

Thereafter, Spain became a secondary theater in the European tragedy, destined for imminent liquidation. Deprived of its revolutionary source, lacking a discourse of its own, exhausted by the violent acts committed by itself and its enemies, Negrin's and Azaña's Republic could conceive of no future other than a world war, in which it would finally find the British and the French on its side. It never actually went that far.[78] Yet the Republic, though defeated, became legendary.

The memory of the Spanish Republic remained precious to those who had lost everything but the honor of a just fight. Although it had incarnated democratic values since July 1936, the Francoist insurrection never held a candle to it in the symbolic domain. The republican camp, as we have seen, embraced European revolutionary romanticism in a whole range of forms—those of Bakunin and Marx, of Sorel and Lenin. The social imagination of 1848 was glorified by the rhetoric of the Spanish Left. Franco, with his coup d'état, endowed this brilliant universe, segmented by diverse ideas and human rivalry, with a semblance of unity. In the interest of that unity, he forsook all democratic practices and imposed the threat of a military dictatorship.

The nationalist general had no spark of what made Fascism fascinating at the time, and his version of dictatorship was oligarchical and old-fashioned. José Primo de Rivero had been a charismatic leader, and the first form of the Falange had been an ideological militia. Franco was a traditional military man, and the second Falange was a party of order. The dictatorship that emerged victorious from the Civil War was closer to a reactionary autocracy based on the Church and the landowners than to a totalitarian power imposed in the name of the popular masses under the flag of social nationalism. Predemocratic as much as antidemocratic, it offered an easy target for its adversaries.

The repertoire presented by Franco's regime was too familiar to make credible its protestations that it was not out to destroy Communism. By reviving the counterrevolutionary Right, hostile to the modern world, it was bound to threaten all liberals. Unlike other Fascist movements, however, it remained incapable of drawing into its fold those who were disappointed with democratic equality or socialism. Francoism owed its particular ferocity more to its espousal of a moral order than to its promise of community. Certainly, little mercy had been shown by any camp, and the anarchists and the Communists had themselves spilled a lot of unnecessary or "innocent" blood. But the Francoist troops bombed or killed in the name of God; they had emblazoned it on their flags, along with eternal Spain, religion, and property. They brought back into the twentieth century a Catholic Middle Ages linked to the social panic of the nineteenth-century bourgeoisie. So their massacres often revived hostile feelings that predated anti-Fascism. Public opinion in traditionally Protestant countries, notably Great Britain and the United States, saw the specter of the Inquisition. In France, part of the Catholic intelligentsia—with Mauriac and Bernanos at the fore—viewed with horror the enlistment of their faith in the service of Francoism.

Finally, what role did the Comintern play in the ideological orchestration of the Spanish Civil War? A capital one, for Münzenberg was at the height of his powers at the time,[79] and for him the event was almost providential. What better proof than Spain of the identity of anti-Fascism and democracy? Mussolini and Hitler rushed to the aid of Franco in order to substitute dictatorship for the Republic; the Soviet intervention was thus ennobled almost automatically as champion of democracy. The little village of Guernica, the age-old home of Basque liberties, was destroyed by German planes of the Condor legion on 26 April 1937: What could have been more emblematic of the conflict? The first major demonstration of a modern air raid revealed the barbarism of a Fascist International and, consequently, the need for anti-Fascist international solidarity. Through the Spanish Civil War, the Soviet Union appeared to be lending a real universal substance to internationalism.

As we have noted, the Soviets intervened in Spain neither as a fraternal power nor even in the name of its exclusive interests or plans. It did so in conformity with its tendency as a totalitarian party-state—less to help the Republic than to take military and political control of it. The

Russians had sold airplanes and arms to Spain, but in the meantime they were liquidating the POUM, assassinating Nin, and filling the republican camp with their own police. Communist anti-Fascism had two faces, neither of which happened to be democratic; the first face, that of solidarity, which had ennobled so many soldiers, perpetually concealed the pursuit of power and the confiscation of liberty.

This is why the legend of the Spanish Civil War, as it was passed from generation to generation, consisted of equal doses of truth and lies. Anti-Fascism had been the standard of the Spanish Revolution before becoming its shroud a year later, in July 1936. A bouquet of democratic and libertarian passions, it wilted from both ambiguous dogma and police practices. It went so far as to kill republican energy under the pretext of organizing it, just as it compromised the republican cause under the guise of defending it. But none of this could be admitted, for then it would be necessary to attribute blame, which could further weaken the republican side. Orwell had hardly returned to England after fighting with the POUM troops when he wrote in a British weekly that the Spanish Civil War had produced "a richer crop of lies than any event since the Great War of 1914–1918."[80] Orwell knew what he was talking about. He was one of the few engagé intellectuals of the century capable of seeing the truth and putting reality before abstraction.[81] He only joined up with the POUM militia on the advice of the small libertarian party he belonged to in England, the Independent Labour Party. He might just as well have joined a Communist battalion, and probably would have preferred it. What opened his eyes, before he was wounded on the Front at Aragon, was witnessing the Communist terror directed at the anarchists and the POUM activists in Barcelona in the spring of 1937. After his release from the hospital he had to go into hiding until he managed to reach France. Alone, or almost alone, among the foreign fighters, and amid the general silence of the left-wing press, Orwell resolved to tell what he had seen. Six months after his July 1937 article, he stated, "A number of people had said to me with varying degrees of frankness that one must not tell the truth about what was happening in Spain and the part played by the communist party because to do so would be to prejudice public opinion against the Spanish government and so aid Franco."[82]

Thus the history of the Spanish Civil War was covered with a blanket of silence and lies that would remain in place throughout the twentieth century.

This is not to say that anti-Fascism, even in its Communist form and among the official militants, did not mobilize a passion for liberty. Quite obviously, the opposite was true: the International Brigades, tightly

controlled by Moscow, did not mouth servile slogans or entertain du-
plicitous thoughts. A wealth of literature demonstrates enthusiasm for
the Spanish cause, even within the Comintern, in the form of combatants' memoirs written after their emancipation from Communism.[83]
One example is the German writer Gustav Regler, who, having fled the
Moscow of Loubianka and the Kamanev trial into the International Brigades, proclaimed: "As long as there are still Fascists, we are all
Spanish."[84]

The militants' "Spanish" enthusiasm in no way altered the reality of
Communists politics, and the Spanish Civil War did nothing to alter its
nature. But the war offered a new arena for the illusion, as well as the
first international battlefield for anti-Fascism. Even for those disillusioned by Communism, it would remain the glory of the just battle
against Franco. Many of them, indeed, happy to have espoused half of
a good cause, had no desire to look at the other half too carefully. So the
taboo on the Spanish Civil War, deliberately maintained by Stalinist
historiographers, found complicity in the fighters' memories. As for
those who chose to break the silence and tell the truth about what Moscow was up to, whether they were anarchists, old dissidents of Bolshevism, victims of the 1937–38 repression, or Comintern members whose
eyes had been opened in Spain, they not only risked blackening their
own history but were accused of helping the cause of the enemy. Communist anti-Fascism profited from the logic of war, which added its
weight in blood to that of class struggle.

Malraux, as always, described the truth and the myths of the Spanish
affair without attempting to distinguish between them. With the first
shot, he immediately perceived the historical ballast borne by that local
conflict, located at the periphery of the European world. Almost twenty
years after the rise of the Russian Soviets in Europe's far East, the Spanish workers' movement had rekindled the flame of the revolution in its
far West. The Bolsheviks, however, had only to leap from war into
Communist dictatorship in order to erase the idea of Russian backwardness from the world's imagination; for the Spanish Republic, reincar-
nating the revolution was not enough, since its image did not conform
to the Soviet model. But here was the Republic, exposed to the aggression of a reactionary general, supported by Mussolini and Hitler; by
planting Fascism squarely on the counterrevolutionary side, the Republic became universal by virtue of its adversary.

By the same token, at least provisionally, the Spanish Republic assumed a place in the center of world affairs. The war of July 1936 concentrated and simplified the political passions of the century. Its armed activity had made those passions heroic, and its anti-Fascism had brought

them up to a European, universal level. It reduced the complexity into two camps, Fascists and anti-Fascists. Malraux certainly suspected a self-serving motive underlying this dichotomy—so dear to the Russians—but he justified it by the imperatives of the war. When participating in the start of the Spanish Civil War, heading a squadron of volunteers, he was still in his Communist period. He was temperamentally inclined to exalt the human will rising up against the tragedy of history. That provisional equilibrium nurtured his writing of a typical book of the era—*L'Espoir* (Hope), an anti-Fascist novel with a pessimistic tone.

The charm of *L'Espoir* lies in its combining the servitude of bearing arms with the liberty of democracy. The plot takes place at the beginning of the war, between 19 July and the victorious defense of Madrid at the end of the year. That was indeed a memorable time, bubbling with revolutionary fervor in the wake of the recent military uprising, and characterized by the heroic disorder of a new beginning, the formation of citizen armies, and even the ephemeral benediction of victory. The French Revolution had only entered the campaign against monarchical Europe three years after its eruption. The Spanish Revolution was all but born with the war, since the months that separated the electoral success from the Francoist insurrection were merely a brief preface, between February and July. So its life was like that of an army, though the spirit that had animated it detested authority. The Spanish revolution is the tormented protagonist of *L'Espoir*, incarnated by the cosmopolitan squadron and the improvised battalions that fought between Toledo and Madrid.

The reason the Spanish Revolution was entitled to public support was not because it was revolutionary. Too many contradictory ideas were jostling under that rubric! To the future fighters who had already begun their battle within the anti-Fascist war, Malraux lent his mental agility through a gallery of argumentative combatants, to whom he listened as if to voices of his own talent. Through him, the century of political messianism found its heroes. Yet the only wisdom that the novelist expressed through their dialogues was something older—the practical advice of action. "The Communists," Garcia says to Hernandez when Alcazar is under siege, "want to do something. You and the anarchists, for different reasons, want to *be* something . . . That's the drama of any revolution like this one. The myths we live under are contradictory: pacifism and the necessity of defense, organization and Christian myths, efficiency and justice, and so forth. We ought to organize them, transform our Apocalypse into an army, or die. That's it."[85] Or, a little further on, "Action can only be conceived of in terms of action."

Nonetheless, Malraux knew very well that in the twentieth century such a Machiavellian formula is worthless unless accompanied by an idea with a name and a touching cause. Could anti-Fascism, a simple negation, possibly be that idea, that cause? This question imbues the novel with a pessimism that is not merely a literary device, for Malraux had no philosophical or political response to it. As far as he was concerned, the fact that the republican forces' war constrained its fighters to retain fraternity among themselves was enough. That the war raised them above themselves through the exercise of noble passions and gratuitous courage was enough. Malraux was at his best when practicing what one might term psychological reporting, describing the many simple men, whether Spanish or foreign volunteers, who rediscovered in the Civil War forgotten or forbidden sentiments. To a European Left that remained profoundly wounded by the souvenirs of 1914–18, the republican Spain depicted in *L'Espoir* reestablished a moral war and a democratic form of heroism.

For Malraux, anti-Fascism was not a revolutionary philosophy. It was the banner of reconciliation between nations and war, that god of the twentieth century. From among the International Brigades, which he immortalized like a war painter, Malraux selected the Comintern's militia; he celebrated the advance guard of the fraternal army as it sought to erase the memories of the fratricidal massacre of 1914:

> Magnin went to the window: still wearing street clothes, but in military shoes, with their stubborn Communist faces and their intellectual-style hairdos, old Poles with Nietzschean mustaches or young men with faces from Soviet films, Germans with shaved heads, Algerians, Italians who looked like Spaniards who accidentally found themselves among the foreigners, English, more picturesque then the others, French who resembled Maurice Thorez or Maurice Chevalier, all of them tense, not because of the efforts of the Madrid teenagers but with the memory of the war that had made them oppose one another, the men of the brigades hammered the narrow street, as sonorous as a hallway. They approached the barracks and began to sing; for the first time in the world, men of all nations, mingled together in combat formation, sang the International.[86]

Thus Malraux gave voice to the left-wing passion for Spain at the moment when Orwell, in *Homage to Catalonia*, was already denouncing it as a lie.[87] Anyone trying to understand the ambiguities of the anti-Fascist war should read these two works together like two prophecies of something that Spain offered only in miniature. The end of the Second World War would find both authors at their posts, in new but similar roles. Malraux would see his 1936 anti-Fascism shattered by the German-Soviet pact of 1939; he would come up with a less fragile version in late Gaullism. Orwell, a melancholy sentinel of truth even at the price of action, would remain the solitary denouncer of the lies of war, blanketed this time under the flowers of victory.

EIGHT

Anti-Fascist Culture

HITLER'S ACCESSION TO POWER IN GERMANY
and the Comintern's anti-Fascist shift profoundly altered the distribution of political power in Europe. The violence of the Nazis and the
Moscow-originated strategy of the Popular Front had polarized relations between the Left and the Right around the issues of Fascism and
Communism, making this period a critical one that would long influence attitudes and feelings. France, thanks both to its tradition and to
its weakness, provides the best observatory. A laboratory for democratic
politics in the nineteenth century, France would continue to play this
role into the twentieth: imprisoned in memories that were revived by
the Bolsheviks, the French did not miss this last chance to relive their
history through a body of doctrines still governed by 1789 and 1793.
But their country was no longer the most powerful in Europe, although
its victories in 1918 allowed it to maintain that illusion; France had become a haven for an exhausted people and a timid bourgeoisie with a
limited political life and a dependent diplomacy. The tendency, characteristic of the age, to internationalize domestic politics was evident in
France. Not that it had been reduced to a mere battlefield for the Communists and Fascists: Communists certainly did not predominate on the
left, and there were very few true Fascists on the right. The Left was,
however, regrouped into the Front populaire—a Communist initiative,
and the Right was generally sympathetic, if not to Fascism, at least to
the anti-Communism of the Fascist regimes. The parties' democratic
fight for power had thus moved closer to the two sources of antidemocratic inspiration, which reinforced each other through their mutual antagonism.

Another justification for a detour through France is the special place
accorded the intellectual aspect of political debates in France. Although
our central concern is not the influence of Communism on thinkers or

writers,[1] but to retrace the mythology of the USSR and Communism in general, at this point in the present history, when Bolshevism was finding its second youth even as it was tasting its first great international political triumphs, a closer look at intellectuals may be instructive. For they alone offer a detailed look at the patchwork of images and ideas that contributed to the new political balance. Of course, to the extent that intellectuals form a distinct social group, intellectuals were certainly not immune to the blindness of the period, nor did they have a clearer vision than others of the future: indeed, they supported deplorable causes in such numbers and with such enthusiasm that twentieth-century history tends to prove the contrary. They were, however, obliged to elaborate their reasoning and consequently to explain its origins and formation, its interconnections and breaks, its logic and contradictions.

This perspective does not exist for other periods, particularly those prior to modern democracy when politics was concentrated in a very few hands and was not imbued with passions akin to those elicited by religion. In the twentieth century, even when reduced to servitude by an omnipotent party, people have been bombarded with the slogans through which "Big Brother" has renewed his basis for total domination over each citizen. On the other hand, when citizens have remained free to choose their own leaders and have been protected by law from abuses of power, they still have to preserve that freedom and collectively to determine its means and limits: individuals and parties pool their ideas and solutions. Since the first peak of ideological overinvestment in politics occurred in the 1930s, let us examine the articulation of ideas, expectations, and passions of that period through the prism of the intellectuals.

The paths of French politics and of French intellectuals have constantly intersected with one another. Since the eighteenth century, writers, philosophers, and artists have played a greater political role in France than in any other European country. This was particularly true of the interwar period. The spectacle of Communism and Fascism castigating parliamentary democracy and the ensuing confrontation as they disputed its last remains presented a new drama to French intellectuals, specialists in the universal. The stage was huge, the plot decisive— nothing less than to change the human condition. One hundred and twenty-eight years after the French Revolution, the Bolsheviks had reappropriated the revolutionaries' liberating project to take it one step further: themselves emancipated from the self-imposed bourgeois limits of the men of 1789, they now set out to emancipate the proletariat and thus all of humanity.

The line at once continuous and broken that links the two revolutions cast a particularly powerful spell over the French Left. October 1917 was linked to 1789 by a vision of historical progress, a sorry version of Marxism taking up where the philosophy of the Enlightenment had left off. It situated the Soviet Union on the path discovered by France, making it the second advance-guard nation more than a century after the first. Those among the French—and there were many of them— who wanted to connect with the new trailblazer of humanity that had emerged from their traces had only to transfer a little pride in the universality of their revolutionary history to the homeland of the proletariat. Doing so provided some consolation for the wretchedness of their current situation.

Fascism was another factor in the Left's motivation to maintain their connection with the good old days through Russian Communism: it revived the counterrevolutionary idea in all its threatening glory. The Bolsheviks had already compared themselves to the Jacobins, and, from 1918 on, the anti-Soviet war of intervention was sufficient to remind the French of the heroics of 1793. Fascism or, in this case, Nazism represented an even more vigorous enemy than the disparate coalition of weak armies brought together or financed by the winners of the First World War. Hitler lent anti-Sovietism the gleam of an ideology and the seduction of power. He conveniently provided the formidable adversary required by the revolutionary spirit, lending substance to its mission. Before being provided with such an imminent menace, Stalin had invented one, justifying his use of the "third phase" diplomacy by the existence of a vast imperialist conspiracy, poised to attack the USSR. From 1933 on, the Nazi danger, which was only too real, offered him an additional reason, which he seized, to clothe the Terror in the Jacobin tradition. References to the great precedent of the First Republic were all the more familiar because the enemy in question was not merely the counterrevolution but Germany, everlasting Germany, barely defeated but already threatening.

France, as a nation with a revolutionary tradition, that is, a democratic and antiliberal one, as distinct from Germany, which was neither democratic nor liberal, or England, which was more liberal than democratic, saw itself as having special connections with the regime of 17 October.

We must beware, however, of obscuring the remarkable universality of the Communism of this period. Its influence was visible everywhere, even in Britain, although there it did not reach down to the working class, despite the efforts of the small British Communist Party, as zealous as its French counterpart in reacting to the same directives. Intellectuals, perhaps less subject to class solidarity, more indignant with their own government, and surely more sensitive to Nazism's threat to culture and to the attractions of the universal, welcomed Communist anti-Fascism. Until 1934–35, as we have seen, the Soviet experience had the sympathy of several major British writers. Yet we cannot accuse a writer such as Bernard Shaw of "anti-Fascist" philo-Sovietism, for his loyalty to the Marxist and then Fabian anticapitalism of his youth, combined with his wish to *épater le bourgeois*, led him to admire Mussolini and Hitler and to esteem Stalin at the same time. On the other hand, the following generation did not grow up with the causes of the socialist Left. Their political awakening arose from hostility to victorious Nazism, which the Tories treated with indulgence.[2]

Many of these young anti-Fascist intellectuals came from upper-class families, and many had cut their teeth in the rarefied air of the Bloomsbury group, the circle that formed around Virginia and Leonard Woolf. One of the best witnesses to this era was Stephen Spender.[3] He was a young, intelligent and sensitive Englishman; a gifted poet, he was indifferent to the political passions of the century until Hitler's appearance. His intellectual trajectory reminds one of Lukács at a decade's remove, as it brought him from ivory-tower aestheticism to a passionate commitment to a new dawn of history. The despondency of the age culminated with Hitler's emergence, but perhaps there was also the glimmer of a promise: like Fascism, Communism was fueled, in the opposite direction, by the idea of a tabula rasa and the end of the bourgeois world. Spender's conversion to Communism was continuous with tradition: "I am a Communist because I am a liberal,"[4] he wrote when he joined the Party, claiming kinship to something best described as English "radicalism" and which extended from Thomas Paine to J. S. Mill, by way of Godwin and Bentham.

He was using "liberal" in its political and even its most libertarian sense, as a lover of liberty and a partisan of maximum liberty—both civil and political—for each individual. Communism was fashioned in such a way that it could crystallize, at least provisionally, both liberal and antiliberal sentiments and could accommodate both adversaries and admirers of the state. Whether taken as a historical reality in the shape of the Soviet regime, or as a philosophical prophecy in the form of humanity no longer alienated, it had a miraculous dual nature. Having ensured that it would remain a utopia even after becoming a state, Communism had to conceal its reality in order to remain an "idea," which is why ideology played such an important role in its operations and propaganda. Hitler added plausibility to the illusion by denigrating, from without, both bourgeois democracy and Communism; it was easy for Spender to turn that double condemnation, traditional in German culture, against the Nazi dictator. By celebrating in tandem the two forms of government that Hitler had denigrated in tandem, he created a "liberal" showcase for the USSR.[5]

Western philo-Sovietism would reach its apogee in Britain with the members of the famous "Cambridge group"[6]—Kim Philby, Guy Burgess, Donald MacLean, Anthony Blunt,[7] and perhaps others whose names we have yet to discover. They were not simply admirers of the Soviet Union; nor were they British Communist Party activists. They went to work for the Soviet spy network and, young as they were, entered directly into a commitment that was both unconditional and irreversible. Their case illustrates the conspiratorial nature of the international Communist movement and the strong devotion it could elicit. The issue of these men's espionage belongs to the history of Communism and is beyond the scope of this book. That of their commitment, however, is germane to our concerns insofar as it provides the most radical example of Western intellectuals' passion for Communism.

In Britain, the Russian Revolution had greater success in universities than in factories. The history of the Cambridge Group is an object lesson in the social isolation of young revolutionaries at British universities in the early 1930s and the particularly abstract nature of their commitment. What made them similar to all those who, in the same period, wanted to be on the front line of the battle against Fascism was their conviction that only the Communist movement offered an anti-Fascist strategy and the means to "guide" the working class. What made them different was that in order to throw their lot in with the proletariat, they chose or accepted an extraordinarily simple path, aristocratic because it was the loftiest—direct service to the country of the proletariat in question. In the series of abstractions that form the intellectual foundation of Communist beliefs, they deliberately situated themselves at the most general level and identified the Soviet state with the international workers' revolution. Having bypassed the intermediary stages of militant activity, they found themselves on an equal footing with universal history.

Their motives were thus free of what is usually found behind espionage when it involves agents working for foreign countries—corruption, blackmail, money. At the time of their recruitment, moreover, none of these young men had anything substantial to reveal to the Soviet secret services. For the NKVD, this group was a convenient investment, whereas the men themselves were acting from political passion. Although we cannot excuse their blindness, we should consider their motivation. Their deliberate extremism that makes their case an interesting one.

The numerous accounts we have of them form a portrait of a milieu. From upper-class rather than rich families, they had been educated in the best schools before meeting at Cambridge within the venerable walls of Trinity College as Britain was reeling from the Great Depression. There they studied history and economics, whose secrets were revealed to them by Maurice Dobb, their chosen mentor, in the light of Marx's *Capital.* University life at that time favored small, elected aristocracies—Cambridge was full of them. Student life coalesced around the Communist conviction and the eccentric style of the English upper classes. These lost children of the British Empire did not appear to be militant Cominternians and shared neither the conventional mores of the Cominternians nor their democratic passion for anonymity. They were also believers, but believers from another place, carrying into the world they sought to enter the manners of the world they wished to overthrow. This surely explains why they did not join the modest British Communist Party but entered the system at the top, through the Soviet Union itself—an aristocratic way of serving the proletariat. The bohemian life, snobbery, homosexuality, whisky, and the tragedy of life all recovered a touch of chivalry in conspiracy. One of Burgess's favorite sayings was that it was better to betray one's country than one's friends.[8]

These young men were the orphans of a Britain that was disappearing before their eyes, the Britain their parents had loved and served. They were surely the first generation in centuries to have had such a strong sense that tradition was waning. World War I had cut Europe loose from its moorings. Like the Weimar intellectuals before them, the Cambridge students had lost track of their history. The Great Depression had destroyed the British economy, which only yesterday had ruled the world. Hitler had taken power in Berlin. In London, the Labour Party had foundered ingloriously in 1931, and the ruling Tories would soon be flirting with Germany's new master. After failing in Germany, Stalin's Soviet Union redirected its efforts toward Paris and London; there it found an influence among intellectuals that Lenin had never had. The Five-Year Plan presented a striking contrast to the decrepit capitalist world, and Soviet anti-Fascism put the British Conservatives and their weakness for Hitler to shame. The Soviet Union, thought of as a substitute for what British greatness had been a century earlier, seemed to be inaugurating a new era in history.

In this promise of historical continuity, British university students found something to counterbalance their disgust for their own class and a confirmation of their certainty that capitalism was in its death throes. Their hatred of the bourgeoisie was a commonplace in their time and among all European intellectuals, but unlike their French and German counterparts, these young Englishmen were in no way drawn to Fascism. Although the British liberal tradition did not protect them from the Stalinist illusion, it did at least immunize them against Nazi mythology. The purpose of their world revolution was not to reconstitute a community but to attain a higher stage of individual emancipation— a goal that fit the anti-Fascist version of Communism of those years like a glove.

The commitment that condemned them to a double life at such a young age can be explained by the international nature of the movement. There had always been two ways to serve the proletarian revolution, one public, and one secret. The young men from Cambridge were recruited as militants at an age at which they could not possibly have known any state secrets. What made them famous in the history of twentieth-century international espionage was their very success, which was largely due to fortunate circumstances, including the amateurishness of the British intelligence services at a time as critical as the war and the postwar period. Had the Cambridge group been less effective, they would be remembered less as spies and more as activists. Extraordinary as it seems today, especially in light of what they later became, their engagement essentially realized the ideas and passions held by many European intellectuals condemned to the prosaic life of a militant or to the condition of fellow traveler. Like them, Philby, MacLean, Burgess, and Blunt believed in the inevitable victory of the Soviet Union and of Communism—and they meant to have their part in it. Reinforced by the Second World War, this certainty would survive Hitler's defeat; after Hitler's fall, they found a new source of nourishment in hatred of America. The fact that one of the greatest European universities, the source of so many important ideas, had provided the USSR with its most devoted and effective agents will remain symbolic of the force of the Communist idea in the twentieth century.

Further evidence may be found in the attraction exercised by Communism, during that same period, in the United States, where the liberties and rights of individuals have always enjoyed an almost sacred respect. Although there was no dominant socialist tradition among the working classes, there was a small, bureaucratized Communist Party, which had already acquired the tormented history of all the Comintern's subsidiaries. In the late 1920s it had expelled both a right-wing and a left-wing opposition—whose Trotskyist affiliation lent it an intellectual profile it did not have in Europe. The "class against class" radicalism promulgated by Moscow during the "third phase" prevented it from mobilizing the deep anxieties of American wage earners in face of the economic crisis; Party militants elicited more violence with their anticapitalist preaching and a few successful infiltrations of the unions. Moreover, in 1935 the "Popular Front" strategy was more appropriate to the American climate of opinion. Gone was the time when President Roosevelt and even Norman Thomas, the 1931 Socialist presidential candidate, were regarded as "Social Fascists." Henceforth, the Communists positioned themselves to the left of the New Deal, where their audience increased until 1939.

The heyday of American Communism was accompanied—as in France but perhaps even more so, to the extent that the popular or electoral influence of the American Communist Party remained incomparably weaker than that of its French counterpart—by a major role in certain universities and among intellectuals and writers. The rich history of this movement has been described in detail both by contemporaries and by later historians.[9] For our present purposes, the relevance of the movement is that it provides yet another illustration of how hatred of Fascism led so many intellectuals to establish a subjective connection between Communism and liberty. At this time, the United States presented what was perhaps the most paradoxical form of the Communist illusion. The most democratic nation in the world, whose political institutions were surrounded by a sort of national cult, had elected and reelected an administration, with a very popular leader, bent on reform and progress; yet many of its intellectuals placed their hopes in the USSR when it came to defending liberty against Fascism, as though anti-Fascism were inseparable from an inevitable tendency toward Communism.

As was the case everywhere, part of this secret attraction could be explained by the simplicity of the message, combined with the exceptional organizational skills of the Communists. The profusion of leagues and associations under their control allowed the Communists to exercise a maximum of influence without diluting their propaganda, which consisted almost exclusively of pro-Sovietism. The true content of this pro-Sovietism, however, was independent of the nature of the regime in question. Its attraction was based on two elements external to the USSR—hostility to Fascism and the critique of capitalism. There was never any question of instituting Communism in the United States; the point was, rather, to defend democracy all over the world. To this quintessential American role, the tragedy of the German Jews lent a striking moral resonance and urgency that was more palpable in New York than in Paris or London. Once Stalin had turned against Hitler, how could anyone be against Stalin's own regime? The American inventory of political evil was patterned on moral law and was not sufficiently complex to contain two antagonistic tyrannies. Moreover, whereas the Soviet

Union had destroyed capitalism, Roosevelt had been content to modify it, a further reason to locate Communism to the left of the New Deal instead of casting it as another enemy of democracy. The Communists themselves set the example by a spectacular rallying to the anti-Fascist alliance. Shortly afterward, the Spanish Civil War would reveal the two camps in confrontation—democracy versus dictatorship. More than three thousand Americans, Communists as well as liberals, for the most part young teachers, set out to fight Franco in the Abraham Lincoln battalion of the International Brigades.

During the 1930s, therefore, the reaction of the American left-wing intellectuals to Communism was similar to that of their European counterparts. They were not inclined to look too closely at the internal situation of the USSR, or to judge the veracity of the confessions made by the accused in the Moscow trials. They would have their own Marxist dissidents, their own Communists thrown out of the Party, their own Trotskyists (who may have shown more resolution and enterprise than anywhere else in the world).[10] Books written during this time, such as *Out of Step*, the memoirs of Sidney Hook (one of the most clear-sighted, if self-righteous, members of this milieu), are filled with the characters of the small New York intellectual scene—the tireless and fanatical militant, the fellow traveler who sometimes had a direct line to Moscow, the Marxist distrustful of the Comintern, the unhappily anti-Soviet Trotskyist, the liberal dazzled by his encounter with the "working class," the pacifist uncertain as to the relationship between anti-Fascism and the war, and so forth—the same cast of characters that was found in France. Which leads us back to the French case, reassured, I hope, of its generality.

We must now consider the era when mass anti-Fascist culture would become definitively left-wing, independent of Communism yet inseparable from it. The period was marked by a sort of intentional ambiguity. Left-wing anti-Fascism had existed, of course, prior to 1934–35; and immediately after the war against Mussolini, among others, it flourished in its Communist, socialist, or liberal form, each nation usually fighting under its own flag. Comintern members of the "third phase" had become expert in accusing its enemies, on the left and on the right, of being Fascists. After 1934, however, the Communists were willing to drop their monopoly on anti-Fascism as long as their new allies were willing to drop their anti-Communism. It was a good deal for the Communists, since they were trading an insubstantial pretension for a priceless advantage. Anti-Fascism now became incompatible with anti-Communism, and any hatred of Hitler coupled with hostility to Stalin was seen as a facade. During the heyday of the "third phase," the Comintern did not allow any positions between the proletarian revolution and Fascism, for even the socialists were considered to be on the Fascist side. After 1935, however, the Cominternians seem to have returned some autonomy to all those intermediary forces, not only to the socialists but to the democrats, the liberals, the "republicans." It was a closely watched freedom, since they controlled the space of anti-Fascism and were still the arbiters of membership. The political universe remained two-dimensional.

The Soviet Union, no longer merely the homeland of the proletariat, also became the bastion of anti-Fascism. Labor internationalism was supposed to grow into democratic internationalism. It was a risky challenge, given what was going on in Moscow and in Russia at large, where the Terror was in full swing, but it worked. The Bolsheviks became expert in organizing trips to the USSR designed to convince selected guests to rally to the Soviet cause.[11] In 1933, as we saw in chapter 5, they got Herriot to testify that he had not seen anything abnormal going on in the Ukraine, from which he had just returned. After Herriot, Pierre Cot. In 1935 it was Romain Rolland's turn.

The author of *Au-dessus de la mêlée (Above the Fray)* was not, like Barbusse, an unconditional friend of the USSR, even though he had been one of the first writers to hail the October Revolution. After the First World War, during the first years of the Soviet regime, Romain Rolland remained one of the great figures in the European intellectual Left, a pacifist and an internationalist devoted to great causes but drawn more to Gandhian nonviolence than to Leninism. He admired the project of the Soviet regime but deplored its means. In June 1927, for example, in response to one of his readers, he stated, "On Bolshevism, I have in no way changed. The bearer of high ideas (or, rather, since thought has never been its forte, the representative of a great cause), Bolshevism has destroyed it (and them) by its narrow sectarianism, its inept intransigence, and its cult of violence. It has given rise to Fascism, which is a sort of reverse Bolshevism."[12] Nonetheless, that same year, at Barbusse's insistence, he agreed to sign an appeal against the "wave of Fascist barbarity," on condition that it should include a condemnation of all forms of Terror.[13] The following year, he renewed his friendship with Gorky just as Gorky was being persuaded to return by Bukharin and Stalin, who would use him mercilessly. He read, gathered information, and the USSR reappeared on his horizon. In 1929 he discouraged Panaït Istrati from publishing his book *Vers l'autre flamme* so as not to give ammunition to the reactionaries: this was emblematic of his decisive leap toward Bolshevism.[14]

Rolland then became a fellow traveler, was promoted by the Party, was massively published in the USSR, and—along with Barbusse, Gide, and eventually Malraux—became the most famous star in the constellation of intellectuals that from 1932–33 onward populated the Association des écrivains et artistes révolutionnaires, the journal *Commune*, the anti-Fascism of Amsterdam-Pleyel, and Münzenberg's various enterprises. In spite of his age, he was quite representative of this group. Unlike Souvarine or Silone before them, this group of writers of such diverse ages and inspirations—Gide, Guéhenno, Jean-Richard Bloch, Vildrac, Malraux, Aragon, Nizan—had not been active in the Communist movement. The crisis of the Bolshevik Party was behind them, Trotsky was in exile, and they had other fish to fry: the Western world was in ruins, Hitler was gaining ground and would soon be in power. Across from them stood the Soviet Union of the Five-Year Plan, the vast construction site of new humanity. The capitalist crisis highlighted the idea of the construction of socialism, which in turn made people forget about the large-scale deportation of peasants. The Nazis' first targets in 1933 were the Communists; how could the first victims of Nazism possibly belong to a system of terror and police like their German executioners? The Nazis, furthermore, belonged to the old world and wanted to save it, whereas the Communists belonged to the new world that they were building. The image of old and new made a radical distinction between the two wills at work; the same image even condemned violence in one place while justifying it elsewhere.[15] Thus fighting Fascism was inseparable from promoting the USSR. It was widely believed during this period that Fascism aimed to absorb the entire bourgeois world, and that the only thing stopping it was the proletarian revolution.

Romain Rolland's trip to Moscow, long delayed for reasons of health, finally took place in July 1935. Although this was the golden age of Franco-Soviet relations, the Laval-Stalin pact having just been signed, it was a grievous time for the citizens of the USSR, since the plan to liquidate tens of thousands of old Bolshevik cadres was now being implemented. Rolland was received like royalty, bombarded with kindness, and assailed by delegations of flatterers staggering under fabricated laudatory speeches, which nonetheless tickled his vanity. The high point of the visit was a two-hour tête-à-tête with Stalin, who also spared no effort and greeted his visitor with the words, "I am happy to chat with the greatest writer in the world."[16] The conversation showcases the two caricatures of the anti-Fascist pantheon, the humanist intellectual and the reasonable dictator.

Each one played his role to the hilt. Romain Rolland assumed his naturally, having played it all his life. He had fought for Dreyfus, and against the First World War; on this day, he took a great leap forward: he became the witness for Communism before the tribunal of history, the universal man through whose mediation the event of October 1917 received, a generation after its birth, a renewal of its contract. Barbusse had been friendly with the Soviet regime for too long to be equally useful. Gide, until then, had not been known for his love of great causes. Stalin had chosen the right man. Considering this incident, which was one among many, one cannot help wondering where the rustic Georgian acquired the psychological penetration that allowed him to anticipate the reactions and sentiments of a star of European literature. Stalin had received a very meager education, had never been out of Russia, spoke only Russian, and had spent his whole life wrangling within the Bolshevik Party; yet he seems to have understood the West, its writers, its politicians, its ins and outs. Few people in the twentieth century possessed such political genius—though in its worst guise.

Romain Rolland took care to pepper his dialogue with critical questions designed to lend more weight to his personality by manifesting his independence: the question of Victor Serge (which was much discussed in Paris)[17]; the death sentence for children under twelve, recently revived after the assassination of Kirov; and the alliance between the USSR and bourgeois France—all issues relating to the distinction between the fellow traveler and the militant. Stalin put these questions to rest with a heavy dose of common sense in the name of class struggle, sharpened by Fascism. He even allowed himself the luxury of taking the role of a moderate, faced with a Soviet public that was clamoring for the heads of Zinoviev and Kamenev, who were allegedly responsible for Kirov's death. The two men bade each other good-bye in a flurry of professions of faith in humanity. The writer returned home with a new life.

In spite of everything, the *Voyage à Moscou* remains one of the best of these somewhat tedious accounts, for it does contain frequent flashes of insight. The rather vain old man who drank deeply of Soviet nectar also sensed that he was arriving in a small world disturbed by profound political crisis, preyed upon by fear, and under police surveillance. Though he did not understand the film that was being projected, he did suspect it was a film. He spent half of his stay in Gorky's *datcha*, and noted that his great Soviet friend, who had been "reconquered" by the Soviet power in 1928, had absolutely no autonomy; he was growing old rather sadly in his gilded prison with a secretary who controlled all communications with the outside world.[18]

If the traveler managed to shield his beliefs from these dangerous

observations, it was because he was already involved in the early Stalinist cult, a new trait in the history of Communism. He had not the
slightest doubt about Trotsky's mistakes, Zinoviev's crimes, the misdeeds of the Fascists, or the wisdom of the Leader. This leader was not
a charismatic one who drew crowds with the magic of collective emotions like the Fascist leaders. He was, rather, an equal among equals,
wise and steadfast, in control of his passions—in short, a figure of reason. Rolland saw Stalin as imbued with rational power, the traditional
image of European thought, by definition ambiguous since it could consist not only of the love of reason but also of a fascination with power.
In any case, the image remained ever after a part of the baggage of admirers of the USSR. Romain Rolland himself, a few years later when he
had awoken from his illusions and his friend Bukharin had been judged
and condemned, dared not confront the pure force of Stalin's regime
with a public declaration.

Rolland's 1935 trip bestowed on the Soviet Union the blessing of
democratic universalism. Through Rolland, the country of Communism ceased to be a distant and violent land in which revolutionary intellectuals battled for power, using obscure vocabulary. It was, instead,
a vast country where, under the direction of an enlightened guide, a
regime had resumed the flame of the French Revolution—the regeneration of humanity. In other words, it was a postrevolutionary order
that had remained true to the revolutionary project whose formula had
eluded the late-eighteenth-century French. It increased its loyal followers by uniting the traditions of the European Left around a shared bottom line, democracy without capitalism.

This image was furthered by the Fascists' announced intention of
putting an end to the principles of 1789. Mussolini and Hitler had never
made a secret of their hatred for the French Revolution and its pretension of rebuilding a society based on individual rights. They mixed both
left- and right-wing critiques of bourgeois individualism, which was
hidden under the mask of rights. The confusion was natural, since this
critique is basically the same from Burke to Marx, pitting social reality
against egalitarian abstraction. But whereas Burke spoke only of traditional society, Marx invented a postindividualist society, redoubling in
the name of history the radical rejection of what had preceded it. In the
same way, both Fascists and Communists could detest the bourgeoisie;
their common passion, however, in no way altered their contradictory
ideas about the objectives of political action. The Fascist "community,"
supported by a negation of 1789, was bound to evoke the counterrevolutionary idea. Communism, in contrast, was presented in the context
of a dialectical continuum (the famous *Aufhebung*) with the Declaration

of the Rights of Man and bourgeois democracy. It sought to realize that promise. This is what Rolland and Gide were saying when they pointed to the Soviet Union as the work site of the future.

This linear vision of contemporary history, torn between reactionary forces, of which the Fascists were the shock troops, and a democratic camp with the USSR as its figurehead, drew less from Marxism than from a belief in human progress centered principally on the French Revolution. Marxism, insofar as it constituted a philosophy, would have little real influence in European universities, until after the Second World War.[19] Soviet policies with the Communist parties in its wake retained only rudiments of Marxism, but the adaptability of those rudiments enabled the Soviets to annex any optimistic historical conception that suited them, in other words, all of the democratic tradition. Thus, even in countries in which the origins and development of democracy were independent of the French Revolution, such as Great Britain and the United States, the influence of an anti-Fascist Soviet Union spread precisely in the name of historical optimism: anyone fighting against Hitler was by the same token fighting for the rights and liberties and hence the emancipation of humanity.

In this way, anti-Fascism purged Soviet Communism of much of the antibourgeois aggressiveness with which Lenin had imbued it in order to separate Bolshevism from Social Democracy. It gave it a facade less repugnant to the West. Whereas Lenin had dissolved the barely elected Constitutional Assembly, Stalin, in 1936, promulgated a Constitution that appeared in line with good principles. The more Eastern his power, the more Western he looked. To isolate Hitler, the Soviet Union drew closer to the democracies. Being still distinct from them, it was a lap ahead on the path to freedom, which is how the Soviets explained Hitler's particular hostility to the USSR. Stalin managed to turn the Nazis' hatred of democracy to his own advantage.

By inscribing the Soviet Union at the top of the list of democratic nations engaged in the battle against the Fascist powers, Stalin gained an enormous advantage—a fierce enemy, deprived of the amenities of freedom, identifiable yet ubiquitous. Since October, the proletarian revolution had been faced with an international bourgeoisie—an abstract monster it exhibited for the detestation of the workers of the world. In one sense, the monster had to be abstract: the Revolution required an adversary as ubiquitous as itself, ready to cross swords anywhere; this lent grandeur and dignity to the battle between the past and the future. The French of the late eighteenth century had described everything that either seemed or actually was hostile to their revolution as "aristocratic." They had been obsessively afraid of an "aristocratic plot." The Russian Bolsheviks' bugbear was the bourgeoisie, something even vaguer: the bourgeoisie could be found wherever anyone was making money. In its international form, it was as universal as capitalism and so abstract that its counterrevolutionary threats had no teeth. The French of 1793 were warring against aristocratic Europe. The post-NEP Russian Revolution was crying out against the imminent aggression of "imperialism." But that imperialism had no name because it had many names, among which Soviet propaganda made no distinction. The adversary of the Communist movement was a faceless menace.

Hitler's accession to power changed everything: he gave the menace a face. Not that Nazism contained all of imperialism, but it did renew the possibility of an interimperialistic war and allowed Stalin to single it out as the principal enemy. Prior to Hitler's victory, Fascism had been nothing more than an antiliberal version of twentieth-century bourgeois domination. Present everywhere, it favored no particular country. There was Mussolini, of course, but Fascist Italy posed no threat to world peace; the Soviet Union, moreover, had relatively good relations with it. In contrast, Hitler had war on his agenda; Stalin was certainly the first to understand this because it led him to the 1934 policy shift. But the operation had other benefits. By establishing terror in Germany, Hitler at last provided the Soviet Revolution with a made-to-order enemy. In Germany, the dictatorship of the bourgeoisie showed its true colors and could no longer hide beneath liberal disguises such as American democracy, British parliamentarianism, or French republicanism. It was revealed by the Nazis for what it was—incapable of assuming its own legality and thrown back on naked violence.

Before Stalin unleashed an even greater terror upon the Soviet Union, Hitlerian terror had served a preventive function. The indignation of the democratic world, being focused on Berlin, was effectively diverted from what would occur in Moscow two years later. This was one of the goals of Dimitrov's agitation and of the countertrial of the Reichstag in 1933. Dimitrov rose from a Comintern staffer to a hero of anti-Fascism. Through him, Communism changed its face. It was defined no longer by what it was but by its opposition to Hitler and, by the same token, to Fascists in general.[20]

It was in this period that the term "Fascist" came into general use in official Soviet language. In order to define Communists, Fascists had to be found everywhere. Stalin's geopolitical fear of Hitler was transposed into the neorevolutionary ideology of new-style Bolshevism. The proletarian revolution became the advance guard of democracy in its fight against Fascism. The enemy was a formidable one, both concrete and concealed; incarnated by Hitler, it existed in all bourgeois countries and even in the Soviet Union, constantly plotting to bring the homeland of socialism, its most formidable adversary, to its knees. This polarization of the political world, typical of the revolutionary credo, explains why Stalinist USSR no longer had any adversaries that were not "Fascists," starting with Trotsky and his supporters, who held the place of honor in the distribution of counterrevolutionary roles. The first name on the list of enemies of the people and anti-Sovietist criminals was that of the "Hitlerian Trotskyist."

To make things clear, it was crucial to rid the designation "Fascist" of any absurdity, and to define it by its role in Stalinist anti-Fascism; this would imply that any adversary or critic of the USSR served Hitler's cause. The most evil of those adversaries or critics were those fighting from within or those who, in exile, continued to communicate with their former partisans. The indomitable Trotsky was the most famous of the former, and he remained loyal even to the first kind of Bolshevism, brandishing Lenin's flag in Stalin's face. In politics, and even more in revolutionary politics, in which ideological legitimacy plays such an important role, the most hated enemy is the closest adversary. One of the functions of the Moscow trials of 1936–38 was to show the world that Trotsky had been in league with Germany and Japan in an extensive plot to destroy the Soviet Union.

The extraordinary credulity of world opinion when faced with such fabrications cannot be attributed solely to the public confessions of the accused, who, as we now know, were performing roles learned under threats and torture. Doubt could be cast on their self-indictments if it were shown that they included facts or meetings that could not have occurred. Such was Trotsky's refutation in the countertrial that the American Left organized under the aegis of John Dewey.[21] But that empirical refutation, the most incontestable of all, also opened up the way for broader questions. If the sworn facts were false and the confessions therefore worthless, what about the regime that had used them for its propaganda and to justify its battles? If Trotsky was innocent, the Left no longer held a monopoly on the morally correct. Thus the fact of taking the mass of confessions for granted had less to do with rational conviction, based on a verification of their content, than with a more or less conscious wish to avoid casting doubt on the Soviet Revolution. Furthermore, it was less costly psychologically to believe the confessions in spite of their implausibility than to doubt them in spite of the show put on by the accused. In the first case, one had to close one's eyes to the "details" in order to maintain the general structure. In the second, one admitted the truth of small, demonstrable facts, and thereafter one could no longer support the whole. Passion supplemented by weakness brought many people to the first alternative: some because they were already Communists or Communist-leaning; others—probably the majority—because they needed to preserve a "good" image of the Soviet Union that would continue to justify the anti-Fascist struggle; others because they were afraid of falling into a reactionary anti-Sovietism; and still others simply because Stalin's USSR had become a great power, allied, moreover, with France. The truth is that the Soviet Union now possessed a great intimidating force and made use of it.

The interest of this affair was not that the anti-Fascist coalition, which had become the Left's universal raison d'être, included a powerful totalitarian state. After all, one can easily imagine a coalition of this sort that would have cohered merely through hostility to Nazi Germany, since fear of Hitler was a sufficient reason to form an alliance. But this was not the case. Before being geopolitical, anti-Fascism was ideological; democracy was emblazoned on its standard. Which democracy? The Soviet state, which was supposed to incarnate the proletariat in power, represented its advance guard. Successor to the bourgeois revolutions, it was carrying forward the message of liberty and equality. As we have seen, Stalin also packaged his domestic policy in democratic anti-Fascism. Zinoviev, Kamenev, Radek, and Bukharin were guilty not merely of weakening political cohesion in the face of Hitler but of conspiring with the Gestapo. Thereafter, those who cast doubt on the crimes to which they had confessed were no longer anti-Fascists but allies of Hitler. The terrible logic of war, which in its patriotic form had made the European extreme Left so indignant during World War I, was once more at work in its ideological form, this time to the benefit of Bolshevism and during peacetime. Anyone who criticized Stalin supported Hitler. The genius of the Georgian was to have caught so many reasonable men in such a simplistic and formidable trap.

Coincidentally, at the very moment when Romain Rolland finally decided to make his pilgrimage to Moscow in June 1935, Souvarine was publishing his tome on Stalin, subtitled *A Historical Overview of Bolshevism*. Begun in 1930, it was the culmination of years of work with many ups and downs. The contract, first signed with a major American publisher, would soon be canceled under the pretext of delays on the part of Souvarine, who was compiling his documentation while simultaneously directing and editing *Critique sociale*.[22] Completed in mid-1934, the manuscript of more than a thousand pages fell like a stone in the prevailing waters. The Franco-Soviet diplomatic rapprochement was under way, orchestrated by the enthusiastic testimonies of the "friends of the USSR," those of the radicals being particularly eloquent. The anti-Fascist union was beginning to take shape. Souvarine had a hard time finding a French publisher. Rejected by Gallimard in spite of Alain's support (which had been mobilized by Simone Weil), he finally found a taker in Plon, despite Gabriel Marcel's opposition.[23] The book finally came out in June 1935, the very month of the Paris "Congress of Writers for the Defense of Culture"—the great anti-Fascist parade produced by Münzenberg. Here was yet another symbolic coincidence.

Souvarine's *Staline* was the first and, for a long time, the only history of the Soviet Union to include the October Revolution. In 1930 the author already had an exceptionally open mind. A former participant in the Communist movement, he possessed the irreplaceable advantage of an inside knowledge of Soviet reality. Like the renegades or those expelled from the Party, he had acquired through the process of disillusionment the disenchanted perspective essential to true analysis. To a greater extent than most of the others, he had centered his life on study. Since the great rupture, all of his activist enterprises with their modest ambitions were characterized by a passion for the truth, in which he had reinvested the flame of his youth. He had undergone a radical conversion from one thing to another while continuing to mobilize the same energy and aggressiveness—first against the bourgeoisie, then against the Communist mystifiers. In writing his book, Souvarine found his vocation.

The book gives us a better understanding of what had immediately distinguished Souvarine from Trotskyist dissidents. Though a latecomer to Bolshevism, Trotsky, as former leader of the Red Army, represented the victorious Bolshevism of October along with Lenin. Even after defeat and in exile he proclaimed that heritage as the whole purpose of his life. Whether in Turkey, Norway, or Mexico, he still felt responsible for the Soviet Union, since he and only he had been Lenin's companion. The proletarian revolution accompanied him into exile. In this heritage lay his greatness, his heroism, his ability to stir others' imaginations. But it was also the origin of his blind spots: bent on exposing the differences between Stalin and Lenin, he could not conceive that they had anything in common. Since he was incapable of criticizing the foundations of the Soviet state, his condemnation of Stalin never went beyond Leninist polemic—the very thing, as it turned out, to divide his few partisans.[24]

Compared to this disaffected prophet, Souvarine was analytical reason itself. His diagnosis of the century was more irreversibly pessimistic: not only had the revolutionary optimism of his youth died in the country that had embodied that optimism, but the country itself had become the quintessential homeland of state lies. So the task at hand was not to start a new revolution from scratch but to try to understand what had happened in Russia. Between 1925 and 1930, Souvarine was still a Communist in his own way; at least, he kept up the pretense as a salve for his solitude and the last link with his past. His book, written between 1930 and 1934, was in no way a political manifesto. The fruit of painstaking research and a vast amount of documentation, it could have been a doctoral thesis if the choice of subject had not been such an unusually courageous one. For Souvarine was no master of the understatement: proceeding from one fact to another, linking up causes and reasons, motives, and justifications, he wrote a fairly classic political history that took into account not only situational constraints but also the role of human decision and responsibility. What made his talent unique was his accurate and fearless judgment as well as his unhesitating exercise of the historian's moral authority. The young veteran of Bolshevism had rediscovered the classical tradition.

I do not wish to extend this discussion of Souvarine's book, which, to judge by its publishing history, had more notoriety than readers.[25] It is enough for our present purposes to point out that the framework he determined for the political history of Bolshevism lasted for a long time and that he had raised the major questions: the relationship between Leninist Communism and the Russian tradition, the true nature of October, the terrorist and bureaucratic degeneration of the Revolution beginning with Lenin, the nature and the causes for Stalin's victory in the struggle for succession, the mystery of its character and animating passions, the extravagant cost of the whole enterprise from the economic and moral points of view. The enigmatic aspect of the 1935 publication was not the book's content but how few waves it made. By virtue of the life he led, Souvarine, though young, belonged to a Communist era that had been more or less obscured by the shift to anti-Fascism. He had known Lenin, the Twenty-One Conditions, the birth of the Comintern and of the French Communist Party, as well as the beginnings of the battle for succession, over which he had no influence, whether by constraint or by lack of knowledge. All this was old hat, since Stalin had won and had redirected the activity of the Comintern against Hitler. Gide was older than Souvarine, but as a latecomer to Communism he was a new figure—and a temporary one—on the anti-Fascist rostrum. Souvarine, in contrast, with his rebellious solitude, had frequented small, marginal groups too weak to protect him but too visible not to leave him exposed. Long a target of the insults of the French Communist Party, which with good reason sensed that he was an indomitable enemy, he had exhausted the public's patience. The Right mistrusted him because he had been a Communist, the Left because he was no longer one. At the time of the *Union sacrée* against Hitler, anti-Communism was not to be tolerated: the Communists did everything they could to denounce the first great work on their history as a renegade's sordid settling of scores.

For democratic opinion, everything that touched on the Soviet Union became increasingly taboo. On the one hand, the USSR was the holder of the patent on revolution, and, on the other, it was continually exposed to reactionary calumnies. So there was a dual reason to regard even friendly critics as hostile a fortiori. The political situation of 1934–36 transformed this moral stumbling block, of which the Communists were the guardians. To get a better idea of the age, let us imagine ourselves at the "Congress of Writers for the Defense of Culture," mentioned earlier. It was in late June 1935 that the cream of the French and European anti-Fascist intelligentsia was mobilized to celebrate—against Hitler but along with the Communists—the cultural values embodied in Soviet humanism. The French were represented by Alain, Rolland, Barbusse, Aragon, Malraux, Gide, Guilloux, and Vildrac; the Germans by Heinrich Mann, Bertolt Brecht, and Johannes Becher; the Russians by Ehrenburg and Alexis Tolstoy; and the British by Aldous Huxley and E. M. Forster.

As with any congress, there was a performance onstage and one behind the scenes. Onstage were the speakers of the day, hugging and kissing, proclaiming great humanistic discourses. Backstage, on the sly, there was a single but major embarrassing event—the problem of Victor Serge. The son of Russian exiles who had settled in Belgium,[26] the young Victor Serge had been active, before 1914, in the anarchist movement; mixed up in the "Bonnot gang" affair, he had served five years in a French prison prior to joining the Soviet Revolution and the Comintern in 1919. Thrown out of the Party for "Trotskyism" in 1928 and arrested soon afterward, he was soon set free, but he did not change his ideas. He then set himself up as a writer in Leningrad and wrote one of the books in Istrati's series, having given up all his illusions about the Stalinist universe. He was arrested again in March 1933 and deported to Orenburg in the Urals. His in-laws, the Russakovs (Serge, like Pierre Pascal, had married one of the Russakovs' daughters), were expelled from Leningrad. His wife, Anita, was also arrested.

Serge was a celebrity in the little French Left, which flew to his defense. Who could better identify with what was happening to him than Rosmer, Pascal, and Souvarine? The first call for his liberation appeared in the eighth issue of the periodical *Critique sociale,* in April 1933, while the Communist press remained silent or sought to disqualify him. Barbusse was silent in *Le Monde;* Aragon, in *Commune.* Rolland and Gide were uncomfortable, and attempted to intervene discreetly at the top without quarreling openly with the Soviet Union. The Victor Serge affair is instructive as one of the first demonstrations of the collective manipulation of anti-Fascist intellectuals by anti-Communist blackmail. Before the Congrès de la Mutualité in June 1935, the organizers realized that people would speak of Victor Serge from the podium, but in devising the program they sought to reduce such discussion to a minimum. Nonetheless, a small group including André Breton, Magdeleine Paz, Charles Plisnier, and Henri Poulaille managed to get Gaetano Salvemini, the great Italian professor banished by Mussolini, onto the dais. "I would not feel as though I had the right to protest against the Gestapo and against the Fascist OVRA if I endeavored to forget about the existence of a Soviet political police. In Germany there are concentration camps, in Italy there are penitentiary islands, and in Soviet Russia there is Siberia—it is in Russia that Victor Serge is prisoner." [27] This theme was taken up the following day by other conspirators, but it was no better received: the congress had been organized not to criticize the USSR but to praise it. A little less than a year later, Victor Serge was authorized to leave Soviet territory for Belgium. This was an exceptional gesture on Stalin's part, probably intended less as a refutation of his adversaries than as a reward to his friends, especially Romain Rolland, by furnishing them with a last decoy.

The most famous participant in the Congrès de la Mutualité to remain silent about the Victor Serge affair was André Gide, then at the height of his literary fame. He did not say much, but he certainly listened. Though not a Communist, he had been an exemplary fellow traveler since the early 1930s. His name alone brought luster to the cause. He had entered the public scene by a route that was aesthetic rather than philosophical, sentimental rather than political. Gide was the quintessential antibourgeois bourgeois author. His art had worked over that territory so thoroughly that he made the general condition of the modern writer into literature that was subversive in a bourgeois way. Born into a prominent Protestant family, Gide was ashamed of his privileged beginnings. A homosexual, he detested the moral hypocrisy of convention; a philosophical wanderer, a latter-day Montaigne, he denounced the violence of the French colonization of Africa. Although he owed his literary accent to Nietzsche, the background of his thought was the Gospel and a Christlike faith, a volatile mixture of revolt and guilt—

the classic path toward a revolutionary utopia. To Gide, individualist, aesthete, and patrician that he was, Communism brought not only real antibourgeois credentials but also the inestimable benefit of a reunion with community. Finally, to the limited extent that we may measure the credulity often found among even the greatest writers, Gide would extend its glory to the level of humanity. When not hidden militants, true fellow travelers often harbored radical misconceptions about their cause, which is why it was such an unstable association. The Cominternians, moreover, had no illusions about such misconceptions and took a strictly instrumental view of them.

Moreover, there were circumstances. Gide, like many of his contemporaries, saw the first Five-Year Plan as the perfect antithesis to capitalist disorder; it was the emergence of reason in history. From there, he had gradually elaborated an image of the USSR as the nation of development, instruction, and culture. He talked with Vaillant-Couturier, the veteran French Communist intellectual, and was friends with Jef Last and Eugène Dabit, both of whom were Communists. In 1932 he still refused to join the Association des écrivains et artistes révolutionnaires, but in 1933 he agreed to serve on the Comité de patronage of *Commune*, the association's review. Hitler's rise to power in Berlin pushed him into the public arena. He attended all the pro-Dimitrov meetings, sat on all the anti-Fascist intellectuals' committees and then on the rostrums of the Front populaire, trying to speak the political language of the unified Left; the artist, however, could always be perceived behind the convert.[28]

The Communists, thinking Gide more committed to their cause than he actually was, were not sufficiently wary of his independent spirit. They did not, however, underestimate his vanity and his other character flaws and continually urged him to spend some time in the Soviet Union. The pilgrimage to Moscow was very much in fashion, and the Soviets had almost perfected the art of receiving prestigious guests. In the summer of 1934, Malraux, Aragon, and Jean-Richard Bloch went to Moscow to participate in the Soviet Writers' Congress, and Malraux continued to make declarations of solidarity with the USSR.[29] Romain Rolland's trip had been a triumph, owing as much to the way it took place as to its propaganda value. The idea was to repeat the operation with a second literary star from the French Communist domain. Cajoled, begged, flattered from all sides, Gide finally gave in: the Soviet government announced that it was printing three hundred thousand postcards bearing his portrait.[30] The author arrived in Moscow with his companion Pierre Herbart, in late June 1936, just one year after

Rolland's trip, and in Leningrad he met with four of his closest friends, who also joined the tour—Jef Last, Eugène Dabit, Louis Guilloux, and the publisher Schiffrin.

A reception fit for a king, a lavish lifestyle, assiduous attention: nothing was left to chance in this strange encounter between the French aesthete and the crude reality of the Soviet Union. Gide and his friends threw themselves into the ceremony and played their assigned role. At the time of their arrival Gorky had recently died, and Gide delivered a totally orthodox funeral oration, which had been touched up by Aragon. But it was not long before he felt he was under surveillance, and what Rolland had accepted as inevitable struck Gide as a servitude. Bukharin, now a pathetic figure, whom Rolland had still managed to see the year before (although, by then, he could no longer speak), was unable to break through the entourage of secret police that isolated him from the outside world. From Pierre Herbart's own account of the trip,[31] it seems clear that Gide reacted to the reception given him with an instinctive mistrust, and that he and his fellow tourists, notwithstanding the obvious entertainment that filled their days, were both suspicious and disappointed.

Gide's book *Retour de l'U.R.S.S.* was already being published by Gallimard at the end of October, as though Gide were in a hurry to free himself from the imposture in which he had participated. Not that the work was written in a tone hostile to the Soviet Union like much of the reactionary literature on the subject. On the contrary, Gide had lost nothing of his delicate touch in handling a burning question. His report even retained traces of naïveté—for example, when he describes the model establishments he had been taken to see. Admittedly, he also made note of the sad monotony of social life, the ugliness of the objects produced, the reestablishment of inequality, the poor quality of art. But the deepest reason for his disappointment was not economic, social, or aesthetic; it had to do with the disappearance of freedom.

In the greetings of the Stakhanovists, the exaggerated politeness of the academicians, and the compliments of the "pioneers," Gide sensed brainwashing, tyranny, and fear. He had made the journey in search of a revolutionary society; yet everywhere he went he found slaves worshiping Stalin. The striking thing about this short work, half masked by the exquisite urbanity of his style, was its testimony that the USSR was not, or was no longer, what it pretended to be; an absolute power was compelling every citizen to say and even to believe the contrary: that it was indeed what it alleged itself to be. "What is now demanded is acquiescence, conformism. What is wanted and required is approbation for all that is done in the USSR; what they are trying to accomplish is that this approbation be not resigned but sincere, even enthusiastic. The most surprising thing is that this is being achieved. On the other hand, the least protest, the least criticism, is punishable by the severest penalty and, moreover, immediately hushed up."

Then comes the most formidable statement in the book: "And I doubt whether the spirit in any other country today, except for Hitler's Germany, is less free, more curbed, more fearful (terrorized), more re-duced to vassalage." [32]

Gide, who left France a fellow traveler, returned comparing Stalin to Hitler, a diagnosis prefiguring that of Ciliga [33] two years later, or, more recently, that of Orwell or Solzhenitsyn: the Soviet Union was the coun-try where lies were generalized and mandatory. Had the author foreseen the scandal that his book would create on the left? Surely. So many people had tried to dissuade him from publishing it that he certainly entertained no illusions in this respect. Indeed, the Communists showed up with their friends and their biggest guns. They really had no choice, because the *Retour de l'U.R.S.S.* owed its success less to its subject than to its author and the curiosity aroused by his about-face. [34] It was the sort of politico-literary event that the French, especially the Parisians, delight in. Here was one of the stars of French literature, one of the most important intellectuals of the Front populaire, attacking Commu-nism while the euphoria of the spring continued.

If we need further evidence that one's attitude toward the Soviet Union was considered the touchstone of the union of left-wing forces, we need only look at the French Communists' reaction to Gide's book, which mirrored the way in which the Spanish Communists adminis-tered *manu militari* in Barcelona shortly afterward. The Spanish Civil War was an aggravating circumstance for Gide, who had no qualms about dividing the democratic camp in face of the enemy. But the book was also indicted by the French Communist Party through both its fel-low travelers and its militants. Georges Friedmann invoked the weight of the Russian past and reproached Gide for being too superficial. Fer-nand Grenier, the head of the French "Friends of the Soviet Union," suspected Trotskyist influences. The workers incriminated the author's bourgeois positions in spite of the fact that other bourgeois, who had made the same trip and were received with less luxury but no less care, described a different USSR.

Gide therefore decided to write a postscript to his book, which came out in June 1937: *Les Retouches à mon Retour de l'U.R.S.S.* He wanted to respond to his adversaries and to his correspondents. In the meantime he had read the literature critical of the USSR that he had neglected during the period of his faith, such as the heavily documented book by

Sir Walter Citrine.[35] He had met heretics, drawn by his nonconformism—Victor Serge, of course, but also M. Yvon, a worker and a former Communist who had lived in the USSR for eleven years and had published a very hostile brochure on the workers' country under Stalin in *La Révolution prolétarienne*.[36] He also met the syndicalist Legay, who had gone to Russia with a delegation of "Friends" but had returned indignant about the living conditions of the Soviet miners.[37] Consequently, the *Retouches* accentuated the break with philo-Communist progressivism. Gide went all the way. For good measure, he added the Moscow trial to the picture along with thousands of deportees: "I see these victims, I hear them, I feel them all around me. Last night, their stifled cries awoke me; today, their silence dictates these lines. No one is intervening in *their* favor. All the right-wing journals use them, moreover, to stir up the regime they execrate; those who hold dear the idea of justice and liberty, those defending Thaelmann, the Barbusses, the Romain Rollands, have said nothing,[38] are saying nothing; and around them the immense proletarian crowd, blinded." [39] A few weeks later, in August 1937, the author of the *Retouches* asked himself in his journal when and how the Communist spirit had ceased to be distinct from the Fascist spirit.[40]

Gide's case provides a French example of the fragility of anti-Fascist Communism in spite of its spectacular popular success. On the one hand, the fight against Hitlerian terror in combination with the Comintern's political shift—remarkably realized by Thorez and his comrades—had brought many democrats and liberals closer to the Communists. On the other, there was Stalin's Soviet Union, which was a potential ally against Hitler and on the side of the Spanish republicans but remained a domain cut off from the civilized world, an unprecedented and mysterious regime, and the object of contradictory and passionate accounts. This ambiguity would have been tolerable for all adversaries of Fascism had their opinion of the Soviet Union not been a precondition of their commitment, but for several reasons it was, primarily because of the Communists. The strategy of the anti-Fascist Popular Fronts was the Communists' idea, and they had no intention of abandoning their control over it. They did not care for governmental responsibility—they rejected it in France—and they could not soft-pedal their connections with the Soviet Union because their movement was centralized in Moscow, with the glorification of the workers' country liberated from capitalist exploitation as its mainspring. So it was especially important to protect that country from an attack by Hitler. What is more, the USSR they were celebrating was accused by its critics, the most perspicacious of whom came from their own ranks, of being no less totalitarian than Nazi Germany. Consequently, the anti-Hitlerian battle was meaningless if necessarily accompanied by a pious or naive pro-Sovietism. The Comintern's anti-Fascism had shifted, but it had not resolved the contradiction embedded in Communism from the beginning: that of an idea that was also a territory.

The founding years of the Soviet regime had produced a first generation of désenchantés—Angelica Balabanova, Pierre Pascal, Souvarine, Monatte, Rosmer; later, at the time of the leftward change in policy during the "third phase," they were joined by Silone, Tasca, Maurin, and Marion. Gide belonged to an even later group, whose disillusionment resulted less from having experienced internal factional battles (although this was the case with Doriot) than from confronting the reality of the Soviet Union under Stalin. They were not so much participants in factional battles—there *were* no more factions—as militants or fellow travelers increasingly uncertain whether one could fight for democracy under the same colors as Stalin: Gide opened up a path between the Front populaire and the German-Soviet nonaggression pact that would be followed, openly or surreptitiously, by Manès Sperber, Louis Fischer, Koestler, Malraux, Friedmann, Nizan, and many others. The compulsory support of the Soviets that the Communists demanded of the anti-Fascists was thus circumscribed by the anti-Fascists themselves.

We would be wrong, however, to consider the debate on the nature of the Soviet regime the only bone of contention between the adversaries of Fascism. There was another, equally charged with emotion, which, moreover, was not unrelated to the Soviet Union—the issue of peace and war.

The Franco-Soviet pact of May 1935, followed by Stalin's public approval of the French national defense budget, threw both the spirit and the power structure of the French Left into confusion. In France, the Communists had never been pacifists, but they had managed to coexist with them, numerous and powerful as they had been since the end of the war. After all, anticapitalism and antimilitarism were passions common to all who actively opposed war. The paranoid fear of a collective attack against the USSR by the imperialist powers that had marked Communist propaganda in the "third phase" had resulted in opposition to the war of intervention in 1918 and 1919. Now, in May 1935, the French Communists, true to form, were applauding Stalin, ready from one day to the next to retract their antimilitarist and antipatriotic proclamations. Would the fight against Hitler be separated from the fight against war? Would it give up the fight for revolution and peace?

The Communists denied this fervently. Yet by emphasizing the particular character of their pacifism, their change of heart provoked a major debate about anti-Fascism. An example of this debate was the "Anti-Fascist Intellectuals' Vigilance Committee,"[41] founded in Paris in the wake of the riot of 6 February 1934. It was a very French phenomenon: its aim was to organize, outside of political parties, the famous "intellectuals" who have played such a particular role in French national history, both as activists and as spokesmen for great causes. The anti-Fascist cause brought other French battles for democracy to mind. Democracy had been destroyed by Hitler both in Germany and in France; it was threatened by the antirepublican leagues. Anti-fascism revived the Dreyfus Affair, for Jews were being persecuted in Germany and anti-Semitism was strong among the French right wing. So the Vigilance Committee sprang from the same collective impetus that would carry the Front populaire, an anticipation of party alliance.

Three men at the intersection of the sciences and the humanities, of university and intellectual life, were the committee's flagbearers: Alain, Paul Rivet, and Paul Langevin. Alain,[42] our World War I antimilitarist artilleryman, had become a national monument through his teaching and his books and had taught philosophy to generations of students at the Lycée Henri IV. He had remained radically hostile to the army and war. As an individualist, however, he was also mistrustful of militant indoctrination, even at the service of a good cause. He was therefore represented on the Vigilance Committee by his good friend, almost his alter ego, the philosopher Michel Alexandre, who was his colleague at Henri IV. Alexandre was an extreme left-wing Jewish pacifist, a partisan of unilateral disarmament who had done his apprenticeship in opposition first to World War I and then to the Treaty of Versailles and the League of Nations; he was willing to excuse certain territorial ambitions on Hitler's part by the injustices of Versailles.

Paul Rivet was a socialist. After leaving the Muséum d'histoire naturelle, he took up ethnography, a field just becoming a legitimate subject in the universities. He helped found the Musée du Trocadéro, which became the Musée de l'homme in 1936, led by a team that included Griaule, Leiris, and Métraux and that opened up the social sciences to non-European societies. Relatively marginal in comparison to Alain owing to his specialty, and not nearly as well known, Rivet was also more sensitive than Alain to the particular perils inherent in Nazi ideology. He was thus at the center of the Committee's political gravity, since the last member of this triumvirate was a Communist sympathizer, the physicist Paul Langevin. Langevin had long distinguished himself in the postwar pacifist campaigns, employing his scientific authority to denounce the destructive and limitless character of modern war. Through Bergery's "Front commun contre le fascisme," he participated in the Amsterdam-Pleyel movement, and from there slid into positions close to those of the Communists, where he would remain.

The composition of the Vigilance Committee mirrored the triangle formed by its sponsors: a few thousand intellectuals ranging over the entire left-wing spectrum. There was a strong Communist or Communist-leaning minority—Aragon, Nizan, Wurmser among the former and Langevin, Joliot-Curie, Romain Rolland, Jean-Richard Bloch among the latter. Next to them were socialists of all hues (André Philip, Colette Audry, André Delmas, Victor Basch, etc.); radicals such as Albert Bayet; independents, professors, writers, and artists (André Breton, Gué-henno, Giono, Ramon Fernandez, Lucien Febvre, Marcel Bataillon, etc.). Their names covered more territory than any of their various parties, and some of these activists were more influential than their parties. Victor Basch was the president of the Ligue des droits de l'homme; Albert Bayet was exceedingly influential in public education; André Delmas was Secretary General of the powerful Syndicat national des instituteurs (the national teachers' union). All these members of the intellectual Left anticipated by several months the anti-Fascist party union. Having learned from the events in 1933 Germany, they were ready to defend freedom in France after February 1934. Furthermore, they set an example for the labor organizations by siding with them early; in 1935 they were grouped under the same flag.

That example soon proved ambiguous, however. The first to point to the positive aspects of the union, the intellectual Left was also the first to reveal the inevitability of disunion. Discord arose not from the definition or the evaluation of the Fascist danger, but from the link between anti-Fascist measures and the fight for peace. As to the former, everyone agreed that Fascism, as illustrated by Germany, was a product of the capitalist crisis as well as the end of democracy. Worried that it would spread to France, people tended to overestimate the risks.

At the start, members of the Vigilance Committee all agreed that anti-Fascism ought not to be the pretext for any war. At the beginning of 1934, in fact, the Communists were still directing their propaganda and energies "against Fascism *and* war." Since Fascism was an evil lurking in all capitalist countries, and since its ultimate triumph would be an imperialist war, there was no essential difference between the two catastrophes: if one were averted, the other would be also. The anti-Fascist was a pacifist, and vice versa. Many of the most influential members of the Vigilance Committee had participated in the Amsterdam-Pleyel movement, where they had had the occasion to hone this common agenda, though at the price of a certain ambiguity.

The 1934–35 shift in Communist policies was supported by a new hypothetical war, neither a conflict between a coalition of imperialists and the USSR nor a simple interimperialist conflict but a confrontation in which the USSR could take the side of the democracies against Nazi Germany, hence a war that could not be described as imperialist. So the anti-Fascists were not duty-bound to avoid war by fighting imperialism in their own countries or by negotiating with the potential adversary; nor was there an obligation, should war arise, to try to stop it. Since the Fascist danger was now embodied by the Nazis, the priority for the anti-Fascists was to resist Hitler rather than to adhere to their traditional pacifism.

When the USSR decided to join the League of Nations, the pacifists still viewed the League merely as an instrument of the victors of World War I. They showed that Hitler was partly justified in his opposition to the Versailles system, for they too condemned Versailles, which they saw as having produced Hitler. When the French Communists became patriots, the pacifists reproached them for abandoning the fight against their own bourgeoisie and returning to anti-German chauvinism. The pacifists regarded prior consent to war with Hitler not only as a regression to the Franco-Russian alliance but as aid to Fascism in the name of anti-Fascism, since nothing realizes the conditions for a Fascist power as war does. Radical pacifism was still undergirded by the experience of 1914–18.

The Vigilance Committee's first debates about international problems brought to light the traditional consensus on the need to revise the Treaty of Versailles and on disarmament. As Italian troops were invading Abyssinia in October 1935, there was still unanimity for imposing economic sanctions against Mussolini. But by the end of the year there was already division between those who advocated negotiations with Hitler over the clauses of Versailles and those who opposed such negotiations. In a public letter of 5 January 1936, Alain wrote to Rivet and Langevin: "On the subject of war and peace, I do not see free men having a common doctrine. Some, without ever realizing it, lean toward a preventive war that would abolish military dictatorships. Others stubbornly seek means to avoid all wars, even a just war." The problem posed by the author was the revision of the Treaty of Versailles, whereas it was no longer an issue for Soviet diplomacy or, consequently, for the Communists. This position was reaffirmed in March, when Hitler's troops reoccupied the Rhineland. For the pacifists, Hitler's action proved the need to reestablish a just international order so as to deprive Hitler of his advantageous role as righter of the wrongs perpetrated on the German people.

The strength of the pacifists' argument lay in what it left unsaid: the accuracy of their suspicion as to the real reasons for the Communist policy shift, which was subordinated to Stalin's diplomatic about-face. Its weakness lay in their casting Hitler as a vulgar Mussolini, as just another nationalistic dictator, and in their failure to perceive the true nature of Nazism. The Communists, on the other hand, gained from their submission to Moscow, turning to their advantage what until then had been a weakness, since the Soviet Union appeared to be headed toward an understanding with France: revolutionary patriotism was a more natural sentiment than revolutionary defeatism. The tension between the two conceptions of anti-Fascism inevitably became acrimonious as the two camps started to accuse each other of being serfs of Moscow or camouflaged pro-Fascists. The final break occurred in June 1936 during the Congrès des comités de vigilance, in the wake of the Front populaire's electoral triumph.

As is often the case, the break resulted from a procedural vote that concealed political disagreement. Defeated, Paul Langevin and his friends left the Committee's headquarters and were replaced by people closer to the pacifists than to the Communists; among these were Marc Delaisi, Jules Isaac, Magdeleine Paz, Jean Guéhenno, Maurice Lacroix, and Marcel Bataillon. They were not as extreme as Alain and Alexandre; most were looking principally for a revision of what had been negotiated at Versailles in order to avoid feeding into Nazi propaganda. Paul Rivet, unable to prevent a split, resigned from the presidency and entered the ranks—provisionally, since he would return to the presidency in January 1937.

Even after the Communists had been pushed out, problems persisted. They were exacerbated by the Spanish Civil War, which revived the division between supporters of the lifting of the arms embargo after the nonintervention fiasco and the radical pacifists entrenched behind their refusal of any form of arms race. The anti-arms-embargo group made a distinction between their rejection of an anti-Fascist military crusade on the one hand and, on the other, the Spanish situation, in which even the indirect absence of aid meant abandoning the Republic to Fascism. But the concern to save the unity of the Front populaire worked in favor of the pacifists. Since World War II, we have all but forgotten about the hold of pacifism over the non-Communist Left in the 1930s: passionate rejection of war was shared by the majority of the Socialist Party, under the auspices of Paul Faure. It was also widely shared by the CGT, and dominated the national teachers' union, which was highly influential in forming public opinion. With the departure of the Communist intellectuals, the Vigilance Committee moved toward pacifism in its most intransigent form: though founded to combat Fascism, it ended up fighting for negotiations with the Fascists. In the summer of 1938, it was one of the hotbeds of militant activism in favor of the Munich agreement. During this time, Rivet and his friends left the committee. It consisted thereafter of "integral pacifists," who would lose their last battle in the summer of 1939.

Interesting for our purposes is that the pacifist extreme Left, which had been wrong about Hitler, was right about Stalin, just as the Communist fellow travelers were right about Hitler but wrong about Stalin. The pacifist extremists took the Nazi dictator for a new Kaiser who could be appeased by the return of a few pieces of his former colonial empire.[43] But they had figured out Stalin's calculations as early as 1935, at the time of his pact with Laval. If the war had become inevitable, better that it should originate in the West. The Front populaire had mingled its two Lefts—or, rather, its two extreme Lefts—in the same fight and in the same victory of the forces of social progress over those of reaction. When it had united its forces in 1934–35, explicit agreement on international policy had not been a precondition of the union. At that time, moreover, as evidenced by the history of the Vigilance Committee, the confrontation was only virtual, since the consequences of the Communist shift appeared only after Stalin's approval of French military expenditures. Not all its consequences were equally felt. As noted, Hitler's reoccupation of the Rhineland on 7 March 1936 did not provoke a reaction from the French Communist Party similar to its July campaign for republican Spain. The Soviet Union was implicated in the second affair but not in the first.

Although the Front populaire had made itself the instrument of emancipation for the nation's popular classes, it had always been too divided to prepare the country for the ordeal that awaited it. As we have seen, however, it was not entirely responsible for that failure; British diplomacy, the state of French public opinion, and Stalin's unreliability were all obstacles to a firm, coherent policy with respect to Hitler. The Front populaire can be blamed for the internal rent in the coalition, concealed by the grandiloquence of international arbitration. Léon Blum experienced that division very personally, as though it were preordained by all that had led him to political action. A pacifist in both heart and mind, a socialist attached to the League of Nations, an Anglophile by tradition, an anti-Bolshevik from the start, and an anti-Nazi above suspicion, the head of the Front populaire government held only strong, if contradictory, convictions. He was not happy either with prior consent to war or with a policy of avoidance at any price, either with intervention in Spain or with nonintervention, either with accelerated rearmament or with Munich. He was certainly the most intelligent witness to the impasse into which victorious France of 1918 had gradually become trapped.

We must therefore abandon the idealized picture of a France in which, during these years, an important anti-Fascist camp, with the Communists out in front, clashed with a more or less pro-Hitler Right already headed for national disaster via its passionate anti-Communism and nourished with arguments by a pacifist intelligentsia destined for "collaboration." The reality was in every way more complex, first because there was no influential "Hitlerian" ideology unless we label the very general attraction exerted by Fascism in France since Mussolini, and second because the fundamental question was how to maintain peace, which must be distinguished from a Fascist-type option. Extreme pacifism did draw a certain number of intellectuals toward Germany: Ramon Fernandez, one of the founding members of the Anti-Fascist Intellectuals' Vigilance Committee, ended up as a "collaborator" during the war. But that was later, and his case was an exception. Until the war, French pacifists, including those who embraced Munich, continued to have their moorings largely on the left.

There remains the multifaceted Communist/anti-Communist question, which usually consisted of the hostile reactions or mistrust elicited by Communist politics, no matter what their orientation, both on the right and in bourgeois public opinion in general. To anti-Communists, the 1934–35 shift aggravated the Communist threat to the social order by extending the influence of the French Communist Party to a victorious Left and to the government itself. The Party could multiply its "republican" promises all it wanted, throw opprobrium on all the various brands of leftism, reach out to Catholics and patriots; yet it continued to be suspected of having in no way altered either its means or its ends. The very suddenness with which it had espoused a policy of national defense, prompted by a few words from Stalin, indicated its lack of autonomy. The same militants who had insulted their country in the name of opposition to the Treaty of Versailles immediately began to mobilize all good Frenchmen against Hitler. What was in doubt was not their spirit of sacrifice but their versatility—their independence and judgment and, hence, the endurance of their new strategy.

Both the strength and the weakness of Communism resided more than ever in its ultimate reality, the Soviet Union. As to its strength, the Bolshevik revolution was supported by a huge state, organized according to new principles and offering a new ideological, political, and military platform to be anti-Fascists in their opposition to Hitler. But in according such a major role to the USSR, the general economy of Communist anti-Fascism showed its weaknesses. The prior acceptance of a war with Nazi Germany on the side of the USSR carried the risk of delivering the small Eastern European countries, especially Poland, to the Red Army; it relied, incautiously, on the solidity of the alliance between the capitalist democracies and Stalin's Soviet Union; and it pre-empted the scenario preferred by many Western diplomats—to point Hitler eastward, accepting the risk of sacrificing the countries that lay between him and the USSR.

As to the nature of the Soviet regime, for many intellectuals it was the crucial factor. If the Soviet Union could be defined by anti-Fascism, or even by radical anti-Fascism (because it was socialist), how could one hesitate to turn to it? What did it matter if it was "totalitarian" or merely dictatorial and, like Hitler, hostile to liberty? Members of the French and the British Right abhorred the Soviet regime without pondering over it; they simply followed their inclinations. But there was a whole chunk of public opinion that reacted in a less simplistic way, especially on the left and in the center: if the Soviet Union claimed to be the advance guard in the fight against Fascism, and if, as the Communists maintained, one had to be pro-Soviet in order to be anti-Fascist, then it was not enough to consider an alliance with the USSR in diplomatic terms, such as expedience. The qualifications of the countries seeking to incarnate the anti-Fascist idea had to be verified. That examination would bring honor to the Left, whereas the Right was more often content simply to condemn.

In the years we are now considering, the USSR was experiencing one of the worst periods in its history, namely, the Great Terror. Gide had divined only the tip of the iceberg. Since his celebrated *Retour*, the great Moscow show trials had exposed the depth of the purge under way between 1936 and 1939, as well as the use of confessions, by which the accused simultaneously demonstrated their guilt and the clairvoyance of their interrogators, spelling their own death. The function of the trials was to polarize politics in the battle between Fascism and anti-Fascism: Trotsky was no longer a dissident or a defeated Bolshevik but an accomplice of the Nazis. The absurdity of what was said in front of these rigged tribunals, which tried only broken men, did not change believers' minds. But in all the racket about the "new humanity" and the joys of collective farming, a dissonance both frail and sharp made itself heard, which could not be extinguished despite all efforts. Most intellectual celebrities did not want to hear about this dissonance, but for the heirs of Pascal, Souvarine, Rosmer, and Silone, the Moscow trials cast a shadow on the country they had loved. Victor Serge, who ended up being deported and was once again hard at work, issued many analyses and warnings. He was one of the first to speak of the system of the Soviet Union as a world of prisons and camps: "Neither the optimistic statistics nor the accounts of tourists traversing Eurasia in sleeping-cars will be able to conceal from us the terrible murmur that rises from the prisons and the slums."[44] In 1938, the Croatian Ante Ciliga, another militant who had escaped from the Soviet work camps, published *Au pays du grand mensonge*,[45] a lengthy report on the Soviet world of concentration camps concealed beneath utopian language. The book was a flop, but it marked out a field that would bring fame to Kravchenko after World War II and to the great dissidents of the 1960s and 1970s. The Moscow trials and the concentration camps set off a new wave of Communist disenchantment from 1937 to 1939, which would be crowned by the German-Soviet nonaggression pact.

Soviet reality came back to haunt the scene of Communist anti-Fascism, threatening to destroy its coherence. If, under the mask of proletarian power, the Soviet Union was hiding a police dictatorship so universal and repressive that the only thing it allowed in public was the solemn approbation of its victims, how could it be made into the standard of the battle against Fascism? This indestructible question constantly dogged the abstract certainty that Stalin, the incarnation of socialism, was the extreme opposite of Hitler, the product of capitalism. Another look at the Ligue des droits de l'homme, French anti-Fascism's best forum,[46] may help us to grasp just how deeply rooted that question was.

The Ligue was born of the battle against a judicial error, the Dreyfus Affair. It brought together an intellectual bourgeoisie of professors and lawyers who, by tradition and profession, were particularly attuned to the defense of human rights in the world; they were closer to 1789 than to 1917, closer to Freemasonry than to Marxism-Leninism. The first Moscow trials, in the summer of 1936, struck this anti-Fascist learned assembly like a thunderbolt at the moment when all eyes were on Spain. Executions in the name of public safety preceded by a secret judicial process would probably have been less disconcerting for these democrats than the Soviet tribunal's condemnation of Lenin's companions in public courts on the basis of implausible confessions. The president of the Ligue, Victor Basch, resolved to raise a protest;[47] the country concerned was, after all, the USSR. A commission of inquiry was established.

The first conclusions of the commission were presented on 18 October 1936 by its spokesman, Raymond Rosenmark, legal counsel to the Ligue.[48] By way of a prologue, Rosenmark first dealt briefly with the irregularities of the Moscow trials in terms of French law: that civilians were judged by a military court, that the preliminary investigation was secret, that there were no defense lawyers and no witnesses, and that the prosecutor, Vishinski, used obscene language. The report itself revolved almost entirely around the confessions, treating them as a legal issue. What made the confessions admissible evidence, and thus credible in spite of their highly exceptional character, was that they had never been retracted during the deposition and the trial, and that all sixteen of the accused had confessed. "It runs contrary to all the historical evidence of criminal justice to assume that, by means of torture or the threat of torture, sixteen out of sixteen innocent people can be made to confess."[49] Nonetheless, the report concluded that more information was needed, insofar as the Moscow trials had revealed the existence of a Nazi conspiracy that had spread to several third-party nations; like revolutionary France in its time, the USSR was targeted by a new set of conspirators. "It would be a negation of the French Revolution, which, according to a famous saying, was a 'bloc,' if we were to deny a nation's right to take strong measures against agitators for civil war, against conspirators with foreign connections."[50]

The commission proceeded with its work, inviting the radical socialist Albert Bayet and the lawyer Maurice Paz to join its three original members—Victor Basch, Mirkine-Guetzevitch (president of the Russian League for the Rights of Man), and Rosenmark. It began to examine the evidence in the second Moscow trial, which had begun in January 1937 against a new batch of old Bolsheviks including Radek and Piatakov. A major public debate took place within the Ligue during its meeting in July of the same year, just after the third trial was held in Moscow. This time, behind closed doors, the leaders of the Red Army were condemned for being accessories to the Hitler-Trotskyist intrigue.

The offensive against the Rosenmark report was led by the old pacifist Félicien Challaye, who, a Communist or a fellow traveler since 1920, had grown hostile toward the USSR in 1935. He denounced the extorted confessions, the extravagance of the charges, and the Ligue's indulgence for the executioners rather than the victims under the guise of impartiality. The Ligue's *Cahiers* went so far as to refuse to publish a refutation of the report by Magdeleine Paz. On the literary side, Challaye was supported by Alain, André Breton, Jean Giono, and Georges Bataille. He was also supported by Georges Pioch, another central figure of the anti-Communist Left who had been one of the leaders of the neophyte French Communist Party during the 1920s. He warned his friends in the Ligue against the two mental devices that threatened to cloud their judgment about the Soviet trials—the analogy with the French Revolution and the blackmail of the anti-Fascist union. This provoked a counterattack on the part of Rosenmark, who continued to maintain that, according to the press, the accused had freely confessed and that the confessions were valid according to French and British jurisprudence.

It fell to the Ligue's president to conclude this thorny debate, punctuated by not always friendly interruptions. Victor Basch enjoyed a great deal of moral authority over his listeners.[51] Not that members of the Ligue were easily led, much less united; impatient with any imposed discipline, most of them were divided within themselves, racked by the contradictions of an anti-Fascism at once triumphant and fragile. Their president came from a place remote from the ambiguous times in which they found themselves. Born in Bratislava to a Hungarian Jewish family fifty years before World War I, he had become a French citizen through his enthusiasm for the Republic and through the Dreyfus Affair. As a professor of German at the Sorbonne in 1906, he had fought for socialism and peace in Jaurès's shadow, and in 1907 he became a member of the Central Committee of the Ligue. In 1914 he was unafraid, for he saw the French cause as justified; yet he was no zealot for going to war. His moral and political homeland had always been the sort of French-style republican universality that Jaurès had managed to incorporate into the socialist future, conceived as a peaceful redeployment of the ideas of the French Revolution by the proletariat. This spirit of synthesis made him a natural to assume the presidency of the Ligue in 1926 and then, especially after 1933, to spearhead the anti-Fascist fight. Having pleaded for a reconciliation with Germany after 1918, he was now once again trapped by history into a democratic crusade against the country whose great writers he had taught for so long. Henceforth, his principal enemy was Hitler. He fought actively for the formation of the Front populaire and for aid to Spain; he controlled a majority within the Ligue, but he would eventually clash with the Ligue's pacifists.

The 1937 debate illustrates both his conviction and his dilemma. He had no sympathy for Communism or for the intolerance of the Bolshevik credo, but neither his experience nor his political vision provided him with the keys to understand them. He tended to perceive that distant world through the ideas that made it accessible to him, and to excuse the elements of that vision that were most contradictory to human rights as the temporary shortcomings of a defensive revolution. After all, were not Lenin's most enthusiastic partisans the most vehement detractors of the Moscow trials? Victor Basch, who had once protested against the terror exercised by Lenin and Trotsky, was cautious about the Moscow trials, as though criticizing the nascent Soviet regime somehow preempted judgment of the Stalinist Terror. We see here another example of a classic procedure, borrowed, incidentally, from the Communists—that of eliminating from the debate over Communism, on account of their excessive partiality, those who were fighting it after having served it.

Those members of the French Left who came into conflict in July 1937 over the Moscow trials were actually arguing about anti-Fascism in France. Throughout the twentieth century and in all of Europe, differences in opinion over the Soviet regime coincided with and revealed more concrete political conflicts over domestic policy. In 1937 France, where the victorious anti-Fascist coalition of 1936 was already riddled with cracks, the question of repression in the USSR threatened the whole spirit of the Front populaire. Félicien Challaye, a veteran of unconditional pacifism, had all the more reason to raise that question because he abhorred the Communists' wish to make anti-Fascism look like a military crusade. Victor Basch reacted in the opposite way, subordinating what he feared was the truth about Stalin to the fight against Hitler.[52] By birth and by profession he belonged to those few, under a hundred thousand of them, who had immediately understood the Hitlerian enterprise: German Jews had been on the front line since 1933. As an adopted son of French democracy who had become one its moral archetypes, he spoke up, unlike many of the refugees driven by Hitler from Germany and then from Austria, condemned to keep silent in a France that had no affection for these prophets of calamity, especially if they were Jewish.

For this reason, Victor Basch balked at destroying the unity of the Front populaire, upon which he had lavished so much care. Even though, as he told everyone, he had serious misgivings about the Moscow trials, he did not like the idea of the debate over the trials, which divided the union against Hitler. Neither could he prevent the debate; the Rosenmark report, which he had approved, was the product of the voluntary half-blindness that reflected the dominant mind-set of the Ligue.[53] A few months later he reassured himself with his favorite quotation, his own words: "Our Revolution too caused the blood of thousands of innocents to be shed; nonetheless, if we democrats were to be asked, If you had the choice, which would you choose, the Revolution along with its crimes, or no crimes and no Revolution? how many of us would choose the second?"[54]

In the meantime, the minority leaders—Challaye, Pioch, Bergery, Michel Alexandre, and Magdeleine Paz, among others—had left the Ligue. Most of them, clear about the Moscow trials, would have preferred to ignore Hitler's aggression. Victor Basch and his majority, clear about Hitler,[55] did not like the idea of condemning the Stalinist regime.

To complete this ideological and political inventory, we must consider a group that has been all but forgotten, though at the time its views were quite widespread among French intellectuals, those who, to varying degrees, viewed both Communism and Fascism with interest or sympathy. This group enters our discussion through a side door, for it was not part of the anti-Fascist coalition in spite of its hostility to the conservative bourgeoisie. Neither right- nor left-wing, it offers a new perspective on Western ambiguities about Soviet Communism.

To judge by what the USSR said about itself, it was the paradise of "real" liberty finally won. To judge by what it actually did, it projected the image of a society in which the individual was entirely subordinated to the state. But this elementary and relatively neutral statement can be understood as either positive or negative: in both cases, it tends to conflate Communism with Fascism, whether to despise them both or, on the contrary, to provide a variety of examples of the same phenomenon: the *Aufhebung* of modern individualism. In contemporary "tyrannies" in their dual guise—to borrow Élie Halévy's words—the liberals abhorred the omnipotence of the party, the end of freedom, the confusion of powers, the cult of the leader. Enemies of liberalism could also continue to admire both sorts of totalitarian regimes for putting an end to individualistic anarchy, restoring a strong central power, and assembling people around a great collective goal. During the 1930s, people who adhered to that line of thought were more numerous, more powerful, and more inclined to write and publish than any before them. Even though such an attitude is still in our midst, it is almost impossible to imagine it in its earlier form: since 1945, Fascism has been banished from humanity for its crimes. History, however, compels us to recognize that Fascism, before becoming a defeated evil, had been, like Communism, a source of hope for many European intellectuals.

Fascism originated as a hostile sibling to Communism; what it borrowed from Communism enabled it to neutralize its rival. When Stalin came, Communism revealed new traits that encouraged this tempting analogy—a nationalist twist, the construction of a new order, the cult of the leader. We have already noted the spell cast by "National Bolshevism" over part of the German Right. Criticism of bourgeois society, however, was so widespread in France that it is still an issue, whether on the intellectual right or left. Action française was the first well-stocked storehouse of antibourgeois politics and served as the schoolroom for most of the interwar period authors. In 1925, one of its pupils, Georges Valois, a follower of Maurras crossbred with "Sorélism," an admirer of Mussolini and probably the first true French Fascist, defined the kinship between Fascism and Communism thus: "No matter which one prevails and absorbs the other, Communism in Russia and Fascism in Italy will have identical results. No Parliament, no democracy, a dictatorship, a nation that shapes itself. When the bourgeoisie has been booted out, the alliance between the state and the people will make everyone conform to the national discipline. . . . Fascism took the best from Action française and from socialism. In Europe it is becoming a synthesis of all the positive antidemocratic movements." [56]

Valois's words were premonitory; a flurry of French works in the same vein followed, preaching the marriage between the revolution and the nation. The French Fascists never gained political autonomy, least of all between 1934 and 1936, when the Communists had succeeded in taking the initiative of the anti-Fascist Popular Fronts. But they do show, in the French context, that even when the Right and the Left were arguing about Fascism, an antiliberal political current persisted, within which the Soviet experience remained a positive point of reference, even to those tempted by Fascism. An example of this current was Drieu La Rochelle, who was tossed about by the twentieth century, unable to find a foothold in it despite of his passion to find its meaning and to play an active role.

Drieu La Rochelle was a friend of Malraux's, though less gifted. Like Malraux, he loved the noise of history, decisive actors, contradictory loyalties, and vague ideas. But Malraux had a nose for the great moments of the century and managed to grab them, turning them into his characters and his books. Drieu La Rochelle did not see those moments coming, missed them, and lost out. He was undone by the Fascist passions that underlay his literary dandyism—his hatred of Jews, Freemasons, members of parliament. A more brilliant talent, or a stronger nature, might have survived his outdated sentiments: but at least Drieu remained one the best witnesses of this ideological state of mind.

Brought into manhood by the First World War, he was involved for a time with Action française and also flirted with surrealism. As a young veteran, both a patriot and a pacifist, he had been friends with Raymond

Lefebvre, one of the founders of French Communism.[57] In his political writings in the 1920s he pleaded for a federation of Europe as the only chance for saving the world's oldest nations, caught between the USSR and the United States, between war and decadence. All his writings of that time were markedly hostile to capitalism and liberal anarchy. In the early 1930s Drieu was still mainly left-wing, close to Bergery and his anti-Fascist "Front commun," but he was increasingly part of that intellectual current which was uncertain as to what separated the Left from the Right and which constantly shifted opinions and actors—antibourgeois, antiliberal, clamoring for national planning and rebirth, but torn between the two poles of Communism and Fascism. When the Front populaire was being formed, Drieu tended toward Fascism but in the name of Communism's ideals: "I have become convinced that Fascism is a necessary stage in the destruction of capitalism. For Fascism does not help capitalism; contrary to the beliefs of the anti-Fascists, contrary to the beliefs of the majority of people who are rallying to Fascism, . . . Fascism creates a transitional civilization, in which capitalism as it existed during its period of great prosperity is brought to a rapid destruction."[58]

During the same year, 1934, with the poor timing that always dogged him, Drieu published a brief work entitled *Socialisme fasciste*.[59] It was a new attempt to designate revolutions as a necessary means of transformation. Europe acquired its historical profile by means of an early wave of "democratic and parliamentary" revolutions set off by seventeenth-century England. October 1917 inaugurated a second series of revolutions, which included those of Mussolini and Hitler. The march on Rome and the Nazi seizure of power were not so much reactions to Bolshevism as derivations of it, just as October had been not "proletarian" but authoritarian, not Marxist but Leninist, establishing the dictatorship not of a class but of a party, and just as Fascist revolutions, necessitated by the crisis in the capitalist economy and parliamentary democracy, were "socialist-leaning and authoritarian," designed to put a political aristocracy in power, grouped around a leader. Stalin, Mussolini, and Hitler were all fighting the same revolutionary and nationalistic battle: "The interests of the nation and the revolution merge in the eyes of Russian youth as in the eyes of the Italian or German youth."[60]

So Drieu translated in his own way the omnipotence of the revolutionary idea over the imagination. Like the Left, he honored revolutions as necessary events possessing a special historical dignity. But in so doing, he was compelled to shift his emphasis from class to party, the era's new divinity. In his view, Bolshevism and Fascism were not separated by the Marxist categories of proletariat and bourgeoisie but were united by the common search for a solution to the "governability" of modern nations. The bourgeoisie was merely an economic class, incapable by definition of forming a political elite. The same was true of the working class; there were no more governing classes than there were revolutionary classes. The revolutions of the twentieth century sought to replace this void by a single party, constituted by deliberate choice, a hothouse for leaders around the great leader. Drieu, lazy and apathetic, shared the obsession of his time—the urge to understand the enigma of political will.

Nevertheless, the kinship between the antidemocratic regimes that had emerged since 1917 did not stop them from going to war against one another. The very opposite happened as they added to yesterday's quarrels the ideological ambitions that are part and parcel of revolutions.

> For Russia, Germany (Hitlerian or not) remains the great neighbor whose technical superiority has not been abolished. And between the semisocialism of the German Fascists and the semi-Fascism of the Russian Communists there exists the same muted familial hatred that existed between the Romanovs' imperialism and that of the Hohenzollerns or the Habsburgs. On both sides, there is the same national base and, on top of that, the same tendency to world evangelism. That is what leads to battle.[61]

In the near future, nothing seemed likely but decadence or the ruin of Western capitalist democracies; they would be succeeded by Hitler's Europe, or Stalin's.

When Drieu wrote this, he was not yet a Fascist, even though, by reading between the lines, we can perceive the defeated man who ten years later (10 June 1944) wrote in his *Journal:* "Looking in the direction of Moscow. As Fascism crumbles, I fix my last thoughts on Communism."[62] But this rather facile prediction is not the most interesting of Drieu's 1934 observations; moreover, the writer's path toward National Socialism was atypical. What was interesting, around 1934–36, was the dual fascination exerted by Fascism and Communism on many intellectuals, who used these ideologies to express their contempt for the bourgeois society in which they lived.

Unlike Drieu, most of these intellectuals were reluctant to commit themselves to Fascism because prewar France, and subsequently wartime France, would be first the adversary and then the victim of Nazi Germany. After the Second World War, not one of them remembered having considered Nazism as a social or political experience worthy of interest. Retrospectively, they all aligned themselves in the polarized area that had been consecrated by the blood spilled—on the right side, of course. The other side was totally criminal. In fact, things did not happen that way, and one need only glance through the political literature of the period, both on the left and on the right, to see how much attention was accorded to the Mussolinian dictatorship and German Nazism. This polemical literature sought to criticize French parliamentarianism rather than to analyze foreign regimes. Instead of listening to what the German Jews pouring into France had to say, the French— Drieu, for example—argued about the ravages or the advantages of liberalism. The debate over Fascism was no better informed than was the debate over Communism, and for the same reasons: real observation played a very limited role.

It is in this light that we must consider the interminable polemic that has dragged on in France at the end of the twentieth century over the politics of left-wing Catholic intellectuals and their journal *Esprit* during those years, a line of thinking that reaches back to Marc Sangnier's *Sillon,* at the beginning of the century. Like that of liberal Catholics in the midnineteenth century, their thinking broke openly with the radically antimodern character of the philosophical and political positions of the Catholic Church, but it went one step further, attempting to initiate a debate with the Marxist Left, including the Communists.

As Daniel Lindenberg understood so well,[63] the Catholic Left extended its curiosity to Marxism through the concept of "community." Conveyed by the Christian tradition, the word refers to a social world in which individual activity is organized in terms of the common good, drawn from the divine will and Christ's sacrifice. In the nineteenth century, it encountered the Romantic critique of modern society: made up of individuals separate from one another, each pursuing his or her own interest, that society is the opposite of a community. The Romantic critique was turned toward the past, nostalgic for the organic Middle Ages, but it was basically no different from the socialist critique, oriented toward the future: both considered modern commercial society to be subverted by bourgeois individualism and thus incapable of founding a true social order. Socialist thinkers merely shifted the solution to the future. They sought to rebuild, on the debris of that individualism, a fraternal world of people associated around a common project. In early nineteenth-century Europe, a certain messianic interpretation of the evangelical promise merged with the revolutionary faith in the regeneration of man: hostile to the bourgeois of 1789, the neo-Catholic Buchez viewed the Jacobin revolution of 1793 as the French prefiguration of the reunion between humanity and community.

A hundred years later, Mounier was drawn to Marxism by the ambition to rebuild a community. Unlike Buchez, however, the editor-in-chief of *Esprit* was disinclined to combine the spiritual and the temporal. Nor did he wish to rebuild a society of corporate and professional status, modeled on the family. His community was to be neither the product of a providential history nor the resurrection of a lost precapitalist order. It corresponded to the most fundamental need of human beings, those creatures of God: the openness to the Other, and the constant search to go beyond oneself. As against capitalist society, that mechanical conglomeration of isolated individuals, Mounier proposed a living and freely constituted community, spiritually active and held together by a creative thrust toward the common good. As a new, "personalist" antibourgeois utopia, the version of the City offered by Mounier and his friends tended toward the left. Though philosophically incompatible with Communism, it shared the Communists' militant spirit and hostility to capitalism. This encouraged dialogue and common undertakings.

But for all that, *Esprit* was not unanimously "anti-Fascist," for Fascism was also part of what Mounier called "the immense communitarian wave that was unfurling over Europe."[64] Fascism too was based on a denunciation of bourgeois individualism and functioned by extolling collective volition. It was a communitarian remodeling of the democracies exhausted by the domination of private interests. The cheapened Nietzscheism in circulation at the time attributed the same status to Communism—a privilege that came with gratuitous adventures pitting will against economic determinism.

The not always favorable but often benevolent attitude of *Esprit* toward the Italian and German Fascist experiences cannot be held for a conversion to Nazism. This attitude could be found among most political groups—except for the Communists—that were hostile to economic liberalism or parliamentary democracy. It was most common in regimes that were enjoying popular success: Mussolini was at the peak of his domestic popularity and his international reputation; the German economy under Hitler was rapidly reviving, in contrast to French stagnation. Thus circumstantial evidence added its weight to the rationales and passions stirred up by ideology. The Italian and German dictatorships seemed to be driving European politics. Sadly, although anti-Semites anywhere could have a weakness for Hitler, one didn't have to be anti-Semitic to be drawn to Fascism. It was enough to be both non-Communist and antiliberal; this defined a vast zone of intellectual opinion, on the right and on the left. I use the term "non-Communist" rather than "anti-Communist" deliberately: for many, antipathy toward

liberalism and rejection of bourgeois hypocrisy, combined with the nihilism that lent the era its tone, were enough to blend an attraction for
Fascism with a weakness for Communism.

A parallel history of Marx and Nietzsche in the context of twentieth-
century France would provide us with a more profound understanding
of French intellectual and moral life than does the contrast between Fascism and anti-Fascism. But it has yet to be written. The history of the
French intelligentsia of the Front populaire, however, illustrates the extent to which political anti-Fascist coalitions hid more than they revealed of the reality of the era. Therein lay their fragility.

To understand what Vincent Descombes has called "the French disarray of 1938,"[65] we should turn to literary criticism or philosophy
rather than to politics, for it was there that the explosion of republican
positivism that followed World War I was most evident, along with the
heterogeneous fragments of an aesthetic nihilism with which it littered
its cultural space. The most beautiful of those fragments, surrealism,
was destroyed from within by its own eclecticism and from without
by its competition with Communism. Surrealism bequeathed Louis
Aragon to the Comintern campaigns, and left André Breton a prophet
without prophecy, a "revolutionary without a revolution,"[66] a great
voice which, from the start, had nothing much to say. It was a sign of
the times that the French writer most suited to the kind of moral mag-
istracy of literature conferred by the national tradition was compelled
to fall silent, or almost silent, at the age of thirty-five. His refusal to lie
was honorable, but it also revealed the narrowness, the fragility, of his
philosophy: when the revolutionary flame was extinguished in Eastern
Europe, he seemed intimidated because history had passed him by. If
he sought to reignite that flame by his own means, what weakness and
what solitude! Breton ought to have remained a remarkable witness to
the twentieth century, even greater, perhaps, through his withdrawal
and his consent to early obscurity. The era had condemned him to measure stoically the failure of his command of ideas; in this sense he was
more realistic than his friend Trotsky, that other indomitable exile who
persisted in belying the contradictions of history.

The surrealist movement died prematurely from having nothing
more to say about the revolution that had been its watchword. It was
broken by Communist blackmail. History, by confiscating its talisman,
had returned its members to the aristocratic freedom natural to writers
and artists, a freedom abrogated by Aragon when he chose a far more
rigorous servitude than that of the bourgeois condition, in which he
might at least have found political roles and major literary genres.
Breton was a king stripped of his realm; the Trotsky of literature, he

became an unemployed genius. He had no control over the remnants of surrealism, which, moreover, had lost the classic majesty of its style: it was antibourgeois anathema, more violent than ever but rid of all political usage, released from canonical forms. Wrapped in bombastic prose, it was now more akin to Nietzsche and Freud than to Marx.

As for Georges Bataille, his hatred of the bourgeoisie inspired brief, peremptory works denouncing the psychological poverty of utilitarian and homogenized man, lost in the universal pedestrianism of economic calculation. The bourgeois has emptied human relations of all that was orgiastic, festive—of all that bore a sacred meaning in the societies described in Marcel Mauss's *The Gift.*[67] The bourgeois no longer wants to "spend" for anyone but himself, surreptitiously, condemned by his very condition to hypocrisy. His abjection is the shame of humanity. The modern society over which he reigns consists of individuals enslaved by the standard of money and therefore strangers to discrimination and passions, especially the prime passion, sexuality. These are all familiar themes; they began with Hegel, of whom Kojève was the Parisian interpreter, and took on a new radicality with Nietzsche and Freud. It was the beginning of a new German obsession in French thought, springing from the still majestic ruins of academic positivism. Bataille offered no very coherent interpretation of the great writers from across the Rhine,[68] but they lent him what was needed to nourish a nihilism of despair.

Bataille's objective was nothing other than the Enlightenment tradition, extended from the revolutionary optimism of the nineteenth century, a combination of Condorcet and Marx. He sought to substitute the dynamic force of despair for the "geometric concept of the future": "the future does not depend on the paltry efforts of a few incorrigibly optimistic unifiers; it is totally dependent on a general disorientation."[69] To him, the age was plunged in wretchedness—the irremediable wretchedness of bourgeois democracies sunken into the incapacity to exist, of revolts directed against that society in the name of life as opposed to inertia: "Any vital force existing today has taken the form of a totalitarian state. . . . Stalin, the shadow and chill cast by his name alone upon any revolutionary hope, along with the horror of the German and Italian police, portrays a humanity where the cries of revolt have become politically negligible, where such cries are now nothing but wrenching and adversity."[70] Written in September 1933 after the rise of Hitler, these lines indicate that the only hope lay in the absolute of despair.

Bataille, then, had nothing in common with anti-Fascism, which he considered a vain undertaking devoid of historical substance, tied to an empty philosophy of progress. The anti-Fascists were "wizards battling storms,"[71] whereas "storms" were the only thing that could budge the moribund foundation of bourgeois society. Both Fascism and Communism were aborted storms, since they ultimately constituted servile societies to be opposed in the name of hatred of the state. But their appearance, that which gave rise to them, and even their complete failure testify once more to the sorry condition of twentieth-century humanity. Communism had engendered the revolt of the proletariat, the only nonbourgeois and hence heterogeneous class. Fascism (to which Bataille would devote a special study that same year),[72] unlike the bourgeois state—an agent of, and subject to, mass society—represented the heterogeneity of power, the return to the sacred aspect of power. Fascist society in effect restored to "royal society" an authority that was inseparably both religious and political, the collective psychological forum indispensable to the heterogeneity of individuals. But that restoration was also a negation of bourgeois society, offering a solution different from proletarian revolution to those classes that were dissociated from the homogeneous society, and thus a popular base for Fascism. "From this potential duality of effervescence results an unprecedented situation. A single society is witness to the formation, concurrently, of two revolutions, which are both hostile to one another and hostile to the established order."[73] The great modern convulsion consist of two movements of separation from the bourgeois condition, movements at once opposing and colluding. They feed each other and mobilize affective forces that simultaneously combine and neutralize each other: witnesses and actors of the interminable subversion that weaves the history of human emancipation without ever completing it.

Before the war, Bataille had never expressed himself better than in his 1933 writings on the great political questions of the time. After a brief reconciliation with Breton in 1935, for the duration of a call to world revolution,[74] he shut himself up in small, ultra-leftist groups—Acéphale, and then the Collège de sociologie—tiny communities of the chosen, who felt called to pursue the secrets of social existence. The Collège de sociologie was frequented between 1938 and 1939 by Benda, Drieu, Benjamin, and Adorno. Its object was "the study of social existence, in all of its manifestations in which the active presence of the sacred reveals itself."[75] Oddly enough, Bataille referred to Durkheim in order to transform his discovery of the "social" as the seat of the religious into the investigative field of a post-Nietzschean nihilism.

But his writings are important not so much for their rigor, which was nonexistent, or their talent, which was mediocre, as for the cold, deadly violence that animated them and for their presaging the end of the Enlightenment world. The gods of republican anti-Fascism were Jean-Jacques Rousseau and Victor Hugo, the fathers and sons of 1789. Soviet

Communism was included in this reassuring filiation: the revolutionary identity preempted the notion that there was a difference between democracy and totalitarianism. Bataille, however, knocked down that house of cards. Neither the Enlightenment nor the French Revolution provided a key to understanding the convulsions of the twentieth century.

One young philosopher, Raymond Aron, was quick to perceive and analyze the rift that had opened up in the European democratic heritage. Without indulging in the desperate absolution of totalitarian regimes that we have seen in Bataille and his friends, Aron began a long, solitary marathon through the French intelligentsia. He had started out, a young *normalien*, as a pacifist-leaning socialist.[76] Dispatched to Germany for a lengthy period in the early 1930s, at the beginning of his professional life, he returned with a clear picture of Hitler's enterprise on the one hand and, on the other, a critique of historical reason.[77] These two things belonged to two different orders of reality, but from the start they formed a mental questionnaire unprecedented at the École normale supérieure, which had formed him. How to oppose Hitler? How to interpret history, and how to relate that interpretation to the truth? The extent to which the latter question was hardly academic in spite of its abstract character can be seen in Aron's defense of his thesis at the Sorbonne in 1938. The candidate belonged not only to a different generation from that of his examiners but also to a different philosophical and moral world, one fostered by Max Weber and Dilthey, exposing the uncertain status of our understanding of the past just as that status was being caught up in the tragedy of history—something Aron grasped before anyone else. In him, the examiners sensed, and feared, the specter of nihilistic anxiety looming up amid convictions about law and progress.[78]

Yet this divided man, this critical philosopher, responded categorically to the first and most urgent questioning about Berlin: resisting Hitler was the absolute priority of the day. But he did not define that battle in the "anti-Fascist" manner of the contemporary Left. Living in the professional milieu of Bouglé, an admirer of Élie Halévy, Aron had no illusions about the Soviet Union and was also critical of the Front populaire.[79] He saw anti-Fascism, with its ambiguous alliances and goals, as rooted in a dead tradition—the historical optimism of the French Revolution and of the nineteenth century, relayed by academic positivism. The most interesting article by the young Raymond Aron on this subject is his paper given before the Société française de philosophie on 17 June 1939, on the eve of the last peacetime summer in Europe.[80]

Aron had titled his paper "Democratic States and Totalitarian States." By "totalitarian," he could only have been referring to Hitler's Germany or Mussolini's Italy. He clearly did not class the USSR in the first category, since one of the theses he develops is that "totalitarian regimes are primarily opposed to democracies and not to Communism." What the Fascist states sought to destroy was not only the political heritage of the nineteenth century but the very spirit of the Western tradition. In this sense, they were "authentically revolutionary," and the favor they had enjoyed in English and French conservative thought could hardly have been "stranger." Faced with the Fascist states, democracies were in a defensive, conservative position: they were in danger of atrophying over a dead heritage that was incapable of granting them new life. "Today, the question is not to save bourgeois, humanitarian, or pacifistic illusions. The excesses of irrationalism do not disqualify—quite to the contrary—the effort needed to cast doubt on progressivism, abstract moralism, or the ideas of 1789. Democratic conservatism, like rationalism, can survive only by renewing itself."[81] For Aron, this was the only way to avoid the catastrophic alternative of Fascism-Communism.

Among those who heard the young philosopher speak that day was Victor Basch. The president of the League of the Rights of Man was a fair approximation of everything the speaker was criticizing—progressivism, pacifism, French-style revolutionary tradition. A courteous conversation ensued between the two men, neither hearing the other. Basch was indignant that Hitler and Mussolini could be honored with the title of revolutionary and that democracies could be described as conservative regimes; such a view was logical for him, since he regarded democracy as essentially revolutionary. But what irritated him the most about Aron's speech was that Aron called into question the principles of 1789, judging them "abstract" and incapable of renewing the democratic spirit. The old Leaguer renewed his pledge of allegiance to the republican faith that had guided his entire existence.

Aron had not meant to attack the ideas of 1789 as ideas; but he did not want French revolutionary universalism to mold the thought and actions of the twentieth-century world. Not only did that universalism fail to enhance understanding of contemporary revolutions, whether Fascist or Communist, but it masked them. On a practical level, it disarmed members of the democracies instead of preparing them for combat. It encouraged rhetoric and moralism, and distracted attention from economic and military realities; it prevented institutional reform, and led to pacifism: these were the negative, though veiled, consequences of the Front populaire and "anti-Fascism." From his first major debate with the French intellectual Left, which was his original milieu, Aron had shown the precise extent of his disagreement and, at the same time, the originality of his critical position. Intellectually, he perceived the twentieth-century revolutions as unique events; his "understanding" of history owed more to Weber than to the French democratic revolutionary vulgate. Politically, he was more democratic than republican, too much of a reformer to belong to the Right, too hostile to the anti-Fascist discourse to belong to the Left, and, for both sides, all too lucid about the coming war.

World War II

THE SECOND WORLD WAR, COMPRISING TWO
successive and contradictory periods, provides a window on the ambiguities of Communist anti-Fascism. From September 1939 to June
1941, Stalin was Hitler's principal ally; from June 1941 to May 1945, his
most determined enemy. It is the second period, authenticated by victory, that has been retained by the selective memory of nations; the first
period, however, must also have its historical due if we are to avoid
solely a winner's version of the past.

The pact signed in Moscow by Ribbentrop and Molotov on 23 August 1939 inaugurated the alliance between the USSR and Nazi Germany. It was presented as an alliance and not just a nonaggression pact
in the midst of the Polish crisis, but the document actually contained a
secret protocol long denied by the Soviets:[1] it revealed the precise extent
of the territorial agreement between the two partners on the eve of the
German troops' crossing of the Polish border. Hitler had put a prior
claim on Lithuania and Western Poland but had conceded that Estonia,
Latvia, Bessarabia, and the part of Poland east of the Narev, Vistula, and
San rivers belonged to the Soviet sphere of influence. The scale of these
anticipated concessions to Soviet expansion shows what Hitler had to
gain from Stalin's about-face: he had a free hand not only in Poland but
in the West.

Hitler entered Poland on 1 September and was at war with Britain
and France two days later. For two more weeks, the time it took for a
speedy deployment of German tanks in the Polish plain, the idea of
continuing an anti-Fascist policy by other means was justifiable and,
moreover, justified, especially by the French Communist Party,[2] since
the German-Soviet nonaggression pact of 23 August, the only public
agreement, was regarded as Stalin's retaliation for the French and British leadership's attempts to isolate him and as a way of gaining time

while remaining outside of the conflict. Even the Soviet troops' entry into Poland on 17 September could, in a pinch, be interpreted as a way of guaranteeing their position. Public opinion was not aware that in eastern Poland, in the wake of the Red Army, the NKVD was doing much the same thing as the SS battalions had done in the wake of the Wehrmacht: liquidating or deporting the Polish elites along with anyone vaguely resembling a potential adversary. Within eight days, Stalin had taken over western Belorussia and the Polish-Ukrainian territories.

On 28 September, Ribbentrop returned to Moscow. There was no longer any doubt about what the Soviets were doing, even without knowledge of the secret protocol on the division of Poland and the re-distribution of populations along ethnic lines.[3] The Nazi minister had signed a veritable treaty of cooperation and friendship with Molotov, topped off by the famous communiqué:

> The government of the Reich and the government of the Soviet Union, by the arrangement signed today, having definitively dealt with the questions raised by the dissolution of the Polish state, and having thus created a basis for a lasting peace in Eastern Europe, express together the opinion that it is in the true interest of all nations to put an end to the state of war that exists between Germany on the one hand and France and Britain on the other. The two governments will thus un-dertake common measures, when necessary, in agreement with other friendly powers, to attain that goal as quickly as possible. If the ef-forts of the two governments are still unsuccessful, the fact will be noted that Britain and France are responsible for the continuation of the war.[4]

It was clear that Hitler would henceforth wage war in the west with the benevolent neutrality of the Soviet Union.

The evolution of Soviet politics left no doubt about that. Stalin, with the blessing of Germany, had immediately made the three small Baltic states into Soviet satellites, prior to annexing them the following year. In the fall of 1939, he still wanted to subjugate Finland, and he inaugu-rated a procedure that he was frequently to employ later on: on the day the Red Army launched a surprise attack on the Finnish border, Radio Moscow announced the creation of a Finnish "democratic government" in that small piece of invaded land, run by Otto Kuusinen, an old Com-intern veteran. This action turned out to be less successful than Hitler's war on Poland, but it clearly demonstrated Stalin's intention to have his share of the first spoils of the world war he had so long predicted, and which he was starting under equally auspicious circumstances.

This prudent but deliberate activism invalidates the time-worn justification of the German-Soviet pact of 23 August: Stalin's turnaround was nothing but tit for tat and a way of foiling western plots to push Hitler toward the Ukraine so as to divert him from the Meuse or the Rhine. Those plots certainly existed and affected British and French policies; in a sense they achieved success with the Munich agreement in September 1938, although they were not—indeed, far from it—solely responsible for the accords. Pacifist western public opinion continually worked against the Czechs, and British and French leaders were probably more myopic than calculating. But we can understand how Stalin, excluded from the meeting in spite of Soviet commitments to Czechoslovakia, considered Munich a dress rehearsal for a pan-imperialist plot against the USSR. This idea had been a quintessential part of the Bolshevik repertory since October 1917, and Stalin's speech at the Eighteenth Bolshevik Party Congress on 10 March 1939 certainly constituted a warning to Western democracies and an overture to Germany. It was not the *first* overture, as we saw in chapter 7. But it is clear that the policy of keeping two irons in the fire, which had surely never left Stalin's mind since 1934, had undergone a serious reorientation, after Munich, in the direction of Germany. Litvinov, the proponent of "collective security," was soon to be replaced by Molotov in the Ministry of Foreign Affairs. Ironically, the choice seems to have been made just as the British Conservatives had finally shed their illusions about Hitler, following the invasion of Czechoslovakia on 15 March 1939: even to them, the war between Germany and the democracies now seemed almost inevitable. As a result, the Soviet position was reinforced.

In the spring of 1939, Stalin had to choose between reaffirming the anti-Fascist policy of collective security or reversing his alliances. He had explored both paths simultaneously and had become increasingly suspicious of the first. The Russian proposition of a tripartite military agreement (USSR, Britain, France) covering all the countries that bordered on the USSR—from the Balkan countries to Romania, including Poland—came up against a Polish and Romanian refusal to accept the Red Army's eventual crossing of their territories for fear that it would never leave. The next installments of that story proved the fears well founded. In fact, Stalin pursued the second option, as confirmed by Molotov's nomination on 4 May. Hitler's perception of the other party's ambitions, which complemented his own, facilitated the negotiations. He, for one, had no trouble wiping Estonia and Poland off the map of Europe if that was the cost of extending Germany to the east and of a free hand in the west. The Polish question, while dividing the "anti-Fascist" camp,[5] brought the Nazis and the Communists together.

Thus, even though the policy of appeasement vis-à-vis Hitler, conducted first by the British Conservatives and then by French leaders, obviously played a role in Russia's diplomatic turnaround concerning Hitler in 1939, that policy does not fully explain it. First of all, Soviet foreign policy between 1934 and 1939 was not patterned entirely on ideological anti-Fascism. Second, the Polish problem, the main stumbling block to a Franco-Anglo-Russian agreement, was not the invention of maniacal anti-Soviet Westerners. Poland had every reason to feel as threatened by Stalin as by Hitler, and France, linked to Poland by a treaty, was in no position to protect its independence if Russian troops were to occupy Polish territory. To protect Poland from Hitler, should British and French leaders agree to its being occupied by Stalin? That question should at least be asked. The anti-Fascist foreign policy of collective security came up against even more serious contradictions than did anti-Fascist domestic policy in countries such as France; the latter created a superficial unity among parties that were basically opposed to one another, whereas the former made adversaries into collaborators. This observation in no way excuses the policy of appeasement, a combination of stupidity and irresponsibility. It does, however, relativize the influence of appeasement by revealing the impasses of the opposite policy. Stalin certainly did not associate the Soviet Union with a unified anti-Nazi front because of ideological passion, a taste for liberty, or even a concern with the European balance of power. His first priority was to protect himself from a German attack and, if possible, to wash away his country's memories of Brest-Litovsk. Hitler, however, when the moment arrived, had more to offer him on these two points than did Chamberlain or Daladier.

The partition of Poland conformed to an old German-Russian tradition of shared domination over Eastern Europe. In the eighteenth and nineteenth centuries, the German share contained both Prussia and Austria, or the German and Austro-Hungarian Empires. In the twentieth century, Hitler had this role all to himself, faced with Stalin, successor to the czars. The work refashioned by the two dictators was also related to their common origin, more recent than the partition of Poland. Both of their respective traditions included the determination to destroy the Europe forged at Versailles, which had been conceived in order to assure the domination of French imperialism over the belt of small states situated between vanquished Germany and the Russia of October 1917.

By joining hands with Hitler, Stalin resumed—if he had ever completely abandoned it—the pre-1933 Bolshevik foreign policy of an alliance with the German extreme Right in the name of the battle against the Versailles system. The situation was all the more favorable for him since by following his own footprints, which were still fairly fresh, he gave the green light to an interimperialist war between Germany, on one side, and Britain and France on the other. The war at that time seemed likely to be lengthy, exhausting for the belligerents, and thus favorable to the consolidation of Soviet power and its territorial expansion. It was already quite a performance to have rubbed out Brest-Litovsk with the help of the same Germany that had dictated its humiliating terms to Lenin!

The question whether Stalin preferred Hitler to the Western democracies, or the other way around, is thus hardly germane. He probably lumped both regimes together under the label of capitalism; the choice he made in August–September 1939 was dictated by circumstance rather than doctrine. The man who had gained control over everything human as well as material within the USSR was offered a new role, thanks to the unexpected offices of the Nazi dictator—that of empire builder, with a piece of Poland as a motivational bonus. In this sense, the Hitler-Stalin pact marked a shift in Stalin's life to ambitions that went beyond the Soviet Union—ambitions that would fill the rest of his life. Despite having switched allies in the meantime, the Stalin of 1939, who had occupied the eastern part of Poland, was no different from the Stalin of 1944, who had "liberated" the western part. Nineteen forty-four was a continuation of 1939: joint tenure with the Nazis was followed by the undivided domination of Moscow over a nation that had shifted westward along with its populations. The autumn of 1939 revealed to the public that Stalin envisioned the expansion of Communism in Europe under the form of an armed exportation of the Soviet regime, supervised by Soviet agents.

One more proof of the true nature of the pact between Hitler and Stalin can be found in the manner in which it was presented and justified in Marxist-Leninist terminology. The ideological character of the Communist world was a boon for historians, for it meant that everything could be explained according to the strange, universalistic idiom that had produced the infallibility of the Party and its leader. Anyone able to crack the code had continuous access to a priceless interpretive instrument, the storehouse of all individual and collective motivations. A capital source, if in calmer times a repetitive and monotonous one, Marxist-Leninist jargon was particularly valuable when things grew turbulent; it seemed almost to become animated and flushed during critical times, when it had to contradict itself and modify the internal economy of its various elements. This was especially true in the fall of 1939, after six years of "anti-Fascist" ideological bombardment.

The German-Soviet pact was, on the face of it, the most difficult political event to fit into Leninist rationalization. Unlike Brest-Litovsk, it had not been dictated by an extreme peril or, like the 1934–35 shift, by a new event (Hitler's dictatorship). It owed everything to circumstances—Hitler's need to neutralize Stalin before setting off the war, the advantage Stalin perceived in the first partition of Eastern Europe. And if more substantial reasons were required, the whole affair between Germany and the USSR in August–September 1939 could be written off in terms of reasons of state. The two great ideocratic dictatorships of the century had finally reached an understanding beyond their ideologies. It was hardly necessary for Hitler to justify himself; it was enough for him to preach nationalism and to enjoy the cynicism of the winner. But Stalin could not cover himself by arguing reasons of state without bringing into question the world vocation of Communism. He could not justify his accord with Hitler without going back on all that militant Communists throughout the world had done and thought since the Leipzig trial. Yet that is what he had to do, since he was still their leader, endowed with a dual character, national and universal. This compulsory exercise is a mine for historians.

The Communist parties reacted to the pact of 23 August first by playing down the brutal novelty of the event, an understandable reaction to receiving bad news. The Communist leaders abroad had not been privy to the secret that was being readied in Moscow. They had registered and transmitted the warning sent by Stalin to London and Paris on 10 March, but this had not caused them to alter in any way the anti-Fascist orientation of their propaganda and activities, which was held to be inviolable. In the days following the news of the pact, they approved Stalin as the artisan of a last maneuver to avoid war (this was already quite a feat), but were still resolved to be on the front line of soldiers fighting Hitler should war break out.[6] This type of declaration did not reduce the public indignation with the Soviet Union elicited by the pact of 23 August; it did, however, reassure the militants by guaranteeing a minimum of continuity in the political line of the Comintern parties. Furthermore, the members of the Moscow International were thinking the same way at the time. On 27 August, in a recently revealed letter,[7] the two highest-ranking members, Dimitrov and Manouilski, wrote to Stalin to ask him what to do about the French Communist Party in Paris: "We believe the position of the Party should always remain the same: to resist the aggression of Fascist Germany. It should support the efforts aimed at reinforcing the defensive potential of France, but, by the same token, it should insist that the Party have the possibility of expressing its opinions openly and be able to develop its activities." A response to this letter was not forthcoming. During the last days of August, Stalin was still wavering over the best way to present to the public what he had just done. On 31 August, at the fourth session of the Supreme Soviet, Molotov was still giving a minimalist interpretation of the pact: necessitated by the pro-Munich policy of the westerners, it did not amount to a reversal of alliances; it simply implied the end of hostilities between Germany and the USSR in the interest of both countries, as well as emphasizing the USSR's decisive international role, especially in all Eastern European matters. Molotov probably phrased his reaction this way so as to prepare the public for what had been stated in black and white in the secret agreement.

On the next day, Poland was invaded, and the rapidity of the German advance, which moved up the deadline for Soviet intervention, forced Stalin to intervene. On 7 September, he received Dimitrov in the presence of Molotov and Zhdanov: this was perhaps the first time he clarified for the Communist movement the philosophical and political implications of the pact. The official summary of his talk, now released from the Comintern archives, is worth citing at length:

> In this interview, Stalin declared that war was occurring between two groups of capitalist countries—poor and rich in terms of colonies, raw materials, etc.—who sought to divide up and dominate the world. We have nothing to say against the fact that they are fighting among themselves as they should be and that they are weakening one another, said Stalin. There is nothing harmful about the situation of the richest capitalist countries being weakened by Germany. Hitler, for one, unconsciously and without wanting to do so, is weakening and undermining the capitalist system.[8]

Stalin declared again that the distinction between Fascism and the democratic regime had been appropriate before the war. "During the war between the imperialist powers, [the distinction] became false. The division of the capitalist countries into Fascist and democratic countries has lost its meaning." He then took a clearly hostile position toward Poland, having characterized it as a Fascist state that oppressed the Ukrainians, the Belorussians, and others.

> Under present conditions, suppression of that state will mean that there will be one less Fascist state. It will not be a bad thing if Poland suffers a defeat and thus enables us to include new territories and new populations in the socialist system.
>   . . . As for the Communist movement, Stalin proposed a renunciation of the slogan of a unified popular front. Communists in capitalist

countries ought to rise up resolutely against their own governments, against the war.

These oral instructions covered just about everything that would constitute the new Communist policy, while revealing that Stalin was to be the boss of the Comintern as well as absolute master of the Soviet Union. Dissociation of the two roles would have been tantamount to a misconception of the Leninist universe. Even as he was affirming the primacy of the interests of the Soviet state over all else, the General Secretary abandoned none of his prerogatives to rule over it in the name of Marxism-Leninism. The price of this lesson was high—nothing less than saying and doing the opposite of what one had been saying and doing since 1934.

Since 1934 or 1935, depending on one's vantage point, the imperialist war that had been rendered inevitable by the rivalries of the capitalist powers was no longer unanimously "imperialist" as in 1914 or during the "third phase" denounced by the Comintern. On the contrary, it set a group of Fascist states, with Hitler's Germany at the fore, against an alliance of democratic states, notably Britain and France, which, even though capitalist, found themselves on the defensive and were consequently less aggressive. One of those states, France, had concluded an alliance with the USSR in 1935: the status of its foreign policy was dignified accordingly: that was the philosophical basis of the anti-Fascist strategy. On 7 September 1939, Stalin put all the belligerents—who were also imperialists—in one category: there was no longer any difference between them. This was not a total return to the "third phase" situation, for at that time the imperialist powers were collectively threatening the Soviet Union. In September 1939 they were warring among themselves, as in 1914, at the risk of weakening one another to the benefit of the USSR. Hence the approval accorded, in spite of everything, to Hitler, who was draining the richest of the imperialists, Great Britain. In Stalin's speeches of autumn 1939, he revived an idea never far from the usual Communist analyses of Fascist Germany, even if unexpressed: that, all things considered, Nazism was an objective ally of the Soviet revolution.

This analysis has logical inconsistencies: Stalin never explained why the imperialist camp chose to weaken itself instead of fighting the common enemy, who was also a mortal enemy. But coherence was beside the point. He sought to tack together, with elements from the Leninist tradition, a new universal interpretation of the situation created by the public and secret agreements of 23 August. The most urgent thing was to put an end to the anti-Fascist strategy, which now characterized the international Communist movement, and the source of its influence; for Communist parties everywhere continued to hark back to it, even while approving the pact. In the short term, this situation was untenable because, given the rapidity of the German advance on Warsaw, Stalin knew he would soon have to order the Red Army to complete the invasion of Poland with a peaceful encounter with the Nazis. How could the French Communists call for their compatriots to take up arms against Hitler on the Rhine when their Soviet big brothers were in league with him east of the Vistula? The answer was to reactivate the idea of an "imperialist war" and, hence, the struggle against war itself: instead of fighting Hitler and Fascism, the militants of "democratic" nations ought henceforth exclusively to target their own bourgeoisies, their own governments.

Was this a return to the Leninist strategy of 1914? Apparently so, like an echo. But Lenin's intention at that time had been to transform the imperialist war into a civil war so as to make it a lever for the proletarian revolution. Stalin would not go that far. The revolution now had a homeland, and instead of dissipating the efforts of the Communist parties in the struggle to overthrow their respective bourgeoisies, in keeping with Lenin's perspective during World War I, what was needed was to unite them in defense of the shared homeland of all workers. It was less a question of "revolutionary defeatism"—a Leninist term never uttered in 1939–40 during the political shift—than of a battle for immediate peace. Paradoxically, the new Communist strategy fell back on the pacifist rallying cry it had so strenuously opposed in the preceding years and which would bring it into harmony with its former adversaries.[9] But in the autumn of 1939 there was nothing pacifist about the Communists' true rationale, which was the unconditional solidarity of all parties with the Soviet Union. That rationale expressed not revolt but submission.

The last major theme in the crucial interview of 7 September between Dimitrov and Stalin was the absolute priority attributed to the Soviet Union in the international Communist configuration. This was not a new idea, for it had emerged with the Comintern, but it took the form of Russian political domination of the movement rather than that of international revolution. Although it gained reality with Stalin's arrival under the banner of "socialism in one country" and the enslavement of the Comintern to the will of one individual, the anti-Fascist shift of 1934–35 had masked with universality the nationalist tendency of the Stalinist dictatorship. In September 1939 the mask fell, along with anti-Fascism, when Stalin found himself about to absorb the eastern third of Poland and then the Baltic states, necessitating a new rationalization for the progress of socialism, which was now assimilated with the USSR's expansion.

In fact, Stalin said nothing about either eastern Poland, the territories lost at Brest-Litovsk that ought to have been reintegrated into the Ukraine, or Soviet Belorussia. He attacked the Polish state as "Fascist" and therefore not worthy of existence—an incoherent attack, since it came after his declaration that the distinction between "Fascist" and "democratic" made no sense, and was accompanied by an agreement with Hitler on the division of Poland. Interestingly, however, it reveals Stalin's extreme oversimplification when considering the "national question": "It will not be a bad thing if Poland suffers a defeat and thus enables us to include new territories and new populations in the socialist system." The future of the "socialist system" henceforth lay entirely within the USSR. In 1944–45, Stalin would modernize his theory without altering its substance. We should bear in mind that from 1939 on, the period when he was renouncing "anti-Fascism," he still laid claim to it for one objective—the Soviet Union's absorption of an independent state. In this sense, his statement on 7 September 1939 was a milestone: following the hidden nationalism of "socialism in one country," he inaugurated the half-revealed nationalism of the "progress of the socialist system" by means of Soviet expansion.

The new political line of the Communist movement was made explicit from the start—two weeks after the 23 August pact, and only a few days after the outbreak of the Second World War. It was not simply a circumstantial adjustment to the anti-Fascist battle caused by the duplicity of the capitalist democracies—something Communist party activists and, indeed, statesmen of many nations would have liked to believe. It was a complete strategic about-face, demonstrated spectacularly by Stalin in the renunciation of anti-Fascism and, more particularly, in the priority given to the fight against Hitler. In this way Stalin recovered certain elements of pre-1934 Bolshevik policy—the assimilation of bourgeois democracy with Fascism, the denunciation of Social Democracy as Social Fascism, the dogged opposition to the imperialist war. But the international situation in the autumn of 1939 was quite new insofar as the imperialist war was no longer a threat to be averted but had already begun. It had rewarded the Soviet state with the liquidation of the Polish state, carried out in agreement with Germany. So the battle cry against the imperialist war, though aimed especially at the British and the French as it had been during the "third phase," led less to revolutionary gesticulation on the part of the Communist parties than to a fundamental test of their subordination to the international home-land of the proletariat.[10] Isolated and, in some cases, illegal, these parties were instructed to confirm that the international proletarian revolution would in future be oriented toward the expansion of the USSR.

The pro-German content of this ideological hodgepodge was avowed more openly from mid-September on, after Stalin had verified the extent to which Hitler had adhered to the letter of his commitments. The Polish affair came off without a hitch, facilitating the German-Soviet joint communiqué of 28 September. Between late September and mid-October, the three Baltic states were constrained to pledge allegiance to the new superpower of Western Europe, for Germany, their traditional "protector," had consented to it beforehand. On 31 October, Molotov proudly outlined the evolution of Soviet foreign policy, in which the new friendship with Germany occupied a major place along with the necessity to return to peace: "If today we speak of the great European powers, Germany finds itself in the situation of a state that aspires to the quickest possible cessation of war and to peace, whereas England and France, which yesterday were still affirming themselves to be against the aggression, were for continuing the war and against making peace. Roles have changed, as you can see." He continued, with extraordinary cynicism: "It will not, as everyone knows, be a matter of reestablishing Poland as it was. It is also insane to continue the present war under the pretext of reestablishing the old Polish state."[11] As always, Molotov was repeating Stalin's words but in an uncoded version. The nonaggression pact of 23 August was indeed the start of an alliance.

Nothing better manifests the extraordinary discipline, unique in the history of humanity, of the multinational political movement that Communism was than the manner in which Stalin's statements to Dimitrov on 7 September became within a few weeks the universal breviary of the movement. The sudden reorientation of such a vast army of militants toward a policy diametrically opposed to the policy of the day before is at once impressive and terrifying. All over the world, Communist parties took note of the Comintern directive of 9 September against the imperialist war and put it into practice. The American Communists sought to keep the United States from joining the Western democracies. The Syrian and Lebanese Communists, who had consented to the French mandate since the Front populaire, turned against French imperialism. The Malayan Communists became anti-British. The Belgian Communists set out once more to encourage neutrality in their country. The British Communists, enthusiastic for war at the beginning of September, were engaged in self-criticism before the month's end, as were the Americans, the Belgians, the French, and so on.

It was in Europe that this curious event was most striking, prompting the clash of the most violent passions. Outside of Europe, in many colonized countries, Hitler and Stalin were easily identified as dictators linked in hatred of the two major colonial democracies of the West. But Europe had been the cradle of Communism and Fascism, the setting for their histories and maneuvers, the place where both regimes cast their spell. The Europeans had just been through the years during which the two regimes had filled the democratic nations' political life with their rivalry and reciprocal insults, sometimes even involving bloody confrontation, as in Spain. Anti-Fascism had lent Communism a Western veneer, and anti-Communism had given Nazism a certificate of civilization. Through their antagonism, the two monstrous regimes of the century had managed to subjugate democratic opinion. The distribution of roles in the war itself had been predetermined.

The war, however, began with a redistribution of those roles. The Europeans watched stupefied as the Soviet Union and Germany divided Poland between them and called for France and Britain to stop their "aggression." Anti-Communism could no longer serve as a rationale for Fascist sympathies; their only remaining justification was an unconditional return to peace. On the other hand, anti-Fascism also ceased to offer a democratic guarantee to Communism. The latter part of this double movement of de-legitimation was more radical than the former, for Hitler, both before and after the German-Soviet pact, continued in his arsenal of propaganda to reserve the possibility of a nominal peace with the West—an idea beloved of Western pacifists. He had been a potential enemy since 1933. When he became a real, if passive, enemy on 3 September, he had not yet fully disqualified the partisans of a new Munich.

Stalin, for his part, had shifted from the role of a potential ally to that of a declared enemy, although he was at war with neither Britain nor France. His switching of camps elicited indignation from all the Western democratic political families—including the anti-Communists, of course, who had only to follow their hearts; from the patriotic Right, since he was helping Hitler; from the pacifists, since he had opened the way for the war; and from the anti-Fascist Left, bitter at having been tricked out of its unified set of convictions and its memories. There is no need to hypothesize a capitalist conspiracy in order to explain how deeply Communism, as an idea and as a regime, fell into discredit in the days and weeks following 23 August 1939; one need only read the Comintern's directives and Molotov's discourses! Nothing in the history of the movement is comparable to the liquidation of its influence. Heaven knows what a trying time that was—the sectarian aridity of the "third phase," the routing of the German Communist Party, the Moscow trials. In the eyes of the European public, however, nothing had dealt a greater blow to Communism's legitimacy than the Hitler-Stalin pact.

Once again, France provides the best vantage point from which to observe this phenomenon, for in that country political passions were fueled in the interwar period by encounters and conflicts between democracy, Communism, and Fascism. There was already a strong Communist Party in France before 1939, proud to have "invented" the Front populaire before receiving the lion's share from that policy in terms of votes and influence. The parliament that issued from the left-wing electoral victory of 1936 continued to function, although the union of left-wing parties had fallen apart. Finding a stable method of governing at the center, under the auspices of the Radicals, proved difficult. The mediocrity of public life contrasted with the texture of ideological passions, for these passions were fueled less from within than from without, exaggerating the scale of domestic quarrels; it was as if national life, deprived of internal energy, had to find its mainspring outside of its borders. Through anti-Fascism, Communism constituted a firm reference for the Left; through anti-Communism, Fascism formed a "magnetic field" for right-wing ideologies; all the while, keeping the peace was the common concern of the nation.

French political passions before World War II, which were as intense as dictated by the national tradition, were for that reason awkward. They lived by proxy off the international situation and the monsters who animated it. So the German-Soviet pact emptied them of their substance, caught them off guard. Anti-Fascism no longer existed in Moscow. Anti-Communism no longer existed in Berlin. Both Stalin and Hitler were responsible for the war. The combination of these three propositions reveals their origin—Stalin's about-face. If the nascent war was an imperialist one like that of 1914, then the title of Marcel Déat's famous article "To die for Danzig?"[12] expressed a refusal on the part of the international proletariat to fight through the mouthpiece of their usual representatives. The Comintern's proclamation that anti-Fascism was a lie deprived many French anti-Nazi activists of their reasons to do battle with Hitler. Pro-Munich France, for its part, outlawed the Communist Party in the name of a war that it too had done everything to avoid, even down to abandoning its international commitments. It acted as though September 1939 was a repetition of August 1914, but it challenged the potential sacrifices of a merely nationalist war, like the previous one, for which it no longer had either the moral or the material means. Even the idea of an anti-Fascist war had ceased to exist since Stalin and Hitler joined hands.

We see most clearly in the French case the extent to which European Communism of that time, in all its variants from the militant to the fellow traveler, had become rooted in anti-Fascism. The French Communist Party had made its way into French political life in 1920 with the promise to Lenin that the "opportunistic" errors of its socialist predecessors—whatever group they belonged to—were over: such was the implication of the membership requirement of the new International. These conditions were imposed on everyone, since everyone, or almost everyone, was responsible for the collapse of 1914, but they were conditions that Lenin felt to be particularly necessary in France. There, Communism had to make a clean break with the bourgeois democratic tradition, Republican rhetoric, and parliamentarianism; to provide for a sector of clandestine activities; to abandon its petty-bourgeois leaders—lawyers and professors—so as to make way for workers fueled by class hatred; and to emphasize everything that now separated it from all the other parties, especially the Socialist Party. So the young Communist Party had spent its time in worker-oriented culture and in pushing revolution, the apogee of which had been the "third phase."

Anti-Fascism brought this narrow focus to a close without canceling out its gains; it carved out a larger space for Communist pedagogy without encroaching on the privileges that this pedagogy had acquired in the worker's domain. For anti-Fascism, as we have seen, constituted a strategy and a discourse with a double foundation. Most obviously, it brought Communism and democracy together in a fight against their common enemy, Hitler. By validating the democratic ancestry of Communism via the French Revolution, anti-Fascism also lent it both a universal and a national content. Hitler wanted both to destroy the values of 1789 and to bring France to its knees. After the Front populaire, the Communists had urged a Front des Français.[13] But their anti-Fascism did not amount to a renunciation of the revolutionary vocation of the "party of the working class." On the contrary, it put the workers on the front line of a battle in which they had found allies but from which they figured they would emerge the sole beneficiaries: the liquidation of Fascism had no true objective besides the end of capitalism, in other words the victory of the proletariat. This perspective enhanced the worthiness of their efforts to end the exile of workers within the nation. Spearheading anti-Fascism, the revolutionary proletariat had made its class struggle into an opportunity for liberty and for safeguarding the national interest.

Such brave memories, glorious as victorious battles, allow us to gauge the shock that the Soviet turnaround of August created among the democratic public, aggravated by the interpretation imposed on the

Comintern parties in September. After a few weeks the French Communist Party was forced to adopt an antinational policy that left it without defenders in the face of the government's repressive measures.[14] It lost all of its public support, the majority of its militants, and many of its elected officials: even the success it had achieved in the preceding period in the name of anti-Fascism aggravated its fall and facilitated its quasi liquidation, since no one remained capable of identifying with its new incarnation, which was the opposite of its old one. The situation looked like August 1914 in reverse. In August 1914, the Socialist Party had abandoned its pacifist commitments in order to join up with the government in wartime. In September 1939, the Communist Party abandoned its patriotic activities and became an outcast of the nation at war.

Only those who understand the true nature of the movement—the primacy of the international as against the national and, in international matters, the first principal of unconditional solidarity with the Soviet Union—can understand the Party's reasoning. Even if public opinion rejected the Communist "betrayal" and the militants abandoned the Comintern parties, the movement's apparatus survived, as could be seen in France and elsewhere. Not that its members had been kept abreast of what was in the works; their only means of preparation were the pamphlets they received from Moscow, which were inadequate. When the day arrived, the cadres were both stunned and docile, aware of the tragic implications that the situation spelled out for their lives and for the world, but they did not balk at the price to be paid, since they saw it as the price of the revolution. At first they had defended the pact of 23 August, but then came the end of anti-Fascism, the partition of Poland, the overt alliance between Stalin and Hitler, and Molotov's speech; to crown it all, they were criticizing themselves for their failure to have figured the whole thing out in August!

The events of the autumn of 1939 all occurred as though the Comintern apparatus met the requirements fixed by Lenin for any revolutionary movement. The collapse of its political influence, the destruction of many of its organizations, and the confusion of its militants had no effect on the faith or discipline of its cadres. The very few dissidents at this level of responsibility were quickly marginalized or liquidated, since they never managed to acquire sufficient numbers, space, or liberty to establish a base for a rival organization. The ordeal revealed that in this respect Stalin had been a good disciple of Lenin: his Comintern, whether in Moscow or the "foreign missions," certainly formed the hard core of militants unconditionally loyal to all of its demands, including self-contradiction in the name of world revolution. They were a small circle—they could even be called an aristocracy—but they were more numerous, more international, yet even more homogeneous and submissive than in Lenin's time. Was this the effect of the Terror or a consequence of its longevity? Both factors worked together to sustain the second Bolshevism, the revolutionary passion combining the security of faith with the lure of power.

World war, having been an involuntary accomplice of Communism, had by midcentury become a weapon for its development. The First World War had brought Communism to power; the Second, which had hardly begun, canceled out the price Russia had paid for the Soviet Union's birth by bringing it territories and populations forcibly abandoned at Brest-Litovsk and even adding part of Poland. In 1920, as the Red Army pushed toward Warsaw, Lenin had already sketched out the military conception of socialism's progress. Stalin picked it up again in 1939–40, in his own way, in an even more primitive version. While the Gestapo was establishing its police regime to the west of Poland, he began a political purge in his eastern section. Hitler rounded up and ordered the assassination not only of the large Jewish minorities but also of tens of thousands of Poles in the name of anti-Semitic and anti-Slavic racism. Stalin deported and murdered in the name of socialism.

The Katyn massacre typified this technique. Beginning in September 1939 in eastern Poland, NKVD squadrons carefully rounded up all present or potential cadres of a national resistance movement—active and reserve officers, some fifteen thousand men, half of them in uniform and the other half consisting of teachers, professors, journalists, lawyers, doctors, and priests. They were distributed among three Soviet concentration camps: Ostachov, Kozielsk, and Starobielsk. All those sent to Kozielsk—just under five thousand—were assassinated in April 1940 in the forest of Katyn, each with one shot in the back of the head.[15] No one knew what had happened to the ten thousand other poor fellows whose bones probably lie somewhere in Russian or Belorussian territory. Lucky were those Poles who, being among the elite, were deported to a Gulag in Siberia or central Asia; in 1941, on the demand of the Polish government in London when Stalin was forced to change camps, hundreds of thousands of them reemerged.

Between September 1939 and the summer of 1940, the Soviet Union concentrated on acquiring new territories, aiming to liquidate the belt of pro-Western states that the victors at Versailles had tried to establish so as to guarantee security to the east of Germany and to the west of the USSR but which, to the contrary, would become German or Russian zones of influence. In spring 1940, after his partial failure in Finland in the preceding winter,[16] Stalin was all the more anxious to put into effect the other provisions of the secret agreements of August 1939, for the Nazis were gaining in strength and prestige by their occupation of Denmark, their invasion of Norway, and, most especially, their crushing of France in June. That same month, with "anti-Soviet" activities in the Baltic states, which had been enfeoffed since the previous autumn, Stalin sent troops in and annexed the states in July and August to form three new Soviet Republics.[17] At the same time, he took back Bessarabia, which Romania had appropriated in 1918, and took as a bonus northern Bukovina, which had never belonged to the Russian Empire and was not part of the secret deal of the previous year. This irritated the Germans, who were very attentive to all that was happening close to their sources of oil.

Until then, the relations between the two totalitarian states had been marked by apparent cordiality, which was part and parcel of a shared cynicism. Stalin had gone so far as forcibly to send back to Nazi Germany several hundred German and Austrian anti-Fascists, many of whom, as former Communists, either were under suspicion or had already been confined in the Gulag archipelago. After the war, Margarete Buber-Neumann, the widow of a former leader of the German Communist Party, recounted the grim odyssey from camp to camp and the crossing of the railroad bridge at Brest-Litovsk, the frontier between the two empires, where she was handed over to an SS officer by an officer of the NKVD.[18] In the economic and commercial sectors, relations were booming, and several agreements had been signed. The two countries aided each other reciprocally in military-industrial matters. In politics, their interests converged. Once the Polish question was out of the way, Hitler wanted to have a free hand to the west, and Stalin stayed out of the conflict while rounding out his "socialism in one country" territories. The two dictators became neighbors to the east across an enormous frontier without any change in the rationale for their alliance.

The crushing defeat of France, however, altered the equilibrium of Europe. Stalin, like many of his contemporaries, had thought the second imperialist war would last roughly as long as the first. He was motivated by self-interest: the longer the war, the better his position, since the belligerents would exhaust themselves while the USSR prudently gained strength, whether in order to intervene directly, or to dissuade the European bourgeoisies from opposing the Communist revolution. A Germany that was too powerful, dominating Europe, did not fit in with his calculations. In any case, the Germans forced their partner of August 1939 to tread very cautiously. Hitler, for his part, had brought

France to its knees but not Britain, which refused to give in. Since *Mein Kampf,* he had always thought he should sew up the West before attacking Russia; so he hesitated in the summer of 1940. From July onward, he was thinking at once of landing in Britain and invading Russia, as Napoleon had planned in 1805.[19] But Keitel dissuaded him from the latter undertaking until fall, since there was not enough time to prepare; and the former plan failed in mid-September, when the German air force proved incapable of taking over British skies. The British landing was soon abandoned, owing to a lack of technical means. But the invasion of Russia was merely postponed, while the Soviet ventures of the summer in Romania made that invasion more likely than ever. Because he could not destroy the USSR in Britain, Hitler would destroy Britain in the USSR, killing two birds with one stone, subjugating the Slavs to the Nazis and depriving Britain of its last potential ally in Europe.[20] In spite of his familiarity with European history, Hitler made the same mistake as Napoleon in 1812, and opened the door to the final catastrophe.

The decision to attack the USSR in 1941 was all but finalized by the summer. The military leadership had been working on it for some time, formally adopting a plan on 18 December 1940. Operation "Barbarossa" was set for the month of May. The plan underlay German policy for eight to ten months before it was carried out. Although Hitler's decision, inspired by the program set out in *Mein Kampf* and the power momentum crowned by the victory in France, seemed hardly surprising, Stalin's beliefs and intentions were more obscure. Despite the exaggerated courtesy of the two allies, he knew he was in a tight spot. It was no longer sufficient to pick up territory on the heels of the Nazi army, entirely oriented toward the west, and to sell his alliance for large, quick windfalls. Hitler had gained control over a huge area of Europe and had recovered access to the east. He was offering his protection to Romania, arbitrating between Hungary and Romania for Transylvania, and making waves in Finland. Stalin played a close game, remaining within the framework of the 1939 agreement. On 12 November, he sent Molotov, his best representative, to Berlin to plead that the texts, that is, the zones of influence, be respected. Ribbentrop, who initiated the encounter, tried to get the USSR to join the members of the recently signed tripartite pact (Germany, Italy, and Japan) so to involve it in the carving up of the British Empire in Asia. But when face to face with Hitler himself, Molotov began to deploy the resources of cynical obstinacy that would make him famous. The Führer's Spenglerian ravings about world politics did not prevent his appeal for observing the rules—in this instance the secret German-Russian agreement on Eastern Europe. A few days later, Stalin clearly expressed an interest in the idea of dividing the world into fourths (with a Soviet priority in northern Iran, Iraq, and eastern Turkey); but nothing could be done about the misunderstanding over Finland and the Balkans.

At the time Hitler was setting the date for Barbarossa, Stalin had every reason to be on his guard; Molotov's behavior in Berlin shows that he was certainly mistrustful from November 1940 on, but this did not stop him from putting all his eggs in one basket. Perhaps, after pocketing the gains of his first policy, he may have toyed with the idea of changing direction. Contemporary Comintern documents, as always, reveal the most about Communist policy, and the directives sent by Moscow to the French Communist Party attest to a shift in the summer of 1940. In conquered, Nazi-occupied France, the Communists attempted first to negotiate with the German authorities so as to be allowed to publish their papers again and to organize the masses against Vichy and the bourgeoisie while the occupying forces looked the other way. This strategy, although in line with the directives of September 1939, risked making the Communists, in the new circumstances of the German triumph, appear too favorable toward the Nazis. So there was a modification, demanded by the International, in the direction of least compliance with the occupation. The Moscow order, fine-tuned on 5 August, was not fiercely anti-Nazi but proscribed any manifestation of collaboration.[21] It obliquely condemned the overtures that had been made toward Abetz for the reappearance of the journal *L'Humanité*, and it recommended that all activities indispensable to the Party, legal (which was thought possible) or illegal, should occur independently of the Germans, though it did not go so far as to preach active resistance to the occupation. Social struggle was the top priority, along with the denunciation of the bourgeois policies of Vichy and a hostile mistrust of the occupying forces. The entire winter of 1940–41 passed under this ambiguity, in which even Stalin himself participated, since he had been consulted about the 5 August document. By the end of the year, his basic tone had hardly changed. As Stalin said to Dimitrov after Molotov's Berlin visit, "Our relations with the Germans are polite on the outside but there is serious friction between us."[22]

If this was the case at the end of 1940, it is difficult to understand why Stalin did not anticipate Hitler's turning against him in June 1941, why he did not believe those who warned him of it, and why the German attack on 22 June 1941 fell like a bolt out of the blue on a badly prepared Red Army. There were many indications of what might occur: Hitler's advance on the Balkans was topped off by the subjection of Bulgaria and the conquest of Yugoslavia and Greece in April. Along the border between Germany and Russia itself, German flights over Soviet territory greatly increased in 1941. Soviet information services had picked up on an amassing of tanks. From Tokyo, at the beginning of the year, an agent named Sorge apprised Stalin of Hitler's decision to attack the USSR; Churchill, desperately in search of an ally, had his ambassador to Moscow pass on the same information in April; the American government followed suit in May. Yet Stalin paid no attention to any of these alerts. In the months leading to 22 June 1941, he seemed deliberately to ignore the warnings, as if he were afraid of arousing German hostility. Soviet shipments of raw materials and foodstuffs to Germany were intensified from January on,[23] and Hitler was careful to maintain reciprocity so as to keep everyone in the dark. When the Japanese foreign minister, Matsuoka, left Moscow on 13 April after signing a non-aggression treaty, Stalin made an impromptu visit to the railroad station to see him off. He asked to shake the hand of the German ambassador, to whom he declared, "We should remain friends, and you should do everything you can to that end." This statement smacks of an attempt to head off fate ten weeks before Barbarossa. But it could also have been a ruse. A little later, in early May, the General Secretary of the Party took Molotov's place as the head of the Soviet government. Further explanatory difficulties ensued, since that deliberate "promotion," even though it probably responded to a prediction of major events and anticipated a new face-to-face with Hitler, did not indicate whether the face-to-face would be peaceful or warlike.

The best proof, indeed the only proof, that Stalin did not believe in an imminent German attack in spite of all the information and warnings was that the Red Army was completely unprepared and was slow to react. Stalin's own behavior was strange: while Molotov announced the invasion over Soviet radio at noon on 22 June, Stalin had withdrawn, exhausted, to his dacha in Kountsevo and did not come out to address the nation until 3 July. These various facts, reported by Khrushchev in his famous report to the Twentieth Congress of the Communist Party in 1956, were interpreted in the light of the incompetence of Khrushchev's predecessor and the pathological isolation in which he had shut himself. Historians, less contemptuous of Stalin's abilities, have generally blamed his mistrust of everything and everybody. According to most historians, the General Secretary believed he was the object of a brainwashing campaign to make him quarrel with Hitler, and so he ignored any seemingly provocative advice. But this explanation does not fit the worsening of Russo-German relations since the summer of 1940; nor does it explain why, in 1940, Stalin had more confidence in Hitler than in Churchill.

A recent book by Victor Suvorov, a defected officer of the GRU (the main intelligence directorate of the Russian Ministry of Defense),[24] has suggested a new key to the mystery. Drawing from Soviet sources, the author seeks to show that when the German attack began, Stalin was in the midst of preparing a similar operation—the invasion of German territory by the Red Army.[25] Suvorov's thesis relies on a study of Soviet military preparations after the occupation of eastern Poland in September 1939; he depicts a Stalin determined to destroy the defensive configuration elaborated in the 1930s along the former eastern border of the USSR, and to replace it with an "all offensive" strategy based on paved roads and a large quantity of light tanks. According to Suvorov, the Hitler-Stalin pact was just one stage of this policy, attempting to use Hitler as an icebreaker to open the way for world revolution. Europe would be unified under the heel of Fascism, the better to be offered up to the Red Army. But the Nazi dictator thwarted the Red dictator: he beat him to the punch by a few weeks or months, thereby benefiting from a nonexistent Soviet defense system. This hypothesis is not entirely absurd;[26] the author is revisiting the old Communist obsession with Fascism as the "supreme stage" of capitalism, that is, the instrument of its liquidation. Yet one can hardly imagine that Stalin was so unrealistic as to envision attacking the Germans, whether in 1941 or 1942, when Hitler was so powerful. The idea that the 1939 pact had brought Stalin not only territory and influence but time as well was perhaps more in keeping with his nature.

To this day there is still no convincing explanation for Stalin's faith in the persistence of his alliance with Hitler and for his panic following 22 June 1941, though evidence may turn up someday in the Soviet archives. One thing, at least, leaves no doubt: it was Hitler and not Stalin who was responsible for the major break that occurred on 22 June 1941 and that would ultimately determine the way World War II was perceived by the public. The rationale behind the war was as clear from the German side as it was obscure or ambiguous from the Soviet side. The invasion of the USSR, though a grave mistake politically, had been deliberately sought and organized according to the program set out almost twenty years earlier in *Mein Kampf.* The occupation of the territory between the Vistula and the Urals in the name of *Lebensraum* for Germany constitutes one of the original and fundamental objectives of Nazism. The only thing surprising about the invasion of June 1941 was that it was undertaken before Hitler had been able to force the British to capitulate; the rest was merely the execution of an ideology, coupled with an underestimation of the adversary's strength. The result was that in marching toward the Urals under the banner of Fascism, the

Wehrmacht lent the war a universal meaning, namely, anti-Fascism. Hence Communism unintentionally recovered the flag it had betrayed; Hitler had left nothing to chance.

In one sense, of course, the war against Fascism had begun not on 22 June 1941 but on 3 September 1939, when Britain and France declared war on Hitler's Germany two days after it had invaded Poland. From then on, the conflict assumed an ideological character. Hatred of the Western plutocracies, the decline of decadent France, the at least partial dismantling of the British Empire all figured in *Mein Kampf,* along with *Lebensraum* to be taken from the Slavs. The war was as inevitable a part of the Nazis' agenda as was the confrontation between the democracies and their enemy—soon to be joined by Mussolini's Italy.

Many other elements contributed to the way World War II was perceived. World War I, still very present, extended its veil of memories up to 1939; it made the revival of the Franco-German conflict look like an interminable quarrel between nations rather than a new battle of ideas. The Western governments that declared war on Germany on 3 September, moreover, were headed by the previous year's signers of the Munich agreement. They did for Poland what they had not done for Czechoslovakia, but not all of them had abandoned the hope of a new compromise with Hitler, once Poland had been beaten.[27] Public opinion, especially in France, had accepted the war more as a fate than as an ideological mission; even the French anti-Fascist Left, as we have seen, rejected the idea of an anti-Fascist crusade before 1939. Only the Communists were preaching such a crusade, but the turnaround of 23 August 1939 transformed them too into combatants against the compromise peace and the "imperialist war," and the terms "anti-Fascist" and "anti-Nazi" disappeared from their literature.[28] When soldiers from the various democracies, left- and right-wing together, marched to battle against Hitler's army in September, it was not to fight Fascism but to defend their respective nations.

Indeed, Hitler's victory over France was not a specifically Fascist one either in its course or even in its objectives. What was new about it, aside from its rapidity, was the predominant use of tanks and aircraft: the battles were in keeping with the laws of war. Hitler found himself fighting with France because of Poland; his grievances against the "hereditary enemy" were more traditional than ideological. He wanted to be the avenger of Rethondes, to take back Alsace-Lorraine, to make the old, overly "civilized" country submit to the renascent Reich. What is more, his wish that Britain should come to Canossa kept him from taking everything away from vanquished France, for if the conditions of the cease-fire were too stringent, the French might be compelled to continue the war up to Casablanca or Algiers, thus reinforcing British determination to fight on. In spite of Mussolini, North Africa and the fleet thus remained in the hands of Vichy. France still administered two-fifths of its territory, and German soldiers were ordered to behave themselves in the three-fifths occupied by them.

Until 1941, only one European nation had been selected as the victim of Nazi terror, delivered up to a systematic destructive enterprise—namely, western Poland. But no one, or almost no one, knew or wanted to know about it; no one even spoke about it, or not loudly enough to reveal the almost savage character of what was under way there. In the meantime, the Bolsheviks were behaving in a similar manner in eastern Poland, making it even more difficult to point a finger at the Nazis. With Hitler's invasion of Russia, however, the time was ripe for a renewal of anti-Fascist sermonizing; Stalin's regime was returned to the camp of democracy, alongside England and eventually the United States, while Soviet territory became the quintessential theater of Nazi barbarism.

Unlike the instructions given in 1940 concerning Western Europe, Hitler's directives to the Wehrmacht on how to maintain its conquest of Russia were highly specific. In France, Hitler had no intention of installing the great millenarian Reich, which was actually to be established in the vast plains east of the Vistula. A glance at the "Table Talks" (the first of which date from the summer of 1941)[29] shows how preoccupied he was with future Germanic agricultural colonization in what he called the "Russian desert." The colonies were to be a productivist utopia, nourished by absolute disdain for the Slavs and by a racism so radical that it legitimated any kind of violence, butchery, or famine against these latter-day "redskins."[30] Hitler's orders to his invading troops—for example, to kill all political commissars that were taken prisoner—went so far beyond the accepted laws of war that he dared not leave their entire execution to Wehrmacht officers and entrusted certain orders—the most criminal ones—to Himmler and the SS, under the direct control of the Führer. In his "special order" of 13 March, Hitler justified both the total character of the war against the USSR and the special assignment of SS troops to "certain tasks" on the grounds of the radical opposition between the two political systems.[31] He thus personally justified the savagery of the battle and lent it ideological significance. On 30 March, in front of 250 officers, he made murdering the enemy a military, national, and political obligation:

Fight against the poison of disintegration. The leaders must be aware of what is at stake. In this battle, they must be the guides. . . . The commissars and members of the GPU are all criminals and must be dealt with as such. . . . The battles will be very different from what they were to the west. To the east, the difficulty will be a guarantee of goodwill for the future. The leaders must be strong enough to overcome their scruples.[32]

After these exhortations to reduce the Slavs to slavery and to liquidate the Communist cadres, Hitler mentioned a third category of enemies of the Reich, a category he spoke of less openly during this period although he had always cast its members as his worst enemies: the Jews. They were implicitly designated in the expression "poison of disintegration"; undoubtedly, in Hitler's eyes, they populated the ranks of political commissars earmarked for liquidation.[33] In speaking to his soldiers, the Führer had several reasons not to put the Jews on the front line of the enemy. The Jews had neither a national territory nor an army: millions of defenseless people, scattered throughout the cities of Eastern Europe, they had nothing of the traditional military enemy about them. To persecute them, in the etymological sense of the term, was hardly a way of achieving military glory such as victory over the Red Army or the liquidation of the USSR would have been. Furthermore, persecution of the Jews had been rampant since September 1939 in what was formerly Poland when it was occupied by German troops. Under the direction of the SS and the Gestapo—the regular army seemed little inclined to take part—huge numbers of Jews were deported to the east, and Jewish communities were forcibly re-ghettoized:[34] this was the only solution found to the problem of driving the Jews not only out of Germany, Austria, and Bohemia, but also out of the Polish territories directly incorporated into the Reich. There was a tragic Jewish concentration in the "General Government" zone,[35] among the tens of thousands of Poles expelled from the western part of their homeland, which had become German. Governor-General Frank repeatedly complained about the overpopulation of undesirables he had to govern, for he was merely an administrative cog in the machine of violence that herded them, along with the gypsies, toward his barren principality. In 1940, the Nazi leaders were still envisaging the definitive expulsion of European Jews from Europe—to Madagascar, for example. The formation of ghettos and the bureaucratic registration of the Jewish population—already between a million and a half to two million—would facilitate their eventual forced emigration.

The idea of an African refuge died as Hitler was mulling over his Russian campaign and briefing his officers on what was expected of them in the late winter and early spring of 1941. So he must have been aware that in marching east, his army would be confronted with the Jewish question again, three or four times as pressing in terms of numbers. The Ukrainian, Belorussian, and Russian Jews formed the largest demographic concentrations of Jewry in Europe, along with the Polish Jews. If the ghetto policy no longer prefaced a general expulsion of the Jews from Europe, it would surely lead to a slowdown in the army's advance, for it was the soldiers who would have to assume the burden of assembling and watching over them. The massacre of the Jews was therefore one of the "special missions" that Hitler assigned to the no less special troops assigned to clear any sworn enemies of the Reich from the lands conquered by the army. After 3 March, following a meeting between Hitler and General Jodl, the special mission of the second wave of invaders to follow the front-line troops—composed of a criminal elite through an inversion of military virtues—was defined thus: "Eradicate the Judeo-Bolshevik intelligentsia, preferably in the actual theater of operations." [36] This euphemism, supposed to attenuate the horrors of what it was ordering, nonetheless said what it meant to say. The prospect for emigration was over. The time for surveillance and roundups was over: now was the time for slaughter. The formation of the four *Einsatzgruppen* (operational forces of intervention—the special units in charge of the liquidation of Jews in the immediate vicinity of the front) foretold the mass executions of the summer and fall of 1941.

If we limit our consideration to German intentions, 22 June 1941 marked a break in the nature of the war, which had turned into an extermination in the name of a racial ideology. This ideology, no doubt, was already present in 1939–40, when the Nazis were deporting the Poles and Polish Jews eastward, but with two differences: in the earlier persecution, atrocious as it was, massacre was not the avowed goal; second, most of the war occurred to the west of Europe, where Hitler's conquests appeared more traditional. The Nazi war, in the full sense of the word, did not reveal its true nature until Hitler gave his instructions in the spring of 1941. It was not the kind of situation that periodically pushes nations into open conflict, subjecting their citizen-soldiers to interminable suffering while offering them a glorious theater in which to display their patriotism. Part and parcel of an ideology far more powerful than nationalism, produced by a deliberate ambition to dominate the world, fighting against an adversary greater than the soldier or the country across the battlefield, pursuing victory all the more fiercely because of its abstract content, the Nazi war as conceived by Hitler would be tragically true to the intentions of its initiator because the German people embraced the same goals. This collective crime, so vast and so meticulously perpetrated by so many individuals, remains almost beyond the imagination.

The Soviet Union was the first theater of the Nazi war, its most visible target, and its most heroic adversary. Since August 1939, virtually all Europeans had abhorred Stalin's homeland, not just his old enemies but his old friends too; the former were vindicated, the latter disillusioned. The Soviet Union had participated in the anti-Polish atrocities and needed no accomplices to subdue the Baltic states by means of executions and massive deportations in the second half of 1940. Then came the invasion of 22 June 1941, which turned the executioner into a victim. From one day to the next, the Soviet Union found itself in the same camp as the British and thus on the side of the democracies and eventually beholden to the United States. Within a few months, Hitler's massive mobilization, the savagery of the Nazi offensive, and the determination of Russian resistance transformed the Soviet Union into the martyr and the hope of European liberty.

This shift was clearly reflected in Winston Churchill's attitude. The old leader, long isolated among British conservatives because of his mistrust of Hitler, was also a veteran of anti-Sovietism. In the spring 1941 he had suffered defeat after defeat: in the Middle East, in Greece, in Crete. His situation was too precarious for him to be choosy about his allies, one of which was the USSR. Alerted by his intelligence services that the Germans were preparing an invasion to the east, he notified Stalin, who did not believe him. But as soon as the attack began, on 22 June, he proclaimed his solidarity with the government he had detested, for it had now become an enemy of the Nazis. Although most of his military advisers believed, as Hitler did, that the Soviet Union would be brought to its knees within a few weeks, Churchill perceived a decisive turning point in a war that Britain had been fighting alone for almost two years. On 12 July, after the rout of the Red Army, the British government signed an agreement with the Soviet government in Moscow that would bind the two nations together until the end of the war; no one was willing to sign a separate peace with Germany. On 2 August, the United States committed itself to both military and economic aid to the USSR. In October, a tripartite agreement of the same sort was signed by the British, the Americans, and the Soviets. The Soviet Union had become an ally and a friend of the two largest liberal democracies in the world even before the most powerful among the three had entered the war. When the Red Army's counterattack at the gates of Moscow marked the first military blow to Nazi power on 6 December, it was all but forgotten that Stalin was a former ally of Hitler's.

Yet they had been allies only a short time ago. The very frontier crossed by German tanks on 22 June 1941 in their eastward rush had been conquered by Stalin in September 1939, with Hitler's complicity over Poland's dead body; yet Stalin was now allied with the Polish émigré government in London! Wars in general, but especially this one, the most universal in history, virtually eliminate choice. They align the past with the present and recognize only two camps; not only soldiers and emotions but ideas and even memories fall into step behind one of the two flags. In the case of the 1941 war between Germany and Russia, this effect was brought to an extreme by the magnitude of the conflict— the millions of men, the deployment of mechanical forces, the rigor of the climate. The entry of the United States and Japan into the war on 8 December, at the crucial moment of the first Russian counterattack, put the final touches to the siege of Moscow, transforming its stakes into universal ones.

Stalin was certainly not the last to understand how the war would affect Soviet politics in general and his dictatorship in particular. Despite his unwillingness to believe any warnings, he already embodied Russian power, in his own despotic and cruel manner, when the conflict occurred. He was responsible for the doctrine of "socialism in one country," the Five-Year Plans, forced industrialization, and the modernization of military equipment. Even though he had killed more of his countrymen than had all of Russia's enemies combined and, furthermore, had liquidated a good portion of the Red Army's managerial staff during the Great Terror in the summer of 1939–40, he represented territorial expansion, following in the footsteps of the czars in the name of "socialism." When, on 3 July 1941, he addressed his "brothers and sisters" to outline a preliminary program of resistance against the enemy, he peppered his discourse with calls to patriotism: he knew better than anyone that the people, as long as they still had the strength to stand, would march against the invader and defend the soil of their homeland, though not the kolkhozy or the Politburo.

Hitler contributed to this national impulse. In places where his troops were met with flowers by villagers counting on the end of rural collectivization, as happened in many Ukrainian kolkhozy, the German soldiers followed orders and soon put a stop to this pointless fraternization; for the Nazis' wartime goal was to destroy the Soviet state in all the conquered territories so as to turn the local populations into free labor for Germany. When a Ukrainian nationalist organization tried to found its own state in Lvov, independent of Moscow, the Wehrmacht arrested its initiators and partisans.[37] It never seriously attempted to support a policy of secession of the Soviet Republics, which in any case would have been negated by the racist conceptions of which the invasion was but the realization. As an ideological war, the Nazi war in Russia paid an ideological price.

This period was to be the only one in the entire history of the Soviet Union in which the totalitarian power was met with a kind of consent, profound if limited, in the patriotism of the people. Even though the government was entirely responsible for the military disarray and the successive defeats that marked the first months of the invasion, it had also destroyed in advance any recourse that the wretched masses might have conceived. People, institutions, churches, traditions: there was nothing left to resist the government. The more obvious its improvidence, the greater its omnipotence, since its national character was yielded up from the depths of defeat. If the government threw a little weight onto the side of the Church so as to make it a better instrument of patriotic sermonizing, it did not let go of any of the NKVD's prerogatives. As the Soviet armies were withdrawing, Robert Conquest tells us, Stalin could not evacuate his prisoners rapidly enough and decided that it was better to shoot them than to leave them in German hands as witnesses.[38]

To the east of the front, deep in the countryside, the war made massive forced labor increasingly necessary. The Gulag would swell during these years with entire deported populations pathologically suspected of treason, such as the Germans of the Volga, or the Kalmouks, or the Chechens. It is true that Stalin plucked out officers when he needed them, like General Rokossovsky, and that he used deportees to form a certain number of regiments from the Gulag. The sinister nature of this patriotism of slavery and the strange sense of collective relaxation created by a terrible war are most vividly rendered by one of the characters in Boris Pasternak's *Doctor Zhivago:*

> You could volunteer for front-line service in a disciplinary battalion, and if you came out alive you were free. After that, attack after attack, mile after mile of electrified barbed wire, mines, mortars, month after month of artillery barrage. They called our company the death squad. It was practically wiped out. How and why I survived, I don't know. And yet—would you believe it—all the utter hell was nothing, it was bliss compared to the horrors of the concentration camp, and not because of the material conditions but for an entirely different reason. . . . It was felt not only by men in your position, in concentration camps, but by absolutely everyone, at home and at the front, and they all took a deep breath and flung themselves into the furnace of this mortal, liberating struggle with real joy, with rapture.[39]

To fight the Nazi invaders under the ghastly conditions to which prison regiments were subject was a privilege for which innumerable *zek* regiments fought throughout the Gulag. At least the war lent some sense to the present and perhaps—who knew?—might lead to the reestablishment of a future.

International democratic opinion lacked the modesty of the "perhaps" so tragically acquired by Soviet citizens. By definition, it had not experienced life in the USSR. The Communist world continued to be more foreign than ever to it. But shared combat imbued that world with a new and far more widespread fraternity which, if distant, was less abstract than ideological fraternity, insofar as people in the west, occupied or engaged in the war, did not grasp the unique horror of the war in the east. They tended to view it along the lines of the 1914–18 precedent, which, in their eyes, had been dreadful enough to preclude a higher rating on the scale of atrocity. They did not grasp the total inhumanity that Nazism had introduced into war in the democratic era. Nonetheless, westerners began to open up maps of the USSR on their kitchen tables so as to trace the front lines and follow the resistance and progress of the Red Army.

There were many reasons why the western nations were indifferent to the extermination of the Jews, including, in varying proportions, anti-Semitism, ignorance of what was going on, and an inability to imagine the systematic turn of mind and the evil genius behind such a diabolical undertaking. The Jews, moreover, were scattered across Europe in their millions, their fates having little influence on the outcome of the war. In contrast, a single nation was perceived behind the Soviet Union, the Russian people, struggling heroically against an invader of their territory and thus weakening Nazi Germany across Europe. On the maps, which looked more familiar with each communiqué, the names of unheard-of cities—Stalingrad, Koursk, Orel, Vitebsk, Minsk—became symbols of a nation that was fighting for liberty. The battle against Nazi Germany put the homeland of October 1917 back in humanity's advance guard.

Although that process occurred primarily through the conduit of a nation at arms against Hitler, it also implied a confirmation of revolutionary universalism. The Soviet Union appeared to have abandoned its mission with the August 1939 pact, but the war of June 1941 made that abandonment seem like a tactical interlude. This retrospective interpretation was facilitated by the secret nature of the territorial distributions decided by Stalin and Hitler. The unprecedented sacrifices consented to by the Red Army in the battle against Germany made it inconceivable that there had ever been even the briefest alliance between Nazism and

Communism. Moreover, we need only forget yesterday to recall the day before. The war harked back to the great and quite recent period when the Communists were at the forefront of the fight against Hitler: now here they were again, their guns in their hands as they had been in Spain but on a higher level. European anti-Fascism found its political constituency through the criticism of what had occurred between the fall of Madrid and the German invasion of Russia. Thanks to that adjustment, it drew renewed strength from the situation as it assumed the dimensions of patriotism and resistance to the occupying force. One result of this unconscious repression was to legitimize the myth that Stalin and the Comintern were capable of decoding the movement of history.

Indeed, Stalin took advantage of his greatest error. He had believed he could fool everyone by the German-Soviet nonagression pact and could leave the belligerents to exhaust themselves to the benefit of the USSR. Then he was betrayed by Hitler and was all but lost. But even before he was saved by his people's attachment to their soil, he had reconstructed the language of his dictatorship along the anti-Fascist lines that had been dropped in 1939. The term "anti-Fascism," which had disappeared from Soviet language after 23 August 1939, made a noisy reappearance in June 1941, along with patriotism. The European Communist parties seized it collectively, now glad to make the required about-face that rejuvenated them by giving them back the means to a policy both democratic and nationalist. It mattered little that, in the final analysis, the about-face had been rendered inevitable by Hitler and not freely decided by Stalin: all Marxists were familiar with the ruse of reason that had used Hitler as a weapon against his own enemies.

From Moscow's point of view, however, this second rehash of anti-Fascism contained contradictions so profound that, although they could be hushed up, prohibited, or imprisoned by Soviet policies, they could never be resolved. They all had the same cause. The war had finally made the USSR, side by side with the western democracies, into a vessel for individual and national freedom. In the end, the Soviets were incapable of transforming the nature of their regime, and the new role and image of the USSR merely became another means of serving the same despot and the same regime.

Modern war tends to give total power to the governments that wage war as long as they are not dishonored by defeat. Stalin was an exception to this (since 1918) frequently cited rule because he had acquired total control over the USSR without having had to engage his country in an external conflict. He had only to keep invoking the imminent threat of war, imperialist plots, and "Hitlerian-Trotskyist" conspiracies. Then came June 1941, and those repeated warnings seemed to be confirmed. What is more, Stalin had the good fortune to live through a real threat to public safety followed by a military recovery at the gates of Moscow and, the next winter, by a formidable victory in the city that bore his name. After that, the war was the most valuable ally of his absolute power. For state organization of the economy, moreover, it was more convenient than peace. It permitted the Russians to benefit from massive American aid. It legitimized primitive relations of authority and provided a rational framework for the unconditional submission of the people and the idolatry of the leader. A demi-god even before the war, Stalin acquired the other half of his divinity at Stalingrad.

The rush of patriotism that called forth the soldiers in the Red Army against the invader did not find freedom waiting on the battlefield. It had saved the national territory but by forging new chains for it. Patriotism had broken Hitler's hold but had deified Stalin. "Faced with two ferocious adversaries," wrote Solzhenitsyn, "they were bound to favor the one who spoke their own language."[40] This interpretation puts too much faith in the notion that there really was a choice, if we recall the contempt and violence to which the Russian and Ukrainian peoples were subjected by the invading forces. But at least it reveals what was hidden beneath the national equivocation that surrounded the Soviet war against Germany. Stalin had counted on a new lease on totalitarian domination since the victory had lent Communism a minimum of national consensus. On the other hand, the finest among those who had fought so courageously against Hitler had viewed the battle as a chance for a civil renaissance, an opportunity and a hope for liberty. Winners of the war, they became the greatest losers as they perpetuated at home the same type of regime they had crushed in Berlin.

And so the German-Russian War, while marking a break in the political line of the Kremlin, harbored the continuation of a totalitarian regime, masked more effectively than ever by anti-Fascism. We can see this reflected in Soviet foreign policy, which remained unchanged before and after 22 June 1941. On the surface, everything had changed. In 1939–40 the Soviet Union had incorporated a piece of Belorussia, the three Baltic states, one-third of Poland, the eastern border of Finland, Bessarabia, and North Bukovina. It matters little that some of these territories had been recuperated from former parts of the Russian Empire, for the annexations were carried out in a Hitlerian fashion, that is, through the superiority of large states over small ones. After 22 June 1941, the Soviet Union, being at war with Hitler, almost naturally became the champion of small nations against the abuse of large ones. Nazi

Germany aspired to occupy and exploit for itself all of Slavic Europe in the name of Aryan superiority. For its part, the USSR made itself into the champion of equality and independence for all nations, an automatic consequence of anti-Fascism. By virtue of its geography and its history, Russia had a particular vocation to apply this program in Slavic Europe, precisely where Hitler was trampling on the idea of nationhood and promoting that of racism.

The recovery of national independence was thus inseparable from the anti-Fascist war. The idea of independence mobilized not only the armies that were fighting against the Wehrmacht but also the clandestine combatants in the resistance movements in occupied Europe. Stalin had incorporated it into his war objectives and into the texts of the international Communist movement. To make more of an effect, he went so far as to dissolve the Comintern on 15 May 1943: What more spectacular proof could he offer than that the various national Communist parties would henceforth be emancipated from the guardianship of Moscow? As always, it did not take him long to grasp the political consequences of the new situation. This was no longer 1939–40; the time for brutal territorial grabs was over. Just as he had patterned his style after that of Hitler, Stalin now adopted the language of his new allies— the language of liberty.

He had no intention of applying its principles, however. He had altered his tactics and language but not his methods or ambitions. Thanks to the war, he remained as much as ever the representative of the Soviet Empire, determined to plant the flag of Communism as far west as possible. But from now on, neither the territorial extension he envisioned (which his armies were gradually carving out) nor the logic of an anti-Hitlerian war could permit bald annexation of new national units into the Soviet Union. The attack of 22 June, moreover, had illustrated the inconveniences of a common frontier with Germany, and the idea of a buffer zone of nonintegrated but satellite republics would ensure greater security for the Russian Republic. So Stalin had an even greater need for local Communist parties that were servile to him, and the dissolution of the Comintern was a decoy for the benefit of his allies in the West. In any case, he kept the former and future upper-level staff of all the European Communist parties on USSR territory—enough personnel to furnish all the politburos anyone could wish for: Romanian, Polish, Hungarian, Bulgarian, Czech, German, and even Italian and French. Wolfgang Leonhard recounts in his memoirs how his sad life as a young German Communist refugee with his mother in the USSR was transformed after 22 June 1941; how in the deepest, darkest republic of

Bashkir he had been enrolled in a school for foreign Communist cadres in anticipation of the great day; and how he found himself, on 30 April 1945, in the company of Grotewohl, Ulbricht, and several others, in the first nonmilitary airplane to land in eastern Prussia after the Red Army, there to found a new German administration.[41]

The case of Poland is symbolic more sadly, for it was the cause of World War II before becoming one of its greatest victims. The starting point of the September 1939 conflict and the first theater of military operations, Poland was continually at the epicenter of the European earthquake; first it was carved up, then it was pillaged and mutilated by Germany and the USSR, and later it became a bone of contention between the USSR and the English-speaking democracies, definitively losing its independence at the end of the war that was supposed to guarantee it. It provides an excellent example of the immutability of Stalin's intentions, before and after 22 June 1941, through a series of contradictory alliances. In 1939 and 1940, the General Secretary had acquired a vast collection of territories in Eastern Europe by negotiating with Hitler. He was still pursuing what Molotov had sought in Berlin in November 1940 — a sort of protectorate over Romania, Bulgaria, Finland, and Turkey; control over the Balkans; and the status of world superpower on a level with Nazi Germany. The new alliances hardly changed this situation, with two exceptions: first, Stalin had extended his ambitions westward with his army's successful campaigns, and, second, he no longer had to negotiate with Hitler but with Churchill and Roosevelt.

The Polish affair shows that Stalin had no more trouble with the democratic leaders than he had had with the Nazi dictator. Although very soon after 22 June he had recognized the Polish government in London—a prelude to the formation of a Polish army on Soviet soil— he refused to include any mention of the Polish-Soviet border in the agreement. He made clear to the British in the fall of 1941 that he wished to retain the territories he had taken from the Germans. Churchill and Roosevelt played for time by delaying the tracing of the frontier until the peace was signed. In the meantime, failing the successful opening of a second European front, which Stalin was noisily demanding, they had to come up with something to give their ally, who, because of what had happened in 1939, they feared would sign a separate peace with Hitler. The democracies' premature concessions to Soviet expansion were the price paid for the state of military unreadiness in which they had been surprised by the war. We must also account for certain illusions: Churchill had few, but Roosevelt had many. The American president was both ignorant and naive about the Soviet Union and its leader. He had such curiously optimistic notions about Stalin that it is difficult to reconcile them with his brilliant handling of domestic affairs. The age, it is true, was conducive to his optimism. Memories of the German-Soviet pact had faded with the years, and the Red Army had paid the heavy price of redemption with its sacrifices. Stalingrad had erased the exchange of niceties between Ribbentrop and Molotov. The war imposed a Manichaean logic, which gradually became an obligatory opinion.

In 1943, the discovery of the mass grave at Katyn complicated the Polish imbroglio by provoking, on the one hand, a rupture between the USSR and the Polish government in London and, on the other, the formation of another Polish team in Moscow, which was a rough draft of the future Communist government. The die was already cast on the Soviet side at the very moment when, at the end of 1943, restoration of national independence and freely elected government were proclaimed as the USSR's war objectives. During the same period, Churchill and Roosevelt accepted the "Curzon line" [42] in Tehran as the eastern border of Poland. This arrangement gave rise to a vast westward displacement of Polish territory to the detriment of millions of Germans who were driven out, implying the future Poland's close dependence on the USSR.

The subsequent history was all but already written; the Soviet military advance to the west made inevitable even the share that had not been consented to beforehand. The insoluble quarrel that set Mikolajczyk, the head of the Polish government in London, against Stalin was quickly settled in August 1944. After a rapid advance, the Red Army made it as far as Praga, a suburb of Warsaw, on the right bank of the Vistula. At the same time, the Polish government in London decided to assert its rights: it set off the insurrection in Warsaw with its clandestine military units. In order to attack the German troops, these units needed help from the Red Army, camped on the other side of the river. But the Russians did not budge. From a distance, the soldiers watched the capitulation of the Polish "National Army" and the destruction of Warsaw. In December, the "Committee for the National Liberation of Poland," which had been formed in Lublin at the urging of the Russians, became Poland's provisional government and was immediately recognized by Moscow. At Yalta, in February 1945, all that Churchill and Roosevelt got from Stalin was the participation of the Poles of London in the provisional government. It was a fake "national union" and did not long survive.

No one, at the time, seemed troubled by the triumph of might over right at the close of a war that had been declared in the name of right against might. In this period, the Communist idea in the twentieth century was at its apogee, triumphant in both facts and minds.

In one of the most moving novels of the century, the Soviet author Vasily Grossman introduces the character of Stalin at the time of Stalingrad. In late November 1942, the General Secretary had just learned of the surrounding of the German Sixth and Fourth Armies by his troops. His eyes closed, he was the first to savor this moment. Grossman reads his thoughts: "This was his hour of triumph. He had not only defeated his current enemy; he had defeated the past. In the village, the grass would grow thicker over the tombs of 1930. The snow and ice of the Arctic Circle would remain dumb and silent. He knew better than anyone that no one condemns a victor."[43]

In the spring of 1945, victory kept its date with Stalingrad. It combined the two gods that make or break historical times: power and ideas. As far as military strength was concerned, it was an absolute victory, in tune with the Allies' commitments not to make a separate peace and not to leave the battlefield before obtaining an unconditional surrender from the enemy. In the realm of ideas, the situation was no less triumphant, marked by the banishing of Fascism from humanity. Insisting on unconditional capitulation may have seemed—and no doubt was—debatable during World War I. But this was not the case in World War II: though defensible under Wilhelm II, the idea of a compromise peace was impossible under Hitler.[44]

Never in history has armed force seemed more legitimate than during the victorious anti-Nazi coalition, wreathed in the triumph of liberty. It was barely permissible to note that this legitimacy had seemed less certain to the Europeans, except for the British, four or five years earlier, when the Germans were winning in Europe and temporarily enjoyed greater strength. Thanks to the victory, the military conflict and the clash of ideas had lost the problematic character they once held in people's minds. To use the vocabulary of the time, history had spoken. Its verdict annulled any earlier doubts.

The Soviet Union had paid more than its share for this unprecedented triumph of democracy—rather late, it is true, since the homeland of Communism did not enter the war until mid-1941 and then only because it was forced to do so by the Nazi attack. Between the summers of 1939 and 1941, Stalin had gone along with Hitler, and he might well have preferred to continue a policy that allowed him to annex eastern Poland, the Baltic States, and Romanian Bessarabia. But once driven into the democratic camp by the German invasion, the Soviet Union had made the heaviest contribution to the victory of 1945 in consensual suffering and spilled blood. It had proved its military strength, its social cohesion, the patriotism of its population. The Red Army was the first to enter Berlin; it occupied Warsaw, Bucharest, Prague, Budapest. It lent Stalin an unassailable negotiating position at the end of the war.

This unexpected advantage was no less political and ideological for all that: Communism had won the war and thus a new lease on history. Not that it had been threatened internally during the prewar period. The Great Terror of the 1930s in the USSR had clearly shown the extent of Stalin's absolute power over the USSR's Communist Party and the Union itself. But the loyalty of the Soviet sister parties, and certainly their influence, had been tested by the dropping of the anti-Fascist line between 1939 and 1941. The victory of 1945 wiped that episode from the people's memory just as it had erased the bad memories of the militants; if any of those memories lingered in the minds of some, the Communist parties would exorcize them with efficiency and total authority.

The image of the Soviet Union, when decked out in all the prestige of power and ideology, had never cast a more potent spell. In the years following October 1917, the Russian Revolution had revived one of the most compelling political images in European culture. That revolutionary idea, however, in its original purity and untainted by history, retained its attraction only among the elites of the working class and in intellectual circles. From the 1930s on, in spite of domestic calamities, the Soviet Union had increased its influence, first as a crisis-proof economic system and then as the democracies' ally against Hitler. But the Hitler-Stalin pact of 1939 had returned the regime of October 1917 to a state of moral and political isolation in Europe. Stalin gained a lot of territory out of the pact, but Communism emerged tainted. The war and the victory of 1945, on the other hand, gave Stalin more prominence than ever before, though for the last time. The Red Army planted its flags with those of the American troops on the banks of the Elbe, having liberated all of Central and Eastern Europe from Nazi oppression; Communism was not only in power but was the incarnation of freedom.

By the same token, the crimes of the regime against the peoples and citizens of the Soviet Union were wiped out not only by victory but by the particular victory over Hitler. Yet the war had done little to temper the regime's arbitrariness or violence. While Stalin had been forced to make regiments out of the *zeks*, he had continued to fill up the Gulag, deporting masses of non-Slav minorities or inhabitants of annexed territories. The time would soon come when he would send hundreds of thousands of Soviet citizens, both those who had been made prisoners by the Germans and those who had fled the USSR, to the Gulag to be liquidated. Like their forebears of 1812, these soldiers had fought with the kind of patriotism that even servitude could not diminish. For the rest, by fighting the Nazi troops, they discovered that Europe had a face even worse than their own regime. Stalin thus benefited not only from the patriotism of servitude but also from that of resistance. Victorious over the Nazis, his army and people sealed or resealed their chains under the abstract banner of liberty.

That banner was invaluable also when borne into the Central and Eastern European countries that had been "liberated," one by one, from Hitler's troops as the Russians advanced. Liberated they were indeed, in one sense. But at what price, and to what end? The Red Army had increasingly pillaged and raped along the way, barely distinguishing between the countries that were supposed to be allies, like Poland, or enemies, like Hungary. The women of Gdansk and those of Budapest had similar memories of such activities. These violent acts could perhaps be attributed to the accumulated suffering and exasperation of battle-weary soldiers. But were they not the first signs of a lasting occupation? The peoples of Eastern Europe, to varying degrees and even when not allied with Hitler (the Poles, for example), had good reason to fear that Stalin intended to continue in 1945 what he had begun in 1939–40: the creation of a protective buffer zone consisting of countries that had been absorbed or made into satellites, as far to the west as possible, in the tracks of the Red Army. The difference is that in 1939–40 Stalin had gone beyond his borders, thanks to complicity with Hitler. In 1945, he drove Hitler out of the Slavic countries and Hungary as a liberator, prior to becoming an occupier himself: history endowed his territorial ambitions with democratic legitimacy. If his army occupied Poland or Czechoslovakia, it was in the name of Polish or Czech independence.

Hitler was thus unwittingly responsible for a formidable increase in the material and psychic strength of Communism, primarily by bequeathing to the postwar world a Communist Europe absurdly extended toward the west, even beyond what its own means would allow it to maintain permanently, more powerful in appearance than in reality, and more inclined to intimidation than to true demonstrations of strength, as postwar diplomacy would bear out. But Hitler had done even more for Stalin. After dishonoring him with the 1939 pact by drawing him into his own schemes for domination, he had given him a chance to buy back his soul with the invasion of 22 June 1941—a move that was both a pretext to a reunion with Russian patriotism and a means of reburnishing Communism with democratic colors.

Because of the emotions it evoked and the blood it spilled, the war engraved attitudes and memories deep into people's hearts. The Soviet Union's emergence from the last global conflict as a democratic super-power had nothing to do with the nature of its regime and everything to do with historical circumstance. Allied with Britain and the United States, the great original democracies, and having lost between twelve and fifteen million of its sons in the fight against the Nazis, it had paid dearly for its new national label of anti-Fascism.

Anti-Fascism: the word foretold what Communism's postwar influence would be. It was not by accident that the Communists had continued to militate under this banner rather than another. They had never wanted any other political arena than this two-dimensional or, rather, bipolar space, the "Fascists" at one pole and themselves at the other. Other forces clustered around each of the poles with varying degrees of seriousness—other strengths, or other weaknesses. The political advantages of the arrangement alone explain the Communists' determination to ensure Fascism's survival through a multitude of imitators, even after they had crushed the regimes that had embodied Fascism. In this way, the identity between Communism and democracy could be perpetuated, and all "bourgeois" governments would be suspected of opening the way to imitators of Mussolini or Hitler. Since the end of Fascism, there has been no Communist policy without its "Fascist menace." This posthumous prophylaxis would have been less bothersome if it had not been used to conceal the nature of the Soviet regime and to invent improbable "Fascists" such as Adenauer, de Gaulle, and Eisenhower.

The reason the anti-Fascist idea made such waves in postwar Europe after losing its point of application was that it prolonged the terrible experience of World War II by labeling and giving a meaning to human suffering. It was sustained by universal memory and also, perhaps, by collective regret, shared to varying degrees but present almost everywhere—regret for not having fought against Mussolini, Hitler, and their ideas. It reinforced a natural tendency to engage in yesterday's battles ex post facto. Unlike World War I, World War II ended with a clear notion as to the identity of the culprits. By defeating Hitler, the Allies had revealed the extraordinary misdeeds that his very defeat had made knowable.

The Nazi regime was held to be a criminal regime both by public opinion and by the international tribunal that met solemnly at Nuremberg to judge and condemn those responsible for it; from November 1945 to October 1946, it took almost a year to examine the grisly list of charges case by case.[45] The Soviet Union had carefully prepared for this unprecedented trial, which was conducted along Anglo-Saxon lines, the human race constituting the prosecutor. The Soviets were all the more anxious to possess a legal certification of Hitler's crimes because they expected that this would highlight the democratic merits of its principal victim, who had also been its principal conqueror. The fact that the Soviets tried to tack Katyn onto the list of horrors committed by the Nazis reveals much about what they expected from the Nuremberg verdict. Defeated on that particular point, they nonetheless received a solemn confirmation of the democratic implications of their victory from the final judgment. In this sense, Nuremberg justice had been a winners' justice, as maintained by its opponents, but this tells only part of the truth; it does not imply that the victors had dispensed no justice.

The enormity of the Nazis' crimes was revealed; it was something that could not be separated from the war deliberately willed by Hitler. It could have been foreseen before 1939, but at that time the crimes were limited to German territory and were, moreover, far below the scale of the Soviet repression of the Ukrainians and Russian ethnic groups during those same years. Although the Allies may have been at least partially aware of the Nazi massacres during the war, those massacres did not become known to the general public until the military collapse and the discovery of the death camps, when the survivors returned in the spring of 1945. The West, during this period, was not yet aware of the most hideous aspect of the Nazi crimes—the extermination of the Jews.[46] When the Jews did not return, they were counted along with the dead of their own countries. When they did return, it was extremely difficult for them to go public with their particular tragedy because the European nations did not like the idea of creating a special category for the Nazis' victims. This was especially true of the Soviet Union, which went so far as to prohibit any mention of the massacres of Russian, Belorussian, or Ukrainian Jews on the monuments commemorating victims of the Nazi crimes committed on Russian soil. Desperately trying to attribute all the crimes of the war to Hitler, the USSR deprived itself of the only argument that would have allowed a distinction to be made between Hitler and Stalin in terms of deliberate massacres—namely, racial genocide. And so the Jews lost everything, even their misfortune; it was an augury that hard times were not yet over.

Anti-Fascism of the 1945 type drew its strength less from an analysis of the war than from the meaning that it gave to war. At the end of the First World War, European nations had fueled their domestic and foreign struggles with the enigma of the war's meaning. At the end of the Second, the victory was interpreted unanimously, even among the vanquished. Germany was in disgrace. The atrocities committed by the

Soviet troops on German soil, the forced westward exodus of twelve to fifteen millions of Germans,[47] and the concomitant death of a good many of them were not even mentioned in the press. The public was barely aware of these matters. The Nazi crimes, publicly sanctioned, formed the showcase for this universal accord, an accord that went beyond the traditional "Woe to the vanquished!" and expressed something beyond guilt for procrastinating too long before joining the fight against Hitler; it lent political condemnation the intransigence of a moral sentiment, relegating Fascism to the domain of absolute evil. Anti-Fascism was less a political position, though it was that too, than a general feeling among the peoples who survived World War II and the moral judgment they drew from it.

It was a feeling and a judgment that would encounter anti-Fascist ideology—the ideology that had gradually been forged during the fight of the European Left against Hitler and Mussolini and had found its promised land in the defense of the Spanish Republic between 1936 and 1939. The Spanish Civil War had crystallized political passions on a European scale. In spite of the final defeat and much bloody internal fighting, the defense of the Spanish Republic had furnished prewar anti-Fascism with a treasure trove of memories and a political tradition—all of which, embellished or made over, would serve as deeds and titles for the self-interested beneficiaries of postwar anti-Fascism.

In the end, the war largely fulfilled the Communist version of the anti-Fascist prophecy: not that it finally extinguished democracy, for the Americans and the British were the principal victors, and the part of Europe they had liberated from the Nazis recovered democratic institutions along with their freedom. The other part of Europe, however, was in the hands of the Red Army, which imposed Soviet regimes and protectorates that reached as far as Budapest and Prague. This was hardly surprising, considering that this sort of territorial expansion, in spite of its exceptional reach, is part and parcel of pure power; for the Europeans and their chancelleries, the idea of an empire emanating from Moscow had been around for a couple of centuries. The real novelty of 1945 was the forms and the ideology assumed by the imperialist thrust: it exported and established Soviet-type societies and regimes in the name of anti-Fascism.

Between 1945 and 1948, in Central and Eastern Europe, coalition governments were replaced by the undivided domination of local Communist parties under the anti-Fascist banner. For those interested less in the instrumental use of anti-Fascism to justify the seizure of power than in anti-Fascism's extraordinary social radiation at the service of

Communism in Western as well as Eastern Europe, this phenomenon requires another type of analysis.

To do this, we must return once more to the war.

The war had no historical equivalent in terms of the nature of the conflict and the forces it brought into play, the two elements mutually reinforcing each other. Because the conflict took on an increasingly ideological character, it mobilized all the great economic powers in the world, culminating in the unconditional surrender of Nazi Germany and Japan. It began in 1939 as a European war between Hitler and the Western democracies; the United States remained out of the conflict, and the German-Soviet nonaggression pact, followed by the partition of Poland and the revelation of a secret alliance, surrounded events with a certain political ambiguity. After June 1941, that ambiguity was dispelled by the German invasion of Russia, making Communism anti-Fascist once again and, hence, democratic. The Japanese attack on Pearl Harbor and the United States' entry into the war completed the picture. Once that picture was established, the public forgot what it owed to circumstances—that is, to the two attacks on victims who had not perceived the imminence of those attacks, let alone their inevitability. The war, which had turned into a world war, now appeared imperative. The ambiguity present at its beginnings served to emphasize the working of historical reason, which had finally distributed forces and roles: liberty versus dictatorship, democracy versus Fascism.

For Europeans, the war had become a kind of a historical tribunal. It had etched the ideological scene in people's minds. It favored the most extreme elements for the same reasons; such is the logic of naked force. By the same token, the war seemed to confirm the two philosophies of historical violence involved in the confrontation—Nazism and Marxism-Leninism. In these circumstances, democracy had less certainty to offer, except in the United States, where it was a national belief. In Europe, where the cause of democracy was intermingled with that of the Communist ally, the term "democratic" had largely shifted to the side of Leninism by the time the fighting ceased.

Indeed, democracy on the continent of Europe had never been the object of a cult free from reticence or fear, especially in the years leading up to World War II. Here we are not speaking of Great Britain, alone among the great European democracies to have actually figured on the side of the victors, and the only one in which a modern society and a government founded on individual freedom had become indefeasible traditions: fortified by its history, Britain might have been able to offer a shared ideal to the Europe it had saved in 1940. It had, however, already been relegated to the second row of the victors and was regarded, as usual, more as an exception than as an example. In continental Europe, the prewar years had been characterized by Fascism and anti-Fascism. The end of the war marked the victory of anti-Fascism rather than of democracy.

France, birthplace of the democratic idea in its revolutionary version, shows us why this was true. In prewar France, several groups, not to be confused with one another but which could combine forces when necessary, were opposed to democracy. The smallest such group consisted of the traditional enemies of the principles of 1789, constantly lying in wait for a chance to be done with the Republic. They were stronger, thanks to Maurras, in the battle of ideas than on the public scene. The other group was larger and more modern but also vaguer in its ideas; it included antiparliamentarianists, nationalists, and even Fascist-leaning advocates of revolution in imitation of Italy or Germany. It participated in right-wing antidemocratic culture to the extent that it disliked the French Revolution, though less than the royalists did, but it also shared the Left's hatred of capitalism; like the socialists and the Communists, it detested the bourgeoisie, and, also like them, it dreamed of a true community beyond individual interests. This passion increasingly characterized the French interwar Left, encouraged by the mounting rivalry between the Socialist and Communist Parties and by their disagreement over the nature of the USSR. That is why the Left, in spite of factual evidence to the contrary, was so passionately attached to the notion that the Fascist adversary was a puppet of capitalism.

This false notion had a price. By concealing the secret link between the political sentiments of the antiparliamentarian Right and those of the revolutionary Left, it weakened democratic culture in its institutional and juridical form to the benefit of the revolutionary idea, whose comeback was all the more victorious because fueled by the great memories of national history. By substituting anti-Fascism for democracy in order to unify the forces at the left and center, it conveniently saved the Left from the possibility of an ulterior subversion by democracy once it had triumphed over Fascism. The socialists adopted this strategy through weakness, since they did not dare renounce the idea of a revolutionary overthrow of bourgeois democracy. The Communists had deliberately invented it because they were counting on that overthrow.

The end of World War II offered anti-Fascism a second political wind by permanently ridding it of its Fascist enemy. Thereafter, anti-Fascism no longer had any rivals in the critique of bourgeois democracy: it held a monopoly on it. The end of World War II was thus even more of a political victory for the Communist idea than for the democratic idea.

Furthermore, the political result of the 1945 victory was to grant anti-Fascism a monopoly on the dominant passion of prewar European politics—hatred of money and of capitalism. In the interwar period this passion was shared by both the revolutionary Left, consisting of the socialist and Communist groups, and the revolutionary Right, the Fascist groups. For the Left, that passion pertained to equality; for the Right, to the nation. Both groups sought a revival of the human community. After 1945, the passion was no longer shared: it remained intact, inseparable from its European form and from the democratic condition of the century, but was entirely invested in the Left. The other path was forbidden.

Is "forbidden" a sufficiently strong word? Since the Crusades, history offers few examples of a political idea defended by armed combat that was subject to such radical interdiction as was the Fascist idea. It had emerged and triumphed, however, in two of the most civilized countries of Europe, Italy and Germany. Before becoming a curse, it had been a ray of hope for many intellectuals, including some of the most distinguished, but by the end of the war it remained only in a demonized form, which would certainly guarantee it a long survival but one dedicated to immortalizing its victors.

Neither the defeat of Fascism not the ideological character of the war are sufficient to explain this fate. Wars do not always destroy the ideas they vanquish; sometimes they even strengthen them. If the only ideological interpreters of Fascism were those who had opposed it, we need to find different and more complicated reasons for the anathema that Fascism became. Some of these reasons have to do with the nature of the doctrine, which celebrated the national and the racial and thus, through exalting the particular, turned democratic universalism, such a strong sentiment in the twentieth century, inside out. In the Nazis' racial exclusivism there was surely something that ran so counter to this sentiment that even mentioning it was shocking. What should one say about the crimes committed in the name of Fascism between 1941 and 1945? They confirmed, in a horrific manner, any doubts raised by the idea of racial superiority. Gradually known to the public in the years following the collapse of the Third Reich, they constituted the moral sanction for the military victory. The Fascist idea was dishonored not only by defeat—in that case it would have survived—but by the final years of Nazism, which defined the idea for ever after.

It matters little that Fascism did not serve to justify comparable crimes elsewhere—in Italy, for example. It even matters little that in Germany, until 1941, the arrests and murders carried out in its name were incomparably less massive than those perpetrated in the name of

the proletarian revolution in the Soviet Union. The last four years of
Nazism henceforth contained the truth of Fascism. They elicited so
much horror that they absorbed the indignation of all the civilized
world. As for less civilized nations, such as the USSR, the fact that they
were major victims as well as major victors sufficed to obscure their own
nature. Germany paid for everyone, and for all the crimes of the twentieth century.

None of this explains why the Communist idea was the greatest beneficiary of the Nazi apocalypse. After all, the contrasting American model
was also available and would progressively, if slowly, make up for lost
terrain in the half-century to follow. We must ask why that model was
so intellectually weak in 1945, in contrast to Marxism-Leninism, among
most of the intelligentsia of Europe, even Western Europe, with the
exception of Germany, which was obviously a case apart.

We have already raised one response to this question: in continental
Europe, where both left- and right-wing political culture were inseparable from dislike of capitalism, the 1945 version of Marxism-Leninism
had the crucial advantage of taking over the entire space of anticapitalism at the very moment when the strategy and notion of anti-Fascism,
of which Marxism-Leninism had been the self-interested if intermittent
instigator, lent it its full democratic dignity by virtue of the victory. This
brought the Communist idea to the providential crossroads at which it
monopolized the critique of capitalism, having formerly managed, only
five years after the Hitler-Stalin pact and at the price of a great deal of
spilled blood, to assume the front line of the democratic fight against
Fascism. If we do not look too closely, World War II appears to confirm
the Marxist definition of anti-Fascism, according to which the definitive
victory over Hitler and his eventual imitators could only be achieved by
uprooting the capitalist economy. As shown by what followed, and as
could have been seen at the time, that idea was absurd. But it was supported by public opinion on two different levels of reality and retained
that support for quite some time, especially in intellectual circles. On
one level, the Communists since 1941 had appeared to be the most radical of anti-Fascist fighters, thanks to the sacrifices they had undergone
and their gift for propaganda. They had thus passed over 1939–41 and
resumed the strategy of the 1930s, which, as far as they were concerned,
facilitated the illusion of anti-Hitlerian continuity. That illusion was so
strong that in 1945 it came to be shared by most of the people who had
denounced the August 1939 pact as treason. The illusion then served as
a delayed bonus for anti-Fascism that worked to the advantage of the
Soviet Union and the Communist parties—a bonus all the more pow-

erful since the enormity of the Nazi crimes after 1941 lent a retrospective veracity to the denunciations of the prewar years.

On the other hand, the collapse of Nazism did not spell the end of the great secular religions of the twentieth century. On the contrary, its radical disappearance left Marxism-Leninism as the sole master, or sole beneficiary, of the religious investments in the battles of the City. The theological-political realm, far from being reduced by the war, had increased its hold over Europeans. Far from marking a break with the laicized messianisms of the prewar period, it ended up as the domination of the Marxist-Leninist philosophy of history in numerous, generally degraded forms. The landscape had been simplified, but its nature was unchanged: the prospect of a revolutionary completion of social humanity was now traced back to a single origin, but it was more obsessive than ever. Liberal democracy offered no such simple and powerful interpretation of the war as the pairing of capitalism and Fascism on the one hand and of anti-Fascism and Communism on the other, pairings that formed part of the mental arsenal first of the Comintern and then of the Cominform. How could liberal democracy surmount a conceptualization of that dreadful century in view of the recent cataclysm whose dimensions gave the lie to the optimism of so many of its thinkers? Adam Smith's "invisible hand" had already left the twentieth century without recourse when faced with the economic catastrophe of 1929, and seemed even more futile the day after the bloody apocalypse of the war. Marxism and Leninism were eager to highlight the tragedy, since it portrayed a dying capitalism with Hitler in the main role. The cascade of abstractions that constitute Marxism-Leninism's sense of history had found avatars that lent it the appearance of truth.

Communist discourse on the war was thus remarkably flexible, acceptable to its hearers. Demonizing the enemy was not really compatible with Marxism and with the idea that people obey the laws of history. But this time it fit with the extraordinary suffering provoked by the war and with the universal indignation elicited by Hitler's crimes. The dead, the deported, the tortured, those who had simply been hungry and cold, in short, all of ruined Europe pointed to the one responsible for its calamities in a language appropriate to its moral state—a discourse on evil and the responsibility for evil, but henceforth concealed in a theology of history. On another level, that theology was attractive to intellectuals as confirmation of the Leninist prediction of the cruelties inseparable from the "supreme phase" of capitalism. It offered them an unlimited field for philosophical speculation about the dialectic of history and liberty, where liberty's only choice, a complex one, was to conform to history.

In this sense, the Second World War completed what the First had begun—the domination of the great political religions over European public opinion—but it annihilated one political religion while crowning and strengthening the other. Victorious, anti-Fascism did not disrupt the moral and political terrain on which it had developed. It deepened the crisis of the democratic idea while appearing to have resolved it. This was the great illusion of the age. It was an illusion from which we are only just emerging, thanks more to the force of circumstance than to intellectual virtue.

Communism at the End of World War II

THE END OF THE SECOND WORLD WAR INAU-
gurated the short period—a dozen or so years—during which Soviet Communism exercised its greatest fascination over the twentieth-century political imagination. Its mythology, as we have seen, had come a long way; though much weakened, it would survive Stalin's death, a distant echo of its glory days. It had never been as influential as it was during the dictator's last years. Because the "cult of personality" had been a defining characteristic of the regime, Khrushchev's denunciation of it in 1956 was particularly dramatic. That date was crucial for postwar Europe: not only did it break the continuity of the Soviet dictatorship; it destroyed the past of a universalistic utopia.

The influence of the USSR after 1945 was similar to that of anti-Fascist Communism between 1935 and 1939, of which it was an extension. The comparison evokes the same retrospective bitterness since both eras were marked by violent repression within the USSR. But the postwar years constituted exceptionally good vintages for the Communist idea because they were accompanied by the most powerful god in history—that of victory. Whereas the First World War had been the cradle of the Soviet Revolution, the Second planted its flags in the very heart of Europe; military success harmonized better with Soviet philosophy than did pacifism. In 1935, Communist anti-Fascism was on the defensive; in 1945, it was triumphant.

That triumph, moreover, was extremely visible to all Europeans and, indeed, to the whole world, for it turned the map of Europe upside down, transforming the global political equilibrium in its most universally perceptible aspect. True, that equilibrium had already been altered in the summer of 1945 by the atomic bombing of Hiroshima and Naga-saki, which introduced a critical disparity of power among the victors. But at the time, the disparity was not seen for what it was by the public at large, for the victors had already decided the major postwar issues. Even after the start of the cold war, the United States, during its brief nuclear monopoly, drew back in horror at the brutality of atomic black-mail. In reality, given the capitulation of the Axis powers after a terrible war in the name of democratic values, the public did not suspect that the victors' alliance was coming apart. What they did seem to see, to varying degrees, was a happy ending and a liberation, for which the Red Army had paid the heaviest price while pocketing the most spectacular gains.

By creating a void in the center of Europe, the collapse of Germany revealed the formidable growth of Russian power. That growth resulted in part from the military battle, which had brought Stalin's army beyond Berlin and all the way to Prague. But it was also the product of the moral and political physiognomy of Europe at the war's end. France, by its 1940 defeat, was no longer among the great powers. It rejoined them through the back door, having recovered the appearances of "rank" rather than any real influence, as General de Gaulle had been all too aware during the war years. Great Britain, for its part, had every reason to figure among the victorious nations, but the victory itself revealed Britain's decline, and Roosevelt did nothing to halt it. As the only great nation that had been at war with Nazi Germany since September 1939, the only power that fought against Hitler from mid-1940 to mid-1941, Britain emerged with honor but in a weakened condition, heroic but anemic, less and less sure of its mastery over the Commonwealth and lacking its traditional capacity as referee in Europe. At the moment when Central Europe was in formation, Western Europe no longer had the means or the moral resources to influence its shape.

Of the three great victors, the United States remained far and away the most powerful economically. On the beaches of Normandy it had organized and accomplished one of the most spectacular military opera-tions in history. After occupying Italy, the Americans liberated France, Belgium, and the Netherlands from Nazi oppression and conquered Germany up to the Elbe, where they joined the Russians. Though tied to Europe by its history, the United States was far from Europe and traditionally refused to involve its soldiers in European conflicts more than was absolutely necessary. Roosevelt, moreover, sincerely believed that the conflict had ended with the crushing of Hitler. Until the day he died in the spring of 1945, during the final days of the war, he main-tained relatively good relations with Stalin, probably due to his illusions about the possibility of a democratic evolution in the USSR after the victory. The division of zones of influence in Europe, which were taking shape between Tehran and Yalta despite his opposition, was less a calculation on Roosevelt's part than a concession to the inevitable, sweetened by his optimistic belief in a modicum of shared ideas among the "anti-Fascist" powers. So the United States itself, soon to become the most determined enemy of Soviet Communism, had once been an accomplice to its influence, even beyond what circumstances had demanded.

The Second World War confirmed what the First had announced— the decline of Europe. The crisis that had produced World War II was so profound that it was no longer possible to masquerade behind the old European "balance of powers." The spirit of the Treaty of Versailles disappeared when the Europe it had created failed. What replaced it was not, as Hitler had hoped, the opposite of Anglo-French domination, that is, German domination, but a precarious joint administration of Europe by two powers at once close and distant.

The power most distant geographically was the closest politically, which went perfectly with the spirit of the Second World War. American democracy needed no other reasons to fight Hitler than loyalty to its British heritage and faith in the liberal and democratic ideas of the Enlightenment. As soon as the United States had overcome its resistance to the very idea of war, those reasons became apparent; American public opinion needed no others. Americans understood that once Hitler was beaten and freedom was triumphant, their soldiers could return home to their peacetime jobs. Russia, on the other hand, in Europe for geographical reasons, had such different customs and political traditions that its European membership was questioned more than any other aspect of its recent history. Since 1917, however, the Communist idea had dispelled much of Russia's foreignness and linked the Russians' sense of mission to Europe. It allowed the new masters of the nation to appropriate the despotic national heritage while presenting their regime as the most advanced form of democracy.

Churchill and, to an even greater extent, Roosevelt contributed to this image of the USSR by forming a major war alliance with Stalin and lending him democratic credentials. Was such a warm celebration of shared ideas really necessary to win the war? Technically not—one could easily imagine a close military alliance and the same material aid from the United States to the USSR without a deluge of proclamations about the "common goals" of the three powerful allies, for those goals never existed. At the end of 1941, Stalin had asked that the borders of June 1941, including the eastern part of former Poland and the Baltic states, be confirmed, as though in switching allies it was natural to retain the gains acquired through the aid of the preceding ally. Was the idea of common objectives really indispensable to public opinion? Maybe not. After all, the French and the British in World War I knew well that their countries were not fighting for the same cause as czarist Russia. In World War II, which had begun with a spectacular demonstration of Soviet political cynicism, the public, even in the United States, might have accepted a clearer definition of the causes defended and the objectives pursued; that, at least, is the impression given by opinion polls carried out in the autumn of 1941, which indicated equal disparagement of Nazi Germany and Soviet Russia, at war since June.[1]

On the other hand, a clear distinction among the objectives of the war might not have survived the spectacle of the Soviet victories, the admiration they aroused, and the pressure they exercised on public opinion. The ideological nature of World War II was unprecedented in history (with the exception of civil wars), for two reasons: it was waged against Hitler, who sought to destroy both democracy and Communism, and it constituted an event both too gigantic and too universal not to have a simple meaning that could also be universal. That explains the force of the patriotic anti-Fascism brandished by Stalin beginning in June 1941. But Roosevelt too had to evoke democracy in order to convince the Americans to join the war, so it became unfashionable to criticize Stalinist Communism. Churchill, in June 1941, had welcomed the serendipitous new Soviet ally with open arms. Alone in the war since the capitulation of France, the British were understandably full of praise for the Kremlin. The American president, probably even more than the British prime minister, believed or wanted to believe that it was possible to share common goals with Stalin. A brilliant politician in domestic affairs, Roosevelt was enough of a patrician to have hoped to reach an understanding about world affairs with Stalin in meetings of the Club of Three; on the other hand, he was sufficiently democratic to have toyed with the hope of a Communist regime loosened up by victory and closer to the New Deal liberal Left's idea of it.[2]

Thus the USSR's democratic passport, which had been stamped by Western authorities so early and so often and under so many and such varied forms, had never been more valid, or more celebrated, than after 1941; it had never been more precious than in 1944 and 1945, when the future of the European landscape was at stake, for it allowed the USSR to disguise its territorial expansion in the idea of democracy. The Soviet ideological arsenal was wonderfully flexible: Stalin had gone to war by channeling the benefits of the Russian nationalist passion toward his own dictatorship. He made the peace by reinventing an internationalist vocation for his victorious troops: the Red Army was portrayed as an impartial missionary of anti-Fascism in the countries it occupied. The peace was merely a continuation of the war in another setting. The secret of postwar Stalinist strategy was to rely on the ideas, passions, and forces released by the war in order to make military victory the springboard for new achievements that would be not only territorial but political.

At the most tragic moment of its history, when plunged most deeply into the war, Europe needed the United States for the second time in the twentieth century. And the United States, one more time, fulfilled its duty as the soldier of democracy. But although Europe needed the United States more than ever at the hour of victory, it retained its old habit of ignoring the American form of government. Future historians will surely be surprised at the paucity of reflections and research on American democracy during the postwar period; it was as if the Europeans' ignorance about the American historical experience, which dated from the era when the United States was still a faraway nation, were becoming even more entrenched at a time when the power of the United States was recognized everywhere. Even World War I had not altered Old Europe's condescending attitude toward the Americans. Here they were again, in 1945, illustrious victors, bearing the American Constitution in the basket of liberty. Nevertheless, Communism rather than democracy was the order of the day.

There are several reasons for this persistent attitude. In general, since the late eighteenth century, Europeans had been used to thinking of their history in terms of discontinuity. They were inclined to interpret their successive regimes in terms of major events, of which the most famous was the French Revolution. American democracy was a social *condition*, whereas democracy in Europe was a subversive force constantly at work in the fabric of history. The Second World War, by transforming the lives of even the humblest citizens, powerfully illustrated the particular historicity of European societies. Even more than the First, it nourished a belief in the omnipotence of will and power. The surviving nations tended to measure their hopes by the yardstick of the suffering they had undergone. They were more eager for revolutionary programs than for constitutional recipes.

Nineteen forty-five reproduced the situation of 1918 in another context and on a far greater scale. Fascism (or, rather, Nazism) had been a European affair, not only because Germany had provided its cradle and its hearth, but because it had conquered Europe and constrained all of its citizens to define themselves in relation to its enterprise of domination. It thus constituted a more general experience, at least vis-à-vis

Europe, than Communism did, for Communism had never existed as a regime east of the Elbe and so was longer able, in the east, to maintain a facade untouched by the reality of its methods. Fascism had neither the same destiny nor the same luck. When defeat came, the blood spilled by Fascism in the name of pure force provoked a reaction against violence on the part of all of its victims, analogous to the violence to which they had been subjected: it was an exercise better suited to Communism than to democracy. As in 1918, the defeated Germany of 1945 pulled together all the vengeful passions elicited by that nation's arrogance, but Hitler's Germany had to pay much more than the traditional price of defeat: it was forced to expiate the idea of racial superiority that it had incarnated with unspeakable barbarity.

Horror of Nazism grew as the war went on; it exploded when the Nazi regime was beaten, not only because the regime had been brought down but because the defeat finally made obvious to everyone what had been going on. The "discovery" of the concentration camps by the public at large was inseparable both from the entry of the allied forces into Germany and from the recovery of a free press. I am not sufficiently optimistic about human nature to ignore the fact that the defeat played a more decisive role than did the "knowledge" factor. Information available during the war was not used or even systematically distributed by the Allies. Moreover, in 1945 the specifically Jewish dimension of the Nazi massacres was largely ignored or hushed up.

Nonetheless, I recall the horrified surprise that gripped Western public opinion at the beginning of the last spring of the war when the first reports of the camps appeared along with the first photographs of the masses of skeletal survivors standing next to huge pits filled with corpses. It was in the latter half of April 1945 that Nazism became the criminal enterprise that the Nuremberg judges, a year later, condemned as such by condemning its commanders. Until 1939, Fascism had been a regime subject to passionate debate with respect to its violence as well its merits. In the West it had had its unconditional adversaries and admirers, but also many witnesses and observers uncertain of their own judgment, who weighed its risks against its advantages and compared its shortcomings with its successes. During the war, military might enabled the Fascists to cover the traces of their crimes, but with defeat they were banished from humanity, made the object of unprecedented public reprobation, and denied the excuse of military necessity. The outcome of the battle was merely an excuse for the Fascists' barbarity.

The nations of Europe naturally tended to re-imagine their past on the basis of what the war had revealed: anti-Fascism became their compulsory patrimony. Even more than the desire to construct or reconstruct democratic states in Europe, it was this negation that unified east and west, for it alone gave the war its most general sense although it prolonged the particular psychological ordeals of the war. Anti-Fascism was both the most abstract and the most concrete expression of the horror just experienced and the total victory that had just put an end to it. The atrocities committed by the Nazis, though they had everywhere assumed the same form, were not at all of the same magnitude to the west and east of Europe. But the war, the German military occupation, national humiliation, the deportation of patriots, and the persecution of the Jews had formed a framework of shared misery, of which Nazism was the common denominator and the sole culprit. The price of peace was no longer, as it had been in Versailles, the abasement of Germany but the extirpation of Nazism. The Germans of 1918, condemned as a nation, had reacted as a nation. The Germans of 1945, condemned as Nazis, were the object of a much more radical and durable opprobrium since they were forced to participate in it. Their only future was anti-Nazism. The ideological form that Hitler had lent their nationalist passions had eradicated their substance. For them, ideological expiation was the only way out of the war.

But it was precisely in this political space, entirely reoccupied by anti-Fascism, that Communism managed to expand its means of influence and fascination; the Red Army's victory and its occupation of a large part of Europe would not have fulfilled that task if they had not entailed a reemergence of that Communist idea which had seduced the West prior to the turnaround of the summer of 1939. A semantic reversal was enough to make this clear: in 1939, the Soviet Union had "invaded" Poland; in 1944, it had "liberated" it. Although, in both cases, it was in fact "occupying"—even more completely in the second than in the first—this terminology demonstrates the chasm of opinion separating the two episodes.

Both the USSR and Communism itself felt at home with anti-Fascism, an old acquaintance that had already been extremely helpful in the prewar years. Its greatest advantage was that it existed only negatively and thus concealed under the pretext of urgency the question of political democracy. In 1945, that urgency no longer existed, for Fascism had been laid to waste. But the urgency survived the circumstances that had made it so crucial; it was carried forward by victory, which exacerbated the passions of the war even as it had reduced their necessity. The Soviet Union had ceased to be anti-Fascist at the most critical moment, in August 1939. But when the victory came, it obscured that desertion by redoubled propaganda and proclamations, to the point that the Fascist danger seemed never more imminent than after it had passed.

Anti-Fascism was all the more valuable an emblem because it gave the revolutionary idea its greatest influence. Like the First World War, the Second put revolution back onto the agenda. The First World War, however, had been conducted in the name of the nation. When it was over, its combatants exhausted, the revolutionaries had to counter nationalistic passions in order to animate their project. They failed in that attempt, even in vanquished Germany. The Second World War, in contrast, had enveloped the war between nations in a war of ideas. Its explicit objective had been to liquidate Fascism; from there, for those who had emerged from it, it was a short path to revolution.

If World War II was a product of Fascism, Fascism itself was a product of capitalism and the bourgeoisie. The socialist movement's long-held conviction that capitalism goes hand in hand with war thus found additional support in this reasoning. From the mid-1930s on, the Comintern had defined Fascism as the most reactionary form of monopolistic capitalism, dominated by finance capital. In this way, Fascism could be classified as the extreme opposite of Soviet-style "socialism" and as its most determined enemy. In 1945, that simplistic interpretation seemed to be confirmed by events. Although it in no way explained those events, it appeared, in its very abstraction, to restitute the disposition of military and political forces at the hour of victory. And it had the advantage of turning that victory into a step toward revolution, that is, toward the abolition of capitalism. Henceforth, for the European Left, the history of the war drew its meaning entirely from Horkheimer's famous phrase: "Those who have nothing to say about capitalism should also be silent about Fascism." The Marxists of the Frankfurt school kept harking back to this false idea, which nonetheless influenced much of the postwar political thought in Europe.[3]

So we must attempt to understand the extraordinary persuasiveness of this idea, going beyond those who, in this case, were going along with general opinion rather than shaping it. Its strength came primarily from the encounter between the trauma of recent historical experience and revolutionary political culture. That war was inseparable from bourgeois domination, which ought to be held responsible, was an old conviction of the socialist Left. But this war had been begun by a dictator who had come to power with the complicity of the German bourgeois parties: this was all it took, in the context of 1945, to make the horror elicited by Nazism rebound not only on the German but also on the European "bourgeoisie." For although German politicians were accused of having created Hitler, the British and the French had signed the Munich agreement. Thus arose "Marxist" rationalization of World

War II, infinitely more powerful than the 1917–18 rationalization of World War I because it derived its force from demonizing the bourgeois. Its simplistic character detracted nothing from it power to convince. It mattered little that Hitler had actually destroyed most of the traditional order of German society and that he had been the fiercest adversary of the West and an erstwhile ally of Stalin, as long as his defeat could still serve to dishonor the thing he had fought in vain—bourgeois democracy.

Paradoxically, the victorious anti-Fascism of the postwar period fed on the images and the passions it held in common with the detested and defeated enemy. On the one hand, it was entirely democratic, defined by the fight against Hitler, his soldiers, and his ideas. On the other, it was antibourgeois and anticapitalist, oriented toward a new type of democracy. That qualification did not necessarily make the Soviet regime into a model, but it did tend to make it preferable to those of the west. In any case, it obscured anything that had made it comparable to Nazism before the war. The Communist movement, moreover, played brilliantly in both keys. Just as the USSR was allied with Britain and the United States, so the Comintern, since 1941, had everywhere revived policies of anti-Fascist unity within "National Fronts." But the Soviets never forgot to emphasize that they were the sole bearers of radical, that is, anticapitalist, anti-Fascism. This negative euphemism sufficed to give the Soviet Union the edge among the allied powers against Hitler.

Hence, the war allowed the socialist homeland alone to retain the greatest role of the democratic repertory: criticism of democracy in the name of democracy. The British and the Americans, gallant warriors against Nazism, were still entrenched in capitalism. Communist anti-Fascism benefited both from its alliance with the United States and from its claim of opening the way to a democracy freed from the power of money. This was sufficient to make people forget, to Stalin's advantage, that the two most constant European anti-Fascists had been neither Communists nor even members of the left wing, but conservatives: Churchill and de Gaulle.[4]

At the end of World War I, the Soviet Union had begun its career in European politics as an icon of the revolutionary idea erected against the imperialist war. But at that time it was backed only by opinion and was powerless to inspire even the humiliated nations in any lasting way. In 1945, as a great victorious state, it added material force to the messianism of the new humanity. World War I had created it. World War II established the USSR on the front line of history by the twofold means of its military strength and the return of the revolutionary idea. Stalin's

Soviet Union, if viewed as the advanced Russification of the Leninist-Soviet model (which had itself already been grafted onto czarist autocracy), had never been more "Russian" than in 1945 or, on a European scale, more "Slavic." This was also the period when it exerted its most vast universalistic influence. Such was Stalin's gift to history, seized by a hair's breadth.

The good fortune that smiled upon Stalin, moreover, extended beyond Europe. To appraise it adequately, we must consider its world consequences, for the Soviet idea, even as it put democratic passions at the service of tyranny, was also capable of mobilizing a European tradition against Europe. By the middle of the twentieth century, the universalization of the world had long progressed through the European conquest of markets and territories. The empires constructed by the West had forcibly spread modern democratic ideas that gave the lie to their policy of colonial domination, which is why the colonized peoples had retained the revolutionary message rather than the liberal promise. The war offered them new possibilities for emancipation, since it weakened—at least relatively—Europe and the West, and because it reaffirmed the universal values of democracy against Hitler. Roosevelt and Stalin, incidentally, made no bones about their anticolonialism. But Roosevelt was president of the greatest capitalist power in the world, designated to be the successor to Western Europe. Stalin, for his part, brandished the standard of Marxism-Leninism against Capital.

That doctrine had everything to please—the respectability of a great philosophical lineage, the democratic stamp of approval, the dignity of "science." Through the success of October 1917, it had proved itself. The USSR exemplified a historical short circuit that promised the non-European world a rapid catching up. Marxism-Leninism was capable of attracting the most sophisticated minds, drawn mainly to Marxism, as well as more primitive ones, more interested in Leninism. To both, it furnished a body of Western ideas capable of unifying antibourgeois emotions in Europe and beyond. German Nazism had enjoyed a good reputation among the various nationalisms of the colonized world, before and after the war, to the extent that it opposed the French and the British empires. But, by the end of the war, the Soviet Union no longer had any anti-Western competitors in Europe. What could be a better conduit for resentment of the elite than the poor, colonized, or dependent countries of the world? It offered both a philosophy and a strategy for emancipation before getting down to the means. In our century, no European doctrinal corpus would be so avidly adopted outside of Europe than Marxism-Leninism—that post-Hegelian philosophy harnessed as a totalitarian ideology.

This ideological bric-a-brac owed its spectacular success to the fact that it offered a universalistic justification of absolute power. Fortified by the Soviet precedent, the tyrant of the second half of the twentieth century drew his legitimacy from an emancipatory ambition: he led his country to socialism via a new version of modern democracy freed of its capitalist liabilities. The formula was broad enough to encompass societies as various as those of Vietnam, Yemen, Poland, or Czechoslovakia. But in all cases it implied the concentration of all power in one party, even if other parties existed nominally, and in a small oligarchy that led that party in the name of historical laws, beginning with the General Secretary. The lie upon which the Soviet regime was constructed tended to universalize itself under the banner of revolution. This phenomenon could take the form of a simple territorial expansion of the USSR, as in the Baltics, or of the creation of sister republics under the auspices of local Communist parties enslaved to Moscow, as in Eastern Europe. But the ideological-political system had a dynamic that went beyond the organization of military conquests or neighborly cooperation. To judge by the attraction it exercised in both the wealthier and the poorer nations of Europe, it was also exportable to a wider, almost unlimited circle; the admiration it elicited from people overseas confirmed its universal character in Europe.

Europe remained and would long remain the part of the world in which the fate of Communism would be played out. A child of European culture, the Marxist-Leninist regime during its heyday had no trouble spreading to countries in Africa and Asia or even, long after the war, to huge countries such as China. Its success testified both to the universality of its language and to the efficacy of its formula for absolute power and also, no doubt, to its ability to cumulate these two advantages and to drape the necessity of a single party in the mantle of historical necessity. It was, however, in Europe that the sort of regime established by Lenin and continued by Stalin in the name of Marxism-Leninism would be judged by the public. Europe was where, first and foremost, Communism had been born and had spread, and where, without ever having been in power, it obtained the consent of so many enlightened voters and minds. The universal attraction of the postwar Communist revolutions outside of Europe came from the Soviet example, which was either imitated or "rejuvenated." But even those secondary forms, Maoism and Castroism, did not long survive as substitution myths for the model in crisis.

Indeed, it was during the immediate postwar period, in Europe—cradle of the Soviet regime and the theater of its exploits—that the future of Communism was decided. The moment of its greatest influence was also the moment of truth: as a form of government, as a power, as an idea.

The domestic history of the USSR in the post–World War II period is peripheral to this essay. We need only note that the war had not altered the nature of the Soviet Union; to the contrary, the victory had aggravated it by enhancing Stalin's prestige and giving him an aura of infallibility. The General Secretary had already accumulated the dual benediction—both international and Russian—inseparable from "socialism in one country." The military leader thus accumulated the glory of the victorious soldier as well. Resigned to live under a dictatorship, the combatants of the terrible war found new ways of justifying their collective servitude. We often assume that they put up a formidable resistance and that their spirit of sacrifice, heroism, and patriotism was comparable to that of their 1812 ancestors, who had also triumphed over a foreign invader. That comparison, in its own way, indicates that the Red Army had defended their homeland, not their regime. Nonetheless, if that regime emerged triumphant from battle, it was not only because it was able to tap into Russian patriotism in the face of Nazi cruelty but also because it had waged war and organized its victory in its own way. The very servitude imposed upon the peoples of the USSR superimposed its effects upon the constraints of military obedience; the war, though patriotic and "anti-Fascist," had also constituted a pursuit of, and then an exacerbation of, the totalitarian experience.

The return to peace in Stalin's USSR was merely a continuation of the war by other means. A striking example was the way in which the Soviet citizens who were abroad when the guns fell silent were "repatriated." These were not just a handful of people but five million, torn from their wretched prewar condition by the even greater misfortune of war. Some were among the huge number taken prisoner by the Wehrmacht, notably between 1941 and 1942; these people suffered wretched conditions in captivity. Others had been requisitioned by the enemy to work in Germany. Still others, either forcibly or voluntarily, collaborated with the Germans or even served in "Vlasov's Army."[5] Finally, there were some who took advantage of the situation in the USSR to flee to the West.

The Yalta agreements made provisions for the repatriation of all Soviet citizens who wished it, along with the forced return of all those who had worn German uniform or had collaborated with the enemy. For Stalin, however, the question went beyond the punishment of traitors. The exit ban from the USSR had been part of the dogma of Soviet domestic policy, and authorization to leave the country had become a huge privilege. Total ignorance as to what was happening abroad was essential to "socialism in one country." Now, at the hour of victory, the bloody upheaval of the war revealed millions of Soviet citizens outside of the triumphant Union; the situation was all the more intolerable because many among them could revitalize the legions of Russian immigrants in the west, thwarting the spectacular advantages that the anti-Fascist war had lent to Soviet propaganda. For Stalin, all Soviet citizens abroad, a fortiori in the west, were suspect—most often regarded as "Fascist"—even if they had been brought in captivity to Germany by the fortunes of war. Soviet prisoners of war had been subjected to terrible cruelty in German camps only to find themselves thrown into Soviet camps when they returned to their native land. Stalin made little distinction between captivity by the enemy, deportation, voluntary emigration, and treason. He intended to recuperate all of them in order to liquidate them, right down to the "White" émigrés of the post–World War I period who by definition had never been "Soviet" subjects.

Tragically, the British, followed by the Americans and the French, exceeded Stalin's demands and went well beyond the Yalta agreements. Of the hordes of men and women whom they turned over, often by force, to the NKVD agents who had come to supervise their return, many had not served Germany. And even those who had would be considered differently by the Americans within five years, not because they had changed their opinion on Nazism, as accused by Soviet propaganda, but because they had discovered that the lost soldiers of Vlasov's armies may have had attenuating circumstances in their dual status as subjects of Stalin and prisoners of Hitler. Solzhenitsyn, with his penchant for living on the edge, describes this situation subtly and powerfully in *The Gulag Archipelago*.

Nicolas Tolstoi has described the heartbreaking scenes, especially in England, caused by forced repatriation.[6] And Heller and Nekrich, after depicting the joyous return of the demobilized Soviet soldiers, point out that

> there were other troop trains heading east as well, but these had sealed doors and barred windows. They too carried Soviet soldiers, but no music or singing came from these tightly locked cattlecars. No one met them at railroad stations. These trains kept traveling day and night. There were also troop ships that pulled up to deserted wharfs to unload former Soviet prisoners of war returning from the Nazi camps. They touched foot on their native soil under heavy guard. Also being returned were those who willingly or otherwise aided the Germans or had worked for them. Among them were some who had never lived in

postrevolutionary Russia but whom the British, American, or French allies had considered Soviet citizens. They were turned over to the Soviet government, to deal with as it saw fit, without trial of any kind.[7]

These two million prisoners, almost all of whom were accused of treason and summarily judged in large groups, would end up in the Gulag camps if not condemned to death and executed.

This collective liquidation was thus nothing like the purges that had occurred in the west for collaboration with the enemy. It indiscriminately included citizens guilty of having served in Vlasov's and other armies, prisoners of war, workers forcefully recruited, accidental or deliberate runaways, and emigrants. There was no justice for anyone, guilty or innocent. This episode shows how the defeat of Nazism had left the other victorious totalitarian state not only intact but omnipotent, in the twofold sense that it had lost nothing of the arbitrary violence it directed against its own citizens and that it managed to make the democratic states accomplices to this violence. That Britain, the United States, and France had openly given up the traditional right to exile in favor of Stalin illustrates better than any other event the formidable power of public opinion that the Soviet Union had garnered since 1941 and crowned with armed victory. The Second World War, unlike the First, did not produce totalitarian states, for they were present at its origin. But by destroying one totalitarian state, it reinforced the other. The elimination of Hitler and Mussolini brought Stalin to his apogee. Stalin undoubtedly had never needed the blessing of western governments to populate his Gulag, but his dictatorship received an extraordinary boost of legitimacy when those governments openly contributed to this sinister task. For the West did not content itself with giving substance to the regime's mythology; it directly abetted its crimes.

It was not, however, the democratic idea itself that gave the USSR its extraordinary sway over world opinion, but the meaning lent by that idea to the victory over Hitler's Germany. The fact that the USSR had paid the highest price for that victory, in alliance with England and the United States, those cradles of freedom, made people forget about the Moscow trials and the toasts exchanged by Molotov and Hitler in 1940. Sophists and simpletons could even drape those shady episodes retrospectively in the gleaming raiments of the final victory: Tukhachevsky's execution and the partition of Poland could now be seen merely as deplorable but necessary means for defeating Hitler. But this very fabrication betrayed the source of the USSR's influence: not love of democracy and liberty, but the judgment of "history."

In this respect, the term "anti-Fascist" remained useful, as during the 1930s, for masking the nature of Soviet Communism. It defined an enemy but not a regime. In 1945, the political simplifications inseparable from the war seemed to have lent it an unequivocal meaning, though they never rid it of ambiguity. But they left a trail of blood. It remained true that the defeat of Nazism was primarily the defeat of Germany. The Germany that had been defeated had been Hitler's Germany, but the country had been invasive in the twentieth century even before Hitler came to power. People either felt favorably toward Germany, like the Hungarians, or resolutely hostile, like the Poles. Nazi ideology did little to alter these earlier dispositions: Hitler's domination of Europe in 1941–42 was perceived as German domination. By the same token, the defeat of Nazism in 1945 was tantamount to a defeat of Germany. The victory of the Soviet Union, anti-Fascist as it may have been, channeled national anti-German passions in Western and Eastern Europe alike.

The Soviets seemed fully aware of this. In all the Allies' discussions about the postwar period after 1943, the Soviets were the most determined to destroy the sources of German power and to pursue the cause pleaded by Clemenceau in 1918–19. They sought more important territorial guarantees than did the French at the time. Not only did they occupy all of Eastern Germany—Pomerania, Prussia, Brandenburg, Saxony, Silesia, and Thuringia–but they were determined to impose a major eastward transfer of the Polish border so as to retain their acquisitions of 1919 and to compensate the Poles with German territories. Their demands for material reparations were so exorbitant that even Churchill thought them unreasonable.[8] In the decisions made at Yalta and Potsdam concerning the guardianship and the division of defeated Germany, the Soviet Union played a key role, to which it was entitled by virtue of its millions of dead and its ravaged territory. What is more, it capitalized on the advantage it had over the British and the Americans of offering survivors a systematic interpretation of the German misdeeds of the twentieth century. Hitler's defeat had convinced public opinion to condemn what had preceded him, casting it ever after as the prehistory of Nazism.

German militarism, responsible for World War I, pillaged Europe twenty-five years later in Nazi uniform. This proposition, which summarizes postwar opinion, was not particularly Marxist; its second element, however, contains a definition of Nazism that could have been Marxist and thus gave a boost to Soviet anti-Nazism. If Hitler was merely the most violent incarnation of German militarism, it was because he "represented" the same economic and social forces that had dominated German history since Bismarck—the alliance of the Prussian junkers and the great industries of the Rhineland.[9] To destroy this hotbed forever required the definitive crushing of both the national and the social forces. Anti-Fascism thus led naturally to the exportation of the revolution, all but engraved in the Red Army's mission.

In one sense, Soviet Communism remained true to the old socialist condemnation of war, that fatal consequence of capitalism, that massacre sought by the sellers of cannons. But this time, in contrast to 1914–18, it also threw its strengths into the balance and came out among the winners. For this reason, from 1941 on, responsibility for World War II was no longer divided between the imperialist powers and came to rest entirely on the shoulders of Hitler's Germany, the offspring of German-style capitalism. This new version of opposing war by means of war was immensely superior to the old one. It made sense of the sacrifices to which the soldiers had consented, whereas revolutionary defeatism forced them to repress even their memories of heroism. It gave pride of place to patriotic sentiments, whereas yesterday's internationalist abstraction tended to discredit them. One of the great secrets of Soviet ideology in 1945 Europe was to associate national passions with revolutionary universalism by means of victory over German militarism. Since Germany, under Bismarck, had become the principal power in Europe, it had accumulated the resentments and hatreds of which Stalin turned out to be the avenger.

This secret power could only be used in doses, which varied according to country and circumstances. Very influential over the Russians, it had little immediate effect on the defeated Germans, who had been subjected to a difficult occupation and an enormous levying of tools and raw materials. The same, though to a lesser extent, was true of Hungary, which had been allied with Germany. But the Soviet Union, which comprised the largest part of Central and East-Central Europe, though feared as a great power, was also viewed as a Slavic big brother when the time came to settle accounts with the German oppressor. The vengeful attitude of the Russians was therefore present among the Bulgarians, the Czechs, and the Serbs. Bulgaria, even though a former German satellite, remained basically pro-Russian. The Czechs recalled how the West had abandoned them at Munich; when victory came, their Communist Party drew a great deal of its strength from the fact that it almost automatically combined patriotism with an attachment to the USSR. As to the peoples of Yugoslavia, who had tragically confronted one another during the war, Tito, with Churchill's support, managed to unite them into a partisan army that would liberate Belgrade side by side with the army of the Soviet general Zhdanov. Could there be a more perfect illustration of the almost providential osmosis that took place during this time between the Soviet regime and the liberation of subjugated nations?

The most interesting case in this respect was that of Poland, since it was the most complex. It was there that the war had begun, in September 1939, and the Poles immediately turned it into tragic fodder for their two patriotic passions—hatred of Germany and hatred of Russia, the two nations that had long been responsible for the carving up of their country. The partition of 1939 had revived bad memories as well as the feeling that Poland was exceptional: it was certainly the only nation in the world to have been subjected to the regimes of both the Gestapo and the NKVD, with each of the persecutors working on his own part of the conquest according to prior agreement. The extreme ardor of the Polish patriots was fueled by the sense that their nation was fragile, and by the melancholic belief that their nation was a chosen one, if only for suffering. Other European nations could "forget" 1939–40 in favor of 1944–45, but not the Poles, for that was when they had once again, and for a long time, lost their homeland. The history of their tragedy, with its Nazi massacres and Soviet deportations, obsessed them all the more because of the errors committed by their own government before the war. In an unforgettable way, it justified their hatred of their two neighboring nations. Their abhorrence of Germany goes without saying. And their fear of Russia survived Hitler's invasion of Russia.

The Poles, long before the Germans informed the whole world of the Katyn massacres, knew that tens of thousands of their people—most of them army officers—had disappeared somewhere in darkest Russia between the fall of 1939 and the spring of 1940. Traditionally hostile to the Russian Empire, they found Soviet Communism an additional reason to fear it. Even the small Polish Communist Party—the bureaucratized child of Rosa Luxemburg that remained a rare locus of Judeo-Polish symbiosis—came into conflict with Moscow, in Moscow: it had been dissolved in 1938 by the Comintern after the majority of the members of its Central Committee in exile were shot.[10] In any case, they would have been excluded the following year from the national consensus concerning the Polish government in exile.

The invasion of the Germans and then the Russians had not broken the Polish state's continuity. Poland had a legal government, formed in France on 30 September 1939 from the most important parties of what had formerly constituted the opposition when the so-called "Colonels' regime" collapsed.[11] The government had an army, which fought first alongside of France and then of England. From London, it directed the resistance in Poland, which began early, was powerful in terms of numbers, and possessed extraordinary courage and efficacy. By driving the Germans forward as it advanced in 1944, the Red Army had created a national and even nationalistic Poland at its doorstep. The "desertion" of the Warsaw insurrection was its first warning shot.

The Polish question would become the Allies' meatiest bone to pick after the war. Remarkably symbolic, it illustrated the contradictory history of the war as well as the impossibility of lasting peace in Europe. The new eastern frontier of Poland was the one drawn by the German-Soviet pact of August 1939 and confirmed by the Russian invasion of mid-September. How could the Polish government in exile, born in opposition to the dismemberment of the homeland, consent to it? The USSR, for its part, could not conceive that, for the price of the soldiers sacrificed since 1941, it would have to let go of its 1939 territorial gains and accept the renaissance of a nationalistic Poland. For all that, the 1939 frontier was almost a replica of the Curzon line, which lent it some historical legitimacy. In any case, as we have seen, the military situation decided the matter. But that did not dispel the sense of failure to which the Mikolajczyk government was subject, for the failure was political as well as military. Stalin relied on the strength of his army, but not exclusively. Democratic world opinion, strongly antipathetic toward Stalin in 1939–40, had shifted to his camp as he changed sides. The opposite occurred among the Poles of London: heroic in 1939, the government-in-exile was but a chimera in 1944. It had concentrated two wars in one, and was still engaged in the first as the second was ending. It remained both anti-Nazi and anti-Soviet when the Soviet Union's recovery of influence had just disarmed anti-Sovietism with anti-Nazism.

Polish-Russian history, therefore, cannot be reduced to a mere capitulation of the Polish government of London when confronted with the Lublin Committee, which had arrived in Russian trucks. Even Polish anti-Sovietism, which was probably the most violent in Europe along with that of the Baltic states, lost some of its vigor with the spirit of the times, so great was the hatred elicited by Nazi Germany. Poland had been periodically chopped away. It had lost three million people, not including the Jews; the nation had gone through a horrible ordeal that could only be compared to that of the Ukraine or Russia. While it saw itself as an outpost of the west in the east, Hitler had seen it as the east of the Slavs; it was ravaged and assassinated as much as for what it thought itself to be as for what it was. Only the Jews ranked below the Poles on the Nazi scale of disdain and hatred. But if the spectacle of their extermination was not enough to extinguish Polish anti-Semitism,

at least the shared misery of the Slavic nations and the victorious deployment of the Red Army would bring people, even in Poland, to put
the hatred of Germany before the fear of Russia. When the Soviet
troops pushed back the Wehrmacht on Polish territory in the latter half
of 1944, they were probably received with mixed sentiments and suspicions, later reinforced by their inaction in face of the national insurrection at Warsaw.[12] The Russians did, however, liberate Poland from Nazi
oppression and put an end to one of the worst periods in the history of
the Polish nation.

The war, as it finally turned out, also made it a taboo to treat the two
traditional enemies of Polish independence on the same footing. This
taboo, self-evident in 1944, would continue to be valid in the following
years, even though Soviet behavior confirmed the pessimistic forecasts
of the British government or of the nationalist members of the domestic
army. It was not enough that the USSR had managed to obtain recognition of the Curzon line from the Allies as well as the victory of the
Lublin Committee over the Poles in London. Since October 1944, the
very day after the defeat of the Warsaw insurgents, the Russians began
to take over a Poland simultaneously liberated and conquered. While
Stalin, with a spectacular reception in Moscow, was showing his support for the Polish Committee for National Liberation, this committee,
aided by the NKVD, immediately began fighting the detachments of
the clandestine army, which had remained loyal to London. The policy
of the fait accompli had been set in motion and would go all the way.[13]
Churchill and Roosevelt had thought Stalin would be satisfied by the
Curzon line, bordering a friendly but free Poland. They were wrong.
"Uncle Joe" could only envision a friendly Poland as a state controlled
from Moscow by means of local puppets.

Yet this new confiscation of Polish independence was favored by
prior events that had worked in the same direction as the disposition of
power. From the outside, international public opinion, struck by the
character and extent of Nazi crimes, tended to assume that Soviet policy
in Poland was meant to guard against an eventual renaissance of German
militarism. In Poland itself this argument had particular relevance to
the nation's new frontiers. In exchange for the land ceded to the USSR
in the east, Poland obtained compensations to the west,[14] including
100,000 square kilometers of German territory. The westward shift of
Polish territory, which resulted in the forced expulsion of millions of
Germans, implied a future German-Polish discord that made the USSR
the guarantor of the new frontiers and thus the indispensable ally of
Poland. This situation allowed the local Communists, who were very
much a minority in their own country because of their dependence

on Moscow, to go along with the anti-German tendency of Polish nationalism.

By progressively annihilating the numerous pockets of military resistance to their regime—the guerrilla war that would continue until 1947—the Polish Communists could continue to claim participation in the anti-Nazi resistance, in which they had in fact played only a marginal role and whose last battalions they had liquidated. By pursuing clandestine combat in the vast Polish forests after the defeat of Germany, the remains of the secret army could be denounced as obeying only partisan motives or, worse still, directives from London or Washington. Thus, the large portion of public opinion that to varying degrees was sympathetic to the struggle against the Soviet takeover of the country was subjected to blackmail: from the beginning of 1946, Mikolajczyk, a Pole in London in a government dominated by Lublin adherents, was accused by Gomulka of being an agent of the West because he opposed the unification of his party with the Socialist-Communist block.[15] Seen thus, the Communists' appropriation of the national theme was obviously instrumental and a lie. But it also held a grain of truth, if we shift our focus from the struggle for power to the period in general.

Germany had been defeated, but our experience of history rarely coincides with the rhythm of events. Defeated, occupied, dishonored, Germany was detested even more than when it had been dominant. The memories of the atrocities committed by its army were still fresh, and the fear evoked by its strength had disappeared. The German capitulation had lent its entire resonance to the theme of the German menace, offering a formidable reinforcement to the European image of the Soviet Union as best illustrated by the Polish case: precisely when the former "domestic army" had switched adversaries, the Polish Communists turned the meaning of its prior combat against the fighters themselves. The domestic army had fought against Nazi oppression; the Communists were continuing the same battle against the German menace.[16]

In pursuit of this cause, they extended the nation's frontiers by expelling millions of Germans from their homes, as far as the lands of Pomerania and East Prussia, which had been the cradle of the Junkers and German militarism. Potential revenge seemed written on this vast expropriation, which gave the new Poland the role of vanguard of world peace. This was one more reason to rid the country of its incompetent traditional shepherds, those petty nobles, those "peasant" leaders and Catholics from another age, who had been incapable of protecting the country against Germany and who now refused reconstruction under the wing of Russia. In spite of Katyn—at the time, many people still had doubts about the Soviets' responsibility for the massacre—the 1945 Communist argument in Poland was by no means devoid of substance, and we would be wrong retrospectively to underestimate its force; that would be tantamount to misjudging the influence of the USSR at the time, even among those European nations least favorable toward the Soviets. Moreover, in view of what was to follow, the Soviet domination of Poland, though much more durable, would never assume the violence of Nazi oppression. Whereas Nazism had preferred to torment non-German European peoples, the most pitiful victims of Bolshevism would turn out to be the Russian themselves, who had given birth to it.

At the hour of victory, beyond its own frontiers, the Communist movement showed an extraordinary capacity to adjust to the USSR's new hegemony over Central and Eastern Europe. On the one hand, its own ideological heritage provided a universalistic interpretation of that hegemony: blaming Nazism on German big capital and its henchmen was enough to turn each of the regimes established under its aegis—in the countries "liberated" by the Red Army—into victories for democracy and peace. The doctrine laid out by the Comintern in the 1930s reached perfection in 1945: the victory of the forces of progress, and tomorrow the victory of socialism, occurred through an extension of the Soviet world.

On the other hand, the military victory allowed the USSR to turn to its own advantage the idea of nationalism, an idea shunted around by the Nazi occupation even among the nations once allied with Germany, such as Romania or Hungary. When Stalin had successfully, and on a grand scale, implemented the policy sketched out prior to the Spanish Civil War, of making satellites out of foreign states, he also found a sufficient amount of anti-German sentiment among survivors to maintain the illusion of a true national restoration. In many European countries, the posthumous legacy of Nazism was the transformation of Communist parties into the champions of recovered liberty.

By latching on to the national idea in this way, the Communist movement garnered to its advantage the two great political passions of twentieth-century democracy: the nation and revolution. After World War I, Fascism mobilized the nationalist passion and turned it against the revolutionary passion incarnated by Bolshevism. At the end of World War II, the defeat of Nazi Germany unleashed the Europeans' nationalistic feelings to the advantage of the Communists, either for assuring their hegemony in armed resistance to the occupying force, as in Yugoslavia, or for having been the forced representatives of the new contract between nation and history, as in Poland. Between these two extremes was a whole series of intermediary cases, but everywhere, to varying degrees, the shock of the war, the momentum of victory, the sense of inevitability, the discrediting of former elites, and the hatred of Germany finally ensured that Soviet Russia would become a nationalistic hope in the very countries it was subjugating.[17] The arrangements decided at Versailles had ingloriously collapsed and, with them, the West's credit. The German domination that followed combined arrogance with violence. Now it was the Russians' turn, draped in the revolutionary idea; their brutal rule would leave people nostalgic for the Austro-Hungarian Empire.

One important group was missing from this resurrection—ephemeral though it may have been—of those subjugated or tormented by Nazi Germany: the Jewish people, who for long had been numerous in these lands, were spread out in an uncertain mosaic of nationalities, and, since 1941, had been the object of the most massive extermination attempt in history, though their tragedy had yet to receive a name at the time. It would be unfair to put all the blame on the Soviet Union, for Churchill and Roosevelt, who since 1943 had had some idea of the extent of the tragedy, said and did nothing about it.[18] And, after the advent of Nazism, Stalin had never shown the least compassion for the Jews and was even, at heart, hostile toward them. Before the war he had deliberately closed Soviet borders to German victims of anti-Semitic persecution.

After the war, Stalin was always suspicious of the hundreds of thousands of Polish Jews who had fled to the USSR from Hitler, first in the fall of 1939, and then in the months following the attack of June 1941. He feared their foreignness both as Jews and as Poles. Tens of thousands of these unfortunate people would end their exodus in the Gulag.[19] A little later, in 1944–45, the Red Army was freeing whole classes and whole nations, but there was no word in its vocabulary for the Jewish tragedy. When the Russians entered Auschwitz in January 1945, no one in the West heard about what they had discovered there. It was not until May, and at the request of the British, that an official report was issued, which, when broadcast, did not include the word "Jew."[20]

For Stalin, the Eastern European nations that had been liberated or occupied by his army were one more reason to deny the Jews their share of the victory over Nazism. Those nations often remained anti-Semitic—a sentiment that had survived the organized massacre of the Jews.[21] It was inseparable from their nationalism. The proportion of Jewish survivors among the "nomenklatura" of the small local Communist parties was already sufficient to heighten those nationalistic sentiments: a kind of overcompensation would compel those leaders to obscure their origins both as the most patriotic of patriots in their respective countries and as the most loyal of those loyal to Moscow in the international Communist movement. Thus Jewish martyrdom would come to be lost in the martyrdom of their nations, and the weight of its misery would be transferred to the account of the Red Army. After Auschwitz and Treblinka, Jewish survivors continued to pay the heavy price of statelessness.

Nations to the west had been liberated from the Germans by the United States Army. These nations were familiar with the Red Army by radio only, and from tales of its exploits from Stalingrad to Berlin. They were unaware not only of the excesses committed by its soldiers, even in friendly nations, but also of the political climate of intimidation that arrived in Red Army trucks. They were all the more inclined to celebrate it because the Soviet Union's success revived many of their own hopes and memories.

The United States, emancipated child of Europe, returned to Europe for the second time in the century to save the West. But America had long ceased to figure among European memories. The Americans had invented a society so original and powerful that it constituted a self-sufficient space of modern democracy, by definition and intention different than anything that had ever existed in Europe and which had, moreover, deliberately kept itself apart as long as possible from European politics. The Americans had always remained loyal to the decision that had defined them as a nation. They left the shores of Europe to found a new social contract across the ocean. That decision, taken by millions of people during the past few centuries, also implied a renunciation of the revolutionary role in Europe; the virtually utopian aspect of American civilization presupposed that Europeans leave Europe. The United States, furthermore, was too permeated with Christian faith and too confident in the spirit of free enterprise to attract those who can only conceive of the future of democracy as something separate from Christianity and capitalism—the myriad children of the French Revolution.

In contrast, the USSR had reestablished itself within that continuum. It had become more than ever the keeper of the revolutionary tradition. To cast it in that role, the European Left did not need to dig deep into its memory but merely to recall the great years of anti-Fascism. The alliance between the Soviet Union and the English-speaking democracies confirmed the strategy of the Popular Fronts on an international scale as well as the dual nature of Communism, uniting the defense of democracy with the fight for revolution. The war had brought its weight in blood to prove this, along with the sanction of force. It had dishonored pacifism, so influential in France and Britain until 1939, which had turned out to be at best impotent, at worst an accomplice to Hitler. That discredit touched both the non–Communist Left and the Right in general, both of whom were guilty of the policy of appeasement with regard to Nazi Germany between 1936 and 1938. The paradox of the postwar moral situation was that Western public opinion seems to have forgotten the Hitler-Stalin pact, remembering only the Munich agreement, which had preceded it. Since people could no longer point a finger at the martyred and victorious USSR, they redirected blame against themselves or, rather, against their leaders, accusing them of trying to escape from an inevitable and just war. After the Soviet victory, the Soviets applied their interpretation of events to all that occurred before it. Thanks to that victory, the Soviet Union incarnated the sense of history not only by virtue of its ideology but by its fallen soldiers and the triumph of its arms. Bolstered by the universal experience of the war against Hitler, its image was strong enough to reshape not only ideas but memories.

In this respect, Western and Eastern Europe were in different situations after 1945. Nazism had been a tragedy for Europe, since it had subjugated almost all of Europe on either side of Germany. All the conquered peoples had been oppressed, though to different degrees, but all were traumatized. Victorious Communism, in contrast, became established only in countries liberated by the Red Army. It did not really touch Europe, except between Warsaw and Prague. In the West, it pursued its course in the imagination, magnified by the 1945 conjunction, independent of all historical reality. In Central and Eastern Europe, the defeat of Hitler exposed the truth of Communism. In Western Europe, it reinforced the Communist illusion. The apparent universality of the movement caused a crack in European consciousness that has yet to finish manifesting its effects.

During this period, Communism no longer had any open enemies in the West; they were in hiding or were silent. "Anti-Fascist" rhetoric had invaded the entire political scene, dragging behind it all of its lies, euphemisms, and unspoken opinions. Any critic of the Soviet Union was by definition banished from it: such criticism constituted a concession to Fascism, if not a step toward its revival. Once again, George Orwell was the most truthful witness of the temporary stupor that overcame public opinion as well as the writer who rebelled the most against the totalitarian bent of the century. Just after the war, on the occasion of a PEN Club meeting to celebrate the tercentenary of Milton's *Areopagitica*, Orwell fulminated that there was less intellectual freedom during his own time than during Milton's.[22] The reasons lay less in persecution than in the evolution of modern societies: the power of money, the state, the increasing passivity of the public, and finally the war, that quintessential instrument for the cretinization of the public. Aside from these hidden adversaries, liberty had open enemies—the totalitarian powers, whose spirit was far from extinguished. Indeed, that spirit was stronger than ever, carried forward by victorious Communism. Orwell, who had not yet written *1984*,[23] had known the importance of lies in Soviet imagery ever since the Spanish Civil War. He felt it more than ever. In spite of the weakness of the small Communist Party in Britain, "Soviet mythology" abounded in British public life; according to that mythology, now independent of its support from the Far Left, Britain had repatriated to the USSR, against their will and unbeknownst to the press, a number of prisoners of war and "displaced people" of Soviet nationality. "The fog of lies and misinformation that surrounds such subjects as the Ukraine famine, the Spanish civil war, Russian policy in Poland, and so forth, is not due entirely to conscious dishonesty, but any writer or journalist who is fully sympathetic to the USSR—sympathetic, that is, in the way the Russians themselves would want him to be—does have to acquiesce in deliberate falsification on important issues."[24]

This falsification was not a transitory phenomenon, as believed or stated by the Communists—allegedly more subtle than the rest—who were trying to recover, but not just yet, the bourgeois concern for truth. For "from the totalitarian point of view history is something to be created rather than learned. A totalitarian state is in effect a theocracy, and its ruling caste, in order to keep its position, has to be thought of as infallible."[25] That is why the orthodoxy spread by the Soviets, even beyond their own frontiers, through the consensual tyranny of self-censure, was even more dangerous than the power of money or bureaucracy. It corrupted the very sources of art and ideas by dishonoring them as disguises for experience. It made literature impossible: that was where humanity voluntarily lost its freedom.

Such was the post–World War II ideological situation that Orwell depicted from London. What then, can be said about Paris?

In the twentieth century, the French have had a hard time living with both victory and defeat. Victorious in 1918, France lacked the moral momentum, the historical vision, the diplomatic talent, the demographic growth, and the military force that would have enabled it to maintain a dominant situation in continental Europe for any length of time. Defeated in 1940, it was incapable of avoiding self-flagellation, the revenge of the Right against the Left under the gaze of the enemy, and the hardly glorious but early and deliberate initiative of anti-Semitic measures. In 1945, France was in an unprecedented situation: it was neither victorious nor beaten, or, rather, it was both victorious and beaten. Thanks to de Gaulle, the armies he managed to muster, and the Resistance, France did obtain—painstakingly and in extremis—a seat at the winners' table on the day of the capitulation. But France had been absent from Yalta or Potsdam. No one had really forgotten that the French had capitulated in June 1940 and had only marginally contributed to the final victory.

The French knew this better than anyone. Was there any nation more accustomed to the fragility of national grandeur and more sensitive to it? Since 1815, a deficit of military glory had burdened French history: Sedan had worsened that frustration, but it had been avenged by Marshals Joffre and Foch. So rapid and complete was the defeat in the spring of 1940 that it brought back, in an extreme form, the sense of national humiliation. The Vichy regime consecrated that defeat under the pretext of tempering it, and the existence of a French government under rather poorly disguised German protection and largely supported, at least at the beginning, by public opinion, limited the reach of de Gaulle's radio appeal of 18 June, both for the immediate situation and for posterity. De Gaulle wanted to ward off the provisional defeat by having the French participate in the final victory. But it was the Americans and the British, not to mention the Russians from the other side of Europe, rather than the French armies who finally erased the defeat made official by Vichy. In 1944, French public opinion was Gaullist, after having supported Vichy in 1940: it was a sign that France had *followed* rather than won the war. The collapse of 1940 was not obscured by the victory of 1944–45, as Sedan had been avenged at the Marne. De Gaulle enabled the French not to think about it, but not to forget or obliterate it either, for the very need to forget is what keeps us from forgetting. The French celebrated their liberation in August 1944, but the victory of 8 May 1945 brought no one out onto the streets.[26] Once again, France emerged from the war a wounded nation, led by its healer.

There was, it is true, an alternative, provided one was on the left. Its hard core, surrounded by a constellation of satellites, was the Communist Party. The Party had played an important role in the Resistance, of which it had been the principal support within the Left, first in isolation and then through an alliance with the other forces, under the more nominal than real authority of General de Gaulle. Many of those who had abandoned de Gaulle in 1939 rejoined him in 1941. Many more, as the war went on, came to admire his actions against the occupying forces and the courage of his militants. Organizational savvy and a gift for manipulation, strong points in the Bolshevik repertory, further helped the Communists; when France was liberated, the French Communist Party appeared so powerful and so "national" that for several weeks at the end of the summer of 1944 its authority seemed to challenge that of the authorities named by de Gaulle.[27]

In the West as well, Communism emerged from the war draped in national colors. In contrast to the East, the absence of the Red Army was a disadvantage in terms of power, but useful to Communist propaganda; for all that related to the Soviet Union, the Red Army maintained a purely imaginary power with no connection to reality. At once a powerful and distant model, the USSR was a liberator in absentia— an ideal situation for the patriotic image of French Communism.

This image was also a trompe l'oeil since the party of 1944–45 remained the same as that of 1939–40 as far as its strategic concepts, its dependence on Moscow, and the majority of its apparatus were concerned. Having changed directions in 1941, it had not altered its nature any more than had the domestic regime of the USSR or the international policies of Stalin. If the French had not managed to forget 1940, neither had the Communist Party, though for different reasons, because 1940 had brought into question both its anti-Fascist tradition and the continuity of its national policy against Germany. That is why it remained the best-kept and most bitterly defended secret of the time: anyone raising it would draw the arrows of a party that had become too nationalistic for the obedience it had manifested four years earlier to the German-Soviet rapprochement, but was now quicker than ever to excommunicate its enemies. In the entire chapter of repressed memories left to the French by the year 1940, Communist politics were secondary compared with the national crisis inaugurated by the collapse of the nation. In 1944, however, that episode took on a hidden dimension all the more important because the Communist Party claimed to represent the essence of national continuity—obviously in contrast to Vichy but also, more subtly, by relation to de Gaulle.

The French case, perhaps more than any other, helps us to understand the strengths and the weaknesses of the patriotic line, with its all but chauvinistic overtones, adopted by the international Communist movement. In a Europe emerging from Nazi oppression, the exaltation of national independence and inseparably anti-German and anti-Nazi feelings allowed the Soviet Union and the local Communist parties to capitalize on the significance of the war and the victory. This notion was all the more beneficial because the spectacular victories of the Germans between 1939 and 1941 had deprived the conquered countries of their political and moral bases. Torn from their pasts, uncertain about the future, unhappy in the present, they had many reasons to reproach their prewar leaders; by the end of the war, they were hating those of them who had sympathized or signed pacts with the Germans. This void opened up a space for the Communist parties that proposed programs to foster national renaissances. The Jacobin tradition furnished them with the means necessary to unify anti-Nazi universalism and anti-German chauvinism. On the other hand, the weakness of this patriotic trumpeting was that it made itself heard through conflictual memories of two kinds: those of the Resistance and those of 1939–40. More recent memories had obscured earlier ones, though none of them were very old. Good memories ousted bad ones. The French Communist Party's attempt to coexist peacefully with the occupying forces sketched out in the summer of 1940 benefited from the collective repression that enveloped that whole accursed year. Intimidation would do the rest.

In a country like France, however, Communism had roots too deep and diverse to fit entirely into the fragile marriage between the idea of nation and the international reality of the movement. In France, as in Italy and in contrast to Britain, Communism had a powerful working-class social base, created over the years by systematic militant action in the name of revolutionary tradition. Since 1936, the French Communist Party had conquered bastions of workers, especially in the Parisian suburbs, among whom the Communists had begun to construct what Annie Kriegel called a "countersociety."[28] In 1936, Communist militants were the ones who supervised the massive strike movement. Though they did not participate in the government, they did constitute a paragovernmental force through their own strength and through the influence of intermediaries. In any case, in a republic that had never paid much attention to its proletariat, the French Communist Party had already won the extraordinary privilege of representing the nation's working class, bringing it historical dignity while fashioning it into the figure of the future. France's originality in the history of Communism was that, from then on, it outfitted its Communist Party in a sort revolutionary respectability: the leadership role of the Party in the working class, the working class in the Front populaire, and the Front populaire in the progress of socialism had all been hypostatized into a series of necessary relationships. The Left had divined the march of history from social and political circumstances thanks to the universalistic tendency of the national genius.

Taking a broad view, we could say that the situation of 1936 was reproduced in 1945, on a larger scale, and magnified by a total victory: Europe was covered with Communist parties, Popular Fronts, anti-capitalist proclamations, and revolutionary engagements. The image of the USSR had reached its zenith. The French Left was back on track. Triumphant anti-Fascism served more than ever to unify the Communists and their allies. It carried both a tactical and a strategic advantage. The former was that anyone who had not taken the side of the alliance was suspected of not being an anti-Fascist, or not being sufficiently anti-Fascist. The latter had to do with objectives: if Fascism was dead, anti-Fascism had still to destroy its roots, which, as the German example had allegedly proved, were located in capitalism itself.

Fascism would thus outlive itself like a latent menace up until the day of the socialist revolution, which was the only thing that could destroy the conditions that had made it possible. The anti-Fascist alliance of 1945 had the advantage over the Popular Front of 1936 in that it opened the way to anticapitalist democracy, conceived as one of the steps toward socialism. This ideological construction, which engendered many byzantine discussions, was intended to do so, in order to escape from the sad analysis of reality. By furnishing a negative object for political action—anti-Fascism and anticapitalism—it simultaneously avoided a debate on democracy and a debate on socialism. It acted as though anti-Fascism necessarily led to the collective appropriation of the means of production, and as though anticapitalism were necessarily democratic. It sought to mask both the revolutionary idea and the democratic idea.

The "revolutionary" obsession had never been more visible in French politics than at the Liberation. It was ubiquitous, and not, as in 1918, linked to a reaction against the war but to the desire to revolutionize the civil order. It was stamped with the ideas and emotions of the twentieth-century wars. The First World War caused the revolutionary passion to grow and prosper in the enemy camps of the Far Left and the Far Right. The Second World War seems to have mobilized that passion among everyone as a consequence of the course of the war. It mattered little that the French had played a passive rather than a leadership role. The misfortunes of post-1940 French history had rendered all the more necessary a break with the past and a new start, so as exorcise the Vichy government.

The universal character of the revolutionary invocation in the literature of that time was striking and had lost nothing of its rhetorical violence: the vocabulary of the Year II, the "punishment of traitors," calls to the nation's energy, and diatribes against egoism were the order of the day. Circumstances brought out, in its left-wing version, the will to break with the Third Republic that Pétain, in a right-wing version, had made use of in 1940. The origins of the idea were even earlier: we have seen how it was manifest in the interwar period in all political families, particularly during the 1930s. But since no one had discovered how to put it into practice, it bounced around in a repertory borrowed from

Fascism and from Communism, sometimes from both simultaneously. In 1940, the idea was especially uncertain, even though it coincided with real popular hostility toward the fallen regime. But this so-called "national" revolution was far from something willed, since it was the outcome of the German victory and the lasting occupation of two-thirds of the country. Nonetheless, even the persecution it had been subjected to under Vichy did not bring the Third Republic any closer to the French Resistance, all things considered. At the Liberation, members of the Resistance too were calling for revolution. For them, recovered independence was no more sufficient than France's participation in the final victory. They wanted to break with a past that predated the Vichy regime, and on its ruins to reinvent not only a republic but a society liberated from the tyranny of money. To accomplish this, however, they had no available ideas other than Communist or Communist-leaning anti-Fascism;[29] they were closer to the past than to the future.

The war had hardly ended when the Fourth Republic began, following in the footsteps of the Third. De Gaulle abandoned the new political movements that emerged from the Resistance when he was unable to make his constitutional ideas prevail. The Christian Democrats, those Johnny-come-latelies who became bourgeois as soon as they set foot in government palaces, brought nothing really new to Republican ideas, whose social horizon they had once dreamed of renewing. As for the Left, the Socialist Party had long been unclear about what it meant by revolution, and the Communists knew all too well. Hence the mediocre institutional compromise of 1946. The "revolutionary" demands manifested with so much passion by the Resistance as something inseparable from national liberation achieved no more results than they had in the 1930s, even though the second version seemed to enjoy broad public support. General de Gaulle blamed the parties for that failure, the parties blamed de Gaulle, the Communist Party blamed the bourgeois parties, the Socialist Party blamed the Communist Party, and so on. But these contradictory accusations were in themselves signs of a more general phenomenon: in spite of its glamour, the revolutionary idea had no more to offer after the war than before. Before the war, it had been caught up in the ambiguities of the relationship between Fascism and Communism. After the debacle of Nazism, it was embodied in a late form of Bolshevism, through passive consent rather than any effort of volition or imagination.

Henceforth, the French were free of the Germans but not from the fatality of history. On the contrary, they hung more than ever onto the idea and the feeling of history, which fueled the primitive Marxism of the time. The victory of the Allies over Hitler had assumed a fatalistic character. Both camps fought each other fiercely, each in the name of a religion of the future. The victors' strength was that they appeared to be carried along by necessity. Of the two beliefs that gave the revolutionary idea its allure—necessity and will—the former had almost absorbed the latter. This explains the often nihilistic or, at any rate, morally inconsistent character of so many contemporary discourses on revolution, a character that shocks one of its most recent historians, Tony Judt, because it was so widespread among French intellectuals and could even be found among Catholic writers.[30] It originated in historical experience and the spirit of the times, which were provisionally more influential than reason or even religion.[31]

We have established an inventory, but we have yet to analyze its circumstances and reasons. This brings us back to the history of Communism in France, which continued to be the repository of the revolutionary idea that made it so powerful and so crippled.

What had become of the various left-wing groups in France of 1944? The war had finally dishonored pacifism, which had been so powerful in 1939, and reduced the influence of the Socialist Party, which was also dishonored by the Munich agreement. Nor could the Radicals and the old Republican standbys of which they were the guardians escape from the general discredit that descended on the Third Republic after the defeat. For the rest, neither the Socialists nor the Radicals, as parties, had played a spectacular role in the Resistance. When the territory of France was liberated in the summer of 1944, French public opinion was leaning more toward the left than at any other time in history but had only one major rallying point—the Communist Party.

The Party had been strengthened by the Red Army's victories and by its role in the Resistance. It shared the people's happy memories of 1936. It had not supported Munich. Circumstances readied it to incarnate the French Left in its most ecumenical version, combining to varying degrees the democratic passion and the revolutionary passion, the republican spirit and Bolshevik "Jacobinism," the taste for liberty and the cult of the state. Just when it was drawing a part of its strength from traditional anti-Germanism, victorious anti-Fascism also gave it an air of unity and a maximum of influence for all these political sentiments together. The French liked this mixture of genres, by which they rendered homage to their tradition with the very word they pretended to be subverting; this in turn furnished a historical basis for their revolutionary preaching.

The Soviet Union was above suspicion because it was the quintessential great power that had prevailed over the Nazis. The too famous Moscow trials were merely proof of a premonitory vigilance against

Hitler's fifth column. The victory, moreover, would allow Stalin's regime to relax its constraints and dictatorship, following the example of the revolutionary Terror of 1793. How could anyone doubt it when even Roosevelt, the other great victor, had thought or at least hoped it was true? The war made the image of the Soviet Union doubly universal and gave the October Revolution a new democratic baptism. The Far Left could continue to admire it, thanks to the battles won by the Red Army, the march of revolutionary violence, and the promise of a radically new society. But Soviet victories also brought the restoration of democracy and even promised a more democratic social order. Prewar polemics on the nature of the Soviet regime were no longer in style, and comparisons with Fascist dictatorships even less so, for circumstances had given the space of its illusion so much elasticity.

Within that space, French Communism unfolded its dual nature, even as it rediscovered, on a higher level, the delights of the Front populaire period, the pleasure of being both governmental and revolutionary, respectable and subversive, national and Stalinist. That pleasure was not reserved for intellectuals, thrilled at the recovery of an identity between the nation, democracy, and revolution. It furnished advance rewards for the efforts of the militants, without waiting for the seizure of power, and compensated leaders for their secret servitude. As to the French, if they were left-wing, they savored precisely the revolutionary part of the Communist image without ceasing to love its reassuring side. Since the French Revolution they had been used to combining their passion for new beginnings with a concern for the continuity of the state. A glance at the collection of constitutional ideas defended by the Communist Party in 1945 and 1946 makes clear that the Party's voters were back to their old habits: the institutional spirit remained that of the Third Republic, rejuvenated by a return to the original model, which was the Convention.

Nonetheless, any reference to bourgeois democracy was mere window dressing. That theater of mementos was but a transition, for the goal was never out of sight: one of the characteristics of Communism is this fixity amid changing circumstances. The Comintern no longer existed, and national independence was the first priority of the Communist parties' programs. But the movement had lost nothing of its ultracentralized character or of the nature of its revolutionary objectives. Stalin, indeed, had become infallible by remaining true to himself, and the cult of which he was the object in the Communist world symbolized the narrow limits of autonomy placed upon the member parties of the former Comintern. Virtually all the heads of parties that were ready to function in their respective countries in 1944–45 had spent the war years in the USSR and were the *missi dominici* of the Supreme Guide. France was no exception to this rule.

Objectively speaking, the revolutionary hope seemed to draw its concrete meaning from the conditions under which Europe had been liberated from the Nazi yoke, that is, the progress of the Red Army. Not that this army imposed the dictatorship of the proletariat in the countries from which it had driven out the Nazi troops. But it did at least impose friendship with the USSR as the primary condition for their domestic regimes while guaranteeing a special role for the local Communist parties, who owed their influence to their authorization. Nothing of this existed in Western Europe. The circumstances of August–September 1944 revealed the limits of the French Communist Party's influence, not only because of de Gaulle but because France had been liberated by the Americans. Even though, apart from Yugoslavia, Communism had its strongest European bases in France and Italy, it was incapable of leading a revolutionary enterprise. So it was weak where it was strong, and strong where it was weak; in both cases, the "proletarian revolution" followed in the footsteps of the Red Army rather than in those of the proletariat's forces. Moreover, it came up against something greater than the bourgeoisie—the United States.

Such was the paradoxical and nonetheless logical consequence of "socialism in one country." When the military victory arrived, it made the USSR the instrument and the beneficiary of "socialism" among its neighbors, to whom it was going to export everything, including political and police training personnel. By the same token, it found its power limited by the other great victor of the war. The mere presence of American troops in Western Europe, the historical seat of bourgeois society, could not explain why the French and the Italian Communist parties had not seized power at the Liberation. Before eventually representing the supreme assurance of the West's fidelity to liberal democracy, the American presence at least constituted a minimal guarantee against the imposition of the Red Army's clients. The idea of revolution had lost its direct connection to the relationship between classes within nations. Henceforth it was accepted in a way that no longer had anything to do with worker internationalism. It was no longer an embodiment of solidarity with the struggle of the proletariats. It adopted the international geography of military power. The ultimate fate of the European working class was no longer related to the relaying of Bolshevism by proletarians in the great European capitalist nations, beginning with Germany, as it had been in the years following October. It was hanging on the fact that the Red Army was camped in Prague. This could have been understood as both a formidable advance and a provisional equilibrium.

In Western Europe, therefore, the revolutionary passion had never been more confused than during the period when it appeared to dominate the public scene. This was clear in both France and Italy. At that time, it had the universal reach of victorious anti-Nazism, which inscribed Communist preaching in the policy line of democracy. Italy had been Fascist, allied with Germany; defeated France had produced the Vichy government. The war, even on the anti-Nazi side, was not an experience that reconciled the French and the Italians to bourgeois democracy. Since it had left standing only one critique of liberalism after liquidating the other, it shifted both public opinions toward the idea of a new democracy, in which the power of the bourgeois and of money would be reduced in the name of the people.

Such an aspiration was not, in itself, necessarily revolutionary, at least in the means envisioned for its realization. It was a kind of dawning because of the retroactive effect of the war, which gave it its meaning: an event of such importance necessarily signaled the opening of new era. How could Hitler's Wagnerian collapse be interpreted as anything but the annunciation of a new order? But what sort of new order? The uncertain proportions of democracy and revolution that had characterized anti-Fascism in 1936 constituted an even more unstable mixture and an overly ambiguous program in 1945. It was too Leninist for the pluralistic elements it retained, and too pluralistic for its Leninist program. It was the hour of "national paths" toward socialism;[32] but that expression, which turned out to be temporary, was more an incantation than a discovery. By its very existence, the new world order forged by the victorious armies gave the lie to the confusion between the democratic and the revolutionary, depriving it of reality.

Such was the sad side of the Liberation era in Western Europe. The return of liberty, due primarily to the work of foreign armies, was celebrated by a concert of soft philosophies and false programs. The philosophies resembled the cult of history, since they proved incapable of analyzing the two figures of a social order that the false programs had pushed to center stage—the Soviet revolution in its Stalinist phase and American-style democracy. Trapped in the ambiguities of anti-Fascism, these programs finally, in an unsaid and often unconscious manner, tended to align themselves with the world order of power. Orwell's diagnosis, though made in London, was a judgment on the whole of Western Europe.

The anti-Nazism of the time did not preclude thinking of Nazism itself. The Jewish genocide may be reconsidered in this light. We have seen how, in the Eastern European nations liberated by the Red Army, the greatest of Nazi crimes was obliterated by the Communist parties in the name of a national renaissance. The Polish Jews that were exterminated were Jewish Poles. The Ukrainian Jews massacred in Babi Yar were Soviet citizens. In France, things did not go quite so far as this official erasure; yet freedom led to results on a lesser scale, comparable to those obtained by ideological orthodoxy. In France too, the Jews were the great forgotten people of the victory.[33] Anti-Fascism, when Communist-dominated, had no place for the massacre of the Jews. The Communists were ill-disposed toward ceding the number one place on Hitler's hate list, a place they had won through a pitched battle, and they numbered many Jewish militants in their ranks. As for anti-Fascism—defined by its lowest common denominator, the democratic sentiment—it accentuated by reaction the abstract universalism of the French tradition, blind to the existence of the Jews as a particular group when that group received the spotlight of unprecedented persecution. That tradition rendered the French particularly indifferent to the fate of foreign Jews on their soil, and they were hardly more attentive when the dimensions of the Jewish hecatomb in the camps became known.[34] More generally, that tradition gave them an excuse for forgetting the anti-Semitic laws passed in the fall of 1940 by Pétain's government and for limiting responsibility for the deportations of French Jews to the crimes of "collaborators." The imaginary transformation of a nation into a people of anti-Nazi *résistants* helped to obscure the philosophical and moral stakes of the war.

ELEVEN

Cold War Communism

THE RESPECT AND ADMIRATION, GAINED FROM
the Red Army's victory over Hitler, that haloed the Communist idea
immediately after World War II did not long remain intact. That moment of confused respectability so foreign to Communism was merely
ephemeral capital with uncertain returns; the history of Communism
was soon to enter a new phase.

This time, Communist history was enmeshed in the world order.
Even in Europe, Stalin encountered only American power. Bolstered by
universal anti-Fascism, he had made a political investment, via "National Fronts" and local Communist parties, in every country in which
his army had had the last word. The coerced rejection by these parties
of the Marshall Plan in July 1947,[1] the subjugation of Poland,[2] and
the Czech coup d'état of February 1948[3] capped off the formation of a
territorial empire bordering ravaged Western Europe, where American
troops stood guard in guilty Germany.

The history of this formation is less vital to my subject than the
manner in which it replicated, on a far greater scale, the two-tiered
command system so typical of socialism. On one hand was the USSR,
its army, its diplomacy, its "services," which would have looked like
any other police state except that it was draped in the ideological garb
of socialism. On the other were the Communist parties, all of whose
leaders were children of the dissolved Comintern that had been replaced
in 1947 by the Cominform, which, though theoretically more flexible,
was in fact similarly omnipotent over its "brother parties."[4] The movement still resembled a highly centralized church, yet maintained the
fiction that its components were autonomous. A single hand directed
both the Soviet Union and the Communist parties in the name of ideological orthodoxy, organizing Soviet domination over the small countries in which the Red Army was stationed, while allowing the parties—

as long as they were led by men who had spent the war in Moscow—to appear to control local political power under the flag of national independence and anti-Fascism. It therefore mattered little whether they were strong, as in Czechoslovakia, or all but nonexistent, as in Romania. The rationale for their domination lay outside of themselves, though they bore its stamp—the language of ideology. The Soviet Union was thus able to constitute a European empire on an unprecedented scale and of a completely new character: never in history had the Russians advanced so far into the west. Never had that advance taken the form of a social idea born in the west and turned against the west. Never had so many and such diverse nations been subjugated through the tyrannical uniformity of ideology. They would even become a "camp"—the camp of "socialism and peace."

The Communist idea merged with imperial power without letting go of anything. Wedded to the cult of force from the start, then limited exclusively to one country, Communism almost naturally found its population base enlarged by the war. It had only to readjust its scale to find itself master not only of increased territory but also, and better yet, of a part of Europe in which it was already furnished with militants, trained well in advance. In the spring of 1947, the long frontier that extended from Lübeck to Trieste through Prague had already cut off from the capitalist world the European nations that had lent a common face to the international revolution. Only those who had experienced or been subjected to it must have been capable of measuring the historic weight of this situation.

The Communist idea's influence over the imagination came from yet another source: the philosophy of war, which had reappeared so rapidly and with such force. People of that time had grown up with memories or tales of 1914 and were emerging from a second global conflict that had cut their lives in two. The end of the First World War had encouraged some hope for a lasting peace, at least for a decade. The Second had barely ended when a Third was threatened—not a vague and distant threat, but an all but inevitable confrontation, proclaimed and experienced as such in both camps and with much fanfare.[5] The general atmosphere in Europe was not one of optimism. The pacifistic idealism of the post–World War I period was dead and buried by 1939. Saturated with violence and tragedy, at once cynical and sentimental, public opinion had in some ways become accustomed to misfortune. Europe, moreover, was more a stake than a player. Its basic role in world power relations only made the weakness of its political will more obvious: its new doctrine was resignation to history.

The causes of and responsibilities for the cold war are beyond our focus.[6] Let us instead consider how quickly almost everyone, everywhere, became resigned to this new conflict, following so closely upon the heels of the other. The early signs were visible even before the fall of Hitler in the Allies' discussions and disagreements about Poland, especially at Yalta. Even if Roosevelt thought he could avoid it, the open contest for European zones of influence had already begun in the final months of the war, as illustrated by the British intervention in Greece and Stalin's intention, no matter what his motives were, to sew up the territory occupied by his army. The Nazi capitulation thus inaugurated a period of anxiety rather than closing a time of pain.

Few conflicts in history have been accompanied by such a sense of fatality as the cold war. On both sides, the leaders not only accepted that fatality but made a philosophy out of it. Stalin did not have to search long in his stock of ideas to come up with a condemnation of imperialism, of which the United States had become the key figure. And Truman endowed the battle against Communism with a "doctrine":[7] an indication that his political talent, which consisted entirely of action, was adjusting to the requirements of the situation and the spirit of the times. The nations of Europe, just emerging from a long ideological war, had no trouble subscribing to the justifications for a new ideological war, following in the tracks of the earlier one, to which each of the camps claimed it was heir. Stalin brandished the menace of a new Fascism, born of American imperialism; he directed the repertory of the anti-Hitler battle against his former ally. Truman, on the other hand, denounced the strength of the Soviet Union, which had taken up where Nazi Germany had left off. There was no question of parrying it with the errors of the Munich policy. The time of Rooseveltian illusions about the "good" evolution of Communism was over: this was war. Thus, the Third World War was put on the tracks of the Second by a mishmash of contradictory analogies and a recycling of contradictory memories. Such was the price of the ambiguity of the anti-Hitler alliance. Europeans resigned themselves, exhausted by all the ideological ferocity and incapable of escaping it except by losing a sense of their own history. Having unified them, the anti-Fascist war now divided them.

This ambiguity was manifest in the way in which the Soviets dealt with the German question. Defeated, crushed, a criminal, Germany of 1945 no longer existed as a political body. Unlike the situation in October–November 1918, even the military collapse had not prompted a part of the German population to rebel against their bad leaders. Yet Germany remained a stake in the struggle for power among its victors— so formidable that the quadripartite military Commission in charge of running it could only work collectively for a few months.[8] Of all the victors, the Soviet Union was the most interested in being paid back in kind. Between 1946 and 1948, it undertook a veritable transfer of the German industrial infrastructure into the Russian zone, dismantling buildings, heavy machinery, and even railroads. But that determination could be cast simply as circumstantial compensation for the immense destruction wrought by the Wehrmacht in Russia and the Ukraine. On the other hand, the anti-Fascist idea, as manipulated by the Soviet military authority, immediately stamped Germany's Eastern zone with particular characteristics.

Not that the denazification set out by the Potsdam Agreements was taken more seriously there than in the Western zone, where the American, British, and French armies were in control. On the contrary, it was on everyone's lips. But in the Russian zone it was seen and applied less as a flurry of inquiries into individuals' past activities than as the collective denial of a national crime. Politics took precedence over law: the German Communist Party, consecrated as the quintessence of anti-Fascism, its leaders having arrived in Moscow on the heels of the Red Army, would finally have its day. It mattered little that it had played no role in the various attempts to overthrow Hitler from within. It owed its prestige less to having been the first group to be persecuted by Hitler in March 1933 then to having been elected by the Soviet victor as a symbol of German working-class resistance to the Nazi dictatorship sought by the bourgeoisie. It was an image of orthodoxy as well as an instrument of power. According to the German Communist Party's version, it is hard to imagine that there had been other prisoners in Hitler's concentration camps besides Communist militants and workers! Once again, ideology exiled the Jews from their own misfortune.[9]

Both exemplary resisters and primary victims, the German Communists were more victims than resisters. They reappeared on the political scene of their country, not as revolutionary victors finally accomplishing the great plan of the twenties, but as militants who had been liberated or brought back by the Red Army, the sole master of the Eastern zone, where their only strength was as the major witnesses of anti-Fascism—but not the only witnesses, since that "victimization" included other authorized parties,[10] starting with the socialists: what counted was that it constituted the only arena of public debate and constrained the actors into a single interpretation. Moreover, the two "workers'" parties would merge in April 1946 with the blessing of the Russian administration. Soviet-style denazification consisted less of punishing and expelling guilty parties than of inserting the German politics it controlled into the tight circle of Sovietism: nothing lay between Nazism and Communism. If one was not allied with the Communists, one was suspected of being nostalgic for or sympathetic to Nazism. And the Communists to be allied with were those who had found refuge in Moscow since and during Hitler's time: they were the only ones the Soviets really trusted.

The German Communist diaspora that had chosen—or had been forced into—exile in the West (in France, Britain, the United States, or Mexico) remained subordinated to the Soviet diaspora, and its history remained almost as obscure as that of the middle-class and aristocratic resistance against Hitler and the plot of 20 July 1944. The only "anti-Fascism" was the one that had grown up in Stalin's shadow; elsewhere, it was rapidly converted against American imperialism and its West German satellite. Adenauer's republic would be denounced as a neo-Nazi regime the moment it introduced German history into Western constitutionalism, whereas Ulbricht's Germany would be considered an ideologically anti-Fascist regime the moment it established a single-party dictatorship under Soviet protection.

That dictatorship left the Germans no choice but to adore not only their conqueror but the regime that had arrived with him. The first requirement was a squaring of the circle: the Red Army had committed numerous atrocities in Eastern Prussia and Pomerania, driving tens of thousands of terrified deserters in front of it. During the entire year that followed, the tracing of the new German-Polish frontiers made the defeat look like a formidable exodus. Upon this uprooted people, who cared only for survival, the conqueror imposed a political catechism of penitence, which formed the ideological basis for the future regime. The German Communists, the only ones who could speak the Soviet language and who had long been gearing up for the role, established themselves at the head of a fragment of their country like a little aristocracy innocent of the national crime since it was made up of victims. But they ruled as a derivative power, for their rule was imposed by the Soviet Union. These heirs to a great worker tradition prostituted it in a foreign adventure of posthumous anti-Fascism, soon to be transformed into an ideology of police power.

The revolution for which Rosa Luxemburg and Liebknecht had died was completed with the force of an occupation army in the silence and guilt of the people. The nationalization of industry and agrarian reform itself, celebrated as the victory of the popular masses, assumed a punitive and bureaucratic tone. It was as though the spirit of German Communism, after being crushed by Nazism, would fare no better after Nazism in turn was crushed. Nonetheless, it eventually managed to maintain an endogenous Marxist culture in the midst of a Sovietized society. Even the most meticulously policed state of the Soviet movement could not discredit Marxism-Leninism in the country in which Marx had been born and Liebknecht had died.

Until becoming two distinct states, the two Germanys were separated by two interpretations and two ways of practicing anti-Fascism. In Western Germany, the renaissance of political life revealed the massive preponderance of anti-Communist parties, including the Social Democrats, since they had remained true to themselves. In view of the final destination of millions of "displaced" Germans, it is easy to understand the unpopularity of Communism in public opinion between 1946 and 1948, to say nothing of the period that followed.[11] In Eastern Europe, the new unified Socialist Party, surrounded by its network of "anti-Fascist" organizations, locked the two "bourgeois" parties into the "Democratic bloc." It was merely an organizational relay of the Soviet military administration charged with celebrating the new Polish frontier, blessing the Russians' economic pillaging of that territory, and justifying the arrests most often made by the Soviet police themselves. From the very start, it assumed the character it would retain up to the end: the party most closely dependent on Moscow since, in the name of anti-Nazism, it was also the almost sacrificial vanguard of victorious Bolshevism in the midst of a conquered people.

The Berlin crisis, the first major alert of the cold war, crystallized the cold war's contradictions. The former capital of Germany, surrounded by the Soviet zone, was given a special status that put it under four-part military administration. There was still an independent Socialist Party there, the same one as in Western Germany, which had held a municipal majority since the election of October 1946. Less than a year later, when the iron curtain fell on Europe, it formed a Western enclave in Sovietized territory, a window to the West—and thus a constant invitation to comparison or flight—and one more reason for the isolation of German Communism, which dropped to record depths of unpopularity.[12] The Soviet blockade of Berlin in the winter of 1948–49 was intended to reduce this sore as a preface to the foundation of a German state in the eastern zone. It may also have been an early attempt, very much in the manner of Stalin, to test the adversary's mettle. The response, in terms of technical performance, was unequivocal—the airlift to Berlin. It was an extraordinary about-face in terms of geography and force, emphasized by geographic identity. At the time, no one needed a long memory in order to recall that Berlin, before becoming the object of American airplanes, had been their target. It had been the capital of a totalitarian empire before becoming a symbol of liberty. The Berliners had changed roles at the same time as the Soviets did, suggesting that

World War III was lurking in the very place where World War II had ended and was even a result of the earlier war since the former Allies disagreed as to its implications.

This German detour helps us to dig deeper into the nature of the Communist idea in the post–World War II war period, and to understand the reorientation it underwent between 1946 and 1948. In 1946 it was already accompanied by the USSR's formidable growth of power, but remained linked to the policies of the anti-Fascist democratic union similar to those the war had illustrated on an international level. By 1948 it was once more on the path to war and revolution, hardening its positions everywhere, faced with imperialism, more intent on constructing fortresses than channels. We are reminded of the constant turns in Communism's history: "war Communism" was succeeded by the New Economic Policy, which was succeeded by the sectarian policies of the "third phase";[13] the Popular Front strategy was succeeded by the Hitler-Stalin Pact. Now, two years after waging war against Hitler alongside the democracies, the Soviet Union closed ranks around itself against imperialism. The confused epic of the war against Hitler was over, as was the time of "national paths toward socialism." The Communist world had become a bloc, or a camp.

The creation of the Cominform in September 1947 set the stage. In an official report, Andrei Zhdanov, one of Stalin's lieutenants, had aligned the entire "socialist camp" on the left, under the control, more absolute than ever, of the Soviet Union, which was threatened by imperialist aggression.[14] The participation of Communist parties in some governments was not sufficient to make them truly "democratic." The "working class," allied with the "laboring masses" and working through the Communist parties, had to play a leading role in those governments. In other words, the only difference between them and the "pure" Soviet regime was that the latter maintained satellite parties within the coalition to which only the Communists held the keys. In order that things be as clear in the west as in the east, the Yugoslavian delegation had been given the responsibility of putting the French and Italian parties on trial, accusing them of having collaborated with bourgeois governments for so long that they had become their flunkies. Thorez and Togliatti—who were mired in opportunism—learned a lesson from the toughest party in the socialist "camp." Neither of them was there, perhaps suspecting that they were in for a disagreeable time. On the French side, it was Jacques Duclos who received the Yugoslavian incursion, thanking them with promises to change in accordance with the rituals of the movement. There is an almost stenographic account of the meeting in Szklarska Porba, a small Polish village close to Wroclaw, by

Eugenio Reale,[15] which deserves to become a classic of the history of Communism, so well does it reveal the violence and servility of the relations that dominated the conclave of affiliated parties.

Was this a revival of the "third phase"? In one sense, yes. Zhdanov's text had a familiar ring about it. It was dominated by the threat of imperialism and the imminent danger of a war against the Soviet Union. So much for theoretical subtleties about interimperialist conflicts and the margin of maneuver they afforded the homeland of socialism: that distinction, which had served as the basis for the strategy of the Popular Fronts and was declared null and void in September 1939, returned in force after June 1941. Now it was out of commission again, for the two most important victors of 1945 were in conflict all over the world. Only one imperialism remained, dominated by American economic and military power and daily losing its hold over Europe and beyond. This is why it was so aggressive and determined to destroy the USSR, advance guard of the people. As between 1927 and 1932, the fight for peace was the order of the day, since it was involved in the defense of the USSR. And Fascism was no longer limited to a few particularly aggressive countries. It was lurking wherever the anti-Soviet war was being prepared, that is, just about everywhere in the capitalist world, primarily in the United States but also in Western Europe, notably in West Germany, where unpunished Nazis were still lurking. The duty of the Cominform parties was to take the lead in this Manichaean fight, in which absolute loyalty to the USSR was to be proclaimed universally. The Social Democrats, when they remained hostile to the Communists, once more became the prime suspects of collusion with imperialism.

The recentering of the international battle was carried out in a setting different from the "third phase." The bloodiest war in history had barely ended when Zhdanov evoked the specter of a third global conflict, haunted by the final image of the second—the atomic mushroom cloud over Hiroshima. Anticipation of tomorrow's horrors went beyond yesterday's worst memories; imagination outpaced memory, constantly feeding from it. Fear of war, even more than after World War I, was supported by a universal fund of emotions, common both to civilians and veterans. Everyone had been touched by the Second World War, and the Third would certainly not distinguish among its victims. A triumph of technology, it would offer no possibility for courage or patriotism. The fight for peace evoked less vehement appeals but gentler and more universal feelings. As in Europe after Versailles, it did not attack national passions or military virtues head-on. It offered a vast asylum for diverse political alternatives, from unconditional solidarity with the Soviet Union to the measure of innocence that could accompany pacifism, including all shades of anti-Americanism. It enveloped revolutionary activism in feelings.

The Soviet Union, though much stronger than it had been during the "third phase," was weak compared to the United States. The Communist idea drew considerable persuasive advantage from this ambiguity. The country in which it was embodied, which had become the greatest power in Europe and the second greatest world power, enjoyed political influence, which gave it its strength, and was reinforced with the moral authority gained from the war against Hitler. But in men and materials it had paid dearly for its victory. Its entire economy needed reconstructing. It had no atomic bomb. So even those who did not believe in the imminence of a war brought on by the United States could understand why Stalin was convinced that it was in the offing and would be inclined to contribute a signature or a vote to even up the disparity of forces regarded as a threat to peace. Communism was liked for both its strength and its weakness. This accumulation of images and confusion of sentiments, so much in evidence among the elites of colonized countries, were not new to Western European public opinion. In democratic politics, fear and compassion make a better couple than one might think.

The conditions surrounding the 1947 turning point prevented it from becoming simply a return to the early Stalinist period Communism. The movement was a reaffirmation of the spirit of "socialism in one country" but extended to Bolshevism in several countries, which endowed it with a simultaneously international and highly centralized character, constructed more firmly than ever around the Soviet bastion, with the battle against the anti-Soviet war as first priority. All the slogans that in 1930 had conjured up the image of a besieged fortress were translated in 1947 into a conquering optimism, as if they had lost their extremist character and been etched in the direct line of democracy. This tells us that Bolshevism had, to paraphrase Lenin, reached its "*supreme* stage"; here, supreme did not imply ultimate, for there would surely be other stages. The term meant that the Soviet system had reached what one might call its "totalitarian maturity": maintaining over the citizens of the USSR a control that had reached an unprecedented level of perfection in human history; extending to several countries in Europe, and soon to China; incarnated by a single leader, adulated as a soldier, a philosopher, and a statesman; and bolstered globally by an ideological influence comparable to the grip of a religion. The Zhdanov report of 1947 represented the apotheosis of that universe— which, in spite of its sinister character, was admired and envied—and gathered into a final chorus all the great tunes of the repertory.

Then the Yugoslav secession occurred, and the very thing the report thought it was inaugurating was in crisis a year later.

The significance of the Yugoslav rupture with the USSR in 1948 lay not so much in the fact that it modified the balance of world power but in what it symbolized. Taken by itself, the rupture had no military consequences. Yugoslavia, a mosaic of small nations, was only a small state; but in breaking with the Stalinist order, Tito inaugurated a genre new to the history of Communism—a schism in national Communism. The Communist movement had certainly had its heretics before that time, and these had even been increasing, generation after generation, in partial consequence of the role played by ideology. With Tito, however, heresy spread not only to an entire party, but to a state. A party could have been dealt with by exterminating its cadres, which is what happened to the Polish Communist Party in 1938; but to reduce a state, war would have to be declared. Such was the price the USSR had to pay for its ambition to be an empire.

Stalin underestimated the Yugoslav Party's ability to resist his pressure. The conflict crystallized around his attempts to control not only the Party but the army, the bureaucracy, and the security forces. This was an old technique, which he had used in all of the satellite countries, and which he topped off with the installation of on-site Soviet advisers. Tito protested, refused to give in, and risked a public rupture, which was given ideological form in the long Cominform "Resolution" of June 1948.

The man who was condemned for "nationalist deviation"—before being cast as an imperialist agent or a Fascist criminal—happened to be the most famous Communist leader in Europe after Stalin. He had led the anti-German guerrilla war at the head of a veritable army. An old Comintern member who had become one of the great figures of World War II, he had appeared to be Stalin's fiercest lieutenant in the vanguard of the Soviet presence in Europe. The Soviet Union had tenaciously supported and defended his demands concerning Corinthia and Trieste. Perhaps Stalin felt threatened by Tito's celebrity; perhaps, inversely, that celebrity had given Tito his nerve. It remains true that the Cominform encyclical lent Tito even more brilliance on the international scene. Well known as a Communist leader, the civil and then military chief of the new Yugoslavia added the glory of an independent Communism to the glory that was already his, while continuing to draw some of his strength from the very thing he had broken with.

Thus began a new chapter in the history of Communism. The barely constituted Soviet empire had survived its first schism—one that was geographically limited but, in political terms, fundamental because it was inevitably accompanied by an ideological confrontation. Finding himself excommunicated, Tito had simultaneously to refute the terms of that excommunication and to turn the accusation of heresy back onto his accusers. He raised to the level of state the hypothesis of a break with Communism, which had been realized by numerous militants over the previous twenty years on an individual level, as they had shifted from excessive loyalty to an ever more categorical hostility to the mother church, while still using the common language. He was constrained by the almost hysterical violence of his prosecutors and diffuse pressure from his new admirers, not to mention the need to find allies. Thus a new Communist territorial pole arose, issuing more from circumstances than from human invention; it was close enough to the old Communist pole in its discourse and ideas to be able to serve as a substitute, and just distant enough to attract all those disaffected with the Communist revolution.

Tito had several imitators, which shows the extent to which the anti-Soviet discourse in Soviet language would, after him, constitute a revolutionary genre. Mao Tse-tung was the most famous to follow suit, but even Enver Hodja's tiny Albania would rise up against Moscow in later years, a pole of European Marxism-Leninism. After 1948, the Communist idea no longer had a single homeland. It became territorialized outside of the Soviet Union. Wherever history located it, and primarily in Yugoslavia, it was condemned in advance to the fate that had struck all messianic promises embodied by a territory or a regime: its life was bound to be more ephemeral than that of the Soviet mythology from which it arose, since it had neither the same seniority, nor the same influence, nor the same means of propaganda.

For a short time, however, Tito's Yugoslavia benefited from its novelty. It lacked the dramatic baggage of memories that had surrounded the history of the Soviet Union until 1941. It emerged from the anti-Fascist war, from the heroic resistance to a Wehrmacht-style guerrilla army; it was born of a coupling of the ideas of nationhood and revolution. It was thus the perfect symbol of a Communism that had been regenerated by anti-Nazism, which enabled it to benefit from past traditions without being burdened by them. The Yugoslav schism provided a fulcrum for the revolutionary passions of those who had discarded Stalinism. Those nostalgic for Lenin, many former partisans of Trotsky, as well as those disappointed by the Soviet Union, found the territory they were missing, so timely was the revolutionary idea. It came to represent the exoticism indispensable to the imagination: after the Russia of October, the poor Balkans were being reborn as the advance guard of European society.

Nonetheless, the schism was limited, more by what it sought to replace than by its own weakness. For, when threatened, the mother church set out to defend itself tooth and nail. Today we can hardly conceive the extreme violence with which the Cominform parties fought the very thing they were actually helping to build—namely, Titoism. The Cominform and the Communist parties leveled the same absurd accusations at Tito that they had showered on Trotsky before Stalin had him assassinated in Mexico City in 1940. Like Tito, Trotsky had defied not so much the Soviet regime as its leader, thus touching something beyond the Soviet regime—its very legitimacy in world history in the person of its only authorized interpreter. By the same token, he had been denounced as a counterrevolutionary, an accomplice of the Nazis, and an eternal conspirator against the USSR. Tito had none of Trotsky's intellectual gifts, even though, like Trotsky, he had the advantage of an important military reputation. But he had a nation behind him, which lent broader resonance to his defiance. The only thing the great exile of Bolshevism had been capable of doing was to collect small factions scattered about the world. The Croatian marshal brought greater means and wider forums to his quarrel.

It was a sign of the times that Tito managed neither to weaken the unity of the Communist world and its empire nor seriously to threaten the ideological legitimacy of Stalin. He could claim to be more loyal to Marxism-Leninism-Stalinism than anyone else, to have accelerated domestic agrarian collectivization, and to have avoided any rapprochement with the West,[16] but the USSR and its satellite countries treated him as a leper, to the point where his personality would soon become central to the trials of "traitors" who had infiltrated the Eastern European Communist parties, just as Trotsky had served as a target for the Moscow trials before World War II. Less than a year after his condemnation by the Cominform, the Rajk trial in Budapest, as François Fejtö has written, was nothing but an "ersatz of the Belgrade trial that could not take place. Rajk was more a witness than a defendant, the principal witness against Tito."[17] The schismatic of Belgrade had become a criminal, certified as such by his "accomplices" in neighboring countries.

Although Tito could not beat Stalin in the field of Marxism-Leninism, where he was fighting on enemy territory at a time when his adversary was at his most powerful, he had raised a problem that could not be laid to rest by repression or terror: the revolt of the nation-states within the Soviet empire. At the end of the war, the USSR had appeared to be the friend of the small nations it had liberated from oppression. That image was never more striking than in Belgrade, in the heart of a Serbia that traditionally looked up to its Russian big brother, and in the capital liberated by an army commanded jointly by Tito and the Soviet general Zhdanov. It was there, however, that less than four years later the first quarrel between yesterday's associates would break out. It was there that Yugoslavia's new leader, an old militant Stalinist and the founder of a particularly repressive regime, would assume the risk of a break with Moscow in the name of national independence. In his case, it mattered little that the reasons of state he was defending against the Russians were those of a federal state containing several small nations, for the idea that energized his unique undertaking was not that of ending Communism in favor of a greater, plurinational democracy, but of affirming the autonomy of the Yugoslav state in relation to the Soviet Union.

The problem posed by Tito as early as 1948 was related only tangentially to the demand for national independence. It was more particularly a demand for political autonomy from Moscow on the part of the new Communist states of Eastern Europe, which had been created in the immediate postwar years. It is almost self-evident that such a demand for autonomy comported a nod to nationalist sentiments; a few years later, this would become clearer in unitary counties such as Poland or Hungary than in federal states such as Yugoslavia. But Tito's quarrel with Moscow showed that the bone of contention was not so much national liberty as individual countries' domestic reasons of state, that is, the power of the local Communist parties in relation to the big brother party in the USSR. In this respect, the Yugoslav schism confirmed the international nature of the Communist system, narrowly centralized from Moscow. But in no way did it alter the nature of the Yugoslav Communist dictatorship. Tito, in his own way, continued to apply "socialism in one country," locked more than ever into Marxism-Leninism. The Soviet empire in its 1946–48 configuration did not last very long, but its disloyal offspring continued to speak its language even as they broke with it. Such is the constraint of ideology: centrifugal elements keep harking back to unity.

So trials were necessary to clear up the ambiguity. Once again, their function was not so much to draw attention to American imperialist plots as to unmask plots in which Communists had played a role. The October Revolution, extending to nations beyond Russia, surrounded by vassal republics, and transformed into an empire, continued to obey the laws that governed its development and devoured its own children. True, it went well beyond this framework, and, by exporting its spirit and its expeditious procedures to neighboring nations, it had begun by striking out at "class enemies." Those nations were still pretending to be democracies liberated from Fascism when they were compelled to expropriate, intimidate, or imprison the partisans of the social or political ancien régime that had remained outside of the National Fronts. The trial and execution of the Bulgarian peasant leader Nicolas Petkov in September of 1947 had been the apogee of the persecutions. But once these "popular democracies" had come under the direct and visible control of the local Communist parties, in 1947–48, they presented even more potential danger to the suspicious Stalin: the Yugoslav example beckoned them toward independence. Like the assassination of Kirov at the end of 1934, it set off the organized terrorism of "revolutionary vigilance."

Stalin did not need this pretext in order to maintain his iron grip on the Soviet Union. According to the most recent statistics available,[18] the population of the Gulag, after declining between 1941 and 1946, began to climb again in 1952–53 to reach levels higher than those of 1939–40. But although the repression continued under full steam, it no longer had the theatrical aspect it had lent to the Moscow trials before the war; it merely continued in an appallingly quotidian way, meticulously concealed from outsiders' eyes and hushed in deathly silence. The Terror, on the other hand, had moved westward, as if its pedagogy were indispensable to the still fragile grafts of Sovietism in the heart of Europe: that was the object of the Rajk trial, which was precisely patterned on the Moscow precedents, even down to the responses. What made things different from the prewar period was the substitution of roles: the Gestapo was played by the CIA, Trotsky by Tito, that of the old Bolsheviks by Rajk and his "accomplices."

The trial, which was a denunciation of the Yugoslav leader, also signified the early Sovietization of the satellite nations. By purging the Communist parties in those countries, having already broken their "bourgeois" opposition, Stalin undertook what since the Comintern period had been called the Bolshevization of those parties, that is, their complete enslavement to his will. From then on, every one of their leaders felt threatened; they could not allow themselves to indulge the nationalistic sentiments of their people, even in a small way. Born of the resistance to Soviet pressures, Tito's rupture ended in speedier Sovietization of the socialist camp. Stalin did nothing about the problems that ensued; he would simply drown Tito in "Bolshevik" orthodoxy.

He thereby condemned himself to worsening the situation. The Soviet Union, so often celebrated for solving the problem of nationalism within its own borders, came up against the outside world. With little difficulty, it had managed to put the entire former czarist empire under the control of Communist totalitarianism. In Eastern and Central Europe, however, it encountered societies that were proud of their membership in Europe and whose heritage did not include submission to the Muscovite bureaucrats. In Budapest and Warsaw, Russia hardly stood for civilization! To these long-suffering nations, which had been liberated and then reconquered and were thus all the more nostalgic for their pasts, the only thing Russia had to offer in order to maintain its yoke was the Communist idea. That idea, rejuvenated by the war and bolstered by the uncertainty of the future, could still seem attractive when freedom returned: once again, it drew the essential part of its ephemeral power from appearing to be the negation of Fascism. But after a few years it had become a part of the dismal logic of Sovietization, suffocating civil society by means of a national police and subordination to Moscow.

The Yugoslav crisis was the first test of Communism's power outside of Russia since October 1917—the first test of the universality of Sovietism. But Sovietism proved incapable of doing anything but reproduce its repressive traits, even in their most spectacular forms, as if its only universal aspect was force, concealed by ideology. The Eastern European nations had always known that Russia had been the last to enter the history of "civilization": now they were experiencing Soviet Communism, which, far from being farther along that path, as it proclaimed, required uniform submission, festooned with obligatory lies. All it could produce was a police state in lieu of a multinational state. In Western Europe it was possible to maintain the cult or the hope of a democratic Communism, or to live in the uncertainty of what was being achieved in its name; east of Prague, however, the idea was struck a mortal blow by the peoples' experience.

Incapable of being associated with liberty, Communism's only chance for survival lay in coexisting with the nationalist sentiment. By 1948–50, however, it had exhausted the credit it had drawn from the generalized hatred of Germany. It was all very well for Soviet propaganda to denounce the allegedly vengeful West Germans, but the time had passed when anti-Germanism could serve to make people in the liberated territories accept or like the Red Army. On the one hand, the scenario of a neo-Nazi Germany's being pushed by the Pentagon into an anti-Soviet war seemed rather unlikely, for it was patently clear that the Red Army had taken up its positions less in order to protect the small nations of Eastern Europe than to create a buffer zone of Communist states totally subjected to the USSR. It was not enough for those states to be "friends of the Soviet Union." It was not even enough for them to be obedient. They had to have the same regime as the USSR, the same institutions, and even the same words to disguise the same nature. The only thing "Communism in one country" could export was itself. Having planted its flags in the mosaic of the European nations that separated it from the West, it was forced to deal with their various traditions. The Soviet Union compelled them to organize themselves, one by one,[19] to conform to its own example, thus compounding national oppression with compulsory adoration of the oppressor-as-model. The situation reproduced colonialism in reverse, since it was confined to Europe: the "Oriental" power of Moscow absorbed even the former territories of the venerable Austro-Hungarian Empire. This reversal indicates the extent of the upheaval caused by the new division of Europe.

Thus the Communist movement, after many twists and turns, encountered once more and in a new configuration its oldest intellectual competitor—nationalism. The twentieth century had begun with the confrontation between the revolutionary passion and nationalist loyalties, a confrontation that had continued long after World War I to be the major component of European political battles. But Stalinism and Nazism corrupted its substance. The former had subjected worker internationalism to the unconditional defense of the Soviet regime. The latter had dishonored nationalism by mixing it with the notion of racial supremacy. World War II at first seemed to have thrived in these ruins, until it found its raison d'être in the anti-Fascist synthesis. But this circumstantial marriage of contradictory ideas, once it was victorious, revealed its contradiction: the union of Stalinism and national independence did not survive the Soviet Union's arrival among the ranks of world superpowers. It treated the countries that had fallen into its military orbit the same way the Comintern had treated the parties that had sworn allegiance to it. At least those parties had submitted voluntarily. Postwar Poland and Romania, however, had had no choice in their national destiny.

This was the background of all the political or judicial "affairs" that, secretly or openly, brought the popular democracies into conflict with their Soviet "protector."[20] Those sad events revealed the inequality of the adversaries, one of which was virtually beaten in advance; Tito was the major exception.[21] Everywhere else, the golden rule of unconditional solidarity with the USSR continued to be applied to militants who had become heads of government, the majority of whom had spent the war years in Moscow. "Applied" is an understatement. This rule was so fundamental and so internalized that it served as a universally accepted criterion in all the purges and as the principal accusation in all trials. During this period it became clear that the apparatchiks trained by the

Comintern were still indispensable to Cominform policy ten or twenty years later. The precise circumstances surrounding these internal crises remain largely unknown. But we do know that, in one way or another, they all had something to do with Soviet reasons of state, that is, with Soviet foreign policy. At the time of the Slánský trial, during Stalin's final years,[22] the prosecutors even resorted to anti-Semitism, alleging that there was an international Zionist plot; it was as though the dictator, before his death, no longer had any scruples about adopting, on a lesser scale, the theme of the greatest tragedy of the century.

Nonetheless, neither the violence, nor the purges, nor the trials could obscure the Tito affair. Having grown to include entire nations, the Communist movement found itself confronted with the illusions it had maintained about its universality. Its lies were exposed by their own reflections. Ideology was no longer sufficient to conceal the domination of a new Russian imperialism: that domination itself only gave rise, on the ruins of old regimes, to a more complete servitude. Internationalism was the mask of force; "popular" democracy was the mask of totalitarianism. The weakness of the system lay in these two distinct yet complementary facts: the first led to the second.

Having rebelled against Stalin, Tito soon had to conceive his own version of Communism. By the logic of national revolt when carried out by former Comintern members, this version necessarily assumed an ideological form, and became "revisionist." It tended to give special weight to what, until then, had simply been individual breaks in the history of Communism. Souvarine and Ruth Fischer had been mere activists in their respective parties and had been condemned or expelled by the Comintern. In one sense, Tito was the victim of the same destiny: after all, both before and after the war, many foreign militants had broken with Moscow—less over questions of liberty than over their margin of independence in deciding which strategy or tactics to apply in their own countries. But these feeble opponents to the Communist movement were compromised, divided, and easy to defeat or, at least, to isolate. Tito said nothing different from what they had said, but through the idea of nationhood he revealed the lies of revolutionary universalism. The damage was irreparable, and even later reconciliation could not affect its reach; on the contrary, it would extend it.

As Tito was shredding the veil of Communist universality, the confrontation between the two former allies was transforming the ideological heritage of the war. Once Hitler and Mussolini had been crushed and had disappeared from the scene, the peace revealed a Europe divided into two camps. Zhdanov had announced this division, as had Churchill and Truman before him.

The disappearance of Fascism automatically simplified the political scene. Soon the only antagonists left were capitalism and socialism, liberal democracy and "popular" democracy, in their living incarnations as the United States of America and the Soviet Union. Each of these modern political ideologies and immanent religions had its territories-elect, which henceforth corresponded strictly to the division of power superimposed on the ideological division.

Anti-Fascism, it is true, survived the death of Hitler and the end of Nazi Germany. The USSR and, following suit, the Cominform made anti-Fascism the center of their propaganda and used it to continue the war by other means. But the constant invocation of the Fascist peril after its disappearance was nothing compared to the democratic safe-conduct provided by the sacrifices and the victories of the Red Army. The very expression "anti-Fascism" was devalued because it was applied to too many cases too soon. Its strength lay in recent memories; it still had too many associations with its original reference to be extended much beyond them and to remain convincing. Demonizing the enemy was no longer a simple matter. The Nazis and their collaborators had been shot or imprisoned. The Communist idea, now deprived of a part of its traditional justification, had to give priority to pleading its own case—not only that of the Soviet regime itself, which had emerged from the war with increased prestige owing to its victory, but also that of the history of the Eastern European nations since that victory. The Soviet Union had extended westward, surrounding itself with a buffer zone of "protected" countries, which put the Communist societies into contact with the Western societies of Europe. It was more powerful, more visible, closer, but for that reason more vulnerable.

I do not mean that it was at a disadvantage in terms of strength simply because it did not have an atomic bomb until 1951. I am sidestepping this aspect of the beginning of the cold war so as to concentrate on the way the cold war affected the Communist idea, an idea brandished more than ever by the USSR. This period provides the best illustration of the way pure power and the visibility of that power were one of Communism's great assets at a time when the twentieth century was prostrate before history. That the Communist idea should be subjected, rapidly or more slowly but inexorably, to the repercussions of the cold war was also the inevitable price to be paid for its narrowly instrumental character. Universalized by armed force, how was it to retain the universality of its idea? Tito's schism illustrated the relevance of this question within the "socialist camp." But what of the territories outside of that camp, that is to say, the west?

There, the idea had not undergone the experience of Sovietism. Let us omit Western Germany from this discussion, for it had become a Federal Republic in 1949 and a refuge for millions of Germans who had fled before the Soviet advance or had been driven from their lands by the Poles, the Czechs, or the Hungarians. The West Germans had nothing more to learn about the violence of the Red Army or the extreme Germanophobia that set the tone in new "popular democratic" states. As a defeated, uprooted, guilty nation, the Federal Republic could manifest its hostility to Slavic Communism only in the silence of the polling booth. But the spectacle offered by the police dictatorship established in the former Soviet zone was open confirmation of its hostile feelings.

In the rest of Western Europe, the Red Army was famous only because of the distant echoes of its victories. The Communist world had moved closer geographically, but remained an object of indirect familiarity, influenced by the favorable opinion left by its victory over Hitler. Churchill and de Gaulle had begun their fight against the Communists very early, each in his own manner and as a function of their respective situations. With the Polish affair in the autumn of 1944, Churchill had realized both his own inability to have any effect on the situation and Stalin's intention to sew up all of Eastern Europe.[23] He knew that the Third World War had begun even before the Second had ended. De Gaulle, during the same period in France, had to put down the French Communist Party so as to reestablish a democratic regime. The Communists would have their revenge in January 1946 by distancing him from power, but their time had already passed. In the years that followed, the two most important anti-Fascists in Europe spearheaded the battle against the postwar Soviet menace.

What they represented would constitute the substance of Western European politics for almost half a century. This was not just a coincidental turning point but a profound, almost organic reaction on the part of Western societies seeking to preserve their independence and their way of life in a two-dimensional international political world. That reaction was not without bitterness since it proved their dependence on the United States. But that dependence also benefited them, for they contributed only a limited amount of financial or military aid. Great Britain, after maintaining the longest fight, had emerged weakened from the war; the armies of postwar France and Italy were incapable of measuring up to those of the USSR. The true guarantee of the balance of forces on either side of the Potsdam border was the presence of American troops in Germany.

Although Western Europe found itself in the "American camp" because of its objective situation, it belonged there by choice. Even in countries with strong Communist parties, such as France and Italy, election results left no doubt of that. The conservative parties were aided by the socialists, or vice versa, and huge majorities were built up in favor of "Atlanticism." Clement Attlee took up where Churchill had left off at Potsdam,[24] as a loyal heir to Churchill's hostility to the USSR. It was during this period that Léon Blum, speaking of the French Communist Party, invented the phrase "foreign nationalist party."[25] The old western democracies were still alive, even if the melancholy atmosphere of the period stemmed in part from a sense of their decline. The American presence in Europe also lent a unique aspect to the ideological battle of the time: whereas before the war the denunciation of the capitalist world by the Communists was aimed either at the parliamentary democracies of Paris and London or at the Fascist states, after the war it centered on the United States. Bourgeois Europe had lost its standing even among its adversaries.

Again, France provides the best perspective from which to understand the particular character assumed by this debate at the time. It was in France, ten or fifteen years earlier, that Communism had appeared for the first time in its victorious version, instigator and advocate of the Front populaire. It was also there that the twenty terrible months of the Hitler-Stalin pact were driven from memory by the French Resistance, to the point where the Communists were positioned as de Gaulle's rivals for several weeks after the Liberation, before unwillingly becoming his allies for a few months. In short, the French Communist Party, though partially Stalinized, had more than merely a strong class reality. It appeared to have cohabited happily with freedom, and it had fought for the nation: 1936 and 1945–46 were its touchstones as well as its great electoral years.

Since 1947, the situation had changed. Ousted from the government by the Socialists,[26] forced by the Cominform a few months later to harden its opposition, it was trapped in the logic of the cold war and forced to evoke its revolutionary mission just as prevailing circumstances were condemning in advance any Soviet-style "revolution." Stalin was digesting—with difficulty—his acquisitions, and Western Europe was moored to America. In France itself, the situation was the opposite of 1936: the Radicals and the Socialists, less numerous at the time, supported the Center and even the Center Right in the name of a foreign policy of defending freedom. United with the entire Left of the Front populaire, the French Communist Party had averted the threat of Fascism and had opened up the way to a coalition of social progress. From 1947 on, isolated in the middle of the political arena, it was battling democratic governments that consisted largely of former Resistance fighters, whom it accused of getting ready for the American war in collaboration with "neo-Fascist" de Gaulle. It offered no alternative ideas and was content to block, with its protesting presence, the normal functioning of alternating governance between Right and Left. It was a return of a Communism that predated "anti-Fascism" but that was enhanced by its victory over Fascism: it was a large, useless force, which success seemed to have rendered too bourgeois to resume the path of revolutionary gesticulation, but which, to the contrary, was being true to its origins and was led by the same men that had been trained during the "third phase." This illustrates yet again the extraordinary character of the Communist movement, whose various parties, despite their growth in size and numbers, so brilliantly continued to obey an international strategy.

For even though a long, losing battle had begun for Western Communist parties, isolated among their adversaries for belonging to the other camp, those adversaries believed the Communists at their apogee. In politics, they now lacked strong enough allies to be anything but followers and were unable to modify the dividing line of the cold war. But they still exerted—and painstakingly maintained—some influence over the public. Thanks to intellectuals, the Communist idea would cast its hottest cinders in Western Europe as it disappeared in the east: in the west it took advantage of its failure; in the east it was the victim of its victory. History proved yet again the polymorphous character of Communism.

This phenomenon, common to all of Western Europe, was particularly clear in France and Italy, where two powerful workers' parties gave intellectual philo-Communism the feeling of being on the side of the people. That feeling was used and abused by the parties in question quite shamelessly and excessively, since it gratified not only the vanity but also the anxiety specific to intellectuals. Their vanity was appeased by the recognition of an imaginary crowd, duly labeled as the tribunal of history by the representatives of the "working class," and their anxiety found an outlet in the desire to be of service. The Communist dons at Oxford and Cambridge had embraced the same historical movement as their French and Italian counterparts but, lacking a large "revolutionary" party, did not receive the same psychological reassurance. They may have needed it less, being children of a more glorious war, which had produced neither a Mussolini nor a June 1940–Vichy combination in their country. For Italian and French intellectuals, the Communist parties, along with a left-wing people, represented vengeance upon yesterday's parties.

Through the war and the Resistance, the Communist idea in the form of anti-Fascism conformed to the national democratic tradition and even constituted its high point. Viewed as a competition between the keepers of that tradition and their adversaries, national history drew its legitimacy from the French Revolution and the Risorgimento. It should not be forgotten, however, that these two events were themselves riddled with conflict and had already revealed the cowardice of a liberal bourgeoisie quick to deny what it had been fighting for. In late eighteenth-century France, the bourgeoisie had been forced to agree to an alliance with the popular classes, only to break with them almost immediately by guillotining Robespierre and opening the way to Thermidorian corruption and Napoleonic despotism. In mid-nineteenth-century Italy it preferred a compromise with the southern land-holding aristocracy and the Piedmontese monarchy to a revolutionary struggle for the emancipation of the people and the nation. A class without energy, always ready to drop liberty in favor of order, it resigned its responsibilities in the twentieth century to the benefit of Fascism. It backed Mussolini in Italy and Pétain in France. Only the "working class" could henceforth take control of the future of the nation. The chain of abstractions substituted for historical actors lent both nobility and necessity to "proletarian" anti-Fascism. It counteracted the popular and revolutionary side of Fascism by reducing it to what it despised: the bourgeois world. It thus recovered for the exclusive benefit of the "anti-Fascist" Left the critique of liberal falseness that the Left had shared with the bourgeoisie fifteen or twenty years earlier. History had chosen between the two pretenders to the reconstruction of the postindividualist social order. By the same token, there had been no better supporters of Mussolini or Pétain than the bourgeoisie. No one hostile to the Communists could possibly be a good democrat or a true anti-Fascist. When weak, the Soviet Union had been cherished like an endangered cause. When powerful, it was to be flattered as if it were an inevitable destiny.

We have encountered throughout this book the belief that gave rise to such amnesiac rationalizations and conformist judgments: it was the religion of history. It was now in its heyday, as though World War II had been its quintessential theater and verdict, accepted beforehand by its participants. For although Marxism had shaped it into a particular doctrine, it was quite generalized in one form or another. Perhaps the most common conviction was that morality in the modern age was totally contained in politics—the sole and ultimate depository of good and evil. Hence the only part of morality that was retained was the good conscience necessary to ideological fanaticism. Militant Communists drew their inner strength from the sense that they were accomplishing history as a supreme good and using force to the right ends. This mixture of genres was seen not seen as a disguise for cynicism but as a categorical imperative to counter "idealism"; many intellectuals—and members of the public at large—used it to justify the violence and crimes of Stalinist Bolshevism, absolving or even celebrating them in the name of the ends to which they were supposed to be merely the means. I remember reading, around 1947, Koestler's *Darkness at Noon* with great excitement, although it did not dissuade me from eventually joining the Communist Party. I admired the idea that the judge and the accused could agree to serve the same cause, the first as executioner and the second as victim. What I liked about this philosophical version of the Moscow trials was the march of historical reason, whose barbarous cult Koestler sought to denounce.

If the spirit of blind consent to the "rational" fait accompli originated in part in the violence that characterized the war, it was also fueled by a sense that the war had not put an end to anything, that it was still going on and may not yet have exhausted its virtues. The cold war was not a war, but it maintained the wartime spirit with a large dose of ideological Manichaeanism, in which Moscow was unrivaled. This was undoubtedly the reason why the great Communist turning point of 1947, a key date in the political life of Western democracies, varied in importance in the intellectual histories of those nations. The Communist parties were no longer in the back alleys of power, but they still exerted widespread intellectual and social influence, notably in France and Italy. In Italy, indeed, the Communist Party occupied the entire left-wing space with the involuntary complicity of a vassalized Pietro Nenni. The cold war had rearranged the governments for whom the Atlantic alliance was the rule. By putting the Communists out of power, it had at least left them the privileges of opposition and the control of grand memories.

Western Communism was no longer vulnerable, as in the past, to the great shifts of the International: it represented a revolution that had become a tradition. Having once again become a class war behind enemy lines, it hung onto all of its democratic and national capital. Born of World War I, it had grown up in opposition to the war. By contrast, it was helped by World War II, until the victors became divided. It lived on its patrimony rather than by its future prospects. The "proletarian revolution" that was its raison d'être was adjourned indefinitely by the international situation, or could not occur without a war. The revolutions that were supposed to have occurred in Eastern Europe were a good indication that their likelihood depended exclusively on geography; all the Communist west had to do was to embellish the account by paying homage to its history. These were strange years, when the propaganda of the new "anti-Fascism" reinvented Hitler in the guise of Adenauer, denounced American democracy in the name of freedom, and wreathed the Soviet empire in memories of the 1848 revolutions.

The pro-Communism of the French intellectuals won laurels which, sad to say, were well deserved. Many books have been written on the subject,[27] and I shall not go into details here. The enthusiasm for Communism was based on the old antiliberal animus that had dominated the Parisian scene in the 1930s in many different forms and within quite diverse traditions. By liquidating Fascism, the war had left the monopoly on that market of ideas to Communism. The total victory galvanized convinced believers, rallied the majority, intimidated those who were wavering, and, moreover, punished the guilty. Consistent with the USSR's role, the victory was more an anti-Fascist than a democratic one and could be celebrated without repressing a faint remaining inclination for the liberal exercise of democracy, so that even those who had changed camps, following history, could retain the same basic sentiments as before. The 1947 break between the former allies thus had little effect on intellectual life, since the conflict of ideas it brought to the forefront of politics had no name in the anti-Fascist repertory.

Added to this picture were particular features of the French tradition—for example, the national habit of conceiving of politics in universal terms, as if it were the natural locus for the emancipation of humanity. During the entire history of the Russian Revolution, the French Revolution had stood as its constant guarantee of legitimacy, confirming the inevitability of revolutions, since the bourgeoisie had resorted to one, and having entailed a short but exemplary period, which served as a model for Lenin. That this connection had long served as a historiographic dogma in France, in spite of the tenuous comparison between the two events, testifies to the extraordinarily abstract way in which the French intelligentsia conceived of the Bolshevik occurrence. Nineteen seventeen had doubled the universalism of 1789. The miraculous thing was that the idea continued to exist, stronger than ever, thirty years after 1917, as if Soviet history had been granted a reprieve in advance. Patterned on the French Revolution, the repressive aspect of the Russian Revolution was attributed to self-defense and thus to something external to its essence, which was, by definition, good. That vision, so typical of the heritage of the French Revolution, relieved the USSR of the burden of proof. It surely helps to explain the Parisian pro-Soviet zeal of that time.

With this ontological dovetailing of the two revolutions, French intellectuals reinvented a collective role for themselves that had been denied their nation by actual history since June 1940. Some had sympathized with the Vichy regime and, in a few spectacular cases, had even sympathized with the Nazis—whether coming from the Right or from pacifism. For those who had opposed Hitler—more and more numerous as the outcome of the war became clear—Gaullism was often suspect. The role played by its founder was that of a providential figure—something quite foreign to the republican tradition. Generals, even de Gaulle, did not pass easily for advocates of democracy and social progress. Even Raymond Aron, who had been in London since June 1940, shared some of these reservations,[28] and Malraux did not become a Gaullist until after the war.[29] On the contrary, anti-Fascism permitted intellectuals to celebrate their reunion with the national revolutionary tradition, which was indissolubly democratic and patriotic. Once again they found themselves in the best seats of the theater of history, like their forebears of 1789 and 1793, and in the role of social prophets that they had held since the eighteenth century. Furthermore, for anyone who wanted it, Marxism-Leninism provided a doctrine for these imaginary reunions, with the idea of a science of history whose secrets were known only by an advance guard.

The right to collective ownership of the revolutionary reference allowed the French both to obscure the national decline and to regain a mission. This, it seems to me, is one of the main reasons for the Communist Party's ability to enchant a great number of French intellectuals. Not that there were no other reasons, even more mechanical ones. In France, as elsewhere, Communism appealed not only to individuals' idealism and ignorance but also to a hidden taste for power, sometimes associated with a masochistic passion for force. In French culture, Aragon was its most famous victim and most accomplished manipulator. But the Party's power to flatter or intimidate was based on a different order of reality. What made it so efficacious at the time was what progressively emptied it of its content in the decades that followed. The Party held the patent on the "October Revolution" label, which, in turn, ordered the universality of the revolutionary tradition. To say that it watched over its treasure is an understatement.

The French case shows us why almost all the major debates on postwar ideas revolved around a single question: the nature of the Soviet regime, which was ardently defended by Communist and progressive intellectuals as an expression of the essence of the socialist revolution. This discussion was as old as the USSR itself but had never been so central. During the Popular Front years, until the complete victory of the Left, it had always been lurking around the public stage, but it occupied a secondary position compared to the fight against Hitler and the question of war or peace. After the victory, the USSR was more anti-Fascist than ever, but the Fascist enemy had been defeated. It was stronger than ever, though also more exposed, faced with the United States and Western Europe. Even during the anti-Communist hysteria led by Senator McCarthy in 1950–54 it was hardly feasible to think of Truman and Eisenhower's America as neo-Nazi, since American soldiers had crossed such great distances to defeat Hitler in France. As for Western Europe, it was remaking its wealth without glory but democratically, under the protection of the United States and, initially, with its aid. Western Germany had joined the constitutional order. The Soviet regime, deprived of a Fascist foil, would find itself on the front line, obliged to make a case not for its origins but for its essence.

At the start of the cold war, the Soviet Union—not yet a nuclear power—hid its military inferiority behind a world campaign for peace. But while pacifists, thanks to the condemnation of the Soviet Union at Versailles, had been almost accidentally pro-Soviet between 1918 and 1935, there was a turnaround after 1945. From then on, critics of the American arms buildup appeared to be condoning the other superpower and its dubious role in mounting international tensions. Although Stalin was no Hitler, Russia had control of Central and Eastern Europe. North Korea's attack on South Korea in June 1950 cast doubt on purely circumstantial explanations of the Soviet peace effort.

The cold war, which in those years had really become a war, set two different political and social systems against each other. It brought the ideological character of the twentieth century to its apex, simplifying the world into two camps, and subsuming the idea of nationhood, to the extent that it remained important, under the idea of an empire or a bloc. Communism necessarily benefited from this division, but more for what it had been, and for what had been constructed in its name, than for what it opposed: it was a world power, victorious in China, visible in Europe as far as Prague, and the apparent bearer of the future, whereas the old Western nations were in decline. It was during the cold war that Communism attained its greatest influence, combined with extreme vulnerability: its existence was countering its very essence. French intellectuals put more stock than ever in its essence, but in doing so they had to swear allegiance to what Kostas Papaioannou called the "cold ideology,"[30] declare that Rajk and Slánský were guilty, deny the existence of concentration camps in the USSR,[31] swear that a "proletarian science" was being born, celebrate Stalin as universal genius, and so on. The pleasure of voluntary servitude was exhausted in these successive exercises, which history, through the mouth of the Party, continued to renew.

This was the beginning of the misunderstanding between Western and Eastern Europe from which we have not yet emerged.[32] The Communist idea reached its zenith in Rome and Paris just at the time when in Warsaw and Budapest it was becoming little more than a mask for Russian oppression. Born of Western philosophy, Communism had reigned in Moscow. Winner of the war, it had extended its reach as far as Leipzig and Prague. In Eastern and Central Europe, its "idea" did not long survive its governance; in Western Europe, however, it blossomed, thanks to the role it had played in the war against Hitler, but without regard for the despotism being established in its name in the east. Thus imposed by the force of people and circumstances, the iron curtain between the two Europes existed in people's minds but not along the confrontational lines of the two camps, separating the Communists in the east from those in the west. In the Central and Eastern European nations, the credit extended to the Communists by the intelligentsia was running dry as early as the 1950s, whereas the majority of Western intellectuals, followed by a vast portion of public opinion, continued to surround postwar Communism with the respect due to the ideas it was supposed to incarnate. Seen from Paris, Rome, or Oxford, the universal validity of the cause was independent of what was happening in Warsaw, Prague, or Budapest. The Western intelligentsia, moreover, had always flattered itself that it had been chosen by a history "more universal" than that of the Poles, the Czechs, or the Hungarians, and so it unwittingly also invested an old superiority complex in the Communist abstraction. It was quite enough that intellectuals were obliged to share their privilege of universality with eccentric Russia: Why should they have to back off in the face of Polish nationalists or reactionary Hungarians?

Abandoned in 1938 to the Germans by the Munich agreement, in 1945 to the USSR and its carving knife by the Yalta and Potsdam agreements, the nations of Eastern and Central Europe were eventually so far forgotten even by Western Europe that they lost their names in the collective designations drawn from Soviet vocabulary—the "popular democracies," the "socialist camp," or simply "Eastern Europe." Unlike the first two abandonments, the third had not been forcibly imposed but had come about through the opium of ideology, which simply suppressed its object. Daladier was aware that he was letting go of Czechoslovakia, and Churchill knew that he was doing the same thing to Poland. The question no longer arose for Western intellectuals, since those states and their neighbors had been reduced to reference points along the road to Soviet socialism. In its extreme form, this blindness was short-lived; but it took a long time to die.

By assuming a central role in world politics, the cold war had hardly modified the great ideological heritage of European politics — or, at least it had done so very slowly. Enhanced by the war and the victory, the image of the Soviet Union had renewed its strength. The ghost of Hitler continued to offer it a democratic guarantee, and Stalin provided it with a raft of good memories.

In the United States, however, the anti-Soviet turn taken by postwar public opinion was so great that it quickly brought on the crises of intolerance and suspicion often hidden in American populism. The Transatlantic aspect of Communist history is not the subject of this book, but its repercussions on the situation in Europe are worth considering.

Communism had never been powerful in the United States, where free enterprise is widely regarded as one of the key constituent elements of liberty. In the 1930s, however, it had put down a few roots, though small ones, as if an interest in Communism were a necessary ingredient of the weltanschauung of a good "liberal" and, even more so, of a "radical"—what Europeans call a left-wing militant. The Great Depression had brought the idea of state economic intervention into fashion, and Hitler's emergence in 1933 had redirected attention, in the form of anti-Fascism, to the problems of Europe. This theme had already made Roosevelt's fortune, first as the inventor of the New Deal and then as Hitler's conqueror. It had, however, also fostered a timid development of a Communist Party, several thousand strong, to the left of "Rooseveltism," which polarized the attention of New York intellectuals. Hence there arose in the pre–World War II United States a microcosm of the peculiar features of Communist politics: a Stalinist and unitary party that was conspiratorial and anti-Fascist and was composed of apparatchiks and idealists—two not necessarily incompatible characteristics. The party had little influence beyond New York and, aside from a handful of union cadres, it touched only a middle class of recent immigrants, including a considerable number of Central and Eastern

European Jews—students, professors, lawyers, and show-business professionals—who had transplanted the Bolshevik legend into their new country, where it had no roots.

The period of the Hitler-Stalin pact had plunged the American Communist Party into an isolation all the more complete since it had reacted like a good Comintern soldier, shifting from one day to the next from anti-Fascism to the "imperialist war." But Hitler's 1941 attack on the USSR put the American Communists back in line with Roosevelt's policy: now they advocated that the United States should enter the war, and later, with great hue and cry, which this time resulted in success, they pushed for the opening of a "second front" in Europe. These were the best years of the tiny American Communist Party's rocky marriage with the United States, for it was drawing its strength from what it was not, determinedly representing the left wing of the Democratic Party and preaching national unity louder than anyone else. Not that public opinion had become, even during the war, pro-Soviet, let alone pro-Communist. The Republican Party and the American Right in general remained staunchly anti-Communist, often attacking the New Deal as an alliance between the liberals, the unions, and the "Reds." The presidential elections of 1944 had occasioned violent attacks along these lines on the outgoing president. During the war, however, the analogy between Hitler and Stalin, which had been a commonplace in the American press during the 1930s,[33] was played down, to the benefit of more optimistic appraisals of at least the future of the USSR. That was the logic of the war, and Roosevelt himself had set the example when he believed victory would lead Stalin to liberalize his dictatorship. How could he have imagined that all the blood spilled fighting Hitler's armies had not been for the cause of liberty?

Nonetheless, conflict with the Soviet Union concerning the new European borders began immediately after the war. Already during the last years of the Roosevelt administration and even more in Truman's first years, American top diplomatic and military personnel were worried about what they saw coming, and in the following years the comparison between Hitler and Stalin reappeared and became widespread.[34] Knowledge of the Soviet regime was quite elementary in the United States at this time; the Hitler-Stalin analogy served as something of a substitute. This was risky, since it cast the Soviet Union in 1946 and 1947 as an aggressor as imminent as Hitler had been in 1938 and 1939 and thus contributed, under the pretext of avoiding another Munich, to a psychosis of inevitable war.

It was when, just after the war, the American Communist Party attained its zenith—a modest zenith, its membership amounting to forty or fifty thousand—that it lacked fertile ground. It had totally failed to popularize the Communist idea in American society, but it had furnished a local accompaniment to the American-Soviet alliance. The acrimonious falling apart of the alliance isolated even the left wing of the Democratic Party. Worse still: Stalin demanded a repudiation of the American Communists' best years. In the spring of 1945, through Jacques Duclos,[35] Stalin condemned their opportunistic policy toward Rooseveltism and their forsaking of class struggle. In the index of deviations, he named this policy "Browderism" after Earl Browder, the former General Secretary of the American Communist party who had been thrown out in February 1946 as a "social imperialist."

Why did Stalin choose the small American Communist Party as the place to announce the revival of "class struggle" more than two years before the creation of the Cominform and the great relaunching of the cold war? American Communism, unlike French or Italian Communism, had neither actual nor potential influence; already feeble, it could hardly be weakened. Its strategic interest, in the new disposition of power, was its location in the heart of imperialism.[36] As far as American Communists were concerned, the "leftward" turn that occurred after Yalta, accentuated by the general realignment of 1947, was not strictly directed at foreign policy objectives. The Party would practice class struggle more or less as before, but its general plan was to have Henry Wallace, a pro-Soviet politician and former vice-president under Roosevelt between 1940 and 1944, run in the elections of 1948 in the name of the Progressive Party, which the Communists controlled.

In November 1948, however, in the midst of the Berlin crisis, the candidate barely exceeded a million votes, and in the following years the new party was little more than a legal facade for persecuted Communists. It had not succeeded in making a serious dent either in the union movement or in democratic public opinion. Even though its 1948 score marked the high point of its influence, it remained—as Dwight Macdonald, one of the most intelligent observers of the period and the prisoner of a rocky love story with the American Far Left, described it[37]—narrowly "Stalinoid" or even "totalitarian-liberal." Macdonald showed how Communism, then so powerful in Paris and Rome, exercised exactly the same fascination in New York but on an extremely reduced scale. Wallace admired the USSR as the great workshop of the future and as yesterday's great ally.[38] He accused Truman of betraying that alliance to follow in the footsteps of the Nazis, turning against the Communists the texts and strategies that had been used against the fifth column during the war. American progressivism too was in the grip of the century that abolished the space between Communism and Fascism.

Macdonald would be crushed under the weight of another simplification—in vogue between 1939 and 1941—according to which Fascism and Communism were merely two periods in the continuing threat to democracy and to the American nation. Hitler had been defeated, but Stalin was more powerful than ever. Because his sole enemy was the United States, Stalin was a more direct menace than Hitler had ever been before the war. "Red Fascism," to revive an expression of the time, went beyond the monstrousness that Nazism had revealed before it was defeated, imposing a presence that Nazism had never had. Even more than Nazism, it had its "fifth column," which was both public and clandestine in the United States. Although the American Communist Party was too weak to initiate policy, it was strong enough to set off a "Red hunt."

The typically American political phenomenon which, between 1950 and 1954, would become "McCarthyism,"[39] named after the senator from Wisconsin who would be its Grand Inquisitor, had its prehistory in the two last years of Truman's first term, and was fostered by the Democratic Party's allying itself to the anti-Communist cause, both at home and abroad. The "Truman Doctrine" and the decree ordering loyalty oaths from Federal employees, though not explicitly related to each other, both date from March 1947. McCarthyism set in motion a threat to the constitutional liberties of American citizens in the name of the defense of the Constitution; it was as though the fear of Communism, this time in the most unanimously liberal democracy in the world, was once again fueling ideological passions opposite yet similar to those of the hated adversary.

McCarthyism was linked primarily to a pathological discovery of power. The war had just ended. The nations of Central and Eastern Europe—associated with the roots and even the memories of so many Americans—were rapidly locked into the Soviet orbit, while freedom in Poland had been defended in vain by Churchill. The United States discovered that it was the only power that could counter the influence of Sovietism, which had become an international system in Europe and elsewhere. Americans were unaccustomed to being engaged in world affairs. They reacted and overreacted to the new situation with ambivalence and excess, with the fear of subversion and the arrogance of power.

Their fear, oddly enough, expressed an accurate intuition about the nature of the enemy, coupled with a false sense of its power. Paranoid fear of a conspiracy against the sovereignty of the people appears in all crises of modern democracy. In the United States, such fears were not entirely baseless, for conspiracy was indeed one of the facets of Communism.[40] But to be as threatening as Americans thought it was, and sufficiently formidable to justify domestic mobilization to protect national security, that conspiracy had to reflect the spectacular international strength of the Communist movement. As representatives of the adversary, the American Communists, long denounced by the Republicans, became more than spies, whether active or potential, after 1949: they were cast as public enemies, supported openly or clandestinely by the connections they had woven over the years. In keeping with the logic of this type of phenomenon—a logic that further solidified public opinion—the accusation was extended to all those who, at one time or another during the 1930s, had followed, listened to, or met Communists. Inquisitions and denunciations criss-crossed America like so many exercises in virtue.

For the anti-Communist crusade was also a crusade of the good. The United States is a country unlike any other: its shared history creates the foundation of its body politic. It is a collectivity of European immigrants whose national identity rests on the ideas of liberty and democracy. The twentieth century was making those ideas not only into the tree of life, in whose shade Americans could pursue life and happiness, but into a treasure that was threatened and that only the Americans could save. America was born as the land blessed by God. In the nineteenth century, it had represented the paradise of the poor. In both its religious version and its degraded form, Democratic messianism was part of its patrimony. So the American mobilization against Communism was like an appeal to destiny. The Americans had come into world affairs accidentally, as a result of their formidable influence, through technical performance rather than an explicit will to dominate. Having discovered their power, they clothed it in a mission that included the *pax americana* of the second half of the twentieth century, and they discovered that the secrets of the American way of life—religion, democracy, free enterprise—were everywhere up against Communism, which was atheistic, despotic, and collectivistic.

McCarthyism renewed the antiliberal violence that had characterized many populist movements in American history. The "people," bearer of the values of the nation, obsessed with the treason of the elites, rallied behind the demagogues. They rediscovered the "nativist" tradition,[41] which was xenophobic and determined to track down anything "un-American" in America, anything that smacked of a cosmopolitanism of which intellectuals were the almost natural forerunners. The social reality of Communism and "progressivism" in the United States provided a special target for the anti-intellectualism underlying the national political character.[42] The paradoxical aspect of the "Red fear" was that in transforming a foreign adversary into a domestic one, it mobilized the isolationist tradition of American public opinion for the cause of an interventionist foreign policy.

That particular chemistry of political passions had already been manifest in the revolutionary tradition, which the American Right professed to abhor: the French Revolution had justified the Terror, at least partially,[43] by invoking the threat to its borders. The Soviet revolution was still obsessed with plots and "imperialist" aggression: twenty years after October, with the Moscow trials, Stalin put the theater of conspiracies back into business in Budapest and Prague. Senator McCarthy drew from the same source, but in a democratic context: his tyranny was only temporary. He manipulated popular emotions fanned by bad news from abroad—the Berlin blockade in 1948, the "loss of China" in 1949,[44] the Korean War in 1950. Among the Americans who cried treason were those isolationists who, in 1940–41, had openly or silently opposed the United States' entry into the war. But the logic of the international context enrolled them in the service of America as a world power; in that service they met more enlightened, more modern, better informed liberals. Indignant as they were about the way in which Stalin had taken over Eastern and Central Europe, anxious as they were about the war in the Far East, they had weighed the new constraints of superpower status and preferred cold war anti-Communism to the ideology of the House Committee on Un-American Activities. It was within this dialectic that a new idea of the United States' mission to the world evolved, along with a consensus on bipartisan foreign policy. Eisenhower, on succeeding Truman in 1952, became the quintessential symbol of the new idea: the military leader of World War II, now called upon to be the political leader in what threatened to be World War III; the reconciler of anti-Fascism and anti-Communism; the man entrusted, in the name of the Republican Party, with the international heritage of Roosevelt, which had already been modified by Truman. Senator McCarthy did not long survive this synthetic electoral hodgepodge. He could not make the hysteria of suspicion last, and in any case his battle against domestic Communism had already been won.

As a whole, the McCarthy episode showed how American democracy, woven of the same political ideas as Western Europe, deployed and employed these ideas in its own way. In addition to economic disparity and differences in objectives and volition, there was now a disparity of power between the European nations and the United States. Western Europeans were not comfortable with the bipolarization of the world, for it emphasized their own decline and their reluctance to pay the human and material price of a vast military program. American protection spared them that price and masked their hesitation to return to the soft pacifism of the 1930s. They found it hard to envision the democratic idea as an anti-Communist crusade, not only because the war was still so recent, but because Truman's America seemed to have confirmed that imperialism, the highest stage of capitalism, was inseparable from Fascist dictatorship.

History would not grant the Cominform a Fascist America: only a total ignorance of American history could allow McCarthyism to be characterized as Fascism. To the Europeans, however, American democracy remained too capitalist not to arouse constant suspicions that it was concealing the domination of money under a discourse of freedom. The United States' world leadership, due to a mixture of circumstances and ambition, had stripped the democratic idea of any Communist connection. It was thus made into pure liberty, an almost religious affirmation of the individual and, hence, separated from the social and vulnerable to the critique of formal rights by actual rights. The ideological crusade of the United States brought Communism and democracy face to face for the first time in the twentieth century, but at the cost of purifying the democratic idea, which was not traditional to Europe. As the American intelligentsia was converting en masse to anti-Communism, most European intellectuals were wondering why. They could not agree that the price to pay for the defense of liberty against Stalin was to extend their blessing to the American cult of free enterprise. It was cheaper for them to be anti-American than anti-Soviet, or to take intellectual comfort in a dual critique that rejected both adversaries. That twofold rejection had only the appearance of impartiality: what was bad about the USSR was attributed not to the system but to circumstances; with the United States, the system was blamed. Cold war pro-Communism was less and less protected by anti-Fascism, but it relied more and more on the anti-capitalist alibi in the almost ideal form provided by the United States.

A good measure of such reliance was the limited political repercussions—reinforced by later cultural success—of initiatives like the "Congress for Cultural Freedom"[45] in France and Italy and, to a lesser degree, in England. The idea originated in the United States, where, in the spring of 1949, in opposition to a Communist-organized "peace" rally in New York, a number of American anti-Communist intellectuals gathered under the aegis of some big names.[46] Almost all were "liberals" or "radicals" indignant at the Cominform's revival of an "anti-Nazi" campaign against the United States. Almost all detested McCarthyism as a perversion of American democracy.

International visibility for this New York initiative was ensured by a meeting between organizational genius and nostalgia for agitprop in the persons of Irving Brown and Arthur Koestler. The purpose was to beat Moscow in the battle of ideas on a large stage, much as Münzenberg had orchestrated grand demonstrations for the "defense of culture"— even the wording was remarkably similar—before World War II.[47] The Communists, moreover, had not lost their touch, and had undertaken many initiatives of this type since the beginning of the cold war.[48]

Koestler had served under Münzenberg. He was consumed by a desire to reverse his course in the service of truth. His bohemian and flamboyant personality, combined with the talents of a first-rate writer, was too literary for a prophet. Nevertheless, he did set the tone for the first meeting of the Congress in Berlin—then a Western enclave in the Communist world—in June 1950, at the beginning of the Korean War. Certain members of his milieu who, like him, had been born at the beginning of the century and, also like him, were former Communists who had survived the great illusion were determined to oppose the war, each in his own style. Ignazio Silone was mainly a witness,[49] whereas Frank Borkenau was a fighter.[50] No one intended to repudiate anti-Fascism but, rather, to prolong its spirit by fighting liberty's other enemy. The assembly that gathered in Berlin held impeccable credentials on this issue; the most illustrious participants were John Dewey, Bertrand Russell, Jacques Maritain, Benedetto Croce, and Karl Jaspers. The others, too, were more left- than right-wing, whether liberals such as Raymond Aron or Hugh Trevor-Roper, or Social Democrats such as Carlo Schmidt or André Philip. This was even more true of the American participants, for in this setting the Left could unflinchingly define itself as both anti-Communist and hostile to McCarthyism. Participants sympathetic to McCarthy, such James Burnham, were rare. A few, like Burnham, had flirted with the Trotskyist or libertarian Far Left, which had produced, among others, the American union leader Irving Brown, the fiery representative to Europe of the American Federation of Labor.[51] In short, the Berlin meeting gathered those who, by free choice, hated the Communists, and formed a battalion bearing the signature of the United States.[52]

In time, the Congress for Cultural Freedom became established among the intellectual milieus of Western Europe, as attested to by the success of its remarkable publications—*Der Monat,* in German, *Encounter,* in English, and *Preuves,* in French. But the militancy that its founders had wanted to give it barely outlasted the Berlin meeting. Neither liberals nor socialists were made for crusades, and Irving Brown's guests had remained free in a way that Münzenberg's had not. Many of them, primarily Trevor-Roper and Russell, but also Silone, were uneasy with Koestler's Manichaeanism. The least one could say was that the intellectual climate of Western Europe was not conducive to it: in France and Italy, anti-Communists were more than ever suspected of Fascist tendencies; McCarthyism had revealed the bad side of America. Having established its headquarters in Paris and organized a brilliant music and arts festival there in 1952, the Congress had landed in a hostile milieu. For the immediate future, it had widened rather than narrowed the gap separating Paris from New York.

Yet the main intellectual contribution to the analysis of Communism during these years came from the United States, though indirectly. It extended into the postwar context the train of German anti-totalitarian thought of the 1930s. Hannah Arendt published *The Origins of Totalitarianism* in 1951.[53] A German Jew, driven out of Germany in 1933, Arendt fled from France to the United States in 1941 and became a U.S. citizen. The significance of her ultimate nationality was that the United States had offered her a political setting where she could live as a citizen, free and without roots. Deliberately "modern," cut off from tradition, she did not cease to be either German or Jewish, and remained both, passionately.[54] The most profound part of her personality was her tender and ardent relationship with *Kultur*, which dated back to her student years when she was studying with Heidegger and Jaspers.[55] She had lifelong contempt—inherited from her teachers—for the French literati, whom she regarded as brilliant, talented, full of ideas, but soulless and indifferent to the truth. She was interested in Zionism, stemming from her hatred for the psychology of the assimilated Jew who wanted so much to be part of an anti-Semitic society. Hitler had condemned her to the fate of Jews—the choice between becoming a parvenu or a pariah. Abhorring the first choice, she embraced the second, which led her to the bohemia of German émigrés in Paris and New York. In New York she met the love of her life, Heinrich Blücher, who was also a pariah but from Bolshevism since he was the alter ego of Heinrich Brandler, the great loser of the German October of 1923.

Amid the world's indifference to the Jewish tragedy, Arendt set herself apart by the passion with which she sought to share, combat, and understand that indifference. Moderation was not in her nature. In Paris, before the war, no one listened to the German Jews for fear that they would drag France into the war. Hannah Arendt worked for Zionist organizations in France; but she returned from a first trip to Palestine, in 1935, uncertain about the general direction of the colonists' project, admiring the colonists' energy but horrified by the social conformity that reigned in the kibbutzim. Her hatred of the nation-state made Jewish nationalism repellent to her. In New York at the beginning of the war, she fought for the creation of a Jewish army to fight Hitler with her unfailing sense of the impracticable; she wanted that army to be independent of the Zionist parties and notables, whereas American Jews could not undertake such a project without appearing to be bad Americans, to say nothing of the hostility that such a thing would arouse among the British. She was, however, one of the first—in early 1943— to raise her voice and alert the public to the hideous plight of the European Jews. She understood better than anyone the terrifying new dimension of what was occurring in Germany—her literary and poetic homeland. She felt as though she had been chosen to be the prophet of the massacre of the Jews by a nation to which she still belonged. Having left Germany once and for all—or so she thought at the time—she remained its witness, as she had once been its child.[56] This existential center of gravity was the background of her tumultuous relations with Zionism.

The Origins of Totalitarianism was conceived in 1943 in an attempt to understand the *unnecessary* character of the massacres of the Jews. At first disbelieving of the unspeakable news from Europe, Arendt bowed to the facts in early 1943. Why had she been incredulous? Because wars were normally between enemies, but "this was different. This was really as though the abyss had opened."[57] Arendt's gift lay at the intersection of current events and philosophy; she could ponder events more deeply than a journalist. The question raised by Hitler's dictatorship, after the horror of the regime, was its novelty. The mystery of Nazism was that it had no precedents either in history itself or in the political typologies of the classic authors. How could one even conceive of it?[58]

By definition, no imaginable "causes" could be assigned to Nazism, for they would reduce the phenomenon to what came before it. The problem was its "origins," and the terrain on which its various elements developed. Arendt's first major culprit was the nation-state as it had emerged in European history, where it had been an intellectual obsession since the sixteenth century. Its high point coincided with the beginnings of its pathology in the second half of the nineteenth century. What Arendt liked about America was that the federal idea was detached from the idea of nationality; this, at least, was her somewhat simplistic notion of it. In the absence of a truly national state and a tradition along the same lines, this arrangement allowed the republican exercise of liberty, whereas in Europe, in the late nineteenth century, nation-states were grappling with problems they could not resolve—anti-Semitism, chauvinistic reactions to the "Jewish question" unresolved by assimilation, and imperialism, the nationalistic form of the universalization of the world. The Nazi state had been a mad, criminal response to the challenges issuing from the 1880s.

From these thoughts emerged the various outlines that Hannah Arendt drew up for the book between 1944 and 1946, in the following sequence: the disintegration of the national state—anti-Semitism—imperialism—racist imperialism (Nazism). She drew her inspiration, without always acknowledging her debt, from German immigrant authors like herself who had been the first historians of the Nazi state—Frank Borkenau, cited above, and, more especially, Franz Neumann, whose *Behemoth* came out in 1942.[59] The term "race-imperialism" as applied to Nazism came from Neumann. His book is the classic documentary study of the structure of the Nazi state. The novelty of Arendt's book was the appearance of the word "totalitarianism" in the final version of her plan in early 1947: anti-Semitism—imperialism—totalitarianism. Her use of the word revived a comparison made during the 1930s that had become taboo since 1945: the association of the two twentieth-century totalitarianisms—Nazi Germany and the Soviet Union.

Arendt's huge, loosely knit book came out in 1951. The first parts were devoted to anti-Semitism and imperialism. They had been written and partially published in article form between 1944 and 1946, when the author was planning to trace only the origins of Nazism. Not that these articles were exclusively about German history: they were concerned more with Europe in general and the subterranean but massive currents that led to the decline of the nation-state, which formed the background to the German catastrophe. For example, modern anti-Semitism, which for Arendt was inseparable from the earlier assimilation of the Jews into the framework of the nation-state, appeared primarily in nineteenth-century Germany and France. In the absence of any specific political shape, imperialism—which was linked to the savage expansionism of the bourgeoisie and led to the pure domination of man over man—was above all a European phenomenon. Arendt spotted the political alliance of "capital and the mob," cemented by a racial ideology, that it produced in France with the Dreyfus Affair, in Victorian England and throughout the British Empire with the idea of the racial superiority of the colonists, and finally, in its continental form, in the pan-German and pan-Slav movements. In the latter case, the crisis of the nation-state attained its extreme point, for the traditional parties and even the nation-states' very legitimacy were brought into question in the name of a racial concept even greater than the nation-state, a concept it was accused of betraying. Although it was easy and even necessary to trace a connection between pan-Germanism and Nazism, the implicit link suggested by Arendt between pan-Slavism and Soviet Communism seems rather arbitrary.

There are really two books in one. The first, including parts one and two, is certainly about the origins of "totalitarianism" but deals almost exclusively with Nazism, since it focuses on the appearance of modern anti-Semitism and ideologies of racial superiority. The second, consisting of part three and written later, in 1948–49,[60] links up again with the contrasting tradition opened up after 1934 by Waldemar Gurian, who was, incidentally, a friend of Arendt's. Here she undertakes a systematic comparison between the Hitlerian and the Stalinist regimes. Both subject matter and conceptual framework are different. In parts one and two, Arendt makes much use of the Marxist Social Democratic tradition from Hilferding to Neumann—the source of the notion of racism as part of the universalization of the world by capital. In part three, the antiliberal and antibourgeois polemic gives way to the analytical denunciation of both left- and right-wing "totalitarian" systems and ideologies. The role of capital disappears in this part of the book. Both Stalinist Russia and Nazi Germany were populated by the uprooted and dehumanized "populace" which, for Arendt, represents the opposite of a free citizenry, even though money was not the source of its dissolution. This comparison is taken up from another angle.[61]

The age of concentration camps was not yet over. This central intuition served as the basis for comparing the two totalitarianisms. Through this gateway to suffering, the European author who was among the first to be struck by the martyrdom of the Jews was also the one most capable of comprehending the suffering of other peoples, beginning with that of the Russians. Her empathy was all the more striking because indifference to the misfortunes of the Russians was widespread in the twentieth century. At the time, literature dealing with the concentration camps—on both sides—was still quite recent. Arendt had read David Rousset's books *L'Univers concentrationnaire* and *Les jours de notre mort*,[62] Eugen Kogon's *Der SS Staat*,[63] an anonymous memoir of the Russian camps entitled *The Dark Side of the Moon*,[64] and, no doubt, the debates over the Kravchenko trial in Paris. To her, the existence of a vast, uprooted population, stripped of rights, submitted to an absolutely arbitrary power, and treated as an object for social experimentation was the distinctive trait of totalitarian societies, since it was something entirely new in history. Despotism, tyranny, and dictatorship had always existed, of course. But totalitarian horror was new insofar as it was carried out by people and exceeded the boundaries of the human order by constituting its absolute negation. Lacking the means of identifying it with any of the known passions, neither the philosophical nor the political tradition had a name for it.

Its cradle was modern democracy or, rather, the degraded form of democracy in which society had become a mere collection of individuals isolated from one another and deprived not only of civic bonds but of class solidarity, and unified only by the pure force of numbers and the elementary emotions invested in a demagogue. It was the pathological end stage of bourgeois individualism, transformed into antibourgeois violence. Politics persisted only in its most primitive form—the need for unity. The citizens' homeland, the natural locus of liberty, had become the instrument for a unique form of subjection that was not only consensual but loudly declaimed. Once established by the masses, the totalitarian dictatorship consolidated the ground from which it had arisen by removing from society all remaining means to autonomy. Hitler destroyed the Länder, the parties, the aristocracy, and the independent associations; he superimposed a one-party apparatus upon all that he had not destroyed. Stalin, heir to a regime in which private property had been banned, managed to liquidate even the peasantry, to say nothing of classes, parties, and so forth. The Bolshevik Party reigned supreme over a universal plebe of atomized individuals. Yet both regimes, right up to the end, enjoyed the support of their terrorized, spellbound peoples.

Ideology supplied the means for democratic humanity to abdicate its destiny to a Leader.[65] For Arendt, "ideology" designated not a collection of ideas and images shared by a particular society at one particular time but a closed system of historical interpretation that denied the importance of any creative action. In a totalitarian society, order was no longer organized by the conventions that regulate social or political relations as a function of the natural laws or the philosophical principles from which they are derived. The only law of that society was the law of history, abolishing any deviation and having no other object than constantly to follow the movement of history as interpreted by the party and, within the party, by the Leader. Terror was its natural instrument. It was not circumstantial, like tyranny, but essential, total, covering the entire domain of political and civil laws disregarded by history in its forward march toward the new humanity. It sought less to crush opposition, which rapidly ceased to exist, than to invent it in order to glorify its course. Determined to counteract divisions within its social body and to abolish even the most private space between individuals, it was exercised in the name of all, for all, over all, as the only force of Law in a lawless world. The concentration camps would reveal the essence of totalitarianism.[66]

The Origins of Totalitarianism, though poorly written and organized, composed of bits and pieces, and covering too many years, remains a work of major importance. It set out to analyze Nazism and ended up with a political theory better suited to Communism; it affirmed the radical novelty of the totalitarian phenomenon while devoting more than half the book to a search for its origins and listing heavily toward the German side. Like Neumann, Arendt combined the old critique of mass democracy with the capitalist genealogy of Fascism, harking back to Gurian's insight into the basic inhumanity of "ideological" regimes but without the contrast of divine transcendence.[67] Confusing, preemptory, contradictory, the book may be forgiven its length and meandering by virtue of the somber violence that permeates it and the brilliance of its third part. It is there that we hear the dark, postwar cantilena—the crimes of the Germans, the Jewish genocide, the catastrophes of liberty, the Soviet camps that outlived the Nazi camps, the war that survived the war. Anti-Nazi, antibourgeois, anti-Soviet, and even anti-Zionist, Arendt assumed, with provocative violence, the figure of a pariah. The time of the book's publication gave her persona a final touch by confiscating, at least provisionally, "her" American Republic, intimidated by a demagogue and swayed by the "populace."

Torn from all her roots, Hannah Arendt was no more a cold-war political writer than she was a left- or right-wing writer. She approved of American foreign policy, while abhorring McCarthyism; she did not go to Berlin in June 1950; she wanted to be a "radical" in the American sense, while banishing Soviet Communism from humanity. Her ambition was of quite another order—to conceptualize the political experience of the twentieth century. In the United States, discussion of the Soviet regime fitted into the discussion of the Nazi regime, which had already proved its lineage. It was fostered by a profusion of Russian and Soviet studies in the major universities, especially at Harvard. In March 1953, two years after the publication of Arendt's book, a symposium was held in Boston on "totalitarianism," to be followed by many others. Presided over by Carl Friedrich,[68] the Boston meeting assembled not the American intellectual Right but the Left, deliberately placing itself outside of the hysterical anti-Communism of the time. Hannah Arendt attended and participated, without giving a paper. But the third part of her book was frequently cited and discussed, for the participants, while accepting the extension of the word "totalitarianism" to the Soviet Union, stopped short at an analysis of already formed regimes that did not go into the question of their "origins." In Friedrich's felicitous words, which both limited and justified the comparison between Hitler and Stalin, "The totalitarian societies are basically alike and they are historically unique; but why they are what they are we do not know."[69] Their particular antecedents, lacking the inevitable character of causality, had finally led, through the hazards of history, to similar societies. This mystery made the totalitarian idea both indispensable and difficult to conceptualize.

Taken as a whole, the European intellectual Left did not even attempt such a conceptualization.[70] Its members were anti-Fascist but not anti-totalitarian. Orwell's observations were never keener than when this old rebellious leftist published his *1984* in 1949. With Stalin's death and the beginning of his succession, history itself would make Hannah Arendt's concern with the origins of totalitarianism impossible to ignore.

TWELVE

The Beginning of the End

STALIN'S PASSING WAS OF A COSMIC ORDER, according to Raymond Abellio:

> Stalin's death occurred in March 1953 under the conjunction of Saturn and Neptune. With his death, Russia lost much more than a hieratic leader; it abandoned the hidden priesthood that it had, until then, exercised over the march of the masses. And just as in India in former times, the king's widows and servants were thrown upon the funeral pyre, so the corpses of the workers of East Berlin, mutilated in the following June by Russian tanks, would accompany the coffin of the last European dictator, marking the end of his reign and a break in time.[1]

A break in time? That is an exaggeration, for the Soviet Union survived Stalin. But it certainly was the end of an era. The death of the Leader reemphasized the paradox of a system allegedly inscribed in the laws of social development yet so dependent on a single person that, when he died, the system lost something essential. The collective panic surrounding his funeral in Moscow, which resulted in several hundred deaths, revealed an anxiety about both past and future. Stalin's death was not the same as Hitler's. The German dictator, who had invented both himself and his regime, committed suicide after his defeat, leaving nothing but ruins behind him. Stalin, in contrast, had been an heir, a victor, an empire builder; he died at the height of his power, a few years after his elevation, on his seventieth birthday, to the status of universal genius.

As Lenin's successor, he profited from the glory of his famous predecessor. He had not been the only pretender to that lineage but, having prevailed by means of ruse and force, he turned it into an almost incontestable title, eclipsing his rivals before eliminating them by assassination, exile, or both as in Trotsky's case. There was, moreover, a solid basis for his right to succession. The one-party system, Bolshevik ideology, terror, and the political police were all inherited from Lenin. He combined them in an "oriental" government, which he crowned with the extermination of the peasantry as "bourgeois"; he had as much right to the original idea as anyone else, and maybe more—his trump card was to have made an ephemeral regime last, prolonging or even relaunching the revolutionary illusion while setting up the regime as a primitive but persuasive chain of authority. Trotsky, too literary to be a terrorist, would surely have foundered in it, and kindly Bukharin would certainly have frittered away the family jewels in a return to moderate capitalism. Stalin made his heritage fruitful by supplementing it with his own genius for politics, controlling the one with the other.

He subsequently won the war, transformed the Soviet Union into an empire and a superpower, and made the Communist idea more influential than it had ever been. His government gained the respectability conferred by victory and strength; his person became the object of universal reverence, feared everywhere, even by those who idolized him. The Soviet Union settled into a more regular routine. Not that it became less arbitrary or despotic, or that mass repression had ended; on the contrary, repression was about to be resumed. But every year, on the anniversary of the October Revolution, the same Kremlin leaders were seated on the rostrum; and the Communist bureaucracy had acquired a "modern" veneer lacking in the prewar party, which, though omnipotent, remained subject to systematic decimation by a shifting group of accomplices grouped around an unpredictable gang leader.

So it might have been expected that the transmission of power in the Soviet Union would occur in a less dramatic and conflictual manner at Stalin's death than it had at Lenin's death. Although the international situation weighed on his potential successors, Stalin paid no attention to it. At no time during the last years of his rule did Stalin seem to have the least interest in organizing his succession. His only obsession was to hang onto his power and, above all, his life by foiling the plots that lurked in his paranoid imagination. As an aging potentate, he continued to live the life of a conspirator and an adventurer, bolstered by absolute power. He surrounded himself with bodyguards and soldiers, having all but ceased to speak in public,[2] constantly changing residences and itineraries, making others taste his food even when it came out of his own kitchen. Even those closest to him, family members or his oldest political colleagues, were not above suspicion.[3] Molotov, the most loyal of them all, whose wife had already been arrested, looked like the next victim. The denunciation of the Jewish doctors' plot[4] in January 1953 illustrated the permanence of the regime's two motivating forces: ideology and terror.

To say that Stalin had no thought of organizing his succession is an understatement. Applying to public life an emotion usually associated with aging, he deliberately acted as if there would be no succession, as if his death, which was inevitable, ought necessarily to bring an era to a close. Failing immortality, the great villains of history have to be content with leaving no descendants. At his death, Stalin necessarily left an enormous void. But he needed to be sure that no one would inherit either his role or his power, since, by definition, no one else was up to the task. I suspect that the reason he made no "testament," as Lenin had done, was not simply because he knew at first hand the vanity of such political dispositions but because he imagined that he, and he alone, had "created the era." That attitude reflects the difference between the two successive leaders and periods of Bolshevism.

Stalin's death immediately aroused a universal emotion that combined memories of the war with fears about the future. Oddly enough, in non-Communist circles homage was rendered not only to the marshal as victor in war but also to the prudence and moderation of his foreign policy.[5] His death, during the seemingly endless Korean war, also created anxiety about world peace—the price of substituting the unknown for the known in a USSR in which power had no limits. But the truth, or at least the beginning of the truth, about Stalin's "era" emerged not from the West but from where Stalin had ruled—the Communist world in general and the Communist Party of the Soviet Union in particular. The internal dialectic of an impossible "succession" produced the first definition of the Stalinist period.

The details of this battle have no relevance here, and their history has yet to be written—one more task for future historians. But we must consider what this battle, in the course of a few years, revealed about Soviet Communism—things that would change millions of minds whose beliefs had never before been touched by even the best-documented critiques and the most reliable witnesses. The first casualty in the battle to succeed Stalin was Soviet mythology.

Because one of the charms of totalitarianism is that it represents a perfect order, the very existence of a battle of succession made waves. The Stalinist regime was a unity, composed of a pyramid of equivalencies, an economy planned according to social reason, a society without class conflict with a single party both guiding and representing it, a presidium of that party, a General Secretary. The human political condition was extinguished by the ever-present falseness of ideology.

Stalin's body was barely cold before politics was reborn in a very narrow circle in its most primitive form, and the tiny oligarchy of heirs initiated a battle for power. It was a rerun of what had begun with Lenin's first paralysis in 1922 and had ended with Stalin's triumph over his rivals between 1927 and 1929. But at that time the Soviet system was still in its infancy, close to the anarchy that had been its cradle; the future of the revolution, that is, the new society, offered a natural framework for the political disagreements of Lenin's companions. By 1953, just a generation later, the Soviet world had found its social footing and its government, universally proclaimed like two faces of the same historical principle. After that, Stalin's companions had few bones left to pick.

Public pronouncements quickly made this situation clear, not only in the realm of economic policy but, more particularly, with respect to the use of terror. These two problems implicitly challenged the authority of the recently deceased man whom the authors of the pronouncements had served and adulated. Lenin's heirs had fought one another to succeed him, while hiding behind the shadow of the founding father. All of them, including Stalin, justified themselves by referring to what he would have done had he lived. By contrast, Stalin's heirs confronted one another over a conditional inheritance, critical of the man who had preceded them. At first the criticism was oblique, for obvious reasons. Stalin had incarnated Communism so completely, both within the USSR and abroad, that the dismantling of his monument entailed great risks; those such as Malenkov, Beria, and Khrushchev were not in the best position to undertake this task, since they had been the principal executors of Stalin's policies. Nonetheless, a certain disavowal of their former omnipotent leader could immediately be heard, couched in a rhetoric clear to those with the proper antennae. After mid-March, Malenkov's emphasis on the "maximal" satisfaction of the needs of the people was an early admission of generalized poverty, especially in the rural areas. References to "collective leadership," accompanied by a preliminary division of functions,[6] presaged a break with earlier practices. Then came the thunderbolt of 4 April: a communiqué from the minister of the interior announced, without comment, that the doctors' "plot" revealed in January had been nothing but a provocation mounted by the former minister of state security.

This laconic communiqué was a landmark not only because of its overt anti-Stalinism but because it pointed to the fundamental debate taking place among Stalin's successors. These were what remained of the old guard, who, like Molotov or Voroshilov, had been in danger since 1949–50. Others, such as Malenkov or Khrushchev, had won their wings during the Terror of the late 1930s and had been coopted by

Stalin into the narrow circle of absolute power, on the ruins of the earlier Bolshevik Party. After World War II, in the climate of the cold war, they had been wary of a resurgence of the great purge, seeing signs of it in the heavy atmosphere of suspicion and repression that pervaded Stalin's last years.[7] Their anxiety was well described by Khrushchev himself a few years later in his famous speech to the Twentieth Congress of the Soviet Communist Party. In that climate, many of them expected to be arrested at any moment, and the doctors' "plot" appeared to be the dreaded signal. They hastened to pronounce the annulment of those charges, as if to show that they no longer wanted to live in fear. By doing so, however, they opened the way not only to hope but to a revision of the past: if the Kremlin doctors were innocent, what about the millions condemned for political crimes before them?

Mutatis mutandis, Stalin's heirs found themselves in a "Thermidorian" situation. Unlike their French predecessors, they did not have the force or the will to kill the tyrant, who was older, bloodier, more powerful, more legitimate, and more of a national figure than Robespierre had been. Nor were they any less dependent ideologically than he, even after Stalin's death. But in two respects the Russian pretenders in 1953 were like the French in the summer of 1794: at least among themselves, they wanted to abolish terror as a means of refereeing their quarrels; and they intended to hold onto power. These two objectives were not easy to reconcile, for in proscribing terror from battles for power, it becomes impossible, on the one hand, to avert a retrospective condemnation of terror, to the detriment of ideology, and, on the other, to retain the advantage of terror against society and to the benefit of a single party. The key to managing this type of situation lay in modulating the extent and speed of their break with the past.

After a few months, the French revolutionaries of 1794 had accepted the logic of 9 Thermidor under public pressure:[8] they had dismantled terrorist legislation, restored liberty, sacrificed those of their own most compromised by Robespierrism, even though that meant maintaining power by rigging elections. Stalin's successors, however, were Bolsheviks, second-generation Bolsheviks for the most part but Bolsheviks nonetheless, who had imbibed hatred for Thermidor with their mothers' milk. The French precedent of 1794 had been the nightmare of October 1917: the Soviet Revolution had continuously sought to dispel the idea that it might one day come to an end, if only with history itself. It was haunted by Thermidor from start to finish, during Kronstadt, at the beginning of the New Economic Policy, and in the internal bureaucratic battles opened up by the paralysis and eventual death of Lenin. Stalin had defeated his last rival, Bukharin, in the name of this inexhaustible cause, since it was consubstantial with the revolutionary project itself: the collectivization of farms and forced industrialization gave it new content. After Stalin's death, his successors, having recently feared for their lives, had to reject his tyranny while maintaining his regime. Their emphasis on "collective leadership" resulted from a compromise on the delicate balance between the two aspects of the administration of the succession. It also expressed their provisional agreement to an anonymous oligarchy: it was in the interest of each member of the administration that none of them be able to profit from the "end" of terror, perhaps to garner a decisive advantage in the struggle for power. The "conspiracy" against Robespierre in July 1794 had also, even after the victory and for the very same reasons, obeyed the same constraint of anonymity.

There was one apparent exception to this rule: the liquidation of Beria. It was this ultimate assassination in the heart of the group of leaders that sealed their resolution to put an end to mutual assassinations. The precise reasons are not known, at least for the present, for lack of witnesses and documents. Beria had been chief of the NKVD since 1939, which made him feared by his colleagues but potentially granted him more popularity, since his job seemed to designate him as the natural inspiration for the decree exonerating the Kremlin doctors and for the break in terror it seemed to symbolize. In fact, that decision had been preceded by amnesty for a million prisoners, personally ordered by Beria, and was followed by an amendment seeking increased rights for non-Russians in the foreign Republics, which also bore his stamp. Finally, according to recent scholarship,[9] Beria's "liberal" intentions extended to foreign policy: it appears he was the first to propose a secret meeting with Tito, and was the author of a document—no less secret—seeking to reestablish private enterprise in the German Democratic Republic by way of preparing the ground for negotiating German reunification. Arrested in June of 1953, Beria was liquidated under mysterious conditions; he disappeared not only from the Party leadership but from Soviet history, according to established procedure.

The last typically Stalinist political assassination therefore struck down one of the most active de-Stalinizers. Since Beria had also been one of Stalin's most effusive sycophants and the meanest of his henchmen, his murder could easily be passed off as the liquidation of the last Stalinist. In any case, it brought all the security organs under the control of the Party, assuring the provisional conspirators their collective leadership. But what is especially interesting about this incident is that it illustrates the narrowness of the channel into which Malenkov, Khrushchev, and a few others tried to push the lifeboat containing the

Bolshevik heritage: the members of this oligarchy were constrained to tolerate one another only because of their individual weaknesses and the memories of shared crimes, which could not be washed away by Beria's blood. They were still the children of Stalin, even as they tried to distinguish themselves from him with priestly prudence, incapable of imagining any other political universe than their own and condemned to work together or lose everything, while each dreamed of being the winner who would take all.

The logic of de-Stalinization, however, when combined with that of the succession, propelled them forward. This was their only common ground. To define it, they all took care to celebrate the foundations of the regime: a legitimism that was part and parcel of the regime's nature and functioning and was all the more indispensable because they were positioning themselves to criticize the forms it had taken. So the second devolution of Bolshevik power—after the one that led from Lenin to Stalin—occurred, like the first, in the veneration of Lenin but, unlike the first, under the sign of a return of the founding father. It implied the suspicion that the Party, under its second historical leader, had been capable of misunderstanding, of misreading, the laws of history. To what extent? How? Why? These questions no longer came from Trotsky or Tito. They came from the holy of holies, debated within the walls of the Kremlin, inevitable but no less dizzying.

Once raised, the questions emerged everywhere, like fissures in the totalitarian world; that was the price of ideology. It was inevitable that the critique of Stalin, implicit in the measures of March and April, would be taken up, like an anxious interrogation, by the hundreds of thousands of prisoners released from the Gulag that summer. The rehabilitation of the "White Shirts" automatically brought calls for the rehabilitation of the countless former enemies of the people who had been arbitrarily condemned or summarily executed. Having glimpsed freedom, how could the millions of *zek*s languishing in labor camps have remained there passively? [10] The desacralizing of the dead Stalin, so soon after the adulation of the live Stalin, opened up a kind of geological fault in the regime, presenting its architects with the uncomfortable choice between a return to the past or a flight toward the future.

The same thing was true of foreign affairs. Contrary to what many Western soothsayers predicted in the days following Stalin's death, his demise put an end to the bitterest period of the cold war, thereby revealing the essential role he had played in it. But while the post-Stalin USSR could quickly sign a truce in Korea, having held the keys to the conflict from the start, the weakening of its domestic regime caused by

the first measures of the spring of 1953 affected Communism throughout the world, beginning with the satellites in Central and Eastern
Europe.

In a minor key, the events of 1953 within the Communist world were
a preview of the scenario that would accompany the collapse of Communism thirty-six years later. In the heart of the system, namely Moscow, the political central command set out to reform Stalin's regime. It
sought to eliminate terror within the Party and to reduce its military
commitments so as to encourage consumption. Difficult as this program was to implement, in the USSR everything, or almost everything,
occurred at the top, within the apparatus, in keeping with the spirit of
the regime. In the satellite countries, on the other hand, the Communist
oligarchies were recent installations, only five or six years old. Kept
under the close control of Moscow and in the hands of Comintern veterans, they were nonetheless old enough to be struck with full force by
the Stalinist critique that came from the east and exposed them to popular uprisings. Away with slogans of rapid industrialization and rural collectivization at any price! Now was the time to forget those Stalinist
plagiaries and to devote oneself to the Malenkov-Khrushchev school.
This meant slowing down the rhythm, giving more room to consumption and less to fear, and liberating or rehabilitating victims of terror. In
Central and Eastern Europe, neither the Stalinist oligarchies nor the
Communist idea itself would easily survive this change in course.

The first signs of crisis emerged in Czechoslovakia in June. A volatile mixture of popular anti-Communist feelings would henceforth
dominate the marketplace of ideas in this part of Europe: labor strikes
for better wages, nationalistic frustrations brought about by Russian
domination or occupation, and liberal and democratic protests against
the one-party system. On 16–17 June, the first major popular anti-
Communist revolt since Kronstadt occurred: all of working-class East
Berlin, protesting the rise of production norms, demanded free elections and booed the Ulbricht-Pieck-Grotewohl trio. On the 18th, Soviet
tanks crushed the insurrection. On the 19th, nineteen "ringleaders"
were condemned to death by Soviet military tribunals and immediately
executed. The paradoxical aspect of the whole affair was that Stalin's
successors in Moscow, busy as they were, each trying to appropriate
the critique of Stalin, inadvertently reinforced Ulbricht, who had been
Stalin's front man in Berlin. By liquidating Beria, they got rid of the
person who had been counted on by those opposing Ulbricht from
within East Germany; by having their tanks open fire on the protesters,
they restored full powers to a major Stalinist. Nineteen thirty-three had

spelled the end of "third phase" Communism in Berlin. Twenty years later, Berlin was the setting for the first failure of the new orientation. So much for the will to reform!

Nonetheless, the extreme centralization of the system, combined with the power of ideology, could not prevent the first signs of "de-Stalinization" in Moscow from endangering the entire Communist order, above all in the satellite republics, where Communism was relatively new and where, in spite of the Terror between 1948 and 1952, civil societies were not sufficiently "Sovietized" to submit quietly to changes imposed from above. In keeping with tradition, the leaders in Moscow tried to establish their disciples everywhere. They put Rákosi out to pasture in Budapest and replaced him with Imre Nagy; not long afterward, in Poland, they released Gomulka from prison. Having done this, however, they left themselves open to two dangers: they compromised the changes they had advocated by putting them in the form of orders from Moscow; and, by opening the door to denunciations of past "errors," they weakened the dictatorships of their affiliated parties in their respective countries as well as dealing a blow to Moscow's absolute authority over those parties.

The end of terror shook up the entire international Communist system. Not that the system was threatened from the outside, for the West made no attempt to take advantage of the situation. What rocked Communism was the questioning of its two fundamental passions—fear and belief. The reduction of the former called into question the foundations of the latter, for in freeing people's minds it forced leaders to revert to the use of terror. It was on these shifting sands that Khrushchev ventured forth in search of an opportunity to eliminate his rivals before it was too late. In February 1955, he managed to replace the "liberal" Malenkov with Bulganin in the position of President of the Ministerial Council, while humiliating Molotov—and Stalin's old guard—in May by presenting his public apology to Tito for the 1948 rupture. But that was not enough. He really seized power in February 1956, at the Twentieth Congress of the Communist Party of the USSR.

Khrushchev's "secret" speech to the Twentieth Congress may be the twentieth century's most important text in the history of Communism, even though Khrushchev was hardly a profound, thorough, or original thinker on the subject. In spite of the secrecy that surrounded the Soviet regime since 1917 and the wall of lies built to protect its myths, the history of the USSR has been the subject of some excellent books. The best, such as Souvarine's *Staline*, were written by dissidents for obvious reasons: only former Communists had both the insider's experience of the system and the ability to analyze the system from the outside. That "outside" should be understood in both a spiritual and a material sense, since the capacity for knowledge was acquired only at the cost of a break, and the ability to publish was subordinated to factors beyond the USSR. But former Communists who became witnesses for the prosecution of the cause they had once served paid a price for their about-face: having once maintained the opposite of what they were now writing, their credibility was limited. Their judgment might have been led astray by passion in both directions, coming and going. This intellectual suspicion was compounded by moral censure for switching camps and friends—a major form of censure in a century when political passions so often assumed the character of a civil war. Thus works on the Soviet Union by former Communists have never enjoyed great authority. As for scholarly histories of the Soviet Union, based on academic research rather than personal experience, these began to appear only in the 1950s, initially in the United States, prompted by the postwar international situation.[11]

In February 1956, the "secret report" appeared and immediately overturned the universal status of the Communist idea. The voice denouncing Stalin's crimes no longer came from the West but from Moscow, and from the holiest of the holy in Moscow—the Kremlin. It belonged not to a Communist who had renounced his vows but to the foremost Communist in the world, the head of the Communist Party of the Soviet Union. Instead of being met with the suspicion that surrounded the pronouncements of former Communists, the report carried the same supreme authority as was attributed to the leader of the system. It drew on a universal force among both Communists and non-Communists. Communists had long been accustomed to taking their leaders at their word, and criticism of Stalin had certainly been meted out to them since March 1953. Nor did Non-Communists have any reason to doubt the "revelations" of the First Secretary of the Central Committee. Although hostile to Communism, they found their opinion and what they already knew confirmed by the report. Even if they were wary of anti-Communism, it was difficult to reject the testimony of someone who had lived through the whole period at Stalin's side and had freely chosen to smear the cause he had been serving. The report was all the more convincing because no one contradicted it. So astonishing—or inconvenient—was the news that for several weeks the debate focused on the authenticity rather than on the content of the report.[12] But once this news had been accepted, the contents of the text became a part of everyone's history of Communism; for the first time since 1917, friends and foes united around the revelations.

Why did Khrushchev create this dangerous unanimity with a critique of Stalin? What made him run the risk of weakening the entire Communist universe? How could he have paid so little heed to the inevitable ravages that such a denunciation of Stalin's crimes would wreak on a movement whose raison d'être was ideology and whose sole religion was the cult of Stalin? Later on, in his memoirs,[13] he would provide his own responses to these questions, and they are convincing. The political atmosphere of the Presidium of the Party, as he reconstructed it, was indeed post-Thermidorian. The liquidation of Beria had not been sufficient to exorcize Stalin's ghost, which haunted all of his successors. Tito had mocked them in 1955, when they sought to blame Beria for the 1948 Soviet-Yugoslav schism. They had protested too much, or too little. Khrushchev, however, wanted to go farther, in spite of Malenkov's reservations and the opposition of the old guard—Voroshilov, Molotov, and Kaganovich.[14] Mikoyan was not opposed to proceeding. In the end, they decided to form a commission of inquiry, directed by Pospelov, one of the "theoreticians" of the Party and director of the Marx-Engels-Lenin Institute from 1949 to 1952. But once the dossier against the dead tyrant was complete, what should be done with it? How should it be used, and should it be used at all?

This was the real issue of the Twentieth Congress, but it was debated only behind the scenes. Everything had the appearance of the classic ritual: a lengthy report, collective leadership, unanimous delegates. But Khrushchev wanted to inform his comrades of the substance of the Pospelov commission's dossier. His desire was surely not without political motivation, related to the struggle for power. By showing the Party that he—one of the major victims of the 1936–39 purges—was spearheading de-Stalinization, the First Secretary thought to consolidate his position both against the old guard and against his principal if already declining rival, Malenkov. He put forward an irrefutable argument: that Stalin's crimes could not remain concealed since the hundreds of thousands of prisoners liberated from the Gulag would surely return to tell of their experiences. In spite of the protests of Molotov, Voroshilov, and Kaganovich, the Presidium yielded to the logic that had been set in motion in 1953. Liberating prisoners was nothing: the hard thing was to hear them out and to respond to their accounts.

As Soviet power devolved, Khrushchev found himself sandwiched between two generations of leaders.[15] He was too young to have served with Stalin during the civil war, as had Kaganovich and Molotov, and too old to have been a pure product of Stalinism, as Brezhnev was. Unlike Malenkov, his contemporary, he had spent most of his career not in Moscow but in the field, in the Ukraine. These features of his existence are not enough to support the assertions in his memoirs that he had been largely ignorant of the massacres committed under Stalin. But they do help to explain why he felt less guilty than Molotov or Malenkov, and why he was less cynical than Brezhnev. As one who had become a member of the Bolshevik Party a few months after October 1917, a simple soldier of the civil war, he was born into politics during the heroic times of Bolshevism, a child of Lenin. Thirty-five years later, this fire still seemed to be burning within him, in spite of all the catastrophes it had brought, and the "return to Lenin," that quasi-obligatory slogan, seemed to express a true hope to him and not a mere tactical retreat. Stalinist Bolshevism in Russia had been dominated by fear. But even in this late era, faith in the Communist ideology had not been weakened. Khrushchev believed in what he said. This enabled him forcefully, and before anyone else, to embody what would henceforth dominate Communist images of a general rehabilitation of the edifice. It also gave him an appeal that he would retain even after his own defeat.

What did he actually say in his famous speech? What exactly happened on the night of 24 February 1956 in the great hall of the Kremlin Grand Palace? When he mounted the rostrum, he must have had the speech ready in his pocket. Bolshevik leaders never improvised, and the matter at hand was so delicate that it made improvisation inconceivable. Khrushchev tells us in his memoirs that Pospelov was in charge of turning his report into a speech,[16] but the text certainly underwent a final polishing by a small committee, and we shall never know exactly what the speaker's own contribution was—though it was undoubtedly an important one. The thorniest problem was to determine just how much of the truth should be revealed so as not to implicate Stalin's successors, the Party, or the regime. To make a break and yet to continue, to reveal and yet to conceal: the secret of the "secret report" lay in the subtle combination of these ingredients in the mouth of a speaker prone to the dramatic.

Stalin was the target of the speech.[17] Malenkov did get a couple of mentions, but as an underling, and in passing. The members of the Presidium were collectively left out, since none of them had been in any position to influence decisions. Beria had paid the price for them all, and once again he was cast as the only bad guy of the lot, described as an "agent in the service of foreign espionage"—a holdover from the Terror among those denouncing it. Stalin's posthumous trial was conducted in a very selective manner. It took support from Lenin's famous testament, reintegrated at last into the Bolshevik heritage, but it legitimized the elimination of Trotsky and Bukharin. It accused the former General Secretary of innumerable arbitrary liquidations, but there was not one word about the atrocities that had accompanied the collectivization of agriculture. There were two reasons for this omission. The first was that the return to Leninism did not condemn the notion of "socialism in one country," the milk on which all the leaders of the Twentieth Congress had been nursed. It was more a matter of returning to the spirit of Lenin within the regime erected by Stalin. The ambiguity of this formula is a good indication of the ambiguity of the whole undertaking. The second reason for the omission can be deduced from the first: through the delegates to the Congress, Khrushchev was addressing the Party and not the society. He could hardly have believed that his discourse would remain confidential; moreover, he was quick to communicate the contents of the text to various Soviet diplomatic organs and affiliated parties. But he had conceived of it as a document internal to the Communist movement. In it, Stalin is accused not of having tortured the peoples of the USSR but of having terrorized, tortured, and assassinated his comrades, beginning with Kirov's assassination in 1934.

In the second half of the speech, however, having said all these dreadful things in front of a shocked audience, Khrushchev went beyond this framework and embarked on a critique of Stalin during the war. Not content with having knocked the statue of the General Secretary from its pedestal, he attacked the military commander, demolishing Stalin's title to legitimacy not only within the oligarchy of the Party but in the order of the nation as well. He denied him the most glorious page ever written by the regime in the history of Russia. Cowardice, incompetence, boastfulness: according to Stalin's successor, these were the "virtues" of the famous war leader who had so celebrated himself and who, at the hour of victory, had eliminated anyone who might have stolen some of the limelight. Worse still: Stalin had used the war to increase his tyranny. He deported whole peoples, far beyond what was required by the military situation. Khrushchev said nothing of the massacres of the Ukrainian peasants during the years of collectivization. But he did raise the deportation of the Kalmuks, the Chechens, and the Balkars; the Ukrainians, he added only half in jest, avoided that fate because they were too numerous. Khrushchev was hardly in a position to talk about totalitarianism, but he evoked its ghost as if to rip from the history of Stalin the most memorable period of his reign: even the great patriotic war furnished an opportunity for the tyrant to forge new chains for the peoples of the Soviet Union.

The most interesting thing about the secret report was Khrushchev's magnification of his initial objective. Like the French Thermidorians, he was trying to cut his losses; he confessed his part in the Terror to lend solemnity to his oath of renunciation. But in doing so he opened up questions that could no longer be closed. The Thermidorians had the same problem. History may one day tell us whether the interpreter remained true to the original script or took liberties with it. What we do know is that the day when the secret report became public, the Communist world lost its bearings rather than entering a new epoch.

Khrushchev described the evil he denounced as the "cult of personality." That term, purely descriptive, does not explain how unprecedented evil could have come out of a party whose militants were supposed to be serving a cause that enveloped and transcended them. The movement of history could have its artisans or its adversaries but not its usurpers. In his own rather primitive manner, the First Secretary had put his finger on the principal contradiction of Bolshevism, already obvious under Lenin but blindingly so under Stalin: under Bolshevism, the importance placed on political volition did not jive with role of the laws of social development; on the other hand, it certainly nurtured the "cult of personality." Since he could not present the contradiction in terms other than Marxist-Leninist ones, Khrushchev threw it to the militants in its raw state, its mystery intact: How could "socialist" society and the absolute power of one person, founded on the police and on terror, be conceived of together?

The contradiction would have been livable, no doubt, if it had remained repressed. But the secret report made it appear as a radical negation because it denounced so vehemently the very thing that had been universally celebrated. The man whose assassinations, arbitrariness, and incompetence were detailed by Khrushchev had been praised as an incomparable genius by those who were condemning him today. The very meaning of the facts had changed: they were now to be presented in a new light, with no real explanation from the specialists as to their earlier meaning. The manipulation of history, an old Stalinist technique, came up against its own limits when functioning in the opposite direction. When going back up the chain of lies, where should one stop? How could one credibly turn the man who had been celebrated as a universal genius into a criminal paranoiac? Stalin had been too important to the Communist movement to be thrown overboard, even publicly. His heirs, companions, and disloyal children could not kill him and emerge unscathed themselves.

The Twentieth Congress of the Soviet Communist Party and the secret report stunningly confirmed something that had been emerging since 1953: that what was now called de-Stalinization had been central to the struggle for succession in Moscow. The very expression "de-Stalinization" implies a renunciation, at least a partial one, of terror, and

Stalin's heirs had sworn upon Beria's corpse never to kill one another as they began to free thousands of *zek*s. But it also meant a "new economic course," more favorable to consumption. Last, and most important, it implied the revision of a very long period in the history of the Soviet Union and the international Communist movement. In just a quarter of a century, Stalin had not only invented a society and a regime but had also fixed their genealogy and canonical doctrines. Although by definition illegal, Communism, thanks to the historical personality of its leader, retained an extraordinary degree of legitimacy. The principal mystery of Stalinist Russia was how it managed to prolong the powerful but fleeting charm of the revolutionary idea to the benefit of a territory and a state through the incarnation of a single man.

How could one attack him retrospectively without affecting that charm? The question was all the more disturbing because the movement was so extensive and varied. The Communist movement had always been international, but before World War II, outside of the USSR, it entailed only parties, whose leaders were carefully chosen for their unconditional loyalty to the "center," regardless of political and ideological vicissitudes. After 1945, the movement also involved foreign governments infiltrated or taken over by Communists, who, as Tito's 1948 breakaway made clear, could be tempted by national independence. And beyond them lay their constituencies, who still recalled their brief encounters with nationhood and liberty at the end of the war. The peoples of the USSR, accustomed to the Russian yoke and lacking a liberal tradition, had long been intoxicated by despotism. There, Stalinism would have a long life. The Poles, the Czechs, the Hungarians, as heirs to a less despotic history, had known only five or six years of servitude when Stalin died.

The Kremlin's margin for maneuver shrank even as its power grew, for de-Stalinization, necessary to Stalin's successors, affected both their legitimacy and that of the entire Communist system. There was an enormous risk that pushing de-Stalinization too far and too hard would imperil both the unity of the movement—which remained organized like an ideological army—and that of the Soviet empire itself. In 1955, the break with Tito had been attributed to Stalin's pathological suspicions; but the chorus of voices denouncing Tito had been so unanimous and vehement since 1948 that reconciliation with him could create only tension and not unity. By the same token, the exportation of the Kremlin's new political line, but done in the old brutal manner, to the various Communist parties inevitably led to internal dissent, particularly dangerous where those parties were in power.

The international apparatus was accustomed to about-faces. This one was different, however: it brought into question not the tactics or the strategy of the movement but its constitutive falseness; it recalled the tone of Trotsky or Souvarine; and it was the result of a new direction, in which the adepts immediately perceived divisions. Rather than having to take their share of the blame for Stalin's Terror, such observers may have been tempted to lie low, waiting for less difficult days before identifying themselves politically. Molotov could be counted on to resist Malenkov; Voroshilov, to resist Khrushchev. For those nostalgic for Stalin, the secret report, served up by the highest Communist authority of the Soviet Union, encouraged them to beat a hasty retreat rather than to attempt a denial or a counteroffensive.

Elsewhere, in the Central and Eastern European countries in which Communist parties had been in power since 1947–48, the liberalization promised by Moscow in the spring of 1953 aroused excessive expectations on the part of the public. This was immediately clear in East Germany, where the workers demonstrated against the norms of planned production but also against Ulbricht and in favor of free elections. Almost everywhere, during the years between Stalin's death and the Twentieth Congress, the "new course" had been symbolized by the superimposition of new leaders upon old ones; but it also gave rise to a general questioning not only of the modalities of the Communist regime but also of its foundations—peasants began to argue against cooperatives, workers against low wages, intellectuals against censorship.

This situation of uncertainty and instability may have prompted Khrushchev to make a decisive break in February 1956. After the secret report, no one could cite Stalin as an authority. The First Secretary certainly had no reason at this time to anticipate the return in force of the loyal followers of the late dictator, unless he thought the ousting of Malenkov in favor of Bulganin the previous year might necessitate a coup on the other side. He may simply have been considering the Soviet situation, as he claims in his memoirs. The Gulag survivors would return and tell their stories. Eliminating the cult of Stalin from Russian history seems to have been more difficult than censuring his role in the Communist International. More radical measures were called for. But it was in the countries that Stalin had controlled only indirectly, and for the fewest years, that the denunciation of his crimes within the USSR would exert the most immediate effects.

In these countries—from Poland to Hungary—people had only just encountered, on a much lesser scale, the arbitrary force and terror inseparable from the "cult of personality." They too had seen Stalin's portrait everywhere. But their societies had not yet been "Sovietized," and not enough time had elapsed for the human political condition to be extinguished. Their peasantries still existed in spite of forced collectivization. The workers had not forgotten the tradition of collective action. The former ruling classes had lain low or made do, and it had not been necessary to exterminate them as in Lenin's Russia. The old world was still very near, and memories of the prewar period had been embellished by postwar actuality. The Poles remained proud of having maintained the Catholic frontier of Europe in face of the Russians. The Hungarians were proud of having been former partners of the Austrians and the Germans against the Slavs. The Czechs had known their time of splendor in the Europe of Versailles. They all remembered independence and their long struggle to achieve it. Soviet oppression had unified them only temporarily against the Soviet Union itself.

That is why de-Stalinization took a more dramatic form on the recent margins of the Soviet empire than it did within the USSR. It brought both the regime and the nation into question. When faced with the delegates to the Twentieth Congress, Khrushchev had little trouble distinguishing between socialist society and the Terror, that is, between the good and the evil deeds of Stalin. But in Warsaw? In Budapest? What eluded the old Ukrainian apparatchik was the same thing that would elude his distant successor Gorbachev more than thirty years later— the power of public opinion. Both were servants of a regime in which an independent public opinion did not exist, and they were blind to its power elsewhere, especially in those countries within their sphere of influence. In 1956 as in 1989, it was as if the two great and only reformers in Soviet history, barely victorious in internal Party battles, had discovered another landscape at their frontiers but still within their empire: what they had undertaken in the calm of Moscow was producing subversive effects in Warsaw, Prague, and Berlin and would continue to do so if left to follow its course. The Soviet regime was all the more impossible to reform since it was relatively recent and relatively European. The imperial structure of the system compromised its potential for evolution at its western periphery.

Khrushchev had secured in advance the territorial heritage of May 1955, when the Warsaw Pact sealed the political and military unity of the Soviet bloc, even providing for "fraternal" mutual aid in case of need. But his secret report worked in the other direction. The Yugoslav party, which greeted it warmly, interpreted it in such a decentralizing way that Khrushchev, though proceeding with the dissolution of the Cominform in April 1956, was soon compelled to reaffirm the leadership role of the Soviet Communist Party.[18] These bureaucratic niceties were followed by the major test of Khrushchevism, in two waves: the Polish affair and the Hungarian revolution—confrontations which, if bureaucratic on the surface, achieved their historical significance by virtue of the Polish and Hungarian nations.

The origin of these conflicts was the internal crisis of the Communist parties set in motion in 1953 by Moscow's renunciation of arbitrary arrests, by the massive freeing of prisoners, and by the first rehabilitations. Each satellite republic had known, in miniature and for a short period, political terror in a public or secret form. Each one, like the Soviet Union, had to account for this terror, rehabilitate the dead, and release those who had been mistakenly imprisoned—some of whom would automatically become candidates for power. In Poland, there were no Rajk- or Slánský-type trials. But Gomulka, General Secretary of the Party, had been dismissed from his position in 1948, thrown out of the Party in 1949, and imprisoned in 1951 for right-wing nationalistic deviation—a charge which, when his liberation became inevitable in 1954, made him into a symbol of both a liberal and a national Communism. Lacking a pluralistic political system, social pressure was exerted from within the Communist Party. The "new course" brought repressed or forbidden questions to light, from the extermination of the leaders of the Polish Communist Party in 1938 [19] to the torture of political prisoners by the state security organs. The same things were happening in Hungary, where Rákosi, Stalin's faithful henchman and the great orchestrator of the Rajk trial, had had to share power since June 1953 with his rival Imre Nagy, who was extremely hostile to his economic policy of industrialization. The compromise was imposed from Moscow: Rákosi managed to remain leader of the Party, while Nagy became head of the government. Thus the Hungarian Party was also the seat of two policies. Unlike the Polish leadership, Rákosi had recuperated full powers in 1955 and postponed payment of his debts until the last possible moment.

The short period between Stalin's death and Khrushchev's secret report, less than three years, shows two quite different faces. On the one hand, everything continued as before, insofar as everything—not only political decisions but all nominations—was initiated by Moscow. On the other hand, since Moscow was no longer Moscow, the entire Communist world was adrift, uncertain of the future. Stalin's death proved what his life had proved: deprived of his extraordinary will, the world he had created lost something fundamental. Only he could have borne, by the mixture of fear and adoration he inspired, the heavy load of lies and terror he left behind him. His successors inherited that load without the will to assume its weight and risks; yet they could not liberate themselves from it completely, much less share the burden among themselves. So the issue of the trials, purges, and terror took center stage in the years when the Communist identity was foundering. It was no longer the enemy who raised this issue; in that case, it would have been inoffensive. It was raised from within by Stalin's companions and was thus very powerful: the victims of Stalinist paranoia were also Communists.

At the Twentieth Congress, Khrushchev, the most courageous and intelligent of Stalin's successors, had lanced the abscess. He had done so in an attempt to control the damage and to clearly separate the heritage assumed from the heritage condemned. That exercise, which had been attempted in small doses since 1953, had not been very successful, and this time, undertaken like a grand historical painting, it was hardly more stabilizing.

The secret report was not a great example of political analysis. This was a failing for which both sides, especially the Marxists, would reproach its author. But it would surely have lost something if it had been more philosophical; its indignant, plain-speaking tone makes it unique among Communist documents. A stranger to empty political rhetoric, as though he had miraculously escaped from that planet of lies, Khrushchev managed to turn this distinction into something universal, which would extend well beyond the circumstances in which he was writing. Reactions to the report immediately made this clear.

In the history of Communism, the second part of 1956 belongs to the Poles and Hungarians. Their experience, above all, signaled the end of the great mythological age of Sovietism in Europe. Since there are many good books on the subject,[20] we need not elaborate on it here. What was new about these two parallel histories was that they manifested the intervention of public opinion and the people in national politics, which was still the monopoly of the Party. In both countries, frustration came to the surface as soon as Stalin died, as did latent agitation. In 1955, the core of organized opposition consisted of intellectuals—journalists, writers, professors, students—most often using for their purposes those official institutions of the regime that were supposed to keep them in line: the Writers' Union, literary magazines, newspapers, schools, and student organizations. Soon a multitude of clubs arose, recalling the great days of 1848. In Budapest, the Petöfi Circle declared war on Rákosi.[21] In Warsaw, student opposition associated itself with the weekly magazine *Po Prostu*, prior to forming a national federation of clubs in April 1956.

Many in this mounting crowd of young people demonstrating in the name of freedom had quite recently been advocating the dictatorship of the proletariat. Although they had condemned democracy as a bourgeois illusion, they now called for the democratization of the regime. At the end of World War II, they had viewed the victory of Bolshevism as a national hope and the emancipation of society; a few years later, as Bolshevism held sway, they watched their countries being enslaved by the Red Army and their societies falling under the surveillance the NKVD. The de-Stalinization under way in Moscow offered a second chance both to their countries and to their faith, for they too were capable of denouncing and deposing the men and institutions that had collaborated with Stalin's agents. Their revolution had occurred not in 1945 or in 1947 but in 1956, adorned in the bright colors of nationhood.

We see here the resurgence—and flexibility—of a certain type of revolutionary optimism once the fascination and the force that had made it a byproduct of Marxism-Leninism had been broken. The people revolting in the summer of 1956 had grown up in an obligatory or consensual lie. The disappearance of that lie was even more liberating for convinced supporters than it was for the acquiescent; the habits of militancy did the rest, lending the whole episode the sense of a revival of honest language. By rising up against Soviet oppression in the name of their own betrayed hopes and flouted liberties, these young people had no intention of returning to the past or of restoring anything. They wanted to save the socialist idea from the disaster brought upon it by the history of the Soviet Union and to renovate the spirit of October in opposition to the tyranny born of October. To stigmatize them, the bureaucrats in power pulled out an old label from the excommunicative vocabulary of Marxist socialism—"revisionists."

The term "revisionists" had been forged at the turn of the century in the polemic between Bernstein and Kautsky in order to condemn Bernstein's theories as contrary to Marxism. It was a gentler term than "renegade," which Lenin would later level at Kautsky when the terminology of disagreement had become more insulting. Even in its early form, "revisionism" implied the idea of both a new and a false interpretation of Marx's doctrine. The revisionist was a heretic who had emerged from the heart of orthodox beliefs and was proposing a new version of them, different from the official interpretations. By 1956, however, the word had lost this clear definition, drawn from a religious analogy. It designated a body of political ideas that belonged more or less to the socialist tradition but could not easily be attributed to a single author or even to a single mentality. The libertarian accent of the revolt was a posthumous vengeance on Lenin for Rosa Luxemburg, but the call to nationalistic sentiments came neither from Lenin nor from Luxemburg. The trial of Stalinism led everyone to reject the "dictatorship of the proletariat," which had produced the dictatorship of the Party. But it rediscovered the dilemmas of democratic pluralism, which Lenin had buried rather than resolved. Should they be dealt with in a reformist manner, as the Social Democrats of Western Europe had done, or in a revolutionary manner, by reinventing the future?

At this junction, the idea of "Councils" reappeared. Dormant since Kronstadt, it arose from the ruins of Polish and Hungarian Bolshevism to terrorize the descendants of Russian Bolshevism. The idea came not only from the revolutionary tradition; it emerged in several factories, first in Warsaw in the spring of 1956, and then taken up in Hungary in the fall. The phenomenon was not really surprising, for it had resonance in the two remaining urban classes that the regime had left at least vaguely conscious of their existence—the workers and the intellectuals. Ironically, those two flanks of Communism—or what were considered its flanks—had become the spearhead of the movement against the Communist dictatorship by adopting the founding commandment of the regime they wished to destroy. The 1956 "Workers' Councils" actually bore little resemblance to the Soviets of Petersburg in 1917. Like their predecessors, they fought for bread and justice, but in Poland they also defended the liberty of the Catholic Church, and both countries fought for national freedom. In Poland and Hungary, patriotic hymns could be heard more often than the *International*. Professors and students now lauded factory workers not as the advance guard of class struggle but as soldiers of freedom and national renaissance.

The Soviet Union repressed the revolt in both countries at roughly the same time, between the end of October and beginning of November 1956, but using different methods. Through its liberal elements, the Polish Communist Party—divided, having lost its Stalinist leader, who had providentially died in Moscow just after the Twentieth Congress—had not lost all contact with the democratic and nationalistic movement. Gomulka, whom the Party had kept in reserve, revealed himself to be the man of the hour at the high point of the crisis: in the famous days of 19 and 20 October 1956, Khrushchev, Molotov, and Kaganovich, accompanied by Marshal Konyev and a constellation of generals, finally agreed—as the lesser of two evils and in exchange for diplomatic and military guarantees—to entrust Gomulka with harnessing the revolutionary movement. The next year proved their calculations to have been correct.

In Budapest, the Russians had been unable to avoid armed intervention. Under Rákosi, the most hated of the Stalinist leaders, the Party had been entirely cut off from the public. The country did not have Poland's historical reasons—fear of Germany—to accept a compromise with Russia. In July, the Soviet leadership could find no one to replace Rákosi except one of his clones, Ernö Gerö. This change was just enough to imbue the agitation with enthusiasm. The situation got out of hand in early October, when all of Budapest participated in the national funeral for Rajk, and it grew even worse in the second half of the month, when the Workers' Councils, the students, the clubs, and the many new organizations that had sprouted up took to the streets and destroyed a monument to Stalin, occupied the state radio station, and massacred agents of the political police. It was too late even for Imre Nagy, Gomulka's Hungarian counterpart, who was caught in the mounting tide of revolutions: after a few days, the insurrection was calling not merely for the nationalization and democratization of Communism but for the withdrawal of Soviet troops, the end of one-party rule, and the reestablishment of democratic pluralism. In the meantime, Nagy, deprived of all material force, had been painfully negotiating with the Soviets to sketch the limits of what he could do. With no hold on the insurgents, he had no influence with the Russians. In the end, from 4 November on, it was the tanks of the Red Army that crushed the popular revolution, at the demand of General Secretary Kádár, who had been substituted for Gerö on 24 October. Kádár had begun by cooperating with Nagy, but on the morning of 4 November he made an about-face and then secretly left for the USSR, where he would form a new "worker and peasant" government. The end of the story could have been written by Stalin: when "order" returned to Hungary, at the cost of methodical repression,[22] Nagy was lured into a trap by the Soviet troops. He was arrested, transported east, tried in secret, and killed with three of his comrades in June 1958.[23]

The crushed Hungarian uprising seemed to bring back the darkest days of Stalinism. To complete the picture, the operation was described as fraternal aid to the Hungarian working class so as to enable it to triumph over the counterrevolution—pure Orwellian language. Nonetheless, to draw a contrast between the "liberal" solution of the Polish crisis and the catastrophic result of the Hungarian insurrection is misleading, not only because both events exemplify Soviet geopolitical success that left the frontiers of the "socialist camp" intact, but, more especially, because the two Communist regimes that emerged from the uprisings of October 1956 would rapidly become more similar to each other than one might have predicted given the conditions of their birth. Gomulka turned out to be less liberal and Kádár less Stalinist than those who had put them in power. Both men were old militants educated in the difficult school of unconditional loyalty to the USSR; both had been imprisoned and, in Kádár's case, even tortured by the totalitarian power they had helped establish in their respective countries. Yet they emerged from the ordeal, after Stalin's death, unswayed in their essential convictions but believing in a less severe "dictatorship of the proletariat" for their children. They were its new face—authoritarian, reliant on the police, sinister, but livable in the most elementary sense of the word: society had recovered a minimum of autonomy from the state. As long as society manifested no public hostility to the state, it no longer had to believe what the state said or applaud what it did. Having triggered the greatest crisis in the history of Communism, de-Stalinization revealed through its prosaic conquerors the limits of its ambitions, in tune with the limits of its potential.

The questions opened up by de-Stalinization, moreover, had arisen more from what its text implied than from its literal content, which was descriptive and historical. By adding the "cult of personality" to Communist vocabulary, Khrushchev added yet another item to the list of deviations; in naming it and in using it to sully Stalin's deeds, he thereby warded it off, according to the rules. But this nominalism did not entirely cover the story revealed by the First Secretary. There was a gap in his "report" between what it told and what it explained: Stalin had played too important a role in the history of Communism and had been too famous as the incarnation of universal history to end up, in the revolutionary memory, the way he was painted by his worst enemies during his lifetime.

The cult of personality according to Khrushchev referred exclusively to the particular paranoia of the man who had made it his means of arbitrary domination. It centered everything inhuman about the regime on one man and his psychology. By denouncing Stalinism in Stalinist terms, Khrushchev killed two birds—the difficulty of the analysis and the pain of the avowal—with one stone. Claude Lefort expressed this well at the time:

> The new leadership, by vigorously stigmatizing the cult of personality, did not even question how it was possible for it to develop; ordinarily, a cult is the product of those who practice it, but the Stalinist cult was presented as something that Stalin had created himself. . . . By all accounts, the present leaders, by virtue of this sort of explanation, had not been members of that famous cult, but had only passed, if one may say so, from the positive rite to the negative rite.[24]

That procedure not only dispensed with any attempt at interpretation but ruled out any specifically Marxist analysis. Khrushchev's report, even while exposing a multitude of atrocious acts and episodes that had been concealed or denied until then, said nothing that allowed a fundamentally new way of considering the past or the future of the Communist movement. As to the past, what it confirmed or revealed was sufficient to disqualify militants and admirers of Communism throughout the world, without offering them the least explanation. It was as if the USSR, alleged homeland of the working class and the promised land of the science of history, could fall under the murderous authority of a tyrant almost accidentally. As to the future, a revival of either Lenin or his principles made no sense and had in fact been part of Stalin's repertory. It defined no new political approach.

Indeed, the fate of the Twentieth Congress and the secret report hinged not on Lenin's heritage but on the administration of the world inherited from Stalin. Nothing that Lenin wrote, and for good reason, could serve as a guide on how to rule over the Soviet empire. In spite of appearances, that very empire, created by Stalin, had obeyed a logic that was posterior and foreign to Leninism, that of "socialism in one country." It had been conceived and entirely organized as a vast rampart round the Soviet Union, made up of nations with regimes identical to its own, and strictly subordinated to its authority, even in matters of domestic politics. The extreme centralization of the Communist movement had never been as ruthless as during the post–World War II years, when "socialism" was extended to several countries as a carbon copy of the Soviet system and an extension of its military preponderance. The USSR was both a besieged fortress and a world superpower, more than ever playing on the dual image of weakness and strength.

Khrushchev's spectacular self-censure in Belgrade, in May 1955, followed by the secret report (in which Tito was "rehabilitated" anew), the dissolution of the Cominform, and the Soviet-Yugoslavian declaration of June 1956,[25] showed that Communist parties and Communist countries intended to renounce their dependency on Moscow. Togliatti, as we have seen, was already speaking of "polycentrism" in an interview that appeared on the very day that Tito and Khrushchev signed the text in Moscow. One week later, however, probably under the pressure of the unsettling news from Poland,[26] The Russians took a step backward: Togliatti was criticized by *Pravda*, which made a point of reiterating the "leadership role" of the USSR in the Communist movement.

This episode reveals the ambiguities or uncertainty of de-Stalinization as to how to organize the international Communist system. There too, Khrushchev's intervention at the Twentieth Congress had a more destabilizing than reforming effect. On the one hand, Togliatti's reunion with Tito was an attempt to constitute a pole relatively independent of Moscow. On the other, the parties with the great-

est reservations about the secret rapport feared a weakening or an explosion of the Communist world. With Thorez and Ulbricht at the fore,
they pressured Khrushchev not to abandon too many of Stalin's international prerogatives. Paradoxically, de-Stalinization, which they did
not like, made their opinions more influential than ever, for by loosening
up the centralization of the international Communist universe, it also
allowed parties nostalgic for the past to have more influence in internal
conclaves or consultations. At the very time when these parties were
lamenting the passing of Comintern or Cominform discipline, they
were nonetheless benefiting from the increase in influence that resulted
from its relaxation.

Thanks to the events of the Twentieth Congress, the Chinese party
had, at long last, won a key position in the international Communist
configuration. That position ensured China's prominence in the world,
the autonomy of the 1949 revolutionary victory, and a great deal of influence for Mao Tse-tung. Although, at the time, Stalin had monopolized the glory of commanding the movement, the Chinese Party was
not enthusiastic about the condemnation of the cult of personality at the
Twentieth Congress. After all, under Stalin, Mao, like all other national
leaders, had enjoyed a "secondary" cult and entertained hopes of assuming the leading role after Stalin. Who deserved it more than the
leader of the Long March? The end of the Korean War in 1954 had
diminished Chinese dependence on the Soviet Union, and Chinese
Communist Party leaders, especially Mao and Chou En-lai, had increased their authority over the decisions of the movement. Khrushchev
paid them a visit in the autumn of 1954. They had encouraged Polish
autonomy, supported Gomulka in the fall, but pushed for the intervention of Soviet tanks in Budapest (along with the Czech, Romanian,
Bulgarian, and East German parties). At the end of the year, in the
29 December issue of the *Peoples' Daily* under a title indicative of the
"theoretical" ambitions of the article, the Chinese leaders published
"New Considerations on the Historical Experience of the Dictatorship of the Proletariat." The article was a response to Tito's speech of
11 November, in which the Yugoslav leader, while conceding the unfortunate necessity for Soviet intervention in Hungary, regretted that
Kádár had not known how to rely upon the "Workers' Councils." The
response of the Chinese paper was that "imperialism" was the basic
cause of the Hungarian insurrection; the article then proceeded to reduce the critique of Stalin to manageable proportions. If there had indeed been, on his part, a tendency toward the "chauvinism of a great
power" and, hence, toward the domination of the neighbor and even of
the brother nation, it remained true that "if one were determined to

speak of Stalinism, one could say that Stalinism was above all Communism, which is Marxism-Leninism." [27]

The Soviet invasion of Hungary, therefore, was followed by comments that more or less explicitly cast doubt on Khrushchev's remarks to the Twentieth Congress. This is not surprising, since the Hungarian insurrection had confronted the entire Communist movement, whether Stalinist or anti-Stalinist, with the question of survival. It had overflowed its banks or, rather, the banks assigned to it by the Twentieth Congress—that of Communism regenerated. For this new Communism had to remain attached to the whole camp, whereas Nagy had evoked a statute of neutrality. And the new Communism still had to keep power in the exclusive hands of the Communist Party or its associates, whereas Nagy had encouraged the revival of political pluralism. For the first time since 1917, there appeared in Budapest the specter of a form of Communism that could be rolled back into capitalism. [28] Even Tito in 1948, expelled and separated from the fold, had never gone so far as to renounce the monopoly of the Party. Nagy, however, had illustrated a precedent even more alarming than nationalistic Communism—namely, suicidal Communism.

The events of 1956 demonstrated the inability of Khrushchev and his friends to redefine any alternative policy in their own camp based on the revelations of the Twentieth Congress. "De-Stalinization" was neither a philosophy, nor a strategy, nor an idea, nor a program. The word's only strength lay in dissolution and a potential for disorder. Understood as a reexamination of the past, it had questioned the two wellsprings of the Soviet regime—ideology and terror. The system had exposed to the anger of the public—or what was left of it—its principal actors, educated in the longest and hardest of schools, at the moment when a modicum of liberty had been restored to their victims. This situation was much more delicate than that of an authoritarian regime seeking to liberalize itself, for this regime was doing something altogether different: it was negating the very thing it had adored and giving the floor to those it had struck down as long as they were willing to give a new, exclusive contract to the party that had victimized them. This clause, which implied maintaining a minimum of terror, kept the critique of Stalin from renewing the repertory of the Communist movement. The insurrection in Budapest had revealed the impasse and narrowed the passage. Mao Tse-tung then sealed it off.

That capital year in the history of Communism had two consequences: the bloc began to disintegrate, and its unified myth lost its credibility.

Khrushchev had hoped for an enlargement of the bloc. As the price of his reconciliation with Tito, he had envisaged the establishment of more equal relations and more honest exchanges between Communist parties; he even thought that along with Yugoslavia—which was friendly again, if touchy about the originality of its regime—a nebula of Third World socialist states of questionable orthodoxy might be formed around the "camp of peace and socialism." Just as de-Stalinization was supposed to reinforce the moral authority of the Soviet Union, so peaceful coexistence would make the Soviet Union the center of the dynamic of progress, whose mission was to shrink away the part of the world that remained under the yoke of imperialism. This was a doubly illusory hypothesis, since the denunciation of Stalin extended the suspicion of the accused to the accusers, and the receding threat of war was eliminating one of the most important reasons for centralization.

By the end of 1956, these associated logics had borne fruit. The Communist world was divided between supporters and adversaries of de-Stalinization. The former ended up, in Hungary, challenging the very foundations of the Communist regime. The latter, by resisting Moscow's new course, compromised the tradition of extreme centralization, whose heyday and instigator they secretly missed. Together, both camps had dug the ditch of "polycentrism."

The general weakening of Moscow's authority was compounded by the increasing influence of revolutionary China and by the personality of Mao—the only Communist since Lenin, along with Tito though of another order, to have seized power by his own means. The other satellite republics had received their power from the Red Army. Tito had seized it single-handedly as soon as the Nazis had collapsed and in spite of Stalin.[29] Mao had always directed the strategy of the Chinese Communist Party independently of Moscow: the sheer size of China gave that independence a formidable potential for disunion. Stalin's successors understood this but could not avert the threat for long without yielding their prerogative in the international Communist movement. Mao had supported them in the Hungarian affair, but not without a few doctrinal reminders that made that support somewhat conditional. At any rate, China was too huge, too populous, too important to be a servile partner in the USSR's international policies. Khrushchev's de-Stalinization would provide the Chinese with ideological space for China's independence as a state.

"Socialism in one country" was thus at an end. In spite of the Yugoslav schism, the system had survived the absorption of the Eastern and Central European nation-states into an empire almost as centralized as the Soviet Union itself. But Stalin's death, followed by "de-Stalinization," had left the field open to centrifugal forces by abandoning the use of terror and inaugurating a margin of ideological flexibility. The movement had begun, naturally enough, at the European periphery of the empire, and soon reached its limits but not its end: the revolts of 1953–56 had left that part of the Communist world, including the Communist parties themselves, with memories that could not be erased. Almost everywhere, and to varying degrees, nationalistic sentiments, the call for democracy, and the desire to improve the standard of living led to separatist currents that the USSR could contain but not eliminate. The USSR, moreover, was more comfortable with "national" types of Communism such as that of Ceauşescu than with "liberal" types such that of Dubcek. And China's overt dissidence, which, beginning in 1960, had its tiny European avatar in Albania, showed that even a shared hostility to "imperialism" was insufficient to maintain the unity of a camp that laid claim not only to the same doctrine but to the same Leninist interpretation of that doctrine.

With the new situation, the Soviet myth came apart at the seams, attacked on both sides of Marxism-Leninism by the Chinese and the Yugoslavs, the Albanians and the Italians. Threatened by plurality, the Communist idea receded. Trotsky had never succeeded in giving political life to left-wing anti-Stalinism. After the Poles and Hungarians, Tito and Mao, minimally united by the shared object of their critiques, would give shape to an anti-Soviet Communism, but only after Stalin's death. The Communist idea remained influential in the world, but its geographical representation was contested. Rome was no longer contained in Rome.

"Revisionism" was the new thing. That word best expresses the statue wobbling on its pedestal. For the Soviet myth it was the beginning of the end, but without a designated successor. In contrast to its first usage, targeted at unorthodox dissidents, it could now be wielded by anyone within a chain of reciprocal accusations, as if even the notion of a model had faded away. Khrushchev had been careful to avoid the risky term, preferring the reassuring affirmation of a return to Leninism, as if the revolution had only tradition left to guide it. But that notion made little sense, for in spite of everything he was a successor rather than a restorer. He was heir to an enormous heritage that included agricultural ruin, bureaucratic industrialization, a new society, a Soviet empire extending as far as Prague, the arms race, the Communist movement frozen in servitude. He had no choice but to return to Lenin, just as Louis XVIII had had no choice in 1814 but to restore the ancien régime. By attacking Stalin, in fact, Khrushchev had unwittingly opened the way to revisionism.

The Yugoslavs had been the first to take that road in 1948, and the

1955 visit of reconciliation had recognized their right to do so. It was a right that they had used, moreover, with moderation, since Milovan Djilas and, after him, Edouard Kardelj had been condemned by Tito for criticizing the political monopoly of the Party.[30] The following year, events in Poland and, even more so, in Hungary had shown the inconsistency of a simple "correction" of past errors. Beyond the Terror, they had exposed the poverty of the workers, the absence of political democracy, and national servitude. In Hungary, "revisionism" went so far as to threaten the regime itself. In both cases, it came up against the exclusive imperatives of geopolitics and Soviet reasons of state. The idea of a socialism reconciled with democracy and the nation was the better able to survive its failure because it had received the spectacular support of intellectuals and workers. It continued to influence Central and Eastern European societies, into the very heart of their Communist parties.

In the following years, to the contrary, Mao and the Chinese Communists were determined to head off the now steady threat to the ideology of the movement, first by helping the Soviets to seal the gap in 1956–57, and then by demanding the privilege of orthodoxy for themselves. Unity was no longer compromised mainly by overstepping the limits traced by the Twentieth Congress. It had been destroyed by the Twentieth Congress itself. Khrushchev himself had become the quintessential "revisionist" in the most classic sense of the word—the grave digger of Communism. The launching of Sputnik did nothing to stave off ideological disintegration, which even had its farcical element when Albania set itself up as the European pillar of "orthodox" Marxism-Leninism. The Communist idea barely outlived the Communist empire and the death of its founder.

The divisive effect of the secret report could also be observed in the West in the two largest Communist parties, the Italian and the French. These two parties were not the closest of friends, but they had followed roughly parallel courses and pursued similar policies; they obeyed the same center, were associated more by force than by affection, and participated in the same battle behind enemy lines.

But Stalin's death had created a new situation.[31] Thorez and Togliatti were Comintern veterans, prestigious leaders not only in their own countries but in Moscow as well. Unconditional disciples of Stalin, they did not have the same reasons to incline their pasts before Malenkov or Khrushchev. They knew enough about Soviet propaganda to figure out what had been brewing in Moscow since 1953 behind the slogans of "collective leadership" and the emphasis on peaceful coexistence. The secret report of February 1956 designated at least a provisional victor of the battle for succession, as well as the cost of membership in his camp—denunciation of the cult of Stalin. The Communist movement had become decentralized de facto as soon as it offered its big barons the hardest decision of their lives—a questioning of their very identity.

Thorez and Togliatti had learned about the secret report in Moscow very soon after its release. They were the heads of parties too powerful and well established in their respective countries to feel threatened by even such a extensive change as this, as was the case in what remained of the American Communists.[32] But how should they maneuver so as to minimize the damage, while dissociating themselves from the "cult of personality" of which they had been the instruments, the imitators, and the beneficiaries? As Marc Lazar has shown, the two leaders adopted similar tactics for two months in the spring of 1956, attempting some preliminary damage control, since the complete transcript of the secret report was not yet known in its entirety, but also recalling Stalin's role in the construction and victory of Soviet socialism. They shared contempt for Khrushchev's amateurism, which exposed them, as well as the entire movement, to foolish risks. After June, however, they took different paths when the "revelations" of the First Secretary, published in their entirety, reached the public. Togliatti gave his famous interview in *Nuovi Argumenti,* placing himself in the "revisionist" wing of Communism with Tito. He sketched out a less narrow interpretation of the "cult of personality" than Khrushchev, blaming the bureaucratic degeneration of the Soviet regime; he supported the idea of a "polycentric" movement.[33] Thorez continued to speak of the report "attributed to comrade Khrushchev," and tried to close the Stalin dossier when it had barely been opened. He drew support from the Soviet leadership's negative reaction to Togliatti's interview. A delegation from the French Communist Party sent to test the waters in Moscow returned bearing the Soviet resolution of 30 June, which was already a retreat from the secret report on Stalin's "errors," underlining, Togliatti to the contrary, the USSR's leadership role in the heart of international Communism.

Both the Italian and the French parties supported the November invasion of Budapest by Russian tanks—the Italians with resignation, the French with relief. As to the Hungarian uprising, the French saw it as merely an imperialist plot, and the Italians also incriminated the Hungarian Communists. Both were familiar with the spirit of revolt among their own intellectuals: the Italians placed more importance on public debate, the French on authoritarian argument in exclusionary procedures. At base, their respective positions were not all that different, since Togliatti rejected the idea of "bourgeois" liberties with as much doctrinal firmness as Thorez, and celebrated "democratic centralism" in the Party with equal intransigence. But in a system of orthodoxy, the least nuance is significant. At the Eighth Congress of the Italian Communist Party in December, Togliatti had only to bring down the old refrain of the "Italian path to socialism" from the attic for his French comrades to declaim, through the voice of Roger Garaudy, the dangers of opportunist deviation.[34] Less than a year after the secret report, even in the West, it seemed that the most obvious effect of de-Stalinization was not a more realistic view of the past but a new configuration of forces. Since Stalin's death, Communism was emancipated less from its lies than from the steel grip that held its various branches together.

A characteristic of Communism, still obvious more than thirty years later during the Gorbachev period, was its inability to change. It tolerated all sorts of ideological tinkering, which allowed for some national diversification. But the continued role of "doctrinal" orthodoxy restrained the scope of such tinkering while making the least nuance absurdly significant. The Communist world had become more divided, while retaining its foundations in a universal lie. Henceforth, there was Russian Communism and Chinese Communism, East German Communism and Yugoslavian Communism, Italian Communism and French Communism, and so forth. Members of the same family, if not all equally close, they all laid claim to the same patrimony and were united by what separated them: Stalin was dead and "revisionists" were everywhere, that is, nowhere. To the weakening central myth, the parties offered respite and the chance for an occasional rebound.

As the interminable process of mending—which would occupy the Western Left until the final disappearance of the Communist regimes—was beginning, a Soviet writer was mourning in his own country. I have mentioned him earlier: his name was Vasily Grossman. In the West, where his books had not yet been translated, no one, at the time, knew who he was. His contemporaries, even in the Soviet Union, were unaware of the depth of the moral crisis that would separate him from Communism and even from Russia between 1952 and 1960, since the book he wrote during that period,[35] which testified to this internal drama, was not published until 1980, and then only in the West. Grossman, therefore, exerted no influence, intellectual or political, on either his Russian or his Western contemporaries. His significance lies less in the posthumous recognition of his talent than in the speed with which he was transformed from a Soviet writer into an anti-Soviet writer. A forerunner of Solzhenitsyn, but with less sparkle, he was the first anti-Soviet author of the postwar period.

Vasily Grossman was a Russian Jew; he was born in Berdichev, in the Jewish heart of the Russian empire, in 1905. After technical studies in

Kiev and later in Moscow, he worked as an engineer for a few years before devoting himself to the literary life, encouraged by Gorky. He began his métier in 1935 with a collection of stories, one of which, "In the City of Berdichev," had been published separately the year before.[36] Its title would lead one to expect a Jewish story, but instead, Grossman introduces a militant Bolshevik woman, Vavilova, into one of the old capitals of Hasidism, as if to dispel the spirit of the place. She is a political commissar in the Red Army at the time when the Polish counter-offensive is threatening the Western Ukraine in 1920. She is pregnant, and gives birth between two battles to a baby, Alyosha; she is then torn between maternal tenderness and her urge to return to battle. The Jews merely provide local color: the quarreling women, the men hesitant to take sides, the narrowness of family life in the shtetl. The inspiration of this short story went along with the spirit of the regime and conformed to its directives: Grossman was not a Judeo-Russian writer but a Soviet writer.

This was not such an uncomfortable situation, once independence had been sacrificed. It was certainly a social "position," and for members of the Writers' Union, material life was relatively easy. Grossman, moreover, was no cynic: a professional in Party themes, an apostle of the Good Cause, he sought to ennoble these compulsory subjects with genuine literary labor, in the tradition of Tolstoy. The civil war, the war of intervention, the Russo-Polish war, production, the kolkhozy, revolution, the Bolsheviks' military and civil heroism—in matter and form, Grossman was a good worker in socialist realism.[37] In contrast to Solzhenitsyn, he was not drawn to the life of a writer by rebelliousness; he took to it as a protected profession, and it was only later that the spirit of revolt gradually penetrated his writing.

The war ought to have affirmed Soviet identity for this Jewish child of the Polish-Ukrainian border. In fact, it threw everything into question. Grossman, as a correspondent of the principal army newspaper, *Krasanaya Zvezsda*, followed the Red Army for four years. He was one of the few intimate observers of the apocalyptic Russo-German front, the terrible retreat of the Red Army, Stalingrad, and the successive thrusts of the counteroffensive that would bring the Soviet flags to Berlin within two years. While acquiring a good feeling for Russian patriotism, Grossman also grasped the horror of what the Nazis had wrought as he traversed the reconquered territories. One of his essays attempts to depict the "hell of Treblinka."[38] The writer arrived at the site of the Nazi concentration camp with the Soviet army, at the beginning of September 1944, a little less than a year after the Germans had "closed" it and attempted to erase all signs of it. But through his eyes, ears, and sixth sense, Grossman divined the enormity of the crime. His article, published in *Znamia* in November, constituted one of the first major texts on the extermination camps of Eastern Poland—Treblinka, Sobibor, Belzec, Birkenau.[39] No other official journalist expressed what was at stake in the anti-Nazi war better than Grossman. He was the only Soviet author able to imagine the Jewish tragedy and having the courage to speak of it.

A short story, which appeared somewhat earlier, also deals with the horror of Nazism. Published in 1943, "The Old Professor" takes place in June 1942 in a small town in the Ukraine, similar to the one in which Grossman was born, at the moment of the German invasion and the imposition of the occupation.[40] The story describes the liquidation of local Jews, who, part way through the story, are driven to a ravine and executed en masse; the old professor, the hero of the story, stoic and wise as a rabbi, explains to his compatriots that they are about to die from "what is happening in the world":

> The Fascists have created an enormous, universal, pan-European penal colony, and in order to make the convicts obey them they have constructed an immense scale of oppression. The Dutch are having a harder time of it than the Danes, the French than the Dutch, and the Czechs than the French; a worse fate is that of the Greeks, Serbs, and Poles, and worse still is that of the Ukrainians and the Russians. These are the degrees on the penal-colony scale. The farther down one goes, the more blood, slavery, and sweat there is. And at the very bottom of this huge, multitiered prison is a chasm to which the Fascists have condemned the Jews. Their fate is meant to terrify all the rest of the European penal colony, so that every fate, no matter how horrible, should appear to be happiness compared to the fate of the Jews. And it seems to me that the sufferings of the Russians and the Ukrainians have now reached such a degree that the time has come to show them that there is a fate even more terrible, even more atrocious. They will say: "Don't complain, be proud, be happy that you are not Jewish!"[41]

Whatever the worth of the professor's argument, it does show that Grossman was one of the very first writers to question the Jewish genocide—not only the violence of the executioners but the anguish of the victims.

> "What can we do?" says Mendel the shirker. "It's fate. A neighbor said to my son: 'Iachka, you don't look Jewish at all, run away from the village.' My Iachka replied, 'I want to look like a Jew; wherever they take my father, I shall go too.'"[42]

Grossman was like that child: he wanted to "look Jewish" in spite of Soviet orthodoxy.[43]

Yet Grossman, unlike Isaak Babel, did not become Judeo-Russian. He aspired to be a Russian writer like Chekhov and Tolstoy, his models. Throughout his life he remained preoccupied with the greatness of the Russian people in the midst of one of the most trying times in its history. Grossman had followed the Red Army to Stalingrad, where his most important work originated. Conceived along the lines of *War and Peace,* the book is a saga with a hundred different characters and interlocking intrigues, but constructed around a central family that sets the scene for the Russian people at war. The battle of Stalingrad is its litmus test, and the martyred city lent its name to the work, which was changed by the authorities to *For a Just Cause*—a title both more opaque and more "Soviet" and used by the postwar authorities to bring the author, now suspect, back into line. Between 1945 and 1952, the huge manuscript went through a difficult period of censorship; first, extracts were published before it was finished, and then, because it said too little about Stalin and too much about the Jews, it was completely blocked for quite a long time.[44] It finally came out in 1952, but in a piecemeal fashion; it was hailed by the public but attacked violently by the press, which was remote-controlled from on high in the Soviet manner. The incident is recounted in detail in the two books on Grossman that have served me for this account.[45]

Was the writer saved by Stalin's death, which occurred not long thereafter? Yes and no. Yes, if we consider that it saved him from the Gulag. No, if we mean that the publication of his book in 1954 reintegrated him into Soviet literature, for he chose the opposite. Isolated, he had sunk into solitude. When *For a Just Cause* finally appeared during the period of "collective leadership," he had begun to rework the book. Under the pretext of writing a second volume devoted to the battle of Stalingrad itself,[46] he produced another version: same subject, same characters, same ambition, but this time free of caution and concessions and bearing a truly Tolstoyan title—*Life and Fate.* "As the Russian tradition teaches us," said Grossman to a friend, "the two substantives must be linked by the conjunction *and*."[47]

What happened to Grossman between *For a Just Cause* and *Life and Fate*? What occurred between the post–World War II period, when Grossman was a suspect author but remained a Soviet Russian, making the rounds of the official periodicals so as to get his book published and entering into compromises with the censors, and the post-Stalinist period, when Grossman, who to all appearances had won the game, went into an internal exile and rewrote another book, having once again become a Russian author? *For a Just Cause* was eventually published, in dribs and drabs, under Stalin. The manuscript for *Life and Fate* was seized by the KGB under Khrushchev, in February 1961 [48]—a paradox that says everything about the progress of freedom in Grossman's land and the contradictions of Khrushchevism.

The subject of *Life and Fate* indicates the source of the author's disenchantment—the war and its concomitant sacrifices and hopes. By mobilizing the primitive, stoic courage of the Russian people for the service of the homeland, the war had also harnessed liberty, since the enemy to be defeated was Hitler's Germany.[49] It thus appeared not only as an anti-Nazi crusade but as a democratic expiation of the regime, obscuring bad memories in the name of freer tomorrows. The hopes of Pasternak or Grossman were no different from Roosevelt's illusions about Stalin: they all thought there was an irresistible logic in the war against Hitler. But things turned out differently, and Stalin's regime emerged unaltered from its victory. Indeed, it added another group to its panoply of hatred and persecution: the Jews, or at least the Jews who managed to survive the Nazi genocide. Soviet anti-Semitism was stronger, and was more encouraged by those in power, after the war than in any other period of the USSR's history. It would culminate in the massive "anti-Zionist" campaign between 1949 and 1953. How could Grossman, a Russian Jew who was the most assiduous witness of the Jewish tragedy, be allowed to appropriate Stalingrad, that monument to the glory of the Stalinist regime?

The war exacerbated the fate of the nation. Won thanks to the extraordinary virtues of a naive people that had put its faith in Stalin, it led to a reinforcement of totalitarian power comparable to that of Nazi Germany. The Russians, including the Russian Jews, ought to have hated their leaders. The war had been a useless sacrifice. This is the despairing tone of *Life and Fate*, one of the saddest books of the twentieth century.

In the book, the war is judged negatively for the slavery it had allowed to triumph but positively for what it had consolidated; it was an admirable war because of the simple heroism displayed by the Russian people, and yet it had no good outcome, since the only possible victors were deplorable ones—Hitler or Stalin. Grossman's dilemma was even more insoluble than that of Stauffenberg, the ringleader of the July 1944 plot against Hitler. In the case of the young German aristocrat, the choice was between defeat of the homeland, a defeat that would nonetheless free it, and victory, which would render it definitively prisoner to the Nazi adventurer along with all of Europe—a dramatic choice, but a feasible one. The path to liberty and goodness led through a national ordeal, but the path did exist. For the author of *Life and Fate*, the Russian people had the choice between captivity under Hitler and captivity under Stalin. What was there to do? There was no question of helping Hitler. Grossman understood what had made Vlasov act, but did not approve of it. The atrocities committed by the Nazi troops in Russia and the Ukraine made the natural duty to fight for the homeland all the more pressing. But by defending Russian soil, the Russians tightened the noose around their own necks; they gave all their strength to the dictatorship and risked exporting that tyranny to all of Europe. There was no good choice; there was only a choice of the lesser of two evils, still a bad choice despite the courage it required. Here was an unhappy people, singled out by the misfortunes of the age, condemned by its virtues to tighten its own shackles.

This misfortune forms the backdrop of *Life and Fate;* it is like a constant murmur on the part of the characters, both soldiers and civilians. They have all come so far that the war at least gives their sufferings some merit. An old Ukrainian peasant, Khristya Chunyak, picks up the dying Semionov, a driver who has been evacuated from a convoy of prisoners taken by the Germans at Stalingrad. He has been starved by the enemy. Khristya remembers having suffered the same treatment at the hands of her own people. Twelve years earlier, she lost her husband in the same way:

> A low wailing hung over the village; the little children kept up a constant, barely audible whine as they crawled about like living skeletons. The men wandered aimlessly around the yards, exhausted by hunger, barely able to breathe, their feet swollen. The women went on searching for something to eat, but everything had already gone— nettles, acorns, and linden leaves, uncured sheepskins, old bones, hooves and horns that had been lying around on the ground. . . . Meanwhile the young men from the city went from house to house, hardly glancing at the dead and dying, searching cellars, digging holes in barns, prodding the ground with iron bars. . . . They were searching for grain hidden away by the kulaks.
>
> One sultry day Vasily Chunyak had breathed his last breath. Just then the young men from the city had come back to the hut. One of them, a man with blue eyes and an accent just like Semionov's, had walked up to the corpse and said:
>
> "They're an obstinate lot, these kulaks. They'd rather die than give in."[50]

The other black year, the height of prewar terror, was 1937, the year of countless unpredictable arrests within the Bolshevik Party—the purge of the all the nation's cadres. *For a Just Cause* devoted a lot of space to the Bolsheviks, but not to their detriment. In *Life and Fate* we find the same characters, heavy with their tragedy. The most complex among them is Krymov, the secretary of the regional committee of Stalingrad, a veteran of the Comintern and its empty rhetoric, who nonetheless is almost arrested in 1937–38. Solitary, dumped by his wife, he discovers a new role for himself at Stalingrad, where he feels out of his element since the people there are being reborn: "There was something good about the relations between people here. There was a true sense of dignity and equality on this clay slope where so much blood had been spilt." [51] As an abstract internationalist, he has lost the use of nationalist language. In the end, he does not escape arrest, even in wartime: a sign that the reign of denunciation remains alive in the Party, and that Stalin's bureaucracy has lost nothing of its absolute power. The bureaucracy will even win the war, draped in nationalism, in place of the true victors.

Anti-Semitism, then, subject to a moral interdiction everywhere after the war, survived and even prospered in Stalin's Soviet Union, encouraged by the state. A Russian patriot, Grossman was obsessed by the Nazis' massacre of the Jews; he was a rarity in a country whose official language recognized only victims of Nazism in general, and where what did exist of a "Russian" opposition to Sovietism tended to reproach the Jews for their participation in the Communist movement. Grossman saw the genocide as the distinctive event of the first half of the twentieth century, a time when—in accordance with philosophies of race and society—"whole sections of the Jewish population were exterminated"; and he adds, "Understandably, the present day remains discreetly silent about this." [52] That silence occurred almost everywhere, but especially in the USSR, where anti-Semitism was in full swing after the war, in the governmental form that it had assumed in Germany. "In totalitarian countries, where society as such no longer exists, there can arise State anti-Semitism. This is a sign that the State is looking for the support of fools, reactionaries and failures, that is seeking to capitalize on the ignorance of the superstitious and the anger of the hungry. The first stage of anti-Semitism is discrimination. . . . The second stage is wholesale destruction." [53]

Grossman's book centers entirely on a comparison between the two totalitarianisms at war against one another, thus depriving the Russian people of a victory since their confrontation contained no camp for liberty. Fighting Communism, Hitler promised a similar, perhaps worse servitude. Fighting Nazism, Stalin sought to extend his absolute power.

Both dictators wanted to destroy what was most noble in human beings, their instinct for liberty. They condemned humanity to the *fate* of enslavement, whereas human *life* consists in being free—as the soldiers who defended Stalingrad were free.

This explains why the camps, which were common to both regimes, were such an important theme—Grossman reflects Hannah Arendt (though he seems not to have read her works) in a fictional way. His story continuously passes from German concentration camps to Soviet camps and back; from the world of the *zeks* in the Siberian taiga to that of the prisoners, Russian and non-Russian, framed by the Nazi miradors. One evening in 1943, behind one of those miradors, in the block in which the old Bolsheviks who are of special interest to the Gestapo are held, one of them, a Soviet commandant who had been taken prisoner at Stalingrad, finds no other explanation for the war than the Fascists' hatred of Communism. He repeats Stalin's argument, directing it at his comrades:

> "Listen, cossacks! Everything's fine! Can't you see that? Every day that the State created by Lenin continues to exist is a death-blow to Fascism. Fascism has no choice: it must either destroy us or perish. The hatred Fascism bears us is yet another proof—a far-reaching proof—of the justice of Lenin's cause. The more the Fascists hate us, the more certain we can be of our own rightness. . . . And in the end we will defeat them." [54]

Later on in the book, in the same camp, Grossman dramatizes the same idea but in a different form: this time the comparison between Hitler and Stalin is made by a Nazi officer. Liss, the commandant of the camp and a thoroughgoing SS man, summons to his office an old Bolshevik militant, Mostovskoy, imprisoned under czarism, a pillar of the Comintern, unconditionally loyal, and nevertheless expelled before the war for having sympathized with Bukharin. Liss speaks to him of the interchangeability of their roles: "When we look one another in the face, we're neither of us just looking at a face we hate—no, we're gazing into a mirror. That's the tragedy of our age. Do you really not recognize yourselves in us—yourselves and the strength of your will? Isn't it true for you too the world *is* your will? Is there anything that can make *you* waver?" [55] In other words, the war being fought by the Nazis has no intellectual or moral sense, in spite of the ideological overinvestment of which it is the object. It feeds on national hatred on both sides, bringing into conflict two different manifestations of the same thing: the party-state. If Hitler's Germany should be victorious, the people will be alone without a partner in the weight of all that hatred. If it should be defeated, Nazism will persist, concealed within the triumph of Communism: then Stalin can even take advantage of hatred of the Jews.

Mostovskoy, disconcerted, is momentarily caught in the confusion of his enemy. He perceives that, in order to refute the SS officer's words, he will have to rehabilitate the ideas and people that he too has learned to despise, and to restore philosophical dignity to morality and religion—in short, to recognize that Christians, Tolstoyans, or even Mensheviks were right to renounce Lenin and Stalin. But this fleeting disorientation gives way to the reality of the situation, bringing him back to his political faith—the precondition for his psychological and moral grounding. Mostovskoy thinks about history, which is on his side. But he finds a surer haven in the friend-enemy relationship, by which he can recover his hatred for the adversary intact.

This scene in *Life and Fate* need not be interpreted as an illustration of the equivalence of evil in the two regimes that fought each other at Stalingrad. The comments on their identity are put into the mouth of the SS officer, who is speaking as a devil's advocate in order to gauge the morale of his enemy.[56] In this way the import of his words is relativized. Moreover, Grossman did not regard the battle of Stalingrad as bringing two equally detestable enemies face to face. On the contrary, the Russian soldiers were there to defend their land, to come to the aid of the country, and to protect freedom; even the Communists were swept up in that just cause, if only temporarily, since they were the ones governing the country. The Red Army's heroism served morality and justice, saving the Bolsheviks from the consequences of their own doctrine. So it is no longer paradoxical that the Russian writer most obsessed with the massacre of European Jews between 1941 and 1945 was the same writer who constantly reworked the parallel between Nazism and Communism. Jewish martyrdom pervades *Life and Fate,* from the ghettos to the gas chambers, defining the Nazi evil as unparalleled and thus highlighting the meaning of the Russian people's fight. But the particular aspect of the Jewish massacre did not rule out comparable aspects of the two regimes' philosophies of power and their negation of liberty. The Russian people's just war in no way canceled out Bolshevik nihilism, concealed beneath the hatred of Nazism. And the victory of the Russian people also rang in the hour of captivity without recourse. The musings of Liss were the prophecies of the author ex post facto.[57]

There is something of Solzhenitsyn in Grossman—the same love of the Russian people, the same compassion for its unjust misfortunes and its betrayed goodness, the same radical condemnation of the Soviet regime and of Bolshevik ideology, the same feel for religion, disaffected in one, Judeo-Christian in the other. And Solzhenitsyn was arrested in uniform, a few months before the end of the war, as though his life reflected, in advance, the absolute pessimism of *Life and Fate*. Better yet: on arriving at the Gulag, he was greeted, along with his fellow prisoners, with cries of "They've brought the Fascists!"[58] These were cries of joy, for it meant freedom for the regular prisoners, who were amnestied by Stalin in honor of the end of the war.

> They had always hated us or at least disdained us, but now the nonpolitical offenders looked upon us almost with love because we had come to take their places. And those same prisoners who had learned, in German captivity, that there is no nation more despised, more abandoned, more alien and unneeded than the Russian, now learned, leaping down from red cattle cars and trucks onto the Russian earth, that even among this outcast people they were the most benighted and grievous of all.[59]

Solzhenitsyn, in a sense, wrote the sequel to *Life and Fate*. Grossman's heroes, having become the *zek*s of the archipelago, were marked with infamy by the power they had saved and stigmatized by the ideology of the enemy they had beaten. So indispensable had anti-Fascism become for the untruth underlying Stalin's power that he now needed post-Fascism. One of the most profound truths of *Life and Fate* is this subtle unveiling of the secret connivance between Nazism and Communism, even in war.

Grossman did not live much beyond the confiscation of his manuscript. He died in 1964, in poverty and in despair at the loss of his book.[60] Of the six categories of burial allowed Soviet writers, he managed barely to obtain the fifth, thanks to his friend Sémion Lipkine[61] and in recognition for the work he had done prior to *Life and Fate*. It was a minimal and yet an excessive privilege, since Grossman was not a Soviet author. Twenty years later, the world would discover a great Russian Jewish writer who was also one of the most profound witnesses to the twentieth century. Thanks to Grossman, in the period opened by the Twentieth Congress, the tradition of the Russian novel was reinvented.

EPILOGUE

There was something accidental about the denunciation of Stalin by his successor. Khrushchev put so much fire into it that one sensed more than political calculation at work in the "secret report" to the Twentieth Congress: it was the voice of someone out to break a taboo and who, carried away by the shocking nature of what he was saying, had lost control of its effects. In one evening, Khrushchev abolished the laws of empty political rhetoric.

But his speech was also part of the logic of necessity or, in other words, of the succession. Of all the regimes strongly identified with the existence of one person, none has ever survived intact the death of the sole authority. Stalin's case was no exception. The devolution of such an exorbitant power onto a single head was not acceptable to any of the presumptive heirs. The shift from that point to the declaration of the regime as illegitimate was facilitated by the "collective leadership" slogan, which sounded better in the annals of Marxism than proclamations of devotion to the Leader. Though useless for interpreting what had already occurred, the doctrine remained indispensable to appropriate the present and the future.

The post-Stalin division of power, therefore, was largely predetermined along the classic lines of change and continuity. What Khrushchev added was a talent quite unexpected in an apparatchik formed by the school of fear and silence—a gift for dramatization and a taste for risk. By the same token, he gave the first succession crisis a foretaste of finality. He denounced the Terror, of which he had been an agent. He abased Stalin, whom he had celebrated. He struck at the past of the regime with so much brutality that he toppled its legend. He needed de-Stalinization to allow Soviet power to devolve to his favor, but by choosing to realize the succession in a discontinuous fashion, he brought its ideological foundations into question. If only by virtue of the supreme authority of the movement, Communists in the USSR and in the world were dispossessed of an essential part of their past, of which they nonetheless remained the offspring. Nothing would be as before.

Not that the system had been shaken to its foundations within the Soviet Union. The leaders' rivalries in no way weakened the dictatorship of the Party over the country. The last-minute execution of Beria elicited no more of a reaction than those of Zinoviev and Bukharin, when the trials were in full swing. Nor did the eviction of Molotov, Malenkov, and Kaganovich from the Central Committee in June 1957, or that of Marshall Zhukov in October, elicit much of a reaction from a dawning "public opinion." And from March 1958 on, Khrushchev, like Stalin, accumulated the two key posts of Prime Minister and First Party Secretary. Through his control of the party, he was furnished with absolute power and would soon be celebrated as an exceptionally wise statesman, regardless of the nature of his initiatives and whims.

His reign brought about no transformation of the regime's political institutions. The Communist Party remained the unique and omnipotent master; the KGB did not tolerate the least opposition. Nor did he institute economic reform: the socialization of all production and exchanges in the hands of power and the bureaucratic administration of the economy remained the cornerstones of society, as attested to by the failure of the First Secretary's vast agricultural projects. As for his foreign policy, it descended in a direct line from Stalin's: the reinforcement and, where possible, the extension of the socialist camp at the expense of imperialism, at the price of major technological developments in the military or, by default, fierce political confrontation—the Berlin Wall, an invention so extravagant that it seemed to have come out of another age, was built in 1961. All over the world, Khrushchev proclaimed that he was as loyal as ever to the ambition of all Bolsheviks—to bury capitalism.

What, then, made him appear so iconoclastic, and how did his historical persona gain its lasting reputation? The answer is simple: he represented the end of political assassinations and mass terror. He had beaten his rivals, but without liquidating them; they, in turn, would take their revenge in 1964 by paying him back in kind. He did nothing to reduce the arbitrariness of the state police. As late as 1957 he instituted a hunt for "parasites," thus providing a target for denunciations and a pretext for the KGB. But the country would no longer be subjected to repression comparable to the martyrdom of the Ukrainian peasantry, the Terror of 1936–38, or the massive deportation of the small ethnic groups. The secret report contained no profession of liberal faith on the

part of Khrushchev, no new political ideas, and no new form of socialism. He had not attacked Stalin's system, or even all of his methods—
only those aspects of the Terror that were abhorrent, universal, and almost mad.

The Soviet Union, under Khrushchev, moved from the totalitarian
stage to the police stage. I am employing these two terms not so much
to define two different states of political society—such precision would
be illusory—as to plot its evolution. It is clear that under Khrushchev,
and after him as well, the USSR retained totalitarian features—the will
of those in power to control thought through language and to have the
people speak exclusively with the vocabulary and slogans imposed from
above. But although that will was still inseparable from the dictatorship
of the Party, which continued to function in the name of Marxism-
Leninism, it was not universally obeyed. Even in public, strange voices
were allowed to be heard, voices thought to have been lost forever.
The regime had lost the almost perfect power it had held over the vast
buzz of self-celebration that had been issuing from the USSR for more
than twenty-five years. Other Soviet citizens began making themselves
heard, telling a different story.

In order to turn the USSR into an airtight space, which nothing
could either leak out of or seep into without the police's prior knowledge, Stalin had taken particular care to subjugate or liquidate the intelligentsia. He had co-opted Gorky, and ordered the assassination of
Mandelstam.[1] Khrushchev, in contrast, needed the intellectuals' support. With de-Stalinization, he stopped short of allowing a rebirth of
the intelligentsia, but he did allow it to resurface. He afforded it a little
public space. Gorbachev did the same, in different circumstances, thirty
years later, no doubt motivated by similar intentions and by the same
appraisal of means. Neither one of them had a great deal of choice in a
society whose foundations had been destroyed. Many of Gorbachev's
interlocutors, moreover, with Sakharov at the fore, had been born
into the opposition under Khrushchev. Through them, Russian society
began to find its voice again, as they showed the way to a moral and
political renaissance.

Not that the intellectuals actually enjoyed freedom of speech, let
alone freedom of publication. At the time of their first attempts to alert
Khrushchev to their increasing opposition to hydrogen bomb testing in
the late 1950s, Sakharov was rebuffed and began his career as a suspect.
The Pasternak "scandal" broke out at the same time. Completed in
1955, *Doctor Zhivago* was published in November 1957, but in Italy.[2]
The Writers' Union, loyal interpreter of the will of those in power, opposed its publication in Moscow. Less than a year later, it received the

Nobel Prize. The reverence accorded the book in the West provoked a hail of insults in the Soviet Union; the author was accused of betraying his country even as he restored to it its own history. The campaign orchestrated by the press and the Party was so intense that Pasternak was compelled to renege on his acceptance of the prize and express his submission in *Pravda*.[3]

But we must not allow the sinister things that the "Pasternak affair" revealed about the Soviet world to obscure the new things that were happening there. First of all, Pasternak was alive, whereas twenty years earlier he would have been arrested, deported, and probably killed. Second, his book was published, whereas formerly the manuscript would have been seized and destroyed. Finally, his case was public, whereas formerly it would have been buried. The torrent of abuse that the Party directed toward him was made of base but strong passions—egalitarianism, nationalism. Pasternak inspired courageous positions and a commitment to liberty, the germ of a timid liberal movement, largely involving recently liberated survivors of the Gulag. Thus, although the Pasternak affair ended in sadness—the writer's isolation in his own country[4]—it nonetheless inaugurated a new period in the relationship between the regime and the society. Persecution, when it no longer killed, gave its prey visibility. When it failed to destroy the literature of its opposition, it made people read it. To a certain extent, Khrushchev needed that literature; this need, in turn, lent a political status even to novels and poetry. The denunciation of the cult of personality had put the intelligentsia in the key role of special witness, a role it would continue to hold.

Thus arose an important if gradual modification in the image of the USSR held by Western intellectuals. Until then, these had only been aware of or familiar with Soviet writers favorable to the regime—who, more often than not, had been sent to meet them on some official mission. Gide, as we have seen, corresponded with Gorky prior to visiting him. Malraux, when one of the big wheels of Cominternian anti-Fascism between 1934 and 1939, received considerable attention from Koltsov and Ehrenburg. The notion of an anti-Soviet, Soviet intellectual was not only unknown but hardly conceivable. The case of Victor Serge, once it was settled, made few waves. The decimation of the Soviet intelligentsia during the 1930s went all but unnoticed in Western Europe. The Right ignored it, for lack of interest; the Left, for lack of perception.

The situation changed with Pasternak, Sakharov, Solzhenitsyn, and all those who would accompany or follow them. The Soviet intellectual was no longer a witness to socialism but a dissident writer. In this reversal, we must not forget the part played by the new situation created by the death of Stalin, the end of the Stalinist myth, the weakening of the dictatorship, and the reemergence of individual voices. According to the ironic law governing this type of situation, it was just when Soviet intellectuals were no longer being exterminated that they found they could arouse sympathy. Once they had recovered their status as thinkers and writers, they also regained the special influence that repression had stripped them of and that had been granted to the celebrators of the regime. Now they were replacing those celebrators with their own image as writers or scholars persecuted for their ideas, fighters for liberty and democracy. These were familiar characters in the West, liberated by the disintegration of Soviet mythology, and they helped that disintegration accelerate and spread. They helped extend the critique of the Moscow regime to all of public opinion, even on the left. Kravchenko had been a mere functionary who deserted his country. Pasternak was a writer wounded by censorship, whose government had forbidden him to accept a Nobel Prize. Banned in Moscow, *Doctor Zhivago* had been published first in Italy and then throughout the world by an extreme left-wing publisher. It had not been necessary for the anti-Communist Right to defend the book: the Communist Left had itself taken the initiative.

We should not push this too far, however. The Italian Communism of the time was the most inclined toward "polycentrism," and, moreover, the decision to publish the book had not been dependent on an editorial decision from the Party. Even though widely hailed as a resurrection of great Russian literature, Pasternak's saga also made many Communists grit their teeth, accustomed as they were to more bracing Soviet texts and little disposed to admire the independence of an author hailed by class adversaries. It is true that Pasternak did not hide his limited admiration for the collapse of October 1917. Nonetheless, because it came as an unexpected confirmation of the secret report, the whole affair constituted an important turning point in the Western view of the USSR. Amazingly, Western opinion tended to cast Pasternak's lot in the terms Khrushchev had used to criticize Stalinist despotism. The very thing that had enabled the poet to return to the literary scene made the return of persecution scandalous. The trickle of liberty regained made visible what totalitarianism had managed to conceal—the distance between the Soviet regime and liberty. Instead of reducing suspicion, the denunciation of Stalin made suspicion universal. If Stalin had perpetrated so many crimes, why should anyone believe his successors, who had served him? During the dictator's time, the disappearance of a number of writers—Pilniak, Babel, Mandelstam—barely caused a ripple in Western opinion. Under Stalin's successors, the banning of a book—crowned in Stockholm, it is true—turned into a universal scandal.

The new visibility of persecution hit all the harder because Khrushchev, in his speech to the Twentieth Congress, seemed to have been promising to end it, and he required a minimum of support from the society at large as a counterweight to the hostility of his rivals in the old Bolshevik guard. So the logic that led to a frontal denunciation of Stalin continued for several years to benefit intellectuals, who were at once beneficiaries, witnesses, and actors in this liberalization. The author of the secret report stopped moving in that direction as a concession to his rivals. He had to go along with them in the Pasternak affair, but had no intention of ending de-Stalinization, which had granted him his title to govern the Party and the nation, and which was fostering a moral and literary renaissance. This explains his zigzagging policy of alternating concessions and repression, depending on the new master's mood and the political situation. The few years preceding and following the Twenty-Second Congress in 1961 witnessed the birth of *samizdat*, the literature from the concentration camps, protest poetry, the fight for civil rights, and free reflection on the Soviet experience—Vasily Grossman, Varlam Chalamov, Eugenia Ginsburg, Vladimir Bukovsky, Aleksandr Solzhenitsyn, Andrei Sakharov. These years also yielded their share of arrests, incarcerations in psychiatric hospitals, and exorbitant condemnations. The fight, at least for the short term, remained totally unequal between a handful of men and the Soviet regime. But with the denunciation of Stalin, the regime itself had cast doubt on the arrests made in its name. Having lost its ideological foundation, repression weakened, though it was still indispensable.

The best account of these years can be found in a section of Solzhenitsyn's memoirs,[5] where he tells how he seized the chance of a lifetime. He was forty in 1958, old enough to be a survivor of the Gulag. He had been identified and arrested in February 1945. The war was not yet over and he was still in uniform. He "took" eight years of camp for having a bad attitude, but, as things turned out, the NKVD had offered him the greatest experience of his life: it added the sense of a providential mission to his passion for writing. Released in 1953, permitted to go home in 1956,[6] rehabilitated in 1957, his genius was fueled almost accidentally by de-Stalinization. He wrote his first books in secret, and by the time the survivors returned and their suffering had ceased to be taboo, he already felt like the new Tolstoy of the Gulag.

Thus Solzhenitsyn could enter the literary pantheon through the official gate—which gave his anti-Soviet preaching unhoped-for influence. As a great writer, a tireless fighter, a prophetic personality, he would soon have become known in any case. But it was through an enormous misunderstanding that his great voice found a provisional forum in an official publication—that was the gift of luck. At the time when Solzhenitsyn submitted *One Day in the Life of Ivan Denisovich*[7] to the journal *Novy Mir*, Khrushchev, in the midst of hostile intrigues with his rival, gave a new anti-Stalinist turn to the Twenty-Second Congress, in the fall of 1961. A few years earlier, he had authorized the persecution of Pasternak, less because of the substance of his work than because of the publication of *Doctor Zhivago* in the West, followed by the intrusion of the Nobel Prize into the closely guarded system of Soviet literature. This time, he personally intervened in *Novy Mir* to authorize the work of someone who had been deported for literature of the very same sort!

No doubt Khrushchev wanted to avoid another Pasternak "affair" at a time when he had particular need of the intelligentsia. But he misjudged both the man and the work. Pasternak was one of the last writers to have escaped from the good old days, and with *Doctor Zhivago* he had returned to the tradition of Russian fiction; he had not shown much regard for the October Revolution, but in the end he had carefully avoided treating the most tragic times in national history in his novel; a son of the ancien régime, he still possessed the grace of understatement and thus a certain prudence. On the other hand, the only society familiar to Solzhenitsyn was the "building of socialism," which had fired his rebellious temperament—a temperament rendered even more violent by his powerful Christian faith. In looking for an ally, the First Secretary came across the most implacably anti-Soviet person he could have found. In seeking to draw literature onto his side, he suddenly made the former prisoner into a "positive hero" of letters, something almost unique in the USSR. For the cardboard "new man" touted during the 1930s and 1940s by the "anti-Fascist" Writers' Congress, Khrushchev unwittingly substituted a genuine hero, as old as the world but whose condition had been renewed by the history of the twentieth century— victim of persecution, prisoner, deportee, in short, a *zek*. The Russian public transformed *One Day in the Life of Ivan Denisovich* into a triumph. Solzhenitsyn immediately became famous in Russia; a little later, his fame spread to the West. This sequence enhanced his glory, for no one could suspect him of being a mere product of anti-Soviet intrigue. The book by the erstwhile *zek* benefited from the same privilege as the secret report of the First Secretary, a few years earlier: since he was listened to and acclaimed in Moscow, he was an irreproachable witness for the West. At least Khrushchev, in denouncing Stalin, had taken care to separate the principle of own his power from the crimes of his predecessor. Solzhenitsyn, however, was at war with the principle itself.

The regime had even more to fear from one of its privileged sons. Sakharov was its most brilliant physicist, prized from an early age for his potential use to the regime, in 1953 a member of the Academy of Sciences at the age of thirty-two, and one of the creators of the Soviet hydrogen bomb. From 1957 on, he was also caught up, in his own way, in de-Stalinization. As his Western European and American colleagues had done fifteen years earlier, he worried about the threat to humanity posed by nuclear tests and the dangers of a nuclear war. This led to a series of confidential notes and rebuffs that would bring Sakharov to increasingly overt opposition. Later, he would explain that the atomic question had always been half scientific and half political and that it had naturally blazed a trail for political questions. No matter what the question, the key was to leave conformism behind. Having made that break, the rest followed naturally.[8] The regime itself contributed to this evolution by gradually pushing the physicist into the small circles of intellectual opposition. Alongside Solzhenitsyn, this would give him moral stature of another kind, no less prestigious and no less familiar to the civilized world than to the world of the accursed writer-prophet— that of the savant fighting for peace and liberty in the name of science and progress.

When Khrushchev was driven from the government, in the fall of 1964, for having acted too impetuously, it was beyond the power of any of his successors to bring back the period when the Soviet Union had been a hermetically sealed territory, from which only the official voice of power could be heard, echoed by millions of subjugated people. From now on, the USSR was a state that no word in any language could adequately describe, but which could best be defined in chronological terms such as "post-totalitarian," meaning sufficiently repressive to fill the prisons and psychiatric hospitals with people who thought incorrectly but no longer capable of inspiring the universal fear that was the condition of universal silence. The remains of loyalty to Stalinist despotism were thwarted by the remains of de-Stalinization. What was left of the Terror no longer had the support of the zeitgeist. The murderers had lost their faith and had become cynical. The victims no longer lived in fear; they protested.

The Brezhnev years, from the mid-1960s on, were probably the least unhappy, in material terms, in Soviet Russian history. But they were also the least legitimate. The Soviet Union invaded Czechoslovakia and occupied Afghanistan. It exiled, imprisoned, and deported its dissidents. It was in the hands of a bureaucracy of corrupt old men. The marriage between the revolutionary idea and its territories was drawing to a close. It had lasted a century.

It was now that the West began burying the Communist idea, a process that would take thirty years. The burial was surrounded by a huge crowd and accompanied by many tears. Even the younger generations participated occasionally, trying to make it look like a renaissance. I would like to have followed that cortège step by step, but it would have made this book too long. Let us content ourselves with an outline.

When the Soviet Union ceased to be a revered model, when even the European Left began listening to the dissidents, though not agreeing with them, the Communist idea exploited several substitute fields. It found new fronts, as we have seen, within the old Stalinist ideocratic empire, in states that had been emancipated less by the death of the despot than by the denunciation of his crimes: either they liberated themselves from Moscow's control by defending Stalin, as in Mao's China, or else they gained a little autonomy by pushing Khrushchevism, like the first Gomulka or the second Kádár. The secret report of 1956 had inevitably opened up these two paths, which modified themselves in due course: in matters of ideological heresy, only the first step counts, and it had been taken by Khrushchev. Since then, moreover, through the dissidents, the USSR itself has let a good many discordant voices be heard, more than one of which harked back to another kind of Communism.

The Communist idea had gained in dimensions what it had lost in unity. It had even gone beyond the geographical heritage of Stalin through Third World independence movements. The French intellectual Far Left briefly believed that the Algerian FLN was a rediscovered partner in a policy of "revolutionary defeatism." That was one way to apply the Leninist schema of 1914 to the situation created by the Algerian nationalists' struggle against the French "bourgeoisie." In a more general way, the battles and wars linked to the emancipation of colonized peoples would rejuvenate the themes of "imperialism, the highest stage of capitalism" by opening up new territories to them, even more distant from Russia than Russia had been from Europe in 1917. At the time, that distance had been erased by the familiarity produced by the circumstances of the war and the idea of the socialist revolution. Half a century later, other factors, of very different orders, contributed to the reduction of that distance: the rapid universalization of the world through technological progress and through the United Nations, the sense of guilt on the part of white peoples, the simplification of world politics into two basic camps. The theory of imperialism came just at the right time to designate the principal link in the capitalist system—that ever-present enemy of the emancipation of peoples, the United

States. The Americans were a nation born of a colonial revolt but were also a nation descended from European civilization; it was in the second role that the United States provided this late version of Leninism with a unified image as adversary.

Hatred of the United States lent a universal shape to the hatred of capital. But it no longer had any special point of application in the adoration or imitation of the USSR. It fed diverse movements and regimes, which were generally channeled by Soviet diplomacy, sometimes infiltrated, often aided materially, but not obliged to pattern their government or language on Moscow. Khrushchev had attempted to reoutline the "socialist camp" with an enlarged base but blander ideology, for which he paid the price at the Twentieth Congress. The Soviet Union had won supplementary political space in the third world, but at the risk of yielding the advantage of revolution to its rivals. China, as we have seen, was the first of these. Khrushchev had more or less brought Tito back into the family, but had lost Mao Tse-tung.

The Chinese president naturally wanted to corner the market on the fascination once exercised by Stalin. Circumstances had changed, and the Chinese leader was no longer borne along by the great wave of anti-Fascism. Chinese history, even recently, even insofar as it had been shared with the West during the Second World War, remains mysterious to the democratic public, which seldom gets excited about things so far out of its grasp. The Communist parties, moreover, were keeping an eye out for trouble. In contrast to Stalinism, in the West, Maoism would remain limited to small groups of students and intellectuals, incapable of even forming parties. It could only remobilize on a very small scale the ideological passion that had been disaffected since the Twentieth Soviet Congress.

As we have seen, Mao's China rapidly distanced itself from "de-Stalinization." It had cloaked its power struggle with the Soviet Union in the old universal language prostituted by Khrushchev—Marxism-Leninism—which had lost its authority. The orphans of Stalinism were to speak that language once again in its Chinese version. Against the "revisionists" of the Kremlin, Mao represented fidelity to tradition: as Trotsky had accused Stalin of betraying Lenin, so Mao accused Khrushchev of betraying Stalin. Nor was the accusation far-fetched. Like Stalin, Mao wanted to make a revolution within the revolution. His Great Leap Forward was similar to the forced march of the first Five-Year Plans, and his Cultural Revolution to "socialism in one country." Both Stalin and Mao tried to destroy the party of which they remained the leaders—Stalin through the police, Mao through the Red Guards. Both had been masters of the Marxist-Leninist catechism, presented in simple, scriptural formulas: *Questions of Leninism, The Little Red Book*—two international bestsellers.

The shift of the revolutionary passion from Stalin to Mao Tse-tung was obscured by the conflict between the Soviet Union and the People's Republic of China, which filled the 1960s and 1970s with its tumult. The Chinese Communist Party's violent hostility toward the USSR concealed what bound it to its hated adversary, which had furnished it with its language, its emotions, and its methods of terrorist domination. Maoism was a curious animal—a kind of anti-Soviet Stalinism for which Khrushchev had provided the opportunity but not the substance. Mao was fighting the Soviet Union with its own language, which he discredited by claiming to speak it better. If "imperialism" was henceforth the principal target of Moscow's "revisionism," what meaning could the words of ideology still have? The extraordinary power of these words over the imagination was revealed in their ability to arouse in the West, among student groups, the fanaticism of Communism's heyday, this time at Mao's service. But this fanaticism was closer to a millenarian heresy than to a religion of history. It reflected the twilight of Marxism-Leninism, not its renaissance. It one-upped Stalinism, but as an illusion about an illusion. It was like a child arriving at the store of the century's ideologies after closing time; an anti-Soviet copy of Sovietism, it was not born to last.

During the same period, "Castroism" was another incarnation of the revolutionary idea in the West. As in Mao's China, it involved a charismatic leader, an intellectual figure chosen by history, leading a popular army to victory. Castro had his own "long march," though it was not as long. It was only at the end of 1958 that he seized power with his guerrilleros. He was too young, too exotic, and too recent to be caught up in the internal battles that divided the Communist world. He had not, like Mao, aroused Khrushchev's wrath; nor, like Khrushchev, had he aroused that of Mao. And his Marxism had a tropical charm unlike the austerity of the Eurasian plains. The ideological pilgrimage to Cuba was all but made into a package tour.[9]

The image of Fidel Castro, seconded by that of Che Guevara, thus added its particular features to the revolutionary kaleidoscope that succeeded Stalinist monolithism. As it had done for Mao, the European Left developed a minor cult for the bearded dictator, in a less hieratic version, more appropriate to the dimensions of the Cuban theater and the good life in the West. If the cult of Mao had been one of the last outbreaks of pure Communist messianism, that of Castro allowed for a less puritanical and authoritarian approach. In Paris, for the disciples of Louis Althusser, Maoist China incarnated the utopia of a poor, austere, and just universe. For Californian students, Cuba under Castro represented a Latin paradise and communitarian warmth. How far we are from the 1930s and the enthusiasm evoked by the Soviet Five-Year Plans! Economic growth no longer counted, compared to such ideas as equality or community. The West was rich, and increasingly so, borne along by economic progress and the consumer society. Contrary to the unanimous predictions of the interwar period, Western capitalism, far from being dead and buried, was flourishing. The Communist utopia fell back on the glorification of poverty, but its audience now consisted only of the children of the wealthy.

This social shift was typical of the time. It was most visible in those Western nations, such as France and Italy, in which the Communist parties maintained their hold over a section of the workers but had little influence on the student movements, which sought their inspiration elsewhere than the USSR. The students, when unfamiliar with the Marxist political tradition, had no reason to exempt the Soviet Union from their criticism of modern bureaucratic oppression. And when they recycled Marxism to incriminate capitalism, they sought new clothes for it, outside of the Muscovite cloakroom. Even as Western Marxism was liberating itself, it was returning to a less risky function than that of a state philosophy; it now served merely to denounce bourgeois society, and it harked back to Marcuse and Gramsci rather than to Zhdanov or Laurent Casanova.[10] The crisis of Marxism-Leninism made Marxism itself appear to have a second wind, at the price of an eclectic interpretation, according to which it could lead either to the resumption of revolutionary radicalism or to a more frequent demand for a kind of anti-bourgeois individualism. The student protests at the end of the 1960s manifested all the various strains of Marxism, in a family portrait from which the bond of shared loyalty to a chosen country had disappeared. The movement now had its source and its heart in something much more diffuse than class or an international strategy: it marked a new political age, in which the working class was losing its messianic role at the same time as the Soviet Union was gradually being stripped of its myth. The hour belonged to an intellectual bohemia divided between self-hatred and the cult of self, a grouping of those who were condemning the existing society rather than calling for a model society. Periodic attempts to meet with the battalions of factory workers were merely holdovers from the past; students found the doors closed. The opposition to capitalism and bourgeois democracy had moved to a new set of actors, references, and registers.

In the West, therefore, everything was conspiring to weaken the myth of the Soviet Union. European societies had entered a period of rapid transformation, propelled by the very capitalist economy they had declared under sentence of death a quarter of a century earlier. They were integrating their workers better than their students; they were weakening class solidarity while sharpening expectations and frustrations. From the de-Stalinization period, European societies retained the Communist idea in the repertory of their political images, but they had extinguished its magic. That magic may have survived in old Cominternist parties, traces of another age, or, in the manner of Trotskyism, traveling aimlessly between scattered groups; but the plurality of models it cited as well as the contradictory policies it embraced were yet another sign that its Soviet embodiment was exhausted. The USSR was more than ever a military superpower at a time when it had already lost much of its utopian function.[11]

None of the substitute images really took the Soviet Union's place in the imaginary order in which it had held such a fundamental position since October 1917. Maoist activism only nourished small terrorist groups, without a real place in opinion. Castro aged much more quickly than October 1917; within only a few years, the young revolutionary hero had turned into a Stalinoid tyrant. In Europe, what was left of Communism's attraction was largely due to the luster it had managed to retain from the great pro-Soviet years—a heritage managed by former Cominform parties with a flair for adjusting to circumstances. It was no longer a matter of celebrating the USSR with triumphalist accents but of protecting its image at the price of inevitable concessions. The homeland of socialism was no longer the ideal regime where material and moral progress, liberty and equality all came into their own together. It was a country that had known the "cult of personality," the full consequences of which had yet to be overcome. That euphemism had allowed the general blessing which, in spite of the mistakes of its heirs, continued to enfold the October Revolution and to be extended to Brezhnev. It was sufficiently abstract to permit the Communist parties a minimal liberty of disavowal, indispensable to the maintenance of the principal thesis: that the Soviet Union incarnated the sense of history—in other words, the essential superiority of socialism over capitalism.

This margin of maneuver allowed the essential elements to be saved, while opening up a bit of space for the idea of a less authoritarian Communism, which could combine greater flexibility in the administration of the economy with a freer political debate and a devolution of power. Thus a kind of debased utopia emerged, drawn from its original form and destined to underline its decline: something that would remain derivative of the Soviet "genre" without a deficit of individual liberties.[12] This squaring of the philosophical circle, reconciling Marxism with the

idea of the "Rights of Man," fit poorly into the historical order, since
the dictatorship of a single party was an instrument common to all ex-
tant Communist regimes. Nonetheless, it formed a basis for the hopes
invested in the relative moderation of Kádár's government in Hungary,
prior to explaining Western enthusiasm for the "Prague Spring." Public
opinion was less taken with the margin of independence that had been
recovered vis-à-vis Moscow than with the "liberal" images of Communism that began to appear; one of the secrets of Dubcek's popularity
among the European Left in 1968 was that he represented the resurgence of liberty within the one-party regime, yet did not leave space for
the new "bourgeois" parties. The Czech episode illustrates the limits
within which even the most liberal "revisionism" evolved. It was not
even altered by Soviet military intervention, for the brief attempt at
"Eurocommunism" during the 1970s was still based on a "soft" version of Soviet Communism, gentle, pacifistic—in other words, Western—but remaining part of the family, another child of the October
revolution.

Such was the form in which the Communist idea sank below the
horizon of history, fashioned by the dual effort to alter its lifestyle and
to keep it loyal to its origins. Freed from the Procrustean bed of Stalinism, it had lost its power but gained flexibility. Having barely escaped
with its life, it still managed to gather those whose memories still tied
them to the old image, as well as those who wanted to give it a new
youth. They all shared, at least, hostility to those who sought to dishonor that past or to prevent a renaissance. Although—or perhaps
because—Communism had become less fanatic in some places, anti-
Communism was still a damnable heresy.

This old taboo had been the most loyal ally of the Communist idea
from the start, since it forbade criticism of the taboo itself. It played a
role similar to that of anti-Fascism in its Cominternian version, guaranteeing the Soviet experience a protection all the more airtight because it
followed a line of reasoning alien to Soviet history and thus independent
of reality. The immunity thus guaranteed to the USSR had found one
of its supports in the fight against Hitler. But its foundation was older,
independent of circumstances, and of a primordial order: since 1917, all
criticisms of the October Revolution had been subject to the accusation
of opposing the emancipation of workers and denying history. This accusation had been a constant means of Communist agitprop, hammered
home, from Lenin to Brezhnev, with the violence of excommunication.
It is difficult to imagine, now that it has disappeared, how and why it
intimidated so many. But we need only remind ourselves how deified
"history" bewitched the minds of the twentieth century. The Commu-

nists managed to capture that bewitchment to their benefit in the name of the "working class." This explains their power to disallow.

Curiously, the deification of history survived the weakening of the Communists and even gained strength and further justification from their decline. Khrushchev destroyed the myth of Stalin, but his belief in the direction of history was unshaken. He dealt a blow to the image of the Soviet Union but spread that of socialism. The society that was supposed to replace capitalism had lost nothing of its need to have diverse models, some of which it had yet to invent. The students in Paris, Berlin, and Rome who criticized the Soviet bureaucracy in 1968 had other versions of socialism in mind. But these children of the capitalism of abundance still consigned capitalism to the trash heap of history, just as the generation of the Great Depression had done thirty-five years earlier. The older generation, with memories of the depression and World War II, could still admire the Soviet Union, but prosperity offered no such resources to their offspring. For young people, however, who hated the market economy for the opposite reasons, the idea of socialism, even though ruined by the Soviet Union, nonetheless served their revolt, since it had got rid of its bad shepherds. In all of its forms— Chinese, Cuban, Albanian, Italian, Czech, Soviet, Cambodian, Sandinistan—Communism had preserved its historical privilege as the grave digger of capitalism.[13]

So the prohibition on anti-Communism at this time was as strict as ever. It gave shape to the minimal orthodoxy that united vague thoughts and idealized policies around a common rejection. The Communist parties watched over it as naturally as they would over a working-class tradition. They were diminished, aged, but still on their feet, loyal to their leaking ship and continuing to draw significant dividends from their mythological capital.[14] They remained strong enough to think they might eventually recuperate the marginal heretics of Maoism nor Castroism, but no longer had the strength to haggle over details.

Student protests did not produce unconditional supporters of the revolution. Instead, as a result of the democratization of the universities and the ideas of 1968, a mostly left-wing middle class emerged. The major legacy of the "events" that occurred at the Sorbonne, at the Free University in Berlin, at the Scuola Normale in Pisa, at Oxford University, and elsewhere was neither Maoism nor Castro-Gueverrism, which were evanescent, but a new bourgeois progressivism, more widespread than the old and with a different spirit. The old sixty-eighters had soon made their peace with the market, publicity, and consumer society, to which many of them took like ducks to water, as if they had denounced the sins of these institutions so as to better adapt to them. But they tried to hang onto the intellectual benefits of the idea of revolution in the midst of their social establishment. For the authors they admired— Marcuse, Foucault, Althusser—totalitarianism only persisted in the bourgeois order. It would be difficult indeed to find a critical analysis of "true socialism" in the twentieth century.

In France, admittedly, the "new philosophers" brought an end to that immunity by finally allowing the concept of totalitarianism to be applied to the history of the Soviet Union.[15] But the French case was unique, owing to the exceptional reception that the publication of the *Gulag Archipelago* received in France.[16] On the other hand, late anti-Stalinism did not stop the flourishing of a compensatory "revisionism," which was aimed at reviving the purged Marxist-Leninist tradition. During the same years when Solzhenitsyn's book was a bestseller in its French edition, the socialist Left joined forces with the oldest Stalinist party in the West in hopes of a renaissance, for they both sought to "break with capitalism." It was an anachronistic union but a fertile one, for it produced the presidency of François Mitterrand, who got caught for a while in the last neo-Bolshevik program of universal history. The Soviet myth had died in intellectual opinion, but survived in a debased form among the people at large, through the revisionist idea and, negatively, through condemnation of anti-Communism.

There is no place where this latter phenomenon was more obvious, during the same period, than in American universities, which offer the perfect setting to observe a taboo typical of the post–1960s generations. In the United States, anti-Communist sentiments had been widely shared in intellectual circles, in unison with the country at large, since the post–World War II years. The student revolts of the sixties, more drawn out and greater in scale than in Europe, broke up the consensus of the cold war. Young people combined their distaste for consumer society with denunciation of the Vietnam War. For the time being, their target was their own country, in a version of Leninist defeatism with the fronts reversed. The privileged children of the universities found themselves supporting revolution, while the labor unions sided with order. The ideas and passions displayed by the students were much more complex than the class hatred that the founder of Bolshevism, following Marx, had considered the engine of revolutionary action. But, more essentially, what emerged from the protests, swept along by a theatrical compassion for Vietnam, was a resurgence of illusionism about the Communist world. A better description might be a "new wave" of illusionism, different from the first, and much more widespread.

The remains of the American Communist Party after McCarthyism had foundered at the time of the Twentieth Congress. The revolutionary activism reborn with the student protests was no longer under Soviet direction. As in Paris, Rome, and Berlin, the references had shifted to Mao, Ho Chi Minh, Castro, Guevara, and, later, Ortega, the hero of "Sandinistan" Nicaragua. But the resurgence of exotic fanaticism touched only tiny minorities and was fleeting. The durable part of the student movement was the reinvention of a "radical" political culture, which saw the United States as less democratic than it claimed to be and the Soviet Union as more democratic than its adversaries believed. The philistines in Washington had tried to cast the two camps as two different types of society, as distinct from one another as liberty from servitude and good from evil. In return, the "radicals," when it was their turn to join university faculties, would teach the following generations about the United States' responsibility for the cold war and about the attenuating circumstances that could be applied to the Soviet Union if we would only take a new look at it.

Let us now turn to the social sciences, for they will lend this essay an air of objectivity by ratifying the social scientist's ambition to find the true causes of social functioning hidden beneath the interminable commentary that every society issues about itself. At this game, the particular ideological character of Soviet society loses its importance. The Soviet Union is a "pluralistic" society like all complex societies. The term "totalitarian," which Hannah Arendt made a part of our vocabulary, loses its pertinence and applicability in relation not only to Brezhnev's USSR but also to Stalin's. The word makes even less sense when it is not the state that is under consideration but social actors. For social scientists supplement their "scientific" qualities with democratic virtues. They combine the "infrastructural" approach with a fondness for the "little man"; they work the fabric of society from bottom to top. Thanks to the social scientists, the USSR was restored to the common context in which societies are judged.

The reader may here have recognized the new type of Sovietology, which, in the United States and Western Europe, took center stage in academia for the last twenty years of the Soviet regime. Like all schools of historiography, it has its good points and its bad, depending on the subject and the writer.[17] My present ambition is not to establish a critical bibliography but to try to describe the spirit common to these works, often put forth as a generational solidarity, especially in the United States, where the social and moral crisis of the 1960s was most profound. The elders—Merle Fainsod, Leonard Schapiro, Richard Pipes, Adam Ulam, Martin Malia, Alain Besançon, Robert Conquest[18]—were suspected of having written cold war Sovietology. The younger generation, more inclined to incriminate their own country, rejected anti-Communism from the opposite end. This meant demonstrating that Stalinism was not only a distinct period but was quite different from the history of Bolshevism; there were certainly many dreadful moments in the history initiated by the October Revolution, but such moments did not condemn the whole of that history since they were not a necessary consequence of it. This was an educated version of the idea—influential at the time—that Communism, including Brezhnev's version, ought to be saved from the crimes committed by Stalin, or, in a more general form, that the regime founded in October 1917 was good in spite of the disasters following its birth, whereas capitalism was bad in spite of the riches it engendered.

By a curious reversal, American professors came to hate the concept of totalitarianism after having studied it and written about it, whereas French intellectuals, at just about the same time, were beginning to study it after having ignored it. But it was American universities that expressed the most general spirit of the times, which was also visible in Italy, Britain, and Germany: in the last two decades of its existence, the Soviet Union, although it had forever lost the extravagant privilege of being a universal model, was still protected by what had survived of its founding promise. The failure of the October Revolution to achieve its goal, recognized by all, had in no way extinguished the Communist idea; it would find other temporary homelands. In the Soviet Union itself, its heritage remained sheltered from the influence it retained: its tragic side could be attributed more to the circumstances of its history than to Lenin or Stalin. Moreover, the modern society that was built in its name was susceptible to resale, to the limited extent that, in emerging from poverty, it rediscovered the star that had shone down on its cradle. The homeland of Marxism-Leninism also found itself under the paradoxical protection of the "revisionist" idea.

During this period, the image of Communism in the West underwent a contradictory evolution: the decline of Soviet mythology in its hard version corresponded to an extension of its soft version. The postwar times had turned around, and the USSR had lost forever its character as a model country, celebrated by Communist parties all over the world. Its partisans became less and less demanding, and were content with a "generally positive" score, paired with a hope for brilliant tomorrows. Because the Soviet Union was no longer the imperfect matrix of a better social order, it offered less ammunition to its adversaries, who were suspected of belonging to an outdated age of political passions. Exhausted as it was, it still furnished support for anticapitalist or anti-imperialist sentiments. If no one, not even the Communists, felt constrained to justify or praise the least of its deeds, the idea that had served as its banner was all the more universally available. Liberated from its obligation to be infallible, the October Revolution recovered some of its features, faded but rejuvenated.

This return to the original promise intersected with the political inclinations of the student generations. These generations had brought the Rights of Man to the fore, in place of class struggle. This done, they anticipated the end of the Soviet Union, since they claimed that the regime born of October was being judged by the tribunal of those very principles that Marx and Lenin had denounced as bourgeois lies. But what they really wanted to do, without knowing it, was something different: they were trying to give a fresh coat of paint to the confrontation between the ideologies of the universal and the particular by means of democratic abstraction. In this game, the Communists were at a disadvantage, since they were in contradiction with their own doctrine, and in legal matters, even late in the century, their score was pathetic. But in the world of moral finalities that formed the universalism of the Rights of Man, they could still make a case for their intentions: they found a retaining wall against history in the ideal kinship that linked them, in their purposes, to a liberal and democratic utopia. Right up to the end, the Soviet Union sheltered its image in what it wished to destroy. On the eve of the implosion of the regime founded by Lenin, anti-Communism was more generally condemned in the West than during the heyday of victorious anti-Fascism.

The last episode in Soviet history provides us with the ultimate demonstration that reformed Communism, socialism with "a human face," is the most universal form of political investment, of which I have been attempting to write the history. Gorbachev closed the chapter of Communist leaders acclaimed by the West.

The manner in which first the Soviet Union and then its empire fell apart remains mysterious. The role played by volition is the most difficult thing to discern; that of objective factors is easier to establish. The continually mounting price of world power and, especially, the arms race exhausted the Soviet economy, which badly needed a major boost. Perhaps historians will one day believe that President Reagan's policies were more efficacious than generally understood by the international press. It remains true that the internal decay of the Soviet Union in the Brezhnev years had reached such a degree that not only the power of the state but also its physical and moral health, supplies, living conditions, and hospitals—in short, the ability of public authorities to meet basic social needs—were in question. A measure of conditions, according to one demographer, was that infant mortality rates had never been higher than during the 1970s.[19]

Individuals, it is true, could live a little better than in the past, which is not saying much, since the regime was at the end of its rope, the party rife with corruption, cynicism, drunkenness, and widespread laziness. A major weakness of a one-party system with full powers over society is that the decline of the party brings on a general decline in the state. Nevertheless, this twilight Bolshevism could probably have survived a little longer and even made it to the end of the century. Although it had lost its faith, it maintained a vast police force, checking to see that people were still speaking the dead language of ideology. Sakharov was well guarded at Gorky. The psychiatric hospitals took care of the dissidents.

Brezhnev's successors, however, especially Andropov and, later, Gorbachev,[20] knew how to distance themselves from him: the risks of this logic had already been demonstrated by Khrushchev and had been the weak point in the dictatorship of the party since Lenin's death. To what extent a concerted program of reform was part of the tacit contract between Andropov, and then Gorbachev, and the majority of the Central Committee, nobody knows. This history remains to be written, and even to be known, since the Soviet Union remained blanketed in silence even on the eve of its dissolution. What is certain, at least, is that it began as a classic succession crisis, each new boss of the Party compelled to take control of the apparatus. Andropov and his immediate successor, Chernenko, did not stay in office long enough to present targets for the man who succeeded them; Brezhnev's men were still the ones to be put down or eliminated if one were to become master. So Gorbachev did as Khrushchev had done after Stalin, and as Brezhnev had done after Khrushchev: he grabbed as much power as he could.

But he did it in a new way. Before Gorbachev, the Party had been the sole means to power. The General Secretary could turn against it, or destroy its very framework and make it over, as Stalin had done in the 1930s. But no one had ever been master of the Soviet Union without having absolute authority over the Communist apparatus. When Khrushchev lost that authority in 1964, he fell. Gorbachev took another route to cement his position. It was not enough for him to remodel the upper levels of the Party; he also drew support from elements outside the Party. The liberation of Sakharov in 1986 indicated that he had changed the rules of the regime.

This tactic was not unlike Mao Tse-tung's launching of the Red

Guards against the Party apparatus. It was intended both to reinvent Communist enthusiasm and to weaken the Communist leaders, Gorbachev's open and potential rivals for the politburo. But things came out differently: everyone stopped responding to orders. The modest step taken toward society, and the relative suspension of police terror, revealed not a mounting of Communism but a vague aspiration toward democracy, which Gorbachev increasingly relied on, both by choice and by necessity. Khrushchev had never brought the Party's political monopoly into question. His distant successor violated that basic rule;[21] threatened, as Khrushchev had been, with being put into the minority on the Central Committee, he reanimated the Parliament and was obliged to seek support from fragments of public opinion such as the intelligentsia. But by weakening his adversaries, he weakened himself, destroying the source of his legitimacy, offering a new field to unexpected rivals. And by dispelling people's fear of speaking out, he suppressed the principle of obedience. Even the mounting economic disorder was in part due to this policy, insofar as such disorder is inseparable from state anarchy. "By suppressing the use of terror," one member of the Soviet Parliament said to me at the time, "Gorbachev had also suppressed confidence." This profound and frightening statement illustrates the fragility and ambiguity of the first and last "President of the Soviet Union": he was too much of a Communist for the freedom he had allowed in.

It is probably too early to know exactly what Gorbachev's intentions were. The only thing we can be sure of is that he did not want to do what he did. There is no reason to assume that he had been a closet anti-Communist, or even a bad Communist, before and after his accession to power. This product of the closed world of Sovietism should probably be taken at his word, as he continually preached the rebirth of Communism through reform. He opened the way to the liquidation of the Eastern European Communist regimes, in the fall of 1989, not because he had deliberately intended to do so but because he refused to spill blood. In the homeland of Bolshevism, he remained loyal to the original idea, renovating and renewing it, but not betraying it. Even his abandoning of the political monopoly of the Party was probably part of a strategy: to collect around him, along with the Communist majority, a large president's party, flanked by a marginalized Right and Left. His goal was something like the Mexican institutional revolutionary party, the loyal guardian of revolutionary legitimacy lost in the night of time. The fact that the project soon appeared to have no substance does not prove that it had never been entertained.

The most remarkable part of this story is not that Gorbachev tried to breathe new life into the Communist idea, but that the West believed him and was enthusiastic about him. Admittedly, many governments had their reservations, in spite of the popularity of the last Soviet leader in the West. No established power likes sudden breaks in situations and custom, and the USSR had for so long been a familiar part of the international scene that no one wanted it to disappear, not even its most constant adversaries.[22] Besides, Gorbachev was pushing for détente and arms reduction; Western financial aid, which had never failed the USSR, became massive when it was no longer a matter of helping to make ends meet but of staving off collapse.[23]

If capitalist governments were eager to help, they were outdone by Western public opinion, which, with the vague but encouraging terms of glasnost and perestroïka, began to celebrate the Soviet Union's promise to conform to the late twentieth-century obsession with "human rights"—to become a society that was less a paradise for the workers, as in the interwar years (for worker messianism hardly existed anymore in the 1980s), than a world of individuals at once free and protected from inequality. Gorbachev's Soviet Union always retained from the original October the benediction of having broken with capitalism, to which it added that of the rediscovery of "rights." What was called "socialism with a human face" in Prague in the spring of 1968 was now embodied by the mother-nation of Communism, which had finally espoused the ambition that the Red Army had destroyed in the womb twenty years earlier.

The last years of the Soviet myth were thus wrapped in a fictitious synthesis between the principles of Bolshevism and those of liberal-democratic pluralism. For Bolshevism was compatible with nationalism, as Stalin had shown all along, even with some autonomy restored to the market—as a temporary expedient, of course—as Lenin had thought to do with the NEP. But Bolshevism had no flexibility whatsoever in matters of ideology and political liberty. It could only hold sway through lies and fear. Even Khrushchev had to kill Nagy. Brezhnev put up with Ceauşescu and Kádár, but not with Dubcek. Gorbachev took up what Nagy and Dubcek had begun, but on a far wider scale, in the center of the empire: the reforms and the renaissance of Bolshevism were mixed with the principles that Bolshevism had sought to destroy in October 1917. He pretended to renovate the communist regime, but had no other ideas than those borrowed from the Western tradition, no other means than those he begged from the major capitalist democracies. His actions contradicted his stated intentions. When reference to the West gradually became a philosophy shared with Sakharov, unifying nomen-klatura and intellectual opposition, there was nothing left of the Communist idea but what it had destroyed. A society had been so badly broken that it had even lost its resources for a Western-style reconstruction, and it had no other resources.

The nations of Eastern and Central Europe, having broken with Moscow in order to rediscover the sources of their own history, immediately understood what was happening. In Russia itself, Gorbachev was still hated as a Communist leader, though he was more like a politician who had sold himself to the West. He acted as though he were still governing the country, but only Western public opinion believed it, credulous as always with respect to the Soviet Union. The Russians felt Gorbachev was presiding over a general disintegration with no foreseeable future, as though to deny once more one of Marxism's last ideas—that societies die only when the elements that are to take their place are ready, formed in the heart of the old world. But nothing like that was happening in Russia. Soviet Communism was disintegrating from within; Gorbachev merely speeded up its death, until his rival, Yeltsin, liquidated it. Born of a revolution, it would die of an involution. But its last leader, despised in Russia, was adored by the West right up to the end. Westerners had a hard time accepting his fall, since it necessarily spelled the end of an illusion that had filled the twentieth century. The Soviet Union left the scene of history before exhausting the patience of its foreign partisans. It left many orphans throughout the world.

By the failure of the regime born of October 1917 and, perhaps even more, by the radical character it assumed, the Communist idea was deprived not only of its chosen ground but also of any recourse: what died before our eyes with Gorbachev's Soviet Union were all the versions of Communism, and even the ambition to humanize it under more favorable conditions. It was as if the greatest path to social happiness ever opened to the modern imagination had been shut off. Communism had never conceived of any other tribunal than that of history, and here it was, condemned by history to vanish from the Earth. It could have lost the cold war and still survived as a regime. It could have engendered rival states, without dying as a principle. It could have presided over the development of diverse societies, which would nonetheless have preserved the original model. One can imagine other fates: it might have worn itself out entirely but have lived on as a body of ideas. But the fate it met left nothing of those ideas. In the space of a few months, the Communist regimes were forced to make way for ideas that the October Revolution had believed it was destroying and replacing: private property, the market, individual rights, "formal" constitutionalism, the separation of powers—the whole panoply of liberal democracy. The failure was total, for it wiped out the original aspiration.

The downfall of Communism has affected not only Communists and Communist sympathizers. For many others it has forced a reconsideration of convictions as old as the Western Left, even of democracy itself, starting with the sense of history by which Marxism-Leninism claimed to give democratic optimism a scientific guarantee. If capitalism has become the future of socialism, if the bourgeois world is what comes after the "proletarian revolution," whatever happened to temporal certainty? The inversion of canonical priorities has undone the dovetailing of epochs on the road to progress. Once again, history has become a tunnel that we enter in darkness, not knowing where our actions will lead, uncertain of our destiny, stripped of the illusory security of a science of what we do. At the end of the twentieth century, deprived of God, we have seen the foundations of deified history crumbling—a disaster that must somehow be averted.

To add to this threat of uncertainty, there is the shock of a closed future. Westerners have become accustomed to investing society with unlimited hope, since that promises freedom and equality for everyone. In order for these qualities to assume their full meaning, it might one day be necessary to go beyond the horizon of capitalism, to go beyond the universe of rich and poor. But the end of Communism has brought the individual back into the antinomy essential to bourgeois democracy. It has revealed, as if something quite new, the complementary and contradictory terms of the liberal equation—individual rights, and the market—thus compromising the very foundation of what has constituted revolutionary messianism for two hundred years. The idea of *another* society has become almost impossible to conceive of, and no one in the world today is offering any advice on the subject or even trying to formulate a new concept. Here we are, condemned to live in the world as it is.

This condition is too austere and contrary to the spirit of modern societies to last. Democracy, by virtue of its existence, creates the need for a world beyond the bourgeoisie and beyond Capital, a world in which a genuine human community can flourish. Throughout this book, the example of the Soviet Union has confirmed democracy's need for a utopia. The idea of Communism, in all its periods, never ceased to protect the history of Communism, right up to the last moment, when the history, by simply stopping, made the idea disappear also, having so long embodied it. But the end of the Soviet world in no way alters the democratic call for another society, and for that very reason we have every reason to believe that the massive failure of Communism will continue to enjoy attenuating circumstances in world opinion, and perhaps even renewed admiration. The Communist idea will not rise again in the form in which it died. The proletarian revolution, Marxist-Leninist science, the ideological election of a party, a territory, or an empire have undoubtedly come to an end along with the Soviet Union. The disappearance of these figures familiar to our century brings our age to a close; it does not, however, spell the end of the democratic repertory.

NOTES

1. This affirmation should be modified according to the particular country concerned; it is, for example, less true of Poland than of Hungary. I was thinking especially of the USSR, upon which everything actually depended, since it was Moscow that had started the wave of disintegration of the Soviet empire.

CHAPTER ONE

1. José Ortega y Gasset, *The Revolt of the Masses* (New York: Norton, 1957), originally published in Spain in 1926 as a series of articles in a Madrid newspaper.

2. Hannah Arendt, *The Origins of Totalitarianism*, vol. 3 (New York: Harcourt Brace & Co., 1951).

CHAPTER TWO

1. James Joll, *The Origins of the First World War* (London: Longman, 1984).

2. Benjamin Constant, "De l'esprit de conquête et de l'usurpation dans leurs rapports avec la civilisation européenne," in *De la liberté chez les Modernes*, edited by Marcel Gauchet (Paris: Hachette, Pluriel, 1980), 118–19.

3. V. I. Lenin, *Imperialism, the Highest Stage of Capitalism* (New York: International Publishers, 1969).

4. Jean-Jacques Becker, *Comment les Français sont entrés dans la guerre: Contribution à l'étude de l'opinion publique (printemps–été 1914)* (Paris: Presses de la Fondation nationale des sciences politiques, 1977).

5. Thomas Mann, *Reflections of a Non-political Man*, translated and introduced by Walter D. Morris (New York: F. Ungar, 1983).

6. The best analysis of this new aspect of the First World War is by Raymond Aron in *Les Guerres en chaîne* (Paris: Gallimard, 1951), chap. 1.

7. Alain [Émile Chartier], *Correspondance avec Élie et Florence Halévy* (Paris: Gallimard, 1957).

8. Letter of 31 January 1917, ibid., 251.

9. Cf. Alain's note of 17 October 1917 on Barbusse's *Le Feu*, which had just appeared: "*Le Feu* seems boring to me. It is told from the standpoint of an officer. Slavery is the evil most aggravated by the war." Ibid., 255.—Trans.

10. "Unfortunately we are governed, and during times like these, by decent folk [*honnêtes gens*]; a cynical sovereign would soon have peace." Letter of 15 March 1915, ibid., 193.

11. A small part of Halévy's correspondence, mostly addressed to Xavier Léon, is included in Alain, *Correspondance*, 322 ff. I was able to consult the rest of Élie Halévy's wartime correspondence (1914–18) among Halévy's papers thanks to the kindness of Mrs. Guy-Loë, to whom I am very grateful.

12. Élie Halévy was the son of Ludovic Halévy, the librettist, and Louise Bréguet, who descended from a Protestant industrial dynasty. He was the brother of Daniel. According to family rules, the two Halévy brothers were raised in the religion of their mother.

13. Élie Halévy's two major works deal with English history: *La formation du radicalisme philosophique*, 3 vols. (Paris: F. Alcan, 1901–4); and *Histoire du peuple anglais au XIXe siècle*, 4 vols. (Paris, Hachette: 1912–32, reissued in 5 vols. 1973–75). See also his Rhodes Memorial Lectures, delivered at Oxford in 1929 and published as *The World Crisis of 1914–1918: An Interpretation* (Oxford: Clarendon Press, 1930).

14. Unpublished letter of 17 November 1914 to Xavier Léon.

15. Unpublished letter of 27 January 1915 to Xavier Léon.

16. Unpublished letter of 3 July 1915 to Xavier Léon. The same idea may be found a few years later in another unpublished letter of 18 September 1917 to Léon: "War and Socialism. The state of war directly benefits State Socialism and, by way of reaction, revolutionary or anarchistic socialism."

17. "I understand why the proletariat would like peace at any price and without more ado, and I understand these crude and uneducated convictions. But I am always surprised by the political frivolity of men of the Challaye school." Unpublished letter of 29 November 1915 to Xavier Léon.

18. Ibid.

19. Letter of 26 November 1914 to Xavier Léon, in Alain, *Correspondance*, 342.

20. In an unpublished letter of 24 March 1916 to Xavier Léon, Halévy wrote, "I keep returning to my theory. The day Jaurès was assassinated and Europe went up in flames, a new era in the history of the world began. It is foolish to think it can be put out in six months."

21. See Alexis de Tocqueville, *Démocratie en Amérique*, pt. 2, bk. 3, chap. 32: "War does not always deliver democratic peoples to military government; but it cannot help but increase immensely, among these peoples, the attributions of civil government; it almost inevitably centralizes the control of all people and the distribution of all things into the hands of civil government. If it does not lead suddenly to despotism by violence, it gradually guides people there by habit."

22. Alain, *Correspondance*, 217.

23. Ibid., 252.

24. Letters to Xavier Léon, 17–27 March 1917, ibid., 363.

25. Élie Halévy to Xavier Léon, 28 March 1917, ibid., 363.

26. Élie Halévy to Xavier Léon, 30 June 1917, ibid., 253.

27. Guillaume Apollinaire, "C'est Lou qu'on la nommait," in *Calligrammes* (Paris, 1917).

28. This term belongs to the postwar political vocabulary. See, e.g., Ernst Jünger, "Die totale Mobilmachung," in *Krieg und Krieger* (1930).

29. Benjamin Constant, *De l'esprit de conquête et de l'usurpation* (Paris, 1814).

30. Jünger, "Die Total Mobilmachung."

31. Léon Werth, *Clavel soldat* (Paris: Editions Viviane Hamy, 1993), 100, 265.

32. On 19 July 1917 the Reichstag voted, 212 to 126, a motion to this effect, which was adopted by the socialists, the centrists, and the Progressive Party against the conservatives and national liberals.

33. At the beginning of 1917, Charles I of Austria sent his brother-in-law, Prince Sixtus de Bourbon-Parma, who served on the side of the Allies, on a peace mission.

Thanks to his contacts with Jules Cambon, the prince was received by Raymond Poincaré in February. But his attempt to open negotiations was blocked by both the Germans and the French, who had obligations to their Romanian and Serbian allies. In early June, Prince Sixtus failed in a second attempt.

34. Cited by Aron, *Les Guerres en chaîne, 33.*

35. Ibid., 33.

36. For a development of this argument, see Henry Kissinger, *Diplomacy* (New York: Simon & Schuster, 1994), 218–45.

37. Jacques Bainville, *Les conséquences économiques de la paix* (Paris, Fayard: 1920, reissued 1941).

38. John M. Keynes, *The Economic Consequences of Peace* (New York: Harcourt, Brace & Howe, 1920); and *Essays in Biography* (New York: Horizon Press, 1951). The first piece in *Essays* ("The Council of Four") is a portrait of the negotiators of the Treaty of Versailles. Keynes was one of the members of the British delegation. Of Clemenceau he wrote: "He felt about France what Pericles felt of Athens—unique value in her, nothing else mattering; but his theory of politics was Bismarck's. He had one illusion—France; and one disillusion—mankind, including Frenchmen and his colleagues not least" (p. 13).

39. Cf. Élie Halévy, "Une interprétation de la crise mondiale de 1914–1918," in *L'Ère des tyrannies* (Paris, Gallimard, 1990), 197: "The problem is to know whether a revolutionary war can end in any other way than in a revolutionary treaty."

40. Kaiser Wilhelm II abdicated on 9 November 1918. On the night of the ninth, the socialist Friedrich Ebert concluded a secret pact with the heads of the Reichswehr against the menace of a Bolshevik-inspired revolution that seemed possible considering the chaotic state of the country (strikes, protest marches, workers' and soldiers' meetings). The militants of the Spartacus League, which founded the German Communist Party between 29 December 1918 and 1 January 1919, planned to seize power. By discharging the Berlin chief of police, who had organized a sort of revolutionary police, on 4 January, the authorities made a show of force. General Noske obtained special powers and brutally put down the Communist insurrection. On 15 January, Rosa Luxemburg was assassinated at the same time as Karl Liebknecht by military officers.

In Hungary, Michel Karolyi's Social-Democratic government (formed in Oct. 1918) allied itself with the Hungarian Communist Party that Béla Kun had created in Moscow. Once the Soviet Republic of Hungary was created, Béla Kun instituted a program imitating that of the Bolsheviks: the nationalization of firms and banks, the confiscation of great properties by cooperatives, the creation of a political police. Unpopular in Hungary, the experiment ended, after 133 days of existence, on 1 August 1919 through the intervention of Romanian troops.

In Bavaria, the socialist Kurt Eisner headed the government from 8 November 1918. He was assassinated on 21 February 1919. In April, a Soviet Republic was proclaimed by the Anarchists and Social Democrats. On 1 May, it came to an end when Berlin sent in troops.

CHAPTER THREE

1. "Dictatorship is rule based directly upon force and unrestricted by any laws." Lenin, *The Proletarian Revolution and the Renegade Karl Kautsky* (Beijing: Foreign Languages Press, 1970), 11.

2. "Enquête sur la situation en Russie," *Bulletin des droits de l'homme* 10, no. 3 (1 February 1919) and nos. 5–6 (1–15 March 1919). These debates were brought to light by Christian Jelen in *L'aveuglement, les socialistes et la naissance du mythe soviétique,* with a foreword by Jean-François Revel (Paris: Flammarion, 1984).

3. The expression "The Revolution is a bloc" was used by Clemenceau during the parliamentary debate of 29 January 1891 prompted by the outlawing of Victorien Sardou's play *Thermidor*.

4. Between the execution of the Dantonists and the fall of Robespierre, or from 3 April to 27 July 1794.

5. Tamara Kondratieva, *Bolcheviks et jacobins* (Paris: Payot, 1989).

6. Ibid.

7. Albert Mathiez (1874–1932) was a historian of the French Revolution and a socialist, but he was not a true Marxist and did not hold with the Hegelian concept of *Aufhebung* as applied to 1789 and 1917.

8. One is reminded here of the passage in the *Social Contract* where Rousseau ponders the work of Peter the Great and the Russian penchant for borrowing and copying: "The Russians shall never be civilized, because they were so too soon. Peter had an imitative genius; he did not possess real genius, the genius that is creative and makes everything out of nothing. Some of the things he did were good, most of them were inappropriate. He saw that his people was barbarous, he did not see that it was not ripe for policing; he wanted to civilize it when he ought to have been hardening it. He wanted first of all to produce Germans or English when he should have begun by producing Russians; he kept his subjects forever from becoming what they could have become by persuading them that they were something they were not." Jean-Jacques Rousseau, *Le Contrat social*, bk. 2, chap. 8.

9. Alphonse Aulard, from 1886 on, held the first chair of the Revolution at the Sorbonne. Republican, radical, and a Freemason, he absolved the French Revolution by "circumstances." He thought the Russian Republic of February was comparable to the French émigrés who sought help from reactionary Europe. He hailed the Russian Revolution as a general case of revolution, a manifestation of the French-type radical experience, whereas, in fact, October was merely the natural continuation of February. He believed this, at least, in 1918–20. In his works after 1920, Aulard recognized this discontinuity and compared the Bolshevik Revolution unfavorably with the French Revolution. The latter had established democracy; the former, dictatorship.

10. At first, the Allies' attitude toward the Bolsheviks was subordinated to the imperatives of the war against the Germans. Symbolic contingents of soldiers were sent to Mourmansk, Arkhangelsk, and Vladivostok to reinforce the embargo. From the summer of 1918 on, they offered conditional aid to Admiral Koltchak in Siberia and to General Denikin in southern Russia. German capitulation modified the situation, but there was no decisive, coherent political policy. Like Clemenceau, Churchill advocated intervention, while Lloyd George favored negotiation. When the naval mutinies occurred in the Black Sea in April 1919, France terminated its intervention in Odessa (which involved 45,000 men). In September, Arkhangelsk and then Mourmansk were evacuated, and in the summer, the British left the Caucasus.

11. The Zimmerwald conference (5–8 September 1915) gathered together socialist partisans of peace "without annexation or indemnities" who were at that time very much in the minority of the different socialist parties. Lenin, who was there, defended the idea of creating a new International. The second "minority" conference was at Kienthal from 24 to 30 April 1916. There, Lenin advocated the withdrawal of all socialists from all governments and the rejection of military funds.

12. Rosa Luxemburg's 1904 article, originally titled "Organizational Problems in Russian Social Democracy," was republished in English under the title *Leninism or Marxism*, with an introduction by B. Wolfe (Ann Arbor: University of Michigan Press, 1934; reprinted by Spartacus, 1946). It was an article on Lenin's 1904 pamphlet *One Step Forward, Two Steps Back*, written in response to critiques by P. Axelrod.

13. Rosa Luxemburg's piece was written in prison; it was published in 1922 by Paul Levi when he broke with Lenin. Published in English as *The Russian Revolution* (New York, 1940).

14. Here I am alluding to Kautsky's critique of Bernstein that he published in 1899 in *Das Neue Zeit* as well as his work of the same year on the agrarian question. See Peter Gay, *The Dilemma of Democratic Socialism: Eduard Bernstein's Challenge to Marx* (New York: Columbia University Press, 1952). In 1899, Eduard Bernstein, the executor of Marx's will, published *The Preconditions of Socialism*, edited and translated by Henry Tudor (Cambridge: Cambridge University Press, 1993), a book in which he brings into question not only the Marxist canon on the evolution of capitalism but also the idea that a brutal rupture with society is a prerequisite for the installation of socialism. Karl Kautsky responded to Bernstein's "revisionism" by publishing *Bernstein und das sozialistische Programm* in 1899. Bernstein's analyses would be rejected by most Social Democrats.

15. *Karl Kautsky, Rosa Luxemburg, Anton Pannekoek: Socialisme, la voie occidentale*, edited and annotated by Henri Weber, translated by Alain Brossat (Paris: Presses universitaires de France, 1983).

16. Karl Kautsky, *The Road to Power*, translated by A. M. Simon (Chicago: Progressive Woman Publications, 1909).

17. Karl Kautsky, *The Dictatorship of the Proletariat*, in *Karl Kautsky: Selected Political Writings*, edited and translated by Patrick Goode (New York: St. Martin's Press), 98–125; *Terrorism and Communism: A Contribution to the Natural History of Revolution* (London: National Labour Press, 1920).

18. Karl Marx, *Critique of the Gotha Program* (New York: International Publishers, 1938). "Between capitalist and communist society lies the period of revolutionary transformation of the one into the other. There corresponds to this also a political transition period in which the State can be nothing but *the revolutionary dictatorship of the proletariat*" (18).

19. Benjamin Constant, *De la force du gouvernement actuel et de la nécessité de s'y rallier* (Paris, 1796), and *Des Effets de la Terreur* (Paris, 1797).

20. V. I. Lenin, *The Proletarian Revolution and the Renegade, Kautsky* (Beijing: Foreign Languages Press, 1975).

21. Boris Souvarine, in his little book *Autour du Congrès de Tours*, points out that those conditions were adapted and modified with respect to the French situation.

22. Annie Kriegel, *Aux origines du communisme français* (Paris and The Hague: Mouton et Cie, 1964), 2 vols.

23. Jacques Sadoul, foreword to Boris Souvarine, *La Troisième Internationale* (Paris: Editions Clarté, 1919).

24. Cited in Jean-Louis Pann, *Boris Souvarine, Le premier désenchanté du communisme* (Paris: Robert Laffont, 1993), 136.

25. Georges Sorel, *Réflexions sur la violence*, with a foreword by Jacques Julliard (Paris: Le Seuil, 1990), Appendix 3, "*pour Lenin*," 296.

26. In May 1920, the administrative commission of the Section française de l'Internationale ouvrière (SFIO) designated Jean Longuet and Marcel Cachin as its delegates to Moscow—two "reconstructors" of the Second International. Longuet was replaced by Louis Frossard. Frossard left with Cachin on 31 May and arrived in Petrograd on 10 June. Cachin had earlier gone to Russia, in April 1917, as an envoy of the House of Deputies' commission on foreign affairs, with the backing of the government.

In early April 1920, Alfred Rosmer, a member of the Committee on the Third International, traveled to Italy, Vienna, and Berlin and from there into Russia. In July, Raymond Lefebvre, another member of the same committee, and the libertarian unionists Marcel Vergeat and Jules Lepetit arrived in Russia. When returning home in early October, these three all disappeared at sea.

27. Mikhail Heller and Aleksandr Nekrich, *Utopia in Power: The History of the Soviet Union from 1917 to the Present,* translated by Phyllis B. Carlos (New York: Summit, 1986); and Richard Pipes, *The Russian Revolution* (New York: Knopf, 1990).

28. I borrow this expression from Michelet, who, in order to describe the state of mind among the French in 1792, refers to the worker or peasant as having "*rentré chez lui.*" *Histoire de la Révolution française* (Paris: Robert Laffont, "Bouquins," 1989), vol. 2, bk. 9, chap. 1,

29. Bertrand Russell, *The Practice and Theory of Bolshevism* (London: G. Allen and Unwin, 1921).

30. *The Autobiography of Bertrand Russell, 1944–69* (New York: Simon and Schuster, 1969), 10.

CHAPTER FOUR

1. Alain Besançon, "La Russie et la Révolution française," in *The French Revolution and the Creation of Modern Political Culture,* vol. 3, ed. François Furet and Mona Ozouf (Oxford: Pergamon Press, 1989), 575–84.

2. See François Furet, *Revolutionary France* (Cambridge, MA: Basil Blackwell, 1991)

3. The term "Leninism" appeared immediately after the death of Lenin (see Boris Souvarine, *Staline,* 307–9). In early April 1924, Joseph Stalin gave a lecture at the University of Sverdlov, which he later published as *The Principles of Leninism.* In 1925, Gregori Zinoviev wrote *Leninism.* The term "Marxism-Leninism" became common with the absolute power of Stalin, who used it in his 1938 *Dialectical Materialism, Historical Materialism.*

4. Pierre Pascal, *Mon journal de Russie,* vol. 1, *1916–1918,* foreword by J. Laloy (Paris: L'Age d'homme, 1975); *En Communisme: Mon journal de Russie,* vol. 2, *1918–1921* (1977); *Mon état d'âme: Mon journal de Russie,* vol. 3, *1922–1926* (1982); *Russie 1927: Mon journal de Russie,* vol. 4 (1982).

5. On Pierre Pascal's Catholicism, which was linked both to Sillon and to the "unionism" cherished by Père Portal, see Régis Ladoux, *Monsieur Portal et les siens,* foreword by Émile Poulat (Paris: Éditions du Cerf, 1985).

6. Pierre Pascal, *Avvakum et les débuts du raskol: La crise religieuse au XVIIe siècle en Russie* (Paris: Librairie Honoré Champion, 1938); *La Vie de l'archiprêtre Avvakum écrite par lui-même . . . ,* translated, with an introduction and notes, by Pierre Pascal (Paris: Gallimard, 1960). On the *raskol,* see Léon Poliakov, *L'Épopée des vieux-croyants* (Paris: Perrin, 1991).

7. Yann Moulier Boutang, *Louis Althusser: Une biographie* (Paris: Grasset, 1992).

8. Secretary of the Socialist Federation of Vienna prior to 1914, Jacques Sadoul (1881–1956) became Undersecretary of State for artillery in the cabinet of Albert Thomas, who then attached him to the French military mission in Russia. Sadoul then attempted to serve as an intermediary between the Allies and the Bolsheviks, hoping that the latter would continue the war against Germany. Having rallied to Bolshevism, he published, under the advice of Lenin, who, incidentally, didn't think much of him, his letters to Albert Thomas. Condemned to death in 1919 by the Paris military tribunal, Sadoul returned to France in 1924; he was acquitted in a second trial. Closely tied to the Soviets, he worked for *Izvestia.*

9. Jacques Sadoul's ambition was to be the sole leader of the French Communist group. In order to eliminate his rivals, he denounced Pierre Pascal to Lenin as a Menshevik sympathizer. An investigation was initiated, and Pascal was forced to de-

fend himself before the Cheka. Sadoul denounced Pascal once again, this time as a Catholic. See Pascal, *Journal* 2: 111-14.

10. Philippe Joseph Benjamin Buchez (1792-1865), with Prosper-Charles Roux, wrote the monumental *Histoire parlementaire de la Révolution française,* which appeared in forty volumes between 1834 and 1838. A former carbonaro and a former Saint-Simonian, he was both a Catholic and a socialist interpreter of the Revolution. In accordance with these two affiliations, he exalted the Jacobins' communitarian messianism, contrasting it to the bourgeois individualism of 1789.

11. Victor Serge, *Souvenirs d'un révolutionnaire* (Paris: Éditions du Seuil, 1951), 153-54.

12. From the materials in his *Journal,* which went so long unpublished, Pierre Pascal later composed a little book of Communist edification. It appeared in late 1920, on the eve of the Tours Congress, and was titled *En Russie rouge: Lettres d'un communiste français* (Petrograd: Éditions de l'Internationale communiste, 1920; Paris: Éditions de la Librairie de l'Humanité, 1921).

13. The Workers' Opposition began in 1919 and was led by Alexander Shliapnikov and Alexandra Kollontai. Its members defended their ideas at the Bolshevik Party's tenth congress as the Kronstadt uprising was occurring. The Workers' Opposition was designed to be the product of the "vanguard of the proletariat, which had not broken its ongoing liaison with the working-class masses organized as unions." The group's ideas about the role of trade unions were rejected by the congress, which forbade all opposition groups within the Party. See Alexandra Kollontai, *L'Opposition ouvrière* (Paris: Éditions du Seuil, 1974).

14. Letter to Rosmer, 24 September 1925; *cf.* Pierre Pascal, *Mon journal de Russie,* vol. 3, 114-16. This letter, erroneously dated 1923, explicitly refers to things that occurred in 1925.

15. Pascal was referring to the London Congress of 1903, in which the Russian Social Democratic Party would virtually break into two large, distinct parts, the majority (Bolsheviks) led by Lenin and the minority (Mensheviks) led by Martov.

16. A revolutionary syndicalist and founder of *La Vie ouvrière* (1909), Pierre Monatte (1881-1960) was one of the very first people to support the Bolshevik Revolution and led the revolutionary faction of the CGT until it split off in 1921. He joined *L'Humanité* in March 1922 but joined the Communist Party only in May 1923. He resigned in 1924 in protest against "Bolshevization" and then founded a new journal, *La Révolution prolétarienne.*

17. In 1933, just back from Soviet Russia, Pierre Pascal joined forces with Boris Souvarine to defend Victor Serge, who had been arrested again. In 1936 he wrote a foreword to a pamphlet by M. Yvon *(Ce qu'est devenue la révolution russe);* the title of his foreword, "Ceux qu'il faut croire" ("Those who must be believed"), indicates the value he placed upon the testimony of this worker, who had lived in the USSR for eleven years. In March 1952, he published in the periodical *Preuves* an article titled "La révolution russe et ses causes," in which he contrasted "the most generous of revolutions" to "that odious system that most brutally gave the lie to all the hopes of 1917." In April 1967, he once again wrote of the distinction between regime and revolution in *La Révolution prolétarienne* ("October and February were a single revolution"). He also participated in a debate organized by the journal *La Table ronde* (nos. 237-38, October/November 1967) with Jean Bruhat, Stanislas Fumet, and Pierre Sorlin on the theme "October 1917, the Russian Revolution and its fate."

18. Boris Souvarine is the subject of a remarkable biography, without which the following pages would not have been possible. Jean-Louis Panné, *Boris Souvarine, le premier désenchanté du communisme* (Paris: Robert Laffont, 1993).

19. Ibid., 60–61.

20. Charles Rappoport, *Une vie révolutionnaire, 1883–1940: Les Mémoires de Charles Rappoport*, edited by H. Goldberg and G. Haupt, foreword by M. Lagana (Paris: Éditions de la maison des sciences de l'homme, 1991).

21. See Boris Souvarine, *Autour du Congrès de Tours* (Paris: Champ libre, 1981), addendum E: the "missi dominici."

22. See the letter Souvarine wrote later, in 1929, to Amédée Dunois, cited by Panné, *Boris Souvarine*, 220. See also Angelica Balabanova, *My Life as a Rebel* (New York: Harper and Bros., 1938).

23. Jules Humbert-Droz, *L'Œil de Moscou à Paris, 1922–1924* (Paris: Julliard, coll. Archives, 1964).

24. Albert Treint (1889–1971) was a schoolteacher who finished the war as a captain. After allying himself with Bolshevism, he became a member of the left wing of the Communist Party. From 1923 on, he was Secretary of the Communist Party and a member of the Comintern Presidium. Close to Zinoviev, he adopted the latter's politics and opposed the other heads of the Party during the "Bolshevization" period. Eventually, after Zinoviev was pushed aside, Treint moved into the opposition himself, animating small oppositional groups before rejoining the SFIO.

25. The Belgian-born Nicolas Lazarevitch (1895–1975) returned to Russia in 1919 but was forced to go to Romania in the summer of the same year. He was in Milan when the factories were occupied in 1920. He then went back to Russia again, where he worked first as a laborer and then as a translator for the Comintern. From that time on, he was critical of the regime. Arrested in 1924 for organizing a group of workers agitating for authentic unions, he was deported in September 1926. Involved with Russian anarchists exiled in France, he was deported to Belgium, where he continued his militant activities. In 1931 he went to Spain and closely followed the social movement there. Returning to France in 1936, he worked as a copyeditor. After the war, still friends with Pierre Pascal and Souvarine, he collaborated with Albert Camus.

26. Panné, *Boris Souvarine*, 166.

27. Georg [György] Lukács, interview published in the *New Left Review*, July–August 1971. Reprinted in Georg Lukács, *Record of a Life*, edited by István Eörsi, translated by Rodney Livingstone (London: Verso Editions, 1983), 181.

28. Saul Bellow, *To Jerusalem and Back* (New York: Avon books, 1977), 162.

29. Arpad Kadarkay, *Georg Lukács: His Life, Thought and Politics* (Oxford: Basil Blackwell, 1991).

30. Cited in ibid., 11.

31. On the early Lukács, the young aesthete of Budapest, see György Markus, "The Life and the Soul: The Young Lukács and the Problem of Culture," in Agnès Heller, ed., *Lukács Reappraised* (New York: Columbia University Press, 1983).

32. Max Weber, *Politik als Beruf* (1917/1919), translated by Simona Draghici as *The Profession of Politics* (Washington, DC: Plutarch Press, 1989); *Wissenschaft als Beruf* (1919).

33. In November 1918, Weber wrote: "We have averted the worst things—the Russian knout. . . . America's world rule was as inevitable as that of Rome after the Punic Wars in ancient times. I hope it will continue not be shared with Russia . . . for the Russian danger has been averted only for now, not forever." From Marianne Weber, *Max Weber*, cited in Kadarkay, *Georg Lukács*, 187–88.

34. Kadarkay, *Georg Lukács*, 205.

35. See chapter 2, note 40, above.

36. *History and Class Consciousness*, translated by Rodney Livingstone (Cambridge, MA: MIT Press, 1968).

37. Victor Serge, *Mémoires d'un révolutionnnaire* (Paris: Éditions du Seuil, 1951), 198. Although Serge dates this meeting in 1928 or 1929, it must have occurred later, because Lukács, along with his wife, moved to Moscow in the spring of 1930. Lukács himself noted the same error in the collection of his autobiographical writings from the end of his life. See "Gelebtes Denken: Notes towards an Autobiography," in Lukács, *Record of a Life*, 143.

38. Georg Lukács, *The Young Hegel: Studies in the Relationship between Dialectics and Economics*, translated by Rodney Livingstone (Cambridge, MA: MIT Press, 1976).

39. Andrew Arato and Paul Breine, *The Young Lukács and the Origins of Western Marxism* (New York: Seabury Press, 1979).

40. On the attraction of despotism for Lukács, see Lee Congdon, *The Young Lukács* (Chapel Hill: University of North Carolina Press, 1983).

41. See Georg Lukács, *The Destruction of Reason* (1954), translated by Peter Palmer (Atlantic Highlands, NJ: Humanities Press, 1981), and, more generally, the Manichaean spirit behind his aesthetics.

42. Leszek Kolakowski, *Main Currents of Marxism: Its Rise, Growth, and Dissolution*, translated by P. S. Falla, vol. 3, *The Breakdown* (Oxford: Clarendon Press, 1978), 253–307.

43. See chapter 12 below, text at note 20.

44. See Kadarkay, *Georg Lukács*, 434–38.

45. Claude Roy, *Somme toute* (Paris: Gallimard Folio, 1976), 139–45.

CHAPTER FIVE

1. This expression was used by Ida Mett in her pamphlet *La Commune de Kronstadt, crépuscule sanglant des Soviets* (Spartacus, 1948).

2. From 1919 on, the nationalistic journalist Wolfgang Kapp forged ties with the military in order to carry out a putsch against the Weimar Republic. With the support of General von Lüttwitz, commander of the troops in Berlin and of the Erhard commando unit, he took action on 13 March 1920. His attempt failed after four days. The German Communist Party remained neutral during these events.

3. Boris Souvarine, *Staline: Aperçu historique du bolshévisme* (Ivréa, 1993), 172.

4. On 9 September 1917, General Kornilov, commander-in-chief of the Russian army, was dismissed by Kerensky. Refusing to submit, he marched on Petrograd. To thwart him, the provisional government relied on the Bolsheviks, who had been functioning clandestinely since the July Days. The Bolsheviks thus gained unhoped-for influence, whereas General Kornilov was abandoned by his troops.

5. The famous land decree that followed October 1917 did not create social ownership of the land. It provided for the redistribution of great landed property to the peasants through the intermediary of local committees and regional peasant soviets. It was drawn entirely from the revolutionary socialist program—a Bolshevik concession intended to cement the alliance between the peasantry and the working class.

6. Stalin's *Principles of Leninism* was frequently republished in Russian and in many foreign languages. It generally figured at the beginning of a larger work, including all of Stalin's later speeches, entitled *Problems of Leninism* (Moscow: Foreign Languages Publishing House, 1947); the Russian version was dated 1938–39.

7. In spite of its biases and inaccuracies, there are few books as informative about the political ways of the Comintern during this period as Ruth Fischer's *Stalin and German Communism: A Study in the Origins of the State Party*, with a preface by Sidney B. Fay (Cambridge, MA: Harvard University Press, 1948).

8. At the time, Lenin had riposted with his idea of the "revolutionary dictatorship of the proletariat and the peasantry," but in fact, since October 1917, Trotsky and he

had been in total agreement that the success of the proletarian revolution in Russia was subordinate to the global or, at least, European revolution.

9. Souvarine, *Staline*, 269. "Com-mendacity" renders Souvarine's French coinage *com-mensonge*.

10. Ruth Fischer, *Stalin and German Communism*, 641.

11. See chapter 6 below, text at note 75.

12. On this "first Bolshevism," see Richard Pipes, *Russia under the Bolshevik Regime* (New York: Knopf, 1993).

13. Panaït Istrati, *Vers l'autre flamme I: Après seize mois dans l'URSS* (Paris: Rieder, 1929); [Victor Serge], *Vers l'autre flamme II: Soviets 1929;* [Boris Souvarine], *Vers l'autre flamme III: La Russie nue.* The first volume of the trilogy was reissued in 1987 (Paris: Gallimard, Folio essais).

14. The son of Russian populists who had taken refuge in Belgium, Victor Serge (1890–1974) was involved in the Bonnot gang affair. After five years in prison, he was deported to Spain, where he participated in the revolutionary movement. Having managed to get to Russia, this libertarian joined up with the Bolsheviks and worked for the Comintern. From 1925 on, he began to distance himself from the Bolsheviks because of the way the regime was evolving and gave his support to the left-wing opposition. Arrested for the first time in 1928, he was banished, along with his wife and son, to Oranienburg in 1933. An international campaign enabled him to leave Russia in 1936. He then published several works on the Soviet Union. A refugee in Marseille in 1940, he managed to reach the Antilles in 1941 and then Mexico. In his last writings, he denounced the "new Russian imperialism."

15. Serge, *Soviets 1929*, 132.

16. A Bolshevik sympathizer prior to the October Revolution, Maksim Gorky (1868–1936) continually denounced Bolshevik undertakings in his journal *New Life*, which was definitively banned by Lenin in July 1918. In 1921 he took refuge in Berlin and thence in Italy, where he remained until May 1928. From 1924 on, in *Lenin and the Russian Peasant*, he paid homage to the founder of the Soviet Union—the first step in his going over to the Soviet side. In 1928 the Soviet authorities organized a triumphant return for his sixtieth birthday. Gorky thus began a new career, that of official writer, who presided over the Association of Soviet Writers and put his pen at the disposal of the regime, exalting its "conquests" and approving its repressive policies. He extolled the practice of rehabilitation through labor and published laudatory reports on the camp on the Solovietski islands (1929) and on the creation of the canal between the White Sea and the Baltic Sea, which cost the lives of many thousands of prisoners. He retained the freedom to go abroad until 1933, after which he was refused all visas.

Corrupted by success, he remained under the strict surveillance of the political police and played a key role in urging French intellectuals, especially Romain Rolland, to support the Soviet regime. After Kirov's assassination in December 1934, he called for the "extermination of the enemy without mercy or pity," thus putting his stamp of approval on the bloody purges. On the last years of Gorky's life, see Vitali Chentalinski, *La Parole ressuscitée: Dans les archives littéraires du K.G.B.* (Paris: Robert Laffont, 1993).

17. Victor Serge, *Soviets 1929*, chap. 16, p. 196.

18. In 1925, Nikolay Ivanovich Bukharin (1888–1938) supported the notion that the economic development of Soviet Russia should be based on the alliance of the proletariat and the peasantry. He wanted the peasants to be guaranteed the possibility of increasing their production through cooperatives and the development of the market. His slogans were aimed at them: "Make yourselves rich, develop your farms," etc. At the time, Stalin supported him, as did Nikolay Oustrialov. See Stephen

Cohen, *Bukharin and the Bolshevik Revolution: A Political Biography, 1888–1938* (New York: Knopf, 1973).

19. Heller and Nekrich, *Utopia in Power.*

20. Oustrialov was a law professor and a figure in the younger party during the February 1917 Revolution, but was then in opposition to the October Revolution in the Kolchak government. After taking refuge in China, he had a change of heart toward the Soviet Union in 1920–21, prompted by Russian patriotism. Later, both outside and within the Soviet Union, he led a "national-Bolshevist" current. He developed, in particular, the idea of a Soviet "Thermidor." See Tamara Kondratieva, *Bolsheviks et Jacobin: Itinéraires des analogies* (Paris: Payot, 1989), 90–109.

21. See Heller and Nekrich, *Utopia in Power,* p. 168, citing N. Valentinov. A Bolshevik from the start, Nicholas Valentinov (1879–1964) broke with Lenin in 1904, after having assiduously sought his company during their exile together in Geneva. In 1953, he explained his philosophical and political differences with Lenin in a book that is essential reading: *Mes rencontres avec Lénine* (Paris: G. Lebovici, 1977). After becoming a Menshevik, he worked in the Superior Council for the National Economy prior to emigrating to France in 1930. He published many articles on the peasant question in the USSR in Souvarine's periodical *Le Contrat Social.*

22. The principal study on the Ukrainian famine written on site was by a German Balt, Edwald Ammende, who at the time was named head of an interdenominational aid group by the Cardinal of Vienna. It was titled *Muß Rußland hungern? Menschen und Völkerschicksale in der Sowjetunion* (Vienna, 1935). There is also *La Famine en Russie: Rapport adressé au gouvernement allemand par le Dr. Otto Schiller* (1933), by an expert on agricultural affairs for the German Embassy in Moscow.

Among literary memories or books of recollections, see Malcolm Muggeridge, *Winter in Moscow* (Boston: Little, Brown, 1934), and *Chronicles of Wasted Time,* vol. 1 (New York: Morrow, 1973); Victor Kravchenko, *J'ai choisi la liberté! La vie publique et privée d'un haut fonctionnaire soviétique* (Paris: Self, 1947); Vassil Barka, *Le Prince jaune* (Paris: Gallimard, 1981); Miron Dolot, *Execution by Hunger: The Hidden Holocaust* (New York: Norton, 1985).

Among historical studies are Vasyl Hryshko, *The Ukrainian Holocaust of 1933,* edited and translated by Marco Carynnyk (Toronto: Bahriany Foundation, 1983), and Robert Conquest, *Harvest of Sorrow: Soviet Collectivization and the Terror Famine* (New York: Oxford U. Press, 1986).

23. Heller and Nekrich, *Utopia in Power,* 235.

24. See Robert Conquest, *The Great Terror* (New York: Macmillan, 1968), appendix F.

25. Ibid., chap. 1.

26. Ibid., 24–26.

27. Panné, *Boris Souvarine,* 199.

28. Karl Kautsky, *Le Bolshévisme dans l'impasse,* translated by Bracke (Paris: Alcan, 1931); reprinted in 1982 (Presses universitaires de France), with a foreword by Henri Weber.

29. Alain Besançon, *Court Traité de soviétologie à l'usage des autorités civiles, militaires et religieuses* (Paris: Hachette, 1976), chap. 2, 61–88.

30. Fred Kupferman, *Au pays des Soviets, le voyage français en Union soviétique, 1917–1939* (Paris: Gallimard-Julliard, 1979), 87–90.

31. Panné, *Boris Souvarine,* 200–202.

32. Prince Gregory Potemkin (1739–91) annexed the Crimea in 1783. There, he organized Catherine II's visit in 1787, building fictitious villages populated by actors disguised as peasants so that she would think Potemkin had conquered a rich and fertile province. After attending a party at the Winter Palace in Saint Petersburg, the

Marquis de Custine wrote: "In despotic countries all the popular diversions seem suspicious to me when compared to those of the Prince. I shall never forget Empress Catherine's trip to the Crimea and the facades of villages appearing here and there, made of painted boards and canvas, a quarter of a league from the road, to convince the triumphant sovereign that the desert was populous under her reign." Custine, *Lettres de Russie*, with a foreword by P. Nora (Paris: Gallimard, 1975), 142–43.

33. Michel Winock, *Histoire politique de la revue "Esprit"* (Paris: Éditions du Seuil, 1975).

34. In 1930, Marcel Déat (1894–1955) published *Perspective socialistes*, a book in which he preached alliance between the working class and the middle class in order to foster a progressive socialization of the economy under the aegis of the government. His theses were rejected by the SFIO, and, in 1933, Déat founded the Parti socialiste de France–Union Jean Jaurès. In 1935 he published *Le Plan français*, written by the Planning Committee he had established. During the Occupation, Déat, who had been a Munich partisan, founded the Rassemblement national populaire, a collaborationist party in which he hoped to concentrate all supporters of Nazi policies. See Philippe Burrin, *La Dérive fasciste: Doriot, Déat, Bergery* (Paris: Éditions du Seuil, 1986), and Marcel Déat, *Mémoires politiques* (Paris: Denoël, 1989).

35. Robert Aron and Arnaud Dandieu, *La Révolution nécessaire* (Paris: Grasset, 1933). In the preface (p. xiii), the authors claim that "the Revolution, which is in the making, and of which the Russian, Italian, and German movements are only incomplete and imperfect precursors, will be realized by France."

36. Ernest Mercier was a *Polytechnicien* and an administrator of the Banque de Paris et des Pays-Bas, president of the Compagnie française des pétroles and of the Union d'électricité. He was also, prior to 1935, one of the supporters of Colonel de La Rocque and founder of a movement called "le Redressement français." *U.R.S.S.: Réflexions par Ernest Mercier, janvier 1936* (Paris: Editions du Centre polytechnicien d'études économiques, February 1936).

37. Charles Beaurepaire, "M. Ernest Mercier fait l'éloge de Staline," *Masses*, nos. 5–6, 25 February 1936.

38. F. A. Warren, *Liberals and Communism: The "Red Decade" revisited* (Bloomington: Indiana University Press, 1966).

39. Founded in 1884 by Sidney and Beatrice Webb, the Fabian Society was named for Fabius Cunctator, "the Temporizer," who led the Roman armies during the Second Punic War. Its members were anti-Marxists and called for a reformist socialism that was to be established gradually. The society became known in 1889 through George Bernard Shaw's *Fabian Essays*. The Fabians tried to influence the Labour Party and the trade unions. In the early 1930s, they were drawn to Soviet Russia. Shaw visited Russia in 1931 and declared upon his return that "the system established in Russia is a Fabian system." After visiting Russia in the same year, Beatrice and Sidney Webb (Sidney was to return to the Soviet Union alone in 1934) published a laudatory description of what they had seen, the two-volume *Soviet Communism: A New Civilization?* (London: Longmans, Green, and Co., 1935).

40. Herbert G. Wells, *Russia in the Shadows* (New York: Doran, 1921).

41. Ibid., 161: "In him I realised that Communism could after all, in spite of Marx, be enormously creative."

42. "Stalin-Wells Talk. The Verbatim Record and a discussion by G. Bernard Shaw, H. G. Wells, J. M. Keynes, Ernst Toller," *New Statesman and Nation*, December 1934.

43. During a meeting after his return to England, Wells declared that there was, at the time, no intellectual liberty in the USSR. This comment was derided by the

German Communist Ernst Toller, then in exile in London. See the discussion on the Wells-Stalin talk, ibid., 27–28.

44. Cited in David Dunn, "A Good Fabian fallen among the Stalinists," *Survey* 28, no. 4 (winter 1984): 28.

45. The MacDonald government had to resign in 1931, proof of the impotence of the Labourites in the face of the economic and social crisis.

46. Bernard Shaw spent ten days in the USSR at the end of July 1931, accompanied by Lord and Lady Astor, in response to a long-standing invitation from the Soviet Writers' Union. He was received with the sort of sumptuous reception reserved for Western intellectual celebrities.

47. "Stalin-Wells Talk," 22.

48. Ibid., 26.

49. J. M. Keynes, "Stalin-Wells Talk," 35.

50. Ibid. Keynes himself, we might note, went to the USSR in 1925 for the bicentenary celebration of the Academy of Sciences of Saint Petersburg. He wrote a short, very critical essay about that trip, published by his Bloomsbury friends: John M. Keynes, *A Short View of Russia* (London: Hogarth Press, 1925).

51. *Soviet Communism: A New Civilization?* In the second edition of the book, published in 1937, the authors removed the question mark from the subtitle.

52. Ibid., "Is the Party a Dictator?" 431.

53. See Dunn, "A good Fabian," 32.

CHAPTER SIX

1. Some of the elements of such a history can be found in Leonard Schapiro, *Totalitarianism* (London: Pall Mall, 1932); Karl Dietrich Bracher, "The Disputed Concept of Totalitarianism, Experience and Actuality," in *Totalitarianism Reconsidered*, edited by Ernest A. Kenze (London: Kennikat Press, 1981); and in Guy Hermet, *Totalitarismes*, edited by Guy Hermet (Paris: coll. Politique comparée, Economica, 1984).

2. Which does not make Tocqueville a theoretician of "totalitarianism" even though he suspected that in modern societies, characterized by the autonomy and equality of individuals, the enslavement of men by the ruling power could take on extreme, unprecedented forms.

3. Mussolini, *Opera*, 21:362. *Cf.* Schapiro, *Totalitarianism*, 13.

4. Jünger, *La Mobilisation totale.*

5. Carl Schmitt, *Der Hüter der Verfassung* (Tübingen: Mohr, 1931), 79. For an English translation, see Ernst Fraenkel, *The Dual State: A Contribution to the Theory of Dictatorship* (Oxford: Oxford University Press, 1941), 60.

6. Published in Élie Halévy, "L'ère des tyrannies," in *Études sur le socialisme et la guerre*, preface by C. Bouglé, epilogue by R. Aron (Paris: Gallimard, 1938), 213–49. Translated by R. K. Webb as *The Era of Tyrannies* (New York: New York University Press, 1966).

7. Used by the philosopher Maurice Blondel, 237.

8. Karl Kautsky, "Marxism and Bolshevism, Democracy and Dictatorship," in *Socialism, Fascism, Communism*, edited by J. Shaplen and D. Shub (New York, 1934), 213.

9. Cited by Henri Weber in "La Théorie du stalinisme dans l'oeuvre de Kautsky," in *Les Interprétations du stalinisme*, edited by Éveline Pisier (Paris: Presses Universitaires de France, 1983), 63.

10. Founded in Vienna in February 1921 by the socialist parties that had left the Second International and were hostile to the Third, the "Internationale 2½" was

composed essentially of Austrians, and eventually dissolved and became part of the Socialist Workers International, the Second International.

11. For more on Hannah Arendt, see the last part of chapter 11.

12. *Historikerstreit* (Atlantic Highlands, NJ: Humanities Press, 1993).

13. Since the 1970s, but especially since the debate that brought German historians to loggerheads over how to interpret Nazism *(Historikerstreit)*, the positions assumed by Ernst Nolte have been the object of so much summary condemnation, in Germany and elsewhere in the West, that he deserves special comment.

To his credit, he has quickly gone beyond the prohibition against putting Communism and Nazism in the same bag—a prohibition more or less generalized in Western Europe, especially in France and Italy, and particularly strict in Germany for obvious reasons, which are still in force. From 1963 on, with his book on Fascism (*Der Faschismus in seiner Epoche;* translated by Leila Vennewitz as *The Three Faces of Fascism* [New York: Holt, Rinehart and Winston, 1966]), Nolte began tracing the outlines of his historical-philosophical interpretation, at once neo-Hegelian and Heideggerian, of the twentieth century. The liberal system, by virtue of its contradictory character and infinite openness to the future, constituted the matrix for two major ideologies: Communism and Fascism. The first, ushered in by Marx, brought modern society's "transcendence" to an extreme. By this the author means the abstraction of democratic universalism, which tears human thought and activity away from the limits of nature and tradition. By contrast, Fascism sought to relieve men from the anxiety of being free and indeterminate beings. Its distant inspiration was drawn from Nietzsche's wish to protect "life" and "culture" from "transcendence."

This explains why we cannot study the two ideologies separately: together they unfold, in a radical way, the contradictions of liberalism, and the twentieth century has been filled with their complementarity and rivalry. But they also have a distinct chronological order: Lenin's victory preceded Mussolini's, to say nothing of Hitler's. The first victory conditioned the other two, in the view of Nolte, who continued to explore this relationship in his books *Die faschistischen Bewegungen* (1966), *Deutschland und der kalte Krieg* (1974), and especially in *Die europaïsche Bürger Krieg 1917–1945* (1987). Ideologically speaking, the universalistic extremism of Bolshevism gave rise to particularistic extremism in Nazism. On a political level, the extermination of the bourgeoisie carried out by Lenin in the name of the abstraction of a classless society created a social panic in that part of Europe most vulnerable to the Communist threat; it brought Hitler and Nazi counterterror to triumph.

Hitler himself, however, was fighting a losing battle against his enemies: he too was caught up in the universal "technological" movement and used the same methods as his adversaries. Just like Stalin, he went flat out for industrialization. He claimed he was vanquishing Judeo-Bolshevism—the two-headed monster of social "transcendence"—but what he really wanted to do was to unify humanity under the domination of the Germanic "race." In this predetermined war, none of the reasons to win remained, and thus Nazism betrayed its original line and logic. These were the terms in which Nolte, in one of his most recent works, *Martin Heidegger: Politik und Geschichte im Leben und Denken* (1992), explains and justifies the brief militant period of Heidegger—who, later on, would be his teacher—for the Nazi cause. According to this view, the philosopher was justified both in his enthusiasm for National Socialism and for his subsequent disenchantment.

It is not difficult to imagine how and why Nolte's books have shocked members of the postwar generations who were imprisoned in their guilt, fearful of weakening the hatred of Fascism by attempting to understand it, or who simply conformed to the spirit of the times. The reasons for the first two responses, at least, are noble. Historians can and must respect them. But historians who imitate them are prevented from seeing the Soviet Terror as one of the fundamental reasons for the popularity of Fascism and Nazism in the 1920s and 1930s. They must turn a blind eye to what Hitler's accession to power owed to the precedent of the Bolshevik victory, to the negative example of pure violence elaborated by Lenin into a system of government, and to the Comintern's obsession with extending the Communist revolution to Germany. When this line of analysis is rejected, it becomes impossible to write the history of Fascism. On a historical order, such a blinkered view is the counterpart of what the Soviet version of anti-Fascism was on a political level. By prohibiting criticism of Communism, this type of historiographical anti-Fascism also blocks the way to an understanding of Fascism. To his credit, Nolte has broken that taboo.

Unfortunately, during the discussion of Nazism with German historians, he weakened his interpretation by exaggerating his thesis: he attempted to cast the Jews as the organized adversaries of Hitler because they were allied with his enemies. Not that he can be called a "negationist." He has expressed horror at the Nazi extermination of the Jews on numerous occasions and at the singularity of the Jewish genocide as an industrial liquidation of a race. He maintains that the Bolsheviks' suppression of the bourgeoisie as a class set the precedent, and that the Gulag was anterior to Auschwitz. But the Jewish genocide, to the extent that it belonged to a contemporary tendency, was for Nolte not just a means toward victory; it retained the horrific particularity of constituting an end in itself, a product of the victory of which the "Final Solution" was the most important aim. True, in a recent essay that attempts to decode Hitler's anti-Semitic paranoia, Nolte appears to find some sort of rationale for it in Chaim Weitzmann's September 1939 appeal to the Jews of the world, in the name of the World Jewish Congress *(Historikerstreit)*, to fight at Britain's side. This argument is both shocking and false.

Such a position can no doubt be attributed to a basic fund of humiliated German nationalism for which Nolte's adversaries have reproached him for twenty years and which in large part motivates his books. But even this charge is not sufficient entirely to discredit a body of work and an interpretation that are among the most profound produced in the second half of the twentieth century.

Cf. Hans Christof Kraus, "L'historiographie philosophique d'Ernst Nolte," in *La Pensée politique* (Paris: Hautes Études–Le Seuil–Gallimard, 1994), 59–87; Alain Renaut, preface to *Ernst Nolte: Les mouvements fascistes* (Paris: Calmann-Lévy, 1969).

14. Ferdinand Lassalle (1825–64) was one of the founders of German socialism. A flamboyant and bohemian character, he started off close to Marx and Engels during the 1849 Revolution in the Rhineland, and then became their rival. Loyal to a set of theories that were more Hegelian than Marxist, he viewed the state as a means to realize the community: the working classes' conquest of the state was the condition for the emancipation of humanity. In 1863, a year before his premature death (in a duel), Lassalle founded the General Association of German Workers. The kind of tactics he practiced and recommended favored the struggle against the liberal bourgeoisie even at the price of an alliance of workers parties with the pre- or antiliberal forces of conservatism—the aristocracy, the army, the monarchy, and the Prussian bureaucracy. This stance led to his famous encounters with Bismarck.

15. *L'Action française,* 15 November 1900, cited in Zeev Sternhell, *La Droite révolutionnaire 1885–1914: Les origines du fascisme* (Paris: Éditions du Seuil, 1978), 359.

16. Charles Maurras, *Dictionnaire politique et critique,* 5:213, cited in Sternhell, ibid., 359.

17. The comparison between Mussolini and Lenin was spun out by Mussolini himself in a long interview in 1932. See Emil Ludwig, *Talks with Mussolini* (Boston: Little, Brown, 1933).

18. André Brissard, *Mussolini* (Paris: Perrin, 1975), 1:85.

19. The *Risorgimento* ("resurrection") was the literary, philosophical, and political movement that, in the mid-nineteenth century, accompanied and supported Italian emancipation and unity.

20. On intellectual antecedents, especially French ones, of Mussolinian Fascism, the classic work is Sternhell's *La Droite révolutionnaire.*

21. These are the terms he employed in an article published in the 18 October 1914 issue of *Avanti,* which signaled his new orientation.

22. Giuseppe Mazzini (1805–72) was one of the great heroes of Romantic Europe, a champion of nationality. He was both a writer and the founder of modern Italy. First a member of the Carbonari, a secret association that staged a failed attempt in 1831 to get Italy to rebel, in 1834 he founded the "Young Europe" movement, which was as political as it was intellectual. He sought to emancipate the oppressed nationalities and to mark that action with a spirit of humanitarian devotion analogous to a religion: Mazzini belonged to the same intellectual family as Michelet and Mickiewicz. In exile in Switzerland, and then in London, he took part in the 1848 Revolution in Italy and was, for a time, one of Garibaldi's troops. He hailed national unity somewhat later, while regretting that it had been constituted under the authority of a king. The last years of his life were darkened by history's refutation of his ideas: nationalism would take the place of nationality and Marx and Bakunin's socialism would replace his religion of humanity.

23. In his 1844 book *Le Speranze d'Italia* (Italy's hopes), Count Balbo set out his conservative theory of Italian unity (no tipping of the European balance) against the revolutionary theories of Mazzini (Italian unity as part of the European revolution of nations, implying the fall of the Hapsburgs). See Federico Chabod, *A History of Italian Fascism* (London: Weidenfeld, 1963).

24. Michel Ostenc, *Intellectuels italiens et fascisme, 1915–1929* (Paris: Payot, 1983), 30–92.

25. Michael A. Ledeen, "Italy: War as a Style of Life," in *The War Generation,* edited by Stephen R. Ward (London: Kennikat Press, 1975), 104–34.

26. For the information in this segment I am much indebted to Renzo de Felice— perhaps the greatest contemporary historian of Italian Fascism—most particularly to his biography of Mussolini as well as two other books of his: *Il fascismo: Le interpretazioni dei contemporanei e degli storici* (Rome: Laterza, 1974), and *Fascism, an Informal Introduction to Its Theory and Practice: An Interview with Michael Ledeen* (New Brunswick, NJ: Transaction Books, 1976).

27. Gustave Le Bon, *La Psychologie des foules* (Paris: Presses universitaires de France, 1990); English translation: *The Crowd* (New York: Viking, 1968). In a later article, Le Bon wrote that the kinship between Lenin and Mussolini was "the evolution of Europe toward diverse forms of dictatorship," *Annales politiques et littéraires,* 1924.

28. Georges Sorel, *Réflexions sur la violence* (Paris: Marcel Rivière, reprinted 1972), foreword by Claude Polin. See "Pour Lénine," ibid., 375–89, the text written by Sorel in September 1919 in support of Lenin. On Sorel's comparison between Lenin and Mussolini, see *Propos de Georges Sorel recueillis par Jean Variot* (Paris: Gallimard, 1935), 66 and 86.

29. Sorel, *Réflexions sur la violence,* 380–84.

30. "Conducteurs de peuples." See *Propos de Georges Sorel,* 86.

31. Ostenc, *Intellectuels italiens et fascisme,* 97–207. On Benedetto Croce, see 242–49.

32. Renzo de Felice, *Mussolini,* vol. 1: *Mussolini il revoluzionario* (1965). See also *An interview with Michael Ledeen,* 43–60.

33. Michael Ledeen, *Universal Fascism: The Theory and Practice of the Fascist International, 1928–1936* (New York: Howard Fertig, 1972).

34. Indeed, in 1797, in chapter 6 of his brochure *Des réactions politiques*, Constant referred to his colleagues who were too inclined to be critical—even in good faith— of the excesses of the Revolution: "Behind these writers, whose intentions are pure but who are dominated by bitter memories or excessive scruples, there marches— with vaster views, better devised means, and better sustained projects—a party by nature Montagnard, but Montagnard for the monarchy." *Écrits et discours politiques,* edited by O. Pozzo di Borgo, 1:49. To this evocation of a counterrevolutionary terror, Joseph de Maistre responded several months later in chapter 10, titled "Des préten- dus dangers d'une contre-révolution," of his *Considérations sur la France.*

35. On this subject, aside from the works of de Felice cited above, see also Angelo Tasca, *Naissance du fascisme: l'Italie de l'armistice à la marche sur Rome* (Paris: Galli- mard, 1938), reissued in 1967 with a foreword by Ignazio Silone.

36. Chabod, *A History of Italian Fascism.*

37. De Felice, *Le Fascisme,* interview by Michael A. Ledeen, 63.

38. Karl Löwith noted that contrast when traveling in Italy in 1934–36. See Karl Löwith, *My Life in Germany before and after 1933: A Report,* translated by Elizabeth King (London: Athlone Press, 1994).

39. See chap. 4, note 4, above.

40. Mussolini's newspaper.

41. Pierre Pascal, *Mon journal de Russie* (see chap. 4, n. 4, above), 4:28–29.

42. On this point I continue to agree with the work of de Felice, cited above. The same idea can be found in Karl Dietrich Bracher, *The German Dictatorship: The Ori- gins, Structure, and Effects of National Socialism,* translated by Jean Steinberg, with an Introduction by Peter Gay (New York: Praeger, 1970), and in Arendt, *Imperialism.* Nolte (*Les Mouvements fascistes,* 93–96), to the contrary, lumps Italian Fascism with the totalitarian regimes insofar as the state had been entirely taken over by Mussolini and his party.

43. Aside from the works already cited, see Meir Michaelis, *Mussolini and the Jews* (Oxford: Clarendon Press, 1978). Mussolini long remained hostile to Hitlerian rac- ism, expressing himself on the subject several times in very hostile terms. He decided to integrate the idea of race into Fascist doctrine only in July 1938, in a diplomatic move. The Italian anti-Semitic laws of 1938–39 were not applied assiduously. The catastrophe of Italian Judaism (which affected 20 percent of the forty thousand Italian Jews, even though six thousand of them emigrated) came after to the fall of Mussolini in July 1943. It was in fact the work of the Germans, who had in the meantime gained control of northern Italy.

44. See Ledeen, *Universal Fascism.*

45. Alan Bullock, *Hitler and Stalin: Parallel Lives* (New York: Alfred Knopf, 1992).

46. On 9 May 1923, a French military tribunal had sentenced Lieutenant Schla- geter, a veteran of the Freikorps and the head of a team of commandos against the French occupation, to death. His execution on 26 May provoked a wave of indigna- tion in Germany.

47. It is almost beside the point that the first volume of the book was written after his Bavarian putsch when he was in prison (1924), and the second shortly after. For it was more of a systematization of Hitler's thought than the text of new orientation. One can easily find the same major themes in his pre-1924 speeches, or the ones that followed.

48. Adolf Hitler, *Mein Kampf* (Munich: Franz Eher, 1925).

49. The best general introduction to the subject is Karl Dieter Bracher's *The Age of Ideologies: A History of Political Thought in the Twentieth Century*, translated by Weald Osiers (New York: St. Martin's Press, 1984).

50. This explains why, a little later, the writers and philosophers of the German revolutionary Right went along with, rather than devoting their ideas and works to, the Nazi victories. Among these were Carl Schmitt, Spengler, and Jünger. The most famous case, however, is Heidegger. By publishing *Being and Time*, the philosopher seemed to be pulling off a philosophical coup d'état in opposition to all tradition. Hatred of modernity and *Zivilisation* assumed the radical form of a negation of Western metaphysics, coupled not only with nostalgia for an "organic" society but with the will to found a new heroic existence, freed from the inauthentic. In his "Rector's Speech," Heidegger himself lent credence to the political analogies that his philosophical poem evoked in the minds of his contemporaries. To extend his benediction to Hitler, the philosopher needed only, in the words of Karl Löwith, "abandon the still quasi-religious isolation, and apply authentic 'existence'—'always particular to each individual'—and the 'duty' *[Müssen]* which follows from it to 'specifically German existence' and its historical destiny, in order thereby to introduce into the general course of German existence the energetic but empty movement of his existential categories ('to decide for oneself'; 'to take stock of oneself in the face of nothingness'; 'wanting one's ownmost destiny'; 'to take responsibility for oneself') and to proceed from there to 'destruction,' now on the terrain of politics." *My Life in Germany before and after 1933*, 32. See also Richard Wolin, *The Politics of Being: The Political Thought of Martin Heidegger* (New York: Columbia University Press, 1990).

51. Oswald Spengler, *Preussentum und Sozialismus* (Munich: C.H. Beck Verlag, 1921).

52. In addition to the Hitler of *Mein Kampf*, a work intended for the general public, and to the Hitler of public speeches, there was also the Hitler of the more or less private "conversations" of Hermann Rauschning's *Hitler Speaks: A Series of Political Conversations with Adolf Hitler on His Real Aims* (London: Thornton Butterworth, 1939); Rauschning, *The Revolution of Nihilism: Warning to the West* (New York: Alliance Book Corp., 1939); and *Hitler's Table Talks: 1941–44, His Private Conversations*, with an Introduction by H. Trevor-Roper (London: Weidenfeld and Nicholson, 1973). See also *The Testament of Adolf Hitler: The Hitler–Borman Documents, February–April 1945* (London: 1961).

53. Pierre-André Taguieff, *La Force du préjugé: Essai sur le racisme et ses doubles* (Paris: Gallimard, 1990).

54. The idea of a natural affinity between liberalism and Bolshevism was a commonplace in German thought of that time. See, for example, Oswald Spengler, *Jahre der Entscheidung* (Oldenburg: G. Stalling, 1933); translated by C. F. Atkinson as *The Hour of Decision* (New York: Alfred A. Knopf, 1934).

55. As far as Hitler was concerned, the Jew was the origin of "democratic" Christianity through Saint Paul, while being responsible for the death of Jesus—doubly guilty, in other words, having killed the Messiah and spread his message; a double enemy, of Christians and anti-Christians. See *Hitler's Secret Conversations*, 62–65.

56. See, for example, Fritz Stern, *The Politics of Cultural Despair: A Study in the Rise of the German Ideology* (Berkeley: University of California Press, 1974).

57. Here, I am merely summing up a section of *Mein Kampf*, especially chapter 11 of the first volume, "People and race," and chapter 13 of the second volume, "German allied policies after the war," where the centrality of the Jewish question in Hitler's global vision can be clearly discerned.

58. Hannah Arendt, *Eichmann in Jerusalem: A Report on the Banality of Evil* (New York: Viking, 1963).

59. For further discussion of this point, see Epilogue, below.

60. Friedrich Meinecke, *The German Catastrophe,* translated by Sidney B. Fay (Cambridge, MA: Harvard University Press, 1950), 52. To be more precise, we might say that Hitler went beyond the intellectual framework of Machiavelli, since for him, as for Stalin, reasons of state were subordinated to the realization of an ideology.

61. Hitler sometimes adopted Bolshevik methods: "I have learnt a great deal from Marxism. . . . I have learnt from their methods. . . . The whole of National Socialism is based on it. . . . [T]he workers' sports clubs, the industrial cells, the mass demonstrations, the propaganda leaflets written specially for the comprehension of the masses; all these new methods of political struggle are essentially Marxist in origin. All I had to do was to take over these methods and adapt them to our purpose." See Rauschning, *Hitler Speaks,* 185.

62. In these lines, my debt to contemporary works on totalitarianism and to Hannah Arendt's book *The Origins of Totalitarianism* (1951) is clear. I am thinking especially of Raymond Aron but also of Claude Lefort and Alain Besançon.

63. Hermann Rauschning, *The Revolution of Nihilism,* pt. 1, chap. 3.

64. Rauschning, *Hitler Speaks,* 134.

65. The treaty of Rapallo (1922) was one of the first major successes of the nascent Soviet diplomacy, establishing a special relationship between Soviet Russia and Weimar Germany—the two pariah states of the Treaty of Versailles. The treaty made Germany the most favored commercial partner of the USSR and also led to clandestine military collaboration between the two countries, by which Germany could begin to counteract the treaty's prohibitions against rearmament.

66. Louis Dupeux, *National-Bolchevisme dans l'Allemagne de Weimar 1919–1933* (Paris: H. Champion, 1979). On Moeller Van den Bruck, see Stern, *The Politics of Despair,* part 3.

67. Karl Radek praised Schlageter during the Third Plenum of the Executive Committee of the Comintern in June 1923: "The fate of this martyr of German nationalism should not be decided in silence nor treated with disdain. . . . This courageous man of the counterrevolution deserves to be honored by us soldiers of the revolution. . . . We shall do everything in order that men like Schlageter, who were ready to die for a great cause, shall not be voyagers into nothingness but voyagers headed toward a better future for all of humanity." *Bulletin communiste,* no. 30 (26 July 1923): 420–21.

68. Founded in December 1919, the German Communist Party (KPD) fused in 1920 with the Independent Socialists (USPD) to form the German United Communist Party (VKPD), which was three hundred thousand members strong. After Paul Lévi was pushed aside for having disapproved the insurrection of March 1921, the Communists were led by H. Brandler and A. Thalheimer, who, after the failure of the German October (1923), were giving way to a new leadership (R. Fisher and A. Maslow). This was the period of the party's "Bolshevization," which was henceforth enfeoffed to Moscow. But Fisher and Maslow were thrown out in 1925 as "Zinovievists." Under the direction of Thaelmann, the German Communist Party applied the line of "class against class," which led the Communists to put National Socialism and Social Democracy on the same level. From 1931 on, Heinz Neumann, who had originally defended this sectarian line without second thoughts, attempted to oppose it. He in turn was thrown out in 1932 and then sent to Moscow, where he was liquidated a few years later. The German Communist Party would continue its policies even after Hitler had taken power.

69. Having made it as leader of the German Communist Party in 1923, Ernst Thaelmann (1886–1944) became a member of the Presidium of the Comintern in 1924. A deputy, he was a candidate for the presidency that same year. Implicated

in 1928 in the Wittorf affair, and maintained at the head of the party by Stalin, he applied the "class against class" policy line that designated the Social Democrats as the first-order adversaries. Arrested in 1933, he was imprisoned, and was executed on 18 August 1944.

70. The SA (Sturm Abteilung: the Brown Shirt stormtroopers) was created in 1921 to ensure the protection of German Nazi Party militants. Supported by former military men, the SA would become a veritable political army (three hundred thousand men by early 1933), commanded from 1931 on by Ernst Röhm. It was banned in April 1932, but the ban was lifted in June by Papen (see n. 72 below). After the Night of the Long Knives (30 June 1934), the SA was liquidated to the benefit of the SS. A former officer, Ernst Röhm (1887–1934) participated in the irregular forces incident and the beer hall putsch in Munich (November 1923). After a dispute with Hitler, he exiled himself to Bolivia in 1925 but returned to Germany in 1930, summoned back by Hitler. After January 1933, he advocated a "second revolution" against the bourgeoisie as a means of moving from the national revolution to a National Socialist revolution.

71. Joseph Goebbels, *Vom Kaiserhof zur Reichskanzlei: eine historische Darstellung in Tagebuchblätter* (Munich: Zentralverlag der N.S.D.A.P.F., 1934).

72. A parliamentarian of the Catholic Center party, Franz von Papen (1879–1969) supported the 1925 candidacy of Marshal Hindenburg against the candidate of his own party. He became chancellor on 1 June 1932, whereupon he lifted the ban on the SA, hoping to include the National Socialists in his majority. After being replaced by Schleicher, he served as an intermediary between Hindenburg and Hitler, acting as Hitler's guarantor in order to convince the old marshal to turn to the leader of the NSDAP.

In November 1918, Kurt von Schleicher (1882–1934) was the liaison between the army and the government. He then clandestinely organized the Reichswehr and negotiated with the Soviets for his training in the USSR. Named head of the political section of the army, he acted as the army's representative, negotiating unsuccessfully with Hitler in the summer of 1932 in hopes of neutralizing him. Having become chancellor on 1 December 1932, he sought to weaken the NSDAP by provoking a split in its ranks. Lacking support from the military, he was forced to resign on 29 January 1933. He was assassinated on 30 June 1934.

73. The question of the financial support of Hitler by German businessmen in the years preceding 1933 has been much studied (especially since it is linked to the Marxist thesis about Nazism, which was seen as a dictatorship of financial capital). The most recent and detailed work on this problem finds that the contribution of the industrial haute bourgeoisie to the Nazis was relatively insignificant. See Henry Asby Turner, *German Big Business and the Rise of Hitler* (New York: Oxford University Press, 1985).

74. Spengler, *The Hour of Decision*, 3.

75. Edward H. Carr, *German-Soviet Relations between the Two World Wars* (Baltimore: Johns Hopkins University Press, 1951); Gustav Hilger and Alfred G. Meyer, *The Incompatible Allies: A Memoir History of German-Soviet Relations, 1918–1941* (New York: Macmillan, 1953).

76. Dupeux, *National-Bolchevisme dans l'Allemagne de Weimar*, esp. 388–427.

77. Here Niekisch was anticipating Ernst Jünger's *Die Arbeiter* (Hamburg: Hanseatische Verlaganstalt, 1932). The Jünger of these years could be considered a subscriber to National Bolshevism, while also on the periphery of pure and simple Nazism. He did not stay there long after 1933.

78. Dupeux, *National-Bolchevisme dans l'Allemagne de Weimar*, 405.

79. The necessity of emancipating technology from its subordination to capital-

ism in order to make it the instrument of the *volkisch* state was a commonplace of the German extreme Right at that time. That emancipation could only find its philosophy in Marxism, a transplant of liberalism, and it was because Stalin renounced that heritage that he could to some extent be its agent in the eyes of the National Bolsheviks. But it was the Nazi state that would fulfill those conditions. See Jeffrey Herf, *Reactionary Modernism: Technology, Culture, and Politics in Weimar and the Third Reich* (Cambridge: Cambridge University Press, 1984).

80. In 1928, the Comintern's Sixth Congress defined the period to come as one of potential revolution, which the Communist Parties were to carry out. The policy of the KPD (German Communist Party) subscribed to this program, which designated Social Democracy as the principal obstacle on the path to revolution and as the accomplice of the Nazis. (At the Eleventh Plenum of the Executive Committee of the Comintern, Ernst Thaelmann said, "In Germany, we now find ourselves in a situation where Social Democracy is deploying the most energy to realize Fascist dictatorship.") The policy favored by the Comintern depended on an entirely submissive clan; that policy was retained until spring 1934.

Under the close control of Moscow, the direction of the KPD would apply "the line"; in August 1931, for example, the Communists, during a referendum on the dissolution of the Prussian Landtag, combined their votes with those of the Nazis against the Social Democratic government. On 3 November 1932, the transport workers of Berlin went on strike, despite the opposition of the union leaders but under the direction of the KPD with the support of the Nazis. The day after the Reichstag elections (6 November), the Nazis called for a resumption of work. In Berlin, the KPD had the highest score, surpassing the Nazis and the Social Democrats. Thanks to their participation in a strike that was accepted by the Communists, the Nazis succeeded in limiting their electoral losses.

81. Marlis Steiner, in *Hitler* (Paris; Fayard, 1991), cites contemporary police reports of wide public approbation.

82. Alla Kirilina, *L'Assassinat de Kirov* (Paris: Éditions du Seuil, 1995). According to Kirilina, neither the local NKVD (Narodny Kommissariat Vnutrennikh Del, "Peoples' Commissariat of Internal Affairs") nor the national NKVD were implicated in Kirov's assassination, which was committed by a lunatic.

83. Jerry Z. Muller, *The Other God That Failed: Hans Freyer and the Deradicalization of German Conservatism* (Princeton: Princeton University Press, 1987). The best testimony about the state of mind of those German professors, written on the spot in 1940, is Löwith's *My Life in Germany before and after 1933*.

84. Waldemar Gurian, *Boshewismus als Weltgefahr* (Lucerne, 1935); translated by E. I. Watkin as *The Future of Bolshevism* (New York: Sheed and Ward, 1936).

Waldemar Gurian was born in 1902 in Saint Petersburg to a bourgeois Jewish family. He was educated in Germany, where his mother had settled in 1909 after the breakup of her marriage and had converted her children to Catholicism. Hannah Arendt, in her eulogy for Gurian in 1955, wrote that he had been the student of Max Scheler and Carl Schmitt. His first works, written between 1925 and 1931, demonstrated his curiosity about the place of the Catholic Church in modern life, concentrating particularly on the French example. A neo-Thomist, this critic of liberalism was no less hostile to an instrumental conception of religion and the Church, such as that of Maurras. The times offered him, and in both of his countries, two aggressively antiliberal and anti-Catholic regimes: Communism and Nazism. This agonizing situation was the pivot of his work, demonstrated for the first time by *The Future of Bolshevism*, which came out in Lucerne in 1935. At that time, Gurian had fled Nazi Germany and taken refuge in Switzerland. There, beginning in October 1934, in collaboration with another German, Otto Knab, an émigré and Catholic, he published a weekly, anti-Nazi pamphlet, poorly duplicated, called *Die Deutschen Briefe*. In 1937, he went to the United States to teach at the University of Notre Dame. There, he pursued an academic career as a specialist on Nazism and Communism, which he analyzed as twin signs of the moral crisis in twentieth-century Europe. For him, Nazism was the German form of Bolshevization. After 1945, he devoted most of his work to analyzing Communist Russia (most notably *Bolshevism: an Introduction to Soviet Communism* [South Bend, IN: University of Notre Dame Press, 1952]). His evolution can be traced through the journal he founded in 1938 and which he edited until his death in 1954, *The Review of Politics*, published by the University of Notre Dame. The January 1955 issue of that journal contains various tributes to his memory, including one by Hannah Arendt, as well as a bibliography of his works.

85. At this point in his analysis, Gurian cites Carl Schmitt, whom he calls "the principal constitutionalist of the National Socialist Reich," and Schmitt's book *Staat, Bewegung, Volk* (State, movement, people) (Hamburg: Hanseatische Verlagsanstalt, 1933). Schmitt explains that the Soviet Union is a type of state characteristic of the contemporary era versus the nineteenth century because the "movement," that is to say, the single party, controlled the state while guiding the people.

86. Gurian, *The Future of Bolshevism*, chap. 5, p. 81.

87. Thomas Mann, *Journal, 1918–1921, 1933–1939*, 27 March 1933. French version edited by C. Schwerin and translated by R. Simon (Paris: Gallimard, 1985); abridged English version, edited by Hermann Kesten and translated by R. and C. Winston (New York: Harry N. Abrams, 1982), 136–37.

88. Ibid., 7 September 1933, p. 169 in English version. It is worth citing the passage in its entirety: "After the antidemocratic upheaval in Russia and the one in Italy—which is intellectually insignificant—Germany comes up with one of her own, which represents the seizure of power by the impoverished and hate-filled petty-bourgeois masses, the class that constitutes its most debased stratum as far as mentality goes. So this is already the third in the series. What distinguishes it from the others? Is the world supposed to be healed by the filthy mysticism, the muddled philosophy of life with which this movement is decked out? Because current changes in political technique and method of government assume the form of a murderous cult of racism and war whose moral and intellectual level is lower than ever before in history? Vindictiveness and megalomania combine to form a threat to the world beside which prewar imperialism was innocence itself."

89. The similarity between Bolshevism and Nazism came up frequently in Mann's journals. For example, on 1 October 1933: "The honor guard of the Storm Troops posted like statues in front of the Feldherrenhalle is a direct and unabashed imitation of the guard the Russians keep in front of Lenin's tomb. It is the 'ideological' arch-enemy they are imitating—as they do in their films—without reflecting, perhaps without even being aware of what they are doing. The similarity in style, the *style of our time*, is far stronger than any rational differences in 'ideology.'" Or again, apropos of the Dimitrov trial, on 24 November 1933: "As I see it, the unconscious meaning of the trial lies in its exposure of the closeness, the kinship, yes, even the identity of National Socialism and communism. Its 'fruit' will be to push to absurdity the hatred between the two camps and their idiotic determination to annihilate each other, when in fact there is no need for such enmity. They are kindred though divergent manifestations of one and the same historical situation, the same political world, and are even less separable than capitalism and Marxism. Symbolic outbreaks like the Reichstag's going up in flames are, we sense, even if we cannot prove it, their joint work."

90. Ibid., 11 September 1939, translated from the French version.

91. Halévy, *The Era of Tyrannies*.

92. This very approving letter from Marcel Mauss to Élie Halévy, which was his contribution to the debate of the *Société de philosophie* ("Your deduction of the two tyrannies, Italian and German, from Bolshevism is absolutely correct."), is cited in the appendix of the *Bulletin de la Société de philosophie*, 234–35. Marcel Mauss was a longtime and perceptive critic of Bolshevism. See his "Appréciation sociologique du bolchevisme" in *Revue de métaphysique et de morale*, January–March 1924.

CHAPTER SEVEN

1. Karl Marx, *18 Brumaire of Louis Bonaparte* (New York: International Publishers, 1984). Marx speaks of the bourgeoisie having had no choice but to elect Bonaparte, preferring despotism over anarchy. On the following day they decried the coup d'état, claiming that only the leader of the tenth of December could save bourgeois society.

2. Even after Hitler came to power, even after the measures he took following the burning of the Reichstag, the Communists continued to view the Nazis' victory as a precursor of the proletarian revolution. *L'Humanité* of 1 April 1933 cited, for example, the following extract from a resolution taken by the Presidium of the Executive Committee of the Communist International at the end of March): "The installation of the open Fascist dictatorship, dispelling all the democratic illusions of the masses and liberating them from the influence of Social Democracy, is accelerating the march of Germany toward the proletarian revolution."

3. See Bullock, *Hitler and Stalin*, vol. 1.

4. Gustav Hilger and Alfred Meyer, *The Incompatible Allies: A History of German-Soviet Relations, 1918–1941* (New York: Macmillan, 1953), 262. See also J. Grunewald, "L'évolution des relations germano-soviétiques de 1933 à 1936," in *Les Relation germano-soviétiques de 1933 à 1939*, edited by J.-B Duroselle (Paris: Armand Colin, 1954).

5. Here I am following Adam B. Ulam's interpretation of the treaty of 1935 in his *Expansion and Coexistence: Soviet Foreign Policy 1917–73* (New York: Praeger), chap. 5.

6. See Besançon, *Court traité de soviétologie*, chap. 2.

7. The opening up of the Comintern archives has allowed us to establish that the French Communist Party was entirely controlled by Moscow through the Comintern and security organs and that all decisions concerning the Party were submitted, via the Comintern, to Stalin himself (see Guillaume Bourgeois, "Comment Staline dirigeait le P.C.F.," *Le Nouvel Observateur*, 5–11 August 1993).

The two key men of the Comintern in Paris were Fried and Togliatti. A Hungarian Jew from Slovakia, Eugen Fried (1900–1943) became a member of the Comintern's bureau of organization during the 1920s. Sent to France in the fall of 1930, and under the supervision of the leaders of the French Communist Party, he took control of a "college of direction," whose function was to watch over the policies followed, and instituted methods of selecting cadres. After 1932, he formed a kind of tandem with Maurice Thorez, becoming Thorez's protector. In 1934, he supported Thorez against Doriot and initiated the turn toward the policy of the *Front populaire*.

Palmire Togliatti (1893–1964), a member of the Italian Communist Party's Central Committee, went to the USSR in 1924 and acceded to the Presidium of the Comintern under the pseudonym of Ercoli. Having thrown his support to Stalin, he became Secretary of the Comintern in 1937 and played an important role in Spain. In 1934 he was dispatched to France to keep an eye on the campaign led by Fried and Thorez. After the war, he became the leader of Italian Communism.

8. The French Communist Party was another name for the French section of the Communist International.

9. Arthur Koestler, *Arrow in the Blue*, vol. 2: *The Invisible Writing* (New York: Macmillan, 1952), chap. 17; Manès Sperber, *Les Visages de l'histoire* (Paris: Odile Jacob, 1990), 85–97.

10. This long letter of 14 July 1937 can be found in *Communism*, no. 38 (1994): 171–89 ("Les Kominterniens 1. Dossier Willi Münzenberg").

11. Arrested during the debacle of May–June 1940, Willi Münzenberg escaped from the internment camp of Chambaran near Lyon with two other inmates, probably in an attempt to get to Switzerland. His body, bearing traces of strangulation, was found a few months later. His companion, Babette Gross, came to the conclusion that he had been assassinated by agents of Stalin. Babette Gross, *Willi Münzenberg: Eine politische Biographie* (Stuttgart, 1967); "Willi Münzenberg, 1889–1940: Un homme contre," Colloque international d'Aix-en-Provence, *Actes*, 26–29 March 1992; Stephen Koch, *Double Lives: Spies and Writers in the Secret Soviet War of Ideas against the West* (New York: Free Press, 1994).

12. See Yves Santamaria, "Le Parti communiste français dans la lutte pour la paix (1932–1936)," dissertation defended in 1989 at the University of Paris 10–Nanterre under the direction of Annie Kriegel. See also idem, "Le comité de lutte contre la guerre dit Amsterdam-Pleyel, 1931–1936," *Communisme*, nos. 18–19 (1988): 71–98.

13. Santamaria, "Le Parti communiste français dans la lutte pour la paix," 1: 159–84.

14. *L'Humanité*, 15 January 1933.

15. A former director of the Krupp firms, Alfred Hugenberg (1887–1951) founded his own business. He bought or took control of half of the German press as well as the information agency of the telegraphic union and the movie firm UFA. A deputy of the German National Party from 1919 on and its president in 1928, Hugenberg formed the Harzburg Front in October 1931 with the National Socialists and the Stahlhelms. Having supported Hitler, he became minister for the Economy and Supplies from January to June 1933.

16. The Night of the Long Knives refers to the massacre ordered by Hitler of Röhm and the heads of the Nazi SA as well as of several dozen other "suspects," such as the General von Schleicher, who had played a key role in Hitler's accession to power. The massacre began on the night of 29–30 June 1934 and continued for forty-eight hours.

17. For the Nazis, the burning of the Reichstag on 28 February 1933 signaled open season on Communists and an exceptional legislation that suspended all constitutional guarantees of individual liberties. Among works on these events are Hans Mommsen, *The Reichstag Fire and Its Political Consequences* (New York: Macmillan, 1985); and Uwe Baches, Karl-Heinz Janssen, Hans Mommsen, Fritz Tobias, and others, *Reichstagbrand: Aufklärung einer historischen Legende* (Munich: Piper, 1986). Today, the fire is considered to have been the act of Marinus van der Lubbe, a young Dutchman, found on the spot by the police, and the guilt attributed to the Nazis is thought to be based on fabricated documents.

18. Koestler, *The Invisible Writing*, 194.

19. Münzenberg's best-known publication on this subject, produced by the publishing house he had just founded, Les Éditions du Carrefour, was the anonymous *Livre brun sur l'incendie du Reichstag et la terreur hitlérienne*. The *Livre brun*, as Koestler commented, "is undoubtedly the work that has exercised the most political influence since Thomas Paine's *Common Sense*."

20. Koestler, *The Invisible Writing*, 194.

21. Ruth Fisher affirmed that Dimitrov's liberation was negotiated between Berlin and Moscow; see *Stalin and German Communism*, 308–9. Margarete Buber-

Neumann thought likewise; see "Le Conspirateur sans mystère," *Preuves* 74, April 1957.

22. Edward H. Carr, *The Twilight of the Comintern, 1930–1935* (London: Macmillan, 1982).

23. The term "Social Fascists" was part of the vocabulary used by the Comintern to designate Social Democratic parties.

24. These events occurred within the context of the Stavisky Affair. On the 6th, the French Communist Party joined in the demonstrations of the Leagues against Daladier, the new president of the Conseil, who had just revoked Chiappe, the prefect of police. But it did so in a distinctive way. On the 9th, the Party demonstrated under its own colors, both against Fascism and against the government. That demonstration was strongly repressed. On the 12th, the day on which the CGT had called a general strike, the two separate demonstrations by the Communists and the socialists merged spontaneously. But the French Communist Party continued to oppose an alliance between the two parties for several months.

25. Philippe Robrieux, *Histoire intérieure du Parti communiste français* (Paris: Fayard, 1980), 1:457.

26. Giulio Ceretti, *Con Togliatti e Thorez: Quarantianni di lotte politiche* (Milan: Feltrinelli, 1973), 168–72.

27. Georges Dimitrov, *Oeuvres choisies*, with a foreword by Maurice Thorez (Paris: Editions sociales, 1952), 37–168.

28. Party Secretary and "boss" of the Leningrad region, Sergei Kirov (1888–1934) advocated a certain moderation when dealing with the opposition. He opposed Stalin in the "Ryutin platform" affair. At the Seventeenth Congress of the PCUS (26 January to 10 February 1934), Kirov was applauded by former members of the opposition who had been reintegrated into the Congress. Three hundred delegates voted against Stalin in the Central Committee elections. Kirov was assassinated on 1 December 1934. Stalin used the murder as a pretext to order the first mass repressions within the Party.

29. The classic work on this subject remains Robert Conquest, *The Great Terror* (London: Macmillan, 1968); new edition, *The Great Terror: A Reassessment* (Oxford: Oxford University Press, 1991).

30. This is Carr's theory in *The Twilight of the Comintern, 1930–1935.*

31. Here we are taking into account the elimination of Doriot in 1934, and the defection of Gitton and Vassart in 1939. For a history of the internal problems of the French Communist Party, see Robrieux, *Histoire intérieure du Parti communiste français*, chap. 6.

32. See above, note 7.

33. This point is no longer contested by historiographers. One of the most useful testimonies on these events, seen from within the French Communist Party, is an account by Cilly Vassart, the wife of one of the Communist leaders of the time, based on the notes left by her husband. Albert Vassart was the organization's Secretary until April 1934, when he replaced Marty (who had vacated the post in December 1933) as representative of the French Communist Party to Moscow. They therefore had front-row seats for the Doriot-Thorez affair as well as for the anti-Fascist shift of the French Communist Party. See C. Vassart, *Le Front populaire en France*, Paris, 1962 (unpublished memoirs).

34. See Robrieux, *Histoire intérieure du Parti communiste français*, 456–57; Vassart, *Le Front populaire en France*, 34.

35. Santamaria, "Le Parti communiste dans la lutte pour la paix"; Thierry Wolton, *Le Grand Recruitment* (Paris: Grasset, 1993).

36. Christian Jelen has written the definitive history of the League of the Rights of Man, *Hitler ou Staline: Le prix de la paix* (Paris: Flammarion, 1988).

37. Jelen, *Hitler ou Staline*, 79.

38. See Stéphane Courtois, "Le système communiste international et la lutte pour la paix, 1917–1939," *Relations internationales*, no. 53 (1988): 5–22.

39. Santamaria, "Le Parti communiste dans la lutte pour la paix," 1:159–99. The context of the International's analysis was the international economic crisis, the Japanese occupation of China, and the tensions in Europe caused by the German "reparations." As is often the case, it was a combination of a profound reflection on the increasing contradictions between the great powers and a delirious interpretation of the "imminence" of an "imperialist" attack against the USSR.

40. In his speeches of 1934–36, Hitler continuously claimed that he wanted peace.

41. Doriot, in an article titled "France will not be a country of slaves," wrote, "For Stalin, we have to serve as a lightning rod for that huge hurricane that Hitler has unleashed on his country. We have to draw this cyclone toward our shores. That is Stalin's goal. . . . An alliance with the Soviets means war. Those who do not understand this have no understanding at all of the situation." *Les Oeuvres françaises*, 1936.

42. This expression comes from Philippe Burrin, *La Dérive fasciste: Doriot, Déat, Bergery, 1933–1945* (Paris: Éditions du Seuil, 1986). On the same subject, see Michel Winock, *Nationalisme, antisémitisme et fascisme en France* (Paris: Éditions du Seuil, Points-Histoire, 1982), 248–92; Antoine Prost, *Les anciens combattants et la société française, 1914–1939*, 3 vols. (Paris: Presses de la Fondation nationale des Sciences politiques, 1977).

43. Ligue des droits de l'homme, *Le Congrès national de 1927*. Systematic transcript of the meetings, 15–17 July 1927, published by the Ligue des droits de l'homme.

44. Here I am thinking especially of Jacob Leib Talmon, *The Origins of Totalitarian Democracy* (London: Secker and Warburg, 1952), and idem, *The Myth of the Nation and the Vision of Revolution* (Berkeley: University of California Press, 1981).

45. This was the most frequent case in nineteenth-century French republican historiography from Michelet to Aulard, with many nuances as to the legitimacy of resorting, even provisionally, to terror.

46. The apparent source of this line of thinking was Buchez.

47. At the first Moscow trial (19–23 August 1936), the sixteen defendants, including G. Zinoviev and L. Kamenev, were condemned to death; they were executed twenty-four hours later. At the second trial (23–30 January 1937), fifteen out of the seventeen defendants, including G. Piatakov and K. Radek, were also condemned and immediately executed. After the third trial (2–13 March 1938), other "old Bolsheviks," of whom Bukharin was the most famous, were liquidated along with Yagoda, the former director of the secret police who had organized the earlier trials. All three trials were characterized by far-fetched accusations supported only by confessions forcibly extracted from the defendants.

48. Jean Bruhat, *Le Châtiment des espions et des traîtres sous la Révolution française* (Paris: Bureau d'éditions, 1937).

49. Ibid., 56.

50. Philippe Burrin, *La Dérive fasciste*, chap. 7, "Les ambiguïtés du frontisme."

51. Christian Jelen, *L'Aveuglement*, with a foreword by Jean-François Revel (Paris: Flammarion, 1984); idem, *Hitler ou Staline*.

52. The Cartel des gauches, which was simply an electoral alliance between the Radicals and the Socialists, won the May 1924 elections. Édouard Herriot invited the Socialists to join his government or to support it on the basis of a ten-point program.

For doctrinal reasons, Léon Blum chose "support without membership." In 1932, the Union des gauches, which had triumphed in the elections, found itself in the same situation, but the Socialists were divided on the membership question, Herriot looking for support more from the Center, while the left wing of his party refused to break with the Socialists.

53. The distinction between the "seizure" and the "exercise" of power was put forward by Léon Blum in defense of the necessity of a Socialist government after the 1936 elections.

54. *Cf.* Marx, *18 Brumaire of Louis Bonaparte*, 121: "But the revolution is thoroughgoing. It is still journeying through purgatory. It does its work methodically. By December 2, 1851, it has completed one half of its preparatory work; it is now completing the other half. First it perfected the parliamentary power, in order to be able to overthrow it. Now [January–March 1852] that it has attained this, it perfects the *executive power*, reduces it to its purest expression, isolates it, sets it up against itself as the sole target, in order to concentrate all its forces of destruction against it, and when it has done this second half of its preliminary work, Europe will leap from its seat and exultantly exclaim: Well grubbed, old mole!"

55. Founded in 1900 by Sun Yat-sen, dissolved in 1913, the Kuomintang (The National People's Party) was revived from 1923 on with the aid of Soviet emissaries. The Chinese Communists, who were the minority, joined it. From 1926 on, at the time of the Kuomintang offensive on North China, the rivalry between the nationalist faction, headed by Chiang Kai-shek, and the Communist faction intensified. In certain regions, the Communists established their own governments. In 1927, the Kuomintang crushed the Communists in Shanghai (in April) and then again in Wuhan (in November). In December, the Communist uprising in Canton was also savagely put down. In Russia, the leftist opposition held Stalin responsible for the failure of Chinese Communism.

56. The Communist Party got 72 candidates elected in the election of April–May 1936, a gain of 62 seats. The SFIO got 146 elected, a gain of 62 seats. The Radicals got 115 elected but with a loss of 43 seats. The relative gains of the Communists were even more marked in terms of votes, since they almost doubled their number, whereas the Socialists reached their ceiling and the Radicals declined.

57. Simone Weil, *La Condition ouvrière*, in *Oeuvres complètes*, book 2, vol. 2 (Paris: Gallimard, 1991).

58. Ibid., 126.

59. In order to stop the factory takeover movement, Léon Blum's government, acting as an arbiter, organized negotiations between the CGT and the bosses. Signed on 8 June 1936, the Matignon accords provided for collective contracts, the readjustment of salaries, and the creation of elected delegates from among the workers in businesses.

60. Weil, *La Condition ouvrière*, 158.

61. Ibid., 158–59.

62. On 2 June 1908, the police intervened in a café in which striking quarriers were gathered, resulting in eight deaths. The CGT called for a general strike for 30 July; that day, new confrontations broke out during a demonstration at Villeneuve-Saint-Georges (four dead, hundreds wounded). In 1911 it was established that the police had infiltrated its agents provocateurs into the most radical sections of the CGT.

63. I am indebted to G. Brenan's *The Spanish Labyrinth* (Cambridge: Cambridge University Press, 1943), in the preparation of this section.

64. José Antonio Primo de Rivera (1903–1936) was the son of Miguel Primo de Rivera, who had established his military regime in Spain from 1923 to 1925. José

Antonio founded the Falange espagñola in October 1933. Elected deputy in the same year, he fought the Republic tirelessly. Arrested in March 1936, he was executed by the republicans in November. The Falange favored a kind of national syndicalism that combined individual and family ownership with trade union ownership, nationalization of credit, agrarian reform, and the creation of an authoritarian state that was capable of fighting regional separatist movements. In April 1937 it became the sole Spanish nationalist party.

65. For example, Burnett Bolloten's book *The Grand Camouflage: The Spanish Civil War and Revolution, 1936–39* (1961), second edition, with an introduction by H. R. Trevor-Roper (New York: Frederick A. Praeger, 1968). Bolloten's last great book was published four years after his death, in 1991, *The Spanish Civil War: Revolution and Counterrevolution* (Chapel Hill: University of North Carolina Press). The great classic on the subject is Hugh Thomas, *The Spanish Civil War* (New York: Simon and Schuster, 1986). See also the very recent work of Pierre Broué, *Staline et la révolution: Le cas espagnol, 1936–1939* (Paris: Fayard, 1993).

66. The POUM was the result of the fusing, completed in September 1935, of Andrés Nin's "Communist Left" and Joaquin Maurin's "Worker and Peasant Bloc." The majority of the militants came from the 1929 expulsion of the Catalonian section from the Spanish Communist Party, when the Comintern imposed its ultra-left policy. Joaquin Maurin (who happened to be Souvarine's brother-in-law) was its leader, but he would spend the entire period of the Civil War in jail. Andrés Nin was a Trotskyist, but he had broken with Trotsky five years earlier along with another POUM leader, Andrade. Strictly speaking, the POUM had nothing of the "Trotskyist" organization about it. But its Stalinist accusers described it as Trotskyist, and part of it stuck. The truth was that the POUM, though not Trotskyist, was very hostile to Stalinism, which it denounced as a "Thermidorian" regime.

67. A Bolshevik since 1917, Alexander Orlov (1895–1973) joined the special services in 1921. Sent to Spain in 1931 for the GPU, he would be responsible for the assassination of Andrés Nin in 1937. Called back to Moscow in July 1938, he defected, and alerted Trotsky to the presence of an NKVD agent in the entourage of his son, Léon Sedov. For more on Orlov, see John Costello and Oleg Tsarev, *Deadly Illusions: The KGB Orlov Dossier Reveals Stalin's Master Spy* (New York: Crown Publishers, 1993). Prior to becoming the head of Soviet services in Spain, Orlov, in 1934 in England, had been at the center of the recruitment of the famous Cambridge network (Philby, MacLean, Burgess, Blunt). He defected to the West in 1938, fearful of being liquidated by Stalin like so many other "Spaniards."

68. George Orwell, *Homage to Catalonia* (London: Secker and Warburg, 1938).

69. Taking its name from the prestigious activist Buenaventura Durruti (1896–1936), the "Friends of Durruti" gathered within the FAI the most radical militants, who saw "social revolution or Fascism" as the only political alternatives. In Barcelona in May 1937, the Friends of Durruti took part in the insurrection started in response to the Communists' attempt to take control of the Generalitat.

70. I am borrowing this expression from the testimony of one of the former heads of the POUM, Julien Gorkin, "Spain: First Test of a People's Democracy," in *The Strategy of Deception*, edited by Jeanne Kirkpatrick (New York: Farrar, Strauss and Co., 1963).

71. See the declaration of José Diaz, the Secretary General of the Spanish Communist Party, in March 1937: "We are fighting for the democratic Republic, for a democratic and parliamentary Republic of a new type and with a profound social content. The struggle taking place in Spain is not aimed at the establishment of a democratic Republic like that of France or of any other capitalist country. No. The democratic Republic for which we are fighting is different. We are fighting to destroy

the material foundations on which reaction and fascism rest; for without their destruction no true political democracy can exist." Cited in Bolloten, *The Spanish Civil War*, 232.

72. Thomas, *The Spanish Civil War*. The same idea can be found in the work of the old Spanish Communist Party leader, Fernando Claudin, *La Crise du mouvement communiste* (Paris: Maspero, 1970): well before the Fascist troops had taken over Barcelona and Madrid, the counterrevolution had silently triumphed in republican Spain.

73. Azaña was the president of the Republic, Negrin the head of the government.

74. Cited in Bolloten, *The Spanish Civil War*, 630.

75. On the value of W. B. Krivitsky's memoirs—*In Stalin's Secret Service* (New York: Harper and Brothers, 1939)—see Bolloten, *The Spanish Civil War*, 105–6, 780–82, notes 43–53.

76. Ibid., 106.

77. Thomas, *The Spanish Civil War*, 339–40. This same idea can be found in Jesus Hernandez, former Communist minister of Negrin, who wrote in his memoirs, "For the man who propounded the greatest socialist lie, the Spanish problem could be clearly stated: By sacrificing the Spanish people, I shall push Hitler toward the West, far from my borders. And the fear of the French and British governments obliges them to act docilely even toward the USSR. On the other hand, with the increasing tension between the Franco-British group and the Nazi Fascists, I shall push them toward war, which will make the USSR the arbiter of the situation." Jesus Hernandez, *Yo fui un ministro de Stalin* (Mexico City, 1952).

78. On 26 January 1939, the nationalists took over Barcelona. The Negrin government, which was still backed by the Communists, took refuge in Valencia. On 5 March 1939, General Miaja deposed Negrin and crushed the Communist resistance. The military junta readied itself to negotiate the surrender of Madrid, which had been taken over without a battle on 28 March. The Civil War was over. General Franco's government was recognized in February by France and Great Britain.

79. Although Münzenberg was at the height of his powers, his influence had begun to decline, for he was already having problems with Moscow, exemplified by the arrest of his protector and friend Radek in September 1936.

80. *New English Weekly*, 29 July 1937, "Spilling the Spanish Beans," cited in Thomas, *The Spanish Civil War*, 817, note 2.

81. Lionel Trilling, "George Orwell and the Politics of Truth," in *The Opposing Self* (New York: Harcourt Brace Jovanovich, 1978), 132–51.

82. Letter to the editor of *Time and Tide*, 5 February 1938. Cited in Thomas, *The Spanish Civil War*, 817.

83. The non-emancipated, by definition, did not have the intellectual freedom to write the truth.

84. Gustav Regler, *Le Glaive et le fourreau* (Paris: Plon, 1960), chapters 11 and 12.

85. André Malraux, *L'Espoir* (Paris: Gallimard, 1937), 249–59.

86. Ibid., chapter 2., p. 325.

87. Orwell wrote *Homage to Catalonia* in the second half of 1937, the year when *L'Espoir* was published.

CHAPTER EIGHT

1. This subject has been treated in depth by, for example, W. Drabovitch, *Les Intellectuels français et le bolchevisme; La Ligue des droits de l'homme; Le néo-marxisme universitaire* (Paris: Les Libertés françaises, 1937), and David Caute, *Communism and the French Intellectuals, 1914–1960* (London: André Deutsch, 1964).

2. Neal Wood, *Communism and British Intellectuals* (New York: Columbia University Press, 1959).

3. Stephen Spender, *World within World* (London: Harold Matson, 1951).

4. Stephen Spender, *Forward from Liberalism* (London: Victor Gollancz, 1937), 202.

5. In a later work, Stephen Spender himself explained how, very soon after he joined the British Communist Party, his eyes were opened to the reality of international Communism and how, from the assimilation of "liberalism" and Communism, he returned to the idea that they were incompatible. His observations on the Spanish Civil War played an important role in this reversal. See Spender's contribution in *Le Dieu des ténèbres* (Paris: Calmann-Lévy, 1950), 247–86.

6. Youri I. Modine, *Mes camarades de Cambridge* (Paris: R. Laffont, 1994); Phillip Knightley, *The Master Spy: The Story of Kim Philby* (London: Deutsch, 1988); Hugh Trevor-Roper, *The Philby Affair* (London: William Kimber, 1968).

7. The fifth man, John Cairncross, did not belong to the same milieu.

8. Andrew Boyle, *The Fourth Man: The Definitive Account of Kim Philby, Guy Burgess, and Donald MacLean and Who Recruited Them to Spy for Russia* (New York: Dial Press, 1979), 283.

9. See for example, Eugene Lyons, *The Red Decade* (New York: Arlington House, 1970); Daniel Aaron, *Writers on the Left: Episodes in American Literary Communism* (New York: Harcourt, Brace and World, 1961); Sidney Hook, *Out of Step: An Unquiet Life in the Twentieth Century* (New York: Carroll and Graf Publishers, 1988); Stephen Koch, *Double Lives* (New York: Free Press, 1994); Theodore Draper, "American Communism Revisited," in *A Present of Things Past* (New York: Hill and Wang, 1990), 117–53); idem, *American Communism and Soviet Russia* (New York: Viking, 1960).

10. Here I am thinking of Jay Lovestone, Sidney Hook, Irving Howe, Edmund Wilson, James Burnham, and Dwight MacDonald, among others, and of the counter-trial of Moscow that this modest American Left managed to set up with the help of the prestigious John Dewey. Western Europe in the 1930s had no equivalent of *The Partisan Review*.

11. Kupferman, *Au pays des Soviets.*

12. Romain Rolland, *Voyage à Moscou: Juin–juillet 1935,* with an Introduction and notes by Bernard Duchatelet (Paris: Albin Michel, 1992), 48.

13. Ibid., 45–46.

14. This was the period (summer of 1929) when Rolland met the "princess" Marie Koudacheva after a long correspondence. Marie Koudacheva, who had espoused the Bolshevik cause in the early twenties, would become Rolland's wife.

15. Gide discussed this very clearly in an opening speech at a demonstration against Fascism organized by the AEAR (Association des écrivains et artistes révolutionnaires) on 21 March 1933: "Why and how I have come to approve of something here that I disapprove of elsewhere is that in German terrorism I see a resumption, a recovery of the most deplorable, detestable past. In the establishment of Soviet society, [I see] an unlimited promise of a future." André Gide, *Littérature engagée* (Paris: Gallimard, 1950), 24. Rolland thought exactly the same thing.

16. The official transcript of Stalin's interview with Romain Rolland, reviewed by both authors, is in the appendix to *Voyage à Moscou,* 237–47.

17. The case of Victor Serge fueled a press campaign in France, and Romain Rolland took it upon himself to plead his case before Yagoda and Stalin. Serge was expelled from the Soviet Union in April 1936.

18. Rolland, *Voyage à Moscou,* 229–32.

19. Cambridge University is an obvious exception. In France, Marxism did not

permeate the universities until after 1945. Between the wars it was more widespread among writers than among professors.

20. This point is well analyzed by Caute, *Communism and the French Intellectuals*, part 2, chap. 2.

21. See note 10 above.

22. Panné, *Souvarine*, 222–26.

23. Ibid., 224.

24. The most lucid writings of Trotsky in exile are the ones devoted to criticism of Comintern policy toward Germany between 1930 and 1933. Trotsky clearly perceived the disastrous consequences of denouncing the Social Democrats as "Social Fascists," along with the tactical concessions to the Nazis. See Leon Trotsky, *Comment vaincre le fascisme: Écrits sur l'Allemagne, 1930–33*, translated from Russian (Paris: Éditions de la Passion, 1993).

25. Boris Souvarine, *Staline: Aperçu historique du bolchevisme* (Paris: Plon, 1935); reprinted in 1937 and 1940, with a new chapter ("La contre-révolution") and a postscript. Translated by C. R. L. James as *Stalin: A Critical Survey of Bolshevism* (London: Secker and Warburg, 1939; Amsterdam: Querido, 1940). The 1940 edition was reprinted in 1977 (Paris: Champ libre), and in 1977 and 1985 with a new foreword and afterword; it was reissued in 1993 (Paris: Ivrea).

By April 1937 the book had sold 6,800 copies. The 1940 French edition was stamped "8th thousand." Panné, *Boris Souvarine*, 225.

26. J.-L. Panné, "L'affaire Victor Serge," *Communisme*, no. 5 (Presses Universitaires de France, 1984), 89–104; Serge, *Mémoires d'un révolutionnaire, 1901–04*.

27. Gaetano Salvemini's speech was printed in the seventh issue of the journal *Les Humbles* (7 July 1935, 5–9), under the title "Pour La liberté de l'esprit."

28. In 1932, André Gide published his *Pages de Journal (1929–1932)* in the *Nouvelle Revue Française (NRF)*. There he revealed his sympathy for the Soviet Union (on 27 July 1931). His enthusiasm was occasionally tempered by the information given him by Pierre Naville, but, over the years his attachment to Communism—by way of his rejection of the capitalist world—deepened. Still, he kept his distance from Communist organizations such as the AEAR until Hitler seized power. Afterward, he ostensibly took the side of the Communist Party; his *Les Caves du Vatican* were serialized in *L'Humanité*, and he participated in the campaigns to free Dimitrov and Thaelmann. His anti-Fascism was the necessary ingredient in his adherence to Communism, which culminated at the Congress of Writers for the Defense of Culture (Paris, 21–25 June 1935), where he defended the Soviet Union against accusations of making everything uniform and of negating individuals' rights.

29. Kupferman, *Au pays des Soviets*, 103. Jean Lacouture, *André Malraux: Une vie dans le siècle* (Paris: Éditions du Seuil, 1973), 170–74.

30. Pierre Daix, "Les Voyages à Moscou: Un demi-siècle d'illusions," *Le Figaro*, 15 June 1992.

31. Pierre Herbart, *En U.R.S.S., 1936* (Paris: Gallimard, 1937). On his return from a trip to China and Indochina as a reporter for Barbusse's newspaper, *Le Monde*, Pierre Herbart (1904–74) joined the Communist Party. He signed on to *L'Humanité* and then, in November 1935, left for Moscow to head the French edition of *Littérature internationale*. His discovery of Soviet society and the trip he made with Gide led him to reconsider his political commitment, but the Spanish Civil War held him back from taking a public stand against Soviet Communism. In 1958, he published a revised view of his stay in Moscow in *La Ligne de force* (Paris: Gallimard, Folio, 1980), a particularly powerful report.

32. André Gide, *Retour de l'U.R.S.S.* (Paris: Gallimard, 1936), 67.

33. Ante Ciliga, *Au pays du grand mensonge* (Paris: Gallimard, 1938; reprinted by Champ libre, 1977). Born in Istria, Ante Ciliga (1898–1992) was an activist in the Croation nationalist movement. He joined the Communist Party after the war, participated in the creation of the Yugoslavian Communist Party and then studied in Prague, Vienna, and Zagreb. In 1922 he became Party Secretary for Croatia. Promoted as member of the Political Bureau, he was arrested and deported. In Vienna he worked in the Comintern Balkan office and was sent to Moscow in the autumn of 1926. During his three years in Moscow and one year in Leningrad, he began to criticize the regime. After three years in jail in Verkney-Ouralsk and two years of exile in Siberia, Ciliga managed to leave the USSR in December 1935 by arguing that he was an Italian national. Settling in Paris, he wrote and published his major book, *Au pays du grand mensonge*. From 1941 on, he began traveling in Europe and was arrested by the Oustachis and imprisoned for six months in the camp in Jasenovac. Freed, he went to Berlin and witnessed the downfall of the Third Reich. After the war, he settled in France and then in Italy, where he published a journal devoted to Yugoslavian problems.

34. According to Kupferman, *Au pays des Soviets*, 182, *Retour de l'U.R.S.S.* was reprinted nine times between 30 October 1936 and 9 September 1937, 146,300 copies in all. *Les Retouches à mon Retour de l'U.R.S.S.*, published in June 1937, would be reprinted only twice, at 48,500 copies. Both books sold only for a brief period.

35. Sir Walter Citrine, *I Search for Truth in the USSR* (New York: E. P. Dutton, 1937).

36. M. Yvon, *Ce qu'est devenue la révolution russe*, the *Révolution prolétarienne* pamphlets (Cannes, 1937). The following year, Gallimard published Yvon's *L'U.R.S.S. telle qu'elle est*, with a preface by André Gide.

37. Kléber Legay, *Un mineur français chez les Russes*, with a foreword by Georges Dumoulin (Paris: Pierre Tisné, 1938). The "good sections" of this book were published in *Le Populaire* of 1937: this was a sign that Léon Blum, a captive of unified action, maintained fewer illusions than ever about the USSR.

38. Barbusse died in Moscow on 30 August 1935.

39. André Gide, *Retouches à mon Retour de l'U.R.S.S.* (Paris: Gallimard, 1937), 66.

40. André Gide, *Journal III, 1889–1939* (Paris: Gallimard, 1939), 1268.

41. Before becoming the "Comité de vigilance des intellectuels antifascistes," the committee was named "Comité d'action antifasciste et de vigilance." See Nicole Furlaud-Racine, "Le Comité de vigilance des intellectuels antifascistes" in *La France sous le gouvernement Daladier d'avril 1938 à septembre 1939*, Colloquium of the Fondation nationale des sciences politiques, 4–6 December 1975.

42. Alain published his book on the war, *Mars ou la guerre jugée*, in 1935. Between 1921 and 1935, he published his "Libres propos" almost without interruption, by his friends Michel and Jeanne Alexandre. From 1935 on, his "propos" appeared in the *Feuilles libres de la quinzaine*.

43. Indeed, there was a debate in the Vigilance Committee in 1937 on the potential effects of such a restitution on the German situation as an appeasing factor in Nazi aggression.

44. Victor Serge, *Seize fusillés à Moscou* (Paris: Spartacus, 1936), 93.

45. See note 33 above.

46. See Jelen, *Hitler ou Staline*.

47. See Victor Basch, "Les procès de Moscou," in the proceedings of the Congrès national de la Ligue des droits de l'homme, 17–19 July 1937, 169.

48. Raymond Rosenmark, "Le procès de Moscou," a report presented in the name of the commission, *Les Cahiers des droits de l'homme*, no. 31 (15 November 1936), 743–50.

49. Ibid., 748.

50. Ibid., 750.

51. On Victor Basch, see Françoise Basch, *Victor Basch: De l'affaire Dreyfus au crime de la Milice* (Paris: Plon, 1994).

52. Julien Benda had a similar type of reaction. In a little-known text that appeared in an ephemeral anti-Fascist and anti-Munich publication, *Les Volontaires*, no. 1 (December 1938), Benda accepted the term "totalitarian" to characterize Communism in contrast to democracy, but gave it a favorable meaning in contrast to Fascism. Fascism and Communism, to him, were two different types of totalitarianism—similar insofar as they both totally subordinated the individual to the state and suppressed liberties, but differing on the question of the goals of social transformation, which belonged exclusively to the Communists. So there was a good as well as a bad kind of totalitarianism. See Julien Benda, "Démocratie et communisme," in *Le fascisme contre l'esprit*, special issue of *Les Volontaires*, no. 5 (April 1939).

53. The Rosenmark report received 1,088 votes as against the 258 votes for Challaye's motion.

54. Basch, "Mise au point," *Les Cahiers des droits de l'homme*, no. 21 (1 November 1937).

55. In the summer of 1938, in the midst of the Sudetenland crisis, Félicien Challaye, on the invitation of the "German Labor Front," took a group tour of Nazi Germany along the lines of the pilgrimages to Soviet Russia. He came back with judgments as indulgent toward the Nazi regime as those held by Communist fellow travelers concerning the Soviet regime. This former Dreyfusard and collaborator on the *Cahiers de la Quinzaine*, this old supporter of Jaurès and onetime fellow traveler of the French Communist Party, determined at the end of his trip what he had believed before his departure: that Hitler's Germany did not want a war.

56. *Popolo d'Italia*, 18 October 1926. Cited in Hamilton, *The Fascist Illusion*.

57. Pierre Andreu and Frédéric Grover, *Pierre Drieu La Rochelle* (Paris, 1979; reprinted by La Table Ronde, 1989). Frédéric Grover, *Drieu La Rochelle (1893–1945)* (Paris: Gallimard, 1979).

58. *La Grande Revue*, March 1934, cited in Hamilton, *The Fascist Illusion*, 235–36.

59. Pierre Drieu La Rochelle, *Socialisme fasciste* (Paris: Gallimard, 1934).

60. Ibid., 149.

61. Drieu La Rochelle, *Socialisme fasciste*, 163.

62. Pierre Drieu La Rochelle, *Journal 1939–1945* (Paris: Gallimard Témoins, 1992), 386.

63. Daniel Lindenberg, "L'homme communautaire," chap. 5 of *Les Années souterraines, 1937–1947* (Paris: La Découverte, 1991).

64. Cited in Lindenberg, *Les Années souterraines*, 209.

65. Vincent Descombes, *Philosophie par gros temps* (Paris: Éditions de Minuit, 1985).

66. This expression comes from the André Thirion's wonderful book, *Révolutionnaires sans révolution* (Paris: Robert Laffont, 1972).

67. Marcel Mauss, *Essai sur le don* (1926); translated by Ian Cunnison as *The Gift: Forms and Functions of Exchange in Archaic Societies*, with an Introduction by E. E. Evans-Pritchard (New York: Norton, 1967). From Mauss's book, Bataille drew the idea of an exchange not tied to economic utility and of a social link founded on pure "expenditure."

68. Descombes, *Philosophie par gros temps*, chap. 4, "La crise française des Lumières."

69. "Le problème de l'État," *La Critique sociale*, no. 9 (September 1933). *La Cri-*

tique sociale was a bimonthly periodical founded by Boris Souvarine in March 1931. It gathered members or sympathizers of the Cercle communiste démocratique around Souvarine and his companion of that time, Colette Peignot. The animating spirit was a nondogmatic Marxist critique of political and literary current events. Simone Weil intermittently participated in the Cercle and in the periodical from 1932 on. The same was true of Georges Bataille, who was even more heterodox (or less Marxist). In 1933, he published three articles in Souvarine's review that are among the most interesting ever written on political thought: "La notion de dépense" in January, "Le problème de l'État" in September, and "La structure psychologique du fascisme" in November. In 1934 *La Critique sociale* was sunk by the financial failure of the publishing house Marcel Rivière.

70. Bataille, "Le problème de l'État."

71. *Bataille,* "La structure psychologique du fascisme," *La Critique sociale,* no. 11 (March 1934).

72. "La structure psychologique du fascisme," *La Critique sociale,* no. 10 (November 1933), and no. 11 (March 1934).

73. Ibid., no. 11.

74. Breton and Bataille, in the fall of 1935, together wrote the declaration of the Contre-Attaque group, an organization that lasted only one year. That manifesto sought to provide a new definition of revolution, one that went beyond the socialization of the means of production and broke free from a national framework. It contained a threefold implicit critique of the Soviet model in demanding an "uncompromising dictatorship of an armed people," insisting on universal revolution, and especially in emphasizing the necessity of subverting "superstructures"; all this bore the mark of Bataille. See Thirion, *Révolutionnaires sans révolution,* 430–31. The manifesto of the Contre-Attaque group is reproduced in *Tracts surréalistes et déclarations collectives (1922–1939)* (Paris: E. Losfeld, 1980), 281–84.

75. Denis Hollier, *Le Collège de sociologie* (Paris: Gallimard, 1979), 24.

76. Jean-François Sirinelli, *Géneration intellectuelle: Khâgneux et normaliens dans l'entre-deux-guerres* (Paris: Presses Universitaires de France, 1994), chap. 13, "Les élèves d'Alain."

77. Nicolas Bavarez, *Raymond Aron* (Paris: Flammarion, 1993).

78. Raymond Aron, *Mémoires* (Paris: Julliard, 1983), chap. 5, 105–6.

79. Ibid., 143–45, and "Raymond Aron 1905–1983: Histoire et politique," *Commentaire,* February 1985, 311–26.

80. This paper, "États démocratiques et États totalitaires," was published only in 1946, in the *Bulletin de la Société française de philosophie,* 40th year, no. 2 (April–May 1946): 41–92. Reprinted in Raymond Aron, *Machiavel et les tyrannies modernes* (Paris: Éditions de Fallois, 1993), 165–83.

81. Aron, *Machiavel et les tyrannies modernes,* 166.

CHAPTER NINE

1. It would be more appropriate to speak of the German-Soviet nonaggression pacts, in the plural, as has been suggested by Stéphane Courtois.

2. After the signing of the Ribbentrop-Molotov accord (23 August 1939), the French Communists voted a patriotic-sounding resolution on 25 August ("If Hitler, in spite of all, sets off a war, even though he knows full well that he will be faced with the French people, with the Communists at the fore . . ."), and then, on 2 September, they voted for war funds and responded to the mobilization orders. On 19 September, in a letter to Léon Blum, Marcel Cachin—in the name of members of parliament—confirmed that orientation. But, at the same time, other Communists put forth a different line of policy, casting the democracies as the parties responsible for Hitler's ag-

gression against Poland. After 1 October (the Communist Party was dissolved on 26 September) it was the denunciation of the Anglo-French "warmongering imperialists" that preponderated, when two Communist deputies (Ramette and Bonte) sent a letter to Herriot notifying him of the next peace propositions on the part of USSR, which had invaded Poland on 17 September. The only "propositions" made were those of Hitler, on 6 October, when he appealed to the democracies to lay down their arms.

3. The idea was that the Germans or Polish-Germans who lived in what would henceforth be Soviet territory should return to the German part of Poland, and that the Ukrainians and Belorussians in the German sector should make the inverse move.

4. Stéphane Courtois, *Le PCF dans la guerre* (Paris: Ramsay, 1980), 50.

5. During the negotiations undertaken by France and Great Britain with the USSR, beginning in May 1939, the Soviets made the signing of a political agreement subject to the signing of a military pact. As soon as the negotiations began on 12 August, the Soviets wanted the British and the French to obtain the right of passage for their troops across Poland and Romania. Marshal Vorochilov made this a prerequisite for the pursuit of negotiations while waiting for the responses of the governments in question. On the 17th, the Soviets and the Germans signed an economic agreement that prefigured the pact of 23 August. That same day, the Polish refused to cede to the Soviet demands.

6. For a description of the French Communist Party's reactions to the German-Soviet nonaggression pact, and the reiterated confirmation of the national union against Hitler during the last week in August and the first half of September, see Courtois, *Le PCF dans la guerre*, chap. 2.

7. Mikhail Narinski, "Le Komintern et le Parti communiste française, 1939–1942," *Communisme*, no. 32–34 (1993): 12.

8. Ibid., 13.

9. Courtois, *Le PCF dans la guerre*, 100–101, nn. 8 and 9.

10. Here and there, however, the adoption of the new line defined by Stalin on 7 September had given rise to slogans such as "revolutionary defeatists"—for example, in the French Communist Party and from the pen of an expert, André Marty. See Philippe Breton, "Le parti, la guerre et la révolution, 1939–1940," *Communisme*, no. 32–34 (1993): 44.

11. Cited by Courtois, *Le PCF dans la guerre*, 88. The entire text of this speech was published in French by the *Cahiers du bolshevisme clandestins* in January 1940. See *Les Cahiers du bolshevisme pendant la campagne 1939–1940, Molotov–Dimitrov–Thorez–Marty*, with a foreword by A. Rossi (Paris: D. Wapler, 1951).

12. "Mourir pour Danzig?" appeared in Marcel Déat's journal *L'Oeuvre*, 4 May 1939.

13. In January 1936, Maurice Thorez launched the slogan "Union of the French nation," reaching out to the Catholics and the Croix-de-Feu militants. At a large meeting on 25 August 1936, he preached a "Front français" for welfare laws, for a domestic struggle against Fascism by means of a union between workers and republicans around the Front populaire, and a real policy of peace, including aid to republican Spain. Then, in October 1937, the French Communist Party supported the slogan of "France for the French." See Philippe Robrieux, *Maurice Thorez: Vie secrète et vie publique* (Paris: Fayard, 1975), 216. After the signing of the Munich agreement (29–30 September 1938), Thorez withdrew the "Union of the French nation" slogan while addressing the Central Committee meeting of 21 November, and simultaneously called for the formation of a "Front français," which was still conceived of as an expansion of the Front populaire, which had become moribund. But when the moment came to vote on the Munich agreement, the Communist Party was the only party that voted against its ratification.

14. We know that at first the French Communist Party justified the German-Soviet pact of 23 August while continuing to reiterate its anti-Hitlerian beliefs. On 2 September, the communist deputies had voted for military aid. On the 6th, the men ready to be called up were sent to their units, with Maurice Thorez at the fore. Notified in mid-September of the new orders of the Comintern on the "imperialist" nature of the war in progress, the Party undertook the shift that was imposed upon it in late September, just when it was outlawed by the government (26 September). This shift would be the object of many articles between October and December, and of self-criticism by the leadership in January 1940. This period of the French Communist Party has been the subject of many works; the ones I have found most useful are A. Rossi, *Les Communistes français pendant la drôle de guerre 1939–1940* (Paris, 1951; reprinted by Albatros in 1972); *Les Cahiers du bolchevisme pendant la campagne 1939–1940;* Courtois, *Le PCF dans la guerre; Le Parti communiste français des années sombres (1938–1941),* edited by J.-P. Azema, A. Prost, and J. P. Rioux (Paris: Éditions du Seuil, 1986); *Les Communistes français de Munich à Châteaubriant (1938–1941),* edited by J.-P. Azema, A. Prost, and J. P. Rioux (Paris: Presses de la Fondation nationale des sciences politiques, 1987); and Philippe Buton, "Le parti, la guerre et la révolution, 1939–1940," *Communisme,* no. 32–34 (1993).

15. The Nazi officials in occupied Poland would reveal the Katyn massacre at the beginning of April 1943, as soon as the mass grave was discovered: this horrible event became a central motif in anti-Soviet propaganda until the end of the war. Three investigatory commissions, one international (organized by Dr. Conti, the head of Germany's health service), one Polish (convoked by the Nazi authorities in Poland but which, under the cover of the Polish Red Cross, informed the Resistance), and one that was specifically German, separately examined the mass grave in the spring and all reached the same conclusion: that the victims had been killed three years earlier, in April or May of 1940, a date that ruled out Nazi responsibility. A Soviet investigation organized by the NKVD in January 1944 came to the opposite conclusion.

Prior to the discovery of the massacre and the above conclusions, the Polish government in London, attempting to reconstitute an army in July 1941 with the Polish citizens who were located in the USSR, noticed that it had no news from fifteen thousand officers who had not responded to the call.

Between 1941 and 1943, the Soviets gave evasive responses to the Polish inquiries. On 14 November 1941, Stalin suggested to the Polish ambassador that the missing officers "had surely fled abroad." The revelation of the Katyn massacre in April 1943 brought a sinister end to Poland's uncertainties, at least as far as fifteen thousand of its officers were concerned; it certainly aggravated Polish-Soviet contentions.

At the Nuremberg Trials, the Soviet prosecutor Roudenko sought unsuccessfully to include Katyn in the inventory of German crimes, in spite of the tribunal's care to reject the testimony of Polish survivors of Anders' and Berling's armies as well as from the Polish domestic resistance. Charges for the responsibility for Katyn were withdrawn from the verdict handed down on 30 September 1946.

In 1948 the Polish published a white paper on the Katyn massacre, with a preface by General Anders, that again presented all the elements of the case against the USSR. For an English version, see *The Crime of Katyn: Facts and Documents* (London: Polish Cultural Foundation, 1965).

On 14 October 1992, President Boris Yeltsin made public the document containing the Soviet Communist Party politburo's decision, signed by Stalin on 5 March 1940, ordering the shooting of 26,000 Poles interned in the USSR after the Soviet attack on Poland in September 1939. See *Le Monde,* 16 October 1992.

On the Katyn Affair in general, see Alexandra Kwiatowska-Viatteau, *Katyn, l'armée polonaise assassinée* (Paris: Complexe, 1982).

16. When he met with Finnish resistance to his ultimatum, Stalin attacked Finland at the end of November 1939. His plan, which was exposed by the formation of a puppet government, included the formation of a republic astride the Russian-Finnish border. The war was difficult and bloody for the Red Army owing to the fierce and clever resistance of the Finnish Army along the Mannerheim line. In March 1940, Finland gained a peace that limited the damages through territorial concessions but, in this way, saved its independence. Stalin's attack on Finland provoked strong anti-Sovietism in the West. The USSR was expelled from the League of Nations in December 1939—the last hope for "collective security" in a bygone era.

17. Jean Cathala, director of the French Institute of Tallin in Estonia since 1929, in *Sans fleur ni fusil* (Paris: Albin Michel, 1981), tells the story of the Soviet troops' entry into Tallin in June 1940 and the integration of the country into the USSR in the summer, following rigged elections in July. He describes the NKVD's gigantic roundup in June (almost one million arrests) in the three Baltic states. Of the USSR takeover he writes: "Sovietization constituted . . . a phenomenon which, to find its equivalent, one must go far back in history. For it was not just a change or loss of sovereignty. It was incorporation into another world: into a world of institutions, of practices and ways of thinking, that had to be accepted as one block, because the spiritual and the temporal, doctrine and the state, the regime and methods of government, the homeland and the party in power were all mixed together in it" (79–80). On likening the Soviets to the SS, Cathala says: "I am not all that sure today that the comparison . . . is accurate: the SS would not have done as well. What Fascism lacked was the geographic space necessary to a concentrational system on a grand scale, a structured power in which the civil society, the political regime, the economy and repression are completely overlapping and, especially, the anchoring, in one state, of mentalities and customs that had been emerging from the beginning of time. National Socialism was incapable of filling that hiatus except with atrocities" (97).

18. Margarete Buber-Neumann, *Under Two Dictators*, trans. Edward Fitzgerald (New York: Dodd Mead, 1951), 165–66.

19. This analogy is noted by Alan Bullock in *Hitler, a Study in Tyranny* (London: Penguin Books, 1990), 597, n. 1.

20. Hitler also thought the destruction of the USSR would reinforce the power of Japan in the Far East, which would focus American concern on that part of the world, thus reducing the United States' solidarity with England and Europe. See *General Halder's Diary*, 31 July 1940, cited by Bullock, *Hitler and Stalin*, 682.

21. For more on this episode and the text of the document intended for the French Communist Party and ratified by the Office of the Executive Committee of the Comintern on 5 August, see Narinski, "Le Komintern et le Parti communiste française. See also, in the same issue of *Communisme* (32–34, 1993), Stéphane Courtois's article "Un été 1940: Les négociations entre le PCF et l'occupant allemand à la lumière des archives de l'Internationale communiste," 85–110.

22. Ibid., 25.

23. A new trade agreement had been signed between Germany and the USSR in January 1941.

24. Victor Suvorov, *Ice-breaker: Who Started the Second World War?* translated by Thomas B. Beattie (New York: Viking Penguin, 1990).

25. Such an invasion was one of the "justifications" offered by Hitler in order to legitimize the calendar of Operation Barbarossa.

26. See René L'Hermitte's letter to *Communisme*, no. 35–37 (1994): 287–90.

27. On the persistence of French pacifism after 3 September 1939 and the anti-Soviet tendency of that pacifism during the "phony war," see the recent work of Louis Crémieux-Brilhac, *Les Français de l'an 40*, 2 vols. (Paris: Gallimard, 1990). *Cf.* vol. 1, *La Guerre, oui ou non?*, chap. 2.

28. Even after 1940, when this literature became (if tacitly) anti-German or, at least, oriented toward the recovery of national independence, it focused on uniting against foreigners or occupying forces. Until June 1941, neither Nazism nor Fascism nor, indeed, democracy was at issue. See Narinski, "Le Komintern et le Parti communiste française."

29. *Hitler's Table Talks, 1941-1944.*

30. Ibid., 68-69, 17 October 1941.

31. Bullock, *Hitler and Stalin*, bk. 3, chap. 11 (the special directive of 13 March 1941 on the war against the USSR).

32. Report submitted by General Halder, army chief of staff, cited by Joachim Fest, *Hitler*, vol. 2 (Paris: Gallimard, 1973), bk. 4, chap. 2, 329-30.

33. Elsewhere, however, Hitler credited Stalin with liquidating the Jewish hold over Bolshevism. See Rauschning, *The Revolution of Nihilism*, 257-58: "In the spring of 1937, before the huge crop of executions in the Russian army, a number of provincial German newspapers were surprisingly busy with Russian events, which were being interpreted as revealing a new development of Nationalism in the Bolshevik State, and its purging of Jewish elements and of doctrinaire revolutionists. There were full accounts of Stalinist anti-Semitism, and much was made of the alleged emergence of the authoritarian idea of a new Tsarism, together with a new Nationalism."

34. Raul Hilberg, *The Destruction of the European Jews* (New York: Holmes and Meier, 1985), chap. 6.

35. The "General Government" to the east of the Polish "incorporated" territories was a triangle, its top near Warsaw and its base running from Krakow to the south of Lvov.

36. Fest, *Hitler*, vol. 7, chap. 2, 329. See also Hilbert, *The Destruction of the European Jews*, p. 243; Gerald Fleming, *Hitler and the Final Solution* (Berkeley: University of California Press, 1984). See also Christopher R. Browning, *Ordinary Men: Reserve Police Battalion 101 and the Final Solution in Poland* (New York: HarperCollins, 1992).

37. Heller and Nekrich, *Utopia in Power*, 335.

38. Conquest, *Harvest of Sorrow*, Epilogue.

39. Boris Pasternak, *Doctor Zhivago* (New York: Pantheon, 1958), 507-8.

40. Aleksandr Solzhenitsyn, "Misconceptions about Russia Are a Threat to America," *Foreign Affairs*, Spring 1980, 818.

41. Wolfgang Leonhard, *Child of the Revolution*, translated by C. M. Woodhouse (Chicago: Henry Regnery, 1958).

42. The problem of the Polish frontiers had been a thorny one for the victorious allies of World War I, who wanted to restore Poland's independence but were uncertain which territories should be included, given the mixed populations of Germans to the west, and of Ukrainians and Belorussians to the east. The so-called Curzon line, named after the British foreign secretary at the time, was traced with the agreement of the French and the Americans in 1919, at Versailles, without consulting the Russians. It located the eastern border of the new Poland along the river Bug. But with the Polish-Soviet war of 1920, it became a dead letter almost immediately. The eventual victory of Pilsudsky, after the Red Army debacle on the Vistula, allowed the Poles to extend their frontier further east by incorporating rural Ukrainian and Belorussian populations.

The Curzon line, or something close to it, resurfaced in August–September 1939 in the secret agreement between Hitler and Stalin, as well as the actual division that ensued. During the war, from 1941 on, it would be at the center of contentions between the Polish government of London and the Soviet Union. Stalin obstinately refused any other Polish-Soviet border than that of September 1939. At Yalta, facing Churchill and Roosevelt, who were urging that the city of Lvov and certain oil fields situated to the east of the Curzon line be nonetheless included in Polish territory, he offered the following response: "They want us to be less Russian than Curzon or Clemenceau!"

43. Vasily Grossman, *Life and Fate*, translated by Robert Chandler (New York: Harper and Row, 1985), 655.

44. George Kennan, *Russia and the West under Lenin and Stalin* (Boston: Little, Brown, 1960).

45. In January 1941, the Allies made a preliminary declaration about war crimes. In October 1942, the British and Americans proposed to the Soviets that an international investigation into the war crimes be established. On 30 October 1943, a conference was held in Moscow, during which the act creating the tribunal was signed. At first, Stalin had wanted to stick to a repression similar to the one he had enacted from 1936 to 1938. The idea of a trial was brought up again at the Potsdam conference (July–August 1945) by President Truman and Judge Robert Jackson. The international tribunal was established to judge crimes against the peace, war crimes, and crimes against humanity. The Nuremberg trials opened on 20 November and ended on 1 October 1946. See Telford Taylor, *The Anatomy of the Nuremberg Trials: A Personal Memoir* (Boston: Little, Brown, 1992).

46. Annette Wieviorka, *Déportation et génocide: Entre la mémoire et l'oubli* (Paris: Plon, 1992).

47. Between six and seven million forced out of Silesia, Pomerania, and eastern Prussia; two to three million from Czechoslovakia; almost two million from Poland and the USSR; and between two and three million from Hungary, Yugoslavia, and Romania.

CHAPTER TEN

1. L. K. Adler and T. G. Paterson, "Red Fascism: The Merger of Nazi Germany and Soviet Russia in the Image of Totalitarianism, 1930–1950," *American Historical Review* 75, no. 4 (April 1970).

2. *The Roosevelt Diplomacy and World War II*, edited by R. Dallek (New York: Holt, Rinehart & Winston, 1970). The best critique of American ignorance about Soviet relations can be found in the first volume of George Kennan's *Memoirs, 1925– 1950* (Boston: Little, Brown, 1967). Kennan was posted, for the second time, to Moscow from 1944 to 1946 as an advisory minister to the American embassy. There, he would become the advocate for the containment policy. In an appendix to the *Memoirs* are some reports from that period, including the famous "telegraphic dissertation," a very long telegram sent on 22 February 1946 about Soviet foreign policy. Henry Kissinger, in *Diplomacy*, chap. 16, "Three Approaches to Peace," analyzes various elements in Roosevelt's attitude toward Stalin during the war. The American president had difficulty bringing his country into the war against Germany in the name of democracy, and that left him no room later to put forward a more nuanced version of the anti-Nazi coalition. Like his predecessor Woodrow Wilson, he shared his fellow citizens' desire to bring home the boys as soon as the war was over as well as the traditional view of European diplomacy, based on the notion of the balance of power. He felt that the war should lead to a peace guaranteed by a directorate consisting of the four victorious powers: the United States, the Soviet Union, Great Britain, and China. Finally, Roosevelt overestimated the strength of Great Britain, which he had

helped to weaken, and wished to confine France to a minor role. Thus his conception—a mixture of Wilsonian idealism and Churchillian realism—depended largely for its realization on Soviet cooperation.

3. Herbert Marcuse, for example, in 1967 was still maintaining that the liberal state's transformation into a totally authoritarian one came about without any change in the social order. He held that liberalism produces the totally authoritarian state as a more developed stage of its evolution, and drew a parallel with the monopolistic period of capitalism. See *Kultur und Gesellschaft* (Frankfurt, 1967), vol. 1, 37.

4. Yet another sign of Churchill and de Gaulle's shared destiny and relative solitude was that they were both compelled, almost at the same moment, to step down from the leadership of their countries as soon as Fascism was defeated.

5. Little is known about Soviet military "collaboration" with the Nazis. It is a quintessentially taboo question in the historiography of the regime. On the German side, the idea has met with only intermittent and fragile support, coming either from anti-Nazi nuclei of the Wehrmacht or, among the Nazis, from those such as Rosenberg who favored parceling out the USSR or from realist politicians such as Goebbels who sought to weaken the adversary. In any case, the atrocities committed behind Soviet lines by the Nazi armies in the name of anti-Slavic racism left little room for this policy to develop.

The first Soviet military formations to don German uniforms were recruited in the summer of 1941 among the tens of thousands taken prisoner in the first months of the war. Their ranks swelled gradually, probably for several reasons, ranging from hostility to Stalin's regime to the simple desire for survival: the living conditions of prisoners of the Red Army in German camps were generally terrible. Those battalions, originally used to combat Soviet "partisans" behind the front, were later regrouped by nationalities to serve in the west, especially in France, to fight internal resistance.

The most serious effort to unify the "Soviet" military forces in the service of Germany was tried in September 1942 by General Vlasov, who had been taken prisoner in July of that year and who, in December, founded the "National Russian Committee" in Smolensk. But for a long time Vlasov, in the name of a national Russian program undermined by his dependent situation and in any case hardly attractive to the national minorities of the USSR, only exercised an illusory authority over the various Soviet-originated military detachments formed by the nationalities. He never managed to get them to the eastern front. Strictly under the orders of the Wehrmacht units, they were essentially assigned to tasks of repression in the west.

Vlasov's mission acquired a little more importance in Nazi policy in the fall of 1944, when the final debacle was taking shape. Himmler agreed to slacken the Russian general's leash; Vlasov then founded the "Committee for the Liberation of the Russian Peoples" in Prague on 14 November. Curiously, the long "Manifesto" that crowned that day constituted a "liberal" anti-Bolshevik program under the patronage of the Nazis! By taking advantage of the massive influx of population chased westward by the advancing Red Army, Vlasov was able to create two armies, comprising some fifty thousand men between them. One army was to distinguish itself in the first days of May 1945 by switching sides and liberating Prague from the SS regiments.

At the end of the war, out of some five million "displaced persons" of Soviet origin, an estimated five hundred thousand or more Soviet citizens of various nationalities served in the Wehrmacht, a number to which we must add Vlasov's two armies of late 1944. The rest was made up of prisoners of war, forced migration workers, deportees pure and simple, and those who had fled to the west for one reason or another at the time of the Soviet Army's counteroffensive. Of the five million men, half of whom found themselves on territory occupied by the Red Army, three million two hundred thousand were repatriated in the summer of 1945. The Allies assumed responsibility for the others, some two million, almost all of whom were sent back to the USSR between 1945 and 1947, like it or not. See George Fischer, *Soviet Opposition to Stalin: A Case Study in World War II* (Cambridge, MA: Harvard University Press, 1952), and Nicolas Bethell, *Le Dernier Secret, 1945: Comment les Alliés livrèrent deux millions de Russes à Staline* (Paris: Le Seuil, 1975).

6. Nicolas Tolstoi, *Victims of Yalta* (London: Hodder and Stoughton, 1977).

7. Heller and Nekrich, *Utopia in Power*, 450.

8. J. P. Nettl, *The Eastern Zone and Soviet Policy in Germany, 1940–50* (Oxford: Oxford University Press, 1951), 43–45; Dennis L. Bark and David R. Gress, *History of Germany since 1945* (Oxford: Basil Blackwell, 1989), part 1.

9. In fact, the political role of these economic and social forces was broken by Hitler. For more on the "democratization" of German society by Nazism, see David Schoenbaum, *Hitler's Social Revolution: Class and Status in Nazi Germany, 1933–1939* (Garden City, NY: Doubleday, 1967).

10. The history of Polish Communism is tumultuous and sad. That of its relations with the Comintern is tragic. Formed in 1918, the Party was primarily, according to Luxemburgian orthodoxy, hostile to Polish independence, since it supported Poland's attachment to the young Soviet republic. That position became rabid in 1920, when the Party supported the Red Army's offensive push toward Warsaw. Prisoner of its excessive antinationalism, prey to internal quarrels, controlled by internationalist militant Jews, the Party had little resonance in Poland and, from 1924 on, provoked Stalin's hatred because of its Trotskyist tendencies. The first cleaning out of its Moscow directors occurred in that year. But this did not prevent another group, two years later, from receiving a new admonition from Stalin for having supported Pilsudski's military coup against the parliamentary regime: this was a tactical error that for thirty years fueled Moscow's contention that the Polish Communist Party had been infiltrated by "Fascist" agents.

Thereafter, however, and until Hitler's rise to power, that party was viewed by the Comintern as little more than an accessory instrument in the service of German politics. It was led, for example, to defend the idea of a revision of the frontiers of Versailles in Upper Silesia and Danzig, against the national interest. It continued to be the object of narrow surveillance and a hunt for Trotskyists (such as Isaac Deutscher, expelled in 1932) periodically directed from Moscow.

Even the 1934–35 shift lent it neither internal space for maneuvering nor minimal respect in Moscow. Even though the absurd propaganda in favor of German revisionism had stopped, the Polish Communist Party was too obviously under the Comintern's thumb and too weak (it had between five and ten thousand members) to convince the Socialist Party and the Bund either of the sincerity of its new patriotism or of the need for their support. Stalin, moreover, feared the effervescence of its factions more than he counted on their utility. In 1934 he began to liquidate several of the Polish leaders, who were in Moscow. In 1937–38 came the great purge. All the Polish Communists present in Moscow were either deported or killed, beginning with the members of the Central Committee. The Party itself was dissolved by the Comintern sometime—we are not sure exactly when—in 1938. The few survivors of Polish Communism owed their lives to the chance of having been arrested earlier in their country and to the shelter offered by Pilsudski's prisons.

We still do not know why the Soviets liquidated the Polish party. It is clear that the Polish Communists had always been suspected of being too Jewish, too Trotskyist, and too Polish—the latter trait favored by the anti-Fascism of the mid-1930s, the time when Stalin was turning toward Hitler. They were, in any case, the first victims of the Soviet-German pact.

For more on Polish Communism, see Nicholas Bethell, *Gomulka: His Poland, His Communism* (New York: Holt, Rinehart & Winston, 1969); M. K. Dziewanowski, *The Communist Party of Poland: An Outline of History*, 2d ed. (Cambridge, MA: Harvard University Press, 1976); and Jan B. de Weydenthal, *The Communists of Poland: An Historical Outline* (Stanford, CA: Hoover Institution Press, 1978).

11. From the 1930s on, Poland was governed, under the authority of Marshal Pilsudski (d. 12 May 1935), by colonels who occupied the key positions in the state, such as Josef Beck in the Department of Foreign Affairs.

12. I draw this observation from the many conversations I have had with Polish friends who witnessed or participated in this period of their history.

13. Krystena Kersten, *The Establishment of Communist Rule in Poland, 1943-1948* (Berkeley: University of California Press, 1991).

14. Provisionally, at the Potsdam Conference. We know that this provisional arrangement was never made official by a definitive peace treaty among the Allies.

15. Kersten, *The Establishment of Communist Rule in Poland*, 245.

16. For a consideration of the ambiguities of postwar Soviet-Polish relations and the condition of Polish enslavement, the most interesting studies are Czeslaw Milosz's *The Seizure of Power* (New York: Farrar, Straus and Giroux, 1982), and *The Captive Mind* (New York: Random House, 1981).

17. Let us not forget that Hungary had been allied with Germany, as had Romania, until the coup d'état of King Michael on 23 August 1944. But even in those countries, the idea of a national renaissance led or supported by the local Communist parties was not simply a product of the Red Army's occupation. See François Fejtö, *Histoire des démocraties populaires* (Paris: Le Seuil, 1975), pt. 1, chap. 5, "Le sort des trois satellites de l'Allemagne."

18. Michael Marrus, *The Holocaust in History* (New York: NAL-Dutton, 1989). See also B. Wasserstein, *Britain and the Jews of Europe, 1939-1945* (Oxford: Oxford University Press, 1979); W. Laqueur, *The Terrible Secret: An Investigation into the Suppression of Information about Hitler's "Final Solution"* (London: Weidenfeld and Nicholson, 1980); D. S. Wyman, *The Abandonment of the Jews: America and the Holocaust, 1941-1945* (New York: Pantheon, 1984).

19. Marrus, *The Holocaust in History*, 172-76. See also M. Marrus, *The Unwanted: European Refugees in the Twentieth Century* (Oxford: Oxford University Press, 1985), 194-200, 241-52.

20. M. Marrus, *The Holocaust in History*, 175-76.

21. Anti-Semitic pogroms persisted in postwar Poland: in Cracow, for example, in August 1945, and in Kielce in July 1946. See Kersten, *The Establishment of Communist Rule in Poland*, pt. 2, 214-20.

22. George Orwell, "The Prevention of Literature," in *Shooting an Elephant and other Essays* (New York: Harcourt Brace, 1950).

23. George Orwell conceived the idea of *1984* in February 1943, but first he finished *Animal Farm*, which was published on 17 August 1945. The death of his wife Eileen and other tasks kept him from finishing *1984* until October 1948; the book was published in early June 1949. Orwell died on 21 January 1950.

24. George Orwell, "The Prevention of Literature," 109.

25. Ibid., 110.

26. Take, for example, the contrast described by Raymond Aron between 11 November 1918 and 8 May 1945: "November 1918 . . . Unless they had seen it, no one could have imagined what Paris was like the day of the Armistice, the day after the Armistice. People embraced in the streets. Everyone: bourgeois, laborers, office workers, young people, old people; it was popular craziness, but joyous

craziness . . . In contrast, in May 1945, Paris was deathly sad. That is how I experienced it. I recall a conversation with Jules Roy that day. He was struck, as I was, by the sadness and lack of hope. It was more the Allies' victory than that of France. There was nothing comparable to the transports of enthusiasm of those days in November 1918." Raymond Aron, *Le Spectateur engagé* (Paris: Julliard, 1981), 110.

For more on the kind of sadness that marked Paris at that time in France, see Malcolm Muggeridge's memoirs, *Chronicles of Wasted Time* (London: Collins, 1973), vol. 2, *The Infernal Grove*, chap. 4, "The Victor's Camp."

27. Philippe Buton, *Les Lendemains qui déchantent: Le Parti communiste français à la Libération* (Paris: Presses de la Fondation des sciences politiques, 1993).

28. Annie Kriegel, *Les Communistes français dans leur premier demi-siècle, 1920– 1970* (Paris: Éditions du Seuil, 1985).

29. The program of the Conseil nationale de la Résistance, adopted on 15 March 1944, shows clearly the point to which revolutionary rhetoric of the domestic resistance borrowed virtually its entire stock of ideas from the Communist repertory. All that is contained in the section that enumerates the measures to be taken immediately after the liberation of the territory are the classical abstractions of anti-Fascism, accompanied by the intention to establish state control of the economy and of society. There is no mention of a new organization of public powers, which had inspired so many projects in the early 1930s and then became the reason for breaking with de Gaulle.

30. Tony Judt, *Past Imperfect: French Intellectuals 1944–1956* (Berkeley: University of California Press, 1992), 39–41.

31. The best commentator on this French political desert was Albert Camus, in his articles in *Combat* between 1944 and 1947, reprinted in *Actuelles, chroniques 1944– 1948* (Paris: Gallimard, 1950).

32. According to Buton (*Les Lendemains qui chantent,* 25–56), Maurice Thorez's declaration of 1946 ("Les progrès de la démocratie à travers le monde . . . permettent d'envisager, pour la marche au socialisme, d'autres chemins que celui suivi par les communistes russes. . . . Nous avons toujours pensé . . . que le peuple de France . . . trouverait lui-même sa voie vers plus de démocratie, de progrès et de justice sociale") in no way modified the strategic goals of the Communists, that is, the establishment of a "popular democracy." It must be seen in relation to the policies elaborated from the mid-1930s at the time of the Spanish Civil War and carried out in the Baltic states from 1939 on.

33. Wieviorka, *Déportation et génocide;* Annie Kriegel, "Les intermittences de la mémoire: de l'histoire immédiate à l'Histoire," *Pardès,* no. 9–10 (1989).

34. Foreign Jewish refugees in France constituted the great majority of Jews deported from France who died in the Nazi camps.

CHAPTER ELEVEN

1. On 5 June 1947, General George Marshall, the American secretary of state, proposed a plan to the European states, including Russia, that would aid them in the reconstruction and restoration of Europe. After the Paris conference, on 12 July, the USSR rejected the American offer, fearing that it would introduce controls upon the economies of the countries it dominated and might bring into question the Soviet strategy for the countries of Eastern and Central Europe. Whereas Czechoslovakia and Poland were ready to accept the Marshall Plan, the USSR forced them to reject it.

2. At the Yalta conference (February 1945), the USSR accepted the principle of

"free, unfettered elections" while simultaneously imprisoning sixteen leaders of the Polish Resistance. On 19 January 1947, the rigged elections gave the majority to a coalition under the thumb of the Communists.

3. In Czechoslovakia, the Communists, who controlled the unions and had infiltrated their agents into the non-Communist parties, began in early 1947 systematically to infiltrate the police. On 13 February 1948, the nomination in Prague of eight Communists to high police posts provoked a crisis between the moderates and Communists in the government coalition. After the resignation of liberal minority ministers, the Communists organized huge meetings all over the country, calling for a purge. On 22 February, the Slovak Party seized power in Bratislava. On 23 February, the opportune discovery of a plot allegedly fomented by the National Socialists allowed the Communists to take complete control of the National Front. A day later, the newspapers and the seats of the liberal parties were occupied. On 25 February, President Beneš, in accepting the resignation of the liberal ministers, yielded to the demands of the Communists, who were henceforth the incontestable holders of power.

4. The dissolution of the Comintern in May 1943 did not mean an interruption in the relations between the Communist parties and the Soviet regime. Deeming it necessary to reorganize its European organization, the Soviets decided to create a Bureau of Information and Liaison, or the Cominform, which was created during an international conference of the European Communist parties in Poland (22–27 September 1947). The constitution of the Cominform was announced on 5 October 1947.

5. Points of reference: Churchill's famous speech of 5 March 1946 at Fulton, denouncing the "iron curtain" that had fallen on Europe; and the founding of the Comintern and the definition of two camps—the imperialists and the socialists—in September 1947.

6. There was of course a major debate about this subject in American historiography when, beginning in the mid-1960s, and in the context of the Vietnam War, a school of "revisionist" historians underlined the role of the United States in starting the cold war. That role was both objective—deduced from an economic analysis and from the expansionism of capitalism, whose means of production found itself without an outlet—and subjective, to the extent that the death of Roosevelt incontestably left the way open for groups less inclined toward the idea of compromise to make the war alliance last. The decision, for example, to drop the atomic bomb on Hiroshima, could be interpreted either as a means to a rapid ending of the war with Japan or as a warning to Stalin. But the weakness of this revisionist historiography is that it is unilateral, and neglects—no small omission—the nature of the Soviet regime and the uniqueness of its foreign policy. For a subtle résumé of the two sides, see B. J. Bernstein, "American Foreign Policy and the Origins of the Cold War," and Arthur Schlesinger, "Origins of the Cold War," in *Twentieth Century America: Recent Interpretations,* edited by B. J. Bernstein and A. J. Matuson (New York: Harcourt Brace Jovanovich, 1972), 344–94 and 409–35. See also J. L. Gassis, "The Tragedy of Cold War History: Reflections on Revisionism, *Foreign Affairs,* January–February 1994.

7. In a speech to the United States Congress on 12 March 1947, which would obtain military loans to Greece and Turkey, President Truman defined a "doctrine" of aid to governments and peoples who were fighting to maintain their "free institutions" against Communism. That doctrine had two faces, an outer one, turned mainly toward Europe, and an inner one, concerned with the United States.

8. France had obtained a German occupation zone in Potsdam. The French military administration was different from those of the Americans and the British because of its reluctance to encourage a redeployment of German political officialdom.

9. The fate reserved, a bit later on in 1951, for Paul Merker, one of the leaders of the Party, was symbolic of the East German Communists' "forgetting" about the Jewish genocide. Paul Merker was an old Comintern militant who had gone through exile in France and the Vernet camp finally to arrive in Mexico in 1942. In Berlin in 1946, he was one of the two major East German Communist leaders, the other one being Franz Dahlen, who had not spent the war in the USSR. A non-Jew, Merker was also the only one who underlined the central character of anti-Semitism in Nazism (an ideological heresy in terms of class struggle), as well as the particular horror of the massacre of the Jews, whereas the official line cast the "working class" as the foremost victim of Nazism. In 1948, he wrote an essay hailing the creation of Israel. He was thrown out of the Central Committee of the SED in August 1950, accused of having contacts with the "American agent" Noel Field. This accusation would also constitute one of the bases for the Slánský trial in Prague in November 1952. In fact, Merker was arrested right afterward as an accomplice to American imperialism and international Zionism. He was tried in a secret court and condemned to eight years' imprisonment. Released in January 1956, he never obtained the rehabilitation he sought in vain until his death in 1969. See Jeffrey Herf, "East German Communists and the Jewish Question," *Journal of Contemporary History* 29, no. 4 (October 1994). On the Jewish question in Poland, see Jean-Charles Szurek, "Le camp-musée d'Auschwitz," in *À l'Est la mémoire retrouvée* (Paris: La Découverte, 1990).

10. At the end of 1945, four parties had received authorization from the Allied military authorities to exercise their activities in four zones: the Communists and the Socialists, as well as two "bourgeois" parties, the Christian Democratic Union and the Liberal Democrats. The latter two parties were particularly weak in the Soviet zone, which was dominated by the "workers'" parties. See J. P. Nettl, *The Eastern Zone and Soviet Policy in Germany, 1945–1950* (Oxford: Oxford University Press, 1951). For a description of Soviet rule in that zone during this period, see Norman Naimark, *The Russians in Germany: A History of the Soviet Zone of Occupation, 1945– 1949* (Cambridge, MA: Harvard University Press, 1995).

11. See Albert O. Hirschman, "Exit, Voice, and the Fate of the German Democratic Republic: An Essay in Conceptual History," *World Politics* 45 (January 1993).

12. See Nettle, *The Eastern Zone*, chap. 4, 107.

13. See above, chap. 5, 155–88.

14. The Secretary of the Central Committee, Andrei Zhdanov (1896–1948), succeeded Kirov in Leningrad. As an apostle of socialist realism, he defended the idea of the mobilization of the arts and letters for the benefit of the regime at the Pan-Soviet Literary Congress in August 1934. A hard-core Stalinist, he entered the Politburo in 1939. During the war, he directed the defense of Leningrad. Promoted to the post of Third Party Secretary in March of 1946, he led a major campaign for the correction of the "ideological line" of the Party in literary and artistic matters and attacked Boris Pasternak, Anna Akhmatova, and Dimitri Shostakovich by way of prelude to a new wave of purges. In September 1947, Stalin sent him to Poland to direct the foundation of the Cominform.

15. Eugenio Reale, *Avec Jacques Duclos au banc des accusés, à la réunion constitutive du Kominform à Szklarska Porba (22–27 septembre 1947)*, translated from the Italian by Pierre Bonuzzi (Paris: Plon, 1958). Eugenio Reale was one of the two leaders of the Italian Communist Party present at the founding meeting of the Cominform. The following year, in 1948, he left the leadership of the Party; in 1952 he resigned from the Central Committee. Hostile to Togliatti and to the subordination of the Party to the USSR, he was expelled on 31 December 1956.

16. I am referring here to the two or three years following his condemnation.

17. François Fejtö, *Histoire des démocraties populaires,* 1: 265. Rajk, who was the Hungarian minister of foreign affairs, having been minister of the interior until the autumn of 1948, was arrested in May 1949, tried in September, condemned to death, and executed. See François Fejtö, "L'affaire Rajk quarante ans plus tard," *Vingtième Siècle,* January–March 1990; and Roger Stéphane, *Rue Laszlo-Rajk: une tragédie hongroise* (Paris: Odile Jacob, 1991).

18. J. Arceh Getty, Gabor T. Rittersporn, and Victor N. Zemskov, "Les victimes de la répression pénale dans l'URSS d'avant-guerre," *Revue d'études slaves* 65, no. 4: 631–70; Nicolas Werth, "Gulag: les chiffres?" *L'Histoire,* September 1993.

19. The Communists' seizures of power in Eastern and Central Europe all happened more or less along the same lines: fortified by the Red Army's support, the Communists led a coalition from which they gradually forced out their adversaries. In October 1944, the Red Army reached Yugoslavia; on 11 November 1945, the National Front took power, and the Republic was declared on the following 29 November. In Bulgaria, the coalition government was replaced by the "Country's Front," presided over by the Cominternian George Dimitrov. The Popular Republic was instituted on 15 September 1946. In Romania, on 27 February 1945, Andrei Vishinski imposed a government made up of the parties of the National Democratic Front, which won the elections of 19 November 1946; King Michael abdicated on 30 December 1947. In Hungary, the Union of Leftist Forces won the elections of August 1947 with 60 percent of the vote, as well as the elections of 1949 with 95.6 percent. On 20 August, the Popular Republic was declared.

20. I am thinking, for example, of Gomulka's exclusion from the Polish Communist Party and his imprisonment in 1949–50; of Clementis, the Czechoslovakian minister of foreign affairs, during the same years; of the Slánský trial in Prague in November 1952; and of Anna Pauker's eviction from Romania, also during this time.

21. Another exception was Kostov, an old Comintern militant from Bulgaria who was tried for "treason" in Sofia in December 1949 and who retracted his confessions and protested the charges.

22. The Slánský trial occurred in Prague, 20–27 November 1952. Rudolf Slánský, former General Secretary of the Czechoslovakian Communist Party, had been arrested the year before and sentenced as the head of a conspiracy against the state. Eleven out of the fourteen accused were Jewish and were designated as such by the charges, which noted the existence of a conspiracy in which "international Zionism" played a central role. Slánský was condemned to death and hanged, along with ten of his fellow defendants. Three others were condemned to life in prison. Two out of those three wrote a history of the trial: Artur London, *The Confession,* translated by A. Hamilton (New York: William Morrow, 1970); Eugen Loebl, *Stalinism in Prague: The Loebl Story* (New York: Grove Press, 1960); and *My Mind on Trial* (New York: Harcourt Brace Jovanovich, 1976).

23. The moment when Churchill felt he had been tricked by Stalin in the Polish affair was perhaps between the interview he had had with the Soviet marshal in Moscow in early October 1944 and the one in Yalta in February 1945. See Roy Douglas, *From War to Cold War, 1942–48* (New York: St. Martin's Press, 1981), chaps. 4–7.

24. The results of the English legislative election of 5 July 1945 were only known three weeks later, when Churchill was already at the Potsdam conference.

25. Léon Blum, *À l'échelle humaine* (Paris: Gallimard, 1945), 105.

26. Following a strike set off in the factories of Renault by militant Trotskyists, the Communist ministers decided to ask for an end to the block on salaries and prices. On 2 May 1947, Paul Ramadier asked the Assembly for a vote of confidence. On the 4th, it adopted an agenda favorable to the government, with the Communists voting

against it. To avoid the collective resignation of the government, Ramadier dismissed the Communist ministers that very evening.

27. See, for example, Jeannine Verdès-Leroux, *Au service du Parti: Le Parti communiste, les intellectuels et la culture (1944–1956)* (Paris: Fayard-Minuit, 1983); David Caute, *The Fellow-Travellers* (London: Weidenfeld and Nicolson, 1973); Pierre Rigoulot, *Les Paupières lourdes: Les Français face au Goulag: aveuglements et indignations*, with a foreword by J. F. Revel (Paris: Editions universitaires, 1991); Tony Judt, *Past Imperfect: French Intellectuals 1944–1956* (Berkeley: University of California Press, 1992).

Raymond Aron's *L'Opium des intellectuels* (Paris: Calmann-Lévy, 1955) remains the most important book on this subject.

28. Aron, *Mémoires*, 182–88. Aron published an article in *France libre* entitled "L'ombre des Bonaparte" (The shadow of the Bonapartes), in which he warned against the resurgence of a "popular Caesarism" that could have tempted General de Gaulle. He discusses that article and what he meant by it in his memoirs (184–86). See also "Raymond Aron, 1905–1983: Histoire et politique," *Commentaire* (Paris: Julliard, 1985), 359–68.

29. Lacouture, *André Malraux*, 320–26. In August 1945, Malraux met General de Gaulle and joined forces with the leader of free France. In 1947, he became a propaganda delegate of the Rassemblement populaire français.

30. Kostas Papaioannou, *L'Idéologie froide* (Paris: J.-J. Pauvert, 1967).

31. I am, of course, referring to the trial won by Victor Kravchenko against the journal *Lettres françaises*, which took place from 24 January to 4 April 1949. See Guillaume Malaurie, *L'Affaire Kravchenko, Paris, 1949, le Goulag en correctionnelle* (Paris: Robert Laffont, 1982).

32. Tony Judt, "The Past is Another Country: Myth and Memory in Post-War Europe," *Daedalus* 71, no. 4 (1992).

33. Adler and Paterson, "Red Fascism," 1046–49.

34. Ibid., 1051–61.

35. Jacques Duclos's letter appeared in the monthly journal of the French Communist Party, the *Cahiers du communisme* of April 1945.

36. I am repeating here the argument advanced by I. Howe and L. Coser in *The American Communist Party: A Critical History* (New York: Praeger, 1962), 442. A similar interpretation of the early alignment of the American Communist Party along the lines of the cold war may be found in Schlesinger, "Origins of the Cold War," 426–27.

37. Dwight Macdonald, "What is Totalitarian Liberalism?" in *Memoirs of a Revolutionist: Essays in Political Criticism* (New York: Farrar, Straus and Cudahy, 1957), 202.

38. Wallace was the author of the following famous words in the spring of 1944 when he was vice-president and was about to take a trip to Soviet Asia: "It is with great anticipation that I approach the Siberian experience. . . . Over 40,000,000 people have taken the place of the 7,000,000—mostly convicts—who miserably existed there under Imperial Russia. So the detractors of Russia must pause before the fact of Soviet Asia of today. . . . I shall see the cities. I shall feel the grandeur that comes when men work wisely with nature." Quoted in Dwight MacDonald, *Henry Wallace: The Man and the Myth* (New York: Vanguard Press, 1948), 103.

39. David Caute, *The Great Fear: The Anti-Communist Purge under Truman and Eisenhower* (New York: Simon and Schuster, 1978); R. M. Fried, *Nightmare in Red: The McCarthy Era in Perspective* (Oxford: Oxford University Press, 1990).

40. I am deliberately leaving aside this aspect of the history of American Communism, which is substantial and is covered by an extensive literature. There is no

longer any doubt that the speed with which the Soviet atomic bomb was developed was due to help from the West. Curiously enough, Senator McCarthy, a perverse demagogue, had a partially accurate idea about the adversary.

41. One of the most famous episodes of American nativism was the Evangelical movement, which was hostile to Catholic immigration. It developed between 1820 and 1830 around the idea of a Popish plot to take over the United States.

42. Richard Hofstadter, *Anti-intellectualism in American Life* (New York: Knopf, 1963).

43. I say "partially" insofar as this rationalization of the Terror was more common among historians of the Revolution than among the revolutionaries themselves. See Mona Ozouf, "Guerre et Terreur dans le discours révolutionnaire, 1892–1894," in *L'École de la France, essais sur la Révolution, l'utopie, l'enseignement* (Paris: Gallimard, 1984).

44. The question of "Who lost China?" was one of the chief accusations leveled by Senator McCarthy's campaign against internal "traitors."

45. It was in Berlin in 1950 that the Kongress für kulturelle Freiheit took place, which inaugurated in Europe the gathering of intellectuals opposed to Soviet totalitarianism. In March 1951, the periodical *Preuves* began publication.

46. See Peter Coleman, *The Liberal Conspiracy: The Congress for Cultural Freedom and the Struggle for the Mind of Postwar Europe* (New York: Free Press, 1989); Edward Shils, "Remembering the Congress for Cultural Freedom," *Encounter*, September 1990; Sidney Hook, *Out of Step: An Unquiet Life in the Twentieth Century* (New York: Harper and Row, 1987), chaps. 26 and 27. Among the "big names" were Albert Einstein, Charlie Chaplin, Paul Robeson, and Leonard Bernstein.

47. The most famous of these demonstrations took place in Paris, in 1935, the first "International Congress for Writers for the Defense of Culture," with illustrious participants such as Gide, Malraux, Benda, Huxley, Heinrich Mann, Brecht, Dreiser, Pasternak, Babel, and Ehrenburg. See chapter 8 above.

48. In September 1948, a huge Peace Congress took place at Wroclaw, formerly Breslau, in Polish Silesia. It was followed by a second one, in Paris, in April 1949. In the meantime, the New York demonstration had taken place in March.

49. Secondo Tranquillo (1900–1978), better known under his pseudonym of Ignazio Silone, was Secretary of the agricultural workers of Abruzzi and an opponent of the war. In Rome, he became Secretary of the Socialist Youth (1919) and then participated in the founding of the Italian Communist Party (1921). Expelled in 1931, he took refuge in Switzerland, where he wrote his first novel, *Fontamara*, which was quite successful. In 1938, he published *L'École des dictateurs*. In 1940 he became a member of the Italian Socialist Party (PSI). Interned in Switzerland in 1947, he returned to Italy in 1944 to become one of the leaders of the PSI. He worked with many periodicals, such as *Preuves* and *Témoins*, and in 1955 he founded *Tempo presente*. He also published essays based on his political experiences, such as *Sortie de secours* and *Le Fascisme*.

50. A Communist until 1929, Frank Borkenau (1900–1957) then went to work at the Institut für Sozialforschung in Frankfurt. After that, he took refuge in London and then, after a sojourn in Panama, went to Spain at the beginning of the Spanish Civil War. In 1937 he published *The Spanish Cockpit* (London: Faber and Faber). Several of his works deal with Communism—*European Communism* (London: Faber and Faber, 1953), and *World Communism: A History of the Communist International*, with a foreword by Raymond Aron (Ann Arbor: University of Michigan Press, 1962).

51. Irving Brown was close to Jay Lovestone, who was one of the great figures of early American Communism in the 1920s and then leader of a dissident group, prior to becoming a rabid anti-Stalinist.

52. The financing of the "Congress for Cultural Freedom" by the CIA, which was funneled through various foundations, was revealed in a series of articles in the *New York Times* in April 1966. This belated scoop, which confirmed a Communist accusation as old as the organization itself, provoked an internal crisis resulting in the dissolution of the Congress in September 1967. It was replaced by the "International Association for Freedom and Culture," which survived until 1979 without ever recovering its predecessor's reputation. See Coleman, *The Liberal Conspiracy*, chaps. 14 and 15.

53. Hannah Arendt, *The Origins of Totalitarianism* (New York: Harcourt, Brace, 1951). That edition was followed by several others, in 1956, 1966, 1968, and in 1973, which were generally augmented by new prefaces. The work was published in France only many years later and in a piecemeal fashion, from 1972 to 1982.

54. This is how she characterized Walter Benjamin in the portrait she wrote of him in *Men in Dark Times* (New York: Harcourt, Brace and World, 1968), 193–206. But the description can equally be applied to Arendt herself.

55. Elisabeth Young-Bruehl, *Hannah Arendt: For Love of the World* (New Haven: Yale University Press, 1982), chap. 2, "Shadows."

56. This becomes abundantly clear in her long correspondence with Karl Jaspers after the war. Hannah Arendt and Karl Jaspers, *Correspondence 1926–1969* (New York: Harcourt, Brace, 1993).

57. Interview with G. Gauss, 28 October 1963. Cited in Young-Bruehl, *Hannah Arendt*, 185.

58. The question, as we have seen, had been posed by European politics, especially in Germany and France during the 1930s (see above, chap. 6). But it was also present in American political science before the United States' entry into World War II. For example, the American Philosophical Society held an academic colloquium in 1940 on the "totalitarian state." Most of the contributions were of the highest order and anticipated ideas usually attributed to Franz Neumann or Hannah Arendt, though the names of their authors have been forgotten. The final paper, presented by a Columbia University professor, J. H. Carlton Hayes, was entitled "The Novelty of Totalitarianism in the History of Western Civilization." It treats both Hitler's Germany and Stalin's USSR. Since I find no citations of this publication in Arendt's book, I have no idea whether she had read it or not. See "Symposium on the Totalitarian State," *Proceedings of the American Philosophical Society* 82 (Philadelphia, 1940): 1–103. On a similar subject, see Frank Borkenau, *The Totalitarian Enemy* (London: Faber and Faber, 1940). The preface of Borkenau's book, dated 1 December 1939, indicates that the comparison between Nazism and Communism had been made necessary by the Hitler-Stalin pact. Certain elements of Borkenau's analysis (the moral nihilism of the two systems, the role of the dissolution of social classes, for example), were also present in Arendt. See Robert A. Skotheim, *Totalitarianism and American Social Thought* (New York: Holt, Rinehart and Winston, 1971).

59. Franz Neumann, *Behemoth: The Structure and Practice of National Socialism, 1933–1944* (Oxford: Oxford University Press, 1942; reprinted 1994).

60. This is what we may surmise from Arendt's correspondence with Jaspers, in which she refers several times to her work on the manuscript.

61. See André Enegren, *La Pensée politique de Hannah Arendt* (Paris: Presses Universitaires de France, 1984); and "Hannah Arendt, 1906–1975, Les Origines du totalitarisme, 1951" in *Dictionnaire des oeuvres politiques*, edited by François Châtelet, Olivier Duhamel, and Évelyne Pisier (Paris: Presses Universitaires de France, 1986).

62. David Rousset, *L'Univers concentrationnaire* (Paris: Le Pavois, 1946), and *Les jours de notre mort* (Paris: Le Pavois, 1947).

63. Eugen Kogon, *Der SS Staat, Das System der deutschen Konzentrationslager*

(Frankfurt, 1946), translated as *The Theory and Practice of Hell: The German Concentration Camps and the System behind Them* (New York: Farrar, Strauss, 1950).

64. *The Dark Side of the Moon,* with a preface by T. S. Eliot (New York: Scribner, 1947).

65. Although this idea could already be found in the 1951 edition of *Origins,* a more precise analysis by Arendt of the "ideological" character of totalitarianism appeared two years later in the July 1953 issue of the *Review of Politics* under the title "Ideology and Terror: A Novel Form of Government." This paper, first presented as a lecture at Notre Dame University, became the thirteenth and final chapter of the 1958 reprint of *Origins.* See Young-Bruehl, *Hannah Arendt,* 251.

66. The first in-depth discussion of Hannah Arendt's book in Europe was Raymond Aron's article "L'Essence du totalitarisme" in *Critique,* 1954. Aron was to return to the subject in his courses at the Sorbonne, which were published under the title *Démocratie et Totalitarisme* (Paris: Gallimard, 1965). He admitted the factual similarities between the Hitlerian and Stalinist regimes, but he did not cast them as two versions of the same thing since they differed on the level of ethical intentionality. For a discussion of the differences between Hannah Arendt and Raymond Aron in the matter of the epistemology of historical knowledge, see Luc Ferry, "Stalinisme et historicisme: La critique du totalitarisme stalinien chez Hannah Arendt et Raymond Aron," in *Les Interprétations du stalinisme,* edited by Évelyne Pisier-Kouchner (Paris: Presses Universitaires de France, 1983), 226–55.

67. For Gurian, as for Eric Voegelin, another German émigré philosopher, totalitarianism was more the product of modern atheism than of the socio-political process. See the Arendt-Voegelin discussion in Gurian's journal, *Review of Politics,* 1952, no. 15. See also "Totalitarianism as a Political Religion," Gurian's contribution to the symposium on totalitarianism organized in March 1953 in Boston, in *Totalitarianism,* edited by C. J. Friedrich (Cambridge, MA: Harvard University Press, 1954), 119–29.

68. *Totalitarianism: Proceedings of a Conference Held at the American Academy of Arts and Sciences, March 1953,* edited by C. J. Friedrich (Cambridge: Harvard University Press, 1954). Carl J. Friedrich (1901–84), born in Germany, emigrated to the United States in 1922, where he was naturalized in 1938. A professor of political science at Harvard, he was one of the leading postwar researchers on Nazi Germany and totalitarianism.

69. Ibid., 60.

70. The outstanding exception to this widespread conformism was, of course, Raymond Aron. The philosopher of the limits of historical comprehension was also the political writer with the greatest analytical capacity for understanding his time. See Nicolas Baverez, *Raymond Aron* (Lyon: Manufacture, 1986).

CHAPTER TWELVE

1. Raymond Abellio, *La Fosse de Babel* (Paris: Gallimard, 1962), 15.

2. He made only one brief appearance at the Nineteenth Congress of the Communist Party of the Soviet Union—the first since 1939—in October 1952.

3. Svetlana Alliluyeva, *Twenty Letters to a Friend* (London: 1967).

4. Jean-Jacques Marie, *Les Derniers Complots de Staline: L'affaire des blouses blanches* (Brussels: Complexe, 1993). The "plot of the White Shirts" was masterminded by the State Security Ministry, and Stalin followed it closely. Nine eminent Soviet doctors—six of whom were Jewish—in charge of caring for top government leaders were arrested, accused of plotting to assassinate their patients. Under physical coercion they admitted everything, including Zhdanov's murder in 1948. The "plot" was revealed to the public on 13 January 1953, prompting an anti-Semitic reaction

which Stalin, had he lived, would probably have liked to dramatize. The doctors were released and rehabilitated one month after Stalin's death.

5. At Stalin's death, the authorities of the democratic countries praised the dictator by recalling the Soviet victory over Nazism. For example, Édouard Herriot declared before the National Assembly: "There is a memory from which we cannot free ourselves: that of the role played by Stalin in the end of the war and the preparation of the victory. We can see this in the ruins of Stalingrad or by studying the battle of Moscow, in which Stalin's military genius sparkled." (The battle was actually conducted by General Joukov.) The Quai d'Orsay made a declaration crediting Stalin with a surprising moderation in foreign affairs: "Although the Soviet government had assumed responsibility for a certain number of operations that endangered peace, we could not lose sight of the fact that Stalin appeared anxious to limit the effects of those operations when they threatened to create irreparable damage."

6. Malenkov gave up his functions at the Secretariat of the Central Committee of the Party on 14 March in order to devote himself to the presidency of the Council of Ministers; thereafter, Khrushchev dominated the Secretariat of the Central Committee and, in September, became titular First Secretary.

7. See Heller and Nekrich, *Utopia in Power,* chap. 9.

8. Bronislaw Baczko, *Comment sortir de la Terreur: Thermidor et la Révolution* (Paris: Flammarion, 1989).

9. Amy Knight, *Beria, Stalin's First Lieutenant* (Princeton: Princeton University Press, 1993).

10. The most important episode in the revolt of the Gulag was that of the camp that depended on the copper mines of Kinguir, in the spring of 1954. Solzhenitsyn gives an account of it in *The Gulag Archipelago.*

11. See, for example, the following studies, all published by Harvard University Press, Cambridge, MA: Richard Pipes, *The Formation of Soviet Russia* (1954); Merle Fainsod, *How Russia is Ruled* (1953, rev. eds. 1963, 1979); *Smolensk under Soviet Rule* (1958); and Leonard Schapiro, *The Origins of the Communist Autocracy* (1954).

12. On the night of 24–25 February 1956, Nikita Khrushchev gave a reading of his report on Stalin's crimes. That document was transmitted to the secretaries of the foreign delegations participating in the Twentieth Congress. On 16 March, the *New York Times* mentioned the report for the first time. On 4 June, the document was published by the American State Department. It had been obtained from Poland, where it had been widely distributed by the Communists. On 6 June, the American Communist Party admitted that the report was authentic. Togliatti, in contrast, described the document (in private) as "insignificant tales"; Thorez and the French Communist Party stuck to the phrase "report attributed to the comrade Khrushchev" and defended Stalin's "*oeuvre.*" The report was nonetheless authenticated indirectly by the minutes of the Twentieth Congress itself, which referred to the famous secret meeting of the famous night in February. Among the Communist nations, Poland was the first country to dare to publish the report in its entirety (*Polityka,* 27 July 1988). See Branko Lazitch, *Le Rapport Khrouchtchev et son histoire* (Paris: Éditions du Seuil, 1976).

13. Nikita Khrushchev, *Khrushchev Remembers* (Boston: Little Brown, 1970).

14. Here, I am following Khrushchev's memoirs.

15. I am grateful to Martin Malia's *The Soviet Tragedy* (New York: Free Press, 1994), 319–20, for this observation.

16. Khrushchev, *Khrushchev Remembers,* chap. 9.

17. See Khrushchev's report in A. Rossi, *Autopsie du stalinisme,* with a postscript by Denis de Rougement (Paris: P. Horay, 1957), 128.

18. In response to an interview with Togliatti published on 20 June 1956 by the

Italian journal *Nuovi Argumenti*, and putting forward the idea of "polycentrism" in the Communist movement, a declaration of the Central Committee of the Communist Party of the USSR, published in *Pravda* on 30 June, nonetheless called for a reinforcement of the ideological unity of international Communism. This same declaration reproached Togliatti for having referred to the "degeneration of Soviet society" as one of the causes of the "cult of personality."

19. The dead were "rehabilitated" by a communiqué issued on 19 February 1956, published simultaneously in Moscow and Warsaw.

20. For the Polish and Hungarian events of 1956, see *1956, Varsovie, Budapest: La deuxième révolution d'Octobre*, edited by Pierre Kende and Krzysztof Pomian (Paris: Éditions du Seuil, 1978); Pierre Broué, Jean-Jacques Marie, and Bela Nagy, *Pologne-Hongrie 1956* (Paris: EDI, 1966; reprinted 1980). On Hungary, see François Fejtö, *1956, Budapest, l'insurrection* (Brussels: Complexe, 1981); Miklos Molnar, *Victoire d'une défaite: Budapest 1956* (Paris: Fayard, 1968); P. Horay, *La Révolte de la Hongrie d'après les émissions des radios hongroises octobre–novembre 1956* (Paris: P. Horay, 1957); *La Révolution hongroise: Histoire du soulèvement d'Octobre* (preceded by "Une révolution antitotalitaire" by Raymond Aron) (Paris: Plon, 1957); and "La révolte de Hongrie," *Les Temps modernes*, January 1957. On Poland, see André Babeau, *Les Conseils ouvriers en Pologne* (Paris: Armand Colin, 1960); "Le socialisme polonais," *Les Temps modernes*, February–March 1957; Krzysztof Pomian, *Pologne: défi à l'impossible?* (Paris: Editions ouvrières, 1982); Terera Toranska, *Oni: Des Staliniens polonais s'expliquent* (Paris: Flammarion, 1986).

21. The Petöfi Circle (named after Sandor Petöfi, 1823–49, a poet who brought about the 1848 uprising of the Hungarian youth for independence) brought together writers and journalists. In the weeks before the 23 October uprising, the Circle played a considerable role in Budapest, preempted by events in Poland.

22. Set off on 2 October 1956, the Hungarian uprising reached a climax on 22 October, when the demonstrators called for a government led by Imre Nagy, which was instituted the following day. From the 25th on, Soviet troops clashed with the "Freedom Fighters"—a spontaneously formed national guard. On the 28th, a cease-fire was ordered by the government, and the Soviets withdrew to the outskirts of Budapest. On the 30th, the Presidium of the PCUS adopted a resolution to crush the uprising by military means. On 1 November, three thousand Soviet tanks invaded Hungary. Nagy attempted to negotiate, but on 3 November the commander of the Hungarian forces, General Maleter, was kidnapped. On the 4th, Budapest was bombarded by artillery fire. The resistance capitulated after three days but continued in the provinces until 14 November. The repression resulted in thousands of casualties, and was followed by thousands of arrests. Two hundred thousand Hungarians emigrated.

23. Having taken refuge in the Yugoslav embassy on 4 November with a few others, including Lukács, Nagy had agreed to leave his shelter when promised immunity by Kádár. His bus was intercepted by Soviet officers.

24. C. Lefort, "Le totalitarisme sans Staline," *Socialisme ou Barbarie*, no. 14 (July–September 1956); reprinted in *Éléments d'une critique de la bureaucratie* (Paris: Gallimard, 1979), 155–235. The quotation is drawn from page 168 of the Gallimard edition. We might note, in contrast to these lines of Lefort, the almost clerical prudence of Sartre in the following comments on Khrushchev, just after the Hungarian disaster: "Yes, one had to know what one wanted, just how far one wanted to go, to undertake reforms without trumpeting them beforehand, but to make them gradually. From this point of view, the most enormous mistake was probably the Khrushchev report, for, in my opinion, the public and solemn denunciation, the detailed exposition of all the crimes of a sacred personality who had for so long represented the

regime, was madness when such frankness was not made possible by the prior and considerable raising of the population's standard of living. . . . But the result was to discover the truth for the masses who were not ready to receive it. When one sees the point to which, here in France, the report has shaken Communist intellectuals and workers, one has an idea of how little prepared the Hungarians, for example, were to understand that awful tale of crimes and weaknesses, unaccompanied by any explanation, any historical analysis, any prudence." *L'Express,* 9 November 1956, cited in Lazitch, *Le Rapport Khrouchtchev et son histoire.*

25. The declaration, signed by Khrushchev and Tito on 20 June 1956, on the occasion of the Yugoslav chief of state's trip to Moscow, mentioned autonomy for each of the developing socialist countries and the need for equality in the dialogue among them.

26. On 28 June the great workers' riot in Poznan occurred, which the Polish army managed to crush. Starting with a demand for higher wages, the demonstration also included anti-Soviet slogans.

27. Fejtö, *Histoire des démocraties populaires,* 2:143.

28. Ibid., 2:127.

29. Controlling the anti-Fascist Committee of the national liberation, Tito and his partisans escaped annihilation thanks to the Italian capitulation in September 1943. In the fall, he received British support when the British abandoned the monarchist Mihailović and his Tchetniks, who had handled the Germans and the Italians with care. In each liberated commune, a popular committee in charge of administration was put into place, and each region was directed by an anti-Fascist council under the surveillance of the Communists. That structure was seconded by one made up of political commissars, who were the link between the liberation army and civil authorities. Tito became master of the country with the arrival of the Red Army, which helped the partisans take Belgrade on 20 October 1944. The war continued until May 1945, the people's army committing massacres in Slovenia, where the Croatians and the Oustachis had taken refuge.

30. Milovan Djilas had emphasized, from 1953 on, the contradiction between the autonomous management of firms and administrations and the existence of a single party of the Leninist type. See *Anatomy of a Moral: The Political Essays of Milovan Djilas,* edited by Abraham Rothberg, with an introduction by Paul Willen (New York: Praeger, 1959).

Edouard Kardelj, vice-president of the Yugoslav state, had singled out the importance of the "Workers' Councils," which the Hungarian revolution had shown to be the best political instruments of a socialist society.

31. Marc Lazar, *Maisons rouges: Les partis communistes français et italien de la Libération à nos jours* (Paris: Aubier, 1992).

32. David A. Shannon, *The Decline of American Communism: A History of the Communist Party of the United States since 1945* (New York: Harcourt, Brace, 1959).

33. This idea was originally a Soviet one, put forward by the Twentieth Congress, though Khrushchev dropped it between February and June 1956.

34. Lazar, *Les Maisons rouges,* 101.

35. Vasily Grossman, *Life and Fate: A Novel,* translated by Robert Chandler (New York: Harper and Row, 1985).

36. Vasily Grossman, *La Route: Nouvelles* (Paris: Julliard–L'Âge d'homme, 1987), 11–26.

37. Grossman's great prewar novel, *Stepan Koltchouguine,* a trilogy of which he finished only the first two volumes, tells the story of a young orphan, a worker from childhood, who becomes a clandestine Bolshevik activist and is deported to Siberia in czarist Russia. In the unfinished volume, he was to become one of the leaders of the

Comintern. See Simon Markish, *Le Cas Grossman* (Paris: Julliard–L'Âge d'homme, 1983), 46–47.

38. A collection of Grossman's war chronicles, *Stalingrad: choses vues*, devoted to the battle of Stalingrad, was published in French as early as 1945, first by Les Éditions de France. At the same time, his long pamphlet on Treblinka came out, *L'Enfer de Treblinka* (Paris: B. Arthaud, 1945). Recently, a new, more substantial collection has been published in French, under the title *Années de guerre*, with a postscript by Alexis Berelowitch (Paris: Autrement, 1993). Unfortunately, passages viewed as too "Stalinist" have been expurgated from that edition. This posthumous treatment is all the more unjustified because Grossman had invested in the anti-Nazi war great hopes for a liberalization of the Soviet regime. See Markish, *Le Cas Grossman*, 54–56.

39. Grossman "divined" rather than observed the hell of Treblinka, because the camp had been destroyed by the Germans after the 2 August 1943 insurrection by the Kommandos responsible for running the death machine. His article is extraordinary, not so much for its documentary precision as for the horrified intuition into what had occurred in those locales, which had since returned to "nature."

40. "The Old Professor" (*"Le vieux professeur"*) is included in *La Roue*, 169–98.

41. Ibid., 183.

42. Ibid., 193.

43. A few months after the publication of "The Old Professor," Grossman would return to the massacres of the Jews in the Ukraine, in an essay dated 12 October 1943, entitled "Ukraine" and published in *Krasnaïa Zvezda* (The Red Star). During this period, Grossman no longer spoke through indirect sources. In the territory reconquered by the Soviet Army in the Ural-Kursk arch, he had seen the massacres of Jews carried out by the Nazis on the left bank of the Dnieper, notably in Babi Yar, near Kiev. But he spoke of this only in passing, so as not to risk censorship. The official line was to avoid bringing attention to the crimes committed against Jews, under the pretext of not feeding the idea in Russia of a war conducted to defend the Jews. Systematic information about the Jewish genocide would be published, however, in the journal *Einkeit* (Unity), which was the mouthpiece of the anti-Fascist Jewish Committee, published in Yiddish and available in Britain and the United States. In this journal in November–December 1943, Grossman published an essay entitled "Ukraine without Jews."

44. Sémion Lipkine, *Le Destin de Vassili Grossman* (Lausanne: L'Âge d'homme, 1989), 28.

45. Markish, *Le Cas Grossman*, 90–94; Lipkine, *Le Destin de Vassili Grossman*, 32–35.

46. The action in *For a Just Cause* takes place between June and September of 1942.

47. Lipkine, *Le Destin de Vassili Grossman*, 44–45.

48. Grossman had entrusted his manuscript to several periodicals. That is how it came into the hands of Souslov, who, when receiving the author several weeks after the KGB raid, had told him he ought to "forget" his novel, adding, "Perhaps it will be published in two or three hundred years."

49. This sentiment was expressed by Pasternak in a very subtle fashion, reversing the traditional relationship between Russia and Germany, in a report written at the front, in September 1943, with the Soviet Third Army, which had just liberated Orel. The report was censored before appearing in the trade union journal *Troud* in November 1943. A censored passage reads: "What is so striking about Hitlerism is that it has deprived Germany of her political primacy. Her dignity has been sacrificed for the sake of playing a derivative role: the country has been forced into becoming

no more than a reactionary footnote to Russian history. If revolutionary Russia had ever had need of a distorting mirror for her features to be reflected in, disfigured by a grimace of hate and incomprehension, then here it is: Germany has set about creating it." Boris Pasternak, "A Journey to the Army," translated by H. Willens, in *Novy Mir: A Selection 1925–1967*, edited by Misha Glenny (London: Jonathan Cape, 1972).

50. *Life and Fate*, 562–63.

51. Ibid., 231.

52. Ibid., 214.

53. Ibid., 487.

54. Ibid., 34.

55. Ibid., 395.

56. Ibid., 471. "And all Liss had wanted was to check out a few ideas in connection with an article he hoped to write: "The Ideology of the Enemy and Their Leaders.""

57. This argument is developed by Markish in *Le Cas Grossman*, 111–12.

58. Aleksandr I. Solzhenitsyn, *The Gulag Archipelago, 1918–1956: An Experiment in Literary Investigation*, translated by Thomas P. Whitney (New York: Harper and Row, 1973–), 187.

59. Ibid.

60. Nonetheless, he did have time to write *Peace Be with You* (which came out of a trip to Armenia), finished in 1963, and an admirable tale, *All Things Pass*, which he also finished shortly before his death and which was published after 1970 in West Germany. As for *Life and Fate*, a typewritten copy of the novel, which had escaped the KGB's raid, arrived in the West in 1974 thanks to André Sakharov, who had microfilmed it and got Efim Etkind to take it "to the West." The complete text would not be published in Russian and French until 1980.

61. Lipkine, *Le Destin de Vassili Grossman*, 123–26.

EPILOGUE

1. Nadezhda Mandelstam, *Hope Against Hope* (New York: Atheneum Books, 1970); Chentalinski, *La Parole ressuscitée*.

2. *Doctor Zhivago* was published by the Italian publisher Feltrinelli. For an account of the whole affair, see *Le Dossier de l'affaire Pasternak: Archives du Comité central et du Politburo*, translated into French by Sophie Benech, with a preface by Jacqueline de Proyart (Paris: Gallimard, 1994).

3. *Pravda*, 1 and 6 November 1958. For more on the nature of these documents, which were a mixture of inevitable concessions (the writer feared he would be expelled from the USSR) and a reaffirmation of his intellectual integrity, see Lazar Fleishman, *Boris Pasternak: The Man and his Politics* (Cambridge, MA: Harvard University Press, 1990), 296–300.

4. Pasternak died on 30 May 1960.

5. Aleksandr Solzhenitsyn, *The Oak and the Calf: Sketches of Literary Life in the Soviet Union*, translated by H. Willets (New York: Harper and Row, 1980).

6. After eight years in the Gulag, Solzhenitsyn had been forced to serve three extra years of exile south of Kazakstan.

7. Aleksandr Solzhenitsyn, *One Day in the Life of Ivan Denisovich*, translated by Gillon Aitken (London: Sphere books, 1974).

8. Andrei Sakharov, "How I came to dissent," *New York Review of Books*, 21 March 1974, 11–17; and *Mémoires* (Paris: Éditions du Seuil, 1990).

9. Jeannine Verdès-Leroux, *La lune et le caudillo: Le rêve des intellectuels et le*

régime cubain, 1959–1971 (Paris: Gallimard, 1989); Paul Hollander, *Political Pilgrims: Travels of Western Intellectuals to the Soviet Union, China, and Cuba* (New York: Harper Colophon Books, 1981).

10. Laurent Casanova, in the immediate post–World War II years, had been in charge of intellectuals in the leadership of the French Communist Party.

11. The USSR seemed to have caught up with and perhaps even surpassed the United States in nuclear armament by the end of the 1960s. The policy of détente, moreover, allowed it to benefit from important loans on the part of Western financial institutions while remaining loyal to the Bolshevik interpretation of détente—which was just another way of increasing the conquests of socialism at the expense of capitalism. This, moreover, is exactly what would happen during 1970s in Vietnam, Laos, Cambodia, Angola, and finally Afghanistan. When Brezhnev and Nixon sealed their new "cooperation" with a treaty in 1972, the Soviet Union and its satellites were at the center of international terrorist logistics.

12. The détente of which the Helsinki accords had been the mistaken symbol projected an image of the USSR on the road to liberty. The final act of the Conference on European Security and Cooperation, signed on 1 August 1975 by thirty-three European nations, the United States, and Canada, endorsed the free circulation of people and ideas, along with the territorial status quo and the development of economic relations. It gave the Soviet dissidents a weapon in their fight for human rights, but in no way altered the pitiless repression to which they were subjected. Most of the incarcerations in psychiatric institutions dated from this period, when the Western public believed it was witnessing a liberalization of the regime. See Vladimir Bukovsky, "Plaidoyer pour une autre détente," *Politique internationale,* fall 1985.

13. The last manifestation of enthusiasm on the part of a section of the Western Left for a reign of terror of the neo-Stalinist (or neo-Maoist) type occurred apropos of the Khmer Rouge revolution between 1975 and 1977.

14. Anyone interested in the idealization of the past and present of the Soviet Union need only look at history and geography high school textbooks on the subject, particularly in France, from the post–World War II period to the 1990s. See Diana Pinto, "L'Amérique dans les manuels d'histoire et géographie," in *Historiens et Géographes,* February 1985, no. 303. Not surprisingly, the enthusiasm of French textbook authors for the Soviet Union lagged behind events and the evolution of intellectual life. It was particularly active in the years following the death of Stalin. See the paper presented by Jacques Dupâquier at a colloquium on the perception of the USSR as transmitted by French textbooks, cited in Jean-François Revel, *La Connaissance inutile* (Paris: Pluriel, 1989), 437–38.

15. André Glucksman, *La Cuisinière et le mangeur d'hommes: Essai sur l'État, le marxisme, les camps de concentration* (Paris: Éditions du Seuil, 1975); Bernard-Henri Lévy, *La Barbarie à visage humain* (Paris: Grasset, 1977). See also Pierre Rigoulot, *Les Paupières lourdes,* 131–50.

16. The French publisher, Les Éditions du Seuil, printed more than a million copies.

17. The most typical—not the best—book of this "school," if the term "school" may be used at all, is that of J. Hough, *The Soviet Union and Social Science Theory* (Cambridge, MA: Harvard University Press, 1977). For similar works, see, for example, Moshe Lewin, *The Making of the Soviet System* (New York: Pantheon, 1985); Leon Haimson, *The Politics of Rural Russia, 1905–1914* (Bloomington: Indiana University Press, 1979); Stephen Cohen, *Rethinking the Soviet Experience* (Oxford: Oxford University Press, 1985).

18. Among the books that set the tone for this type of Sovietology are Merle Fainsod, *How Russia is Ruled* (Cambridge, MA: Harvard University Press, 1953);

idem, *Smolensk under Soviet Rule* (Cambridge, MA: Harvard University Press, 1958); Karl Friedrich and Zbigniew Brzezinski, *Totalitarian Dictatorship and Autocracy* (Cambridge, MA: Harvard University Press, 1956); Leonard Schapiro, *The Origins of the Communist Autocracy* (Cambridge, MA: Harvard University Press, 1954); Adam Ulam, *The Bolsheviks: The Intellectual and Political History of the Triumph of Communism in Russia* (New York: Macmillan, 1965); Robert Conquest, *The Great Terror* (New York: Macmillan, 1968); Alain Besançon, *Les Origines intellectuels du léninisme* (Paris: Calmann Lévy, 1977).

After spearheading "Gorbachevism," which seemed to validate the thesis of a "pluralistic" Soviet Union on the road to reform, the revisionist school was put on the defensive by the implosion of the regime. See "The Strange Death of Soviet Communism," *The National Interest*, no. 31 (Spring 1993), part 2, "Sins of the Scholars," by Richard Pipes, Martin Malia, Robert Conquest, William Odom, and Peter Rutland.

19. Emmanuel Todd, *La Chute finale: Essai sur la décomposition de la sphère soviétique* (Paris: Robert Laffont, 1976). See also two papers given by the American demographer Murray Feshback in April 1978 ("Population and Manpower Trends in the USSR") and in July 1983 ("Soviet Population, Labor Force, and Health"). These papers were discussed by Seymour Martin Lipset and Bence Gyorgy at a meeting of the American Sociological Association in Pittsburgh, August 1992.

20. When Brezhnev died on 10 November 1982, he was replaced as General Secretary of the Party by Andropov of the KGB, who was reputed to be a "modernizer." Andropov died on 9 February 1984, however, and was succeeded by an old Brezhnev-type apparatchik, Chernenko. He in turn died on 10 March 1985.

21. The freeing of Sakharov, in 1986, was the first step in this direction; the Central Committee vote in February 1990 to end the political monopoly of the Party was the last.

22. Jacek Kuron, one of the great Polish dissidents who became a minister, said later that in certain Western politicians he could see "a nostalgia for the old world order and the Soviet Union. Some of them would even be ready to reconstruct the USSR so that they could once again have their government orders." *Polityka*, 26 March 1993.

23. The best description of the unconditional "Gorbachevism" of Western governments and public opinions is in Jean-François Revel's *Le Regain démocratique* (Paris: Fayard, 1992), part 2.

INDEX

Abellio, Raymond, 438
Abraham Lincoln battalion, 274
Abyssinia, 212, 294
Acéphale, 311
Action française, 164, 304
Adenauer, Konrad, 400, 419
Adorno, Theodor, 311
Afghanistan, 486
agricultural collectivization, 143–46, 198, 341, 449–50
Akhmatova, Anna, 549 n.14
Alain: and Alexandre, 229; at Congress of Writers for the Defense of Culture, 285; in Ligue debate on Moscow trials, 301; *Mars ou la guerre jugée*, 536 n.42; "Propos," 536 n.42; on Russian Revolution, 53; and Souvarine's *Staline*, 283; and Vigilance Committee, 292; on war and peace, 294; on World War I, 49–50, 52–53
Albania, 406, 465, 466
Alexandre, Jeanne, 536 n.42
Alexandre, Michel, 229, 292, 303, 536 n.42
Algeria, 487
Althusser, Louis, 100, 489, 494
America. *See* United States
American Communist Party. *See* Communist Party (American)
American Revolution, 9
Ammende, Edwald, 515 n.22
Amsterdam-Pleyel movement: bourgeois pacifism as target of, 219; as failing to draw a crowd, 219; fight for peace associated with anti-Fascism in, 231; and French anti-Fascism, 226; imminence of anti-Soviet war as underlying, 230; International Congress against Fascism and War, 213, 215; Langevin in, 293; Monzie and Cot in, 227; and Rolland, 276; Salle

Pleyel meeting, 219; Vigilance Committee members in, 294
anarchism: restoring order in Spanish loyalist cities, 250; socialists defeat in Spain, 255; in Spain, 249, 250; Spanish Communist strategy contrasted with that of, 253. *See also* anarcho-syndicalism
anarcho-syndicalism: and Souvarine, 112; and Spanish Popular Front, 245; in Third Republic workers' movement, 243. *See also* revolutionary syndicalism
Andropov, Yuri, 498, 561 n.20
Années de guerre (Grossman), 558 n.38
anti-Americanism, 404, 429
anticolonialism, 370–71, 487–88
anti-Communism: of American Right, 424; and anti-Fascism becoming incompatible, 274–75, 285; in British foreign policy, 247; condemned in American universities, 494; on eve of collapse of Soviet Union, 497; Hitler as incarnation of, 196; and Italian Fascism, 174, 177, 179; McCarthyism, 421, 426–29; Nazism lent veneer of civilization by, 326; on Stalin's switching camps, 326; as still taboo in 1960s, 492–93; in West Germany, 401; younger Sovietologists rejecting, 496
anti-Fascism: and anti-Communism becoming incompatible, 274–75, 285; Aron on, 312; Bataille on, 310–11; and Blum's leadership of the Popular Front, 239–40; during cold war, 400, 413–15; and Communism, 209–65; Communism lent a Western veneer by, 326, 328; Communist Party making a duplicate of itself in, 240; comparison of Fascism and Communism prevented by, 160, 181; as compulsory for Europe after the war, 366–67; core ideology of, 237; culture of, 266–314;

transformation, 344; Japanese nonaggression treaty, 334; Kirov murder, 202, 223, 277, 450, 514 n.16, 529 n.28; Kronstadt mutiny, 90, 95, 104, 126; League of Nations expels, 541 n.16; League of Nations joined by, 212, 219, 224, 232, 294; as losing its foreignness in anti-Fascism, 222; loyalty to, 99–124; Marshall Plan rejected by, 547 n.1; as moving closer to the democracies to isolate Hitler, 279; nationalism used after World War II, 381–82; nationalities stripped of autonomy, 137; "new course," 453, 455; and Nuremberg trials, 352–53, 543 n.45; as pluralistic, 495; Poland invaded in 1920, 330, 545 n.10; Poland invaded in 1939, 319, 330, 337; Poland liberated by, 351, 367, 379; Poland taken over by, 380–81; as pole of Communist revolution, 58; postwar debates revolving around nature of, 420–21; postwar image of, 350–52, 383–88, 391–92; postwar influence of, 361–62, 369–71; on postwar settlement, 375; primacy in international Communism, 323; radical students compare United States with, 495; Rapallo Treaty, 192, 198, 218, 225, 523 n.65; rapprochement with France, 212–13, 230–31; recognition of, 146–55; relations with Germany in 1920s, 198; repatriation of Soviet citizens after the war, 372–74, 544 n.5; as Revolutionary France's successor, 67; Rolland's visit to, 276–78; Shaw on, 152–53, 516 n.39; Soviet-Yugoslav declaration of 1956, 461, 557 n.25; Spanish Republic supported by, 245–46, 247, 251–52, 255, 260–62; as superpower, 352, 461, 491, 560 n.11; as taboo for democratic opinion, 285; territorial expansion disguised as democracy, 364–65; terror as pillar of, 202; in Third World independence movements, 487–88; Tito's break with, 405–10, 452; totalitarian maturity of, 404; tripartite agreement with Britain and United States, 340; trips to, 275; and United States as opposed in cold war, 413, 424–31; United States as stronger than, 404, 421; and United States in joint domination of Europe, 363; as universalizing itself under banner of revolution, 371; Warsaw Pact, 454; the Webbs' visit to, 154–55; Wells on, 150–52, 516 n.43; Western financial aid to, 500; Western students criticizing, 490; World War II as not changing nature of regime, 372; World War II's costs to, 349–50, 352, 374. See also Brest-Litovsk, Treaty of; de-Stalinization; dissidents; Five-Year

Plan; Franco-Soviet Treaty of Assistance; German-Soviet pact of 1939; Gulag, the; Moscow show trials of 1936–38; New Economic Policy; Soviet secret police; succession; Workers' Opposition; and leaders by name (Brezhnev, Leonid; Bukharin, Nikolay Ivanovich; Gorbachev, Mikhail; Kamenev, Lev; Khrushchev, Nikita; Lenin, Vladimir Ilyich; Molotov, Vyacheslav; Stalin, Joseph; Trotsky, Leon; Zinoviev, Gregori)
Sovkhozes, 144
Spain: anarchist movement in, 249; as Catholic, aristocratic, and poor, 248; Communist Party, 249, 250, 252, 253, 255, 256–57; as at periphery of European politics, 248; Primo de Rivera, 248, 259, 531 n.64. See also Spanish Civil War
Spanish Civil War, 245–65; Americans in, 274; anti-Fascist memories provided by, 354; Blum's nonintervention policy, 240, 246, 247, 248; British nonintervention policy, 246–47, 257–58; Comintern's role in, 260; July military insurrection, 249–51; as key event of 1930s, 247; legend of, 261–62; Malraux on, 262, 263–65; Orwell on, 261, 264–65; and pacifism, 295; repression of Catalonian Left, 254–55; Stalin's aims and strategy in, 251–55, 258; as testing ground for World War II, 256. See also Falangists; Franco, Francisco; International Brigades; Spanish Republic
Spanish Republic: apparatus of repression of, 255–56; Blum government as abandoning, 246, 247; Bolsheviks contrasted with, 262; Communist control of administration of, 253; military insurrection confronting, 249–51; revolutionary romanticism of, 259; Soviet Union supporting, 245–46, 247, 251–52, 255, 260–62. See also Popular Front (Spanish)
Spartacus League, 79, 214, 507 n.40
Spender, Stephen, 269, 534 n.5
Spengler, Oswald, 187, 192, 194, 203, 522 n.50
Sperber, Manès, 214, 291
Stalin, Joseph: address on German invasion, 341; American Communist Party criticized by, 425; American imperialism as cold war philosophy of, 398; as anti-colonialist, 370; anti-Fascism renounced by, 321–24; belligerent complicity with Hitler, 161; on "building socialism" in Soviet Union, 142–43; Bukharin and the Right defeated by, 141, 142; and Churchill, 347; collectivization of agriculture, 143–46; Comintern controlled by, 211,

CPSIA information can be obtained
at www.ICGtesting.com
Printed in the USA
BVHW040807030221
599225BV00059B/2081

9 780226 273419